W9-AUD-713

The Gift of Love

One Year New Testament
Daily Devotional for Couples

Star Song
PUBLISHING GROUP

Nashville, Tennessee

Copyright © 1993 by Star Song Publishing Group
All rights reserved. First Edition.

No part of this publication may be reproduced, stored in a retrieval system, or transmitted in any form by any means, electronic, mechanical, photocopy, recording, or otherwise, without the prior written permission of the publisher, except for brief quotations in critical reviews or articles.

The scripture text of *The Gift of Love* is from *The Living Bible* copyright © 1971 by Tyndale House Publishers, Wheaton, Illinois 60189. Used by permission. All rights reserved. *The Living Bible* is a compilation of the Scripture portions previously published by Tyndale House Publishers under the following titles: *Living Letters,* 1962; *Living Prophecies,* 1965; *Living Gospels,* 1966; *Living Psalms and Proverbs,* 1967; *Living Lessons of Life and Love,* 1968; *Living Books of Moses,* 1969; *Living History of Israel,* 1970. Some material has also been taken from the *Life Application Bible,* copyright © 1988, 1989, 1990, 1991 by Tyndale House Publishers Inc., Wheaton, Illinois 60189. New Testament Life Application Notes and Bible Helps © 1986 owned by assignment to Tyndale House Publishers, Inc. Used by permission. All rights reserved.

Life Application and *The One Year New Testament* are registered trademarks of Tyndale House Publishers, Inc.

ISBN 1-56233-050-0

Star Song Publishing Group, a division of Jubilee Communications, Inc.
2325 Crestmoor, Nashville, Tennessee 37215.

Printed in the United States of America.

The
Gift
of Love

The Ancestors of Jesus

These are the ancestors of Jesus Christ, a descendant of King David and of Abraham:

²Abraham was the father of Isaac; Isaac was the father of Jacob; Jacob was the father of Judah and his brothers.
³Judah was the father of Perez and Zerah (Tamar was their mother); Perez was the father of Hezron; Hezron was the father of Aram;
⁴Aram was the father of Amminadab; Amminadab was the father of Nahshon; Nahshon was the father of Salmon;
⁵Salmon was the father of Boaz (Rahab was his mother); Boaz was the father of Obed (Ruth was his mother); Obed was the father of Jesse;
⁶Jesse was the father of King David. David was the father of Solomon (his mother was the widow of Uriah);
⁷Solomon was the father of Rehoboam; Rehoboam was the father of Abijah; Abijah was the father of Asa;
⁸Asa was the father of Jehoshaphat; Jehoshaphat was the father of Joram; Joram was the father of Uzziah;
⁹Uzziah was the father of Jotham; Jotham was the father of Ahaz; Ahaz was the father of Hezekiah;
¹⁰Hezekiah was the father of Manasseh; Manasseh was the father of Amos; Amos was the father of Josiah;
¹¹Josiah was the father of Jechoniah and his brothers (born at the time of the exile to Babylon).
¹²After the exile:
Jechoniah was the father of Shealtiel; Shealtiel was the father of Zerubbabel;
¹³Zerubbabel was the father of Abiud; Abiud was the father of Eliakim; Eliakim was the father of Azor;
¹⁴Azor was the father of Zadok; Zadok was the father of Achim; Achim was the father of Eliud;
¹⁵Eliud was the father of Eleazar; Eleazar was the father of Matthan; Matthan was the father of Jacob;
¹⁶Jacob was the father of Joseph (who was the husband of Mary, the mother of Jesus Christ the Messiah).
¹⁷These are fourteen of the generations from Abraham to King David; and fourteen from King David's time to the exile; and fourteen from the exile to Christ.

The Good News Is about Jesus Christ
ᦆ Romans 1:1-7 ᦅ

Dear friends in Rome: ¹This letter is from Paul, Jesus Christ's slave, chosen to be a missionary, and sent out to preach God's Good News. ²This Good News was promised long ago by God's prophets in the Old Testament. ³It is the Good News about his Son, Jesus Christ our Lord, who came as a human baby, born into King David's royal family line; ⁴and by being raised from the dead he was proved to be the mighty Son of God, with the holy nature of God himself.

⁵And now, through Christ, all the kindness of God has been poured out upon us undeserving sinners; and now he is sending us out around the world to tell all people everywhere the great things God has done for them, so that they, too, will believe and obey him.

⁶,⁷And you, dear friends in Rome, are among those he dearly loves; you, too, are invited by Jesus Christ to be God's very own—yes, his holy people. May all God's mercies and peace be yours from God our Father and from Jesus Christ our Lord.

Proverbs for Today
ᦆ 1:1-6 ᦅ

These are the proverbs of King Solomon of Israel, David's son: He wrote them to teach his people how to live—how to act in every circumstance, for he wanted them to be understanding, just and fair in everything they did. "I want to make the simple-minded wise!" he said. "I want to warn young men about some problems they will face. I want those already wise to become the wiser and become leaders by exploring the depths of meaning in these nuggets of truth."

———————— ❧ KEY VERSE ❧ ————————

And now, through Christ, all the kindness of God has been poured out upon us undeserving sinners; and now he is sending us out around the world to tell all people everywhere the great things God has done for them, so that they, too, will believe and obey him.—*Romans 1:5*

———————— ❧ REFLECTION ❧ ————————

Long after people have forgotten that the organist hit a flat instead of a sharp during the opening of the "Wedding March" or that the Maid of Honor had a coffee stain on her gown or that the cake had just a little too much baking soda in it, they will remember that each of you made a vow to love, honor, and cherish the other for as long as you both shall live. From that day forth, your friends and family began to think of you not as "Bob" or "Mary" but as "Bob-and-Mary"—a couple who will share the rest of their lives together as one.

Allow your marriage to reflect the forgiveness of Christ by showing kindness toward each other and by being an example of his mercy to those around you. In an age of rising divorce rates and dysfunctional families, a Christian couple whose marriage is rooted in prayer and the Word of God will demonstrate to friends and family his love, his kindness, and his goodness.

———————— ❧ MEDITATION ❧ ————————

Heavenly Father, we submit our marriage to you. Forgive us of any habits or attitudes we have that are not pleasing in your sight or that don't bring glory to you. Help us to spend less energy thinking about ourselves and our desires and more time focusing on you and the great work that you are doing in our lives. ❧

JANUARY 2 ————————————

Jesus Is Born in Bethlehem
❧ Matthew 1:18–25 ❧

These are the facts concerning the birth of Jesus Christ: His mother, Mary, was engaged to be married to Joseph. But while she was still a virgin she became pregnant by the Holy Spirit. [19]Then Joseph, her fiancé, being a man of stern principle, decided to break the engagement but to do it quietly, as he didn't want to publicly disgrace her.

[20]As he lay awake considering this, he fell into a dream, and saw an angel standing beside him. "Joseph, son of David," the angel said, "don't hesitate to take Mary as your wife! For the child within her has been conceived by the Holy Spirit. [21]And she will have a Son, and you shall name him Jesus (meaning 'Savior'), for he will save his people from their sins. [22]This will fulfill God's message through his prophets—

[23]*'Listen! The virgin shall conceive a child!* She shall give birth to a Son, and he shall be called "Emmanuel" (meaning "God is with us").'"

[24]When Joseph awoke, he did as the angel commanded, and brought Mary home to be his wife, [25]but she remained a virgin until her Son was born; and Joseph named him "Jesus."

Paul's Desire to Visit the Church in Rome
❧ Romans 1:8–15 ❧

Let me say first of all that wherever I go I hear you being talked about! For your faith in God is becoming known around the world. How I thank God through Jesus Christ for this good report, and for each one of you. [9]God knows how often I pray for you. Day and night I bring you and your needs in prayer to the one I serve with all my might, telling others the Good News about his Son.

¹⁰And one of the things I keep on praying for is the opportunity, God willing, to come at last to see you and, if possible, that I will have a safe trip. ¹¹,¹²For I long to visit you so that I can impart to you the faith that will help your church grow strong in the Lord. Then, too, I need your help, for I want not only to share my faith with you but to be encouraged by yours: Each of us will be a blessing to the other.

¹³I want you to know, dear brothers, that I planned to come many times before (but was prevented) so that I could work among you and see good results, just as I have among the other Gentile churches. ¹⁴For I owe a great debt to you and to everyone else, both to civilized people and uncivilized alike; yes, to the educated and uneducated alike. ¹⁵So, to the fullest extent of my ability, I am ready to come also to you in Rome to preach God's Good News.

Proverbs for Today
◌§ 1:7–9 §◌

How does a man become wise? The first step is to trust and reverence the Lord! Only fools refuse to be taught. Listen to your father and mother. What you learn from them will stand you in good stead; it will gain you many honors.

◌ KEY VERSE ◌

For I long to visit you so that I can impart to you the faith that will help your church grow strong in the Lord. Then, too, I need your help, for I want not only to share my faith with you but to be encouraged by yours: Each of us will be a blessing to the other.—*Romans 1:11–12*

◌ REFLECTION ◌

A common theme in situation comedies on television is for a husband or wife to come home after a bad day at work and begin to take his or her frustrations out on the other members of their family. Over the course of the next thirty minutes everyone becomes angry at the person who started the whole thing until something happens that makes them all realize how silly they've been. Right before the credits roll they vow never to fight again—a promise that lasts until the following week or until the show is canceled, whichever comes first.

Although Paul was writing to the Christians in Rome, his words ring true in the lives of couples today. Encouraging your spouse is one of the greatest privileges of married life. If your husband or wife is going through a difficult time, regardless of the circumstances, be a spiritual blessing by listening to his or her problems and praying together until God resolves the situation.

◌ MEDITATION ◌

Heavenly Father, guide us in our adventure of spiritual openness with one another. Give us the words to say that will encourage each of us to live according to your promises and your divine will. Let each of us be a blessing to the other. §◌

JANUARY 3

Visitors from Eastern Lands
◌§ Matthew 2:1–12 §◌

Jesus was born in the town of Bethlehem, in Judea, during the reign of King Herod.

At about that time some astrologers from eastern lands arrived in Jerusalem, asking, ²"Where is the newborn King of the Jews? for we have seen his star in far-off eastern lands, and have come to worship him."

³King Herod was deeply disturbed by their question, and all Jerusalem was filled with rumors. ⁴He called a meeting of the Jewish religious leaders.

"Did the prophets tell us where the Messiah would be born?" he asked.

⁵"Yes, in Bethlehem," they said, "for this is what the prophet Micah wrote:

> ⁶"O little town of Bethlehem, you are not just an unimportant Judean village, for a Governor shall rise from you to rule my people Israel.'"

⁷Then Herod sent a private message to the astrologers, asking them to come to see him; at this meeting he found out from them the exact time when they first saw the star. Then he told them, ⁸"Go to Bethlehem and search for the child. And when you find him, come back and tell me so that I can go and worship him too!"

⁹After this interview the astrologers started out again. And look! The star appeared to them again, standing over Bethlehem. ¹⁰Their joy knew no bounds!

¹¹Entering the house where the baby and Mary his mother were, they threw themselves down before him, worshiping. Then they opened their presents and gave him gold, frankincense and myrrh. ¹²But when they returned to their own land, they didn't go through Jerusalem to report to Herod, for God had warned them in a dream to go home another way.

Paul Declares the Power of the Gospel
⊸ Romans 1:16–19 ⊱

For I am not ashamed of this Good News about Christ. It is God's powerful method of bringing all who believe it to heaven. This message was preached first to the Jews alone, but now everyone is invited to come to God in this same way. ¹⁷This Good News tells us that God makes us ready for heaven—makes us right in God's sight—when we put our faith and trust in Christ to save us. This is accomplished from start to finish by faith. As the Scripture says it, "The man who finds life will find it through trusting God."

¹⁸But God shows his anger from heaven against all sinful, evil men who push away the truth from them. ¹⁹For the truth about God is known to them instinctively; God has put this knowledge in their hearts.

Proverbs for Today
⊸ 1:10–19 ⊱

If young toughs tell you, "Come and join us"—turn your back on them! "We'll hide and rob and kill," they say. "Good or bad, we'll treat them all alike. And the loot we'll get! All kinds of stuff! Come on, throw in your lot with us; we'll split with you in equal shares." Don't do it, son! Stay far from men like that, for crime is their way of life, and murder is their specialty. When a bird sees a trap being set, it stays away, but not these men; they trap themselves! They lay a booby trap for their own lives. Such is the fate of all who live by violence and murder. They will die a violent death.

⊸ KEY VERSE ⊱

After this interview the astrologers started out again. And look! The star appeared to them again, standing over Bethlehem. Their joy knew no bounds! Entering the house where the baby and Mary, his mother, were, they threw themselves down before him, worshiping. Then they opened their presents and gave him gold, frankincense, and myrrh.—*Matthew 2:9–11*

⊸ REFLECTION ⊱

The wise men experienced a boundless joy when they came to worship Jesus. Unfortunately, many Christians act as though their faith is a chore that must be performed once a week rather than a privilege to be experienced each moment of the day.

A loss of joy can happen in a marriage as well. Dedicate a portion of your day to worship the Lord together. Rekindle the joy that Jesus brings into your lives when you offer your marriage to him. Worship is not limited to a church building; allow your home to become a sanctuary for his presence.

⊸ MEDITATION ⊱

Heavenly Father, we worship you today and thank you for the eternal gift of salvation that you have given us in your Son, Jesus Christ. Like the wise men who traveled a great distance to bring you their finest treasures, we offer you our lives and our marriage. ⊱

Mary and Joseph Flee to Egypt
◆§ Matthew 2:13–23 §◆

After the astrologers were gone, an angel of the Lord appeared to Joseph in a dream. "Get up and flee to Egypt with the baby and his mother," the angel said, "and stay there until I tell you to return, for King Herod is going to try to kill the child." [14]That same night he left for Egypt with Mary and the baby, [15]and stayed there until King Herod's death. This fulfilled the prophet's prediction,

"I have called my Son from Egypt."

[16]Herod was furious when he learned that the astrologers had disobeyed him. Sending soldiers to Bethlehem, he ordered them to kill every baby boy two years old and under, both in the town and on the nearby farms, for the astrologers had told him the star first appeared to them two years before. [17]This brutal action of Herod's fulfilled the prophecy of Jeremiah,

[18]"Screams of anguish come from Ramah,
　Weeping unrestrained;
　Rachel weeping for her children,
　Uncomforted—
　For they are dead."

[19]When Herod died, an angel of the Lord appeared in a dream to Joseph in Egypt, and told him, [20]"Get up and take the baby and his mother back to Israel, for those who were trying to kill the child are dead."

[21]So he returned immediately to Israel with Jesus and his mother. [22]But on the way he was frightened to learn that the new king was Herod's son, Archelaus. Then, in another dream, he was warned not to go to Judea, so they went to Galilee instead, [23]and lived in Nazareth. This fulfilled the prediction of the prophets concerning the Messiah,

"He shall be called a Nazarene."

The Depravity of Human Beings
◆§ Romans 1:20–32 §◆

Since earliest times men have seen the earth and sky and all God made, and have known of his existence and great eternal power. So they will have no excuse [when they stand before God at Judgment Day].

[21]Yes, they knew about him all right, but they wouldn't admit it or worship him or even thank him for all his daily care. And after awhile they began to think up silly ideas of what God was like and what he wanted them to do. The result was that their foolish minds became dark and confused. [22]Claiming themselves to be wise without God, they became utter fools instead. [23]And then, instead of worshiping the glorious, ever-living God, they took wood and stone and made idols for themselves, carving them to look like mere birds and animals and snakes and puny men.

[24]So God let them go ahead into every sort of sex sin, and do whatever they wanted to—yes, vile and sinful things with each other's bodies. [25]Instead of believing what they knew was the truth about God, they deliberately chose to believe lies. So they prayed to the things God made, but wouldn't obey the blessed God who made these things.

[26]That is why God let go of them and let them do all these evil things, so that even their women turned against God's natural plan for them and indulged in sex sin with each other. [27]And the men, instead of having a normal sex relationship with women, burned with lust for each other, men doing shameful things with other men and, as a result, getting paid within their own souls with the penalty they so richly deserved.

[28]So it was that when they gave God up and would not even acknowledge him, God gave them up to doing everything their evil minds could think of. [29]Their lives became full of every kind of wickedness and sin, of greed and hate, envy, murder, fighting, lying, bitterness, and gossip. [30]They were backbiters, haters of God, insolent, proud braggarts, always thinking of new ways of sinning and continually being disobedient to their parents. [31]They tried to misunderstand, broke their promises, and were heartless—without pity. [32]They were fully aware of God's death penalty for these

crimes, yet they went right ahead and did them anyway, and encouraged others to do them, too.

Proverbs for Today
⇥§ 1:20–23 §⇤

Wisdom shouts in the streets for a hearing. She calls out to the crowds along Main Street, and to the judges in their courts, and to everyone in all the land: "You simpletons!" she cries. "How long will you go on being fools? How long will you scoff at wisdom and fight the facts? Come here and listen to me! I'll pour out the spirit of wisdom upon you, and make you wise.

_____ ● **KEY VERSE** ● _____

After they were gone, an angel of the Lord appeared to Joseph in a dream. "Get up and flee to Egypt with the baby and his mother," the angel said, "and stay there until I tell you to return, for King Herod is going to try to kill the child." That same night he left for Egypt with Mary and the baby, and stayed there until King Herod's death. This fulfilled the prophet's prediction, "I have called my Son from Egypt."—*Matthew 2:13–15*

_____ ● **REFLECTION** ● _____

Joseph is known as a man who obeyed God swiftly and without asking questions. His obedience fulfilled many Old Testament prophecies concerning the birth of God's Son and our Savior, Jesus Christ.

Has God asked you to do something as a couple? In an intimate relationship, such as marriage, people and responsibilities can complicate your life—tempting you to disobey God's guidance because you are afraid of what may happen. Facing these people and situations will be much easier if we listen to God and obey him with open hearts and a positive attitude.

_____ ● **MEDITATION** ● _____

Heavenly Father, soften our hearts so that we can more clearly hear your voice of instruction in our lives. Give us the courage to act immediately and without excuses. §⇤

JANUARY 5 _____

John the Baptist Preaches Repentance
⇥§ Matthew 3:1–12 §⇤

While Mary, Joseph, and Jesus were living in Nazareth, John the Baptist began preaching out in the Judean wilderness. His constant theme was, ²"Turn from your sins . . . turn to God . . . for the Kingdom of Heaven is coming soon." ³Isaiah the prophet had told about John's ministry centuries before! He had written,

"I hear a shout from the wilderness, 'Prepare a road for the Lord—straighten out the path where he will walk.'"

⁴John's clothing was woven from camel's hair and he wore a leather belt; his food was locusts and wild honey. ⁵People from Jerusalem and from all over the Jordan Valley, and, in fact, from every section of Judea went out to the wilderness to hear him preach, ⁶and when they confessed their sins, he baptized them in the Jordan River.

⁷But when he saw many Pharisees and Sadducees coming to be baptized, he denounced them.

"You sons of snakes!" he warned. "Who said that you could escape the coming wrath of God? ⁸Before being baptized, prove that you have turned from sin by doing worthy deeds. ⁹Don't try to get by as you are, thinking, 'We are safe for we are Jews—descendants of Abraham.' That proves nothing. God can change these stones here into Jews!

¹⁰"And even now the axe of God's judgment is poised to chop down every unproductive tree. They will be chopped and burned.

¹¹"With water I baptize those who repent of their sins; but someone else is coming, far greater than I am, so great that I am not worthy to carry

his shoes! He shall baptize you with the Holy Spirit and with fire. ¹²He will separate the chaff from the grain, burning the chaff with never-ending fire, and storing away the grain.''

God's Judgment on Sin
✑ Romans 2:1–16 ઠ✒

''Well,'' you may be saying, ''what terrible people you have been talking about!'' But wait a minute! You are just as bad. When you say they are wicked and should be punished, you are talking about yourselves, for you do these very same things. ²And we know that God, in justice, will punish anyone who does such things as these. ³Do you think that God will judge and condemn others for doing them and overlook you when you do them, too? ⁴Don't you realize how patient he is being with you? Or don't you care? Can't you see that he has been waiting all this time without punishing you, to give you time to turn from your sin? His kindness is meant to lead you to repentance.

⁵But no, you won't listen; and so you are saving up terrible punishment for yourselves because of your stubbornness in refusing to turn from your sin; for there is going to come a day of wrath when God will be the just Judge of all the world. ⁶He will give each one whatever his deeds deserve. ⁷He will give eternal life to those who patiently do the will of God, seeking for the unseen glory and honor and eternal life that he offers. ⁸But he will terribly punish those who fight against the truth of God and walk in evil ways—God's anger will be poured out upon them. ⁹There will be sorrow and suffering for Jews and Gentiles alike who keep on sinning. ¹⁰But there will be glory and honor and peace from God for all who obey him, whether they are Jews or Gentiles. ¹¹For God treats everyone the same.

¹²⁻¹⁵He will punish sin wherever it is found. He will punish the heathen when they sin, even though they never had God's written laws, for down in their hearts they know right from wrong. God's laws are written within them; their own conscience accuses them, or sometimes excuses them. And God will punish the Jews for sinning because

they have his written laws but don't obey them. They know what is right but don't do it. After all, salvation is not given to those who know what to do, unless they do it. ¹⁶The day will surely come when at God's command Jesus Christ will judge the secret lives of everyone, their inmost thoughts and motives; this is all part of God's great plan which I proclaim.

Proverbs for Today
✑ 1:24–28 ઠ✒

I have called you so often but still you won't come. I have pleaded, but all in vain. For you have spurned my counsel and reproof. Some day you'll be in trouble, and I'll laugh! Mock me, will you?—I'll mock you! When a storm of terror surrounds you, and when you are engulfed by anguish and distress, then I will not answer your cry for help. It will be too late though you search for me ever so anxiously.

_____ ✑ **KEY VERSE** ઠ✒ _____

''Well,'' you may be saying, ''what terrible people you have been talking about!'' But wait a minute! You are just as bad. When you say they are wicked and should be punished, you are talking about yourselves, for you do these very same things. And we know that God, in justice, will punish anyone who does such things as these. Do you think that God will judge and condemn others for doing them and overlook you when you do them, too? Don't you realize how patient he is being with you? Or don't you care? Can't you see that he has been waiting all this time without punishing you, to give you time to turn from your sin? His kindness is meant to lead you to repentance.—***Romans 2:1–4***

_____ ✑ **REFLECTION** ઠ✒ _____

Have you ever noticed how the people you don't know very well seem to be perfect? Have you also observed that the person who shares your hearth and home has an assortment of deficiencies you can recite effortlessly and in alphabetical order at a moment's notice? Paul warns us about the danger of judging the sins of another person while at the same time ignoring our own sinful nature. The next time you get the urge to nag or criticize your mate, surprise him or her instead with a confession of your own weaknesses. The results will be astonishing for both of you.

───────── ◈ **MEDITATION** ◈ ─────────

Heavenly Father, fill our marriage with the kind of love that frees us to openly admit our faults to each other. We ask, in turn, that you will also place in our hearts an attitude of forgiveness whenever we are confronted with our partner's shortcomings. ෨

JANUARY 6 ───────────────

John Baptizes Jesus
◄§ Matthew 3:13–17 §►

Then Jesus went from Galilee to the Jordan River to be baptized there by John. [14]John didn't want to do it.

"This isn't proper," he said. "I am the one who needs to be baptized by you."

[15]But Jesus said, "Please do it, for I must do all that is right." So then John baptized him.

[16]After his baptism, as soon as Jesus came up out of the water, the heavens were opened to him and he saw the Spirit of God coming down in the form of a dove. [17]And a voice from heaven said, "This is my beloved Son, and I am wonderfully pleased with him."

Paul's Warning to Jews
◄§ Romans 2:17–29 §►

You Jews think all is well between yourselves and God because he gave his laws to you; you brag that you are his special friends. [18]Yes, you know what he wants; you know right from wrong and favor the right because you have been taught his laws from earliest youth. [19]You are so sure of the way to God that you could point it out to a blind man. You think of yourselves as beacon lights, directing men who are lost in darkness to God. [20]You think that you can guide the simple and teach even children the affairs of God, for you really know his laws, which are full of all knowledge and truth.

[21]Yes, you teach others—then why don't you teach yourselves? You tell others not to steal—do *you* steal? [22]You say it is wrong to commit adultery—do *you* do it? You say, "Don't pray to idols," and then make money your god instead.

[23]You are so proud of knowing God's laws, *but you dishonor him by breaking them.* [24]No wonder the Scriptures say that the world speaks evil of God because of you.

[25]Being a Jew is worth something if you obey God's laws; but if you don't, then you are no better off than the heathen. [26]And if the heathen obey God's laws, won't God give them all the rights and honors he planned to give the Jews? [27]In fact, those heathen will be much better off than you Jews who know so much about God and have his promises but don't obey his laws.

[28]For you are not real Jews just because you were born of Jewish parents or because you have gone through the Jewish initiation ceremony of circumcision. [29]No, a real Jew is anyone whose heart is right with God. For God is not looking for those who cut their bodies in actual body circumcision, but he is looking for those with changed hearts and minds. Whoever has that kind of change in his life will get his praise from God, even if not from you.

Proverbs for Today
◄§ 1:29–33 §►

"For you closed your eyes to the facts and did not choose to reverence and trust the Lord, and you turned your back on me, spurning my advice. That is why you must eat the bitter fruit of having your own way, and experience the full terrors of the pathway you have chosen. For you turned away from me—to death; your own complacency will kill you. Fools! But all who listen to me shall live in peace and safety, unafraid.''

But all who listen to me shall live in peace and safety, unafraid.—*Proverbs 1:33*

_____ ◈ REFLECTION ◈ _____

Everyone from nutritionists to grandmothers have said for years that the most important meal of the day is breakfast. For a lot of people, however, breakfast is also the time to read the daily newspaper. Thus, in addition to toast, cereal, and coffee, these poor souls begin their morning with a large dose of bad news about the economy and frightening statistics about the rising crime rate. It's no wonder that stores have trouble keeping antacid tablets in stock.

News about the family isn't much better these days. Even couples who have been married for decades find themselves jumping on the divorce bandwagon. It makes you wonder if there is hope for modern marriages. Well, put away your nerve pills because the answer is yes. Although most couples eventually will be faced with challenges and uncertainties, God is always faithful to meet our needs if we turn our problems over to him. Submit any difficulties you are having in your marriage to God today. Not only will your breakfast taste better, but you'll also discover that life isn't so bleak after all.

_____ ◈ MEDITATION ◈ _____

Heavenly Father, we turn our cares and concerns over to you. We ask you to give us the peace that comes from knowing that you will tend to our every need. Forgive our sins and help us to turn away from those things that have caused problems in our relationship. ❧

JANUARY 7

Satan Tempts Jesus in the Wilderness
❧ Matthew 4:1–11 ❧

Then Jesus was led out into the wilderness by the Holy Spirit, to be tempted there by Satan. [2]For forty days and forty nights he ate nothing and became very hungry. [3]Then Satan tempted him to get food by changing stones into loaves of bread.

"It will prove you are the Son of God," he said.

[4]But Jesus told him, "No! For the Scriptures tell us that bread won't feed men's souls: obedience to every word of God is what we need."

[5]Then Satan took him to Jerusalem to the roof of the Temple. [6]"Jump off," he said, "and prove you are the Son of God; for the Scriptures declare, 'God will send his angels to keep you from harm,' . . . they will prevent you from smashing on the rocks below."

[7]Jesus retorted, "It also says not to put the Lord your God to a foolish test!"

[8]Next Satan took him to the peak of a very high mountain and showed him the nations of the world and all their glory. [9]"I'll give it all to you," he said, "if you will only kneel and worship me."

[10]"Get out of here, Satan," Jesus told him. "The Scriptures say, 'Worship only the Lord God. Obey only him.'"

[11]Then Satan went away, and angels came and cared for Jesus.

The Advantage of Being Jewish
❧ Romans 3:1–8 ❧

Then what's the use of being a Jew? Are there any special benefits for them from God? Is there any value in the Jewish circumcision ceremony? [2]Yes, being a Jew has many advantages.

First of all, God trusted them with his laws [so that they could know and do his will]. [3]True, some of them were unfaithful, but just because they broke their promises to God, does that mean God will break his promises? [4]Of course not! Though everyone else in the world is a liar, God is not. Do you remember what the book of Psalms says about this? That God's words will always prove true and right, no matter who questions them.

5"But," some say, "our breaking faith with God is good, our sins serve a good purpose, for people will notice how good God is when they see how bad we are. Is it fair, then, for him to punish us when our sins are helping him?" (That is the way some people talk.) 6God forbid! Then what kind of God would he be, to overlook sin? How could he ever condemn anyone? 7For he could not judge and condemn me as a sinner if my dishonesty brought him glory by pointing up his honesty in contrast to my lies. 8If you follow through with that idea you come to this: the worse we are, the better God likes it! But the damnation of those who say such things is just. Yet some claim that this is what I preach!

Proverbs for Today
⋖§ 2:1–5 ⸂⸃

Every young man who listens to me and obeys my instructions will be given wisdom and good sense. Yes, if you want better insight and discernment, and are searching for them as you would for lost money or hidden treasure, then wisdom will be given you, and knowledge of God himself; you will soon learn the importance of reverence for the Lord and of trusting him.

⋖§ KEY VERSE ⸂⸃
Though everyone else in the world is a liar, God is not. Do you remember what the book of Psalms says about this? That God's words will always prove true and right, no matter who questions them. —*Romans 3:4*

⋖§ REFLECTION ⸂⸃
Our society condones many things that God's Word clearly defines as sin. This conflict between God's Word and the world's standards can cloud our thinking and cause us to lose the focus we need to keep our relationship holy before him.

The next time you become angry with your spouse, ask these questions: Am I angry because I am thinking only of myself? Am I angry because the world's standards are not being met? Am I angry because I am not obeying God's Word? If you answered yes to either of the first two questions, you need to confess your sin to your spouse and to God. Ask both of them for forgiveness. If you answered in the affirmative to the third question, you need to turn as a couple to God's Word and pray that he will help both of you seek his plan for your lives. Then rededicate your hearts and your home to him.

⋖§ MEDITATION ⸂⸃
Heavenly Father, forgive us when we shape our marriage around the lies of this world. Help us to stay focused on your Word so that we will understand and know your truth. ⸂⸃

JANUARY 8

The Kingdom of Heaven Is Near

When Jesus heard that John had been arrested, he left Judea and returned home to Nazareth in Galilee; but soon he moved to Capernaum, beside the Lake of Galilee, close to Zebulun and Naphtali. 14This fulfilled Isaiah's prophecy:

15,16"The land of Zebulun and the land of Naphtali, beside the Lake, and the countryside beyond the Jordan River, and Upper Galilee where so many foreigners live—there the people who sat in darkness have seen a great Light; they sat in the land of death, and the Light broke through upon them."

17From then on, Jesus began to preach, "Turn from sin, and turn to God, for the Kingdom of Heaven is near."

18One day as he was walking along the beach beside the Lake of Galilee, he saw two brothers—Simon, also called Peter, and Andrew—out in a boat fishing with a net, for they were commercial fishermen.

¹⁹Jesus called out, "Come along with me and I will show you how to fish for the souls of men!" ²⁰And they left their nets at once and went with him.

²¹A little farther up the beach he saw two other brothers, James and John, sitting in a boat with their father Zebedee, mending their nets; and he called to them to come too. ²²At once they stopped their work and, leaving their father behind, went with him.

²³Jesus traveled all through Galilee teaching in the Jewish synagogues, everywhere preaching the Good News about the Kingdom of Heaven. And he healed every kind of sickness and disease. ²⁴The report of his miracles spread far beyond the borders of Galilee so that sick folk were soon coming to be healed from as far away as Syria. And whatever their illness and pain, or if they were possessed by demons, or were insane, or paralyzed—he healed them all. ²⁵Enormous crowds followed him wherever he went—people from Galilee, and the Ten Cities, and Jerusalem, and from all over Judea, and even from across the Jordan River.

All People Are Sinners
⋦ Romans 3:9–19 ⋧

Well, then, are we Jews *better* than others? No, not at all, for we have already shown that all men alike are sinners, whether Jews or Gentiles. ¹⁰As the Scriptures say,

"No one is good—no one in all the world is innocent."

¹¹No one has ever really followed God's paths, or even truly wanted to.

¹²Every one has turned away; all have gone wrong. No one anywhere has kept on doing what is right; not one.

¹³Their talk is foul and filthy like the stench from an open grave. Their tongues are loaded with lies. Everything they say has in it the sting and poison of deadly snakes.

¹⁴Their mouths are full of cursing and bitterness.

¹⁵They are quick to kill, hating anyone who disagrees with them.

¹⁶Wherever they go they leave misery and trouble behind them, ¹⁷and they have never known what it is to feel secure or enjoy God's blessing.

¹⁸They care nothing about God nor what he thinks of them.

¹⁹So the judgment of God lies very heavily upon the Jews, for they are responsible to keep God's laws instead of doing all these evil things; not one of them has any excuse; in fact, all the world stands hushed and guilty before Almighty God.

Proverbs for Today
⋦ 2:6–15 ⋧

For the Lord grants wisdom! His every word is a treasure of knowledge and understanding. He grants good sense to the godly—his saints. He is their shield, protecting them and guarding their pathway. He shows how to distinguish right from wrong, how to find the right decision every time. For wisdom and truth will enter the very center of your being, filling your life with joy. You will be given the sense to stay away from evil men who want you to be their partners in crime—men who turn from God's ways to walk down dark and evil paths, and exult in doing wrong, for they thoroughly enjoy their sins. Everything they do is crooked and wrong.

⋧ KEY VERSE ⋦

For the Lord grants wisdom! His every word is a treasure of knowledge and understanding. He grants good sense to the godly—his saints. He is their shield, protecting them and guarding their pathway. He shows how to distinguish right from wrong, how to find the right decision every time. For wisdom and truth will enter the very center of your being, filling your life with joy. —*Proverbs 2:6–10*

⋧ REFLECTION ⋦

Every decision you make in life has consequences. This is true in marriage. Whether it's accepting a new job, attending a different church, or even something as mundane as buying a new car, your choices will affect the lives of each member of your family.

Christians don't have to make decisions in a vacuum and then worry if the decisions will negatively affect a loved one. If we earnestly seek God's guidance and diligently study his Word, God will direct our steps and keep us from harm. If you are about to make an important decision, rest on the promise that God will reveal his plan for your life. Remember that wisdom does not come naturally; it must be sought daily in an ongoing relationship with our Creator.

☙ MEDITATION ☙

Heavenly Father, help us to search for your will for our lives so diligently that it becomes the basis for each decision we make. Bless our home and fill it with your peace. ☙

JANUARY 9

The Sermon on the Mount—the Beatitudes
☙ Matthew 5:1–16 ☙

One day as the crowds were gathering, Jesus went up the hillside with his disciples and sat down and taught them there.

[3]"Humble men are very fortunate!" he told them, "for the Kingdom of Heaven is given to them. [4]Those who mourn are fortunate! for they shall be comforted. [5]The meek and lowly are fortunate! for the whole wide world belongs to them.

[6]"Happy are those who long to be just and good, for they shall be completely satisfied. [7]Happy are the kind and merciful, for they shall be shown mercy. [8]Happy are those whose hearts are pure, for they shall see God. [9]Happy are those who strive for peace—they shall be called the sons of God. [10]Happy are those who are persecuted because they are good, for the Kingdom of Heaven is theirs.

[11]"When you are reviled and persecuted and lied about because you are my followers—wonderful! [12]Be *happy* about it! Be *very glad!* for a *tremendous reward* awaits you up in heaven. And remember, the ancient prophets were persecuted too.

[13]"You are the world's seasoning, to make it tolerable. If you lose your flavor, what will happen to the world? And you yourselves will be thrown out and trampled underfoot as worthless. [14]You are the world's light—a city on a hill, glowing in the night for all to see. [15,16]Don't hide your light! Let it shine for all; let your good deeds glow for all to see, so that they will praise your heavenly Father.

Salvation Is by Faith in Jesus Christ
☙ Romans 3:20–31 ☙

Now do you see it? No one can ever be made right in God's sight by doing what the law commands. For the more we know of God's laws, the clearer it becomes that we aren't obeying them; his laws serve only to make us see that we are sinners.

[21,22]But now God has shown us a different way to heaven —not by "being good enough" and trying to keep his laws, but by a new way (though not new, really, for the Scriptures told about it long ago). Now God says he will accept and acquit us— declare us "not guilty"—if we trust Jesus Christ to take away our sins. And we all can be saved in this same way, by coming to Christ, no matter who we are or what we have been like. [23]Yes, all have sinned; all fall short of God's glorious ideal; [24]yet now God declares us "not guilty" of offending him if we trust in Jesus Christ, who in his kindness freely takes away our sins.

[25]For God sent Christ Jesus to take the punishment for our sins and to end all God's anger against us. He used Christ's blood and our faith as the means of saving us from his wrath. In this way he was being entirely fair, even though he did not punish those who sinned in former times. For he was looking forward to the time when Christ would come and take away those sins. [26]And now in these days also he can receive sinners in this same way, because Jesus took away their sins.

But isn't this unfair for God to let criminals go

free, and say that they are innocent? No, for he does it on the basis of their trust in Jesus who took away their sins.

²⁷Then what can we boast about doing, to earn our salvation? Nothing at all. Why? Because our acquittal is not based on our good deeds; it is based on what Christ has done and our faith in him. ²⁸So it is that we are saved by faith in Christ and not by the good things we do.

²⁹And does God save only the Jews in this way? No, the Gentiles, too, may come to him in this same manner. ³⁰God treats us all the same; all, whether Jews or Gentiles, are acquitted if they have faith. ³¹Well then, if we are saved by faith, does this mean that we no longer need obey God's laws? Just the opposite! In fact, only when we trust Jesus can we truly obey him.

Proverbs for Today
◄§ 2:16–22 §►

Only wisdom from the Lord can save a man from the flattery of prostitutes; these girls have abandoned their husbands and flouted the laws of God. Their houses lie along the road to death and hell. The men who enter them are doomed. None of these men will ever be the same again. Follow the steps of the godly instead, and stay on the right path, for only good men enjoy life to the full; evil men lose the good things they might have had, and they themselves shall be destroyed.

◄§ KEY VERSE §►

You are the world's light—a city on a hill, glowing in the night for all to see.—*Matthew 5:14*

◄§ REFLECTION §►

If you live in or have ever visited a coastal community, you've probably seen one of the most charming architectural structures ever designed—the lighthouse. These sturdy towers do more than pose quaintly for postcard photographers, however. Their beacons warn sailors when they are coming too close to a shoreline and protect them from destructive reefs and other hazardous obstructions.

The light that Jesus speaks of glows from within the hearts of his followers and welcomes others to accept his gift of salvation. When people look at your marriage, do they see Christ's influence on your lives? If not, it's time to examine your relationship and rededicate your marriage to him. Only then will you reflect the light that Jesus wants you to share with others. It will shine through everything you do.

◄§ MEDITATION §►

Heavenly Father, we seek forgiveness for any sins in our marriage that diminish your light in our lives. Keep us aware of the darkness in which others dwell so that we can help illuminate their path to your Kingdom. §►

JANUARY 10

The Sermon on the Mount—Jesus Has Come to Fulfill the Law
◄§ Matthew 5:17–48 §►

"Don't misunderstand why I have come—it isn't to cancel the laws of Moses and the warnings of the prophets. No, I came to fulfill them, and to make them all come true. ¹⁸With all the earnestness I have I say: Every law in the Book will continue until its purpose is achieved. ¹⁹And so if anyone breaks the least commandment, and teaches others to, he shall be the least in the Kingdom of Heaven. But those who teach God's laws *and obey them* shall be great in the Kingdom of Heaven.

²⁰"But I warn you—unless your goodness is greater than that of the Pharisees and other Jewish leaders, you can't get into the Kingdom of Heaven at all!

²¹"Under the laws of Moses the rule was, 'If you murder, you must die.' ²²But I have added to that

rule, and tell you that if you are only *angry,* even in your own home, you are in danger of judgment! If you call your friend an idiot, you are in danger of being brought before the court. And if you curse him, you are in danger of the fires of hell.

²³"So if you are standing before the altar in the Temple, offering a sacrifice to God, and suddenly remember that a friend has something against you, ²⁴leave your sacrifice there beside the altar and go and apologize and be reconciled to him, and then come and offer your sacrifice to God. ²⁵Come to terms quickly with your enemy before it is too late and he drags you into court and you are thrown into a debtor's cell, ²⁶for you will stay there until you have paid the last penny.

²⁷"The laws of Moses said, 'You shall not commit adultery.' ²⁸But I say: Anyone who even looks at a woman with lust in his eye has already committed adultery with her in his heart. ²⁹So if your eye—even if it is your best eye!—causes you to lust, gouge it out and throw it away. Better for part of you to be destroyed than for all of you to be cast into hell. ³⁰And if your hand—even your right hand—causes you to sin, cut it off and throw it away. Better that than find yourself in hell.

³¹"The law of Moses says, 'If anyone wants to be rid of his wife, he can divorce her merely by giving her a letter of dismissal.' ³²But I say that a man who divorces his wife, except for fornication, causes her to commit adultery if she marries again. And he who marries her commits adultery.

³³"Again, the law of Moses says, 'You shall not break your vows to God, but must fulfill them all.' ³⁴But I say: Don't make any vows! And even to say, 'By heavens!' is a sacred vow to God, for the heavens are God's throne. ³⁵And if you say 'By the earth!' it is a sacred vow, for the earth is his footstool. And don't swear 'By Jerusalem!' for Jerusalem is the capital of the great King. ³⁶Don't even swear 'By my head!' for you can't turn one hair white or black. ³⁷Say just a simple 'Yes, I will' or 'No, I won't.' Your word is enough. To strengthen your promise with a vow shows that something is wrong.

³⁸"The law of Moses says, 'If a man gouges out another's eye, he must pay with his own eye. If a tooth gets knocked out, knock out the tooth of the one who did it.' ³⁹But I say: Don't resist violence! If you are slapped on one cheek, turn the other too. ⁴⁰If you are ordered to court, and your shirt is taken from you, give your coat too. ⁴¹If the military demand that you carry their gear for a mile, carry it two. ⁴²Give to those who ask, and don't turn away from those who want to borrow.

⁴³"There is a saying, 'Love your *friends* and hate your enemies.' ⁴⁴But I say: Love your *enemies!* Pray for those who *persecute* you! ⁴⁵In that way you will be acting as true sons of your Father in heaven. For he gives his sunlight to both the evil and the good, and sends rain on the just and on the unjust too. ⁴⁶If you love only those who love you, what good is that? Even scoundrels do that much. ⁴⁷If you are friendly only to your friends, how are you different from anyone else? Even the heathen do that. ⁴⁸But you are to be perfect, even as your Father in heaven is perfect.

Abraham Was Justified by Faith
⊰§ Romans 4:1–12 ৡ►

Abraham was, humanly speaking, the founder of our Jewish nation. What were his experiences concerning this question of being saved by faith? Was it because of his good deeds that God accepted him? If so, then he would have something to boast about. But from God's point of view Abraham had no basis at all for pride. ³For the Scriptures tell us Abraham *believed God,* and that is why God canceled his sins and declared him "not guilty."

⁴,⁵But didn't he earn his right to heaven by all the good things he did? No, for being saved is a gift; if a person could earn it by being good, then it wouldn't be free—but it is! It is *given* to those who do *not* work for it. For God declares sinners to be good in his sight if they have faith in Christ to save them from God's wrath.

⁶King David spoke of this, describing the happiness of an undeserving sinner who is declared "not guilty" by God. ⁷"Blessed, and to be envied," he said, "are those whose sins are forgiven and put out of sight. ⁸Yes, what joy there is for anyone whose sins are no longer counted against him by the Lord."

⁹Now then, the question: Is this blessing given only to those who have faith in Christ but also keep

the Jewish laws, or is the blessing also given to those who do not keep the Jewish rules, but only trust in Christ? Well, what about Abraham? We say that he received these blessings through his faith. Was it by faith alone? Or because he also kept the Jewish rules?

¹⁰For the answer to that question, answer this one: *When* did God give this blessing to Abraham? It was *before he became a Jew*—before he went through the Jewish initiation ceremony of circumcision.

¹¹It wasn't until later on, *after* God had promised to bless him *because of his faith,* that he was circumcised. The circumcision ceremony was a sign that Abraham already had faith and that God had already accepted him and declared him just and good in his sight—before the ceremony took place. So Abraham is the spiritual father of those who believe and are saved without obeying Jewish laws. We see, then, that those who do not keep these rules are justified by God through faith. ¹²And Abraham is also the spiritual father of those Jews who have been circumcised. They can see from his example that it is not this ceremony that saves them, for Abraham found favor with God by faith alone, *before he was circumcised.*

Proverbs for Today
❧ 3:1–6 ❧

My son, never forget the things I've taught you. If you want a long and satisfying life, closely follow my instructions. Never tire of loyalty and kindness. Hold these virtues tightly. Write them deep within your heart. If you want favor with both God and man, and a reputation for good judgment and common sense, then trust the Lord completely; don't ever trust yourself. In everything you do, put God

first, and he will direct you and crown your efforts with success.

❧ KEY VERSE ❧

Under the laws of Moses the rule was, "If you murder, you must die." But I have added to that rule and tell you that if you are only *angry,* even in your own home, you are in danger of judgment! If you call your friend an idiot, you are in danger of being brought before the court. And if you curse him, you are in danger of the fires of hell.—*Matthew 5:21–22*

❧ REFLECTION ❧

Few forces in nature are more destructive than human anger. It ruins friendships, careers, and marriages. In fact, anger is such a sinful and damaging emotion that Jesus compared it to murder!

Check into the anger in your home. Do you allow your dislike for someone to fester like a sore and isolate you from friends and family? Is your hostility directed toward the one you pledged to love and honor before the throne of God? Confess your sin to those against whom you harbor ill feelings and ask God to forgive you for this deadly transgression. If this person is your spouse, seek the guidance of a pastor or Christian counselor. Left unchecked, anger will destroy your marriage and damage your relationship with God.

❧ MEDITATION ❧

Heavenly Father, please forgive us for any angry feelings we have toward one another. Help us to develop attitudes that are pleasing to you. ❧

JANUARY 11

The Sermon on the Mount—
Religious Hypocrisy

"Take care! Don't do your good deeds publicly, to be admired, for then you will lose the reward

from your Father in heaven. ²When you give a gift to a beggar, don't shout about it as the hypocrites do—blowing trumpets in the synagogues and streets to call attention to their acts of charity! I tell you in all earnestness, they have received all the reward they will ever get. ³But when you do a kindness to someone, do it secretly—don't tell your left hand what your right hand is doing. ⁴And your Father who knows all secrets will reward you.

⁵"And now about prayer. When you pray, don't be like the hypocrites who pretend piety by praying publicly on street corners and in the synagogues where everyone can see them. Truly, that is all the reward they will ever get. ⁶But when you pray, go away by yourself, all alone, and shut the door behind you and pray to your Father secretly, and your Father, who knows your secrets, will reward you.

⁷,⁸"Don't recite the same prayer over and over as the heathen do, who think prayers are answered only by repeating them again and again. Remember, your Father knows exactly what you need even before you ask him!

⁹"Pray along these lines: 'Our Father in heaven, we honor your holy name. ¹⁰We ask that your kingdom will come now. May your will be done here on earth, just as it is in heaven. ¹¹Give us our food again today, as usual, ¹²and forgive us our sins, just as we have forgiven those who have sinned against us. ¹³Don't bring us into temptation, but deliver us from the Evil One. Amen.' ¹⁴,¹⁵Your heavenly Father will forgive you if you forgive those who sin against you; but if *you* refuse to forgive *them, he* will not forgive *you*.

¹⁶"And now about fasting. When you fast, declining your food for a spiritual purpose, don't do it publicly, as the hypocrites do, who try to look wan and disheveled so people will feel sorry for them. Truly, that is the only reward they will ever get. ¹⁷But when you fast, put on festive clothing, ¹⁸so that no one will suspect you are hungry, except your Father who knows every secret. And he will reward you.

Salvation Is the Free Gift of God
◄§ Romans 4:13–17 §►

It is clear, then, that God's promise to give the whole earth to Abraham and his descendants was not because Abraham obeyed God's laws but because he trusted God to keep his promise. ¹⁴So if you still claim that God's blessings go to those who are "good enough," then you are saying that God's

promises to those who have faith are meaningless, and faith is foolish. ¹⁵But the fact of the matter is this: when we try to gain God's blessing and salvation by keeping his laws we always end up under his anger, for we always fail to keep them. The only way we can keep from breaking laws is not to have any to break!

¹⁶So God's blessings are given to us by faith, as a free gift; we are certain to get them whether or not we follow Jewish customs if we have faith like Abraham's, for Abraham is the father of us all when it comes to these matters of faith. ¹⁷That is what the Scriptures mean when they say that God made Abraham the father of many nations. God will accept all people in every nation who trust God as Abraham did. And this promise is from God himself, who makes the dead live again and speaks of future events with as much certainty as though they were already past.

Proverbs for Today
◄§ 3:7–8 §►

Don't be conceited, sure of your own wisdom. Instead, trust and reverence the Lord, and turn your back on evil; when you do that, then you will be given renewed health and vitality.

────────── ◄§ KEY VERSE §► ──────────

Don't be conceited, sure of your own wisdom. Instead, trust and reverence the Lord, and turn your back on evil; when you do that, then you will be given renewed health and vitality.—*Proverbs 3:7–8*

────────── ◄§ REFLECTION §► ──────────

Young couples often believe that they alone possess true wisdom. This attitude usually reflects four years of higher education and the "discovery" that previous generations foolishly made a mess of the world.

On the other hand, many older couples also have a false sense of their own wisdom. They feel that insight comes from the "school of hard knocks" and that a lifetime of experiences help them to know intuitively what to do in any given situation.

Actually, both attitudes are ridiculous. God is the only true source of wisdom. If you want to make wise decisions, place your trust in the Lord by relying constantly on his Word and turning to him daily in prayer.

_____ ◈ MEDITATION ◈ _____

Heavenly Father, protect us from our vanity. Help us not to rely on a false and destructive sense of our own discernment. Guide us through the reading of your Word so that we will understand your wisdom for our lives. ᕯ

JANUARY 12

The Sermon on the Mount— Store Your Treasures in Heaven
ᕯ Matthew 6:19–34 ᕯ

"Don't store up treasures here on earth where they can erode away or may be stolen. [20]Store them in heaven where they will never lose their value, and are safe from thieves. [21]If your profits are in heaven your heart will be there too.

[22]"If your eye is pure, there will be sunshine in your soul. [23]But if your eye is clouded with evil thoughts and desires, you are in deep spiritual darkness. And oh, how deep that darkness can be!

[24]"You cannot serve two masters: God and money. For you will hate one and love the other, or else the other way around.

[25]"So my counsel is: Don't worry about *things*—food, drink, and clothes. For you already have life and a body—and they are far more important than what to eat and wear. [26]Look at the birds! They don't worry about what to eat—they don't need to sow or reap or store up food—for your heavenly Father feeds them. And you are far more valuable to him than they are. [27]Will all your worries add a single moment to your life?

[28]"And why worry about your clothes? Look at the field lilies! They don't worry about theirs. [29]Yet King Solomon in all his glory was not clothed as beautifully as they. [30]And if God cares so wonderfully for flowers that are here today and gone tomorrow, won't he more surely care for you, O men of little faith?

[31,32]"So don't worry at all about having enough food and clothing. Why be like the heathen? For they take pride in all these things and are deeply concerned about them. But your heavenly Father already knows perfectly well that you need them, [33]and he will give them to you if you give him first place in your life and live as he wants you to.

[34]"So don't be anxious about tomorrow. God will take care of your tomorrow too. Live one day at a time.

Abraham Believed God's Promise
ᕯ Romans 4:18–25 ᕯ

So, when God told Abraham that he would give him a son who would have many descendants and become a great nation, Abraham believed God even though such a promise just couldn't come to pass! [19]And because his faith was strong, he didn't worry about the fact that he was too old to be a father, at the age of one hundred, and that Sarah his wife, at ninety, was also much too old to have a baby.

[20]But Abraham never doubted. He believed God, for his faith and trust grew ever stronger, and he praised God for this blessing even before it happened. [21]He was completely sure that God was well able to do anything he promised. [22]And because of Abraham's faith God forgave his sins and declared him "not guilty."

[23]Now this wonderful statement—that he was accepted and approved through his faith—wasn't just for Abraham's benefit. [24]It was for us, too, assuring us that God will accept us in the same way he accepted Abraham—when we believe the promises of God who brought back Jesus our Lord from the dead. [25]He died for our sins and rose again to make us right with God, filling us with God's goodness.

Proverbs for Today
◄§ 3:9–10 ě►

Honor the Lord by giving him the first part of all your income, and he will fill your barns with wheat and barley and overflow your wine vats with the finest wines.

—————— ◄ **KEY VERSE** ◈ ——————

You cannot serve two masters: God and money. For you will hate one and love the other, or else the other way around.—*Matthew 6:24*

—————— ◈ **REFLECTION** ◈ ——————

Money is often a source of many conflicts in marriage. It is easy to understand why this happens. Everyone needs money for food, clothing, shelter, and other necessities. Yet money is anything but a security blanket. It can be stolen. We can lose our jobs. A fire or other disaster can quickly wipe out our possessions and other assets.

The only true source of security is Jesus Christ. Who is your master? How much time do you spend each day thinking about money? Do you devote as much energy to praying and reading God's Word? Make a vow to place your trust in the One who will see you through any crisis and will provide for your every need.

—————— ◈ **MEDITATION** ◈ ——————

Heavenly Father, keep our eyes focused on eternal life rather than the cares of this world. We release our concerns about tomorrow to you and dedicate this day to your service. ě►

JANUARY 13 _____

The Sermon on the Mount—Don't Criticize
◄§ Matthew 7:1–5 ě►

''Don't criticize, and then you won't be criticized. ²For others will treat you as you treat them. ³And why worry about a speck in the eye of a brother when you have a board in your own? ⁴Should you say, 'Friend, let me help you get that speck out of your eye,' when you can't even see because of the board in your own? ⁵Hypocrite! First get rid of the board. Then you can see to help your brother.

Trials Are a Part of God's Redemptive Purpose
◄§ Romans 5:1–5 ě►

So now, since we have been made right in God's sight by faith in his promises, we can have real peace with him because of what Jesus Christ our Lord has done for us. ²For because of our faith, he has brought us into this place of highest privilege where we now stand, and we confidently and joyfully look forward to actually becoming all that God has had in mind for us to be.

³We can rejoice, too, when we run into problems and trials for we know that they are good for us—they help us learn to be patient. ⁴And patience develops strength of character in us and helps us trust God more each time we use it until finally our hope and faith are strong and steady. ⁵Then, when that happens, we are able to hold our heads high no matter what happens and know that all is well, for we know how dearly God loves us, and we feel this warm love everywhere within us because God has given us the Holy Spirit to fill our hearts with his love.

Proverbs for Today
◄§ 3:11–12 ě►

Young man, do not resent it when God chastens and corrects you, for his punishment is proof of his love. Just as a father punishes a son he delights in to make him better, so the Lord corrects you.

—————— ◈ **KEY VERSE** ◈ ——————

We can rejoice, too, when we run into problems and trials for we know that they are good for us—they help us learn to be patient.—*Romans 5:3*

Many people believe that, if God really loved the world, then he wouldn't allow sorrow and pain—especially for those who follow him. But Paul tells us to rejoice in the midst of our trials and tribulations. Why? Because not only does God grant us peace in the face of adversity, he also teaches us how to be stronger, more faithful, and better equipped to face even greater challenges.

The next time you and your spouse encounter a problem, ask yourselves these questions: How can our marriage grow closer as a result of this situation? Is God trying to teach us something that will help us later? Have we placed our faith completely in him and his certain deliverance? When you learn to rejoice during the bad times, the good times will bring an even deeper sense of thanksgiving.

◦ MEDITATION ◦

Heavenly Father, we thank you for the challenges we are facing. Help us to rejoice when things do not go as we had planned. ◦

JANUARY 14

The Sermon on the Mount—The Golden Rule
◦ Matthew 7:6–12 ◦

"Don't give holy things to depraved men. Don't give pearls to swine! They will trample the pearls and turn and attack you.

[7]"Ask, and you will be given what you ask for. Seek, and you will find. Knock, and the door will be opened. [8]For everyone who asks, receives. Anyone who seeks, finds. If only you will knock, the door will open. [9]If a child asks his father for a loaf of bread, will he be given a stone instead? [10]If he asks for fish, will he be given a poisonous snake? Of course not! [11]And if you hardhearted, sinful men know how to give good gifts to your children, won't your Father in heaven even more certainly give good gifts to those who ask him for them?

[12]"Do for others what you want them to do for you. This is the teaching of the laws of Moses in a nutshell.

God's Mercy Toward Sinners
◦ Romans 5:6–11 ◦

When we were utterly helpless with no way of escape, Christ came at just the right time and died for us sinners who had no use for him. [7]Even if we were good, we really wouldn't expect anyone to die for us, though, of course, that might be barely possible. [8]But God showed his great love for us by sending Christ to die for us while we were still sinners. [9]And since by his blood he did all this for us as sinners, how much more will he do for us now that he has declared us not guilty? Now he will save us from all of God's wrath to come. [10]And since, when we were his enemies, we were brought back to God by the death of his Son, what blessings he must have for us now that we are his friends, and he is living within us!

[11]Now we rejoice in our wonderful new relationship with God—all because of what our Lord Jesus Christ has done in dying for our sins—making us friends of God.

Proverbs for Today
◦ 3:13–15 ◦

The man who knows right from wrong and has good judgment and common sense is happier than the man who is immensely rich! For such wisdom is far more valuable than precious jewels. Nothing else compares with it.

◦ KEY VERSE ◦

The man who knows right from wrong and has good judgment and common sense is happier than the man who is immensely rich!—*Proverbs 3:13*

Scripture tells us that King Solomon was the wisest and wealthiest person who ever lived. When we examine his life, this verse takes on even greater significance. Although Solomon had wealth beyond measure, he was a tragic figure who didn't rely on the wisdom God had given him.

Many Christian couples fall prey to the same snares that trapped Solomon. Focusing their time and attention on material gain, they justify their actions with shallow logic and misguided values. Despite the trappings of success, they are as despondent and unsatisfied as non-Christians they encounter each day. God wants to bless your marriage with happiness, good judgment, and a strong moral sense. Accept his richest blessings today.

◦ MEDITATION ◦

Heavenly Father, forgive us for our sin of discontent. Help us to purge ourselves of those things that strip us of true happiness. Provide us with a strong sense of what is right and wrong. ◦

JANUARY 15

The Sermon on the Mount— Enter by the Narrow Way
◦ Matthew 7:13–29 ◦

"Heaven can be entered only through the narrow gate! The highway to hell is broad, and its gate is wide enough for all the multitudes who choose its easy way. [14]But the Gateway to Life is small, and the road is narrow, and only a few ever find it.

[15]"Beware of false teachers who come disguised as harmless sheep, but are wolves and will tear you apart. [16]You can detect them by the way they act, just as you can identify a tree by its fruit. You need never confuse grapevines with thorn bushes or figs with thistles. [17]Different kinds of fruit trees can quickly be identified by examining their fruit. [18]A variety that produces delicious fruit never produces an inedible kind. And a tree producing an inedible kind can't produce what is good. [19]So the trees having the inedible fruit are chopped down and thrown on the fire. [20]Yes, the way to identify a tree or a person is by the kind of fruit produced.

[21]"Not all who sound religious are really godly people. They may refer to me as 'Lord,' but still won't get to heaven. For the decisive question is whether they obey my Father in heaven. [22]At the Judgment many will tell me, 'Lord, Lord, we told others about you and used your name to cast out demons and to do many other great miracles.' [23]But I will reply, 'You have never been mine. Go away, for your deeds are evil.'

[24]"All who listen to my instructions and follow them are wise, like a man who builds his house on solid rock. [25]Though the rain comes in torrents, and the floods rise and the storm winds beat against his house, it won't collapse, for it is built on rock.

[26]"But those who hear my instructions and ignore them are foolish, like a man who builds his house on sand. [27]For when the rains and floods come, and storm winds beat against his house, it will fall with a mighty crash." [28]The crowds were amazed at Jesus' sermons, [29]for he taught as one who had great authority, and not as their Jewish leaders.

Jesus and Adam
◦ Romans 5:12–19 ◦

When Adam sinned, sin entered the entire human race. His sin spread death throughout all the world, so everything began to grow old and die, for all sinned. [13][We know that it was Adam's sin that caused this] because although, of course, people were sinning from the time of Adam until Moses, God did not in those days judge them guilty of death for breaking his laws—because he had not yet given his laws to them, nor told them what he wanted them to do. [14]So when their bodies died it was not for their own sins since they themselves had never disobeyed God's special law against eating the forbidden fruit, as Adam had.

What a contrast between Adam and Christ who was yet to come! [15]And what a difference between man's sin and God's forgiveness!

For this one man, Adam, brought death to many through his *sin*. But this one man, Jesus Christ, brought forgiveness to many through God's *mercy*. [16]Adam's *one* sin brought the penalty of death to many, while Christ freely takes away *many* sins and gives glorious life instead. [17]The sin of this one man, Adam, caused *death to be king over all,* but all who will take God's gift of forgiveness and acquittal are *kings of life* because of this one man, Jesus Christ. [18]Yes, Adam's *sin* brought *punishment* to all, but Christ's *righteousness* makes men *right with God,* so that they can live. [19]Adam caused many to be sinners because he *disobeyed* God, and Christ caused many to be made acceptable to God because he *obeyed*.

Proverbs for Today
⧼ 3:16–18 ⧽

Wisdom gives: a long, good life, riches, honor, pleasure, peace, wisdom is a tree of life to those who eat her fruit; happy is the man who keeps on eating it.

All who listen to my instructions and follow them are wise, like a man who builds his house on solid rock. Though the rain comes in torrents, and the floods rise and the storm winds beat against his house, it won't collapse, for it is built on rock. —*Matthew 7:24–25*

✎ REFLECTION ✎

Have you ever seen a house after it has been toppled by a hurricane or tornado? The destructive power of fierce winds and torrential rain is awesome. Strong timbers snap like match sticks while floors designed to withstand the weight of heavy appliances crumble like dry cereal.

Although Jesus was referring to the moral underpinning upon which we should build our lives, his parable can also apply to the foundation for a good marriage. When a husband and wife actively seek God's wisdom and obey his commandments, their marriage will survive intact against the gale force of the world's cares and temptations. If you build your marriage on the solid rock of Jesus Christ, you will always have a shelter from the storm.

✎ MEDITATION ✎

Heavenly Father, we ask that you will help us build our marriage upon the things that cannot be destroyed or broken. We thank you for your unwavering goodness and mercy to us, and we pray that you will be glorified in our home. ⧽

JANUARY 16

Jesus Performs Miracles of Healing
⧼ Matthew 8:1–17 ⧽

Large crowds followed Jesus as he came down the hillside.

[2]*Look! A leper is approaching. He kneels before him, worshiping. "Sir," the leper pleads, "if you want to, you can heal me."*

[3]*Jesus touches the man. "I want to," he says. "Be healed." And instantly the leprosy disappears.*

[4]*Then Jesus says to him, "Don't stop to talk to anyone; go right over to the priest to be examined; and take with you the offering required by Moses' law for lepers who are healed—a public testimony of your cure."*

[5,6]When Jesus arrived in Capernaum, a Roman army captain came and pled with him to come to his home and heal his servant boy who was in bed paralyzed and racked with pain.

[7]"Yes," Jesus said, "I will come and heal him."

8,9Then the officer said, "Sir, I am not worthy to have you in my home; [and it isn't necessary for you to come]. If you will only stand here and say, 'Be healed,' my servant will get well! I know, because I am under the authority of my superior officers and I have authority over my soldiers, and I say to one, 'Go,' and he goes, and to another, 'Come,' and he comes, and to my slave boy, 'Do this or that,' and he does it. And I know you have authority to tell his sickness to go—and it will go!"

10Jesus stood there amazed! Turning to the crowd he said, "I haven't seen faith like this in all the land of Israel! 11And I tell you this, that many Gentiles [like this Roman officer], shall come from all over the world and sit down in the Kingdom of Heaven with Abraham, Isaac, and Jacob. 12And many an Israelite—those for whom the Kingdom was prepared—shall be cast into outer darkness, into the place of weeping and torment."

13Then Jesus said to the Roman officer, "Go on home. What you have believed has happened!" And the boy was healed that same hour!

14When Jesus arrived at Peter's house, Peter's mother-in-law was in bed with a high fever. 15But when Jesus touched her hand, the fever left her; and she got up and prepared a meal for them!

16That evening several demon-possessed people were brought to Jesus; and when he spoke a single word, all the demons fled; and all the sick were healed. 17This fulfilled the prophecy of Isaiah, "He took our sicknesses and bore our diseases."

Sin's Power over Us Is Broken
Romans 5:20—6:11

The Ten Commandments were given so that all could see the extent of their failure to obey God's laws. But the more we see our sinfulness, the more we see God's abounding grace forgiving us. 21Before, sin ruled over all men and brought them to death, but now God's kindness rules instead, giving us right standing with God and resulting in eternal life through Jesus Christ our Lord.

6:1Well then, shall we keep on sinning so that God can keep on showing us more and more kindness and forgiveness?

2,3Of course not! Should we keep on sinning when we don't have to? For sin's power over us was broken when we became Christians and were baptized to become a part of Jesus Christ; through his death the power of your sinful nature was shattered. 4Your old sin-loving nature was buried with him by baptism when he died, and when God the Father, with glorious power, brought him back to life again, you were given his wonderful new life to enjoy.

5For you have become a part of him, and so you died with him, so to speak, when he died; and now you share his new life, and shall rise as he did. 6Your old evil desires were nailed to the cross with him; that part of you that loves to sin was crushed and fatally wounded, so that your sin-loving body is no longer under sin's control, no longer needs to be a slave to sin; 7for when you are deadened to sin you are freed from all its allure and its power over you. 8And since your old sin-loving nature "died" with Christ, we know that you will share his new life. 9Christ rose from the dead and will never die again. Death no longer has any power over him. 10He died once for all to end sin's power, but now he lives forever in unbroken fellowship with God. 11So look upon your old sin nature as dead and unresponsive to sin, and instead be alive to God, alert to him, through Jesus Christ our Lord.

Proverbs for Today
3:19–20

The Lord's wisdom founded the earth; his understanding established all the universe and space. The deep fountains of the earth were broken open by his knowledge, and the skies poured down rain.

————————— KEY VERSE —————————

Look! A leper is approaching. He kneels before him, worshiping. "Sir," the leper pleads, "if you want to, you can heal me." Jesus touches the man. "I want to," he says. "Be healed." And instantly the leprosy disappears. Then Jesus says to him, "Don't stop to talk to anyone; go right over to the priest to be examined; and take with you the offering required by Moses' law for lepers who are healed—a public testimony of your cure."—*Matthew 8:2–4*

REFLECTION

To be a leper in ancient times meant that you were a permanent outcast from society. Because there was no cure, the only way to combat the disease was to isolate infected ones from the rest of the population. For most people, separation was probably as bad emotionally as leprosy was physically. They could no longer embrace their family or care for their loved ones. Essentially it was a living death.

A sinful nature often becomes a form of spiritual leprosy. It acts like a fatal, contagious disease by separating families and destroying marriages. Is there a sinful habit in your life that is coming between you and your spouse? Just as Christ healed a man of his fatal condition over 2,000 years ago, he can wipe away your sin and restore your marriage. Ask Christ to cure the disease that is ravaging your family.

MEDITATION

Heavenly Father, we are sinful creatures in constant need of your forgiveness and healing. Reveal any sin in our lives that is separating us from you and from each other. Forgive us of that sin and heal our marriage.

JANUARY 17

Follow Jesus Now
Matthew 8:18–22

When Jesus noticed how large the crowd was growing, he instructed his disciples to get ready to cross to the other side of the lake.

¹⁹Just then one of the Jewish religious teachers said to him, "Teacher, I will follow you no matter where you go!"

²⁰But Jesus said, "Foxes have dens and birds have nests, but I, the Messiah, have no home of my own—no place to lay my head."

²¹Another of his disciples said, "Sir, when my father is dead, then I will follow you."

²²But Jesus told him, "Follow me *now!* Let those who are spiritually dead care for their own dead."

No Longer Allow Sin to Be Your Master
Romans 6:12–23

Do not let sin control your puny body any longer; do not give in to its sinful desires. ¹³Do not let any part of your bodies become tools of wickedness, to be used for sinning; but give yourselves completely to God—every part of you—for you are back from death and you want to be tools in the hands of God, to be used for his good purposes.

¹⁴Sin need never again be your master, for now you are no longer tied to the law where sin enslaves you, but you are free under God's favor and mercy.

¹⁵Does this mean that now we can go ahead and sin and not worry about it? (For our salvation does not depend on keeping the law, but on receiving God's grace!) Of course not!

¹⁶Don't you realize that you can choose your own master? You can choose sin (with death) or else obedience (with acquittal). The one to whom you offer yourself—he will take you and be your master and you will be his slave. ¹⁷Thank God that though you once chose to be slaves of sin, now you have obeyed with all your heart the teaching to which God has committed you. ¹⁸And now you are free from your old master, sin; and you have become slaves to your new master, righteousness.

¹⁹I speak this way, using the illustration of slaves and masters, because it is easy to understand: just as you used to be slaves to all kinds of sin, so now you must let yourselves be slaves to all that is right and holy.

²⁰In those days when you were slaves of sin you didn't bother much with goodness. ²¹And what was the result? Evidently not good, since you are ashamed now even to think about those things you used to do, for all of them end in eternal doom.

²²But now you are free from the power of sin and are slaves of God, and his benefits to you include holiness and everlasting life. ²³For the wages of sin is death, but the free gift of God is eternal life through Jesus Christ our Lord.

Proverbs for Today
§ 3:21–26 ❧

Have two goals: wisdom—that is, knowing and doing right—and common sense. Don't let them slip away, for they fill you with living energy, and bring you honor and respect. They keep you safe from defeat and disaster and from stumbling off the trail. With them on guard you can sleep without fear; you need not be afraid of disaster or the plots of wicked men, for the Lord is with you; he protects you.

❧ KEY VERSE ❧

And now you are free from your old master, sin; and you have become slaves to your new master, righteousness.—*Romans 6:18*

❧ REFLECTION ❧

When we haven't fully dedicated our lives to God, we can find it difficult to break free of a sin committed so frequently that it becomes a habit. Often these habits are so powerful that they control our lives and destroy those around us. If you have a sin that has become a comfortable habit, confess it before God right now so that your partner is not weakened in his or her faith.

❧ MEDITATION ❧

Heavenly Father, fill us with your righteousness and break the cycle of sin in our lives. Create new habits in us that are holy and pleasing to you. ❧

JANUARY 18

Jesus Demonstrates His Power over Nature and Demons
§ Matthew 8:23–34 ❧

Then Jesus got into a boat and started across the lake with his disciples. ²⁴Suddenly a terrible storm came up, with waves higher than the boat. But Jesus was asleep.

²⁵The disciples went to him and wakened him, shouting, "Lord, save us! We're sinking!"

²⁶But Jesus answered, "O you men of little faith! Why are you so frightened?" Then he stood up and rebuked the wind and waves, and the storm subsided and all was calm. ²⁷The disciples just sat there, awed! "Who is this," they asked themselves, "that even the winds and the sea obey him?"

²⁸When they arrived on the other side of the lake, in the country of the Gadarenes, two men with demons in them met him. They lived in a cemetery and were so dangerous that no one could go through that area.

²⁹They began screaming at him, "What do you want with us, O Son of God? You have no right to torment us yet."

³⁰A herd of pigs was feeding in the distance, ³¹so the demons begged, "If you cast us out, send us into that herd of pigs."

³²"All right," Jesus told them. "Begone."

And they came out of the men and entered the pigs, and the whole herd rushed over a cliff and drowned in the water below. ³³The herdsmen fled to the nearest city with the story of what had happened, ³⁴and the entire population came rushing out to see Jesus, and begged him to go away and leave them alone.

An Illustration from the Law
§ Romans 7:1–6 ❧

Don't you understand yet, dear Jewish brothers in Christ, that when a person dies the law no longer holds him in its power?

²Let me illustrate: when a woman marries, the law binds her to her husband as long as he is alive. But if he dies, she is no longer bound to him; the laws of marriage no longer apply to her. ³Then she can marry someone else if she wants to. That would be wrong while he was alive, but it is perfectly all right after he dies.

⁴Your "husband," your master, used to be the Jewish law; but you "died," as it were, with Christ on the cross; and since you are "dead," you are no longer "married to the law," and it has no more control over you. Then you came back to life again when Christ did, and are a new person. And now you are "married," so to speak, to the one who rose from the dead, so that you can produce good fruit, that is, good deeds for God. ⁵When your old nature was still active, sinful desires were at work within you, making you want to do whatever God said not to, and producing sinful deeds, the rotting fruit of death. ⁶But now you need no longer worry about the Jewish laws and customs because you "died" while in their captivity, and now you can really serve God; not in the old way, mechanically obeying a set of rules, but in the new way, [with all of your hearts and minds].

Proverbs for Today
~§ 3:27–32 §~

Don't withhold repayment of your debts. Don't say "some other time," if you can pay now.

□ Don't plot against your neighbor; he is trusting you. Don't get into needless fights. □ Don't envy violent men. Don't copy their ways. For such men are an abomination to the Lord, but he gives his friendship to the godly.

_____ ❧ **KEY VERSE** ❧ _____

But Jesus answered, "O you men of little faith! Why are you so frightened?" Then he stood up and rebuked the wind and waves, and the storm subsided and all was calm.—*Matthew 8:26*

_____ ❧ **REFLECTION** ❧ _____

Sometimes the most destructive forces in a marriage are not those found within the relationship; they are outside pressures that seem threatening and inescapable. Just as Christ was able to rebuke the wind and the waves that frightened his disciples, so too is he able to calm the storms that endanger your family.

When the cares of the world loom around you and you feel as if your marriage is sinking into a never-ending cycle of despair, don't be afraid. Christ is always faithful and will never leave you.

_____ ❧ **MEDITATION** ❧ _____

Heavenly Father, when the storms of life overwhelm us, keep our faith strong. Forgive us for our fear and allow us to accept your gift of peace. §~

JANUARY 19

Jesus Heals a Paralytic
~§ Matthew 9:1–8 §~

So Jesus climbed into a boat and went across the lake to Capernaum, his home town.

²Soon some men brought him a paralyzed boy on a mat. When Jesus saw their faith, he said to the sick boy, "Cheer up, son! For I have forgiven your sins!"

³"Blasphemy! This man is saying he is God!" ex-

claimed some of the religious leaders to themselves.

⁴Jesus knew what they were thinking and asked them, "Why are you thinking such evil thoughts? ⁵,⁶I, the Messiah, have the authority on earth to forgive sins. But talk is cheap—anybody could say that. So I'll prove it to you by healing this man." Then, turning to the paralyzed man, he commanded, "Pick up your stretcher and go on home, for you are healed."

⁷And the boy jumped up and left!

[8]A chill of fear swept through the crowd as they saw this happen right before their eyes. How they praised God for giving such authority to a man!

God's Law Reveals Our Sin
Romans 7:7–14

Well then, am I suggesting that these laws of God are evil? Of course not! No, the law is not sinful but it was the law that showed me my sin. I would never have known the sin in my heart—the evil desires that are hidden there—if the law had not said, ''You must not have evil desires in your heart.'' [8]But sin used this law against evil desires by reminding me that such desires are wrong and arousing all kinds of forbidden desires within me! Only if there were no laws to break would there be no sinning.

[9]That is why I felt fine so long as I did not understand what the law really demanded. But when I learned the truth, I realized that I had broken the law and was a sinner, doomed to die. [10]So as far as I was concerned, the good law which was supposed to show me the way of life resulted instead in my being given the death penalty. [11]Sin fooled me by taking the good laws of God and using them to make me guilty of death. [12]But still, you see, the law itself was wholly right and good.

[13]But how can that be? Didn't the law cause my doom? How then can it be good? No, it was sin, devilish stuff that it is, that used what was good to bring about my condemnation. So you can see how cunning and deadly and damnable it is. For it uses God's good laws for its own evil purposes.

[14]The law is good, then, and the trouble is not there but with *me*, because I am sold into slavery with Sin as my owner.

Proverbs for Today
3:33–35

The curse of God is on the wicked, but his blessing is on the upright. The Lord mocks at mockers, but helps the humble. The wise are promoted to honor, but fools are promoted to shame!

❧ KEY VERSE ❧

But how can that be? Didn't the law cause my doom? How then can it be good? No, it was sin, devilish stuff that it is, that used what was good to bring about my condemnation. So you can see how cunning and deadly and damnable it is. For it uses God's good laws for its own evil purposes.—*Romans 7:13*

❧ REFLECTION ❧

Many people feel that they have to be in control of every situation. Unfortunately, this attitude doesn't go away when they get home. In fact, it's often intensified in an intimate relationship.

Sometimes piety is used to control a spouse. The problem, of course, doesn't lie with God's laws but with our own sinful nature. God must be the one in charge—not us. God promises to rebuild and renew our relationships when we place him in charge of our lives. Allow God to be the one who is in control of your marriage. When you do this, both of you will be equal partners before him.

❧ MEDITATION ❧

Heavenly Father, we submit our marriage and our lives to you. Take control of our human desires and aspirations and make us loving partners for your glory and service. ❧

JANUARY 20

Jesus Calls Matthew to Be His Disciple
Matthew 9:9–13

As Jesus was going on down the road, he saw a tax collector, Matthew, sitting at a tax collection booth.

''Come and be my disciple,'' Jesus said to him, and Matthew jumped up and went along with him.

[10]Later, as Jesus and his disciples were eating dinner [at Matthew's house], there were many notorious swindlers there as guests!

[11]The Pharisees were indignant. "Why does your teacher associate with men like that?"

[12]"Because people who are well don't need a doctor! It's the sick people who do!" was Jesus' reply. [13]Then he added, "Now go away and learn the meaning of this verse of Scripture,

'It isn't your sacrifices and your gifts I want—I want you to be merciful.'

For I have come to urge sinners, not the self-righteous, back to God."

The New and the Old Nature Are at War
⋖§ Romans 7:15–25 §⋗

I don't understand myself at all, for I really want to do what is right, but I can't. I do what I don't want to—what I hate. [16]I know perfectly well that what I am doing is wrong, and my bad conscience proves that I agree with these laws I am breaking. [17]But I can't help myself, because I'm no longer doing it. It is sin inside me that is stronger than I am that makes me do these evil things.

[18]I know I am rotten through and through so far as my old sinful nature is concerned. No matter which way I turn I can't make myself do right. I want to but I can't. [19]When I want to do good, I don't; and when I try not to do wrong, I do it anyway. [20]Now if I am doing what I don't want to, it is plain where the trouble is: sin still has me in its evil grasp.

[21]It seems to be a fact of life that when I want to do what is right, I inevitably do what is wrong. [22]I love to do God's will so far as my new nature is concerned; [23,24,25]but there is something else deep within me, in my lower nature, that is at war with my mind and wins the fight and makes me a slave to the sin that is still within me. In my mind I want to be God's willing servant but instead I find myself still enslaved to sin.

So you see how it is: my new life tells me to do right, but the old nature that is still inside me loves to sin. Oh, what a terrible predicament I'm in!

Who will free me from my slavery to this deadly lower nature? Thank God! It has been done by Jesus Christ our Lord. He has set me free.

Proverbs for Today
⋖§ 4:1–6 §⋗

Young men, listen to me as you would to your father. Listen, and grow wise, for I speak the truth—don't turn away. For I, too, was once a son, tenderly loved by my mother as an only child, and the companion of my father. He told me never to forget his words. "If you follow them," he said, "you will have a long and happy life. *Learn to be wise*," he said, "*and develop good judgment and common sense! I cannot overemphasize this point.*" Cling to wisdom—she will protect you. Love her—she will guard you.

⋒ KEY VERSE ⋒

Then he added, "Now go away and learn the meaning of this verse of Scripture, 'It isn't your sacrifices and your gifts I want—I want you to be merciful.' For I have come to urge sinners, not the self-righteous, back to God."—*Matthew 9:13*

⋒ REFLECTION ⋒

Undoubtedly you have heard about a husband who gives his wife a dozen roses or a wife who fixes her husband a special candlelight dinner after doing something that he or she regrets. While these gestures are signs of remorse for wrong actions, they don't get at the root of the problem. Giving a gift does not mean that our hearts have truly changed. Don't become like the Pharisees and offer token gestures that are meaningless. Give your spouse the gifts that truly demonstrate your love: kindness, understanding, and, above all, mercy.

⋒ MEDITATION ⋒

Heavenly Father, just as you have shown mercy to us as sinners may we show mercy toward each other. §⋗

JANUARY 21

The Bridegroom and His Friends
Matthew 9:14–17

One day the disciples of John the Baptist came to Jesus and asked him, "Why don't your disciples fast as we do and as the Pharisees do?"

[15]"Should the bridegroom's friends mourn and go without food while he is with them?" Jesus asked. "But the time is coming when I will be taken from them. Time enough then for them to refuse to eat.

[16]"And who would patch an old garment with unshrunk cloth? For the patch would tear away and make the hole worse. [17]And who would use old wineskins to store new wine? For the old skins would burst with the pressure, and the wine would be spilled and skins ruined. Only new wineskins are used to store new wine. That way both are preserved."

There Is No Condemnation in Christ
Romans 8:1–11

So there is now no condemnation awaiting those who belong to Christ Jesus. [2]For the power of the life-giving Spirit—and this power is mine through Christ Jesus—has freed me from the vicious circle of sin and death. [3]We aren't saved from sin's grasp by knowing the commandments of God, because we can't and don't keep them, but God put into effect a different plan to save us. He sent his own Son in a human body like ours—except that ours are sinful—and destroyed sin's control over us by giving himself as a sacrifice for our sins. [4]So now we can obey God's laws if we follow after the Holy Spirit and no longer obey the old evil nature within us.

[5]Those who let themselves be controlled by their lower natures live only to please themselves, but those who follow after the Holy Spirit find themselves doing those things that please God. [6]Following after the Holy Spirit leads to life and peace, but following after the old nature leads to death, [7]because the old sinful nature within us is against God. It never did obey God's laws and it never will. [8]That's why those who are still under the control of their old sinful selves, bent on following their old evil desires, can never please God.

[9]But you are not like that. You are controlled by your new nature if you have the Spirit of God living in you. (And remember that if anyone doesn't have the Spirit of Christ living in him, he is not a Christian at all.) [10]Yet, even though Christ lives within you, your body will die because of sin; but your spirit will live, for Christ has pardoned it. [11]And if the Spirit of God, who raised up Jesus from the dead, lives in you, he will make your dying bodies live again after you die, by means of this same Holy Spirit living within you.

Proverbs for Today
4:7–10

Getting wisdom is the most important thing you can do! And with your wisdom, develop common sense and good judgment. If you exalt wisdom, she will exalt you. Hold her fast and she will lead you to great honor; she will place a beautiful crown upon your head. My son, listen to me and do as I say, and you will have a long, good life.

⊸ KEY VERSE ⊸

Those who let themselves be controlled by their lower natures live only to please themselves, but those who follow after the Holy Spirit find themselves doing those things that please God.—*Romans 8:5*

⊸ REFLECTION ⊸

We live in a culture where we're told that our interests and desires should not be subject to anyone else—if we want something, we deserve to have it. A good marriage involves thinking first of someone other than yourself. Don't make your spouse a second-class citizen in your home. Treat him or her with the same love and respect that you want in return.

⊸ MEDITATION ⊸

Heavenly Father, allow us to die to the self as we live first for you and then for each other.

Jesus Performs Miracles of Healing
⮜ Matthew 9:18–26 ⮞

As Jesus was saying this, the rabbi of the local synagogue came and worshiped him. "My little daughter has just died," he said, "but you can bring her back to life again if you will only come and touch her."

[19] As Jesus and the disciples were going to the rabbi's home, [20] a woman who had been sick for twelve years with internal bleeding came up behind him and touched a tassel of his robe, [21] for she thought, "If I only touch him, I will be healed."

[22] Jesus turned around and spoke to her. "Daughter," he said, "all is well! Your faith has healed you." And the woman was well from that moment.

[23] When Jesus arrived at the rabbi's home and saw the noisy crowds and heard the funeral music, [24] he said, "Get them out, for the little girl isn't dead; she is only sleeping!" Then how they all scoffed and sneered at him!

[25] When the crowd was finally outside, Jesus went in where the little girl was lying and took her by the hand, and she jumped up and was all right again! [26] The report of this wonderful miracle swept the entire countryside.

The Life of the Spirit
⮜ Romans 8:12–23 ⮞

So, dear brothers, you have no obligations whatever to your old sinful nature to do what it begs you to do. [13] For if you keep on following it you are lost and will perish, but if through the power of the Holy Spirit you crush it and its evil deeds, you shall live. [14] For all who are led by the Spirit of God are sons of God.

[15] And so we should not be like cringing, fearful slaves, but we should behave like God's very own children, adopted into the bosom of his family, and calling to him, "Father, Father." [16] For his Holy Spirit speaks to us deep in our hearts, and tells us that we really are God's children. [17] And since we are his children, we will share his treasures—for all God gives to his Son Jesus is now ours too. But if we are to share his glory, we must also share his suffering.

[18] Yet what we suffer now is nothing compared to the glory he will give us later. [19] For all creation is waiting patiently and hopefully for that future day when God will resurrect his children. [20,21] For on that day thorns and thistles, sin, death, and decay—the things that overcame the world against its will at God's command—will all disappear, and the world around us will share in the glorious freedom from sin which God's children enjoy.

[22] For we know that even the things of nature, like animals and plants, suffer in sickness and death as they await this great event. [23] And even we Christians, although we have the Holy Spirit within us as a foretaste of future glory, also groan to be released from pain and suffering. We, too, wait anxiously for that day when God will give us our full rights as his children, including the new bodies he has promised us—bodies that will never be sick again and will never die.

Proverbs for Today
⮜ 4:11–13 ⮞

I would have you learn this great fact: that a life of doing right is the wisest life there is. If you live that kind of life, you'll not limp or stumble as you run. Carry out my instructions; don't forget them, for they will lead you to real living.

⮜ KEY VERSE ⮞

So, dear brothers, you have no obligations whatever to your old sinful nature to do what it begs you to do. For if you keep on following it you are lost and will perish, but if through the power of the Holy Spirit you crush it and its evil deeds, you shall live.—*Romans 8:12–13*

According to God's Word, when a couple is united in marriage they become as one person. While this is certainly true, it's also true that a "couple" is made up of individuals—each with two or more decades of personality traits and habits that have become ingrained and are difficult to change overnight. Let go of anything from your past that hinders your marriage, especially those attitudes, feelings, and activities that are sinful in God's eyes.

━━━━━━━━━━ ✍ MEDITATION ✍ ━━━━━━

Heavenly Father, we release the control of our old sinful nature over to you. Take away any impure thoughts and habits that separate us from you and from each other. ✍

JANUARY 23

Jesus Gives Sight to the Blind and Casts Out Demons
✍ Matthew 9:27–38 ✍

As Jesus was leaving her home, two blind men followed along behind, shouting, "O Son of King David, have mercy on us."

[28]They went right into the house where he was staying, and Jesus asked them, "Do you believe I can make you see?"

"Yes, Lord," they told him, "we do."

[29]Then he touched their eyes and said, "Because of your faith it will happen."

[30]And suddenly they could see! Jesus sternly warned them not to tell anyone about it, [31]but instead they spread his fame all over the town.

[32]Leaving that place, Jesus met a man who couldn't speak because a demon was inside him. [33]So Jesus cast out the demon, and instantly the man could talk. How the crowds marveled! "Never in all our lives have we seen anything like this," they exclaimed.

[34]But the Pharisees said, "The reason he can cast out demons is that he is demon-possessed himself—possessed by Satan, the demon king!"

[35]Jesus traveled around through all the cities and villages of that area, teaching in the Jewish synagogues and announcing the Good News about the Kingdom. And wherever he went he healed people of every sort of illness. [36]And what pity he felt for the crowds that came, because their problems were so great and they didn't know what to do or where to go for help. They were like sheep without a shepherd.

[37]"The harvest is so great, and the workers are so few," he told his disciples. [38]"So pray to the one in charge of the harvesting, and ask him to recruit more workers for his harvest fields."

The Holy Spirit Intercedes for Us
✍ Romans 8:24–32 ✍

We are saved by trusting. And trusting means looking forward to getting something we don't yet have—for a man who already has something doesn't need to hope and trust that he will get it. [25]But if we must keep trusting God for something that hasn't happened yet, it teaches us to wait patiently and confidently.

[26]And in the same way—by our faith—the Holy Spirit helps us with our daily problems and in our praying. For we don't even know what we should pray for, nor how to pray as we should; but the Holy Spirit prays for us with such feeling that it cannot be expressed in words. [27]And the Father who knows all hearts knows, of course, what the Spirit is saying as he pleads for us in harmony with God's own will. [28]And we know that all that happens to us is working for our good if we love God and are fitting into his plans.

[29]For from the very beginning God decided that those who came to him—and all along he knew who would—should become like his Son, so that his Son would be the First, with many brothers.

³⁰And having chosen us, he called us to come to him; and when we came, he declared us "not guilty," filled us with Christ's goodness, gave us right standing with himself, and promised us his glory.

³¹What can we ever say to such wonderful things as these? If God is on our side, who can ever be against us? ³²Since he did not spare even his own Son for us but gave him up for us all, won't he also surely give us everything else?

Proverbs for Today
◆§ 4:14–19 §◆

Don't do as the wicked do. Avoid their haunts—turn away, go somewhere else, for evil men can't sleep until they've done their evil deed for the day. They can't rest unless they cause someone to stumble and fall. They eat and drink wickedness and violence! But the good man walks along in the ever-brightening light of God's favor; the dawn gives way to morning splendor, while the evil man gropes and stumbles in the dark.

◆ KEY VERSE ◆

And in the same way—by our faith—the Holy Spirit helps us with our daily problems and in our praying. For we don't even know what we should pray for, nor how to pray as we should; but the Holy Spirit prays for us with such feeling that it cannot be expressed in words.—*Romans 8:26*

◆ REFLECTION ◆

Have you ever wanted to tell your spouse something but didn't quite know what to say? As our Creator, God recognizes our needs and weaknesses better than we understand them ourselves. If a marriage is to be built on a foundation of trust, then we should feel free to express our feelings to our partner. When you have difficulty telling your husband or wife something, ask the Lord to strengthen you and give you the right words to say. Then together turn to God in prayer.

◆ MEDITATION ◆

Heavenly Father, help us accept the things that happen to us—knowing that they fit into your plan for our lives. ◆

JANUARY 24

Jesus Commissions the Twelve
◆§ Matthew 10:1–18 §◆

Jesus called his twelve disciples to him, and gave them authority to cast out evil spirits and to heal every kind of sickness and disease.
^{2,3,4}Here are the names of his twelve disciples:

Simon (also called Peter),
Andrew (Peter's brother),
James (Zebedee's son),
John (James' brother),
Philip,
Bartholomew,
Thomas,
Matthew (the tax collector),
James (Alphaeus' son),
Thaddaeus,

Simon (a member of "The Zealots," a subversive political party),
Judas Iscariot (the one who betrayed him).

⁵Jesus sent them out with these instructions: "Don't go to the Gentiles or the Samaritans, ⁶but only to the people of Israel—God's lost sheep. ⁷Go and announce to them that the Kingdom of Heaven is near. ⁸Heal the sick, raise the dead, cure the lepers, and cast out demons. Give as freely as you have received!

⁹"Don't take any money with you; ¹⁰don't even carry a duffle bag with extra clothes and shoes, or even a walking stick; for those you help should feed and care for you. ¹¹Whenever you enter a city or village, search for a godly man and stay in his home until you leave for the next town. ¹²When you ask

permission to stay, be friendly, [13]and if it turns out to be a godly home, give it your blessing; if not, keep the blessing. [14]Any city or home that doesn't welcome you—shake off the dust of that place from your feet as you leave. [15]Truly, the wicked cities of Sodom and Gomorrah will be better off at Judgment Day than they.

[16]"I am sending you out as sheep among wolves. Be as wary as serpents and harmless as doves. [17]But beware! For you will be arrested and tried, and whipped in the synagogues. [18]Yes, and you must stand trial before governors and kings for my sake. This will give you the opportunity to tell them about me, yes, to witness to the world.

Nothing Can Separate Us from the Love of God
Romans 8:33–39

Who dares accuse us whom God has chosen for his own? Will God? No! He is the one who has forgiven us and given us right standing with himself.

[34]Who then will condemn us? Will Christ? *No!* For he is the one who died for us and came back to life again for us and is sitting at the place of highest honor next to God, pleading for us there in heaven.

[35]Who then can ever keep Christ's love from us? When we have trouble or calamity, when we are hunted down or destroyed, is it because he doesn't love us anymore? And if we are hungry, or penniless, or in danger, or threatened with death, has God deserted us?

[36]No, for the Scriptures tell us that for his sake we must be ready to face death at every moment of the day—we are like sheep awaiting slaughter; [37]but despite all this, overwhelming victory is ours through Christ who loved us enough to die for us. [38]For I am convinced that nothing can ever separate us from his love. Death can't, and life can't. The angels won't, and all the powers of hell itself cannot keep God's love away. Our fears for today, our worries about tomorrow, [39]or where we are—high above the sky, or in the deepest ocean—nothing will ever be able to separate us from the love of God demonstrated by our Lord Jesus Christ when he died for us.

Proverbs for Today
4:20–27

Listen, son of mine, to what I say. Listen carefully. Keep these thoughts ever in mind; let them penetrate deep within your heart, for they will mean real life for you, and radiant health.

Above all else, guard your affections. For they influence everything else in your life. Spurn the careless kiss of a prostitute. Stay far from her. Look straight ahead; don't even turn your head to look. Watch your step. Stick to the path and be safe. Don't sidetrack; pull back your foot from danger.

KEY VERSE

Above all else, guard your affections. For they influence everything else in your life.—*Proverbs 4:23*

REFLECTION

You may have heard the well-worn maxim about the three most important rules for purchasing a house: "Location! Location! Location!" What's the point? If something is important, it can't be overstated.

When it comes to marriage, never forget the important rule "Guard your affections! Guard your affections! Guard your affections!" Make your home a place for holy living. Keep your mind focused on the things that matter and don't be swayed by meaningless desires.

MEDITATION

Heavenly Father, sanctify our marriage and keep our hearts focused on you and on each other.

Take Up Your Cross and Follow Jesus
⋅§ Matthew 10:19—11:1 §⋅

"When you are arrested, don't worry about what to say at your trial, for you will be given the right words at the right time. [20]For it won't be you doing the talking—it will be the Spirit of your heavenly Father speaking through you!

[21]"Brother shall betray brother to death, and fathers shall betray their own children. And children shall rise against their parents and cause their deaths. [22]Everyone shall hate you because you belong to me. But all of you who endure to the end shall be saved.

[23]"When you are persecuted in one city, flee to the next! I will return before you have reached them all!

[24]"A student is not greater than his teacher. A servant is not above his master. [25]The student shares his teacher's fate. The servant shares his master's! And since I, the master of the household, have been called 'Satan,' how much more will you! [26]But don't be afraid of those who threaten you. For the time is coming when the truth will be revealed: their secret plots will become public information.

[27]"What I tell you now in the gloom, shout abroad when daybreak comes. What I whisper in your ears, proclaim from the housetops!

[28]"Don't be afraid of those who can kill only your bodies—but can't touch your souls! Fear only God who can destroy both soul and body in hell. [29]Not one sparrow (What do they cost? Two for a penny?) can fall to the ground without your Father knowing it. [30]And the very hairs of your head are all numbered. [31]So don't worry! You are more valuable to him than many sparrows.

[32]"If anyone publicly acknowledges me as his friend, I will openly acknowledge him as my friend before my Father in heaven. [33]But if anyone publicly denies me, I will openly deny him before my Father in heaven.

[34]"Don't imagine that I came to bring peace to the earth! No, rather, a sword. [35]I have come to set a man against his father, and a daughter against her mother, and a daughter-in-law against her mother-in-law— [36]a man's worst enemies will be right in his own home! [37]If you love your father and mother more than you love me, you are not worthy of being mine; or if you love your son or daughter more than me, you are not worthy of being mine. [38]If you refuse to take up your cross and follow me, you are not worthy of being mine.

[39]"If you cling to your life, you will lose it; but if you give it up for me, you will save it.

[40]"Those who welcome you are welcoming me. And when they welcome me they are welcoming God who sent me. [41]If you welcome a prophet because he is a man of God, you will be given the same reward a prophet gets. And if you welcome good and godly men because of their godliness, you will be given a reward like theirs.

[42]"And if, as my representatives, you give even a cup of cold water to a little child, you will surely be rewarded."

[11:1]When Jesus had finished giving these instructions to his twelve disciples, he went off preaching in the cities where they were scheduled to go.

Paul's Longing for the Salvation of the Jews
⋅§ Romans 9:1–5 §⋅

Oh, Israel, my people! Oh, my Jewish brothers! How I long for you to come to Christ. My heart is heavy within me and I grieve bitterly day and night because of you. Christ knows and the Holy Spirit knows that it is no mere pretense when I say that I would be willing to be forever damned if that would save you. [4]God has given you so much, but still you will not listen to him. He took you as his own special, chosen people and led you along with a bright cloud of glory and told you how very much he wanted to bless you. He gave you his rules for daily life so you would know what he wanted you to do. He let you worship him, and gave you mighty promises. [5]Great men of God were your fathers, and Christ himself was one of you, a Jew so far as his human nature is concerned, he who now rules over all things. Praise God forever!

Proverbs for Today
◄§ 5:1–6 §►

Listen to me, my son! I know what I am saying; *listen!* Watch yourself, lest you be indiscreet and betray some vital information. For the lips of a prostitute are as sweet as honey, and smooth flattery is her stock in trade. But afterwards only a bitter conscience is left to you, sharp as a double-edged sword. She leads you down to death and hell. For she does not know the path to life. She staggers down a crooked trail, and doesn't even realize where it leads.

◄§ KEY VERSE §►

Don't be afraid of those who can kill only your bodies—but can't touch your souls! Fear only God who can destroy both soul and body in hell. Not one sparrow (What do they cost? Two for a penny?) can fall to the ground without your Father knowing it.—*Matthew 10:28–29*

◄§ REFLECTION §►

Whom do you fear in this world? If your boss asks you to do something dishonest, do you go along because you are afraid of losing your job? Do you hesitate to share your opinions with others because they might belittle your convictions? Don't make decisions based on what seems logical according to the world's standards but rather on what is found in God's Word. A strong marriage can withstand any challenge because you always have a faithful partner to lean on when others threaten you. God is the only one you need to please. Serve him gladly and without fear of what others will say or do.

◄§ MEDITATION §►

Heavenly Father, help us to consider you and you alone when faced with conflict from others. We thank you for the gift of marriage and the courage we receive from having someone with whom to share our challenges. §►

JANUARY 26

Jesus Endorses John the Baptist's Ministry
◄§ Matthew 11:2–19 §►

John the Baptist, who was now in prison, heard about all the miracles the Messiah was doing, so he sent his disciples to ask Jesus, ³"Are you really the one we are waiting for, or shall we keep on looking?"

⁴Jesus told them, "Go back to John and tell him about the miracles you've seen me do— ⁵the blind people I've healed, and the lame people now walking without help, and the cured lepers, and the deaf who hear, and the dead raised to life; and tell him about my preaching the Good News to the poor. ⁶Then give him this message, 'Blessed are those who don't doubt me.'"

⁷When John's disciples had gone, Jesus began talking about him to the crowds. "When you went out into the barren wilderness to see John, what did you expect him to be like? Grass blowing in the wind? ⁸Or were you expecting to see a man dressed as a prince in a palace? ⁹Or a prophet of God? Yes, and he is more than just a prophet. ¹⁰For John is the man mentioned in the Scriptures—a messenger to precede me, to announce my coming, and prepare people to receive me.

¹¹"Truly, of all men ever born, none shines more brightly than John the Baptist. And yet, even the lesser lights in the Kingdom of Heaven will be greater than he is! ¹²And from the time John the Baptist began preaching and baptizing until now, ardent multitudes have been crowding toward the Kingdom of Heaven, ¹³for all the laws and prophets looked forward [to the Messiah]. Then John appeared, ¹⁴and if you are willing to understand what I mean, he is Elijah, the one the prophets said would come [at the time the Kingdom begins]. ¹⁵If ever you were willing to listen, listen now!

¹⁶"What shall I say about this nation? These peo-

ple are like children playing, who say to their little friends, [17]"We played wedding and you weren't happy, so we played funeral but you weren't sad.' [18]For John the Baptist doesn't even drink wine and often goes without food, and you say, 'He's crazy.' [19]And I, the Messiah, feast and drink, and you complain that I am 'a glutton and a drinking man, and hang around with the worst sort of sinners!' But brilliant men like you can justify your every inconsistency!"

God Shows Mercy to Whomever He Wants
Romans 9:6–18

Well then, has God failed to fulfill his promises to the Jews? No! [For these promises are only to those who are truly Jews.] And not everyone born into a Jewish family is truly a Jew! [7]Just the fact that they come from Abraham doesn't make them truly Abraham's children. For the Scriptures say that the promises apply only to Abraham's son Isaac and Isaac's descendants, though Abraham had other children too. [8]This means that not all of Abraham's children are children of God, but only those who believe the promise of salvation which he made to Abraham.

[9]For God had promised, "Next year I will give you and Sarah a son." [10-13]And years later, when this son, Isaac, was grown up and married, and Rebecca his wife was about to bear him twin children, God told her that Esau, the child born first, would be a servant to Jacob, his twin brother. In the words of the Scripture, "I chose to bless Jacob, but not Esau." And God said this before the children were even born, before they had done anything either good or bad. This proves that God was doing what he had decided from the beginning; it was not because of what the children did but because of what God wanted and chose.

[14]Was God being unfair? Of course not. [15]For God had said to Moses, "If I want to be kind to someone, I will. And I will take pity on anyone I want to." [16]And so God's blessings are not given just because someone decides to have them or works hard to get them. They are given because God takes pity on those he wants to.

[17]Pharaoh, king of Egypt, was an example of this fact. For God told him he had given him the kingdom of Egypt for the very purpose of displaying the awesome power of God against him: so that all the world would hear about God's glorious name. [18]So you see, God is kind to some just because he wants to be, and he makes some refuse to listen.

Proverbs for Today
5:7–14

Young men, listen to me, and never forget what I'm about to say: *Run from her! Don't go near her house,* lest you fall to her temptation and lose your honor, and give the remainder of your life to the cruel and merciless; lest strangers obtain your wealth, and you become a slave of foreigners. Lest afterwards you groan in anguish and in shame, when syphilis consumes your body, and you say, "Oh, if only I had listened! If only I had not demanded my own way! Oh, why wouldn't I take advice? Why was I so stupid? For now I must face public disgrace."

KEY VERSE

And I, the Messiah, feast and drink, and you complain that I am "a glutton and a drinking man, and hang around with the worst sort of sinners!" But brilliant men like you can justify your every inconsistency!—*Matthew 11:19*

REFLECTION

Fat grams. Cholesterol count. Caloric intake. Aerobic minutes. Standing heart rate. There was a time when people in the church knew the page number of their favorite hymn or tried to memorize a certain number of Scripture verses each year. Today, Christians, like non-Christians, are more in tune with their physical health than they are with their spiritual well-being. While it is important to eat right and stay fit, we should never forget that our physical bodies will someday pass from this earth, regardless of how well we take care of them. On the other hand, our souls will live forever and should be fed and nurtured accordingly each day. Tomorrow when you and your spouse get up early to go to a local gym or fix a healthy breakfast, be sure you set aside equal time to feed and strengthen your relationship with God.

❦ MEDITATION ❦

Heavenly Father, we ask that you will keep our minds focused each day on things that are truly meaningful. Help us to be more concerned about our eternal home than our temporal bodies. ❧

JANUARY 27

Jesus Denounces Unrepentant Cities
❧ Matthew 11:20–30 ❧

Then Jesus began to pour out his denunciations against the cities where he had done most of his miracles, because they hadn't turned to God.

[21] "Woe to you, Chorazin, and woe to you, Bethsaida! For if the miracles I did in your streets had been done in wicked Tyre and Sidon their people would have repented long ago in shame and humility. [22] Truly, Tyre and Sidon will be better off on the Judgment Day than you! [23] And Capernaum, though highly honored, shall go down to hell! For if the marvelous miracles I did in you had been done in Sodom, it would still be here today. [24] Truly, Sodom will be better off at the Judgment Day than you."

[25] And Jesus prayed this prayer: "O Father, Lord of heaven and earth, thank you for hiding the truth from those who think themselves so wise, and for revealing it to little children. [26] Yes, Father, for it pleased you to do it this way! . . .

[27] "Everything has been entrusted to me by my Father. Only the Father knows the Son, and the Father is known only by the Son and by those to whom the Son reveals him. [28] Come to me and I will give you rest—all of you who work so hard beneath a heavy yoke. [29,30] Wear my yoke—for it fits perfectly—and let me teach you; for I am gentle and humble, and you shall find rest for your souls; for I give you only light burdens."

God's Decisions Are Just and Merciful
❧ Romans 9:19–26 ❧

Well then, why does God blame them for not listening? Haven't they done what he made them do?

[20] No, don't say that. Who are you to criticize God? Should the thing made say to the one who made it, "Why have you made me like this?" [21] When a man makes a jar out of clay, doesn't he have a right to use the same lump of clay to make one jar beautiful, to be used for holding flowers, and another to throw garbage into? [22] Does not God have a perfect right to show his fury and power against those who are fit only for destruction, those he has been patient with for all this time? [23,24] And he has a right to take others such as ourselves, who have been made for pouring the riches of his glory into, whether we are Jews or Gentiles, and to be kind to us so that everyone can see how very great his glory is.

[25] Remember what the prophecy of Hosea says? There God says that he will find other children for himself (who are not from his Jewish family) and will love them, though no one had ever loved them before. [26] And the heathen, of whom it once was said, "You are not my people," shall be called "sons of the Living God."

Proverbs for Today
❧ 5:15–21 ❧

Drink from your own well, my son—be faithful and true to your wife. Why should you beget children with women of the street? Why share your children with those outside your home? Be happy, yes, rejoice in the wife of your youth. Let her breasts and tender embrace satisfy you. Let her love alone fill you with delight. Why delight yourself with prostitutes, embracing what isn't yours? *For God is closely watching you,* and he weighs carefully everything you do.

Come to me and I will give you rest—all of you who work so hard beneath a heavy yoke. Wear my yoke—for it fits perfectly—and let me teach you; for I am gentle and humble, and you shall find rest for your souls; for I give you only light burdens.—*Matthew 11:28–30*

◦§ REFLECTION ◦

If you and your spouse were to break your day into twenty-four one-hour segments, what percentage of time would be spent getting ready for work, traveling to work, working, driving home, unwinding, eating, going to bed, and sleeping? If you're like most couples, the figure will be very close to 100 percent. It's no wonder that marriages drift apart, marriage counseling is a booming industry, and divorces are at an all-time high. People are too tired to make the effort to spend time learning about, appreciating, and loving their spouses. Give the burden of time management in your marriage to the Lord and ask him to help both of you find rest from the cares of the world in your relationship with each other.

◦§ MEDITATION ◦

Heavenly Father, as we rest in you today, help us learn to be like your Son, Jesus Christ—gentle and humble toward each. ◦

JANUARY 28

Jesus Teaches about the Sabbath
◦§ Matthew 12:1–21 ◦

About that time, Jesus was walking one day through some grainfields with his disciples. It was on the Sabbath, the Jewish day of worship, and his disciples were hungry; so they began breaking off heads of wheat and eating the grain.

²But some Pharisees saw them do it and protested, "Your disciples are breaking the law. They are harvesting on the Sabbath."

³But Jesus said to them, "Haven't you ever read what King David did when he and his friends were hungry? ⁴He went into the Temple and they ate the special bread permitted to the priests alone. That was breaking the law too. ⁵And haven't you ever read in the law of Moses how the priests on duty in the Temple may work on the Sabbath? ⁶And truly, one is here who is greater than the Temple! ⁷But if you had known the meaning of this Scripture verse, 'I want you to be merciful more than I want your offerings,' you would not have condemned those who aren't guilty! ⁸For I, the Messiah, am master even of the Sabbath."

⁹Then he went over to the synagogue, ¹⁰and noticed there a man with a deformed hand. The Phar-isees asked Jesus, "Is it legal to work by healing on the Sabbath day?" (They were, of course, hoping he would say "Yes," so they could arrest him!) ¹¹This was his answer: "If you had just one sheep, and it fell into a well on the Sabbath, would you work to rescue it that day? Of course you would. ¹²And how much more valuable is a person than a sheep! Yes, it is right to do good on the Sabbath." ¹³Then he said to the man, "Stretch out your arm." And as he did, his hand became normal, just like the other one!

¹⁴Then the Pharisees called a meeting to plot Jesus' arrest and death.

¹⁵But he knew what they were planning, and left the synagogue, with many following him. He healed all the sick among them, ¹⁶but he cautioned them against spreading the news about his miracles. ¹⁷This fulfilled the prophecy of Isaiah concerning him:

¹⁸"Look at my Servant.
See my Chosen One.
He is my Beloved, in whom my soul delights.
I will put my Spirit upon him,
And he will judge the nations.

¹⁹He does not fight nor shout;
   He does not raise his voice!
²⁰He does not crush the weak,
   Or quench the smallest hope;
   He will end all conflict with his final victory,
²¹And his name shall be the hope
   Of all the world."

The Rock of Stumbling
⋅§ Romans 9:27–33 §⋅

Isaiah the prophet cried out concerning the Jews that though there would be millions of them, only a small number would ever be saved. ²⁸"For the Lord will execute his sentence upon the earth, quickly ending his dealings, justly cutting them short."

²⁹And Isaiah says in another place that except for God's mercy all the Jews would be destroyed—all of them—just as everyone in the cities of Sodom and Gomorrah perished.

³⁰Well then, what shall we say about these things? Just this, that God has given the Gentiles the opportunity to be acquitted by faith, even though they had not been really seeking God. ³¹But the Jews, who tried so hard to get right with God by keeping his laws, never succeeded. ³²Why not? Because they were trying to be saved by keeping the law and being good instead of by depending on faith. They have stumbled over the great stumbling stone. ³³God warned them of this in the Scriptures when he said, "I have put a Rock in the path of the Jews, and many will stumble over him (Jesus). Those who believe in him will never be disappointed."

Proverbs for Today
⋅§ 5:22–23 §⋅

The wicked man is doomed by his own sins; they are ropes that catch and hold him. He shall die because he will not listen to the truth; he has let himself be led away into incredible folly.

⋅ KEY VERSE ⋅

The wicked man is doomed by his own sins; they are ropes that catch and hold him.—*Proverbs 5:22*

⋅ REFLECTION ⋅

Whom do you blame in your marriage when something goes wrong? Is it your mother-in-law? Your spouse? Your children? The "inner child" your dysfunctional parents created against your will? When you compare what Scripture says with the comments, books, and articles offered by psychologists, marriage counselors, and talk show hosts, you discover entirely different perspectives. While popular opinion believes that people are not guilty for the things they do—that they are entirely the work of those who unfairly influence them—Scripture declares that individuals alone are responsible and are accountable for their sins. Have you accused your marriage partner of causing you to stumble morally or influencing you to do something you know is wrong? You alone are responsible for your moral failures. Ask God to forgive you of your sins and turn to him as the sole source of moral guidance in your marriage.

⋅ MEDITATION ⋅

Heavenly Father, forgive us of our sins and help us to not build destructive habits in our marriage that will hinder our relationship with you. §⋅

JANUARY 29 _____

The Kingdom of God Has Come with Power

Then a demon-possessed man—he was both blind and unable to talk—was brought to Jesus, and Jesus healed him so that he could both speak and see. ²³The crowd was amazed. "Maybe Jesus is the Messiah!" they exclaimed.

²⁴But when the Pharisees heard about the miracle

they said, "He can cast out demons because he is Satan, king of devils."

²⁵Jesus knew their thoughts and replied, "A divided kingdom ends in ruin. A city or home divided against itself cannot stand. ²⁶And if Satan is casting out Satan, he is fighting himself, and destroying his own kingdom. ²⁷And if, as you claim, I am casting out demons by invoking the powers of Satan, then what power do your own people use when they cast them out? Let them answer your accusation! ²⁸But if I am casting out demons by the Spirit of God, then the Kingdom of God has arrived among you. ²⁹One cannot rob Satan's kingdom without first binding Satan. Only then can his demons be cast out! ³⁰Anyone who isn't helping me is harming me.

³¹,³²"Even blasphemy against me or any other sin, can be forgiven—all except one: speaking against the Holy Spirit shall never be forgiven, either in this world or in the world to come.

³³"A tree is identified by its fruit. A tree from a select variety produces good fruit; poor varieties don't. ³⁴You brood of snakes! How could evil men like you speak what is good and right? For a man's heart determines his speech. ³⁵A good man's speech reveals the rich treasures within him. An evil-hearted man is filled with venom, and his speech reveals it. ³⁶And I tell you this, that you must give account on Judgment Day for every idle word you speak. ³⁷Your words now reflect your fate then: either you will be justified by them or you will be condemned."

We Are Reconciled to God through Faith in Christ
⋅§ Romans 10:1–12 §⋅

Dear brothers, the longing of my heart and my prayer is that the Jewish people might be saved. ²I know what enthusiasm they have for the honor of God, but it is misdirected zeal. ³For they don't understand that Christ has died to make them right with God. Instead they are trying to make themselves good enough to gain God's favor by keeping the Jewish laws and customs, but that is not God's way of salvation. ⁴They don't understand that Christ gives to those who trust in him everything they are trying to get by keeping his laws. He ends all of that.

⁵For Moses wrote that if a person could be perfectly good and hold out against temptation all his life and never sin once, only then could he be pardoned and saved. ⁶But the salvation that comes through faith says, "You don't need to search the heavens to find Christ and bring him down to help you," and, ⁷"You don't need to go among the dead to bring Christ back to life again."

⁸For salvation that comes from trusting Christ—which is what we preach—is already within easy reach of each of us; in fact, it is as near as our own hearts and mouths. ⁹For if you tell others with your own mouth that Jesus Christ is your Lord, and believe in your own heart that God has raised him from the dead, you will be saved. ¹⁰For it is by believing in his heart that a man becomes right with God; and with his mouth he tells others of his faith, confirming his salvation.

¹¹For the Scriptures tell us that no one who believes in Christ will ever be disappointed. ¹²Jew and Gentile are the same in this respect: they all have the same Lord who generously gives his riches to all those who ask him for them.

Proverbs for Today
⋅§ 6:1–5 §⋅

Son, if you endorse a note for someone you hardly know, guaranteeing his debt, you are in serious trouble. You may have trapped yourself by your agreement. Quick! Get out of it if you possibly can! Swallow your pride; don't let embarrassment stand in the way. Go and beg to have your name erased. Don't put it off. Do it now. Don't rest until you do. If you can get out of this trap you have saved yourself like a deer that escapes from a hunter, or a bird from the net.

☙ KEY VERSE ☙

Jesus knew their thoughts and replied, "A divided kingdom ends in ruin. A city or home divided against itself cannot stand."—*Matthew 12:25*

If you've ever done yard work, you know that it's a lot easier to break one stick over your leg than it is two. This is true of human relationships as well. Whether it's a sports team, a company, a city, or a nation, the more harmony that exists among the individual members that make up the group, the more they are able to accomplish and the stronger they are when faced with adversity.

This is especially true in a marriage. When a couple works together in loving support of one another, nothing can separate them. But when a couple works against each other—when they complain to their friends about their spouse or continually point out each other's faults—they will soon be broken apart as easily as a single twig. Become your partner's best friend and ally. Together you will find joy in each other and you will be able to accomplish great things for the undivided Kingdom of God.

Heavenly Father, help us to live together in complete harmony and to dedicate our marriage to be loving and nurturing lifetime partners for one another. ❧

JANUARY 30

The Sign of Jonah the Prophet
⊸§ Matthew 12:38–50 §⊷

One day some of the Jewish leaders, including some Pharisees, came to Jesus asking him to show them a miracle.

[39,40]But Jesus replied, "Only an evil, faithless nation would ask for further proof; and none will be given except what happened to Jonah the prophet! For as Jonah was in the great fish for three days and three nights, so I, the Messiah, shall be in the heart of the earth three days and three nights. [41]The men of Nineveh shall arise against this nation at the judgment and condemn you. For when Jonah preached to them, they repented and turned to God from all their evil ways. And now a greater than Jonah is here—and you refuse to believe him. [42]The Queen of Sheba shall rise against this nation in the judgment, and condemn it; for she came from a distant land to hear the wisdom of Solomon; and now a greater than Solomon is here—and you refuse to believe him.

[43,44,45]"This evil nation is like a man possessed by a demon. For if the demon leaves, it goes into the deserts for a while, seeking rest but finding none. Then it says, 'I will return to the man I came from.' So it returns and finds the man's heart clean but empty! Then the demon finds seven other spirits more evil than itself, and all enter the man and live in him. And so he is worse off than before."

[46,47]As Jesus was speaking in a crowded house his mother and brothers were outside, wanting to talk with him. When someone told him they were there, [48]he remarked, "Who is my mother? Who are my brothers?" [49]He pointed to his disciples. "Look!" he said, "these are my mother and brothers." [50]Then he added, "Anyone who obeys my Father in heaven is my brother, sister and mother!"

All Who Believe the Good News Will Be Saved
⊸§ Romans 10:13–21 §⊷

Anyone who calls upon the name of the Lord will be saved.

[14]But how shall they ask him to save them unless they believe in him? And how can they believe in him if they have never heard about him? And how can they hear about him unless someone tells them? [15]And how will anyone go and tell them unless someone sends him? That is what the Scriptures are talking about when they say, "How beautiful are the feet of those who preach the Gospel of peace with God and bring glad tidings of good things." In other words, how welcome are those who come preaching God's Good News!

[16]But not everyone who hears the Good News has welcomed it, for Isaiah the prophet said, "Lord, who has believed me when I told them?" [17]Yet faith comes from listening to this Good News—the Good News about Christ.

[18]But what about the Jews? Have they heard God's Word? Yes, for it has gone wherever they are; the Good News has been told to the ends of the earth. [19]And did they understand [that God would give his salvation to others if they refused to take it]? Yes, for even back in the time of Moses, God had said that he would make his people jealous and try to wake them up by giving his salvation to the foolish heathen nations. [20]And later on Isaiah said boldly that God would be found by people who weren't even looking for him. [21]In the meantime, he keeps on reaching out his hands to the Jews, but they keep arguing and refusing to come.

Proverbs for Today
§ 6:6–11 §

Take a lesson from the ants, you lazy fellow. Learn from their ways and be wise! For though they have no king to make them work, yet they labor hard all summer, gathering food for the winter. But you—all you do is sleep. When will you wake up? "Let me sleep a little longer!" Sure, just a little more! And as you sleep, poverty creeps upon you like a robber and destroys you; want attacks you in full armor.

KEY VERSE
And how will anyone go and tell them unless someone sends him? That is what the Scriptures are talking about when they say, "How beautiful are the feet of those who preach the Gospel of peace with God and bring glad tidings of good things." In other words, how welcome are those who come preaching God's Good News!—*Romans 10:15*

REFLECTION

In addition to describing the relationship God wants to have with us and specific rules for holy living, Scripture is also filled with the most exquisite word images found in literature. Thanks to Madison Avenue, when people talk about what lies beneath their ankles they usually refer to suede leather, air pumps, steel reinforced toes, Velcro, high heels, or designer labels. Feet have become a mere afterthought to the materials designed to protect them. Yet this Scripture weaves together two images that make shoe commercials frivolous by comparison—the miracle of the human body and the glory of God's message of salvation As a couple, allow your feet to be more than a tool for keeping your loafers stretched and flexible. Let them be vehicles for bringing the Good News of Christ to others.

MEDITATION

Heavenly Father, we submit our entire bodies to your service. Use our hands to comfort those in distress, our mouths to preach your Word, and our feet to carry us forth into the world as we are guided by your Holy Spirit. §

JANUARY 31

The Parable of the Soils
§ Matthew 13:1–23 §

Later that same day, Jesus left the house and went down to the shore, [2,3]where an immense crowd soon gathered. He got into a boat and taught from it while the people listened on the beach. He used many illustrations such as this one in his sermon:

"A farmer was sowing grain in his fields. [4]As he scattered the seed across the ground, some fell beside a path, and the birds came and ate it. [5]And some fell on rocky soil where there was little depth of earth; the plants sprang up quickly enough in the shallow soil, [6]but the hot sun soon scorched them and they withered and died, for they had so little root. [7]Other seeds fell among thorns, and the thorns choked out the tender blades. [8]But some fell on good soil, and produced a crop that was thirty, sixty, and even a hundred times as much as he had planted. [9]If you have ears, listen!"

[10]His disciples came and asked him, "Why do you always use these hard-to-understand illustrations?"

[11]Then he explained to them that only they were permitted to understand about the Kingdom of Heaven, and others were not.

[12,13]"For to him who has will more be given," he told them, "and he will have great plenty; but from him who has not, even the little he has will be taken away. That is why I use these illustrations, so people will hear and see but not understand.

[14]"This fulfills the prophecy of Isaiah:

'They hear, but don't understand; they look, but don't see! [15]For their hearts are fat and heavy, and their ears are dull, and they have closed their eyes in sleep, [16]so they won't see and hear and understand and turn to God again, and let me heal them.'

But blessed are your eyes, for they see; and your ears, for they hear. [17]Many a prophet and godly man has longed to see what you have seen, and hear what you have heard, but couldn't.

[18]"Now here is the explanation of the story I told about the farmer planting grain: [19]The hard path where some of the seeds fell represents the heart of a person who hears the Good News about the Kingdom and doesn't understand it; then Satan comes and snatches away the seeds from his heart. [20]The shallow, rocky soil represents the heart of a man who hears the message and receives it with real joy, [21]but he doesn't have much depth in his life, and the seeds don't root very deeply, and after a while when trouble comes, or persecution begins because of his beliefs, his enthusiasm fades, and he drops out. [22]The ground covered with thistles represents a man who hears the message, but the cares of this life and his longing for money choke out God's Word, and he does less and less for God. [23]The good ground represents the heart of a man

who listens to the message and understands it and goes out and brings thirty, sixty, or even a hundred others into the Kingdom."

God Has Not Rejected the Jews
৵§ Romans 11:1-6 ৡৰ

I ask then, has God rejected and deserted his people the Jews? Oh no, not at all. Remember that I myself am a Jew, a descendant of Abraham and a member of Benjamin's family.

[2,3]No, God has not discarded his own people whom he chose from the very beginning. Do you remember what the Scriptures say about this? Elijah the prophet was complaining to God about the Jews, telling God how they had killed the prophets and torn down God's altars; Elijah claimed that he was the only one left in all the land who still loved God, and now they were trying to kill him too.

[4]And do you remember how God replied? God said, "No, you are not the only one left. I have seven thousand others besides you who still love me and have not bowed down to idols!"

[5]It is the same today. Not all the Jews have turned away from God; there are a few being saved as a result of God's kindness in choosing them. [6]And if it is by God's kindness, then it is not by their being good enough. For in that case the free gift would no longer be free—it isn't free when it is earned.

Proverbs for Today
৵§ 6:12-15 ৡৰ

Let me describe for you a worthless and a wicked man; first, he is a constant liar; he signals his true intentions to his friends with eyes and feet and fingers. He is always thinking up new schemes to swindle people. He stirs up trouble everywhere. But he will be destroyed suddenly, broken beyond hope of healing.

———————— ৵ KEY VERSE ৡ ————————

The shallow, rocky soil represents the heart of a man who hears the message and receives it with real joy, but he doesn't have much depth in his life, and the seeds don't root very deeply, and after a while when trouble comes, or persecution begins because of his beliefs, his enthusiasm fades, and he drops out.—*Matthew 13:20–21*

❧ REFLECTION ❧

Paper. Tin. Diamond. Silver. Gold. We use different symbols to represent the number of years a couple has shared their lives together in holy matrimony. One symbol we don't use is the earth beneath our feet. In fact, if you compared someone's marriage to common dirt, the chances are quite good that your name will be mud from then on as far as they're concerned. Still, the parable of the soils that Christ used to describe the reactions of different people to his Word can also be applied to a married couple. Most marriages begin with great enthusiasm and joy. But, while some become stronger in the face of adversities and challenges, others weaken and die. Whether you will be celebrating your first or your fifty-first anniversary this year, make sure you secure the roots of your marriage each day by demonstrating through words and actions the love you feel for your partner.

❧ MEDITATION ❧

Heavenly Father, bind our hearts together in love so that the roots of our marriage will be deep and lasting. ❧

FEBRUARY 1

Illustrations of the Kingdom of Heaven
❧ Matthew 13:24–35 ❧

Here is another illustration Jesus used: "The Kingdom of Heaven is like a farmer sowing good seed in his field; [25]but one night as he slept, his enemy came and sowed thistles among the wheat. [26]When the crop began to grow, the thistles grew too.

[27]"The farmer's men came and told him, 'Sir, the field where you planted that choice seed is full of thistles!'

[28]"'An enemy has done it,' he exclaimed.

"'Shall we pull out the thistles?' they asked.

[29]"'No,' he replied. 'You'll hurt the wheat if you do. [30]Let both grow together until the harvest, and I will tell the reapers to sort out the thistles and burn them, and put the wheat in the barn.'"

[31,32]Here is another of his illustrations: "The Kingdom of Heaven is like a tiny mustard seed planted in a field. It is the smallest of all seeds, but becomes the largest of plants, and grows into a tree where birds can come and find shelter."

[33]He also used this example:

"The Kingdom of Heaven can be compared to a woman making bread. She takes a measure of flour and mixes in the yeast until it permeates every part of the dough."

[34,35]Jesus constantly used these illustrations when speaking to the crowds. In fact, because the prophets said that he would use so many, he never spoke to them without at least one illustration. For it had been prophesied, "I will talk in parables; I will explain mysteries hidden since the beginning of time."

A Stumbling Block to Jews
❧ Romans 11:7–12 ❧

So this is the situation: Most of the Jews have not found the favor of God they are looking for. A few have—the ones God has picked out—but the eyes of the others have been blinded. [8]This is what our Scriptures refer to when they say that God has put them to sleep, shutting their eyes and ears so that they do not understand what we are talking about when we tell them of Christ. And so it is to this very day.

[9]King David spoke of this same thing when he said, "Let their good food and other blessings trap them into thinking all is well between themselves and God. Let these good things boomerang on them and fall back upon their heads to justly crush them. [10]Let their eyes be dim," he said, "so that they cannot see, and let them walk bent-backed forever with a heavy load."

[11]Does this mean that God has rejected his Jewish people forever? Of course not! His purpose was to make his salvation available to the Gentiles, and then the Jews would be jealous and begin to want God's salvation for themselves. [12]Now if the whole world became rich as a result of God's offer of salvation, when the Jews stumbled over it and turned it down, think how much greater a blessing the world will share in later on when the Jews, too, come to Christ.

Proverbs for Today
<§ 6:16–19 §>

For there are six things the Lord hates—no, seven: haughtiness, lying, murdering, plotting evil, eagerness to do wrong, a false witness, sowing discord among brothers.

————————⋅ KEY VERSE ⋅————————

Here is another of his illustrations: "The Kingdom of Heaven is like a tiny mustard seed planted in a field. It is the smallest of all seeds but becomes the largest of plants, and grows into a tree where birds can come and find shelter."—*Matthew 13:31–32*

————————⋅ REFLECTION ⋅————————

Everyone has a specific concept of what their ideal house would look like. Some people dream of a stately mansion with majestic pillars and a large wooden door that opens to reveal tastefully decorated rooms and a beautiful winding staircase. Others long for a rustic cedar lodge with a huge stone fireplace and hardwood floors.

Regardless of whether you currently live in a small cottage or a two-bedroom apartment, be content with what you have and where you live. If you fill your home with love, it will be a sanctuary that meets your every need and where friends and relatives will long to visit.

————————⋅ MEDITATION ⋅————————

Heavenly Father, help us to make our house a home where we find peace and contentment and where your Word is proclaimed to others. §>

FEBRUARY 2 ————————————————

Jesus Explains the Parable
of the Thistles and Wheat
<§ Matthew 13:36–43 §>

Then, leaving the crowds outside, Jesus went into the house. His disciples asked him to explain to them the illustration of the thistles and the wheat.

[37]"All right," he said, "I am the farmer who sows the choice seed. [38]The field is the world, and the seed represents the people of the Kingdom; the thistles are the people belonging to Satan. [39]The enemy who sowed the thistles among the wheat is the devil; the harvest is the end of the world, and the reapers are the angels.

[40]"Just as in this story the thistles are separated and burned, so shall it be at the end of the world: [41]I will send my angels and they will separate out of the Kingdom every temptation and all who are evil, [42]and throw them into the furnace and burn them. There shall be weeping and gnashing of teeth. [43]Then the godly shall shine as the sun in their Father's Kingdom. Let those with ears, listen!

God Has Grafted the Gentiles
into His Family Tree
<§ Romans 11:13–21 §>

As you know, God has appointed me as a special messenger to you Gentiles. I lay great stress on this and remind the Jews about it as often as I can, [14]so that if possible I can make them want what you Gentiles have and in that way save some of them. [15]And how wonderful it will be when they become Christians! When God turned away from them it meant that he turned to the rest of the world to offer his salvation; and now it is even more wonderful when the Jews come to Christ. It will be like dead people coming back to life. ¹⁶And since Abraham and the prophets are God's people, their children will be too. For if the roots of the tree are holy, the branches will be too.

¹⁷But some of these branches from Abraham's tree, some of the Jews, have been broken off. And you Gentiles who were branches from, we might say, a wild olive tree, were grafted in. So now you, too, receive the blessing God has promised Abraham and his children, sharing in God's rich nourishment of his own special olive tree.

¹⁸But you must be careful not to brag about being put in to replace the branches that were broken off. Remember that you are important only because you are now a part of God's tree; you are just a branch, not a root.

¹⁹"Well," you may be saying, "those branches were broken off to make room for me so I must be pretty good."

²⁰Watch out! Remember that those branches, the Jews, were broken off because they didn't believe God, and you are there only because you do. Do not be proud; be humble and grateful—and careful. ²¹For if God did not spare the branches he put there in the first place, he won't spare you either.

Proverbs for Today
◄§ 6:20–26 §►

Young man, obey your father and your mother. Take to heart all of their advice; keep in mind everything they tell you. Every day and all night long their counsel will lead you and save you from harm; when you wake up in the morning, let their instructions guide you into the new day. For their advice is a beam of light directed into the dark corners of your mind to warn you of danger and to give you a good life. Their counsel will keep you far away from prostitutes with all their flatteries, and unfaithful wives of other men. Don't lust for their beauty. Don't let their coyness seduce you. For a prostitute will bring a man to poverty, and an adulteress may cost him his very life.

◄ KEY VERSE ◈

For a prostitute will bring a man to poverty, and an adulteress may cost him his very life.—*Proverbs 6:26*

◄ REFLECTION ◈

In his relentless battle against the human soul, Satan tries to destroy us by perverting our natural desires. Some people are tempted by material possessions; others by their appetite for food. Unfortunately, the Devil uses one of the most beautiful gifts God has given us—our sexuality—to ruin many marriage relationships. Don't allow him to pervert your need for intimacy. Flee from situations that will compromise your marriage vows, and pray for God's protection from temptation.

◄ MEDITATION ◈

Heavenly Father, we thank you for creating us as sexual beings. We pray that you will remove any impure thoughts we have and place in our hearts a desire only for each other. §►

FEBRUARY 3

Illustrations of the Kingdom of Heaven
◄§ Matthew 13:44–58 §►

"The Kingdom of Heaven is like a treasure a man discovered in a field. In his excitement, he sold everything he owned to get enough money to buy the field—and get the treasure, too!

⁴⁵"Again, the Kingdom of Heaven is like a pearl merchant on the lookout for choice pearls. ⁴⁶He discovered a real bargain—a pearl of great value—and sold everything he owned to purchase it!

⁴⁷,⁴⁸"Again, the Kingdom of Heaven can be illustrated by a fisherman—he casts a net into the water and gathers in fish of every kind, valuable and worthless. When the net is full, he drags it up onto the beach and sits down and sorts out the edible ones into crates and throws the others away. ⁴⁹That is the way it will be at the end of the world—the

angels will come and separate the wicked people from the godly, ⁵⁰casting the wicked into the fire; there shall be weeping and gnashing of teeth. ⁵¹Do you understand?"

"Yes," they said, "we do."

⁵²Then he added, "Those experts in Jewish law who are now my disciples have double treasures—from the Old Testament as well as from the New!"

⁵³,⁵⁴When Jesus had finished giving these illustrations, he returned to his home town, Nazareth in Galilee, and taught there in the synagogue and astonished everyone with his wisdom and his miracles.

⁵⁵"How is this possible?" the people exclaimed. "He's just a carpenter's son, and we know Mary his mother and his brothers—James, Joseph, Simon, and Judas. ⁵⁶And his sisters—they all live here. How can he be so great?" ⁵⁷And they became angry with him!

Then Jesus told them, "A prophet is honored everywhere except in his own country, and among his own people!" ⁵⁸And so he did only a few great miracles there, because of their unbelief.

The Kindness and Severity of God
◄§ Romans 11:22–27 §►

Notice how God is both kind and severe. He is very hard on those who disobey, but very good to you if you continue to love and trust him. But if you don't, you too will be cut off. ²³On the other hand, if the Jews leave their unbelief behind them and come back to God, God will graft them back into the tree again. He has the power to do it.

²⁴For if God was willing to take you who were so far away from him—being part of a wild olive tree—and graft you into his own good tree—a very unusual thing to do—don't you see that he will be far more ready to put the Jews back again, who were there in the first place?

²⁵I want you to know about this truth from God, dear brothers, so that you will not feel proud and start bragging. Yes, it is true that some of the Jews have set themselves against the Gospel now, but this will last only until all of you Gentiles have come to Christ—those of you who will. ²⁶And then all Israel will be saved.

Do you remember what the prophets said about this? "There shall come out of Zion a Deliverer, and he shall turn the Jews from all ungodliness. ²⁷At that time I will take away their sins, just as I promised."

Proverbs for Today
◄§ 6:27–35 §►

Can a man hold fire against his chest and not be burned? Can he walk on hot coals and not blister his feet? So it is with the man who commits adultery with another's wife. He shall not go unpunished for this sin. Excuses might even be found for a thief, if he steals when he is starving! But even so, he is fined seven times as much as he stole, though it may mean selling everything in his house to pay it back. But the man who commits adultery is an utter fool, for he destroys his own soul. Wounds and constant disgrace are his lot, for the woman's husband will be furious in his jealousy, and he will have no mercy on you in his day of vengeance. You won't be able to buy him off no matter what you offer.

────────◄ **KEY VERSE** ►────────

The Kingdom of Heaven is like a treasure a man discovered in a field. In his excitement, he sold everything he owned to get enough money to buy the field—and get the treasure, too!—*Matthew 13:44*

────────◄ **REFLECTION** ►────────

Have you ever been swept up in the momentum created by a hot new fad? One day you're a normal, sane person who goes to work, putters in the garden, and shops for groceries. The next day you can't stop talking or thinking about a new board game, or a hit song, or the latest ice cream flavor. The thing about fads is that their meteoric rise in popularity is exceeded only by their speedy fall to the end of a discount table. Fads, as their name suggests, are meaningless. Their only long-term benefit is to the company that markets them.

Actually, in the scope of eternity, everything is faddish. Everything, that is, except the kingdom of heaven. Are you placing emphasis in your marriage on the things that really matter? Do you spend more time finding new places for knick-knacks than you do reading God's Word and praying together? Evaluate your priorities as a couple and begin building a home where eternal things matter most.

❧ MEDITATION ❧

Heavenly Father, place in our hearts a desire for things that are truly meaningful. Help us to keep our thoughts focused on eternity and on your Kingdom. ❧

FEBRUARY 4

King Herod Beheads John the Baptist
❧ Matthew 14:1–13 ❧

When King Herod heard about Jesus, [2]he said to his men, "This must be John the Baptist, come back to life again. That is why he can do these miracles." [3]For Herod had arrested John and chained him in prison at the demand of his wife Herodias, his brother Philip's ex-wife, [4]because John had told him it was wrong for him to marry her. [5]He would have killed John but was afraid of a riot, for all the people believed John was a prophet.

[6]But at a birthday party for Herod, Herodias' daughter performed a dance that greatly pleased him, [7]so he vowed to give her anything she wanted. [8]Consequently, at her mother's urging, the girl asked for John the Baptist's head on a tray.

[9]The king was grieved, but because of his oath, and because he didn't want to back down in front of his guests, he issued the necessary orders.

[10]So John was beheaded in the prison, [11]and his head was brought on a tray and given to the girl, who took it to her mother.

[12]Then John's disciples came for his body and buried it, and came to tell Jesus what had happened.

[13]As soon as Jesus heard the news, he went off by himself in a boat to a remote area to be alone. But the crowds saw where he was headed, and followed by land from many villages.

God Will Not Go Back on His Promises
❧ Romans 11:28–36 ❧

Now many of the Jews are enemies of the Gospel. They hate it. But this has been a benefit to you, for it has resulted in God's giving his gifts to you Gentiles. Yet the Jews are still beloved of God because of his promises to Abraham, Isaac, and Jacob. [29]For God's gifts and his call can never be withdrawn; he will never go back on his promises. [30]Once you were rebels against God, but when the Jews refused his gifts God was merciful to you instead. [31]And now the Jews are the rebels, but some day they, too, will share in God's mercy upon you. [32]For God has given them all up to sin so that he could have mercy upon all alike.

[33]Oh, what a wonderful God we have! How great are his wisdom and knowledge and riches! How impossible it is for us to understand his decisions and his methods! [34]For who among us can know the mind of the Lord? Who knows enough to be his counselor and guide? [35]And who could ever offer to the Lord enough to induce him to act? [36]For everything comes from God alone. Everything lives by his power, and everything is for his glory. To him be glory evermore.

Proverbs for Today
❧ 7:1–5 ❧

Follow my advice, my son; always keep it in mind and stick to it. Obey me and live! Guard my words as your most precious possession. Write them down, and also keep them deep within your heart. Love wisdom like a sweetheart; make her a beloved member of your family. Let her hold you back from affairs with other women—from listening to their flattery.

◦ KEY VERSE ◦

For God's gifts and his call can never be withdrawn; he will never go back on his promises.—*Romans 11:29*

◦ REFLECTION ◦

Do you or your spouse have a unique gift or talent? Can one of you write beautiful letters that your families love to read? Is your spouse a great storyteller whose tales bring a room full of people together in rapt attention? Or are you both musically inclined and frequently asked to sing during the Sunday morning worship service at your church? God gives each of us special abilities that can be used to further his Kingdom and reveal his glory. Encourage one another and seek God's wisdom for how you can use your gifts to serve.

◦ MEDITATION ◦

Heavenly Father, thank you for making each of us unique and for giving us special abilities to share the Good News of salvation. Help us to see how we can best serve your Kingdom. ❧

FEBRUARY 5

The Feeding of the Five Thousand
◦§ Matthew 14:14–21 §◦

So when Jesus came out of the wilderness, a vast crowd was waiting for him and he pitied them and healed their sick.

[15]That evening the disciples came to him and said, "It is already past time for supper, and there is nothing to eat here in the desert; send the crowds away so they can go to the villages and buy some food."

[16]But Jesus replied, "That isn't necessary—you feed them!"

[17]"What!" they exclaimed. "We have exactly five small loaves of bread and two fish!"

[18]"Bring them here," he said.

[19]Then he told the people to sit down on the grass; and he took the five loaves and two fish, looked up into the sky and asked God's blessing on the meal, then broke the loaves apart and gave them to the disciples to place before the people. [20]And everyone ate until full! And when the scraps were picked up afterwards, there were twelve basketfuls left over! [21](About 5,000 men were in the crowd that day, besides all the women and children.)

A Living Sacrifice to God
◦§ Romans 12:1–5 §◦

And so, dear brothers, I plead with you to give your bodies to God. Let them be a living sacrifice, holy—the kind he can accept. When you think of what he has done for you, is this too much to ask? [2]Don't copy the behavior and customs of this world, but be a new and different person with a fresh newness in all you do and think. Then you will learn from your own experience how his ways will really satisfy you.

[3]As God's messenger I give each of you God's warning: Be honest in your estimate of yourselves, measuring your value by how much faith God has given you. [4,5]Just as there are many parts to our bodies, so it is with Christ's body. We are all parts of it, and it takes every one of us to make it complete, for we each have different work to do. So we belong to each other, and each needs all the others.

Proverbs for Today
◦§ 7:6–23 §◦

I was looking out the window of my house one day, and saw a simple-minded lad, a young man lacking common sense, walking at twilight down the street to the house of this wayward girl, a prostitute. She approached him, saucy and pert, and dressed seductively. She was the brash, coarse type, seen often in the streets and markets, soliciting at every corner for men to be her lovers. She put her arms around him and kissed him, and with a saucy look she said, "I was just coming to look for you and here you are! Come home with me and I'll fix you a wonderful dinner, and after that—well, my bed is spread with lovely, colored sheets of finest linen imported from Egypt, perfumed with myrrh, aloes and cinnamon. Come on, let's take our fill of love until morning, for my husband is away on a long trip. He has taken a wallet full of money with him, and won't return for several days." So she seduced him with her pretty speech, her coaxing and her wheedling, until he yielded to her. He couldn't resist her flattery. He followed her as an ox going to the butcher, or as a stag that is trapped, waiting to be killed with an arrow through its heart. He was as a bird flying into a snare, not knowing the fate awaiting it there.

────────────⊸ KEY VERSE ⊷────────────

And so, dear brothers, I plead with you to give your bodies to God. Let them be a living sacrifice, holy—the kind he can accept. When you think of what he has done for you, is this too much to ask? Don't copy the behavior and customs of this world, but be a new and different person with a fresh newness in all you do and think. Then you will learn from your own experience how his ways will really satisfy you.—*Romans 12:1–2*

────────────⊸ REFLECTION ⊷────────────

The human body is a marvelous instrument. Despite the incredible scientific advances that have been made in this century, researchers still have not unlocked all the secrets of the tiny cell—let alone explain the infinite complexities of the brain. It's no wonder God wants us to treat our bodies as holy and blameless before him. As our Creator, he knows just how special we are. Encourage one another to think on things that are pure and to engage in activities that will be pleasing to him.

────────────⊸ MEDITATION ⊷────────────

Heavenly Father, we offer our bodies as living sacrifices to you. Help us to focus our hearts and minds on those things that are pleasing in your sight. ❧

FEBRUARY 6

Jesus Walks on the Water
⊸§ Matthew 14:22–36 §⊷

Immediately after this, Jesus told his disciples to get into their boat and cross to the other side of the lake while he stayed to get the people started home. [23,24]Then afterwards he went up into the hills to pray. Night fell, and out on the lake the disciples were in trouble. For the wind had risen and they were fighting heavy seas.

[25]About four o'clock in the morning Jesus came to them, walking on the water! [26]They screamed in terror, for they thought he was a ghost.

[27]But Jesus immediately spoke to them, reassuring them. "Don't be afraid!" he said.

[28]Then Peter called to him: "Sir, if it is really you, tell me to come over to you, walking on the water."

[29]"All right," the Lord said, "come along!"

So Peter went over the side of the boat and walked on the water toward Jesus. [30]But when he looked around at the high waves, he was terrified and began to sink. "Save me, Lord!" he shouted.

[31]Instantly Jesus reached out his hand and rescued him. "O man of little faith," Jesus said. "Why did you doubt me?" [32]And when they had climbed back into the boat, the wind stopped.

[33]The others sat there, awestruck. "You really are the Son of God!" they exclaimed.

34They landed at Gennesaret. 35The news of their arrival spread quickly throughout the city, and soon people were rushing around, telling everyone to bring in their sick to be healed. 36The sick begged him to let them touch even the tassel of his robe, and all who did were healed.

Gifts Are Given to Serve Others
Romans 12:6–13

God has given each of us the ability to do certain things well. So if God has given you the ability to prophesy, then prophesy whenever you can—as often as your faith is strong enough to receive a message from God. 7If your gift is that of serving others, serve them well. If you are a teacher, do a good job of teaching. 8If you are a preacher, see to it that your sermons are strong and helpful. If God has given you money, be generous in helping others with it. If God has given you administrative ability and put you in charge of the work of others, take the responsibility seriously. Those who offer comfort to the sorrowing should do so with Christian cheer.

9Don't just pretend that you love others: really love them. Hate what is wrong. Stand on the side of the good. 10Love each other with brotherly affection and take delight in honoring each other. 11Never be lazy in your work but serve the Lord enthusiastically.

12Be glad for all God is planning for you. Be patient in trouble, and prayerful always. 13When God's children are in need, you be the one to help them out. And get into the habit of inviting guests home for dinner or, if they need lodging, for the night.

Proverbs for Today
7:24–27

Listen to me, young men, and not only listen but obey; don't let your desires get out of hand; don't let yourself think about her. Don't go near her; stay away from where she walks, lest she tempt you and seduce you. For she has been the ruin of multitudes—a vast host of men have been her victims. If you want to find the road to hell, look for her house.

KEY VERSE

God has given each of us the ability to do certain things well. So if God has given you the ability to prophesy, then prophesy whenever you can—as often as your faith is strong enough to receive a message from God.—*Romans 12:6*

REFLECTION

If you're married to someone who is involved in full- or part-time ministry—whether it's serving as a pastor, worship leader, or Sunday school teacher—you know the depth of his or her commitment to the church and the amount of time spent each week working for the kingdom. It's your duty to encourage and help as much as possible. If she is involved in a visitation ministry, go with her whenever you can. If he's a youth pastor, then volunteer to be a driver and chaperon during a retreat. Intercede in prayer on a daily basis. Not only will you be supportive, you will share in each other's lives and strengthen your marriage.

MEDITATION

Heavenly Father, thank you for the responsibilities you have given us. We pray for everyone who serves your Kingdom and pray that their ministry will encourage others to follow you.

Righteousness Is a Matter of the Heart
‹§ Matthew 15:1–20 §›

Some Pharisees and other Jewish leaders now arrived from Jerusalem to interview Jesus.

[2]"Why do your disciples disobey the ancient Jewish traditions?" they demanded. "For they ignore our ritual of ceremonial handwashing before they eat." [3]He replied, "And why do your traditions violate the direct commandments of God? [4]For instance, God's law is 'Honor your father and mother; anyone who reviles his parents must die.' [5,6]But you say, 'Even if your parents are in need, you may give their support money to the church instead.' And so, by your man-made rule, you nullify the direct command of God to honor and care for your parents. [7]You hypocrites! Well did Isaiah prophesy of you, [8]'These people say they honor me, but their hearts are far away. [9]Their worship is worthless, for they teach their man-made laws instead of those from God.'"

[10]Then Jesus called to the crowds and said, "Listen to what I say and try to understand: [11]You aren't made unholy by eating non-kosher food! It is what you *say* and *think* that makes you unclean."

[12]Then the disciples came and told him, "You offended the Pharisees by that remark."

[13,14]Jesus replied, "Every plant not planted by my Father shall be rooted up, so ignore them. They are blind guides leading the blind, and both will fall into a ditch."

[15]Then Peter asked Jesus to explain what he meant when he said that people are not defiled by non-kosher food.

[16]"Don't you understand?" Jesus asked him. [17]"Don't you see that anything you eat passes through the digestive tract and out again? [18]But evil words come from an evil heart, and defile the man who says them. [19]For from the heart come evil thoughts, murder, adultery, fornication, theft, lying and slander. [20]These are what defile; but there is no spiritual defilement from eating without first going through the ritual of ceremonial handwashing!"

Conquer Evil by Doing Good
‹§ Romans 12:14–21 §›

If someone mistreats you because you are a Christian, don't curse him; pray that God will bless him. [15]When others are happy, be happy with them. If they are sad, share their sorrow. [16]Work happily together. Don't try to act big. Don't try to get into the good graces of important people, but enjoy the company of ordinary folks. And don't think you know it all!

[17]Never pay back evil for evil. Do things in such a way that everyone can see you are honest clear through. [18]Don't quarrel with anyone. Be at peace with everyone, just as much as possible.

[19]Dear friends, never avenge yourselves. Leave that to God, for he has said that he will repay those who deserve it. [Don't take the law into your own hands.] [20]Instead, feed your enemy if he is hungry. If he is thirsty give him something to drink and you will be "heaping coals of fire on his head." In other words, he will feel ashamed of himself for what he has done to you. [21]Don't let evil get the upper hand but conquer evil by doing good.

Proverbs for Today
‹§ 8:1–10 §›

Can't you hear the voice of wisdom? She is standing at the city gates and at every fork in the road, and at the door of every house. Listen to what she says: "Listen, men!" she calls. "How foolish and naive you are! Let me give you understanding. O foolish ones, let me show you common sense! Listen to me! For I have important information for you. Everything I say is right and true, for I hate lies and every kind of deception. My advice is wholesome and good. There is nothing of evil in it. My words are plain and clear to anyone with half a mind—if it is only open! My instruction is far more valuable than silver or gold."

‹ KEY VERSE ›

Work happily together. Don't try to act big. Don't try to get into the good graces of important people, but enjoy the company of ordinary folks. And don't think you know it all!—*Romans 12:16*

Jesus gave two commandments concerning attitudes and human relationships that many people—even Christians—regularly ignore. One is not to act important or to impose personal opinions on others. The other is not to ignore anyone who isn't wealthy or in a position of authority. Often the two commandments go hand in hand; disobeying one can lead to disobeying the other.

As a couple, you can have a tremendous ministry to someone society has rejected. Be a friend to the friendless, a comfort to the sick, and an encouragement to anyone who is discouraged and alone. And remember, Christ said that those who are first now will be last in his Kingdom. Someday the people everyone thinks are great will be humbled before him. Don't be one of them.

———— ❧ **MEDITATION** ❧ ————

Heavenly Father, help us to control our pride and our attitudes toward other people. Forgive us when we gravitate toward someone solely because that person is rich and powerful. Keep our perspectives pure and focused on your commandments. ❧

FEBRUARY 8 ————

Jesus Heals a Canaanite Woman's Daughter
❧ Matthew 15:21–28 ❧

Jesus then left that part of the country and walked the fifty miles to Tyre and Sidon.

22A woman from Canaan who was living there came to him, pleading, "Have mercy on me, O Lord, King David's Son! For my daughter has a demon within her, and it torments her constantly."

23But Jesus gave her no reply—not even a word. Then his disciples urged him to send her away. "Tell her to get going," they said, "for she is bothering us with all her begging."

24Then he said to the woman, "I was sent to help the Jews—the lost sheep of Israel—not the Gentiles."

25But she came and worshiped him and pled again, "Sir, help me!"

26"It doesn't seem right to take bread from the children and throw it to the dogs," he said.

27"Yes, it is!" she replied, "for even the puppies beneath the table are permitted to eat the crumbs that fall."

28"Woman," Jesus told her, "your faith is large, and your request is granted." And her daughter was healed right then.

Obedience to the Government
❧ Romans 13:1–7 ❧

Obey the government, for God is the one who has put it there. There is no government anywhere that God has not placed in power. 2So those who refuse to obey the laws of the land are refusing to obey God, and punishment will follow. 3For the policeman does not frighten people who are doing right; but those doing evil will always fear him. So if you don't want to be afraid, keep the laws and you will get along well. 4The policeman is sent by God to help you. But if you are doing something wrong, of course you should be afraid, for he will have you punished. He is sent by God for that very purpose. 5Obey the laws, then, for two reasons: first, to keep from being punished, and second, just because you know you should.

6Pay your taxes too, for these same two reasons. For government workers need to be paid so that they can keep on doing God's work, serving you. 7Pay everyone whatever he ought to have: pay your taxes and import duties gladly, obey those over you, and give honor and respect to all those to whom it is due.

Proverbs for Today
⋘ 8:11–13 ⋙

For the value of wisdom is far above rubies; nothing can be compared with it. Wisdom and good judgment live together, for wisdom knows where to discover knowledge and understanding. If anyone respects and fears God, he will hate evil. For wisdom hates pride, arrogance, corruption and deceit of every kind.

⋘ KEY VERSE ⋙

If anyone respects and fears God, he will hate evil. For wisdom hates pride, arrogance, corruption, and deceit of every kind.—*Proverbs 8:13*

⋘ REFLECTION ⋙

Have you ever had an experience like the following? You pass an old college roommate on the street—someone you haven't seen for years. Neither of you have to be any place in particular for a while so you spend the next hour in a diner drinking coffee and catching up on each other's lives. Before long you realize something has changed about your friend. The kind, gracious person you knew as a teenager has become a bitter and angry adult. She says negative things about mutual acquaintances and boasts of her accomplishments. By the time you part, you wish you hadn't seen her so you could remember her as she was.

Scripture tells us that the only truly good and sinless person who ever lived was Jesus Christ. The righteousness of everyone else is like "filthy rags." It doesn't matter how sweet and generous you are: if your heart is not filled with the presence of the Holy Spirit, disappointments and negative influences will eventually harden your heart and corrupt your attitudes.

As a couple, ask God to be the most important influence in your lives. If you submit yourselves to him, the first thing old friends will notice when you become reacquainted is the dynamic presence of the Holy Spirit and how he has changed you for the better.

⋘ MEDITATION ⋙

Heavenly Father, we want you to be the most significant influence in our marriage. Protect us from negative thoughts and attitudes that will stifle your presence in our lives. ⋙

FEBRUARY 9

The Feeding of the Four Thousand
⋘ Matthew 15:29–39 ⋙

Jesus now returned to the Sea of Galilee, and climbed a hill and sat there. [30]And a vast crowd brought him their lame, blind, maimed, and those who couldn't speak, and many others, and laid them before Jesus, and he healed them all. [31]What a spectacle it was! Those who hadn't been able to say a word before were talking excitedly, and those with missing arms and legs had new ones; the crippled were walking and jumping around, and those who had been blind were gazing about them! The crowds just marveled, and praised the God of Israel.

[32]Then Jesus called his disciples to him and said, "I pity these people—they've been here with me for three days now, and have nothing left to eat; I don't want to send them away hungry or they will faint along the road."

[33]The disciples replied, "And where would we get enough here in the desert for all this mob to eat?"

[34]Jesus asked them, "How much food do you have?" And they replied, "Seven loaves of bread and a few small fish!"

[35]Then Jesus told all of the people to sit down on the ground, [36]and he took the seven loaves and the fish, and gave thanks to God for them, and divided them into pieces, and gave them to the disciples who presented them to the crowd. [37,38]And every-

one ate until full—4,000 men besides the women and children! And afterwards, when the scraps were picked up, there were seven basketfuls left over!

[39]Then Jesus sent the people home and got into the boat and crossed to Magadan.

Loving Others Is a Sure Way to Obey God
Romans 13:8–14

Pay all your debts except the debt of love for others—never finish paying that! For if you love them, you will be obeying all of God's laws, fulfilling all his requirements. [9]If you love your neighbor as much as you love yourself you will not want to harm or cheat him, or kill him or steal from him. And you won't sin with his wife or want what is his, or do anything else the Ten Commandments say is wrong. All ten are wrapped up in this one, to love your neighbor as you love yourself. [10]Love does no wrong to anyone. That's why it fully satisfies all of God's requirements. It is the only law you need.

[11]Another reason for right living is this: you know how late it is; time is running out. Wake up, for the coming of the Lord is nearer now than when we first believed. [12,13]The night is far gone, the day of his return will soon be here. So quit the evil deeds of darkness and put on the armor of right living, as we who live in the daylight should! Be decent and true in everything you do so that all can approve your behavior. Don't spend your time in wild parties and getting drunk or in adultery and lust, or fighting, or jealousy. [14]But ask the Lord Jesus Christ to help you live as you should, and don't make plans to enjoy evil.

Proverbs for Today
8:14–26

"I, Wisdom, give good advice and common sense. Because of my strength, kings reign in power, and rulers make just laws. I love all who love me. Those who search for me shall surely find me. Unending riches, honor, justice and righteousness are mine to distribute. My gifts are better than the purest gold or sterling silver! My paths are those of justice and right. Those who love and follow me are indeed wealthy. I fill their treasuries. The Lord

formed me in the beginning, before he created anything else. From ages past, I am. I existed before the earth began. I lived before the oceans were created, before the springs bubbled forth their waters onto the earth; before the mountains and the hills were made. Yes, I was born before God made the earth and fields, and the first handfuls of soil.

KEY VERSE

What a spectacle it was! Those who hadn't been able to say a word before were talking excitedly, and those with missing arms and legs had new ones; the crippled were walking and jumping around, and those who had been blind were gazing about them! The crowds just marveled, and praised the God of Israel.—*Matthew 15:31*

REFLECTION

Imagine what it must have been like for the people Jesus healed of their physical impairments. Remember that this was a time when physicians couldn't perform surgery on someone with a heart defect. They weren't able to correct a person's eyesight with glasses or contacts. They didn't have vaccines for diseases like polio or chemotherapy for cancer. No wonder the people Jesus touched and made whole rejoiced and praised God. He was their only source of hope.

Today, if it is his will for their lives, God still miraculously cures people of their physical problems. But, more important, he offers to everyone deliverance from the pain and anguish caused by our fallen condition. Turn to him as a couple and pray that he will forgive you of your sins and heal the spiritual brokenness in your lives. When you do, God will indeed perform a miracle and free you from bondage.

MEDITATION

Heavenly Father, we recognize you as the Great Physician and believe that you are able to cure, if it is your will, any sickness or other health problem we are suffering. We also know that your grace is sufficient to heal all of our spiritual wounds and we ask that you will restore us and make us whole.

Beware of the Teachings
of the Pharisees and Sadducees
❧ Matthew 16:1–12 ❧

One day the Pharisees and Sadducees came to test Jesus' claim of being the Messiah by asking him to show them some great demonstrations in the skies. [2,3]He replied, ''You are good at reading the weather signs of the skies—red sky tonight means fair weather tomorrow; red sky in the morning means foul weather all day—but you can't read the obvious signs of the times! [4]This evil, unbelieving nation is asking for some strange sign in the heavens, but no further proof will be given except the miracle that happened to Jonah.'' Then Jesus walked out on them.

[5]Arriving across the lake, the disciples discovered they had forgotten to bring any food.

[6]''Watch out!'' Jesus warned them; ''beware of the yeast of the Pharisees and Sadducees.''

[7]They thought he was saying this because they had forgotten to bring bread.

[8]Jesus knew what they were thinking and told them, ''O men of little faith! Why are you so worried about having no food? [9]Won't you ever understand? Don't you remember at all the 5,000 I fed with five loaves, and the basketfuls left over? [10]Don't you remember the 4,000 I fed, and all that was left? [11]How could you even think I was talking about food? But again I say, 'Beware of the yeast of the Pharisees and Sadducees.' ''

[12]Then at last they understood that by ''yeast'' he meant the *wrong teaching* of the Pharisees and Sadducees.

God Is Master over the
Weak and Strong Believer
❧ Romans 14:1–4 ❧

Give a warm welcome to any brother who wants to join you, even though his faith is weak. Don't criticize him for having different ideas from yours about what is right and wrong. [2]For instance, don't argue with him about whether or not to eat meat that has been offered to idols. You may believe there is no harm in this, but the faith of others is weaker; they think it is wrong, and will go without any meat at all and eat vegetables rather than eat that kind of meat. [3]Those who think it is all right to eat such meat must not look down on those who won't. And if you are one of those who won't, don't find fault with those who do. For God has accepted them to be his children. [4]They are God's servants, not yours. They are responsible to him, not to you. Let him tell them whether they are right or wrong. And God is able to make them do as they should.

Proverbs for Today
❧ 8:27–32 ❧

''I was there when he established the heavens and formed the great springs in the depths of the oceans. I was there when he set the limits of the seas and gave them his instructions not to spread beyond their boundaries. I was there when he made the blueprint for the earth and oceans. I was the craftsman at his side. I was his constant delight, rejoicing always in his presence. And how happy I was with what he created—his wide world and all his family of mankind! And so, young men, listen to me, for how happy are all who follow my instructions.

────── ❧ KEY VERSE ❧ ──────

Jesus knew what they were thinking and told them, ''O men of little faith! Why are you so worried about having no food? Won't you ever understand? Don't you remember at all the five thousand I fed with five loaves, and the basketfuls left over?'' —*Matthew 16:8–9*

────── ❧ REFLECTION ❧ ──────

It's Monday evening. Neither of you get paid until Friday. You have two ice cream sandwiches, a jar of mustard, six grapes, and half a roll of breath mints to eat. Both of your cars need gas and your rent is due the following morning. If you're like most couples, at some point in your marriage you've struggled through a week like this. If you haven't, then don't be too critical of the disciples for their lack of faith. It's hard not to be discouraged when you don't have enough to meet your needs.

Yet, as Jesus said, don't let your anxiety cause you to lose faith. While we can't expect God to help us when we foolishly spend more than we earn on expensive clothes or frivolous entertainment, he will forgive us and help us not make the same mis-

takes again. If your situation is not caused by careless living, then ask God to help you find a new job or a cheaper place to live. Whatever will help you the most, God will provide the answers and meet your needs.

⊸ MEDITATION ⊸

Heavenly Father, help us to maintain our faith in you during difficult times. We know that you are able to meet our every need. Please reveal your plan for resolving our dilemmas. ॐ

FEBRUARY 11

Jesus Predicts His Own Death
⊸§ Matthew 16:13–28 ॐ

When Jesus came to Caesarea Philippi, he asked his disciples, "Who are the people saying I am?"

[14]"Well," they replied, "some say John the Baptist; some, Elijah; some, Jeremiah or one of the other prophets."

[15]Then he asked them, "Who do *you* think I am?"

[16]Simon Peter answered, "The Christ, the Messiah, the Son of the living God."

[17]"God has blessed you, Simon, son of Jonah," Jesus said, "for my Father in heaven has personally revealed this to you—this is not from any human source. [18]You are Peter, a stone; and upon this rock I will build my church; and all the powers of hell shall not prevail against it. [19]And I will give you the keys of the Kingdom of Heaven; whatever doors you lock on earth shall be locked in heaven; and whatever doors you open on earth shall be open in heaven!"

[20]Then he warned the disciples against telling others that he was the Messiah.

[21]From then on Jesus began to speak plainly to his disciples about going to Jerusalem, and what would happen to him there—that he would suffer at the hands of the Jewish leaders, that he would be killed, and that three days later he would be raised to life again.

[22]But Peter took him aside to remonstrate with

him. "Heaven forbid, sir," he said. "This is not going to happen to you!"

[23]Jesus turned on Peter and said, "Get away from me, you Satan! You are a dangerous trap to me. You are thinking merely from a human point of view, and not from God's."

[24]Then Jesus said to the disciples, "If anyone wants to be a follower of mine, let him deny himself and take up his cross and follow me. [25]For anyone who keeps his life for himself shall lose it; and anyone who loses his life for me shall find it again. [26]What profit is there if you gain the whole world— and lose eternal life? What can be compared with the value of eternal life? [27]For I, the Son of Mankind, shall come with my angels in the glory of my Father and judge each person according to his deeds. [28]And some of you standing right here now will certainly live to see me coming in my Kingdom."

Jesus Is Our Lord in Both Life and Death
⊸§ Romans 14:5–9 ॐ

Some think that Christians should observe the Jewish holidays as special days to worship God, but others say it is wrong and foolish to go to all that trouble, for every day alike belongs to God. On questions of this kind everyone must decide for himself. [6]If you have special days for worshiping the Lord, you are trying to honor him; you are doing a good thing. So is the person who eats meat that has been offered to idols; he is thankful to the Lord for it; he is doing right. And the person who won't touch such meat, he, too, is anxious to please the Lord, and is thankful. ⁷We are not our own bosses to live or die as we ourselves might choose. ⁸Living or dying we follow the Lord. Either way we are his. ⁹Christ died and rose again for this very purpose, so that he can be our Lord both while we live and when we die.

Proverbs for Today
◄§ 8:33–36 §►

"Listen to my counsel—oh, don't refuse it—and be wise. Happy is the man who is so anxious to be with me that he watches for me daily at my gates, or waits for me outside my home! For whoever finds me finds life and wins approval from the Lord. But the one who misses me has injured himself irreparably. Those who refuse me show that they love death."

◄ KEY VERSE ◄

We are not our own bosses to live or die as we ourselves might choose.—*Romans 14:7*

◄ REFLECTION ◄

Everyone has someone to whom they must answer in their workplace. Even if you own a company, you are responsible to your employees, a group of shareholders, or to the bank that has loaned you money. Whether or not your supervisor is a pleasant, agreeable person, he or she still expects you to perform your duties to the utmost of your ability. If you fail too often, the chances are very good that you will soon be looking for other employment.

In your personal life it's important that your ultimate authority, or "boss," be the one who created you. As a couple, seek God's guidance on a daily basis. If you make a mistake he won't hold it against you. Unlike those who control your paycheck, he is always willing to forgive you for your shortcomings and welcome you back into his arms. Don't be afraid to confess your sins and turn everything over to him.

◄ MEDITATION ◄

Heavenly Father, we acknowledge you as the Lord of our lives. Guide us in all of our steps and lead us along your path of righteousness. §►

FEBRUARY 12

Jesus Is Transfigured on the Mountain
◄§ Matthew 17:1–13 §►

Six days later Jesus took Peter, James, and his brother John to the top of a high and lonely hill, ²and as they watched, his appearance changed so that his face shone like the sun and his clothing became dazzling white.

³Suddenly Moses and Elijah appeared and were talking with him. ⁴Peter blurted out, "Sir, it's wonderful that we can be here! If you want me to, I'll make three shelters, one for you and one for Moses and one for Elijah."

⁵But even as he said it, a bright cloud came over them, and a voice from the cloud said, *"This* is my beloved Son, and I am wonderfully pleased with him. Obey *him."*

⁶At this the disciples fell face downward to the ground, terribly frightened. ⁷Jesus came over and touched them. "Get up," he said, "don't be afraid."

⁸And when they looked, only Jesus was with them.

⁹As they were going down the mountain, Jesus commanded them not to tell anyone what they had seen until after he had risen from the dead.

¹⁰His disciples asked, "Why do the Jewish leaders insist Elijah must return before the Messiah comes?"

¹¹Jesus replied, "They are right. Elijah must come and set everything in order. ¹²And, in fact, he has already come, but he wasn't recognized, and was badly mistreated by many. And I, the Messiah, shall also suffer at their hands."

[13]Then the disciples realized he was speaking of John the Baptist.

Be Sensitive to Others
Romans 14:10–16

You have no right to criticize your brother or look down on him. Remember, each of us will stand personally before the Judgment Seat of God. [11]For it is written, "As I live," says the Lord, "every knee shall bow to me and every tongue confess to God." [12]Yes, each of us will give an account of himself to God.

[13]So don't criticize each other any more. Try instead to live in such a way that you will never make your brother stumble by letting him see you doing something he thinks is wrong.

[14]As for myself, I am perfectly sure on the authority of the Lord Jesus that there is nothing really wrong with eating meat that has been offered to idols. But if someone believes it is wrong, then he shouldn't do it because for him it is wrong. [15]And if your brother is bothered by what you eat, you are not acting in love if you go ahead and eat it. Don't let your eating ruin someone for whom Christ died. [16]Don't do anything that will cause criticism against yourself even though you know that what you do is right.

Proverbs for Today
9:1–6

Wisdom has built a palace supported on seven pillars, and has prepared a great banquet, and mixed the wines, and sent out her maidens inviting all to come. She calls from the busiest intersections in the city, "Come, you simple ones without good judgment; come to wisdom's banquet and drink the wines that I have mixed. Leave behind your foolishness and begin to live; learn how to be wise."

KEY VERSE

So don't criticize each other anymore. Try instead to live in such a way that you will never make your brother stumble by letting him see you doing something he thinks is wrong.—*Romans 14:13*

REFLECTION

There are three basic reactions when you discover that your husband or wife is doing something foolish or sinful: you can join in the unwise choices; you can turn away and say harsh, negative things; or you can explain why you believe what is being done is wrong and pray that God will help him or her listen and appreciate your honesty.

When you get married, the most important person in your life is your spouse. His or her influence can either strengthen or diminish your character. Try to be a positive example and don't become bitter or judgmental when your spouse makes a mistake.

MEDITATION

Heavenly Father, help us be an encouragement and support for one another. Keep our minds and hearts focused on you as the only true source of wisdom.

FEBRUARY 13

Jesus Heals a Demon–Possessed Boy
Matthew 17:14–21

When Jesus, Peter, James, and John arrived at the bottom of the hill, a huge crowd was waiting for them. A man came and knelt before Jesus and said, [15]"Sir, have mercy on my son, for he is mentally deranged, and in great trouble, for he often falls into the fire or into the water; [16]so I brought him to your disciples, but they couldn't cure him."

[17]Jesus replied, "Oh, you stubborn, faithless people! How long shall I bear with you? Bring him here to me." [18]Then Jesus rebuked the demon in the boy and it left him, and from that moment the boy was well.

[19]Afterwards the disciples asked Jesus privately, "Why couldn't we cast that demon out?"

²⁰"Because of your little faith," Jesus told them. "For if you had faith even as small as a tiny mustard seed you could say to this mountain, 'Move!' and it would go far away. Nothing would be impossible. ²¹But this kind of demon won't leave unless you have prayed and gone without food."

Live to Build Each Other Up
◄§ Romans 14:17–23 §►

For, after all, the important thing for us as Christians is not what we eat or drink but stirring up goodness and peace and joy from the Holy Spirit. ¹⁸If you let Christ be Lord in these affairs, God will be glad; and so will others. ¹⁹In this way aim for harmony in the church and try to build each other up.

²⁰Don't undo the work of God for a chunk of meat. Remember, there is nothing wrong with the meat, but it is wrong to eat it if it makes another stumble. ²¹The right thing to do is to quit eating meat or drinking wine or doing anything else that offends your brother or makes him sin. ²²You may know that there is nothing wrong with what you do, even from God's point of view, but keep it to yourself; don't flaunt your faith in front of others who might be hurt by it. In this situation, happy is the man who does not sin by doing what he knows is right. ²³But anyone who believes that something he wants to do is wrong shouldn't do it. He sins if he does, for he thinks it is wrong, and so for him it *is* wrong. Anything that is done apart from what he feels is right is sin.

Proverbs for Today
◄§ 9:7–8 §►

If you rebuke a mocker, you will only get a smart retort; yes, he will snarl at you. So don't bother with him; he will only hate you for trying to help him. But a wise man, when rebuked, will love you all the more.

———— ❧ KEY VERSE ❧ ————

For, after all, the important thing for us as Christians is not what we eat or drink but stirring up goodness and peace and joy from the Holy Spirit.—*Romans 14:17*

———— ❧ REFLECTION ❧ ————

When people become Christians, they often reject many of their old habits and interests and replace them with more wholesome activities. Smoking and alcohol abuse can be exchanged for exercise and a healthy diet. Noisy evenings in front of the television munching on fast food can be exchanged for enjoyable dinnertime discussions of the day's events.

Unfortunately, many Christian couples don't examine their lives beyond the physical changes they have made. They continue to practice many of the same spiritual sins. They gossip or say hurtful things or become jealous when someone else succeeds. While it's important to change your way of life and take care of the bodies God has given you, don't forget to ask him to change your hearts as well. Then you will become examples of the love Jesus showed when he gave his life for our salvation.

———— ❧ MEDITATION ❧ ————

Heavenly Father, we pray that you will remove all the bad habits we have accumulated over our lives—not just the ones that people immediately see. Make us pure and blameless in your sight. §►

FEBRUARY 14

A Coin to Pay Taxes
◄§ Matthew 17:22–27 §►

One day while Jesus and the disciples were still in Galilee, Jesus told them, "I am going to be betrayed into the power of those who will kill me, and on the third day afterwards I will be brought back to life again." And the disciples' hearts were filled with sorrow and dread.

²⁴On their arrival in Capernaum, the Temple tax collectors came to Peter and asked him, "Doesn't your master pay taxes?"

[25] "Of course he does," Peter replied.

Then he went into the house to talk to Jesus about it, but before he had a chance to speak, Jesus asked him, "What do you think, Peter? Do kings levy assessments against their own people, or against conquered foreigners?"

[26,27] "Against the foreigners," Peter replied.

"Well, then," Jesus said, "the citizens are free! However, we don't want to offend them, so go down to the shore and throw in a line, and open the mouth of the first fish you catch. You will find a coin to cover the taxes for both of us; take it and pay them."

Adopt the Attitude of Christ
Romans 15:1–6

Even if we believe that it makes no difference to the Lord whether we do these things, still we cannot just go ahead and do them to please ourselves; for we must bear the "burden" of being considerate of the doubts and fears of others—of those who feel these things are wrong. Let's please the other fellow, not ourselves, and do what is for his good and thus build him up in the Lord. [3] Christ didn't please himself. As the Psalmist said, "He came for the very purpose of suffering under the insults of those who were against the Lord." [4] These things that were written in the Scriptures so long ago are to teach us patience and to encourage us, so that we will look forward expectantly to the time when God will conquer sin and death.

[5] May God who gives patience, steadiness, and encouragement help you to live in complete harmony with each other—each with the attitude of Christ toward the other. [6] And then all of us can praise the Lord together with one voice, giving glory to God, the Father of our Lord Jesus Christ.

Proverbs for Today
9:9–10

Teach a wise man, and he will be the wiser; teach a good man, and he will learn more. *For the reverence and fear of God are basic to all wisdom. Knowing God results in every other kind of understanding.*

KEY VERSE

May God who gives patience, steadiness, and encouragement help you to live in complete harmony with each other—each with the attitude of Christ toward the other. And then all of us can praise the Lord together with one voice, giving glory to God, the Father of our Lord Jesus Christ. —*Romans 15:5–6*

REFLECTION

Boxes of candy. Flowers. Perfumed cards. Candlelight dinners. Other than Christmas, no other holiday inspires couples to shop for gifts that express their love for one another like the one dedicated to Saint Valentine. While his life is shrouded in mystery, legend says that this third-century Christian priest was martyred for his faith and that his love for those he ministered to was absolute and unwavering.

This Valentine's Day, in addition to the candy, flowers, and candlelight dinner, offer a gift to your spouse that won't wilt or grow stale. Promise to be faithful, steadfast, loving, and kind, today and always. Then, as a couple, make the same vow to your Heavenly Father. Tell about his goodness and mercy, and share the gift of salvation with others.

MEDITATION

Heavenly Father, thank you for the love we can share with one another. We pray that our feelings will be an inspiration and encouragement to others and that they will see you in our lives.

How to Be Great in the Kingdom of God
⊷§ Matthew 18:1–20 ໐⊷

About that time the disciples came to Jesus to ask which of them would be greatest in the Kingdom of Heaven!

²Jesus called a small child over to him and set the little fellow down among them, ³and said, ''Unless you turn to God from your sins and become as little children, you will never get into the Kingdom of Heaven. ⁴Therefore anyone who humbles himself as this little child, is the greatest in the Kingdom of Heaven. ⁵And any of you who welcomes a little child like this because you are mine, is welcoming me and caring for me. ⁶But if any of you causes one of these little ones who trusts in me to lose his faith, it would be better for you to have a rock tied to your neck and be thrown into the sea.

⁷''Woe upon the world for all its evils. Temptation to do wrong is inevitable, but woe to the man who does the tempting. ⁸So if your hand or foot causes you to sin, cut it off and throw it away. Better to enter heaven crippled than to be in hell with both of your hands and feet. ⁹And if your eye causes you to sin, gouge it out and throw it away. Better to enter heaven with one eye than to be in hell with two.

¹⁰''Beware that you don't look down upon a single one of these little children. For I tell you that in heaven their angels have constant access to my Father. ¹¹And I, the Messiah, came to save the lost.

¹²''If a man has a hundred sheep, and one wanders away and is lost, what will he do? Won't he leave the ninety-nine others and go out into the hills to search for the lost one? ¹³And if he finds it, he will rejoice over it more than over the ninety-nine others safe at home! ¹⁴Just so, it is not my Father's will that even one of these little ones should perish.

¹⁵''If a brother sins against you, go to him privately and confront him with his fault. If he listens and confesses it, you have won back a brother. ¹⁶But if not, then take one or two others with you and go back to him again, proving everything you

say by these witnesses. ¹⁷If he still refuses to listen, then take your case to the church, and if the church's verdict favors you, but he won't accept it, then the church should excommunicate him. ¹⁸And I tell you this—whatever you bind on earth is bound in heaven, and whatever you free on earth will be freed in heaven.

¹⁹''I also tell you this—if two of you agree down here on earth concerning anything you ask for, my Father in heaven will do it for you. ²⁰For where two or three gather together because they are mine, I will be right there among them.''

Gentiles Should Rejoice in God's Grace
⊷§ Romans 15:7–17 ໐⊷

So, warmly welcome each other into the church, just as Christ has warmly welcomed you; then God will be glorified. ⁸Remember that Jesus Christ came to show that God is true to his promises and to help the Jews. ⁹And remember that he came also that the Gentiles might be saved and give glory to God for his mercies to them. That is what the Psalmist meant when he wrote: ''I will praise you among the Gentiles, and sing to your name.''

¹⁰And in another place, ''Be glad, O you Gentiles, along with his people the Jews.''

¹¹And yet again, ''Praise the Lord, O you Gentiles, let everyone praise him.''

¹²And the prophet Isaiah said, ''There shall be an Heir in the house of Jesse, and he will be King over the Gentiles; they will pin their hopes on him alone.''

¹³So I pray for you Gentiles that God who gives you hope will keep you happy and full of peace as you believe in him. I pray that God will help you overflow with hope in him through the Holy Spirit's power within you.

¹⁴I know that you are wise and good, my brothers, and that you know these things so well that you are able to teach others all about them. ¹⁵,¹⁶But even so I have been bold enough to emphasize some of these points, knowing that all you need is this reminder from me; for I am, by God's

grace, a special messenger from Jesus Christ to you Gentiles, bringing you the Gospel and offering you up as a fragrant sacrifice to God; for you have been made pure and pleasing to him by the Holy Spirit. [17]So it is right for me to be a little proud of all Christ Jesus has done through me.

Proverbs for Today
≈§ 9:11–12 §≈

"I, Wisdom, will make the hours of your day more profitable and the years of your life more fruitful." Wisdom is its own reward, and if you scorn her, you hurt only yourself.

——————— ✍ KEY VERSE ✍ ———————

I also tell you this—if two of you agree down here on earth concerning anything you ask for, my Father in heaven will do it for you. For where two or three gather together because they are mine, I will be right there among them.—*Matthew 18:19–20*

——————— ✍ REFLECTION ✍ ———————

When you repeated the words "I do" in front of your family and friends, you made a pact that binds you together with another person for life. From that day forth, you had to start weighing the needs and feelings of someone else before making a decision. God wants all married couples to be in agreement about their attitudes, their convictions, and their faith. If you and your spouse work together to create a harmonious marriage in which each supports and loves the other unconditionally, God will honor your prayers and meet your needs.

——————— ✍ MEDITATION ✍ ———————

Heavenly Father, we come before you as a couple united in our love for each other and our desire to serve you. Bless our marriage and our lives together. §≈

FEBRUARY 16

Jesus Teaches on Forgiveness
≈§ Matthew 18:21–35 §≈

Then Peter came to Jesus and asked, "Sir, how often should I forgive a brother who sins against me? Seven times?"

[22]"No!" Jesus replied, "seventy times seven!

[23]"The Kingdom of Heaven can be compared to a king who decided to bring his accounts up to date. [24]In the process, one of his debtors was brought in who owed him $10,000,000! [25]He couldn't pay, so the king ordered him sold for the debt, also his wife and children and everything he had.

[26]"But the man fell down before the king, his face in the dust, and said, 'Oh, sir, be patient with me and I will pay it all.'

[27]"Then the king was filled with pity for him and released him and forgave his debt.

[28]"But when the man left the king, he went to a man who owed him $2,000 and grabbed him by the throat and demanded instant payment.

[29]"The man fell down before him and begged him to give him a little time. 'Be patient and I will pay it,' he pled.

[30]"But his creditor wouldn't wait. He had the man arrested and jailed until the debt would be paid in full.

[31]"Then the man's friends went to the king and told him what had happened. [32]And the king called before him the man he had forgiven and said, 'You evil-hearted wretch! Here I forgave you all that tremendous debt, just because you asked me to— [33]shouldn't you have mercy on others, just as I had mercy on you?'

[34]"Then the angry king sent the man to the torture chamber until he had paid every last penny due. [35]So shall my heavenly Father do to you if you refuse to truly forgive your brothers."

Paul, Apostle to the Gentiles
≈§ Romans 15:18–22 §≈

I dare not judge how effectively he has used others, but I know this: he has used me to win the

Gentiles to God. ¹⁹I have won them by my message and by the good way I have lived before them, and by the miracles done through me as signs from God—all by the Holy Spirit's power. In this way I have preached the full Gospel of Christ all the way from Jerusalem clear over into Illyricum.

²⁰But all the while my ambition has been to go still farther, preaching where the name of Christ has never yet been heard, rather than where a church has already been started by someone else. ²¹I have been following the plan spoken of in the Scriptures where Isaiah says that those who have never heard the name of Christ before will see and understand. ²²In fact that is the very reason I have been so long in coming to visit you.

Proverbs for Today
⋖§ 9:13–18 §⋗

A prostitute is loud and brash, and never has enough of lust and shame. She sits at the door of her house or stands at the street corners of the city, whispering to men going by, and to those minding their own business. "Come home with me," she urges simpletons. "Stolen melons are the sweetest; stolen apples taste the best!" But they don't realize that her former guests are now citizens of hell.

✺ KEY VERSE ✺

Then Peter came to him and asked, "Sir, how often should I forgive a brother who sins against me? Seven times?" "No!" Jesus replied, "Seventy times seven!"—*Matthew 18:21–22*

✺ REFLECTION ✺

"You always hurt the one you love." On the surface this well-known phrase doesn't make any sense. Why would a person try to make someone they care for unhappy? The truth is, few people truly *want* to hurt a loved one. Usually their unkind or hurtful actions or words are the result of job pressures, financial burdens, or other problems.

If your spouse has done something to upset you, remember to follow the example of Christ and offer your compassion, love, and forgiveness rather than anger and bitterness. If you do, you will relieve rather than escalate the situation. On the other hand, of course, if you have sinned against your husband or wife, ask for forgiveness and ask God to help you never to repeat your foolish actions.

✺ MEDITATION ✺

Heavenly Father, just as you have forgiven us countless times for our transgressions, help us to forgive one another when we have been sinned against. Help us, also, to place our spouse's needs first. §⋗

FEBRUARY 17

Jesus Teaches about Divorce
⋖§ Matthew 19:1–12 §⋗

After Jesus had finished this address, he left Galilee and circled back to Judea from across the Jordan River. ²Vast crowds followed him, and he healed their sick. ³Some Pharisees came to interview him, and tried to trap him into saying something that would ruin him.

"Do you permit divorce?" they asked.

⁴"Don't you read the Scriptures?" he replied. "In them it is written that at the beginning God created man and woman, ^{5,6}and that a man should leave his father and mother, and be forever united to his wife. The two shall become one—no longer two, but one! And no man may divorce what God has joined together."

⁷"Then, why," they asked, "did Moses say a man may divorce his wife by merely writing her a letter of dismissal?"

⁸Jesus replied, "Moses did that in recognition of your hard and evil hearts, but it was not what God had originally intended. ⁹And I tell you this, that anyone who divorces his wife, except for fornication, and marries another, commits adultery."

¹⁰Jesus' disciples then said to him, "If that is how it is, it is better not to marry!"

¹¹"Not everyone can accept this statement," Jesus said. "Only those whom God helps. ¹²Some are born without the ability to marry, and some are disabled by men, and some refuse to marry for the sake of the Kingdom of Heaven. Let anyone who can, accept my statement."

The Collection for the Jerusalem Church
⋙ Romans 15:23–33 ⋘

But now at last I am through with my work here, and I am ready to come after all these long years of waiting. ²⁴For I am planning to take a trip to Spain, and when I do, I will stop off there in Rome; and after we have had a good time together for a little while, you can send me on my way again.

²⁵But before I come, I must go down to Jerusalem to take a gift to the Jewish Christians there. ²⁶For you see, the Christians in Macedonia and Achaia have taken up an offering for those in Jerusalem who are going through such hard times. ²⁷They were very glad to do this, for they feel that they owe a real debt to the Jerusalem Christians. Why? Because the news about Christ came to these Gentiles from the church in Jerusalem. And since they received this wonderful spiritual gift of the Gospel from there, they feel that the least they can do in return is to give some material aid. ²⁸As soon as I have delivered this money and completed this good deed of theirs, I will come to see you on my way to Spain. ²⁹And I am sure that when I come the Lord will give me a great blessing for you.

³⁰Will you be my prayer partners? For the Lord Jesus Christ's sake, and because of your love for me—given to you by the Holy Spirit—pray much with me for my work. ³¹Pray that I will be protected in Jerusalem from those who are not Christians. Pray also that the Christians there will be willing to accept the money I am bringing them. ³²Then I will be able to come to you with a happy heart by the will of God, and we can refresh each other.

³³And now may our God, who gives peace, be with you all. Amen.

Proverbs for Today
⋙ 10:1–2 ⋘

Happy is the man with a level-headed son; sad the mother of a rebel. ☐ Ill-gotten gain brings no lasting happiness; right living does.

⋙ KEY VERSE ⋘

Ill-gotten gain brings no lasting happiness; right living does.—*Proverbs 10:2*

⋙ REFLECTION ⋘

Remember when you were a child and desperately wanted the latest toy or game or piece of sporting equipment—the one all your friends had gotten for Christmas or for their birthday? You wanted it so badly that you were even willing to steal it; nothing else seemed important and you just knew you'd never be happy unless you got what you wanted. Soon childhood turned into adolescence and then adulthood. Along the way, new interests captured your thoughts and previous desires seemed trivial by comparison. Unfortunately, many people will do anything for these fleeting pleasures. The bitter irony is that the more greedy they become and the more aggressively they acquire, the more miserable their lives become.

The Bible tells us that we are to save up our treasures in heaven, where their value is never corrupted. As a couple, don't spend your time plotting ways to get some material possession at any price. Soon these things will seem as meaningless as a long-forgotten and broken toy. Work together to achieve something truly valuable—contentment with what you have and a lifetime of service to God and an eternity in his presence.

⋙ MEDITATION ⋘

Heavenly Father, we thank you for what we have and ask that you will continue to bless us with the abundance of your grace and mercy in our lives. ⋘

⋙ 64 ⋘

Jesus Blesses the Little Children
◄§ Matthew 19:13–15 §►

Little children were brought for Jesus to lay his hands on them and pray. But the disciples scolded those who brought them. "Don't bother him," they said.

¹⁴But Jesus said, "Let the little children come to me, and don't prevent them. For of such is the Kingdom of Heaven." ¹⁵And he put his hands on their heads and blessed them before he left.

Paul Greets His Friends at Rome
◄§ Romans 16:1–16 §►

Phoebe, a dear Christian woman from the town of Cenchreae, will be coming to see you soon. She has worked hard in the church there. Receive her as your sister in the Lord, giving her a warm Christian welcome. Help her in every way you can, for she has helped many in their needs, including me. ³Tell Priscilla and Aquila "hello." They have been my fellow workers in the affairs of Christ Jesus. ⁴In fact, they risked their lives for me; and I am not the only one who is thankful to them: so are all the Gentile churches.

⁵Please give my greetings to all those who meet to worship in their home. Greet my good friend Epaenetus. He was the very first person to become a Christian in Asia. ⁶Remember me to Mary, too, who has worked so hard to help us. ⁷Then there are Andronicus and Junias, my relatives who were in prison with me. They are respected by the apostles, and became Christians before I did. Please give them my greetings. ⁸Say "hello" to Ampliatus, whom I love as one of God's own children, ⁹and Urbanus, our fellow worker, and beloved Stachys.

¹⁰Then there is Apelles, a good man whom the Lord approves; greet him for me. And give my best regards to those working at the house of Aristobulus. ¹¹Remember me to Herodion my relative. Re-member me to the Christian slaves over at Narcissus House. ¹²Say "hello" to Tryphaena and Tryphosa, the Lord's workers, and to dear Persis, who has worked so hard for the Lord. ¹³Greet Rufus for me, whom the Lord picked out to be his very own; and also his dear mother who has been such a mother to me. ¹⁴And please give my greetings to Asyncritus, Phlegon, Hermes, Patrobas, Hermas, and the other brothers who are with them. ¹⁵Give my love to Philologus, Julia, Nereus and his sister, and to Olympas, and all the Christians who are with them. ¹⁶Shake hands warmly with each other. All the churches here send you their greetings.

Proverbs for Today
◄§ 10:3–4 §►

The Lord will not let a good man starve to death, nor will he let the wicked man's riches continue forever. ☐ Lazy men are soon poor; hard workers get rich.

KEY VERSE

Shake hands warmly with each other. All the churches here send you their greetings.—*Romans 16:16*

REFLECTION

Have you ever been somewhere and felt completely out of place? Unless somebody makes an effort to help you feel comfortable, the chances are quite good you'll never want to return. This is what many people experience when they go to a church for the first time. Everyone seems to know each other, have a regular pew where they sit, and have plans together after church. There seems to be no room for anyone else.

As a couple, you have an opportunity to help others feel welcome when they are new to your church. Suggest a class they might enjoy. Invite them out to lunch after the service. Call them up during the week and tell them how much you enjoyed getting to know them. You'll not only be helping your church continue to grow, you may be developing friendships that will last a lifetime.

MEDITATION

Heavenly Father, help us to notice others when they visit our church. Place within us an empathy for their needs and show us how we can be their friends so they will feel comfortable and welcome.

FEBRUARY 19

Jesus and the Rich Man
Matthew 19:16–30

Someone came to Jesus with this question: "Good master, what must I do to have eternal life?"

[17]"When you call me good you are calling me God," Jesus replied, "for God alone is truly good. But to answer your question, you can get to heaven if you keep the commandments."

[18]"Which ones?" the man asked.

And Jesus replied, "Don't kill, don't commit adultery, don't steal, don't lie, [19]honor your father and mother, and love your neighbor as yourself!"

[20]"I've always obeyed every one of them," the youth replied. "What else must I do?"

[21]Jesus told him, "If you want to be perfect, go and sell everything you have and give the money to the poor, and you will have treasure in heaven; and come, follow me." [22]But when the young man heard this, he went away sadly, for he was very rich.

[23]Then Jesus said to his disciples, "It is almost impossible for a rich man to get into the Kingdom of Heaven. [24]I say it again—it is easier for a camel to go through the eye of a needle than for a rich man to enter the Kingdom of God!"

[25]This remark confounded the disciples. "Then who in the world can be saved?" they asked.

[26]Jesus looked at them intently and said, "Humanly speaking, no one. But with God, everything is possible."

[27]Then Peter said to him, "We left everything to follow you. What will we get out of it?"

[28]And Jesus replied, "When I, the Messiah, shall sit upon my glorious throne in the Kingdom, you my disciples shall certainly sit on twelve thrones judging the twelve tribes of Israel. [29]And anyone who gives up his home, brothers, sisters, father, mother, wife, children, or property, to follow me, shall receive a hundred times as much in return, and shall have eternal life. [30]But many who are first now will be last then; and some who are last now will be first then."

Avoid Divisive People
Romans 16:17–27

And now there is one more thing to say before I end this letter. Stay away from those who cause divisions and are upsetting people's faith, teaching things about Christ that are contrary to what you have been taught. [18]Such teachers are not working for our Lord Jesus, but only want gain for themselves. They are good speakers, and simple-minded people are often fooled by them. [19]But everyone knows that you stand loyal and true. This makes me very happy. I want you always to remain very clear about what is right, and to stay innocent of any wrong. [20]The God of peace will soon crush Satan under your feet. The blessings from our Lord Jesus Christ be upon you.

[21]Timothy my fellow-worker, and Lucius and Jason and Sosipater, my relatives, send you their good wishes. [22]I, Tertius, the one who is writing this letter for Paul, send my greetings too, as a Christian brother. [23]Gaius says to say "hello" to you for him. I am his guest, and the church meets here in his home. Erastus, the city treasurer, sends you his greetings and so does Quartus, a Christian brother.

²⁴Goodbye. May the grace of our Lord Jesus Christ be with you all.

²⁵,²⁶,²⁷I commit you to God, who is able to make you strong and steady in the Lord, just as the Gospel says, and just as I have told you. This is God's plan of salvation for you Gentiles, kept secret from the beginning of time. But now as the prophets foretold and as God commands, this message is being preached everywhere, so that people all around the world will have faith in Christ and obey him. To God, who alone is wise, be the glory forever through Jesus Christ our Lord. Amen.

Sincerely,
Paul

Proverbs for Today
⋖§ 10:5 §⋗

A wise youth makes hay while the sun shines, but what a shame to see a lad who sleeps away his hour of opportunity.

─────── ✐ KEY VERSE ✐ ───────

Stay away from those who cause divisions and are upsetting people's faith, teaching things about Christ that are contrary to what you have been taught.—*Romans 16:17*

─────── ✐ REFLECTION ✐ ───────

There are few experiences more enjoyable than listening to gifted speakers. Whether they are lecturing in a classroom, telling a story at a party, or delivering a sermon on Sunday morning, their ability to communicate can hold the attention of a small gathering or large group—and they always leave their listeners wanting to hear more. Unfortunately, many eloquent people become enraptured with their ability to hold an audience spellbound and start believing that style is more important than substance.

This attitude is especially dangerous in the church, where a pastor, worship leader, or Sunday school teacher has been given the responsibility of explaining and interpreting the Word of God. If his or her interest in exercising an ability to sway others is greater than the commitment to prayerfully studying the Scriptures, division and corruption in a congregation often result.

As a couple, read and study your Bible together each day. Turn to the works of trusted and godly scholars who will help you dig deeper into difficult verses. And, most important, pray that God will reveal himself to you through his Word. By doing this faithfully, you will know when others are preaching heresy and will be able to defend the truth against their eloquent but false claims.

─────── ✐ MEDITATION ✐ ───────

Heavenly Father, keep our hearts and minds focused on the truths of your Word. Help us to see beyond the messenger so that we can discern the content of the message. §⋗

FEBRUARY 20

The Parable of the Field Workers
⋖§ Matthew 20:1–19 §⋗

Here is another illustration of the Kingdom of Heaven. "The owner of an estate went out early one morning to hire workers for his harvest field. ²He agreed to pay them $20 a day and sent them out to work.

³"A couple of hours later he was passing a hiring hall and saw some men standing around waiting for jobs, ⁴so he sent them also into his fields, telling them he would pay them whatever was right at the end of the day. ⁵At noon and again around three o'clock in the afternoon he did the same thing.

⁶"At five o'clock that evening he was in town again and saw some more men standing around and asked them, 'Why haven't you been working today?'

[7]" 'Because no one hired us,' they replied.

" 'Then go on out and join the others in my fields,' he told them.

[8]"That evening he told the paymaster to call the men in and pay them, beginning with the last men first. [9]When the men hired at five o'clock were paid, each received $20. [10]So when the men hired earlier came to get theirs, they assumed they would receive much more. But they, too, were paid $20.

[11,12]"They protested, 'Those fellows worked only one hour, and yet you've paid them just as much as those of us who worked all day in the scorching heat.'

[13]" 'Friend,' he answered one of them, 'I did you no wrong! Didn't you agree to work all day for $20? [14]Take it and go. It is my desire to pay all the same; [15]is it against the law to give away my money if I want to? Should you be angry because I am kind?' [16]And so it is that the last shall be first, and the first, last."

[17]As Jesus was on the way to Jerusalem, he took the twelve disciples aside, [18]and talked to them about what would happen to him when they arrived.

"I will be betrayed to the chief priests and other Jewish leaders, and they will condemn me to die. [19]And they will hand me over to the Roman government, and I will be mocked and crucified, and the third day I will rise to life again."

God's Gifts to the Corinthian Church
◄§ 1 Corinthians 1:1–9 ε►

From: Paul, chosen by God to be Jesus Christ's missionary, and from brother Sosthenes.

[2]*To:* The Christians in Corinth, invited by God to be his people and made acceptable to him by Christ Jesus. *And to:* All Christians everywhere—whoever calls upon the name of Jesus Christ, our Lord and theirs.

[3]May God our Father and the Lord Jesus Christ give you all of his blessings, and great peace of heart and mind.

[4]I can never stop thanking God for all the wonderful gifts he has given you, now that you are Christ's: [5]he has enriched your whole life. He has helped you speak out for him and has given you a full understanding of the truth; [6]what I told you Christ could do for you has happened! [7]Now you have every grace and blessing; every spiritual gift and power for doing his will are yours during this time of waiting for the return of our Lord Jesus Christ. [8]And he guarantees right up to the end that you will be counted free from all sin and guilt on that day when he returns. [9]God will surely do this for you, for he always does just what he says, and he is the one who invited you into this wonderful friendship with his Son, even Christ our Lord.

Proverbs for Today
◄§ 10:6–7 ε►

The good man is covered with blessings from head to foot, but an evil man inwardly curses his luck. We all have happy memories of good men gone to their reward, but the names of wicked men stink after them.

◄§ KEY VERSE ε►

Now you have every grace and blessing; every spiritual gift and power for doing his will are yours during this time of waiting for the return of our Lord Jesus Christ.—*1 Corinthians 1:7*

◄§ REFLECTION ε►

In this verse Paul refers to the many gifts that had been given to the church in Corinth. Its members were capable of doing great things for the Kingdom of God and could have been powerful witnesses in their wicked city. Unfortunately they became proud of their gifts and began arguing over which were better and whether one gift made a person more spiritual than another. Of course, every gift was important because they were designed to complement each other. However, because the Corinthians chose to be proud of what God had given them rather than use it to proclaim the gospel message, the church began to quarrel and split.

In a marriage, even though both people have become one in the eyes of God, each person has a unique and special gift they can use to minister to others. If your talent seems more exciting or brings more acclaim than the abilities of your spouse, don't become proud and haughty. Like the Corinthians, you will only produce jealousy and anger in your relationship, attitudes that can lead to separation. Encourage each other and work together, using the gifts God has graciously bestowed on you in the manner he intended.

Heavenly Father, help us to remember that you are the giver of all good things and that our gifts and abilities come from your generous hand. Use us to magnify your glory and not our own. ◞

FEBRUARY 21

The True Leader Is a Servant
◞ Matthew 20:20–28 ◟

Then the mother of James and John, the sons of Zebedee, brought her sons to Jesus and respectfully asked a favor.

²¹"What is your request?" he asked. She replied, "In your Kingdom, will you let my two sons sit on two thrones next to yours?"

²²But Jesus told her, "You don't know what you are asking!" Then he turned to James and John and asked them, "Are you able to drink from the terrible cup I am about to drink from?"

"Yes," they replied, "we are able!"

²³"You shall indeed drink from it," he told them. "But I have no right to say who will sit on the thrones next to mine. Those places are reserved for the persons my Father selects."

²⁴The other ten disciples were indignant when they heard what James and John had asked for.

²⁵But Jesus called them together and said, "Among the heathen, kings are tyrants and each minor official lords it over those beneath him. ²⁶But among you it is quite different. Anyone wanting to be a leader among you must be your servant. ²⁷And if you want to be right at the top, you must serve like a slave. ²⁸Your attitude must be like my own, for I, the Messiah, did not come to be served, but to serve, and to give my life as a ransom for many."

Divisions within the Corinthian Church
◞ 1 Corinthians 1:10–17 ◟

But, dear brothers, I beg you in the name of the Lord Jesus Christ to stop arguing among your-

selves. Let there be real harmony so that there won't be splits in the church. I plead with you to be of one mind, united in thought and purpose. ¹¹For some of those who live at Chloe's house have told me of your arguments and quarrels, dear brothers. ¹²Some of you are saying, "I am a follower of Paul"; and others say that they are for Apollos or for Peter; and some that they alone are the true followers of Christ. ¹³And so, in effect, you have broken Christ into many pieces.

But did I, Paul, die for your sins? Were any of you baptized in my name? ¹⁴I am so thankful now that I didn't baptize any of you except Crispus and Gaius. ¹⁵For now no one can think that I have been trying to start something new, beginning a "Church of Paul." ¹⁶Oh, yes, and I baptized the family of Stephanas. I don't remember ever baptizing anyone else. ¹⁷For Christ didn't send me to baptize, but to preach the Gospel; and even my preaching sounds poor, for I do not fill my sermons with profound words and high sounding ideas, for fear of diluting the mighty power there is in the simple message of the cross of Christ.

Proverbs for Today
◞ 10:8–9 ◟

The wise man is glad to be instructed, but a self-sufficient fool falls flat on his face. A good man has firm footing, but a crook will slip and fall.

But, dear brothers, I beg you in the name of the Lord Jesus Christ to stop arguing among yourselves. Let there be real harmony so that there won't be splits in the church. I plead with you to be of one mind, united in thought and purpose. —*1 Corinthians 1:10*

The words of Paul in this verse are very personal. He doesn't say "To whom it may concern" or even "Dear church in Corinth." Instead he refers to them as "brothers." His words are those of one family member to another. If there is a conflict in your relationship, don't try to get the upper hand by referring to your spouse in derogatory terms.

This will only escalate the situation and create long-term scars of bitterness. Instead, speak to one another in love—despite your disagreements. You will discover that your arguments seem less and less important and will become more and more infrequent.

—&& MEDITATION &&—

Heavenly Father, forgive us when we say things to one another that are intentionally hurtful. Help us to always speak in love, even when we disagree, so that we can remain "united in thought and purpose" in service to you. ❧

FEBRUARY 22

Jesus Heals Two Blind Men
—§ Matthew 20:29–34 §—

As Jesus and the disciples left the city of Jericho, a vast crowd surged along behind.

[30]Two blind men were sitting beside the road and when they heard that Jesus was coming that way, they began shouting, "Sir, King David's Son, have mercy on us!"

[31]The crowd told them to be quiet, but they only yelled the louder.

[32,33]When Jesus came to the place where they were he stopped in the road and called, "What do you want me to do for you?"

"Sir," they said, "we want to see!"

[34]Jesus was moved with pity for them and touched their eyes. And instantly they could see, and followed him.

The "Foolishness" of God
—§ 1 Corinthians 1:18–25 §—

I know very well how foolish it sounds to those who are lost, when they hear that Jesus died to save them. But we who are saved recognize this message as the very power of God. [19]For God says, "I will destroy all human plans of salvation no matter how wise they seem to be, and ignore the best ideas of men, even the most brilliant of them."

[20]So what about these wise men, these scholars, these brilliant debaters of this world's great affairs? God has made them all look foolish, and shown their wisdom to be useless nonsense. [21]For God in his wisdom saw to it that the world would never find God through human brilliance, and then he stepped in and saved all those who believed his message, which the world calls foolish and silly. [22]It seems foolish to the Jews because they want a sign from heaven as proof that what is preached is true; and it is foolish to the Gentiles because they believe only what agrees with their philosophy and seems wise to them. [23]So when we preach about Christ dying to save them, the Jews are offended and the Gentiles say it's all nonsense. [24]But God has opened the eyes of those called to salvation, both Jews and Gentiles, to see that Christ is the mighty power of God to save them; Christ himself is the center of God's wise plan for their salvation. [25]This so-called "foolish" plan of God is far wiser than the wisest plan of the wisest man, and God in his weakness— Christ dying on the cross—is far stronger than any man.

Proverbs for Today
&§ 10:10 &>

Winking at sin leads to sorrow; bold reproof leads to peace.

&> KEY VERSE &<

Winking at sin leads to sorrow; bold reproof leads to peace.—*Proverbs 10:10*

&> REFLECTION &<

Do you remember the first time you saw a horror film on late-night television as a child? You didn't notice that the picture was grainy, the sound fuzzy, the plot inconsistent, and the sets thrown together. The plastic fangs and overacted shrieks seemed all too real, and you spent the night shivering under your covers and catching your breath at the slightest sound. It seems strange, doesn't it, that if you saw the same movie today it would have no effect on you other than to inspire a nostalgic smile? Over the years, you have seen so many horrifying things, both real and fictional, that your sense of apprehension has been numbed. In other words, if they want to make you jump today, Hollywood directors will have to invent "new and improved" ways to scare you.

The same is true with sin. Repeated exposure to a sinful attitude or habit soon leads to acceptance and, frequently, participation. This cycle happens all too often in a marriage when one spouse does or says things the other knows are wrong. Soon familiarity leads to consent until both are guilty of the same sin.

Don't fall victim to this destructive spiral. If your spouse has a sinful habit, confront him or her in love. If your spouse refuses to listen, pray for God's guidance and, if necessary, seek help from a pastor or Christian counselor. The one thing God asks us never to do when confronted with sin is to tolerate it.

&> MEDITATION &<

Heavenly Father, we pray that you will forgive us of our sins and ask that you will help us not to be a negative influence on each other but rather a mutual source of moral and spiritual encouragement. &>

FEBRUARY 23

Jesus' Triumphal Entry into Jerusalem
&§ Matthew 21:1-17 &>

As Jesus and the disciples approached Jerusalem, and were near the town of Bethphage on the Mount of Olives, Jesus sent two of them into the village ahead.

²"Just as you enter," he said, "you will see a donkey tied there, with its colt beside it. Untie them and bring them here. ³If anyone asks you what you are doing, just say, 'The Master needs them,' and there will be no trouble."

⁴This was done to fulfill the ancient prophecy, ⁵"Tell Jerusalem her King is coming to her, riding humbly on a donkey's colt!"

⁶The two disciples did as Jesus said, ⁷and brought the animals to him and threw their garments over the colt for him to ride on. ⁸And some in the crowd threw down their coats along the road ahead of him, and others cut branches from the trees and spread them out before him.

⁹Then the crowds surged on ahead and pressed along behind, shouting, "God bless King David's Son!" . . . "God's Man is here!" . . . Bless him, Lord!" . . . "Praise God in highest heaven!"

¹⁰The entire city of Jerusalem was stirred as he entered. "Who is this?" they asked.

¹¹And the crowds replied, "It's Jesus, the prophet from Nazareth up in Galilee."

¹²Jesus went into the Temple, drove out the merchants, and knocked over the moneychangers' tables and the stalls of those selling doves.

¹³"The Scriptures say my Temple is a place of

prayer," he declared, "but you have turned it into a den of thieves."

[14]And now the blind and crippled came to him and he healed them there in the Temple. [15]But when the chief priests and other Jewish leaders saw these wonderful miracles, and heard even the little children in the Temple shouting, "God bless the Son of David," they were disturbed and indignant and asked him, "Do you hear what these children are saying?"

[16]"Yes," Jesus replied. "Didn't you ever read the Scriptures? For they say, 'Even little babies shall praise him!'"

[17]Then he returned to Bethany, where he stayed overnight.

The Foolish Will Shame the Wise
1 Corinthians 1:26–31

Notice among yourselves, dear brothers, that few of you who follow Christ have big names or power or wealth. [27]Instead, God has deliberately chosen to use ideas the world considers foolish and of little worth in order to shame those people considered by the world as wise and great. [28]He has chosen a plan despised by the world, counted as nothing at all, and used it to bring down to nothing those the world considers great, [29]so that no one anywhere can ever brag in the presence of God.

[30]For it is from God alone that you have your life through Christ Jesus. He showed us God's plan of salvation; he was the one who made us acceptable to God; he made us pure and holy and gave himself to purchase our salvation. [31]As it says in the Scriptures, "If anyone is going to boast, let him boast only of what the Lord has done."

Proverbs for Today
10:11–12

There is living truth in what a good man says, but the mouth of the evil man is filled with curses. □ Hatred stirs old quarrels, but love overlooks insults.

KEY VERSE

Notice among yourselves, dear brothers, that few of you who follow Christ have big names or power or wealth.—*1 Corinthians 1:26*

REFLECTION

Fame . . . power . . . wealth. These are the human attributes and distinctions that our culture admires and glorifies. Those who possess any of these characteristics are accepted anywhere and are always treated with special care. They are also considered ideal marriage partners because their prestige and glory reflect on those around them.

God cherishes qualities in a person that have absolutely nothing to do with superficial, human values. Don't criticize your spouse because he or she isn't the most successful or attractive or popular person you know. Look with God's perspective. Is he kind? Is she generous? Does he share the love of Christ with others? These are the qualities that make a person truly great. Tell your husband or wife what you admire most about his or her character, and encourage faithfulness to God's definition of greatness.

MEDITATION

Heavenly Father, keep our perspective on eternal values. Help us not to judge each other according to the world's meaningless standards.

FEBRUARY 24

The Cursing of the Fig Tree
§ Matthew 21:18–22 §

In the morning, as Jesus was returning to Jerusalem, he was hungry, [19]and noticed a fig tree beside the road. He went over to see if there were any figs, but there were only leaves. Then he said to it, "Never bear fruit again!" And soon the fig tree withered up.

[20]The disciples were utterly amazed and asked, "How did the fig tree wither so quickly?"

[21]Then Jesus told them, "Truly, if you have faith, and don't doubt, you can do things like this and much more. You can even say to this Mount of Olives, 'Move over into the ocean,' and it will. [22]You can get anything—*anything* you ask for in prayer—if you believe."

The Preaching of the Cross
§ 1 Corinthians 2:1–10 §

Dear brothers, even when I first came to you I didn't use lofty words and brilliant ideas to tell you God's message. [2]For I decided that I would speak only of Jesus Christ and his death on the cross. [3]I came to you in weakness—timid and trembling. [4]And my preaching was very plain, not with a lot of oratory and human wisdom, but the Holy Spirit's power was in my words, proving to those who heard them that the message was from God. [5]I did this because I wanted your faith to stand firmly upon God, not on man's great ideas.

[6]Yet when I am among mature Christians I do speak with words of great wisdom, but not the kind that comes from here on earth, and not the kind that appeals to the great men of this world, who are doomed to fall. [7]Our words are wise because they are from God, telling of God's wise plan to bring us into the glories of heaven. This plan was hidden in former times, though it was made for our benefit before the world began. [8]But the great men of the world have not understood it; if they had, they never would have crucified the Lord of Glory. [9]That is what is meant by the Scriptures which say that no mere man has ever seen, heard or even imagined what wonderful things God has ready for those who love the Lord. [10]But we know about these things because God has sent his Spirit to tell us, and his Spirit searches out and shows us all of God's deepest secrets.

Proverbs for Today
§ 10:13–14 §

Men with common sense are admired as counselors; those without it are beaten as servants. □ A wise man holds his tongue. Only a fool blurts out everything he knows; that only leads to sorrow and trouble.

KEY VERSE

A wise man holds his tongue. Only a fool blurts out everything he knows; that only leads to sorrow and trouble.—*Proverbs 10:14*

REFLECTION

It's not an accident that a person who has many friends is also someone who doesn't share opinions about everyone and everything. A great conversationalist is someone who is a great listener.

The same is true in marriage. Don't feel as if you have to make value judgments about every event in your life or comment on whether you like or dislike the people you meet. Idle chatter and thoughtless remarks can often lead to hurt feelings, bitter attitudes, and other serious consequences. Think before you state a strong opinion. It's better to be a silent peace keeper than a loud troublemaker.

MEDITATION

Heavenly Father, forgive us for making offhand comments that keep us from achieving harmony in our home and fellowship with others. May our tongues be instruments of praise that tell others the Good News of your salvation. §

FEBRUARY 25

The Parable of the Disloyal Tenants
◄§ Matthew 21:23–46 §►

When Jesus had returned to the Temple and was teaching, the chief priests and other Jewish leaders came up to him and demanded to know by whose authority he had thrown out the merchants the day before.

[24]"I'll tell you if you answer one question first," Jesus replied. [25]"Was John the Baptist sent from God, or not?"

They talked it over among themselves. "If we say, 'From God,'" they said, "then he will ask why we didn't believe what John said. [26]And if we deny that God sent him, we'll be mobbed, for the crowd all think he was a prophet." [27]So they finally replied, "We don't know!"

And Jesus said, "Then I won't answer your question either.

[28]"But what do you think about this? A man with two sons told the older boy, 'Son, go out and work on the farm today.' [29]'I won't,' he answered, but later he changed his mind and went. [30]Then the father told the youngest, 'You go!' and he said, 'Yes, sir, I will.' But he didn't. [31]Which of the two was obeying his father?"

They replied, "The first, of course."

Then Jesus explained his meaning: "Surely evil men and prostitutes will get into the Kingdom before you do. [32]For John the Baptist told you to repent and turn to God, and you wouldn't, while very evil men and prostitutes did. And even when you saw this happening, you refused to repent, and so you couldn't believe.

[33]"Now listen to this story: A certain landowner planted a vineyard with a hedge around it, and built a platform for the watchman, then leased the vineyard to some farmers on a sharecrop basis, and went away to live in another country.

[34]"At the time of the grape harvest he sent his agents to the farmers to collect his share. [35]But the farmers attacked his men, beat one, killed one and stoned another.

[36]"Then he sent a larger group of his men to collect for him, but the results were the same. [37]Finally the owner sent his son, thinking they would surely respect him.

[38]"But when these farmers saw the son coming they said among themselves, 'Here comes the heir to this estate; come on, let's kill him and get it for ourselves!' [39]So they dragged him out of the vineyard and killed him.

[40]"When the owner returns, what do you think he will do to those farmers?"

[41]The Jewish leaders replied, "He will put the wicked men to a horrible death, and lease the vineyard to others who will pay him promptly."

[42]Then Jesus asked them, "Didn't you ever read in the Scriptures: 'The stone rejected by the builders has been made the honored cornerstone; how remarkable! what an amazing thing the Lord has done'?

[43]"What I mean is that the Kingdom of God shall be taken away from you, and given to a nation that will give God his share of the crop. [44]All who stumble on this rock of truth shall be broken, but those it falls on will be scattered as dust."

[45]When the chief priests and other Jewish leaders realized that Jesus was talking about them—that they were the farmers in his story— [46]they wanted to get rid of him, but were afraid to try because of the crowds, for they accepted Jesus as a prophet.

The Spirit Gives Us Wisdom
◄§ 1 Corinthians 2:11–16 §►

No one can really know what anyone else is thinking, or what he is really like, except that person himself. And no one can know God's thoughts except God's own Spirit. [12]And God has actually given us his Spirit (not the world's spirit) to tell us about the wonderful free gifts of grace and blessing that God has given us. [13]In telling you about these gifts we have even used the very words given to us by the Holy Spirit, not words that we as men might choose. So we use the Holy Spirit's words to explain the Holy Spirit's facts. [14]But the man who isn't a Christian can't understand and can't accept these thoughts from God, which the Holy Spirit teaches us. They sound foolish to him, because only those who have the Holy Spirit within them can understand what the Holy Spirit means. Others just can't take it in. ¹⁵But the spiritual man has insight into everything, and that bothers and baffles the man of the world, who can't understand him at all. ¹⁶How could he? For certainly he has never been one to know the Lord's thoughts, or to discuss them with him, or to move the hands of God by prayer. But, strange as it seems, we Christians actually do have within us a portion of the very thoughts and mind of Christ.

Proverbs for Today
◆§ 10:15–16 §◆

The rich man's wealth is his only strength. The poor man's poverty is his only curse. □ The good man's earnings advance the cause of righteousness. The evil man squanders his on sin.

◆ KEY VERSE ◆

No one can really know what anyone else is thinking, or what he is really like, except that person himself. And no one can know God's thoughts except God's own Spirit.—*1 Corinthians 2:11*

◆ REFLECTION ◆

If you have ever watched a courtroom drama on television, you know that someone will invariably ask the defendant, "What were you thinking when you committed the crime?" If you have ever read a biography about a president of the United States, you know that the author will speculate at some point, "What was he thinking when he made the decision that changed the course of history?" If you have ever watched an interview with an athlete who made a crucial error, you know the reporter will probably ask, "What in the world were you thinking when you threw away your team's chance to win?"

Most of us are curious about what makes other people tick. We want to understand why a person decided to do one thing when another action would have been easier or smarter. If the person won't, or can't, tell us, we begin to theorize and come to our own conclusions.

The Bible tells us that to guess what others are thinking and then judge them on that basis is wrong. This is especially true in marriage. Don't become angry with your spouse because of feelings and attitudes you are convinced that he or she holds. Instead, ask him or her to share his or her thoughts with you. You will create a strong marriage based on trust and honesty rather than a weak relationship built on secrecy and suspicion.

◆ MEDITATION ◆

Heavenly Father, help us keep our hearts and minds pure and blameless before you and with each other. Forgive us when we judge too quickly. May our marriage encourage us to share our deepest thoughts and feelings. §◆

FEBRUARY 26

The Parable of the Wedding Dinner
◆§ Matthew 22:1–14 §◆

Jesus told several other stories to show what the Kingdom of Heaven is like.

"For instance," he said, "it can be illustrated by the story of a king who prepared a great wedding dinner for his son. ³Many guests were invited, and when the banquet was ready he sent messengers to notify everyone that it was time to come. But all refused! ⁴So he sent other servants to tell them, 'Everything is ready and the roast is in the oven. Hurry!'

⁵"But the guests he had invited merely laughed and went on about their business, one to his farm, another to his store; ⁶others beat up his messengers and treated them shamefully, even killing some of them.

⁷"Then the angry king sent out his army and de-

stroyed the murderers and burned their city. [8]And he said to his servants, 'The wedding feast is ready, and the guests I invited aren't worthy of the honor. [9]Now go out to the street corners and invite everyone you see.'

[10]"So the servants did, and brought in all they could find, good and bad alike; and the banquet hall was filled with guests. [11]But when the king came in to meet the guests he noticed a man who wasn't wearing the wedding robe [provided for him].

[12]" 'Friend,' he asked, 'how does it happen that you are here without a wedding robe?' And the man had no reply.

[13]"Then the king said to his aides, 'Bind him hand and foot and throw him out into the outer darkness where there is weeping and gnashing of teeth.' [14]For many are called, but few are chosen.' "

Paul Rebukes Divisive Church Members
⋞ 1 Corinthians 3:1–9 ⋟

Dear brothers, I have been talking to you as though you were still just babies in the Christian life, who are not following the Lord, but your own desires; I cannot talk to you as I would to healthy Christians, who are filled with the Spirit. [2]I have had to feed you with milk and not with solid food, because you couldn't digest anything stronger. And even now you still have to be fed on milk. [3]For you are still only baby Christians, controlled by your own desires, not God's. When you are jealous of one another and divide up into quarreling groups, doesn't that prove you are still babies, wanting your own way? In fact, you are acting like people who don't belong to the Lord at all. [4]There you are, quarreling about whether I am greater than Apollos, and dividing the church. Doesn't this show how little you have grown in the Lord?

[5]Who am I, and who is Apollos, that we should be the cause of a quarrel? Why, we're just God's servants, each of us with certain special abilities, and with our help you believed. [6]My work was to plant the seed in your hearts, and Apollos' work was to water it, but it was God, not we, who made the garden grow in your hearts. [7]The person who does the planting or watering isn't very important, but God is important because he is the one who makes things grow. [8]Apollos and I are working as a team, with the same aim, though each of us will be rewarded for his own hard work. [9]We are only God's co-workers. You are *God's* garden, not ours; you are *God's* building, not ours.

Proverbs for Today
⋞ 10:17 ⋟

Anyone willing to be corrected is on the pathway to life. Anyone refusing has lost his chance.

๏ KEY VERSE ๏

Apollos and I are working as a team, with the same aim, though each of us will be rewarded for his own hard work.—*1 Corinthians 3:8*

๏ REFLECTION ๏

Teams are created for a variety of reasons and purposes. There are baseball teams composed of a group of athletes whose main ambition is to win more baseball games than their opponents, business teams within a company whose function is to develop and achieve a specific corporate goal, and political teams whose members attempt to win the election of their party's candidates.

The common denominator is that a group of people achieved a common goal that would have been impossible if each member of the team had worked alone. Marriage demands the same unified spirit. While your rewards may be different, ultimately you will both have much more successful and satisfying lives if you work as a harmonious team and try to help and support each other.

๏ MEDITATION ๏

Heavenly Father, we thank you for our marriage and ask that you will help us be loving, nurturing, supportive partners to one another. ⋟

Jesus Answers the Pharisees and the Sadducees
᪗ Matthew 22:15–46 ᪘

Then the Pharisees met together to try to think of some way to trap Jesus into saying something for which they could arrest him. [16]They decided to send some of their men along with the Herodians to ask him this question: "Sir, we know you are very honest and teach the truth regardless of the consequences, without fear or favor. [17]Now tell us, is it right to pay taxes to the Roman government or not?"

[18]But Jesus saw what they were after. "You hypocrites!" he exclaimed. "Who are you trying to fool with your trick questions? [19]Here, show me a coin." And they handed him a penny.

[20]"Whose picture is stamped on it?" he asked them. "And whose name is this beneath the picture?"

[21]"Caesar's," they replied.

"Well, then," he said, "give it to Caesar if it is his, and give God everything that belongs to God."

[22]His reply surprised and baffled them and they went away.

[23]But that same day some of the Sadducees, who say there is no resurrection after death, came to him and asked, [24]"Sir, Moses said that if a man died without children, his brother should marry the widow and their children would get all the dead man's property. [25]Well, we had among us a family of seven brothers. The first of these men married and then died, without children, so his widow became the second brother's wife. [26]This brother also died without children, and the wife was passed to the next brother, and so on until she had been the wife of each of them. [27]And then she also died. [28]So whose wife will she be in the resurrection? For she was the wife of all seven of them!"

[29]But Jesus said, "Your error is caused by your ignorance of the Scriptures and of God's power! [30]For in the resurrection there is no marriage; everyone is as the angels in heaven. [31]But now, as to whether there is a resurrection of the dead—don't you ever read the Scriptures? Don't you realize that God was speaking directly to you when he said, [32]'I

am the God of Abraham, Isaac, and Jacob'? So God is not the God of the dead, but of the *living*."

[33]The crowds were profoundly impressed by his answers— [34,35]but not the Pharisees! When they heard that he had routed the Sadducees with his reply, they thought up a fresh question of their own to ask him. One of them, a lawyer, spoke up: [36]"Sir, which is the most important command in the laws of Moses?"

[37]Jesus replied, "'Love the Lord your God with all your heart, soul, and mind.' [38,39]This is the first and greatest commandment. The second most important is similar: 'Love your neighbor as much as you love yourself.' [40]All the other commandments and all the demands of the prophets stem from these two laws and are fulfilled if you obey them. Keep only these and you will find that you are obeying all the others."

[41]Then, surrounded by the Pharisees, he asked them a question: [42]"What about the Messiah? Whose son is he?" "The son of David," they replied.

[43]"Then why does David, speaking under the inspiration of the Holy Spirit, call him 'Lord'?" Jesus asked. "For David said,

[44]'God said to my Lord, Sit at my right hand until I put your enemies beneath your feet.'
[45]Since David called him 'Lord,' how can he be merely his son?"
[46]They had no answer. And after that no one dared ask him any more questions.

Everyone's Work Will Be Judged by God
᪗ 1 Corinthians 3:10–17 ᪘

God, in his kindness, has taught me how to be an expert builder. I have laid the foundation and Apollos has built on it. But he who builds on the foundation must be very careful. [11]And no one can ever lay any other real foundation than that one we already have—Jesus Christ. [12]But there are various kinds of materials that can be used to build on that foundation. Some use gold and silver and jewels; and some build with sticks, and hay, or even straw! [13]There is going to come a time of testing at Christ's

Judgment Day to see what kind of material each builder has used. Everyone's work will be put through the fire so that all can see whether or not it keeps its value, and what was really accomplished. ¹⁴Then every workman who has built on the foundation with the right materials, and whose work still stands, will get his pay. ¹⁵But if the house he has built burns up, he will have a great loss. He himself will be saved, but like a man escaping through a wall of flames.

¹⁶Don't you realize that all of you together are the house of God, and that the Spirit of God lives among you in his house? ¹⁷If anyone defiles and spoils God's home, God will destroy him. For God's home is holy and clean, and you are that home.

Proverbs for Today
◄§ 10:18 §►

To hide hatred is to be a liar; to slander is to be a fool.

───────── ◢ KEY VERSE ◣ ─────────

Don't you realize that all of you together are the house of God, and that the Spirit of God lives among you in his house? If anyone defiles and spoils God's home, God will destroy him. For God's home is holy and clean, and you are that home.—*1 Corinthians 3:16–17*

───────── ◢ REFLECTION ◣ ─────────

In this verse, Paul refers to the church as the "house of God." Just as you would be upset if someone came into your home and physically destroyed it, God becomes angry with those who spiritually defile his house. If a church member uses his or her financial position or status in the community to achieve personal goals that are contrary to God's plan, usually the church splits, new members become discouraged and quit attending, and the person who instigated the conflict becomes part of another congregation where he or she resumes a career as a troublemaker.

What happens in the church is a model for what will take place in your home if each of you care only about your own desires and forget about placing the Holy Spirit in charge of your lives. Ultimately, you will be in constant tension that will tear your marriage apart. However, if you make your home a place where God's Word is held in reverence and you welcome God with your actions and through your prayers, he will honor you as a couple and bless your marriage and your family.

───────── ◢ MEDITATION ◣ ─────────

Heavenly Father, we pray for harmony in our home and ask that you will guide our lives and our marriage. §►

FEBRUARY 28

Jesus Condemns the Religious Leaders
◄§ Matthew 23:1–12 §►

Then Jesus said to the crowds, and to his disciples, ²"You would think these Jewish leaders and these Pharisees were Moses, the way they keep making up so many laws! ³And of course you should obey their every whim! It may be all right to do what they say, but above anything else, *don't follow their example.* For they don't do what they tell you to do. ⁴They load you with impossible demands that they themselves don't even try to keep.

⁵"Everything they do is done for show. They act holy by wearing on their arms little prayer boxes with Scripture verses inside, and by lengthening the memorial fringes of their robes. ⁶And how they love to sit at the head table at banquets, and in the reserved pews in the synagogue! ⁷How they enjoy the deference paid them on the streets, and to be called 'Rabbi' and 'Master'! ⁸Don't ever let anyone call you that. For only God is your Rabbi and all of you are on the same level, as brothers. ⁹And don't address anyone here on earth as 'Father,' for only God in heaven should be addressed like that. ¹⁰And

don't be called 'Master,' for only one is your master, even the Messiah.

[11]"The more lowly your service to others, the greater you are. To be the greatest, be a servant. [12]But those who think themselves great shall be disappointed and humbled; and those who humble themselves shall be exalted.

The "Foolishness" of God
◄§ 1 Corinthians 3:18–23 §►

Stop fooling yourselves. If you count yourself above average in intelligence, as judged by this world's standards, you had better put this all aside and be a fool rather than let it hold you back from the true wisdom from above. [19]For the wisdom of this world is foolishness to God. As it says in the book of Job, God uses man's own brilliance to trap him; he stumbles over his own "wisdom" and falls. [20]And again, in the book of Psalms, we are told that the Lord knows full well how the human mind reasons, and how foolish and futile it is.

[21]So don't be proud of following the wise men of this world. For God has already given you everything you need. [22]He has given you Paul and Apollos and Peter as your helpers. He has given you the whole world to use, and life and even death are your servants. He has given you all of the present and all of the future. All are yours, [23]and you belong to Christ, and Christ is God's.

Proverbs for Today
◄§ 10:19 §►

Don't talk so much. You keep putting your foot in your mouth. Be sensible and turn off the flow!

◄ KEY VERSE §►

Don't talk so much. You keep putting your foot in your mouth. Be sensible and turn off the flow! —*Proverbs 10:19*

◄ REFLECTION §►

The Bible warns us frequently about the use and misuse of the tongue. It even compares the tongue to a weapon that can kill. The key to keeping a reign on the tongue is to *listen* instead. When you speak, ask an open-ended question that gets the *other* person talking. And then wait; listen; give the person a long enough silence to say his or her piece. Spend today asking open-ended questions and waiting for the other person to answer fully.

If speaking without thinking is destroying your home, try the reverse for a change: listening. You might save the life of something very precious— your marriage.

◄ MEDITATION §►

Heavenly Father, purify our thoughts so that the words we speak are uplifting and affirming. §►

MARCH 1

Jesus Denounces the Pharisees
◄§ Matthew 23:13–39 §►

"Woe to you, Pharisees, and you other religious leaders. Hypocrites! For you won't let others enter the Kingdom of Heaven, and won't go in yourselves. And you pretend to be holy, with all your long, public prayers in the streets, while you are evicting widows from their homes. Hypocrites! [15]Yes, woe upon you hypocrites. For you go to all lengths to make one convert, and then turn him into twice the son of hell you are yourselves. [16]Blind guides! Woe upon you! For your rule is that to swear 'By God's Temple' means nothing—you can break that oath, but to swear 'By the gold in the Temple' is binding! [17]Blind fools! Which is greater, the gold, or the Temple that sanctifies the gold? [18]And you say that to take an oath 'By the altar' can be broken, but to swear 'By the gifts on the altar' is binding! [19]Blind! For which is greater, the gift on the altar, or the altar itself that sanctifies the gift? [20]When you swear 'By the altar' you are swearing by it and everything on it, [21]and when you swear

'By the Temple' you are swearing by it, and by God who lives in it. [22]And when you swear 'By heavens' you are swearing by the Throne of God and by God himself.

[23]"Yes, woe upon you, Pharisees, and you other religious leaders—hypocrites! For you tithe down to the last mint leaf in your garden, but ignore the important things—justice and mercy and faith. Yes, you should tithe, but you shouldn't leave the more important things undone. [24]Blind guides! You strain out a gnat and swallow a camel.

[25]"Woe to you, Pharisees, and you religious leaders—hypocrites! You are so careful to polish the outside of the cup, but the inside is foul with extortion and greed. [26]Blind Pharisees! First cleanse the inside of the cup, and then the whole cup will be clean.

[27]"Woe to you, Pharisees, and you religious leaders! You are like beautiful mausoleums—full of dead men's bones, and of foulness and corruption. [28]You try to look like saintly men, but underneath those pious robes of yours are hearts besmirched with every sort of hypocrisy and sin.

[29,30]"Yes, woe to you, Pharisees, and you religious leaders—hypocrites! For you build monuments to the prophets killed by your fathers and lay flowers on the graves of the godly men they destroyed, and say, 'We certainly would never have acted as our fathers did.'

[31]"In saying that, you are accusing yourselves of being the sons of wicked men. [32]And you are following in their steps, filling up the full measure of their evil. [33]Snakes! Sons of vipers! How shall you escape the judgment of hell?

[34]"I will send you prophets, and wise men, and inspired writers, and you will kill some by crucifixion, and rip open the backs of others with whips in your synagogues, and hound them from city to city, [35]so that you will become guilty of all the blood of murdered godly men from righteous Abel to Zechariah (son of Barachiah), slain by you in the Temple between the altar and the sanctuary. [36]Yes, all the accumulated judgment of the centuries shall break upon the heads of this very generation.

[37]"O Jerusalem, Jerusalem, the city that kills the prophets, and stones all those God sends to her! How often I have wanted to gather your children together as a hen gathers her chicks beneath her wings, but you wouldn't let me. [38]And now your house is left to you, desolate. [39]For I tell you this, you will never see me again until you are ready to welcome the one sent to you from God.''

Paul and Apollos—Servants of Christ
⋐ 1 Corinthians 4:1–7 ⋑

So Apollos and I should be looked upon as Christ's servants who distribute God's blessings by explaining God's secrets. [2]Now the most important thing about a servant is that he does just what his master tells him to. [3]What about me? Have I been a good servant? Well, I don't worry over what you think about this, or what anyone else thinks. I don't even trust my own judgment on this point. [4]My conscience is clear, but even that isn't final proof. It is the Lord himself who must examine me and decide.

[5]So be careful not to jump to conclusions before the Lord returns as to whether someone is a good servant or not. When the Lord comes, he will turn on the light so that everyone can see exactly what each one of us is really like, deep down in our hearts. Then everyone will know why we have been doing the Lord's work. At that time God will give to each one whatever praise is coming to him.

[6]I have used Apollos and myself as examples to illustrate what I have been saying: that you must not have favorites. You must not be proud of one of God's teachers more than another. [7]What are you so puffed up about? What do you have that God hasn't given you? And if all you have is from God, why act as though you are so great, and as though you have accomplished something on your own?

Proverbs for Today
⋐ 10:20–21 ⋑

When a good man speaks, he is worth listening to, but the words of fools are a dime a dozen. A godly man gives good advice, but a rebel is destroyed by lack of common sense.

Woe to you, Pharisees, and you religious leaders! You are like beautiful mausoleums—full of dead men's bones, and of foulness and corruption. —*Matthew 23:27*

──────── ✍ REFLECTION ✍ ────────

Does the following sound like a typical Saturday at your house? You both get up and throw on your work clothes. One of you mows the lawn while the other weeds the flower bed. You dust, vacuum, clean the bathroom, mop the kitchen floor, and, finally, collapse into bed. The next Saturday, bright and early, you start the whole process over again.

It's as important to keep a clean life as it is a clean house. We're unwilling to live among physical dirt; we should be unwilling to live with compromises and inconsistencies in our marriages as well. Is your marriage like a mausoleum—appearing beautiful to others, yet empty of love and intimacy in the privacy of your home? If so, clean up the inside—work to treat each other as king and queen, just the way you do in public.

──────── ✍ MEDITATION ✍ ────────

Heavenly Father, help us to focus on what is important in life and to spend less time fretting over nonessentials. ✍

MARCH 2

Jesus Preaches about the End of the Age
✍ Matthew 24:1–31 ✍

As Jesus was leaving the Temple grounds, his disciples came along and wanted to take him on a tour of the various Temple buildings.

[2]But he told them, "All these buildings will be knocked down, with not one stone left on top of another!"

[3]"When will this happen?" the disciples asked him later, as he sat on the slopes of the Mount of Olives. "What events will signal your return, and the end of the world?"

[4]Jesus told them, "Don't let anyone fool you. [5]For many will come claiming to be the Messiah, and will lead many astray. [6]When you hear of wars beginning, this does not signal my return; these must come, but the end is not yet. [7]The nations and kingdoms of the earth will rise against each other and there will be famines and earthquakes in many places. [8]But all this will be only the beginning of the horrors to come.

[9]"Then you will be tortured and killed and hated all over the world because you are mine, [10]and many of you shall fall back into sin and betray and hate each other. [11]And many false prophets will appear and lead many astray. [12]Sin will be rampant every-

where and will cool the love of many. [13]But those enduring to the end shall be saved.

[14]"And the Good News about the Kingdom will be preached throughout the whole world, so that all nations will hear it, and then, finally, the end will come.

[15]"So, when you see the horrible thing (told about by Daniel the prophet) standing in a holy place (Note to the reader: You know what is meant!), [16]then those in Judea must flee into the Judean hills. [17]Those on their porches must not even go inside to pack before they flee. [18]Those in the fields should not return to their homes for their clothes.

[19]"And woe to pregnant women and to those with babies in those days. [20]And pray that your flight will not be in winter, or on the Sabbath. [21]For there will be persecution such as the world has never before seen in all its history, and will never see again.

[22]"In fact, unless those days are shortened, all mankind will perish. But they will be shortened for the sake of God's chosen people.

[23]"Then if anyone tells you, 'The Messiah has arrived at such and such a place, or has appeared here or there,' don't believe it. [24]For false Christs shall

arise, and false prophets, and will do wonderful miracles, so that if it were possible, even God's chosen ones would be deceived. [25]See, I have warned you.

[26]"So if someone tells you the Messiah has returned and is out in the desert, don't bother to go and look. Or, that he is hiding at a certain place, don't believe it! [27]For as the lightning flashes across the sky from east to west, so shall my coming be, when I, the Messiah, return. [28]And wherever the carcass is, there the vultures will gather.

[29]"Immediately after the persecution of those days the sun will be darkened, and the moon will not give light, and the stars will seem to fall from the heavens, and the powers overshadowing the earth will be convulsed.

[30]"And then at last the signal of my coming will appear in the heavens and there will be deep mourning all around the earth. And the nations of the world will see me arrive in the clouds of heaven, with power and great glory. [31]And I shall send forth my angels with the sound of a mighty trumpet blast, and they shall gather my chosen ones from the farthest ends of the earth and heaven.

The Corinthians' Pride and the Humility of Servants
ᴥ§ 1 Corinthians 4:8–13 ᶜᴥ

You seem to think you already have all the spiritual food you need. You are full and spiritually contented, rich kings on your thrones, leaving us far behind! I wish you really were already on your thrones, for when that time comes you can be sure that we will be there, too, reigning with you. [9]Sometimes I think God has put us apostles at the very end of the line, like prisoners soon to be killed, put on display at the end of a victor's parade, to be stared at by men and angels alike.

[10]Religion has made us foolish, you say, but of course you are all such wise and sensible Christians! We are weak, but not you! You are well thought of, while we are laughed at. [11]To this very hour we have gone hungry and thirsty, without even enough clothes to keep us warm. We have been kicked around without homes of our own. [12]We have worked wearily with our hands to earn our living. We have blessed those who cursed us. We have been patient with those who injured us. [13]We have replied quietly when evil things have been said about us. Yet right up to the present moment we are like dirt under foot, like garbage.

Proverbs for Today
ᴥ§ 10:22 ᶜᴥ

The Lord's blessing is our greatest wealth. All our work adds nothing to it!

--------- ᴥ **KEY VERSE** ᴥ ---------

The Lord's blessing is our greatest wealth. All our work adds nothing to it!—*Proverbs 10:22*

--------- ᴥ **REFLECTION** ᴥ ---------

"Social Security Benefits Slashed." "Fewer and Fewer Couples Are Prepared for Retirement." "Economists Warn of an Uncertain Future for Tomorrow's Senior Citizens."

It seems like a week doesn't pass without headlines like these plastered across the front pages of newspapers and magazines. With dire predictions staring us in the face on a regular basis, it's easy to lose sight of where our real security lies. It isn't our jobs—we can lose them tomorrow. It isn't our health—sickness can strike suddenly and without warning. It isn't our money—ask anyone who lived during the Depression.

Our only true source of security comes from the Lord and the many blessings he freely gives. Nothing we do can add to these blessings other than to trust in him at all times. Whatever worries and cares you have as a couple, give them over to the Lord today. He will gladly provide for your every need.

--------- ᴥ **MEDITATION** ᴥ ---------

Heavenly Father, together we turn all of our cares and concerns over to you and place our future completely in your hands. ᶜᴥ

Be Prepared for the Lord's Coming
§ Matthew 24:32–51 §

"Now learn a lesson from the fig tree. When her branch is tender and the leaves begin to sprout, you know that summer is almost here. ³³Just so, when you see all these things beginning to happen, you can know that my return is near, even at the doors. ³⁴Then at last this age will come to its close.

³⁵"Heaven and earth will disappear, but my words remain forever. ³⁶But no one knows the date and hour when the end will be—not even the angels. No, nor even God's Son. Only the Father knows.

³⁷,³⁸"The world will be at ease —banquets and parties and weddings—just as it was in Noah's time before the sudden coming of the flood; ³⁹people wouldn't believe what was going to happen until the flood actually arrived and took them all away. So shall my coming be.

⁴⁰"Two men will be working together in the fields, and one will be taken, the other left. ⁴¹Two women will be going about their household tasks; one will be taken, the other left.

⁴²"So be prepared, for you don't know what day your Lord is coming.

⁴³"Just as a man can prevent trouble from thieves by keeping watch for them, ⁴⁴so you can avoid trouble by always being ready for my unannounced return.

⁴⁵"Are you a wise and faithful servant of the Lord? Have I given you the task of managing my household, to feed my children day by day? ⁴⁶Blessings on you if I return and find you faithfully doing your work. ⁴⁷I will put such faithful ones in charge of everything I own!

⁴⁸"But if you are evil and say to yourself, 'My Lord won't be coming for a while,' ⁴⁹and begin oppressing your fellow servants, partying and getting drunk, ⁵⁰your Lord will arrive unannounced and unexpected, ⁵¹and severely whip you and send you off to the judgment of the hypocrites; there will be weeping and gnashing of teeth.

Paul Counsels His Beloved Children
§ 1 Corinthians 4:14–21 §

I am not writing about these things to make you ashamed, but to warn and counsel you as beloved children. ¹⁵For although you may have ten thousand others to teach you about Christ, remember that you have only me as your father. For I was the one who brought you to Christ when I preached the Gospel to you. ¹⁶So I beg you to follow my example, and do as I do.

¹⁷That is the very reason why I am sending Timothy—to help you do this. For he is one of those I won to Christ, a beloved and trustworthy child in the Lord. He will remind you of what I teach in all the churches wherever I go.

¹⁸I know that some of you will have become proud, thinking that I am afraid to come to deal with you. ¹⁹But I will come, and soon, if the Lord will let me, and then I'll find out whether these proud men are just big talkers or whether they really have God's power. ²⁰The Kingdom of God is not just talking; it is living by God's power. ²¹Which do you choose? Shall I come with punishment and scolding, or shall I come with quiet love and gentleness?

Proverbs for Today
§ 10:23 §

A fool's fun is being bad; a wise man's fun is being wise!

KEY VERSE

Are you a wise and faithful servant of the Lord? Have I given you the task of managing my household, to feed my children day by day? Blessings on you if I return and find you faithfully doing your work.—*Matthew 24:45–46*

REFLECTION

Many Christian couples feel that if they don't serve as pastors at a local church or haven't been called to a foreign mission field, they can't really be full-time ministers. Yet Jesus compared Christian service to the management of a home. In a home someone cooks the meals, someone takes out the trash, someone pays the bills, and someone gives the dog a bath each week. In a well-run house, responsibilities are divided up evenly and fairly so that each person contributes his or her fair share and one person doesn't have to do everything.

The same is true in the church. Each member of a congregation should have specific duties that help further that church's work. Someone needs to visit the sick, someone needs to teach the young adult Sunday school class, someone needs to clean up after banquets, and someone needs to lead the choir.

If each of us meet our day-to-day responsibilities of maintaining the house of God, we are faithfully doing the Lord's work.

As a couple, you can offer your services in a variety of ways. If you aren't already involved in your church, ask your pastor what needs to be done. If you are filling a need, make sure you meet your responsibilities. Just as you wouldn't want your spouse to leave all his or her chores for you to do, don't place someone in the uncomfortable position of doing your job and his or hers too at church.

─────── ✐ MEDITATION ✐ ───────

Heavenly Father, help us to meet the responsibilities you have given us in both our church and our home. ❧

MARCH 4 ─────────────────

The Parable of the Ten Bridesmaids
❧ Matthew 25:1–13 ❧

"The Kingdom of Heaven can be illustrated by the story of ten bridesmaids who took their lamps and went to meet the bridegroom. [2,3,4]But only five of them were wise enough to fill their lamps with oil, while the other five were foolish and forgot.

[5,6]"So, when the bridegroom was delayed, they lay down to rest until midnight, when they were roused by the shout, 'The bridegroom is coming! Come out and welcome him!'

[7,8]"All the girls jumped up and trimmed their lamps. Then the five who hadn't any oil begged the others to share with them, for their lamps were going out.

[9]"But the others replied, 'We haven't enough. Go instead to the shops and buy some for yourselves.'

[10]"But while they were gone, the bridegroom came, and those who were ready went in with him to the marriage feast, and the door was locked.

[11]"Later, when the other five returned, they stood outside, calling, 'Sir, open the door for us!'

[12]"But he called back, 'Go away! It is too late!'

[13]"So stay awake and be prepared, for you do not know the date or moment of my return.

Paul Condemns Immorality in the Church
❧ 1 Corinthians 5:1–8 ❧

Everyone is talking about the terrible thing that has happened there among you, something so evil that even the heathen don't do it: you have a man in your church who is living in sin with his father's wife. [2]And are you still so conceited, so "spiritual"? Why aren't you mourning in sorrow and shame, and seeing to it that this man is removed from your membership?

[3,4]Although I am not there with you, I have been thinking a lot about this, and in the name of the Lord Jesus Christ I have already decided what to do, just as though I were there. You are to call a meeting of the church—and the power of the Lord Jesus will be with you as you meet, and I will be there in spirit— [5]and cast out this man from the fellowship of the church and into Satan's hands, to punish him, in the hope that his soul will be saved when our Lord Jesus Christ returns.

[6]What a terrible thing it is that you are boasting about your purity, and yet you let this sort of thing

go on. Don't you realize that if even one person is allowed to go on sinning, soon all will be affected? [7]Remove this evil cancer—this wicked person—from among you, so that you can stay pure. Christ, God's Lamb, has been slain for us. [8]So let us feast upon him and grow strong in the Christian life, leaving entirely behind us the cancerous old life with all its hatreds and wickedness. Let us feast instead upon the pure bread of honor and sincerity and truth.

Proverbs for Today
◄§ 10:24–25 §►

The wicked man's fears will all come true, and so will the good man's hopes. Disaster strikes like a cyclone and the wicked are whirled away. But the good man has a strong anchor.

_____◄ KEY VERSE ◄_____

Disaster strikes like a cyclone and the wicked are whirled away. But the good man has a strong anchor.—*Proverbs 10:25*

_____◄ REFLECTION ◄_____

Laying a solid foundation is just as important for building a good marriage as it is for constructing a sturdy house. A godly relationship, grounded in Scripture, can stand up to any conflict or adversity. As Christians, be confident that nothing will destroy your marriage and don't fret over minor disagreements or conflicts. God brought you together for a purpose and will stand with you every day of your lives together.

_____◄ MEDITATION ◄_____

Heavenly Father, help us to anchor our marriage in you and your Word. ɞ►

MARCH 5

Faithfulness in the Kingdom of Heaven
◄§ Matthew 25:14–30 §►

"Again, the Kingdom of Heaven can be illustrated by the story of a man going into another country, who called together his servants and loaned them money to invest for him while he was gone.

[15]"He gave $5,000 to one, $2,000 to another, and $1,000 to the last—dividing it in proportion to their abilities—and then left on his trip. [16]The man who received the $5,000 began immediately to buy and sell with it and soon earned another $5,000. [17]The man with $2,000 went right to work, too, and earned another $2,000.

[18]"But the man who received the $1,000 dug a hole in the ground and hid the money for safekeeping.

[19]"After a long time their master returned from his trip and called them to him to account for his money. [20]The man to whom he had entrusted the $5,000 brought him $10,000.

[21]"His master praised him for good work. 'You have been faithful in handling this small amount,' he told him, 'so now I will give you many more responsibilities. Begin the joyous tasks I have assigned to you.'

[22]"Next came the man who had received the $2,000, with the report, 'Sir, you gave me $2,000 to use, and I have doubled it.'

[23]"'Good work,' his master said. 'You are a good and faithful servant. You have been faithful over this small amount, so now I will give you much more.'

[24,25]"Then the man with the $1,000 came and said, 'Sir, I knew you were a hard man, and I was afraid you would rob me of what I earned, so I hid your money in the earth and here it is!'

[26]"But his master replied, 'Wicked man! Lazy slave! Since you knew I would demand your profit,

27you should at least have put my money into the bank so I could have some interest. 28Take the money from this man and give it to the man with the $10,000. 29For the man who uses well what he is given shall be given more, and he shall have abundance. But from the man who is unfaithful, even what little responsibility he has shall be taken from him. 30And throw the useless servant out into outer darkness: there shall be weeping and gnashing of teeth.'

Be in the World, Not of the World
1 Corinthians 5:9–13

When I wrote to you before I said not to mix with evil people. 10But when I said that I wasn't talking about unbelievers who live in sexual sin, or are greedy cheats and thieves and idol worshipers. For you can't live in this world without being with people like that. 11What I meant was that you are not to keep company with anyone who claims to be a brother Christian but indulges in sexual sins, or is greedy, or is a swindler, or worships idols, or is a drunkard, or abusive. Don't even eat lunch with such a person.

12It isn't our job to judge outsiders. But it certainly is our job to judge and deal strongly with those who are members of the church, and who are sinning in these ways. 13God alone is the Judge of those on the outside. But you yourselves must deal with this man and put him out of your church.

Proverbs for Today
10:26

A lazy fellow is a pain to his employers—like smoke in their eyes or vinegar that sets the teeth on edge.

KEY VERSE

For the man who uses well what he is given shall be given more, and he shall have abundance. But from the man who is unfaithful, even what little responsibility he has shall be taken from him. —*Matthew 25:29*

REFLECTION

Did Margaret Mitchell write *Gone with the Wind* without first learning that a verb and its subject must agree? Did Albert Einstein postulate the theory of relativity without first understanding the laws of physics? Did Arnold Palmer learn how to sink a twenty-foot putt without first figuring out how to get the ball from the tee to the green? The answer to each of these questions is, of course, no. Yet many people quickly become frustrated and give up if they can't excel at something immediately. They set unrealistic goals that defeat and discourage them.

God doesn't place that kind of pressure on his children. He expects us to do our best with the tasks he gives us and, if we prove our willingness to persevere and succeed, he will offer us additional responsibilities. Don't become discouraged if you aren't currently achieving the success you would like with the ministry God has given you. Encourage one another, press ahead, and welcome the challenges that are before you. Soon you will find yourself with new and more exciting opportunities to serve the Lord.

MEDITATION

Heavenly Father, help us to persevere in the tasks you have given us, and to be content with small steps of progress. And may you get the glory for all the successes we enjoy.

The Separation of the Sheep from the Goats
✑§ Matthew 25:31–46 ৡ

"But when I, the Messiah, shall come in my glory, and all the angels with me, then I shall sit upon my throne of glory. [32]And all the nations shall be gathered before me. And I will separate the people as a shepherd separates the sheep from the goats, [33]and place the sheep at my right hand, and the goats at my left.

[34]"Then I, the King, shall say to those at my right, 'Come, blessed of my Father, into the Kingdom prepared for you from the founding of the world. [35]For I was hungry and you fed me; I was thirsty and you gave me water; I was a stranger and you invited me into your homes; [36]naked and you clothed me; sick and in prison, and you visited me.'

[37]"Then these righteous ones will reply, 'Sir, when did we ever see you hungry and feed you? Or thirsty and give you anything to drink? [38]Or a stranger, and help you? Or naked, and clothe you? [39]When did we ever see you sick or in prison, and visit you?'

[40]"And I, the King, will tell them, 'When you did it to these my brothers you were doing it to me!' [41]Then I will turn to those on my left and say, 'Away with you, you cursed ones, into the eternal fire prepared for the devil and his demons. [42]For I was hungry and you wouldn't feed me; thirsty, and you wouldn't give me anything to drink; [43]a stranger, and you refused me hospitality; naked, and you wouldn't clothe me; sick, and in prison, and you didn't visit me.'

[44]"Then they will reply, 'Lord, when did we ever see you hungry or thirsty or a stranger or naked or sick or in prison, and not help you?'

[45]"And I will answer, 'When you refused to help the least of these my brothers, you were refusing help to me.'

[46]"And they shall go away into eternal punishment; but the righteous into everlasting life."

Believers Should Not Sue Each Other
✑§ 1 Corinthians 6:1–9a ৡ

How is it that when you have something against another Christian, you "go to law" and ask a heathen court to decide the matter instead of taking it to other Christians to decide which of you is right? [2]Don't you know that some day we Christians are going to judge and govern the world? So why can't you decide even these little things among yourselves? [3]Don't you realize that we Christians will judge and reward the very angels in heaven? So you should be able to decide your problems down here on earth easily enough. [4]Why then go to outside judges who are not even Christians? [5]I am trying to make you ashamed. Isn't there anyone in all the church who is wise enough to decide these arguments? [6]But, instead, one Christian sues another and accuses his Christian brother in front of unbelievers.

[7]To have such lawsuits at all is a real defeat for you as Christians. Why not just accept mistreatment and leave it at that? It would be far more honoring to the Lord to let yourselves be cheated. [8]But, instead, you yourselves are the ones who do wrong, cheating others, even your own brothers.

[9]Don't you know that those doing such things have no share in the Kingdom of God?

Proverbs for Today
✑§ 10:27–28 ৡ

Reverence for God adds hours to each day; so how can the wicked expect a long, good life? □ The hope of good men is eternal happiness; the hopes of evil men are all in vain.

✑ KEY VERSE ৡ

To have such lawsuits at all is a real defeat for you as Christians. Why not just accept mistreatment and leave it at that? It would be far more honoring to the Lord to let yourselves be cheated.—*1 Corinthians 6:7*

Scripture often says things that completely contradict the attitudes and mores of our culture. In fact, some verses seem so foreign to our modern sensibilities that they are often dismissed as irrelevant for today's Christians. Yet God never contradicts himself. This passage from 1 Corinthians is in complete harmony with verses that declare we should demonstrate love and forgiveness at all times, regardless of the circumstances.

If you or your spouse has been cheated or mis-treated, ask the Lord to help you forgive the offending party. Then turn to the Holy Spirit and to Scripture for guidance on how you should resolve the situation. Remember that you each have a higher law to which you must be faithful. Never use secular standards as an excuse for vengeance.

_____ ❧ **MEDITATION** ❧ _____

Heavenly Father, help us to forgive those who have betrayed our trust and caused us to suffer loss. We pray that their eyes will be opened and that they will turn to you and seek repentance. ❧

MARCH 7 _____

The Priests Plot Jesus' Death
❧ Matthew 26:1–16 ❧

When Jesus had finished this talk with his disciples, he told them,

"As you know, the Passover celebration begins in two days, and I shall be betrayed and crucified."

³At that very moment the chief priests and other Jewish officials were meeting at the residence of Caiaphas the High Priest, ⁴to discuss ways of capturing Jesus quietly, and killing him. ⁵"But not during the Passover celebration," they agreed, "for there would be a riot."

⁶Jesus now proceeded to Bethany, to the home of Simon the leper. ⁷While he was eating, a woman came in with a bottle of very expensive perfume, and poured it over his head.

⁸,⁹The disciples were indignant. "What a waste of good money," they said. "Why, she could have sold it for a fortune and given it to the poor."

¹⁰Jesus knew what they were thinking, and said, "Why are you criticizing her? For she has done a good thing to me. ¹¹You will always have the poor among you, but you won't always have me. ¹²She has poured this perfume on me to prepare my body for burial. ¹³And she will always be remembered for this deed. The story of what she has done will be told throughout the whole world, wherever the Good News is preached."

¹⁴Then Judas Iscariot, one of the twelve apostles, went to the chief priests, ¹⁵and asked, "How much will you pay me to get Jesus into your hands?" And they gave him thirty silver coins. ¹⁶From that time on, Judas watched for an opportunity to betray Jesus to them.

Christ's Blood Has Washed Away All Our Sins
❧ 1 Corinthians 6:9b–13a ❧

Don't fool yourselves. Those who live immoral lives, who are idol worshipers, adulterers or homosexuals—will have no share in his Kingdom. Neither will thieves or greedy people, drunkards, slanderers, or robbers. ¹¹There was a time when some of you were just like that but now your sins are washed away, and you are set apart for God, and he has accepted you because of what the Lord Jesus Christ and the Spirit of our God have done for you. ¹²I can do anything I want to if Christ has not said no, but some of these things aren't good for me. Even if I am allowed to do them, I'll refuse to if I think they might get such a grip on me that I can't easily stop when I want to. ¹³For instance, take the matter of eating. God has given us an appetite for food and stomachs to digest it. But that doesn't mean we should eat more than we need. Don't think of eating as important, because some day God will do away with both stomachs and food.

Proverbs for Today
⊷§ 10:29–30 §⊷

God protects the upright but destroys the wicked. The good shall never lose God's blessings, but the wicked shall lose everything.

⊷ KEY VERSE ⊷

Then Judas Iscariot, one of the twelve apostles, went to the chief priests and asked, "How much will you pay me to get Jesus into your hands?" And they gave him thirty silver coins. From that time on, Judas watched for an opportunity to betray Jesus to them.—*Matthew 26:14–16*

⊷ REFLECTION ⊷

What would it take for you to betray Christ? This seems like a terrible question, yet so many Christians regularly forsake the Savior for their own glory—and for much less than thirty pieces of silver. They deny their faith to gain acceptance at work; they become pious and look down on their unsaved neighbors so they can feel better about themselves; they start rumors about their pastor so they can gain power in their church.

Judas used a seemingly innocent kiss to betray Jesus. He chose a very intimate gesture to commit an evil and heinous sin. Are there insignificant acts you commit as a couple that are, in reality, betrayals of the one who died for you? Examine your attitudes and actions carefully, and resist the temptation of turning your back on Jesus to achieve personal gain.

⊷ MEDITATION ⊷

Heavenly Father, forgive us for the times we place our own desires and egos above our faith in you. §⊷

MARCH 8

The Last Supper
⊷§ Matthew 26:17–35 §⊷

On the first day of the Passover ceremonies, when bread made with yeast was purged from every Jewish home, the disciples came to Jesus and asked, "Where shall we plan to eat the Passover?"

[18]He replied, "Go into the city and see Mr. So-and-So, and tell him, 'Our Master says, my time has come, and I will eat the Passover meal with my disciples at your house.'" [19]So the disciples did as he told them, and prepared the supper there.

[20,21]That evening as he sat eating with the Twelve, he said, "One of you will betray me."

[22]Sorrow chilled their hearts, and each one asked, "Am I the one?"

[23]He replied, "It is the one I served first. [24]For I must die just as was prophesied, but woe to the man by whom I am betrayed. Far better for that one if he had never been born."

[25]Judas, too, had asked him, "Rabbi, am I the one?" And Jesus had told him, "Yes."

[26]As they were eating, Jesus took a small loaf of bread and blessed it and broke it apart and gave it to the disciples and said, "Take it and eat it, for this is my body."

[27]And he took a cup of wine and gave thanks for it and gave it to them and said, "Each one drink from it, [28]for this is my blood, sealing the New Covenant. It is poured out to forgive the sins of multitudes. [29]Mark my words—I will not drink this wine again until the day I drink it new with you in my Father's Kingdom."

[30]And when they had sung a hymn, they went out to the Mount of Olives.

[31]Then Jesus said to them, "Tonight you will all

desert me. For it is written in the Scriptures that God will smite the Shepherd, and the sheep of the flock will be scattered. [32]But after I have been brought back to life again I will go to Galilee, and meet you there."

[33]Peter declared, "If everyone else deserts you, I won't."

[34]Jesus told him, "The truth is that this very night, before the cock crows at dawn, you will deny me three times!"

[35]"I would die first!" Peter insisted. And all the other disciples said the same thing.

The Body Is the Home of the Holy Spirit
1 Corinthians 6:13b–20

But sexual sin is never right: our bodies were not made for that, but for the Lord, and the Lord wants to fill our bodies with himself. [14]And God is going to raise our bodies from the dead by his power just as he raised up the Lord Jesus Christ. [15]Don't you realize that your bodies are actually parts and members of Christ? So should I take part of Christ and join him to a prostitute? Never! [16]And don't you know that if a man joins himself to a prostitute she becomes a part of him and he becomes a part of her? For God tells us in the Scripture that in his sight the two become one person. [17]But if you give yourself to the Lord, you and Christ are joined together as one person.

[18]That is why I say to run from sex sin. No other sin affects the body as this one does. When you sin this sin it is against your own body. [19]Haven't you yet learned that your body is the home of the Holy Spirit God gave you, and that he lives within you? Your own body does not belong to you. [20]For God has bought you with a great price. So use every part of your body to give glory back to God, because he owns it.

Proverbs for Today
10:31–32

The good man gives wise advice, but the liar's counsel is shunned. The upright speak what is helpful; the wicked speak rebellion.

KEY VERSE

But sexual sin is never right: our bodies were not made for that but for the Lord, and the Lord wants to fill our bodies with himself. —*1 Corinthians 6:13b*

REFLECTION

One of the fascinating things about baking is that a bowl filled with ingredients that taste terrible by themselves can be mixed together and become a delicious cake. Of course, you can't throw just anything into the batter and get the same results. If you replace sugar, flour, and eggs with salt, mustard powder, and vinegar you will end up with a lethal combination that wouldn't even be fit for a landfill.

The same is true with what you pour into your marriage. God wants to fill you both with his righteousness, holiness, and mercy. If you replace that with impure lusts, jealousy, and spite, the joyful lives that God intended for you will become bitter and wasted. Allow the Holy Spirit to fill your lives with his goodness and purity, and pray that he will help you savor each moment of your lives together.

MEDITATION

Heavenly Father, we thank you for our marriage and ask that you will help us remove anything from our lives that can potentially taint our relationship.

Jesus Is Betrayed at Gethsemane
◄§ Matthew 26:36–56 §►

Then Jesus brought them to a garden grove, Gethsemane, and told them to sit down and wait while he went on ahead to pray. [37]He took Peter with him and Zebedee's two sons James and John, and began to be filled with anguish and despair.

[38]Then he told them, "My soul is crushed with horror and sadness to the point of death . . . stay here . . . stay awake with me."

[39]He went forward a little, and fell face downward on the ground, and prayed, "My Father! If it is possible, let this cup be taken away from me. But I want your will, not mine."

[40]Then he returned to the three disciples and found them asleep. "Peter," he called, "couldn't you even stay awake with me one hour? [41]Keep alert and pray. Otherwise temptation will overpower you. For the spirit indeed is willing, but how weak the body is!"

[42]Again he left them and prayed, "My Father! If this cup cannot go away until I drink it all, your will be done."

[43]He returned to them again and found them sleeping, for their eyes were heavy, [44]so he went back to prayer the third time, saying the same things again.

[45]Then he came to the disciples and said, "Sleep on now and take your rest . . . but no! The time has come! I am betrayed into the hands of evil men! [46]Up! Let's be going! Look! Here comes the man who is betraying me!"

[47]At that very moment while he was still speaking, Judas, one of the Twelve, arrived with a great crowd armed with swords and clubs, sent by the Jewish leaders. [48]Judas had told them to arrest the man he greeted, for that would be the one they were after. [49]So now Judas came straight to Jesus and said, "Hello, Master!" and embraced him in friendly fashion.

[50]Jesus said, "My friend, go ahead and do what you have come for." Then the others grabbed him.

[51]One of the men with Jesus pulled out a sword and slashed off the ear of the High Priest's servant.

[52]"Put away your sword," Jesus told him. "Those using swords will get killed. [53]Don't you realize that I could ask my Father for thousands of angels to protect us, and he would send them instantly? [54]But if I did, how would the Scriptures be fulfilled that describe what is happening now?" [55]Then Jesus spoke to the crowd. "Am I some dangerous criminal," he asked, "that you had to arm yourselves with swords and clubs before you could arrest me? I was with you teaching daily in the Temple and you didn't stop me then. [56]But this is all happening to fulfill the words of the prophets as recorded in the Scriptures."

At that point, all the disciples deserted him and fled.

Paul's Advice to Married Couples
◄§ 1 Corinthians 7:1–9 §►

Now about those questions you asked in your last letter: my answer is that if you do not marry, it is good. [2]But usually it is best to be married, each man having his own wife, and each woman having her own husband, because otherwise you might fall back into sin.

[3]The man should give his wife all that is her right as a married woman, and the wife should do the same for her husband: [4]for a girl who marries no longer has full right to her own body, for her husband then has his rights to it, too; and in the same way the husband no longer has full right to his own body, for it belongs also to his wife. [5]So do not refuse these rights to each other. The only exception to this rule would be the agreement of both husband and wife to refrain from the rights of marriage for a limited time, so that they can give themselves more completely to prayer. Afterwards, they should come together again so that Satan won't be able to tempt them because of their lack of self-control.

[6]I'm not saying you *must* marry; but you certainly *may* if you wish. [7]I wish everyone could get

along without marrying, just as I do. But we are not all the same. God gives some the gift of a husband or wife, and others he gives the gift of being able to stay happily unmarried. [8]So I say to those who aren't married, and to widows—better to stay unmarried if you can, just as I am. [9]But if you can't control yourselves, go ahead and marry. It is better to marry than to burn with lust.

Proverbs for Today
◦§ 11:1–3 §◦

The Lord hates cheating and delights in honesty. □ Proud men end in shame, but the meek become wise. □ A good man is guided by his honesty; the evil man is destroyed by his dishonesty.

◦ KEY VERSE ◦

The man should give his wife all that is her right as a married woman, and the wife should do the same for her husband: for a girl who marries no longer has full right to her own body, for her husband then has his rights to it, too; and in the same way the husband no longer has full right to his own body, for it belongs also to his wife.—*1 Corinthians 7:3–4*

◦ REFLECTION ◦

Sex and sexuality have been so perverted by the movie, print, and music industries that it's sometimes easy to forget that physical intimacy between a husband and wife is one of the most beautiful acts ordained by God. The pleasure that comes from sex is a wonderful gift that was intended to draw a couple closer together in love, not shame them for their passion. Try to please your mate sexually, for this pleases God. As Christians, you should give your bodies freely to one another and never forget that physical love represents the spiritual bond that unites you.

◦ MEDITATION ◦

Heavenly Father, we thank you for the intimacy of marriage and the passion we feel for one another. ❧

MARCH 10

Jesus Appears before the Jewish Supreme Court
◦§ Matthew 26:57–75 §◦

Then the mob led Jesus to the home of Caiaphas the High Priest, where all the Jewish leaders were gathering. [58]Meanwhile, Peter was following far to the rear, and came to the courtyard of the High Priest's house and went in and sat with the soldiers, and waited to see what was going to be done to Jesus.

[59]The chief priests and, in fact, the entire Jewish Supreme Court assembled there and looked for witnesses who would lie about Jesus, in order to build a case against him that would result in a death sentence. [60,61]But even though they found many who agreed to be false witnesses, these always contradicted each other.

Finally two men were found who declared, "This man said, 'I am able to destroy the Temple of God and rebuild it in three days.'"

[62]Then the High Priest stood up and said to Jesus, "Well, what about it? Did you say that, or didn't you?" [63]But Jesus remained silent.

Then the High Priest said to him, "I demand in the name of the living God that you tell us whether you claim to be the Messiah, the Son of God."

[64]"Yes," Jesus said, "I am. And in the future you will see me, the Messiah, sitting at the right hand of God and returning on the clouds of heaven."

[65,66]Then the High Priest tore at his own clothing, shouting, "Blasphemy! What need have we for other witnesses? You have all heard him say it! What is your verdict?"

They shouted, "Death!—Death!—Death!"

[67]Then they spat in his face and struck him and

some slapped him, [68]saying, "Prophesy to us, you Messiah! Who struck you that time?"

[69]Meanwhile, as Peter was sitting in the courtyard a girl came over and said to him, "You were with Jesus, for both of you are from Galilee."

[70]But Peter denied it loudly. "I don't even know what you are talking about," he angrily declared.

[71]Later, out by the gate, another girl noticed him and said to those standing around, "This man was with Jesus—from Nazareth."

[72]Again Peter denied it, this time with an oath. "I don't even know the man," he said.

[73]But after a while the men who had been standing there came over to him and said, "We know you are one of his disciples, for we can tell by your Galilean accent."

[74]Peter began to curse and swear. "I don't even know the man," he said.

And immediately the cock crowed. [75]Then Peter remembered what Jesus had said, "Before the cock crows, you will deny me three times." And he went away, crying bitterly.

Paul's Advice on Divorce
1 Corinthians 7:10–17

Now, for those who are married I have a command, not just a suggestion. And it is not a command from me, for this is what the Lord himself has said: A wife must not leave her husband. [11]But if she is separated from him, let her remain single or else go back to him. And the husband must not divorce his wife.

[12]Here I want to add some suggestions of my own. These are not direct commands from the Lord, but they seem right to me: If a Christian has a wife who is not a Christian, but she wants to stay with him anyway, he must not leave her or divorce her. [13]And if a Christian woman has a husband who isn't a Christian, and he wants her to stay with him, she must not leave him. [14]For perhaps the husband who isn't a Christian may become a Christian with the help of his Christian wife. And the wife who isn't a Christian may become a Christian with the help of her Christian husband. Otherwise, if the family separates, the children might never come to know the Lord; whereas a united family may, in God's plan, result in the children's salvation.

[15]But if the husband or wife who isn't a Christian is eager to leave, it is permitted. In such cases the Christian husband or wife should not insist that the other stay, for God wants his children to live in peace and harmony. [16]For, after all, there is no assurance to you wives that your husbands will be converted if they stay; and the same may be said to you husbands concerning your wives.

[17]But be sure in deciding these matters that you are living as God intended, marrying or not marrying in accordance with God's direction and help, and accepting whatever situation God has put you into. This is my rule for all the churches.

Proverbs for Today
11:4

Your riches won't help you on Judgment Day; only righteousness counts then.

❧ KEY VERSE ❧

But be sure in deciding these matters that you are living as God intended, marrying or not marrying in accordance with God's direction and help, and accepting whatever situation God has put you into. This is my rule for all the churches.—*1 Corinthians 7:17*

❧ REFLECTION ❧

Rich or poor, healthy or sick, young or old; it doesn't matter what station in life you find yourself if you're a Christian. You can rest in the knowledge that you are where God wants you and be confident that he will make your life meaningful if you let him. Accept whatever situation God has put you into, and seek his direction on how as a couple you can work together for his Kingdom.

❧ MEDITATION ❧

Heavenly Father, give us the wisdom and insight to see beyond our immediate situation and remember that you are in control of our lives and our futures. ❧

MARCH 11

Judas Returns the Thirty Pieces of Silver
Matthew 27:1–10

When it was morning, the chief priests and Jewish leaders met again to discuss how to induce the Roman government to sentence Jesus to death. [2]Then they sent him in chains to Pilate, the Roman governor.

[3]About that time Judas, who betrayed him, when he saw that Jesus had been condemned to die, changed his mind and deeply regretted what he had done, and brought back the money to the chief priests and other Jewish leaders.

[4]"I have sinned," he declared, "for I have betrayed an innocent man."

"That's your problem," they retorted.

[5]Then he threw the money onto the floor of the Temple and went out and hanged himself. [6]The chief priests picked the money up. "We can't put it in the collection," they said, "since it's against our laws to accept money paid for murder."

[7]They talked it over and finally decided to buy a certain field where the clay was used by potters, and to make it into a cemetery for foreigners who died in Jerusalem. [8]That is why the cemetery is still called "The Field of Blood."

[9]This fulfilled the prophecy of Jeremiah which says,

"They took the thirty pieces of silver—the price at which he was valued by the people of Israel— [10]and purchased a field from the potters as the Lord directed me."

We Have Been Bought with a Price
1 Corinthians 7:18–24

For instance, a man who already has gone through the Jewish ceremony of circumcision before he became a Christian shouldn't worry about it; and if he hasn't been circumcised, he shouldn't do it now. [19]For it doesn't make any difference at all whether a Christian has gone through this ceremony or not. But it makes a lot of difference whether he is pleasing God and keeping God's commandments. That is the important thing.

[20]Usually a person should keep on with the work he was doing when God called him. [21]Are you a slave? Don't let that worry you—but of course, if you get a chance to be free, take it. [22]If the Lord calls you, and you are a slave, remember that Christ has set you free from the awful power of sin; and if he has called you and you are free, remember that you are now a slave of Christ. [23]You have been bought and paid for by Christ, so you belong to him—be free now from all these earthly prides and fears. [24]So, dear brothers, whatever situation a person is in when he becomes a Christian, let him stay there, for now the Lord is there to help him.

Proverbs for Today
11:5–6

Good people are directed by their honesty; the wicked shall fall beneath their load of sins. The good man's goodness delivers him; the evil man's treachery is his undoing.

KEY VERSE

For it doesn't make any difference at all whether a Christian has gone through this ceremony or not. But it makes a lot of difference whether he is pleasing God and keeping God's commandments. That is the important thing.—*1 Corinthians 7:19*

REFLECTION

In this verse Paul was specifically addressing the ceremony of circumcision because it had become a stumbling block for the Corinthian church. Yet any type of ritual can become a spiritual hindrance if it replaces what is truly meaningful in life. For instance, if you sacrifice your prayer time each evening for a ball game or substitute conversation with your spouse in the morning for the newspaper, you have replaced an activity that pleases God with a meaningless ritual.

Don't allow your marriage to become mechanical and filled with activities that do nothing to strengthen your commitment to each other and your relationship with the Lord. Remember what Paul says: The important thing is to please God and keep his commandments!

❦ MEDITATION ❦

Heavenly Father, we ask that you will remove any stumbling blocks from our lives that can hinder not only our faith in you but also our relationship with each other. ❧

MARCH 12

Jesus Appears before Pilate
❦ Matthew 27:11–30 ❧

Now Jesus was standing before Pilate, the Roman governor. "Are you the Jews' Messiah?" the governor asked him.

"Yes," Jesus replied.

¹²But when the chief priests and other Jewish leaders made their many accusations against him, Jesus remained silent.

¹³"Don't you hear what they are saying?" Pilate demanded.

¹⁴But Jesus said nothing, much to the governor's surprise.

¹⁵Now the governor's custom was to release one Jewish prisoner each year during the Passover celebration—anyone they wanted. ¹⁶This year there was a particularly notorious criminal in jail named Barabbas, ¹⁷and as the crowds gathered before Pilate's house that morning he asked them, "Which shall I release to you—Barabbas, or Jesus your Messiah?" ¹⁸For he knew very well that the Jewish leaders had arrested Jesus out of envy because of his popularity with the people.

¹⁹Just then, as he was presiding over the court, Pilate's wife sent him this message: "Leave that good man alone; for I had a terrible nightmare concerning him last night."

²⁰Meanwhile the chief priests and Jewish officials persuaded the crowds to ask for Barabbas' release, and for Jesus' death. ²¹So when the governor asked again, "Which of these two shall I release to you?" the crowd shouted back their reply: "Barabbas!"

²²"Then what shall I do with Jesus, your Messiah?" Pilate asked.

And they shouted, "Crucify him!"

²³"Why?" Pilate demanded. "What has he done wrong?" But they kept shouting, "Crucify! Crucify!"

²⁴When Pilate saw that he wasn't getting anywhere, and that a riot was developing, he sent for a bowl of water and washed his hands before the crowd, saying, "I am innocent of the blood of this good man. The responsibility is yours!"

²⁵And the mob yelled back, "His blood be on us and on our children!"

²⁶Then Pilate released Barabbas to them. And after he had whipped Jesus, he gave him to the Roman soldiers to take away and crucify.

²⁷But first they took him into the armory and called out the entire contingent. ²⁸They stripped him and put a scarlet robe on him, ²⁹and made a crown from long thorns and put it on his head, and placed a stick in his right hand as a scepter and knelt before him in mockery. "Hail, King of the Jews," they yelled. ³⁰And they spat on him and grabbed the stick and beat him on the head with it.

Paul's Advice to Unmarried Women
❦ 1 Corinthians 7:25–31 ❧

Now I will try to answer your other question. What about girls who are not yet married? Should they be permitted to do so? In answer to this question, I have no special command for them from the Lord. But the Lord in his kindness has given me wisdom that can be trusted, and I will be glad to tell you what I think.

²⁶Here is the problem: We Christians are facing great dangers to our lives at present. In times like

these I think it is best for a person to remain unmarried. ²⁷Of course, if you already are married, don't separate because of this. But if you aren't, don't rush into it at this time. ²⁸But if you men decide to go ahead anyway and get married now, it is all right; and if a girl gets married in times like these, it is no sin. However, marriage will bring extra problems that I wish you didn't have to face right now.

²⁹The important thing to remember is that our remaining time is very short, [and so are our opportunities for doing the Lord's work]. For that reason those who have wives should stay as free as possible for the Lord; ³⁰happiness or sadness or wealth should not keep anyone from doing God's work. ³¹Those in frequent contact with the exciting things the world offers should make good use of their opportunities without stopping to enjoy them; for the world in its present form will soon be gone.

Proverbs for Today
◄§ 11:7 §►

When an evil man dies, his hopes all perish, for they are based upon this earthly life.

◄ KEY VERSE ►

The important thing to remember is that our remaining time is very short, [and so are our opportunities for doing the Lord's work]. For that reason those who have wives should stay as free as possible

for the Lord; happiness or sadness or wealth should not keep anyone from doing God's work.—*1 Corinthians 7:29–30*

◄ REFLECTION ►

Do you remember your first day of school? What did you wear to your senior prom? Where did you go on your first date? It doesn't matter how long it has been since these momentous events occurred in your life, the memories are probably as fresh as if they happened yesterday. Our time on earth is very brief—regardless of how long we live—and the number of significant activities in which we can engage are limited.

Paul reminds us of this fact by saying that, since our time is short, we should use it as effectively as possible. The excuses we make for not doing the Lord's work are meaningless. If, as a couple, you are looking for reasons to turn your backs on God, you will never be rich enough, or settled in your careers enough, or satisfy enough of the responsibilities to your families to accomplish his will for your lives. Allow God to help you work through your excuses and resolve the conflicts in your marriage so you can begin serving him today.

◄ MEDITATION ►

Heavenly Father, help us never to forget that our lives will pass in the blink of an eye and that we must live each day with our minds focused on eternity. §►

MARCH 13

The Crucifixion of Jesus
◄§ Matthew 27:31–56 §►

After the mockery, they took off the robe and put Jesus' own garment on him again, and took him out to crucify him.

³²As they were on the way to the execution grounds they came across a man from Cyrene, in Africa—Simon was his name—and forced him to carry Jesus' cross. ³³Then they went out to an area

known as Golgotha, that is, "Skull Hill," ³⁴where the soldiers gave him drugged wine to drink; but when he had tasted it, he refused.

³⁵After the crucifixion, the soldiers threw dice to divide up his clothes among themselves. ³⁶Then they sat around and watched him as he hung there. ³⁷And they put a sign above his head, "This is Jesus, the King of the Jews."

³⁸Two robbers were also crucified there that morning, one on either side of him. ³⁹And the peo-

ple passing by hurled abuse, shaking their heads at him and saying, 40"So! You can destroy the Temple and build it again in three days, can you? Well, then, come on down from the cross if you are the Son of God!"

41,42,43And the chief priests and Jewish leaders also mocked him. "He saved others," they scoffed, "but he can't save himself! So you are the King of Israel, are you? Come down from the cross and we'll believe you! He trusted God—let God show his approval by delivering him! Didn't he say, 'I am God's Son'?"

44And the robbers also threw the same in his teeth.

45That afternoon, the whole earth was covered with darkness for three hours, from noon until three o'clock.

46About three o'clock, Jesus shouted, "Eli, Eli, lama sabachthani?" which means, "My God, my God, why have you forsaken me?"

47Some of the bystanders misunderstood and thought he was calling for Elijah. 48One of them ran and filled a sponge with sour wine and put it on a stick and held it up to him to drink. 49But the rest said, "Leave him alone. Let's see whether Elijah will come and save him."

50Then Jesus shouted out again, dismissed his spirit, and died.

51And look! The curtain secluding the Holiest Place in the Temple was split apart from top to bottom; and the earth shook, and rocks broke, 52and tombs opened, and many godly men and women who had died came back to life again. 53After Jesus' resurrection, they left the cemetery and went into Jerusalem, and appeared to many people there.

54The soldiers at the crucifixion and their sergeant were terribly frightened by the earthquake and all that happened. They exclaimed, "Surely this was God's Son."

55And many women who had come down from Galilee with Jesus to care for him were watching from a distance. 56Among them were Mary Magdalene and Mary the mother of James and Joseph, and the mother of James and John (the sons of Zebedee).

Paul's Advice to Unmarried Men
⋖§ 1 Corinthians 7:32–40 §⋗

In all you do, I want you to be free from worry. An unmarried man can spend his time doing the Lord's work and thinking how to please him. 33But a married man can't do that so well; he has to think about his earthly responsibilities and how to please his wife. 34His interests are divided. It is the same with a girl who marries. She faces the same problem. A girl who is not married is anxious to please the Lord in all she is and does. But a married woman must consider other things such as housekeeping and the likes and dislikes of her husband.

35I am saying this to help you, not to try to keep you from marrying. I want you to do whatever will help you serve the Lord best, with as few other things as possible to distract your attention from him.

36But if anyone feels he ought to marry because he has trouble controlling his passions, it is all right, it is not a sin; let him marry. 37But if a man has the willpower not to marry and decides that he doesn't need to and won't, he has made a wise decision. 38So the person who marries does well, and the person who doesn't marry does even better.

39The wife is part of her husband as long as he lives; if her husband dies, then she may marry again, but only if she marries a Christian. 40But in my opinion she will be happier if she doesn't marry again; and I think I am giving you counsel from God's Spirit when I say this.

Proverbs for Today
⋖§ 11:8 §⋗

God rescues good men from danger while letting the wicked fall into it.

───────── ⋗ KEY VERSE ⋖ ─────────

I am saying this to help you, not to try to keep you from marrying. I want you to do whatever will help you serve the Lord best, with as few other things as possible to distract your attention from him.
—*1 Corinthians 7:35*

While it's true that God has ordained marriage as a good and holy relationship between a man and woman, it's also true that our first responsibility as Christians is to God, not our spouse. This is why Paul said that it is better for some people not to marry. By dividing their loyalties, they will be less effective servants in the kingdom of God.

Don't allow your marriage to become a detriment to your spiritual walk with the Lord. Instead, ask God to help each of you be an asset to the other. If you are focused as one body, then together you can do greater things for him than either of you could alone.

·¶ MEDITATION ·¶

Heavenly Father, we commit our marriage to you and offer our lives to your service. ·¶

MARCH 14

Jesus' Burial
·¶ Matthew 27:57–66 ·¶

When evening came, a rich man from Arimathea named Joseph, one of Jesus' followers, [58]went to Pilate and asked for Jesus' body. And Pilate issued an order to release it to him. [59]Joseph took the body and wrapped it in a clean linen cloth, [60]and placed it in his own new rock-hewn tomb, and rolled a great stone across the entrance as he left. [61]Both Mary Magdalene and the other Mary were sitting nearby watching.

[62]The next day—at the close of the first day of the Passover ceremonies—the chief priests and Pharisees went to Pilate, [63]and told him, "Sir, that liar once said, 'After three days I will come back to life again.' [64]So we request an order from you sealing the tomb until the third day, to prevent his disciples from coming and stealing his body and then telling everyone he came back to life! If that happens we'll be worse off than we were at first."

[65]"Use your own Temple police," Pilate told them. "They can guard it safely enough."

[66]So they sealed the stone and posted guards to protect it from intrusion.

Teaching about Food Offered to Idols
·¶ 1 Corinthians 8:1–13 ·¶

Next is your question about eating food that has been sacrificed to idols. On this question everyone feels that only his answer is the right one! But although being a "know-it-all" makes us feel important, what is really needed to build the church is love. [2]If anyone thinks he knows all the answers, he is just showing his ignorance. [3]But the person who truly loves God is the one who is open to God's knowledge.

[4]So now, what about it? Should we eat meat that has been sacrificed to idols? Well, we all know that an idol is not really a god, and that there is only one God, and no other. [5]According to some people, there are a great many gods, both in heaven and on earth. [6]But we know that there is only one God, the Father, who created all things and made us to be his own; and one Lord Jesus Christ, who made everything and gives us life.

[7]However, some Christians don't realize this. All their lives they have been used to thinking of idols as alive, and have believed that food offered to the idols is really being offered to actual gods. So when they eat such food it bothers them and hurts their tender consciences. [8]Just remember that God doesn't care whether we eat it or not. We are no worse off if we don't eat it, and no better off if we do. [9]But be careful not to use your freedom to eat it, lest you cause some Christian brother to sin whose conscience is weaker than yours.

[10]You see, this is what may happen: Someone who thinks it is wrong to eat this food will see you eating at a temple restaurant, for you know there is no harm in it. Then he will become bold enough to do it too, although all the time he still feels it is

wrong. [11]So because you "know it is all right to do it," you will be responsible for causing great spiritual damage to a brother with a tender conscience for whom Christ died. [12]And it is a sin against Christ to sin against your brother by encouraging him to do something he thinks is wrong. [13]So if eating meat offered to idols is going to make my brother sin, I'll not eat any of it as long as I live, because I don't want to do this to him.

Proverbs for Today
◄§ 11:9–11 §►

Evil words destroy. Godly skill rebuilds. ☐ The whole city celebrates a good man's success—and also the godless man's death. ☐ The good influence of godly citizens causes a city to prosper, but the moral decay of the wicked drives it downhill.

───────── ◄ KEY VERSE ◄ ─────────

And it is a sin against Christ to sin against your brother by encouraging him to do something he thinks is wrong.—*1 Corinthians 8:12*

───────── ◄ REFLECTION ◄ ─────────

The Bible has specific rules for proper conduct. We know that we shouldn't take the Lord's name in vain or steal or commit adultery. Yet there are many activities that are not addressed directly in Scripture that are considered improper by some Christians. These include the use of tobacco products, going to movies, or swimming in mixed company. There are other equally committed Christians, however, who see nothing wrong with any of these practices.

It's relatively easy for two people to have different standards and convictions in how they express their faith, even in a marriage. This verse helps us head off potential conflict by telling us to respect one another's convictions. If your spouse believes that a particular activity is sinful but you don't, refrain from doing it anyway. It's better to eliminate meaningless activities from your life completely—even those you enjoy—than to cause your husband or wife to compromise his or her convictions in an effort to please you.

───────── ◄ MEDITATION ◄ ─────────

Heavenly Father, help us to be a source of encouragement to each other and to refrain from any activity that will be a hindrance to our marriage. §►

MARCH 15

Jesus Rises from the Grave
◄§ Matthew 28:1–15 §►

Early on Sunday morning, as the new day was dawning, Mary Magdalene and the other Mary went out to the tomb.

[2]Suddenly there was a great earthquake; for an angel of the Lord came down from heaven and rolled aside the stone and sat on it. [3]His face shone like lightning and his clothing was a brilliant white. [4]The guards shook with fear when they saw him, and fell into a dead faint.

[5]Then the angel spoke to the women. "Don't be frightened!" he said. "I know you are looking for Jesus, who was crucified, [6]but he isn't here! For he has come back to life again, just as he said he would. Come in and see where his body was lying. . . . [7]And now, go quickly and tell his disciples that he has risen from the dead, and that he is going to Galilee to meet them there. That is my message to them."

[8]The women ran from the tomb, badly frightened, but also filled with joy, and rushed to find the disciples to give them the angel's message. [9]And as they were running, suddenly Jesus was there in front of them!

"Good morning!" he said. And they fell to the

ground before him, holding his feet and worshiping him.

[10]Then Jesus said to them, "Don't be frightened! Go tell my brothers to leave at once for Galilee, to meet me there."

[11]As the women were on the way into the city, some of the Temple police who had been guarding the tomb went to the chief priests and told them what had happened. [12,13]A meeting of all the Jewish leaders was called, and it was decided to bribe the police to say they had all been asleep when Jesus' disciples came during the night and stole his body.

[14]"If the governor hears about it," the Council promised, "we'll stand up for you and everything will be all right."

[15]So the police accepted the bribe and said what they were told to. Their story spread widely among the Jews, and is still believed by them to this very day.

The Rights of an Apostle
1 Corinthians 9:1–10

I am an apostle, God's messenger, responsible to no mere man. I am one who has actually seen Jesus our Lord with my own eyes. And your changed lives are the result of my hard work for him. [2]If in the opinion of others, I am not an apostle, I certainly am to you, for you have been won to Christ through me. [3]This is my answer to those who question my rights.

[4]Or don't I have any rights at all? Can't I claim the same privilege the other apostles have of being a guest in your homes? [5]If I had a wife, and if she were a believer, couldn't I bring her along on these trips just as the other disciples do, and as the Lord's brothers do, and as Peter does? [6]And must Barnabas and I alone keep working for our living, while you supply these others? [7]What soldier in the army has to pay his own expenses? And have you ever heard of a farmer who harvests his crop and doesn't have the right to eat some of it? What shepherd takes care of a flock of sheep and goats and isn't allowed to drink some of the milk? [8]And I'm not merely quoting the opinions of men as to what is right. I'm telling you what God's law says. [9]For in the law God gave to Moses he said that you must not put a muzzle on an ox to keep it from eating when it is treading out the wheat. Do you suppose God was thinking only about oxen when he said this? [10]Wasn't he also thinking about us? Of course he was. He said this to show us that Christian workers should be paid by those they help. Those who do the plowing and threshing should expect some share of the harvest.

Proverbs for Today
11:12–13

To quarrel with a neighbor is foolish; a man with good sense holds his tongue. □ A gossip goes around spreading rumors, while a trustworthy man tries to quiet them.

❧ KEY VERSE ❧

Then Jesus said to them, "Don't be frightened! Go tell my brothers to leave at once for Galilee, to meet me there."—*Matthew 28:10*

❧ REFLECTION ❧

Jesus told the two women to find the disciples and tell them to meet him in Galilee. Although frightened, they didn't allow their anxiety to keep them from doing what the Lord asked.

There are many circumstances that may hinder us emotionally from willingly doing God's will. Some Christians are married to unbelievers who have negative feelings toward the church. Others are timid about sharing their faith with unsaved friends and coworkers because they don't want to be ridiculed. Ask God to give you the courage and wisdom to tell others about him. Whether you are sharing the Good News of salvation with a husband or wife or, as a couple, you are ministering to a neighbor, he will provide you with the ability and the opportunity to proclaim his message.

❧ MEDITATION ❧

Heavenly Father, we ask that you will not only give us the chance to witness to our friends and neighbors but also provide us with both the courage to speak and the wisdom to say the right things. ❧

Jesus Commissions His Disciples
§ Matthew 28:16–20 §

Then the eleven disciples left for Galilee, going to the mountain where Jesus had said they would find him. [17]There they met him and worshiped him—but some of them weren't sure it really was Jesus!

[18]He told his disciples, "I have been given all authority in heaven and earth. [19]Therefore go and make disciples in all the nations, baptizing them into the name of the Father and of the Son and of the Holy Spirit, [20]and then teach these new disciples to obey all the commands I have given you; and be sure of this—that I am with you always, even to the end of the world."

The Good News Preached without Compensation
§ 1 Corinthians 9:11–18 §

We have planted good spiritual seed in your souls. Is it too much to ask, in return, for mere food and clothing? [12]You give them to others who preach to you, and you should. But shouldn't we have an even greater right to them? Yet we have *never* used this right, but supply our own needs without your help. We have never demanded payment of any kind for fear that, if we did, you might be less interested in our message to you from Christ.

[13]Don't you realize that God told those working in his temple to take for their own needs some of the food brought there as gifts to him? And those who work at the altar of God get a share of the food that is brought by those offering it to the Lord. [14]In the same way the Lord has given orders that those who preach the Gospel should be supported by those who accept it.

[15]Yet I have never asked you for one penny. And I am not writing this to hint that I would like to start now. In fact, I would rather die of hunger than lose the satisfaction I get from preaching to you without charge. [16]For just preaching the Gospel isn't any special credit to me—I couldn't keep from preaching it if I wanted to. I would be utterly miserable. Woe unto me if I don't.

[17]If I were volunteering my services of my own free will, then the Lord would give me a special reward; but that is not the situation, for God has picked me out and given me this sacred trust and I have no choice. [18]Under this circumstance, what is my pay? It is the special joy I get from preaching the Good News without expense to anyone, never demanding my rights.

Proverbs for Today
§ 11:14 §

Without wise leadership, a nation is in trouble; but with good counselors there is safety.

KEY VERSE

Without wise leadership, a nation is in trouble; but with good counselors there is safety.—*Proverbs 11:14*

REFLECTION

Throughout Scripture, God admonishes his people to seek wise counsel when confronted with difficulties. As a couple, whether you are engaged or have just celebrated your golden wedding anniversary, you need to have regular fellowship with trustworthy and dedicated Christians who are willing to pray with you before making important decisions or during periods of stress and uncertainty. If you and your spouse don't have an individual or couple like this in your lives, ask God to provide someone. Just as he placed Nathan in King David's life, he will bring a godly person to you.

MEDITATION

Heavenly Father, we ask that you bring godly people into our lives so that they can encourage us when our faith is shaken and pray with us during times of uncertainty. §

MARCH 17

John the Baptist Prepares the Way for Jesus
§ Mark 1:1–8 §

Here begins the wonderful story of Jesus the Messiah, the Son of God.

²In the book written by the prophet Isaiah, God announced that he would send his Son to earth, and that a special messenger would arrive first to prepare the world for his coming.

³"This messenger will live out in the barren wilderness," Isaiah said, "and will proclaim that everyone must straighten out his life to be ready for the Lord's arrival."

⁴This messenger was John the Baptist. He lived in the wilderness and taught that all should be baptized as a public announcement of their decision to turn their backs on sin, so that God could forgive them. ⁵People from Jerusalem and from all over Judea traveled out into the Judean wastelands to see and hear John, and when they confessed their sins he baptized them in the Jordan River. ⁶His clothes were woven from camel's hair and he wore a leather belt; locusts and wild honey were his food. ⁷Here is a sample of his preaching:

"Someone is coming soon who is far greater than I am, so much greater that I am not even worthy to be his slave. ⁸I baptize you with water but he will baptize you with God's Holy Spirit!"

Common Ground—the Context for Evangelism
§ 1 Corinthians 9:19–27 §

And this has a real advantage: I am not bound to obey anyone just because he pays my salary; yet I have freely and happily become a servant of any and all so that I can win them to Christ. ²⁰When I am with the Jews I seem as one of them so that they will listen to the Gospel and I can win them to Christ. When I am with Gentiles who follow Jewish customs and ceremonies I don't argue, even though I don't agree, because I want to help them. ²¹When with the heathen I agree with them as much as I can, except of course that I must always do what is right as a Christian. And so, by agreeing, I can win their confidence and help them too.

²²When I am with those whose consciences bother them easily, I don't act as though I know it all and don't say they are foolish; the result is that they are willing to let me help them. Yes, whatever a person is like, I try to find common ground with him so that he will let me tell him about Christ and let Christ save him. ²³I do this to get the Gospel to them and also for the blessing I myself receive when I see them come to Christ.

²⁴In a race, everyone runs but only one person gets first prize. So run your race to win. ²⁵To win the contest you must deny yourselves many things that would keep you from doing your best. An athlete goes to all this trouble just to win a blue ribbon or a silver cup, but we do it for a heavenly reward that never disappears. ²⁶So I run straight to the goal with purpose in every step. I fight to win. I'm not just shadow-boxing or playing around. ²⁷Like an athlete I punish my body, treating it roughly, training it to do what it should, not what it wants to. Otherwise I fear that after enlisting others for the race, I myself might be declared unfit and ordered to stand aside.

Proverbs for Today
§ 11:15 §

Be sure you know a person well before you vouch for his credit! Better refuse than suffer later.

✍ KEY VERSE ✍

When I am with those whose consciences bother them easily, I don't act as though I know it all and don't say they are foolish; the result is that they are willing to let me help them. Yes, whatever a person is like, I try to find common ground with him so that he will let me tell him about Christ and let Christ save him.—*1 Corinthians 9:22*

✍ REFLECTION ✍

One of the most valuable traits a person can have is the skill and desire to understand and have sympathy for another person's point of view. Whether the environment is a board room, court room, or living room, the ability to seek common ground makes each party involved feel vital and appreciated. It doesn't mean that anyone compromises his or her convictions; it just makes the opportunity for a peaceful solution more likely.

Christian couples need to find common ground when they have disagreements in order to more easily solve their problems. If you and your spouse are having difficulty resolving a situation, don't resort to name calling or accusations. Instead, turn to God's Word and pray that the Holy Spirit will open both of your hearts to his guidance and direction.

◦ MEDITATION ◦

Heavenly Father, help us find peaceful solutions to our problems and give us the insight and patience we need to see each other's point of view. ε

MARCH 18

Jesus' Baptism and Temptation
◦§ Mark 1:9–13 ε

Then one day Jesus came from Nazareth in Galilee, and was baptized by John there in the Jordan River. ¹⁰The moment Jesus came up out of the water, he saw the heavens open and the Holy Spirit in the form of a dove descending on him, ¹¹and a voice from heaven said, "You are my beloved Son; you are my Delight."

¹²,¹³Immediately the Holy Spirit urged Jesus into the desert. There, for forty days, alone except for desert animals, he was subjected to Satan's temptations to sin. And afterwards the angels came and cared for him.

An Example for Christians
◦§ 1 Corinthians 10:1–14 ε

For we must never forget, dear brothers, what happened to our people in the wilderness long ago. God guided them by sending a cloud that moved along ahead of them; and he brought them all safely through the waters of the Red Sea. ²This might be called their "baptism"—baptized both in sea and cloud!—as followers of Moses—their commitment to him as their leader. ³,⁴And by a miracle God sent them food to eat and water to drink there in the desert; they drank the water that Christ gave them. He was there with them as a mighty Rock of spiritual refreshment. ⁵Yet after all this most of them did not obey God, and he destroyed them in the wilderness.

⁶From this lesson we are warned that we must not desire evil things as they did, ⁷nor worship idols as they did. (The Scriptures tell us, "The people sat down to eat and drink and then got up to dance" in worship of the golden calf.)

⁸Another lesson for us is what happened when some of them sinned with other men's wives, and 23,000 fell dead in one day. ⁹And don't try the Lord's patience—they did, and died from snake bites. ¹⁰And don't murmur against God and his dealings with you, as some of them did, for that is why God sent his Angel to destroy them.

¹¹All these things happened to them as examples—as object lessons to us—to warn us against doing the same things; they were written down so that we could read about them and learn from them in these last days as the world nears its end.

¹²So be careful. If you are thinking, "Oh, I would never behave like that"—let this be a warning to you. For you too may fall into sin. ¹³But remember this—the wrong desires that come into your life aren't anything new and different. Many others have faced exactly the same problems before you. And no temptation is irresistible. You can trust God to keep the temptation from becoming so strong that you can't stand up against it, for he has promised this and will do what he says. He will show you how to escape temptation's power so that you can bear up patiently against it.

¹⁴So, dear friends, carefully avoid idol-worship of every kind.

Proverbs for Today
◄§ 11:16–17 §►

Honor goes to kind and gracious women, mere money to cruel men. □ Your own soul is nourished when you are kind; it is destroyed when you are cruel.

───────◄ **KEY VERSE** ►───────

But remember this—the wrong desires that come into your life aren't anything new and different. Many others have faced exactly the same problems before you. And no temptation is irresistible. You can trust God to keep the temptation from becoming so strong that you can't stand up against it, for he has promised this and will do what he says. He will show you how to escape temptation's power so that you can bear up patiently against it.—*1 Corinthians 10:13*

───────◄ **REFLECTION** ►───────

Jesus Christ was the only sinless and perfect human being who ever lived. Yet even he faced temptation. Even he had to resist Satan's offer to reject the laws of God. Yet God gave him the means to resist.

It is exactly the same for us as well. Even devout Christian couples will face Satan's attempts to trip them up. It's important for us to be on guard against those temptations—to be wary of tempting situations, and to resist them when they come. But it's also important to remember that with every temptation, God provides a way out.

Satan will bring temptations into your marriage—temptations that threaten to destroy the union God has given you. Expect them despite your Christian faith. Expect also that God will help you during those times, taking care of your needs and making you a stronger person in the process, if you will take the route of escape he has provided.

───────◄ **MEDITATION** ►───────

Heavenly Father, there is no human relationship that is as important as the one we have with each other. Help us to stick close to each other, to be wary of temptations, and always to take the ways of escape you provide. §►

MARCH 19 _____

Jesus Calls His First Disciples
◄§ Mark 1:14–20 §►

Later on, after John was arrested by King Herod, Jesus went to Galilee to preach God's Good News. [15]"At last the time has come!" he announced. "God's Kingdom is near! Turn from your sins and act on this glorious news!"

[16]One day as Jesus was walking along the shores of the Sea of Galilee, he saw Simon and his brother Andrew fishing with nets, for they were commercial fishermen. [17]Jesus called out to them, "Come, follow me! And I will make you fishermen for the souls of men!" [18]At once they left their nets and went along with him.

[19]A little farther up the beach, he saw Zebedee's sons, James and John, in a boat mending their nets. [20]He called them too, and immediately they left their father Zebedee in the boat with the hired men and went with him.

Communion—Sharing in the Lord's Death
◄§ 1 Corinthians 10:15–22 §►

You are intelligent people. Look now and see for yourselves whether what I am about to say is true. [16]When we ask the Lord's blessing upon our drinking from the cup of wine at the Lord's Table, this means, doesn't it, that all who drink it are sharing together the blessing of Christ's blood? And when we break off pieces of the bread from the loaf to eat there together, this shows that we are sharing together in the benefits of his body. [17]No matter how many of us there are, we all eat from the same loaf, showing that we are all parts of the one body

◄§ 104 §►

of Christ. [18]And the Jewish people, all who eat the sacrifices, are united by that act.

[19]What am I trying to say? Am I saying that the idols to whom the heathen bring sacrifices are really alive and are real gods, and that these sacrifices are of some value? No, not at all. [20]What I am saying is that those who offer food to these idols are united together in sacrificing to demons, certainly not to God. And I don't want any of you to be partners with demons when you eat the same food, along with the heathen, that has been offered to these idols. [21]You cannot drink from the cup at the Lord's Table and at Satan's table, too. You cannot eat bread both at the Lord's Table and at Satan's table.

[22]What? Are you tempting the Lord to be angry with you? Are you stronger than he is?

Proverbs for Today
◄§ 11:18–19 §►

The evil man gets rich for the moment, but the good man's reward lasts forever. The good man finds life; the evil man, death.

───────── ◄ KEY VERSE ► ─────────

The good man finds life; the evil man, death.
—*Proverbs 11:19*

───────── ◄ REFLECTION ► ─────────

Do you envy people you work with or see on the news who seem to effortlessly acquire worldly success? If the intent of their hearts is evil, they deserve your prayers, not your respect. The Bible says that their lives will end in destruction.

As a couple, keep your hearts and minds focused on Jesus Christ. Only then will you find true success. The riches and glory of those who live only to please themselves is fleeting and meaningless when compared to the eternal rewards awaiting those who commit their lives in faithful service to the Lord.

───────── ◄ MEDITATION ► ─────────

Heavenly Father, help us to replace our human desires for respect and material success with a keen hunger for righteousness and a love for those around us. §►

MARCH 20

Jesus Demonstrates His Authority
◄§ Mark 1:21–28 §►

Jesus and his companions now arrived at the town of Capernaum and on Saturday morning went into the Jewish place of worship—the synagogue—where he preached. [22]The congregation was surprised at his sermon because he spoke as an authority, and didn't try to prove his points by quoting others—quite unlike what they were used to hearing!

[23]A man possessed by a demon was present and began shouting, [24]"Why are you bothering us, Jesus of Nazareth—have you come to destroy us demons? I know who you are—the holy Son of God!"

[25]Jesus curtly commanded the demon to say no more and to come out of the man. [26]At that the evil spirit screamed and convulsed the man violently and left him. [27]Amazement gripped the audience and they began discussing what had happened.

"What sort of new religion is this?" they asked excitedly. "Why, even evil spirits obey his orders!"

[28]The news of what he had done spread quickly through that entire area of Galilee.

Do All to the Glory of God
◄§ 1 Corinthians 10:23—11:1 §►

You are certainly free to eat food offered to idols if you want to; it's not against God's laws to eat such meat, but that doesn't mean that you should go ahead and do it. It may be perfectly legal, but it may not be best and helpful. ²⁴Don't think only of yourself. Try to think of the other fellow, too, and what is best for him.

²⁵Here's what you should do. Take any meat you want that is sold at the market. Don't ask whether or not it was offered to idols, lest the answer hurt your conscience. ²⁶For the earth and every good thing in it belongs to the Lord and is yours to enjoy.

²⁷If someone who isn't a Christian asks you out to dinner, go ahead; accept the invitation if you want to. Eat whatever is on the table and don't ask any questions about it. Then you won't know whether or not it has been used as a sacrifice to idols, and you won't risk having a bad conscience over eating it. ²⁸But if someone warns you that this meat has been offered to idols, then don't eat it for the sake of the man who told you, and of his conscience. ²⁹In this case *his* feeling about it is the important thing, not yours.

But why, you may ask, must I be guided and limited by what someone else thinks? ³⁰If I can thank God for the food and enjoy it, why let someone spoil everything just because he thinks I am wrong? ³¹Well, I'll tell you why. It is because you must do everything for the glory of God, even your eating and drinking. ³²So don't be a stumbling block to anyone, whether they are Jews or Gentiles or Christians. ³³That is the plan I follow, too. I try to please everyone in everything I do, not doing what I like or what is best for me, but what is best for them, so that they may be saved.

¹¹·¹And you should follow my example, just as I follow Christ's.

Proverbs for Today
◄§ 11:20–21 §►

The Lord hates the stubborn but delights in those who are good. You can be very sure the evil man will not go unpunished forever. And you can also be very sure God will rescue the children of the godly.

_____ ◢ **KEY VERSE** ◣ _____

But why, you may ask, must I be guided and limited by what someone else thinks? If I can thank God for the food and enjoy it, why let someone spoil everything just because he thinks I am wrong? Well, I'll tell you why. It is because you must do everything for the glory of God, even your eating and drinking. —*1 Corinthians 10:29–31*

_____ ◢ **REFLECTION** ◣ _____

The unofficial anthem of modern culture is, "Do whatever you want as long as it doesn't keep others from fulfilling their own desires." God's Word presents a far different set of values for Christians to live by. We are to obey his laws and place him first in our lives. We are also to think of others before we consider our own needs.

You have been created in the image of God and, as Christians, must act accordingly. Keep your marriage focused on the standards God has established for his people. Ignore the "wisdom" of the world, for it is foolishness in God's eyes.

_____ ◢ **MEDITATION** ◣ _____

Heavenly Father, we dedicate our lives to your honor and glory and ask that you will forgive us when we allow our pride and selfish desires to keep us from doing your will. §►

Jesus Casts Out Demons and Heals Many
Mark 1:29–39

Then, leaving the synagogue, Jesus and his disciples went over to Simon and Andrew's home, where they found Simon's mother-in-law sick in bed with a high fever. They told Jesus about her right away. ³¹He went to her bedside, and as he took her by the hand and helped her to sit up, the fever suddenly left, and she got up and prepared dinner for them!

^{32,33}By sunset the courtyard was filled with the sick and demon-possessed, brought to him for healing; and a huge crowd of people from all over the city of Capernaum gathered outside the door to watch. ³⁴So Jesus healed great numbers of sick folk that evening and ordered many demons to come out of their victims. (But he refused to allow the demons to speak, because they knew who he was.)

³⁵The next morning he was up long before daybreak and went out alone into the wilderness to pray.

^{36,37}Later, Simon and the others went out to find him, and told him, "Everyone is asking for you."

³⁸But he replied, "We must go on to other towns as well, and give my message to them too, for that is why I came."

³⁹So he traveled throughout the province of Galilee, preaching in the synagogues and releasing many from the power of demons.

Women in the Church
1 Corinthians 11:2–16

I am so glad, dear brothers, that you have been remembering and doing everything I taught you. ³But there is one matter I want to remind you about: that a wife is responsible to her husband, her husband is responsible to Christ, and Christ is responsible to God. ⁴That is why, if a man refuses to remove his hat while praying or preaching, he dishonors Christ. ⁵And that is why a woman who publicly prays or prophesies without a covering on her head dishonors her husband [for her covering is a sign of her subjection to him]. ⁶Yes, if she refuses to wear a head covering, then she should cut off all her hair. And if it is shameful for a woman to have her head shaved, then she should wear a covering. ⁷But a man should not wear anything on his head [when worshiping, for his hat is a sign of subjection to men].

God's glory is man made in his image, and man's glory is the woman. ⁸The first man didn't come from woman, but the first woman came out of man. ⁹And Adam, the first man, was not made for Eve's benefit, but Eve was made for Adam. ¹⁰So a woman should wear a covering on her head as a sign that she is under man's authority, a fact for all the angels to notice and rejoice in.

¹¹But remember that in God's plan men and women need each other. ¹²For although the first woman came out of man, all men have been born from women ever since, and both men and women come from God their Creator.

¹³What do you yourselves really think about this? Is it right for a woman to pray in public without covering her head? ^{14,15}Doesn't even instinct itself teach us that women's heads should be covered? For women are proud of their long hair, while a man with long hair tends to be ashamed. ¹⁶But if anyone wants to argue about this, all I can say is that we never teach anything else than this—that a woman should wear a covering when prophesying or praying publicly in the church, and all the churches feel the same way about it.

Proverbs for Today
11:22

A beautiful woman lacking discretion and modesty is like a fine gold ring in a pig's snout.

✎ KEY VERSE ✎

But remember that in God's plan men and women need each other.—*1 Corinthians 11:11*

Much has been made over the past two decades about the so-called battle of the sexes. Many sociologists and secular marriage counselors believe that the differences between men and women are so significant that conflicts are not only inevitable, they are also healthy.

The Bible paints a far different picture about God's plan for the sexes. From creation we were designed to complement each other. Our natural affection is for the opposite sex. Take delight in your spouse and thank God daily for bringing the two of you together.

◈ MEDITATION ◈

Heavenly Father, we thank you for our marriage and ask that you will continue strengthening our love for each other and blessing our lives together. ❧

MARCH 22

Jesus Heals a Leper
◄§ Mark 1:40–45 ❧

Once a leper came and knelt in front of Jesus and begged to be healed. "If you want to, you can make me well again," he pled.

[41]And Jesus, moved with pity, touched him and said, "I want to! Be healed!" [42]Immediately the leprosy was gone—the man was healed!

[43,44]Jesus then told him sternly, "Go and be examined immediately by the Jewish priest. Don't stop to speak to anyone along the way. Take along the offering prescribed by Moses for a leper who is healed, so that everyone will have proof that you are well again."

[45]But as the man went on his way he began to shout the good news that he was healed; as a result, such throngs soon surrounded Jesus that he couldn't publicly enter a city anywhere, but had to stay out in the barren wastelands. And people from everywhere came to him there.

Gluttony at Communion Services
◄§ 1 Corinthians 11:17–22 ❧

Next on my list of items to write you about is something else I cannot agree with. For it sounds as if more harm than good is done when you meet together for your communion services. [18]Everyone keeps telling me about the arguing that goes on in these meetings, and the divisions developing among you, and I can just about believe it. [19]But I suppose you feel this is necessary so that you who are always right will become known and recognized!

[20]When you come together to eat, it isn't the Lord's Supper you are eating, [21]but your own. For I am told that everyone hastily gobbles all the food he can without waiting to share with the others, so that one doesn't get enough and goes hungry while another has too much to drink and gets drunk. [22]What? Is this really true? Can't you do your eating and drinking at home, to avoid disgracing the church and shaming those who are poor and can bring no food? What am I supposed to say about these things? Do you want me to praise you? Well, I certainly do not!

Proverbs for Today
◄§ 11:23 ❧

The good man can look forward to happiness, while the wicked can expect only wrath.

◈ KEY VERSE ◈

Everyone keeps telling me about the arguing that goes on in these meetings, and the divisions developing among you, and I can just about believe it. But I suppose you feel this is necessary so that you who are always right will become known and recognized!—*1 Corinthians 11:18–19*

Sometimes people are disagreeable and unkind because they have an uncontrollable need to always get the upper hand in relationships. They aren't happy until the other person concedes and lets them have their way. This attitude is not only boring and obnoxious, it's also sinful.

Paul tells us that it is better to demonstrate love toward each other than it is to have the last word.

A successful marriage is based on mutual respect in which each partner listens to and values the convictions and ideas of the other.

_____ ◦§ MEDITATION §◦ _____

Heavenly Father, forgive us when we do things that cause strife in our marriage. Help us to replace our pride and selfish ambitions with a desire for a peaceful and loving home. ❧

MARCH 23

Jesus Heals a Paralytic
◦§ Mark 2:1–12 §◦

Several days later Jesus returned to Capernaum, and the news of his arrival spread quickly through the city. [2]Soon the house where he was staying was so packed with visitors that there wasn't room for a single person more, not even outside the door. And he preached the Word to them. [3]Four men arrived carrying a paralyzed man on a stretcher. [4]They couldn't get to Jesus through the crowd, so they dug through the clay roof above his head and lowered the sick man on his stretcher, right down in front of Jesus.

[5]When Jesus saw how strongly they believed that he would help, Jesus said to the sick man, "Son, your sins are forgiven!"

[6]But some of the Jewish religious leaders said to themselves as they sat there, [7]"What? This is blasphemy! Does he think he is God? For only God can forgive sins."

[8]Jesus could read their minds and said to them at once, "Why does this bother you? [9,10,11]I, the Messiah, have the authority on earth to forgive sins. But talk is cheap—anybody could say that. So I'll prove it to you by healing this man." Then, turning to the paralyzed man, he commanded, "Pick up your stretcher and go on home, for you are healed!"

[12]The man jumped up, took the stretcher, and pushed his way through the stunned onlookers! Then how they praised God. "We've never seen anything like this before!" they all exclaimed.

Share in the Lord's Table in a Worthy Manner
◦§ 1 Corinthians 11:23–34 §◦

For this is what the Lord himself has said about his Table, and I have passed it on to you before: That on the night when Judas betrayed him, the Lord Jesus took bread, [24]and when he had given thanks to God for it, he broke it and gave it to his disciples and said, "Take this and eat it. This is my body, which is given for you. Do this to remember me." [25]In the same way, he took the cup of wine after supper, saying, "This cup is the new agreement between God and you that has been established and set in motion by my blood. Do this in remembrance of me whenever you drink it." [26]For every time you eat this bread and drink this cup you are re-telling the message of the Lord's death, that he has died for you. Do this until he comes again.

[27]So if anyone eats this bread and drinks from this cup of the Lord in an unworthy manner, he is guilty of sin against the body and the blood of the Lord. [28]That is why a man should examine himself carefully before eating the bread and drinking from the cup. [29]For if he eats the bread and drinks from the cup unworthily, not thinking about the body of Christ and what it means, he is eating and drinking God's judgment upon himself; for he is trifling with the death of Christ. [30]That is why many of you are weak and sick, and some have even died.

[31]But if you carefully examine yourselves before eating you will not need to be judged and punished. [32]Yet, when we are judged and punished by the Lord, it is so that we will not be condemned with the rest of the world. [33]So, dear brothers, when you gather for the Lord's Supper—the communion service—wait for each other; [34]if anyone is really hungry he should eat at home so that he won't bring punishment upon himself when you meet together.

I'll talk to you about the other matters after I arrive.

Proverbs for Today
⋖§ 11:24–26 §⋗

It is possible to give away and become richer! It is also possible to hold on too tightly and lose everything. Yes, the liberal man shall be rich! By watering others, he waters himself. People curse the man who holds his grain for higher prices, but they bless the man who sells it to them in their time of need.

⋖ KEY VERSE §⋗

It is possible to give away and become richer! It is also possible to hold on too tightly and lose everything.—*Proverbs 11:24*

⋖ REFLECTION §⋗

Surveys consistently reveal that the vast majority of people believe that greed is wrong. Yet these same studies show that an even greater percentage of individuals want to own a nicer house and make more money. This contradiction demonstrates the tension that exists in the hearts of most people when it comes to possessions. They want to be generous and charitable with others, but they just don't want to do anything that will jeopardize their own standard of living.

Christians know that all that we have is a gift from God. Don't hang on to what you really don't own in the first place. Give freely to the work of God's Kingdom and trust him to provide for your needs. The peace and joy that come from sharing with others will bring far greater rewards than mere temporal wealth.

⋖ MEDITATION §⋗

Heavenly Father, we thank you for all the many blessings and gifts you have freely bestowed upon us and our marriage. Reveal to us ways we can be equally generous with others who have less than we do. §⋗

MARCH 24

Jesus Calls Levi to Be His Disciple
⋖§ Mark 2:13–17 §⋗

Then Jesus went out to the seashore again, and preached to the crowds that gathered around him. [14]As he was walking up the beach he saw Levi, the son of Alphaeus, sitting at his tax collection booth. "Come with me," Jesus told him. "Come be my disciple."

And Levi jumped to his feet and went along.

[15]That night Levi invited his fellow tax collectors and many other notorious sinners to be his dinner guests so that they could meet Jesus and his disciples. (There were many men of this type among the crowds that followed him.) [16]But when some of the Jewish religious leaders saw him eating with these men of ill repute, they said to his disciples, "How can he stand it, to eat with such scum?"

[17]When Jesus heard what they were saying, he told them, "Sick people need the doctor, not healthy ones! I haven't come to tell good people to repent, but the bad ones."

Judging the Truthfulness of a Message
⋖§ 1 Corinthians 12:1–3 §⋗

And now, brothers, I want to write about the special abilities the Holy Spirit gives to each of you, for I don't want any misunderstanding about them. ²You will remember that before you became Christians you went around from one idol to another, not one of which could speak a single word. ³But now you are meeting people who claim to speak messages from the Spirit of God. How can you know whether they are really inspired by God or whether they are fakes? Here is the test: no one speaking by the power of the Spirit of God can curse Jesus, and no one can say, "Jesus is Lord," and really mean it, unless the Holy Spirit is helping him.

Proverbs for Today
≈§ 11:27 §≈

If you search for good you will find God's favor; if you search for evil you will find his curse.

◦ KEY VERSE ◦

But now you are meeting people who claim to speak messages from the Spirit of God. How can you know whether they are really inspired by God or whether they are fakes? Here is the test: no one speaking by the power of the Spirit of God can

curse Jesus, and no one can say, "Jesus is Lord," and really mean it, unless the Holy Spirit is helping him.—*1 Corinthians 12:3*

◦ REFLECTION ◦

If there was ever an occupation for which there is an abundance of candidates it is writing an advice column. The world seems filled with people who are ready, willing, and eager to share their opinions with anyone who crosses their paths.

While it is important to seek the counsel of wise and godly people, it is also imperative that you test their advice against the Word of God. If what they tell you contradicts the laws that God has established for his people, turn your back on what they have to say. And, if either of you are asked to share your opinion with another person or couple, turn first to the Scriptures so that you don't become a stumbling block to him or her.

◦ MEDITATION ◦

Heavenly Father, bless us with wise and godly friends with whom we can have regular fellowship and who can help us grow in our faith. §≈

MARCH 25

The Bridegroom and His Friends
≈§ Mark 2:18–22 §≈

John's disciples and the Jewish leaders sometimes fasted, that is, went without food as part of their religion. One day some people came to Jesus and asked why his disciples didn't do this too.
¹⁹Jesus replied, "Do friends of the bridegroom refuse to eat at the wedding feast? Should they be sad while he is with them? ²⁰But some day he will be taken away from them, and then they will mourn. ²¹[Besides, going without food is part of the old way of doing things.] It is like patching an old garment with unshrunk cloth! What happens? The patch pulls away and leaves the hole worse than before. ²²You know better than to put new wine into old wineskins. They would burst. The wine would be

spilled out and the wineskins ruined. New wine needs fresh wineskins."

Spiritual Gifts in the Church
≈§ 1 Corinthians 12:4–11 §≈

Now God gives us many kinds of special abilities, but it is the same Holy Spirit who is the source of them all. ⁵There are different kinds of service to God, but it is the same Lord we are serving. ⁶There are many ways in which God works in our lives, but it is the same God who does the work in and through all of us who are his. ⁷The Holy Spirit displays God's power through each of us as a means of helping the entire church.

⁸To one person the Spirit gives the ability to give wise advice; someone else may be especially good

at studying and teaching, and this is his gift from the same Spirit. [9]He gives special faith to another, and to someone else the power to heal the sick. [10]He gives power for doing miracles to some, and to others power to prophesy and preach. He gives someone else the power to know whether evil spirits are speaking through those who claim to be giving God's messages—or whether it is really the Spirit of God who is speaking. Still another person is able to speak in languages he never learned; and others, who do not know the language either, are given power to understand what he is saying. [11]It is the same and only Holy Spirit who gives all these gifts and powers, deciding which each one of us should have.

Proverbs for Today
◅§ 11:28 §▻

Trust in your money and down you go! Trust in God and flourish as a tree!

────────◦ KEY VERSE ◦────────

You know better than to put new wine into old wineskins. They would burst. The wine would be spilled out and the wineskins ruined. New wine needs fresh wineskins.—*Mark 2:22*

────────◦ REFLECTION ◦────────

Jesus used many different analogies and parables during his ministry to explain difficult theological concepts to his followers. This familiar metaphor was used by Christ to describe the condition of the Pharisees' hearts and their unwillingness to accept God's divine order rather than their own man-made laws.

If God is trying to work in your marriage and is asking you to accept his will for your lives, don't become rigid and turn away from him. Allow the Holy Spirit to perform a new work in you. The changes he will create in your marriage will bring great joy and peace to your home and will make you increasingly eager to know more about his abundant plan for each of you.

────────◦ MEDITATION ◦────────

Heavenly Father, share with us the design you have for our lives and prepare our hearts so that we will be able to understand and willingly accept your divine and perfect plan. §▻

MARCH 26 _____

Jesus Has Authority over the Sabbath
◅§ Mark 2:23–3:6 §▻

Another time, on a Sabbath day as Jesus and his disciples were walking through the fields, the disciples were breaking off heads of wheat and eating the grain.

[24]Some of the Jewish religious leaders said to Jesus, "They shouldn't be doing that! It's against our laws to work by harvesting grain on the Sabbath."

[25,26]But Jesus replied, "Didn't you ever hear about the time King David and his companions were hungry, and he went into the house of God—Abiathar was High Priest then—and they ate the special bread only priests were allowed to eat? That was against the law too. [27]But the Sabbath was made to benefit man, and not man to benefit the Sabbath. [28]And I, the Messiah, have authority even to decide what men can do on Sabbath days!"

[3:1]While in Capernaum Jesus went over to the synagogue again, and noticed a man there with a deformed hand.

[2]Since it was the Sabbath, Jesus' enemies watched him closely. Would he heal the man's hand? If he did, they planned to arrest him!

[3]Jesus asked the man to come and stand in front of the congregation. [4]Then turning to his enemies he asked, "Is it all right to do kind deeds on Sabbath days? Or is this a day for doing harm? Is it a

day to save lives or to destroy them?'' But they wouldn't answer him. [5]Looking around at them angrily, for he was deeply disturbed by their indifference to human need, he said to the man, ''Reach out your hand.'' He did, and instantly his hand was healed!

[6]At once the Pharisees went away and met with the Herodians to discuss plans for killing Jesus.

The Body of Christ Has Many Parts
◄§ 1 Corinthians 12:12–18 ᠑►

Our bodies have many parts, but the many parts make up only one body when they are all put together. So it is with the ''body'' of Christ. [13]Each of us is a part of the one body of Christ. Some of us are Jews, some are Gentiles, some are slaves and some are free. But the Holy Spirit has fitted us all together into one body. We have been baptized into Christ's body by the one Spirit, and have all been given that same Holy Spirit.

[14]Yes, the body has many parts, not just one part. [15]If the foot says, ''I am not a part of the body because I am not a hand,'' that does not make it any less a part of the body. [16]And what would you think if you heard an ear say, ''I am not part of the body because I am only an ear, and not an eye''? Would that make it any less a part of the body? [17]Suppose the whole body were an eye—then how would you hear? Or if your whole body were just one big ear, how could you smell anything?

[18]But that isn't the way God has made us. He has made many parts for our bodies and has put each part just where he wants it.

Proverbs for Today
◄§ 11:29–31 ᠑►

The fool who provokes his family to anger and resentment will finally have nothing worthwhile left. He shall be the servant of a wiser man. □ Godly men are growing a tree that bears life-giving fruit, and all who win souls are wise. □ Even the godly shall be rewarded here on earth; how much more the wicked!

───────────◄§ KEY VERSE ᠑►───────────

The fool who provokes his family to anger and resentment will finally have nothing worthwhile left. He shall be the servant of a wiser man.—*Proverbs 11:29*

───────────◄§ REFLECTION ᠑►───────────

When you live with someone for a long time, you begin to learn which buttons to push that will make him or her angry, defensive, or insecure. The Bible states that only a foolish person will use this knowledge to gain the upper hand in a relationship. These buttons are much like the one frequently mentioned in spy novels that triggers the countdown to launch a nuclear arsenal. Once pushed, the only thing left standing are smoldering ruins. For the sake of your marriage, your family, and your own serenity, don't push them! Like a good ambassador, always look for ways to arrive at peaceful solutions.

───────────◄§ MEDITATION ᠑►───────────

Heavenly Father, forgive us when we knowingly provoke each other to anger. Help us both to have a deep and abiding desire for peace and harmony in our home. ᠑►

MARCH 27

Jesus Chooses His Twelve Disciples
◄§ Mark 3:7–19 ᠑►

Meanwhile, Jesus and his disciples withdrew to the beach, followed by a huge crowd from all over Galilee, Judea, Jerusalem, Idumea, from beyond the Jordan River, and even from as far away as Tyre and Sidon. For the news about his miracles had spread far and wide and vast numbers came to see him for themselves.

[9]He instructed his disciples to bring around a boat and to have it standing ready to rescue him in case he was crowded off the beach. [10]For there had been many healings that day and as a result great numbers of sick people were crowding around him, trying to touch him.

[11]And whenever those possessed by demons caught sight of him they would fall down before him shrieking, "You are the Son of God!" [12]But he strictly warned them not to make him known.

[13]Afterwards he went up into the hills and summoned certain ones he chose, inviting them to come and join him there; and they did. [14,15]Then he selected twelve of them to be his regular companions and to go out to preach and to cast out demons. [16-19]These are the names of the twelve he chose:

Simon (he renamed him "Peter"),
James and John (the sons of Zebedee, but Jesus called them "Sons of Thunder"),
Andrew,
Philip,
Bartholomew,
Matthew,
Thomas,
James (the son of Alphaeus),
Thaddaeus,
Simon (a member of a political party advocating violent overthrow of the Roman government),
Judas Iscariot (who later betrayed him).

All Parts of the Body Are Necessary
1 Corinthians 12:19–27

What a strange thing a body would be if it had only one part! [20]So he has made many parts, but still there is only one body.

[21]The eye can never say to the hand, "I don't need you." The head can't say to the feet, "I don't need you."

[22]And some of the parts that seem weakest and least important are really the most necessary. [23]Yes, we are especially glad to have some parts that seem rather odd! And we carefully protect from the eyes of others those parts that should not be seen, [24]while of course the parts that may be seen do not require this special care. So God has put the body together in such a way that extra honor and care are given to those parts that might otherwise seem less important. [25]This makes for happiness among the parts, so that the parts have the same care for each other that they do for themselves. [26]If one part suffers, all parts suffer with it, and if one part is honored, all the parts are glad.

[27]Now here is what I am trying to say: All of you together are the one body of Christ and each one of you is a separate and necessary part of it.

Proverbs for Today
12:1

To learn, you must want to be taught. To refuse reproof is stupid.

KEY VERSE

What a strange thing a body would be if it had only one part! So he has made many parts, but still there is only one body. —*1 Corinthians 12:19–20*

REFLECTION

This verse tells us about the different roles people play in the church. Each of these roles—from the pastor to the person who sets up the coffee pot every Sunday morning—is important. If a congregation is to fulfill its commission to spread the Good News of salvation to the world, every role must be filled.

This message is also applicable to the roles two people serve in a marriage. Each of you is equally important, and you both bring specific skills and strengths to your relationship. Lean on each other's strengths. Together you can be a dynamic unit in which each person provides support and encouragement to the other.

MEDITATION

Heavenly Father, we thank you for our individual strengths and ask that we can encourage each other in our roles as Christians and as husband and wife.

The Kingdom of God and the Kingdom of Satan
✑ Mark 3:20–35 ✒

When Jesus returned to the house where he was staying, the crowds began to gather again, and soon it was so full of visitors that he couldn't even find time to eat. [21]When his friends heard what was happening they came to try to take him home with them.

"He's out of his mind," they said.

[22]But the Jewish teachers of religion who had arrived from Jerusalem said, "His trouble is that he's possessed by Satan, king of demons. That's why demons obey him."

[23]Jesus summoned these men and asked them (using proverbs they all understood), "How can Satan cast out Satan? [24]A kingdom divided against itself will collapse. [25]A home filled with strife and division destroys itself. [26]And if Satan is fighting against himself, how can he accomplish anything? He would never survive. [27][Satan must be bound before his demons are cast out], just as a strong man must be tied up before his house can be ransacked and his property robbed.

[28]"I solemnly declare that any sin of man can be forgiven, even blasphemy against me; [29]but blasphemy against the Holy Spirit can never be forgiven. It is an eternal sin."

[30]He told them this because they were saying he did his miracles by Satan's power [instead of acknowledging it was by the Holy Spirit's power].

[31,32]Now his mother and brothers arrived at the crowded house where he was teaching, and they sent word for him to come out and talk with them. "Your mother and brothers are outside and want to see you," he was told.

[33]He replied, "Who is my mother? Who are my brothers?" [34]Looking at those around him he said, "These are my mother and brothers! [35]Anyone who does God's will is my brother, and my sister, and my mother."

The Gifts of the Spirit
✑ 1 Corinthians 12:28–31 ✒

Here is a list of some of the parts he has placed in his Church, which is his body:

Apostles,
Prophets—those who preach God's Word,
Teachers,
Those who do miracles,
Those who have the gift of healing;
Those who can help others,
Those who can get others to work together,
Those who speak in languages they have never
 learned.

[29]Is everyone an apostle? Of course not. Is everyone a preacher? No. Are all teachers? Does everyone have the power to do miracles? [30]Can everyone heal the sick? Of course not. Does God give all of us the ability to speak in languages we've never learned? Can just anyone understand and translate what those are saying who have that gift of foreign speech? [31]No, but try your best to have the more important of these gifts.

First, however, let me tell you about something else that is better than any of them!

Proverbs for Today
✑ 12:2–3 ✒

The Lord blesses good men and condemns the wicked. Wickedness never brings real success; only the godly have that.

✑ KEY VERSE ✒

He replied, "Who is my mother? Who are my brothers?" Looking at those around him he said, "These are my mother and brothers! Anyone who does God's will is my brother, and my sister, and my mother."—*Mark 3:33–35*

✑ REFLECTION ✒

Much has been made lately about the meaning and significance of families. Everyone from politicians to soap manufacturers are using a particular definition of "family" to advance their personal agenda. It's true that families are important. Very important. Traditional families must be protected and preserved for the sake of future generations. Yet we must never forget that, as Christians, we are part of a much bigger and even more important family: the family of God. As you strive to meet the needs of your earthly family, remember that your primary allegiance is to your Heavenly Father and his Kingdom.

MEDITATION

Heavenly Father, we thank you for each other and the family you have helped us to establish. We also thank you for our extended Christian family and pray for the well-being of all our brothers and sisters in the Lord around the world.

MARCH 29

The Parable of the Soils
Mark 4:1–20

Once again an immense crowd gathered around Jesus on the beach as he was teaching, so he got into a boat and sat down and talked from there. ²His usual method of teaching was to tell the people stories. One of them went like this:

³"Listen! A farmer decided to sow some grain. As he scattered it across his field, ⁴some of it fell on a path, and the birds came and picked it off the hard ground and ate it. ⁵,⁶Some fell on thin soil with underlying rock. It grew up quickly enough, but soon wilted beneath the hot sun and died because the roots had no nourishment in the shallow soil. ⁷Other seeds fell among thorns that shot up and crowded the young plants so that they produced no grain. ⁸But some of the seeds fell into good soil and yielded thirty times as much as he had planted—some of it even sixty or a hundred times as much! ⁹If you have ears, listen!"

¹⁰Afterwards, when he was alone with the twelve and with his other disciples, they asked him, "What does your story mean?"

¹¹,¹²He replied, "You are permitted to know some truths about the kingdom of God that are hidden to those outside the kingdom:

'Though they see and hear, they will not
understand or turn to God, or be forgiven for
their sins.'

¹³But if you can't understand *this* simple illustration, what will you do about all the others I am going to tell?

¹⁴"The farmer I talked about is anyone who brings God's message to others, trying to plant good seed within their lives. ¹⁵The hard pathway, where some of the seed fell, represents the hard hearts of some of those who hear God's message; Satan comes at once to try to make them forget it. ¹⁶The rocky soil represents the hearts of those who hear the message with joy, ¹⁷but, like young plants in such soil, their roots don't go very deep, and though at first they get along fine, as soon as persecution begins, they wilt.

¹⁸"The thorny ground represents the hearts of people who listen to the Good News and receive it, ¹⁹but all too quickly the attractions of this world and the delights of wealth, and the search for success and lure of nice things come in and crowd out God's message from their hearts, so that no crop is produced.

²⁰"But the good soil represents the hearts of those who truly accept God's message and produce a plentiful harvest for God—thirty, sixty, or even a hundred times as much as was planted in their hearts."

The Characteristics of Love
1 Corinthians 13:1–7

If I had the gift of being able to speak in other languages without learning them, and could speak in every language there is in all of heaven and earth, but didn't love others, I would only be making noise. [2]If I had the gift of prophecy and knew all about what is going to happen in the future, knew everything about *everything*, but didn't love others, what good would it do? Even if I had the gift of faith so that I could speak to a mountain and make it move, I would still be worth nothing at all without love. [3]If I gave everything I have to poor people, and if I were burned alive for preaching the Gospel but didn't love others, it would be of no value whatever.

[4]Love is very patient and kind, never jealous or envious, never boastful or proud, [5]never haughty or selfish or rude. Love does not demand its own way. It is not irritable or touchy. It does not hold grudges and will hardly even notice when others do it wrong. [6]It is never glad about injustice, but rejoices whenever truth wins out. [7]If you love someone you will be loyal to him no matter what the cost. You will always believe in him, always expect the best of him, and always stand your ground in defending him.

Proverbs for Today
❧ 12:4 ❧

A worthy wife is her husband's joy and crown; the other kind corrodes his strength and tears down everything he does.

❧ KEY VERSE ❧

If you love someone, you will be loyal to him no matter what the cost. You will always believe in him, always expect the best of him, and always stand your ground in defending him.—*1 Corinthians 13:7*

❧ REFLECTION ❧

A word that is used frequently when people refer to a married couple is commitment. "They really seem like a very committed couple." "Their commitment to each other was apparent after he lost his job." "Her illness really tested their commitment."

While it's true that commitment is an important part of a successful marriage, the most important ingredient is love. You can be committed to a job but not love it. You can be committed to paying your taxes but not feel any affection for your W2 form. The same is true for a married couple. Commitment will serve you during the best and worst of times. But love will transcend the mundane activities of your lives together and ensure that you will forsake all others for the one you vowed to cherish as long you both live.

❧ MEDITATION ❧

Heavenly Father, our love for each other is exceeded only by our love for you. We thank you that you have given each of us the perfect partner and pray that you will continue to bless our lives together. ❧

MARCH 30

Illustrations of the Kingdom of God
❧ Mark 4:21–34 ❧

Then Jesus asked them, "When someone lights a lamp, does he put a box over it to shut out the light? Of course not! The light couldn't be seen or used. A lamp is placed on a stand to shine and be useful.

[22]"All that is now hidden will someday come to light. [23]If you have ears, listen! [24]And be sure to put into practice what you hear. The more you do this, the more you will understand what I tell you. [25]To him who has shall be given; from him who has not shall be taken away even what he has.

[26]"Here is another story illustrating what the Kingdom of God is like:

"A farmer sowed his field, [27]and went away, and as the days went by, the seeds grew and grew without his help. [28]For the soil made the seeds grow.

First a leaf-blade pushed through, and later the wheat-heads formed and finally the grain ripened, [29]and then the farmer came at once with his sickle and harvested it."

[30]Jesus asked, "How can I describe the Kingdom of God? What story shall I use to illustrate it? [31,32]It is like a tiny mustard seed! Though this is one of the smallest of seeds, yet it grows to become one of the largest of plants, with long branches where birds can build their nests and be sheltered."

[33]He used many such illustrations to teach the people as much as they were ready to understand. [34]In fact, he taught only by illustrations in his public teaching, but afterwards, when he was alone with his disciples, he would explain his meaning to them.

Love Is the Greatest Gift
1 Corinthians 13:8–13

All the special gifts and powers from God will someday come to an end, but love goes on forever. Someday prophecy, and speaking in unknown languages, and special knowledge—these gifts will disappear. [9]Now we know so little, even with our special gifts, and the preaching of those most gifted is still so poor. [10]But when we have been made perfect and complete, then the need for these inadequate special gifts will come to an end, and they will disappear.

[11]It's like this: when I was a child I spoke and thought and reasoned as a child does. But when I became a man my thoughts grew far beyond those of my childhood, and now I have put away the childish things. [12]In the same way, we can see and understand only a little about God now, as if we were peering at his reflection in a poor mirror; but someday we are going to see him in his completeness, face to face. Now all that I know is hazy and blurred, but then I will see everything clearly, just as clearly as God sees into my heart right now.

[13]There are three things that remain—faith, hope, and love—and the greatest of these is love.

Proverbs for Today
12:5–7

A good man's mind is filled with honest thoughts; an evil man's mind is crammed with lies. □ The wicked accuse; the godly defend. The wicked shall perish; the godly shall stand.

KEY VERSE

In the same way, we can see and understand only a little about God now, as if we were peering at his reflection in a poor mirror; but someday we are going to see him in his completeness, face to face. Now all that I know is hazy and blurred, but then I will see everything clearly, just as clearly as God sees into my heart right now.—*1 Corinthians 13:12*

REFLECTION

God's revelation to his people is progressive. The deeper the relationship you and your spouse have with the Lord, the more he will reveal himself to you. In this verse, Paul shares God's promise that someday, when we get to Heaven, God will show us his complete glory and we will understand everything perfectly that now seems confusing.

A marriage is also built on "progressive revelation." One of the joys of married life is the chance to completely know another person. By sharing in each other's hopes, fears, triumphs, and tragedies, the love and devotion a couple have for one another will grow and mature. Remember, just as you don't have to completely understand the ways of God to serve him faithfully, you also don't have to figure out such mysteries as why your spouse puts syrup on cottage cheese to love him or her with all your heart.

MEDITATION

Heavenly Father, we ask that you will walk with us throughout our lives and continue to reveal yourself to us as our faith grows. We also pray that you will rekindle daily our desire to know one another in a deeper way so that our love will continue to grow and mature.

Jesus Calms the Storm
✥ Mark 4:35–41 ✥

As evening fell, Jesus said to his disciples, "Let's cross to the other side of the lake." [36]So they took him just as he was and started out, leaving the crowds behind (though other boats followed). [37]But soon a terrible storm arose. High waves began to break into the boat until it was nearly full of water and about to sink. [38]Jesus was asleep at the back of the boat with his head on a cushion. Frantically they wakened him, shouting, "Teacher, don't you even care that we are all about to drown?"

[39]Then he rebuked the wind and said to the sea, "Quiet down!" And the wind fell, and there was a great calm!

[40]And he asked them, "Why were you so fearful? Don't you even yet have confidence in me?"

[41]And they were filled with awe and said among themselves, "Who is this man, that even the winds and seas obey him?"

Prophecy and Tongues
✥ 1 Corinthians 14:1–5 ✥

Let love be your greatest aim; nevertheless, ask also for the special abilities the Holy Spirit gives, and especially the gift of prophecy, being able to preach the messages of God.

[2]But if your gift is that of being able to "speak in tongues," that is, to speak in languages you haven't learned, you will be talking to God but not to others, since they won't be able to understand you. You will be speaking by the power of the Spirit but it will all be a secret. [3]But one who prophesies, preaching the messages of God, is helping others grow in the Lord, encouraging and comforting them. [4]So a person "speaking in tongues" helps himself grow spiritually, but one who prophesies, preaching messages from God, helps the entire church grow in holiness and happiness.

[5]I wish you all had the gift of "speaking in tongues" but, even more, I wish you were all able to prophesy, preaching God's messages, for that is a greater and more useful power than to speak in unknown languages—unless, of course, you can tell everyone afterwards what you were saying, so that they can get some good out of it too.

Proverbs for Today
✥ 12:8–9 ✥

Everyone admires a man with good sense, but a man with a warped mind is despised. □ It is better to get your hands dirty—and eat, than to be too proud to work—and starve.

✥ KEY VERSE ✥

And they were filled with awe and said among themselves, "Who is this man, that even the winds and seas obey him?"—*Mark 4:41*

✥ REFLECTION ✥

Life is unpredictable. Each day we are confronted with decisions and events that cause us anxiety and uncertainty. One of the great comforts of the Christian life is knowing we can rest in the assurance that God is in complete control. Just as Jesus said that our Heavenly Father is even concerned about the sparrow that falls from its nest, we are guaranteed that he cares about us infinitely more.

If you and your spouse are going through a time of hardship or indecision, turn your cares over to the Lord. If he can calm the winds and seas, he is more than able and willing to meet your needs and reveal his will for your lives.

✥ MEDITATION ✥

Heavenly Father, even though our lives are unpredictable, we are thankful that they are in your hands and that you will guide and protect us if we live faithfully according to your will.

Jesus Casts Out Demons
⌁ Mark 5:1–20 ⌁

When Jesus and his disciples arrived at the other side of the lake a demon-possessed man ran out from a graveyard, just as Jesus was climbing from the boat.

3,4This man lived among the gravestones, and had such strength that whenever he was put into handcuffs and shackles—as he often was—he snapped the handcuffs from his wrists and smashed the shackles and walked away. No one was strong enough to control him. 5All day long and through the night he would wander among the tombs and in the wild hills, screaming and cutting himself with sharp pieces of stone.

6When Jesus was still far out on the water, the man had seen him and had run to meet him, and fell down before him.

7,8Then Jesus spoke to the demon within the man and said, "Come out, you evil spirit."

It gave a terrible scream, shrieking, "What are you going to do to me, Jesus, Son of the Most High God? For God's sake, don't torture me!"

9"What is your name?" Jesus asked, and the demon replied, "Legion, for there are many of us here within this man."

10Then the demons begged him again and again not to send them to some distant land.

11Now as it happened there was a huge herd of hogs rooting around on the hill above the lake. 12"Send us into those hogs," the demons begged.

13And Jesus gave them permission. Then the evil spirits came out of the man and entered the hogs, and the entire herd plunged down the steep hillside into the lake and drowned.

14The herdsmen fled to the nearby towns and countryside, spreading the news as they ran. Everyone rushed out to see for themselves. 15And a large crowd soon gathered where Jesus was; but as they saw the man sitting there, fully clothed and perfectly sane, they were frightened. 16Those who saw what happened were telling everyone about it, 17and the crowd began pleading with Jesus to go

away and leave them alone! 18So he got back into the boat. The man who had been possessed by the demons begged Jesus to let him go along. 19But Jesus said no.

"Go home to your friends," he told him, "and tell them what wonderful things God has done for you; and how merciful he has been."

20So the man started off to visit the Ten Towns of that region and began to tell everyone about the great things Jesus had done for him; and they were awestruck by his story.

The Need for Understanding in the Church
⌁ 1 Corinthians 14:6–12 ⌁

Dear friends, even if I myself should come to you talking in some language you don't understand, how would that help you? But if I speak plainly what God has revealed to me, and tell you the things I know, and what is going to happen, and the great truths of God's Word—that is what you need; that is what will help you. 7Even musical instruments—the flute, for instance, or the harp—are examples of the need for speaking in plain, simple English rather than in unknown languages. For no one will recognize the tune the flute is playing unless each note is sounded clearly. 8And if the army bugler doesn't play the right notes, how will the soldiers know that they are being called to battle? 9In the same way, if you talk to a person in some language he doesn't understand, how will he know what you mean? You might as well be talking to an empty room.

10I suppose that there are hundreds of different languages in the world, and all are excellent for those who understand them, 11but to me they mean nothing. A person talking to me in one of these languages will be a stranger to me and I will be a stranger to him. 12Since you are so anxious to have special gifts from the Holy Spirit, ask him for the very best, for those that will be of real help to the whole church.

Proverbs for Today

A good man is concerned for the welfare of his animals, but even the kindness of godless men is cruel.

KEY VERSE

"Go home to your friends," he told him, "and tell them what wonderful things God has done for you; and how merciful he has been."—*Mark 5:19b*

REFLECTION

This man had been demon possessed but now was a living example of Jesus' power. He wanted to go with Jesus, but Jesus told him to go home and share his story.

If you have experienced Jesus' power in your marriage, both of you can be a living example to other married couples. Are you, like this man, willing to share how God has helped you and your relationship? What lessons have you learned that you can share with other couples? Just as we would tell others about a doctor who cured a physical disease, we should tell about the ways Christ cures our selfish ways in marriage.

MEDITATION

Heavenly Father, we thank you for all the many blessings you have given us. We pray that we will be a witness of your goodness to others. §§-

APRIL 2

Jesus Performs Miracles of Healing
-§ Mark 5:21–43 §§-

When Jesus had gone across by boat to the other side of the lake, a vast crowd gathered around him on the shore.

22The leader of the local synagogue, whose name was Jairus, came and fell down before him, 23pleading with him to heal his little daughter.

"She is at the point of death," he said in desperation. "Please come and place your hands on her and make her live."

24Jesus went with him, and the crowd thronged behind. 25In the crowd was a woman who had been sick for twelve years with a hemorrhage. 26She had suffered much from many doctors through the years and had become poor from paying them, and was no better but, in fact, was worse. 27She had heard all about the wonderful miracles Jesus did, and that is why she came up behind him through the crowd and touched his clothes.

28For she thought to herself, "If I can just touch his clothing, I will be healed." 29And sure enough, as soon as she had touched him, the bleeding stopped and she knew she was well!

30Jesus realized at once that healing power had gone out from him, so he turned around in the crowd and asked, "Who touched my clothes?"

31His disciples said to him, "All this crowd pressing around you, and you ask who touched you?"

32But he kept on looking around to see who it was who had done it. 33Then the frightened woman, trembling at the realization of what had happened to her, came and fell at his feet and told him what she had done. 34And he said to her, "Daughter, your faith has made you well; go in peace, healed of your disease."

35While he was still talking to her, messengers arrived from Jairus' home with the news that it was too late—his daughter was dead and there was no point in Jesus' coming now. 36But Jesus ignored their comments and said to Jairus, "Don't be afraid. Just trust me."

37Then Jesus halted the crowd and wouldn't let anyone go on with him to Jairus' home except Peter and James and John. 38When they arrived, Jesus saw that all was in great confusion, with unrestrained weeping and wailing. 39He went inside and spoke to the people.

"Why all this weeping and commotion?" he asked. "The child isn't dead; she is only asleep!"

[40]They laughed at him in bitter derision, but he told them all to leave, and taking the little girl's father and mother and his three disciples, he went into the room where she was lying.

[41,42]Taking her by the hand he said to her, "Get up, little girl!" (She was twelve years old.) And she jumped up and walked around! Her parents just couldn't get over it. [43]Jesus instructed them very earnestly not to tell what had happened, and told them to give her something to eat.

Pray for the Ability to Interpret
◄§ 1 Corinthians 14:13–17 ᴈ►

If someone is given the gift of speaking in unknown tongues, he should pray also for the gift of knowing what he has said, so that he can tell people afterwards, plainly. [14]For if I pray in a language I don't understand, my spirit is praying but I don't know what I am saying.

[15]Well, then, what shall I do? I will do both. I will pray in unknown tongues and also in ordinary language that everyone understands. I will sing in unknown tongues and also in ordinary language, so that I can understand the praise I am giving; [16]for if you praise and thank God with the spirit alone, speaking in another language, how can those who don't understand you be praising God along with you? How can they join you in giving thanks when they don't know what you are saying? [17]You will be giving thanks very nicely, no doubt, but the other people present won't be helped.

Proverbs for Today
◄§ 12:11 ᴈ►

Hard work means prosperity; only a fool idles away his time.

◄● KEY VERSE ●

She thought to herself, "If I can just touch his clothing, I will be healed." And sure enough, as soon as she had touched him, the bleeding stopped and she knew she was well!—*Mark 5:28–29*

◄● REFLECTION ●

This woman had an incurable condition causing her to bleed constantly. This may have been menstrual or uterine disorder which would have made her ritually unclean (Leviticus 15:25–27) and excluded her from most social contact with other Jews. She desperately wanted Jesus to heal her, but she knew her bleeding would cause Jesus to be "unclean" under Jewish law if she touched him. Still, she reached out by faith and was healed.

Sometimes you may feel that problems in your marriage will keep you from God. Or perhaps you feel that you are not worthy to approach God. But God is always ready to help; we should never allow our fear or sin to keep us from approaching him. Coming to God for help is the first step in healing our broken relationships.

◄● MEDITATION ●

Heavenly Father, we come to you, honestly submitting each specific problem we are having in our marriage to you and asking that you will grant us the peace and wisdom we need to solve them. ᴈ►

APRIL 3

A Prophet Is not Honored in His Hometown
◄§ Mark 6:1–6 ᴈ►

Soon afterwards Jesus left that section of the country and returned with his disciples to Nazareth, his home town. [2,3]The next Sabbath he went to the synagogue to teach, and the people were astonished at his wisdom and his miracles because he was just a local man like themselves.

"He's no better than we are," they said. "He's just a carpenter, Mary's boy, and a brother of James and Joseph, Judas and Simon. And his sisters live right here among us." And they were offended!

[4]Then Jesus told them, "A prophet is honored everywhere except in his home town and among his relatives and by his own family." [5]And because of their unbelief he couldn't do any mighty miracles among them except to place his hands on a few sick people and heal them. [6]And he could hardly accept the fact that they wouldn't believe in him.

Then he went out among the villages, teaching.

Tongues Is a Sign to Unbelievers
1 Corinthians 14:18–25

I thank God that I "speak in tongues" privately more than any of the rest of you. [19]But in public worship I would much rather speak five words that people can understand and be helped by, than ten thousand words while "speaking in tongues" in an unknown language.

[20]Dear brothers, don't be childish in your understanding of these things. Be innocent babies when it comes to planning evil, but be men of intelligence in understanding matters of this kind. [21]We are told in the ancient Scriptures that God would send men from other lands to speak in foreign languages to his people, but even then they would not listen. [22]So you see that being able to "speak in tongues" is not a sign to God's children concerning his power, but is a sign to the unsaved. However, prophecy (preaching the deep truths of God) is what the Christians need, and unbelievers aren't yet ready for it. [23]Even so, if an unsaved person, or someone who doesn't have these gifts, comes to church and hears you all talking in other languages, he is likely to think you are crazy. [24]But if you prophesy, preaching God's Word, [even though such preaching is mostly for believers] and an unsaved person or a new Christian comes in who does not understand about these things, all these sermons will convince him of the fact that he is a sinner, and his conscience will be pricked by everything he hears. [25]As he listens, his secret thoughts will be laid bare and he will fall down on his knees and worship God, declaring that God is really there among you.

Proverbs for Today
12:12–14

Crooks are jealous of each other's loot, while good men long to help each other. □ Lies will get any man into trouble, but honesty is its own defense. Telling the truth gives a man great satisfaction, and hard work returns many blessings to him.

KEY VERSE

Lies will get any man into trouble, but honesty is its own defense.—*Proverbs 12:13*

REFLECTION

This verse has a simple point: the facts will always support what the honest person says. Dishonest people need to invent a defense. They need to twist the facts to support the claims they make. But for someone who always tells the truth, the facts—plain and unvarnished—give an unshakable defense. If you want a life that is free from worry, be sure always to tell the truth—especially to your spouse. If you find you always have to defend your actions to your husband or wife, perhaps your honesty is less than it should be.

MEDITATION

Heavenly Father, help us to be honest in our words and forthright in our actions so that there will never be any deceit in our marriage or in our dealings with other people.

APRIL 4

Jesus Commissions the Twelve Disciples
ఆ§ Mark 6:7–13 ぞ

And Jesus called his twelve disciples together and sent them out two by two, with power to cast out demons. [8,9]He told them to take nothing with them except their walking sticks—no food, no knapsack, no money, not even an extra pair of shoes or a change of clothes.

[10]"Stay at one home in each village—don't shift around from house to house while you are there," he said. [11]"And whenever a village won't accept you or listen to you, shake off the dust from your feet as you leave; it is a sign that you have abandoned it to its fate."

[12]So the disciples went out, telling everyone they met to turn from sin. [13]And they cast out many demons, and healed many sick people, anointing them with olive oil.

Use Your Gifts to Build Each Other Up
ఆ§ 1 Corinthians 14:26–33 ぞ

Well, my brothers, let's add up what I am saying. When you meet together some will sing, another will teach, or tell some special information God has given him, or speak in an unknown language, or tell what someone else is saying who is speaking in the unknown language, but everything that is done must be useful to all, and build them up in the Lord. [27]No more than two or three should speak in an unknown language, and they must speak one at a time, and someone must be ready to interpret what they are saying. [28]But if no one is present who can interpret, they must not speak out loud. They must talk silently to themselves and to God in the unknown language but not publicly. [29,30]Two or three may prophesy, one at a time, if they have the gift, while all the others listen. But if, while someone is prophesying, someone else receives a message or idea from the Lord, the one who is speaking should stop. [31]In this way all who

have the gift of prophecy can speak, one after the other, and everyone will learn and be encouraged and helped. [32]Remember that a person who has a message from God has the power to stop himself or wait his turn. [33]God is not one who likes things to be disorderly and upset. He likes harmony, and he finds it in all the other churches.

Proverbs for Today
ఆ§ 12:15–17 ぞ

A fool thinks he needs no advice, but a wise man listens to others. □ A fool is quick-tempered; a wise man stays cool when insulted. □ A good man is known by his truthfulness; a false man by deceit and lies.

―――――ఆ KEY VERSE ఆ―――――

Jesus called his twelve disciples together and sent them out two by two, with power to cast out demons.—*Mark 6:7*

―――――ఆ REFLECTION ఆ―――――

The disciples were sent out in pairs. Individually they could have reached more areas of the country, but this was not Christ's plan. One advantage in going out by twos was that they could strengthen and inspire each other along the way, especially when they faced rejection. God meets many of our needs through others. This can be especially true in a marriage. In God's gift of marriage we have a source of encouragement when times are tough; a partner with whom to share our hopes and dreams. Treat your spouse as a life-long traveling companion. Be there for each other at every step of the way.

―――――ఆ MEDITATION ఆ―――――

Heavenly Father, we thank you for our marriage and ask that you will help us be a source of strength for each other, regardless of the circumstances. ぞ

The Story of John the Baptist's Death
◦§ Mark 6:14–29 §◦

King Herod soon heard about Jesus, for his miracles were talked about everywhere. The king thought Jesus was John the Baptist come back to life again. So the people were saying, "No wonder he can do such miracles." [15]Others thought Jesus was Elijah the ancient prophet, now returned to life again; still others claimed he was a new prophet like the great ones of the past.

[16]"No," Herod said, "it is John, the man I beheaded. He has come back from the dead."

[17,18]For Herod had sent soldiers to arrest and imprison John because he kept saying it was wrong for the king to marry Herodias, his brother Philip's wife. [19]Herodias wanted John killed in revenge, but without Herod's approval she was powerless. [20]And Herod respected John, knowing that he was a good and holy man, and so he kept him under his protection. Herod was disturbed whenever he talked with John, but even so he liked to listen to him.

[21]Herodias' chance finally came. It was Herod's birthday and he gave a stag party for his palace aides, army officers, and the leading citizens of Galilee. [22,23]Then Herodias' daughter came in and danced before them and greatly pleased them all.

"Ask me for anything you like," the king vowed, "even half of my kingdom, and I will give it to you!"

[24]She went out and consulted her mother, who told her, "Ask for John the Baptist's head!"

[25]So she hurried back to the king and told him, "I want the head of John the Baptist—right now—on a tray!"

[26]Then the king was sorry, but he was embarrassed to break his oath in front of his guests. [27]So he sent one of his bodyguards to the prison to cut off John's head and bring it to him. The soldier killed John in the prison, [28]and brought back his head on a tray, and gave it to the girl and she took it to her mother.

[29]When John's disciples heard what had happened, they came for his body and buried it in a tomb.

Let There Be Order in Christian Meetings
◦§ 1 Corinthians 14:34–40 §◦

Women should be silent during the church meetings. They are not to take part in the discussion, for they are subordinate to men as the Scriptures also declare. [35]If they have any questions to ask, let them ask their husbands at home, for it is improper for women to express their opinions in church meetings.

[36]You disagree? And do you think that the knowledge of God's will begins and ends with you Corinthians? Well, you are mistaken! [37]You who claim to have the gift of prophecy or any other special ability from the Holy Spirit should be the first to realize that what I am saying is a commandment from the Lord himself. [38]But if anyone still disagrees—well, we will leave him in his ignorance.

[39]So, my fellow believers, long to be prophets so that you can preach God's message plainly; and never say it is wrong to "speak in tongues"; [40]however, be sure that everything is done properly in a good and orderly way.

Proverbs for Today
◦§ 12:18 §◦

Some people like to make cutting remarks, but the words of the wise soothe and heal.

_____◦ KEY VERSE ◦_____

Women should be silent during the church meetings. They are not to take part in the discussion, for they are subordinate to men as the Scriptures also declare. If they have any questions to ask, let them ask their husbands at home, for it is improper for women to express their opinions in church meetings.—*1 Corinthians 14:34–35*

◈ REFLECTION ◈

Do these verses mean that women should not speak in church services today? It is clear from 1 Corinthians 11:5 that women can pray and prophesy in the church, apparently in public meetings. It is also clear in chapters 12 through 14 that women have spiritual gifts, and they are encouraged to exercise them in the body of Christ. In other words, women have much to contribute and should participate in worship services.

In the Corinthian culture, women were not allowed to confront men in public. Apparently some of the women who had become Christians thought their Christian freedom gave them the right to speak up in public worship and question the men. This was causing division in the church. In addition, women of that day did not receive formal religious education as the men did. Women may have been raising questions in church that could have more easily been answered at home without disrupting the worship service. To promote unity, Paul was asking the women not to flaunt their Christian freedom at an inappropriate time. The purpose of Paul's words here was to promote unity, not to teach us about women's role in the church.

Just as the Corinthian wives used their faith inappropriately to obtain unwarranted freedom, Christian husbands today should not use verses from Scripture taken out of context as an excuse to force their wives to submit to their will. As a Christian couple, your first responsibility is to love and care for each other, not to look for excuses always to get your way. The Golden Rule—treating others as we would like to be treated—applies to the way we relate to everyone, including our spouses.

◈ MEDITATION ◈

Heavenly Father, help us always to be mindful of each other's needs. We pray that the way we react to each other will always be motivated by love rather than selfish desires. ❧

APRIL 6

The Feeding of the Five Thousand
◈ Mark 6:30–44 ◈

The apostles now returned to Jesus from their tour and told him all they had done and what they had said to the people they visited.

³¹Then Jesus suggested, "Let's get away from the crowds for a while and rest." For so many people were coming and going that they scarcely had time to eat. ³²So they left by boat for a quieter spot. ³³But many people saw them leaving and ran on ahead along the shore and met them as they landed. ³⁴So the usual vast crowd was there as he stepped from the boat; and he had pity on them because they were like sheep without a shepherd, and he taught them many things they needed to know.

³⁵,³⁶Late in the afternoon his disciples came to him and said, "Tell the people to go away to the nearby villages and farms and buy themselves some food, for there is nothing to eat here in this desolate spot, and it is getting late."

³⁷But Jesus said, *"You* feed them."

"With what?" they asked. "It would take a fortune to buy food for all this crowd!"

³⁸"How much food do we have?" he asked. "Go and find out."

They came back to report that there were five loaves of bread and two fish. ³⁹,⁴⁰Then Jesus told the crowd to sit down, and soon colorful groups of fifty or a hundred each were sitting on the green grass.

⁴¹He took the five loaves and two fish and looking up to heaven, gave thanks for the food. Breaking the loaves into pieces, he gave some of the bread and fish to each disciple to place before the people. ⁴²And the crowd ate until they could hold no more!

43,44 There were about 5,000 men there for that meal, and afterwards twelve basketfuls of scraps were picked up off the grass!

The Resurrection Appearances of the Lord
◄§ 1 Corinthians 15:1–11 §►

Now let me remind you, brothers, of what the Gospel really is, for it has not changed—it is the same Good News I preached to you before. You welcomed it then and still do now, for your faith is squarely built upon this wonderful message; ²and it is this Good News that saves you if you still firmly believe it, unless of course you never really believed it in the first place.

³I passed on to you right from the first what had been told to me, that Christ died for our sins just as the Scriptures said he would, ⁴and that he was buried, and that three days afterwards he arose from the grave just as the prophets foretold. ⁵He was seen by Peter and later by the rest of "the Twelve." ⁶After that he was seen by more than five hundred Christian brothers at one time, most of whom are still alive, though some have died by now. ⁷Then James saw him and later all the apostles. ⁸Last of all I saw him too, long after the others, as though I had been born almost too late for this. ⁹For I am the least worthy of all the apostles, and I shouldn't even be called an apostle at all after the way I treated the church of God.

¹⁰But whatever I am now it is all because God poured out such kindness and grace upon me—and not without results: for I have worked harder than all the other apostles, yet actually I wasn't doing it, but God working in me, to bless me. ¹¹It makes no difference who worked the hardest, I or they; the important thing is that we preached the Gospel to you, and you believed it.

Proverbs for Today
◄§ 12:19–20 §►

Truth stands the test of time; lies are soon exposed. Deceit fills hearts that are plotting for evil; joy fills hearts that are planning for good!

◄ KEY VERSE ◄

It makes no difference who worked the hardest, I or they; the important thing is that we preached the Gospel to you and you believed it.—*1 Corinthians 15:11*

◄ REFLECTION ◄

Paul spoke of working harder than the other apostles. This is not a prideful statement because he knew that his power came from God (1 Corinthians 15:9) and that it didn't matter who worked hardest (1 Corinthians 15:11). Because of his prominent position as a Pharisee, Paul's conversion made him the object of even greater persecution than the other apostles; thus he had to work harder to preach the same message.

Marriage is not always a fifty-fifty relationship. Sometimes one spouse earns much more money than the other, or is particularly gifted in a way that brings more acclaim and honor than the other. Don't allow insecurity on the one hand or pride on the other to create petty jealousies in your marriage. Each of you has something to contribute. Support and encourage each other, and you will be happy, loving, and equal partners throughout life.

◄ MEDITATION ◄

Heavenly Father, we ask that you will help us to work together for your Kingdom, and that each of us will be able to use his or her unique gifts and talents for your glory. §►

APRIL 7

Jesus Walks on the Water
⋖§ Mark 6:45–56 §⋗

Immediately after this Jesus instructed his disciples to get back into the boat and strike out across the lake to Bethsaida, where he would join them later. He himself would stay and tell the crowds good-bye and get them started home.

[46]Afterwards he went up into the hills to pray. [47]During the night, as the disciples in their boat were out in the middle of the lake, and he was alone on land, [48]he saw that they were in serious trouble, rowing hard and struggling against the wind and waves.

About three o'clock in the morning he walked out to them on the water. He started past them, [49]but when they saw something walking along beside them they screamed in terror, thinking it was a ghost, [50]for they all saw him.

But he spoke to them at once. "It's all right," he said. "It is I! Don't be afraid." [51]Then he climbed into the boat and the wind stopped!

They just sat there, unable to take it in! [52]For they still didn't realize who he was, even after the miracle the evening before! For they didn't want to believe!

[53]When they arrived at Gennesaret on the other side of the lake they moored the boat, [54]and climbed out.

The people standing around there recognized him at once, [55]and ran throughout the whole area to spread the news of his arrival, and began carrying sick folks to him on mats and stretchers. [56]Wherever he went—in villages and cities, and out on the farms—they laid the sick in the market plazas and streets, and begged him to let them at least touch the fringes of his clothes; and as many as touched him were healed.

The Resurrection—the Foundation of Faith
⋖§ 1 Corinthians 15:12–20 §⋗

But tell me this! Since you believe what we preach, that *Christ* rose from the dead, why are some of you saying that dead people will never come back to life again? [13]For if there is no resurrection of the dead, then Christ must still be dead. [14]And if he is still dead, then all our preaching is useless and your trust in God is empty, worthless, hopeless; [15]and we apostles are all liars because we have said that God raised Christ from the grave, and of course that isn't true if the dead do not come back to life again. [16]If they don't, then Christ is still dead, [17]and you are very foolish to keep on trusting God to save you, and you are still under condemnation for your sins; [18]in that case all Christians who have died are lost! [19]And if being a Christian is of value to us only now in this life, we are the most miserable of creatures.

[20]But the fact is that Christ did actually rise from the dead, and has become the first of millions who will come back to life again some day.

Proverbs for Today
⋖§ 12:21–23 §⋗

No real harm befalls the good, but there is constant trouble for the wicked. □ God delights in those who keep their promises, and abhors those who don't. □ A wise man doesn't display his knowledge, but a fool displays his foolishness.

⋖ KEY VERSE ⋗

If being a Christian is of value to us only now in this life, we are the most miserable of creatures. —*1 Corinthians 15:19*

⋖ REFLECTION ⋗

Why did Paul say people would be miserable if Christianity had only earthly value? In Paul's day, Christian faith often brought a person persecution, ostracism from family, and, in many cases, poverty. There were few tangible benefits to being a Christian in that society. It was certainly not a step up the social or career ladder.

While the consequences of being a Christian are not as drastic for most people today, it still takes a lot of courage and commitment to stand for convictions that others laugh at, or (worse) find offensive. As a Christian couple, you should comfort each other when neighbors, coworkers, or even family taunt or harass you for your faith or convictions. Remember that some day you will spend eternity with the One who died for your sins so that you might have eternal life.

───────── ✐ MEDITATION ✐ ─────────

Heavenly Father, we pray that you will help us see beyond what others say about our love for you and keep our thoughts on the glorious day when we will be united with you in Heaven. ✌

APRIL 8

Inner Purity
✐ Mark 7:1–23 ✌

One day some Jewish religious leaders arrived from Jerusalem to investigate Jesus, [2]and noticed that some of his disciples failed to follow the usual Jewish rituals before eating. [3](For the Jews, especially the Pharisees, will never eat until they have sprinkled their arms to the elbows, as required by their ancient traditions. [4]So when they come home from the market they must always sprinkle themselves in this way before touching any food. This is but one of many examples of laws and regulations they have clung to for centuries, and still follow, such as their ceremony of cleansing for pots, pans and dishes.)

[5]So the religious leaders asked him, "Why don't your disciples follow our age-old customs? For they eat without first performing the washing ceremony."

[6,7]Jesus replied, "You bunch of hypocrites! Isaiah the prophet described you very well when he said, 'These people speak very prettily about the Lord but they have no love for him at all. Their worship is a farce, for they claim that God commands the people to obey their petty rules.' How right Isaiah was! [8]For you ignore God's specific orders and substitute your own traditions. [9]You are simply rejecting God's laws and trampling them under your feet for the sake of tradition.

[10]For instance, Moses gave you this law from God: 'Honor your father and mother.' And he said that anyone who speaks against his father or mother must die. [11]But you say it is perfectly all right for a man to disregard his needy parents, telling them, 'Sorry, I can't help you! For I have given to God what I could have given to you.' [12,13]And so you break the law of God in order to protect your man-made tradition. And this is only one example. There are many, many others."

[14]Then Jesus called to the crowd to come and hear. "All of you listen," he said, "and try to understand. [15,16]Your souls aren't harmed by what you eat, but by what you think and say!"

[17]Then he went into a house to get away from the crowds, and his disciples asked him what he meant by the statement he had just made.

[18]"Don't you understand either?" he asked. "Can't you see that what you eat won't harm your soul? [19]For food doesn't come in contact with your heart, but only passes through the digestive system." (By saying this he showed that every kind of food is kosher.)

[20]And then he added, "It is the thought-life that pollutes. [21]For from within, out of men's hearts, come evil thoughts of lust, theft, murder, adultery, [22]wanting what belongs to others, wickedness, deceit, lewdness, envy, slander, pride, and all other folly. [23]All these vile things come from within; they are what pollute you and make you unfit for God."

Death Will Be Defeated in the End
✐ 1 Corinthians 15:21–28 ✌

Death came into the world because of what one man (Adam) did, and it is because of what this other man (Christ) has done that now there is the resurrection from the dead. [22]Everyone dies because all of us are related to Adam, being members of his sinful race, and wherever there is sin, death results. But all who are related to Christ will rise again. [23]Each, however, in his own turn: Christ rose first; then when Christ comes back, all his people will become alive again.

[24]After that the end will come when he will turn the Kingdom over to God the Father, having put down all enemies of every kind. [25]For Christ will be King until he has defeated all his enemies, [26]including the last enemy—death. This too must be defeated and ended. [27]For the rule and authority over all things has been given to Christ by his Father; except, of course, Christ does not rule over the Father himself, who gave him this power to rule. [28]When Christ has finally won the battle against all his enemies, then he, the Son of God, will put himself also under his Father's orders, so that God who has given him the victory over everything else will be utterly supreme.

Proverbs for Today
⋅§ 12:24 ⋅

Work hard and become a leader; be lazy and never succeed.

_____ ◦ KEY VERSE ◦ _____

"Your souls aren't harmed by what you eat, but by what you think and say!"—*Mark 7:15–16*

_____ ◦ REFLECTION ◦ _____

Do you worry more about what is in the food that you and your spouse eat each day than what you put in your hearts and minds? As they interpreted the dietary laws in Leviticus 11, the Jews believed they could be clean before God because of what they did not eat. But Jesus pointed out that sin actually begins in the attitudes and intentions of the inner person. He did not downgrade the law, but he paved the way for the change made clear in Acts 10:9–29 when God removed the cultural restrictions on food. We are not pure because of outward acts—we become pure on the inside as Christ renews our minds and conforms us to his image (see Romans 8:29).

_____ ◦ MEDITATION ◦ _____

Heavenly Father, teach us to fill our hearts and minds only with what is pure and holy. ⋅

APRIL 9

Jesus Demonstrates His Redemptive Power
⋅§ Mark 7:24–37 ⋅

Then Jesus left Galilee and went to the region of Tyre and Sidon, and tried to keep it a secret that he was there, but couldn't. For as usual the news of his arrival spread fast.

[25]Right away a woman came to him whose little girl was possessed by a demon. She had heard about Jesus and now she came and fell at his feet, [26]and pled with him to release her child from the demon's control. (But she was Syrophoenician—a "despised Gentile!")

[27]Jesus told her, "First I should help my own family—the Jews. It isn't right to take the children's food and throw it to the dogs."

[28]She replied, "That's true, sir, but even the puppies under the table are given some scraps from the children's plates."

[29]"Good!" he said, "You have answered well—so well that I have healed your little girl. Go on home, for the demon has left her!"

[30]And when she arrived home, her little girl was lying quietly in bed, and the demon was gone.

[31]From Tyre he went to Sidon, then back to the Sea of Galilee by way of the Ten Towns. [32]A deaf man with a speech impediment was brought to him, and everyone begged Jesus to lay his hands on the man and heal him.

³³Jesus led him away from the crowd and put his fingers into the man's ears, then spat and touched the man's tongue with the spittle. ³⁴Then, looking up to heaven, he sighed and commanded, "Open!" ³⁵Instantly the man could hear perfectly and speak plainly!

³⁶Jesus told the crowd not to spread the news, but the more he forbade them, the more they made it known, ³⁷for they were overcome with utter amazement. Again and again they said, "Everything he does is wonderful; he even corrects deafness and stammering!"

True Meaning in Daily Life
◄§ 1 Corinthians 15:29–34 §►

If the dead will not come back to life again, then what point is there in people being baptized for those who are gone? Why do it unless you believe that the dead will some day rise again?

³⁰And why should we ourselves be continually risking our lives, facing death hour by hour? ³¹For it is a fact that I face death daily; that is as true as my pride in your growth in the Lord. ³²And what value was there in fighting wild beasts—those men of Ephesus—if it was only for what I gain in this life down here? If we will never live again after we die, then we might as well go and have ourselves a good time: let us eat, drink, and be merry. What's the difference? For tomorrow we die, and that ends everything!

³³Don't be fooled by those who say such things. If you listen to them you will start acting like them. ³⁴Get some sense and quit your sinning. For to your shame I say it, some of you are not even Christians at all and have never really known God.

Proverbs for Today
◄§ 12:25 §►

Anxious hearts are very heavy but a word of encouragement does wonders!

◢ KEY VERSE ◣

Anxious hearts are very heavy, but a word of encouragement does wonders!—*Proverbs 12:25*

◢ REFLECTION ◣

When your husband or wife insults you, it is natural to respond with unkind words. But that solves nothing and only encourages trouble. Instead, "keep your cool" and answer slowly and quietly. Your positive response will achieve positive results. On the other hand, if you have done or said something that has hurt or offended your spouse, don't become defensive or make excuses for your actions. Ask him or her to forgive you and to explain why your words hurt so much. You will be opening up a constructive line of dialogue that will strengthen your marriage and reduce the chances of future flare-ups.

◢ MEDITATION ◣

Heavenly Father, we pray that you will quiet our hearts when we become angry, so that we won't say something in the heat of the moment that will bring ongoing conflict into our marriage. §►

APRIL 10

The Feeding of the Four Thousand
◄§ Mark 8:1–9 §►

One day about this time as another great crowd gathered, the people ran out of food again. Jesus called his disciples to discuss the situation.

"I pity these people," he said, "for they have been here three days, and have nothing left to eat. ³And if I send them home without feeding them, they will faint along the road! For some of them have come a long distance."

⁴"Are we supposed to find food for them here in the desert?" his disciples scoffed.

⁵"How many loaves of bread do you have?" he asked.

"Seven," they replied. ⁶So he told the crowd to

sit down on the ground. Then he took the seven loaves, thanked God for them, broke them into pieces and passed them to his disciples; and the disciples placed them before the people. [7]A few small fish were found, too, so Jesus also blessed these and told the disciples to serve them.

[8,9]And the whole crowd ate until they were full, and afterwards he sent them home. There were about 4,000 people in the crowd that day and when the scraps were picked up after the meal, there were seven very large basketfuls left over!

Earthly Analogies for the Resurrection Body
◄§ 1 Corinthians 15:35–44 §►

But someone may ask, "How will the dead be brought back to life again? What kind of bodies will they have?" [36]What a foolish question! You will find the answer in your own garden! When you put a seed into the ground it doesn't grow into a plant unless it "dies" first. [37]And when the green shoot comes up out of the seed, it is very different from the seed you first planted. For all you put into the ground is a dry little seed of wheat, or whatever it is you are planting, [38]then God gives it a beautiful new body—just the kind he wants it to have; a different kind of plant grows from each kind of seed. [39]And just as there are different kinds of seeds and plants, so also there are different kinds of flesh. Humans, animals, fish, and birds are all different.

[40]The angels in heaven have bodies far different from ours, and the beauty and the glory of their bodies is different from the beauty and the glory of ours. [41]The sun has one kind of glory while the moon and stars have another kind. And the stars differ from each other in their beauty and brightness.

[42]In the same way, our earthly bodies which die and decay are different from the bodies we shall have when we come back to life again, for they will never die. [43]The bodies we have now embarrass us for they become sick and die; but they will be full of glory when we come back to life again. Yes, they are weak, dying bodies now, but when we live again they will be full of strength. [44]They are just human bodies at death, but when they come back to life they will be superhuman bodies. For just as there are natural, human bodies, there are also supernatural, spiritual bodies.

Proverbs for Today
◄§ 12:26 §►

The good man asks advice from friends; the wicked plunge ahead—and fall.

◄ KEY VERSE ◄

"I pity these people," he said, "for they have been here three days and have nothing left to eat. And if I send them home without feeding them, they will faint along the road! For some of them have come a long distance."—*Mark 8:2–3*

◄ REFLECTION ◄

Do you ever think God is so busy with important matters that he can't possibly be aware of your needs? Just as Jesus was concerned about these faithful followers who needed food, he also cares about our daily needs. At another time Jesus said, "Don't worry at all about having enough food and clothing. Your heavenly Father already knows perfectly well that you need them" (Matthew 6:31–32). Do either of you have concerns that you think would not interest God? There is no problem too large for him to handle and no need too small to escape his interest.

◄ MEDITATION ◄

Heavenly Father, we turn our cares and needs over to you, knowing that you will answer our prayers in your perfect timing. We also thank you for the many prayers you have already answered and the blessings you provide for us daily. §►

Beware of the Teaching of Herod and the Pharisees
∽§ Mark 8:10–21 §∼

Immediately after this Jesus got into a boat with his disciples and came to the region of Dalmanutha. [11]When the local Jewish leaders learned of his arrival they came to argue with him.

"Do a miracle for us," they said. "Make something happen in the sky. Then we will believe in you."

[12]He sighed deeply when he heard this and he said, "Certainly not. How many more miracles do you people need?"

[13]So he got back into the boat and left them, and crossed to the other side of the lake. [14]But the disciples had forgotten to stock up on food before they left, and had only one loaf of bread in the boat.

[15]As they were crossing, Jesus said to them very solemnly, "Beware of the yeast of King Herod and of the Pharisees."

[16]"What does he mean?" the disciples asked each other. They finally decided that he must be talking about their forgetting to bring bread.

[17]Jesus realized what they were discussing and said, "No, that isn't it at all! Can't you understand? Are your hearts too hard to take it in? [18]'Your eyes are to see with—why don't you look? Why don't you open your ears and listen?' Don't you remember anything at all?

[19]"What about the 5,000 men I fed with five loaves of bread? How many basketfuls of scraps did you pick up afterwards?"

"Twelve," they said.

[20]"And when I fed the 4,000 with seven loaves, how much was left?"

"Seven basketfuls," they said.

[21]"And yet you think I'm worried that we have no bread?"

Adam Versus Christ
∽§ 1 Corinthians 15:45–49 §∼

The Scriptures tell us that the first man, Adam, was given a natural, human body but Christ is more than that, for he was life-giving Spirit.

[46]First, then, we have these human bodies and later on God gives us spiritual, heavenly bodies. [47]Adam was made from the dust of the earth, but Christ came from heaven above. [48]Every human being has a body just like Adam's, made of dust, but all who become Christ's will have the same kind of body as his—a body from heaven. [49]Just as each of us now has a body like Adam's, so we shall some day have a body like Christ's.

Proverbs for Today
∽§ 12:27–28 §∼

A lazy man won't even dress the game he gets while hunting, but the diligent man makes good use of everything he finds. ☐ The path of the godly leads to life. So why fear death?

❧ KEY VERSE ☙

" 'Your eyes are to see with—why don't you look? Why don't you open your ears and listen?' Don't you remember anything at all?"—*Mark 8:18*

❧ REFLECTION ☙

How could the disciples experience so many of Jesus' miracles and yet be so slow to comprehend his identity? They had already seen Jesus feed over 5,000 people with five loaves and two fish, yet now they doubted whether he could feed another large group.

People today are also slow to catch on. Although Christ has brought both of you through trials and temptations in the past, you may be slow to believe that he can do it in the future. Don't be like the disciples. Remember what Christ has done for you, and have faith that he can help you today too.

❧ MEDITATION ☙

Heavenly Father, we thank you and praise you for the wonderful things you have done in our marriage. We also ask that you will forgive us when the circumstances of our lives weaken our faith. Help us to believe in your power! §∼

APRIL 12

A Blind Man Has His Sight Restored
ᕦ Mark 8:22–26 ᕤ

When Jesus and his disciples arrived at Bethsaida, some people brought a blind man to him and begged him to touch and heal him. [23]Jesus took the blind man by the hand and led him out of the village, and spat upon his eyes, and laid his hands over them.

"Can you see anything now?" Jesus asked him.

[24]The man looked around. "Yes!" he said, "I see men! But I can't see them very clearly; they look like tree trunks walking around!"

[25]Then Jesus placed his hands over the man's eyes again and as the man stared intently, his sight was completely restored, and he saw everything clearly, drinking in the sights around him.

[26]Jesus sent him home to his family. "Don't even go back to the village first," he said.

Transformation in the Twinkling of an Eye
ᕦ 1 Corinthians 15:50–58 ᕤ

I tell you this, my brothers: an earthly body made of flesh and blood cannot get into God's Kingdom. These perishable bodies of ours are not the right kind to live forever.

[51]But I am telling you this strange and wonderful secret: we shall not all die, but we shall all be given new bodies! [52]It will all happen in a moment, in the twinkling of an eye, when the last trumpet is blown. For there will be a trumpet blast from the sky and all the Christians who have died will suddenly become alive, with new bodies that will never, never die; and then we who are still alive shall suddenly have new bodies too. [53]For our earthly bodies, the ones we have now that can die, must be transformed into heavenly bodies that cannot perish but will live forever.

[54]When this happens, then at last this Scripture will come true—"Death is swallowed up in victory." [55,56]O death, where then your victory? Where then your sting? For sin—the sting that causes death—will all be gone; and the law, which reveals our sins, will no longer be our judge. [57]How we thank God for all of this! It is he who makes us victorious through Jesus Christ our Lord!

[58]So, my dear brothers, since future victory is sure, be strong and steady, always abounding in the Lord's work, for you know that nothing you do for the Lord is ever wasted as it would be if there were no resurrection.

Proverbs for Today
ᕦ 13:1 ᕤ

A wise youth accepts his father's rebuke; a young mocker doesn't.

KEY VERSE

So, my dear brothers, since future victory is sure, be strong and steady, always abounding in the Lord's work, for you know that nothing you do for the Lord is ever wasted as it would be if there were no resurrection.—*1 Corinthians 15:58*

REFLECTION

Paul said that because of the resurrection, nothing we do is wasted. Sometimes we hesitate to do good because we don't see immediate results. But if we can maintain a Heavenly perspective, we will understand that we don't often see the good that comes from our efforts. Truly believing that Christ has won the ultimate victory will affect the way we live right now. Don't let discouragement over an apparent lack of results keep either of you from working for Christ and his Kingdom. In every situation, ask each other, "Is this what Christ would have us do?" If you both strive to do the right thing in your marriage and in your relationships with others, your actions will always have eternal benefits.

MEDITATION

Heavenly Father, help us keep a proper perspective on everything we do and say. Help us remember that the things we don't see or understand will be clear to us when we stand in your presence. ❧

Peter's Confession
❧ Mark 8:27–38 ❧

Jesus and his disciples now left Galilee and went out to the villages of Caesarea Philippi. As they were walking along he asked them, "Who do the people think I am? What are they saying about me?"

²⁸"Some of them think you are John the Baptist," the disciples replied, "and others say you are Elijah or some other ancient prophet come back to life again."

²⁹Then he asked, "Who do you think I am?" Peter replied, "You are the Messiah." ³⁰But Jesus warned them not to tell anyone!

³¹Then he began to tell them about the terrible things he would suffer, and that he would be rejected by the elders and the Chief Priests and the other Jewish leaders—and be killed, and that he would rise again three days afterwards. ³²He talked about it quite frankly with them, so Peter took him aside and chided him. "You shouldn't say things like that," he told Jesus.

³³Jesus turned and looked at his disciples and then said to Peter very sternly, "Satan, get behind me! You are looking at this only from a human point of view and not from God's."

³⁴Then he called his disciples and the crowds to come over and listen. "If any of you wants to be my follower," he told them, "you must put aside your own pleasures and shoulder your cross, and follow me closely. ³⁵If you insist on saving your life, you will lose it. Only those who throw away their lives for my sake and for the sake of the Good News will ever know what it means to really live.

³⁶"And how does a man benefit if he gains the whole world and loses his soul in the process? ³⁷For is anything worth more than his soul? ³⁸And anyone who is ashamed of me and my message in these days of unbelief and sin, I, the Messiah, will be ashamed of him when I return in the glory of my Father, with the holy angels."

The Jerusalem Church Collection
❧ 1 Corinthians 16:1–9 ❧

Now here are the directions about the money you are collecting to send to the Christians in Jerusalem; (and, by the way, these are the same directions I gave to the churches in Galatia). ²On every Lord's Day each of you should put aside something from what you have earned during the week, and use it for this offering. The amount depends on how much the Lord has helped you earn. Don't wait until I get there and then try to collect it all at once. ³When I come I will send your loving gift with a letter to Jerusalem, to be taken there by trustworthy messengers you yourselves will choose. ⁴And if it seems wise for me to go along too, then we can travel together.

⁵I am coming to visit you after I have been to Macedonia first, but I will be staying there only for a little while. ⁶It could be that I will stay longer with you, perhaps all winter, and then you can send me on to my next destination. ⁷This time I don't want to make just a passing visit and then go right on; I want to come and stay awhile, if the Lord will let me. ⁸I will be staying here at Ephesus until the holiday of Pentecost, ⁹for there is a wide open door for me to preach and teach here. So much is happening, but there are many enemies.

Proverbs for Today

The good man wins his case by careful argument; the evil-minded only wants to fight. □ Self-control means controlling the tongue! A quick retort can ruin everything.

❧ KEY VERSE ❧

"And how does a man benefit if he gains the whole world and loses his soul in the process?"—*Mark 8:36*

❧ 135 ❧

Many people spend their lives seeking pleasure. Jesus said, however, that possessions, position, and power are meaningless and worthless. Whatever we have on earth is only temporary and cannot be exchanged for our souls. If you each work hard at getting what only you yourself want, you might eventually have a pleasurable life. In the end, however, you will find it hollow and empty . . . and possibly separate. *As a couple,* are you willing to make the pursuit of God more important than the selfish pursuit of pleasure? Follow Jesus to know what it means to live in this life and to have life eternal as well.

—⁌ MEDITATION ⁌—

Heavenly Father, we ask that you will help us sort through our priorities so that we will focus on what is truly meaningful—our eternal lives with you. ⁓

APRIL 14

The Transfiguration of Jesus
⁌ Mark 9:1–13 ⁌

Jesus went on to say to his disciples, "Some of you who are standing here right now will live to see the Kingdom of God arrive in great power!"

[2]Six days later Jesus took Peter, James and John to the top of a mountain. No one else was there.

Suddenly his face began to shine with glory, [3]and his clothing became dazzling white, far more glorious than any earthly process could ever make it! [4]Then Elijah and Moses appeared and began talking with Jesus!

[5]"Teacher, this is wonderful!" Peter exclaimed. "We will make three shelters here, one for each of you. . . ."

[6]He said this just to be talking, for he didn't know what else to say and they were all terribly frightened.

[7]But while he was still speaking these words, a cloud covered them, blotting out the sun, and a voice from the cloud said, *"This is my beloved Son. Listen to him."*

[8]Then suddenly they looked around and Moses and Elijah were gone, and only Jesus was with them.

[9]As they descended the mountainside he told them never to mention what they had seen until after he had risen from the dead. [10]So they kept it to themselves, but often talked about it, and wondered what he meant by "rising from the dead."

[11]Now they began asking him about something the Jewish religious leaders often spoke of, that Elijah must return [before the Messiah could come]. [12,13]Jesus agreed that Elijah must come first and prepare the way—and that he had, in fact, already come! And that he had been terribly mistreated, just as the prophets had predicted. Then Jesus asked them what the prophets could have been talking about when they predicted that the Messiah would suffer and be treated with utter contempt.

Paul's Final Instructions
⁌ 1 Corinthians 16:10–18 ⁌

If Timothy comes make him feel at home, for he is doing the Lord's work just as I am. [11]Don't let anyone despise or ignore him [because he is young], but send him back to me happy with his time among you; I am looking forward to seeing him soon, along with the others who are returning.

[12]I begged Apollos to visit you along with the others, but he thought that it was not at all God's will for him to go now; he will be seeing you later on when he has the opportunity.

[13]Keep your eyes open for spiritual danger; stand true to the Lord; act like men; be strong; [14]and whatever you do, do it with kindness and love.

¹⁵Do you remember Stephanas and his family? They were the first to become Christians in Greece and they are spending their lives helping and serving Christians everywhere. ¹⁶Please follow their instructions and do everything you can to help them as well as all others like them who work hard at your side with such real devotion. ¹⁷I am so glad that Stephanas, Fortunatus, and Achaicus have arrived here for a visit. They have been making up for the help you aren't here to give me. ¹⁸They have cheered me greatly and have been a wonderful encouragement to me, as I am sure they were to you, too. I hope you properly appreciate the work of such men as these.

Proverbs for Today
◄§ 13:4 §►

Lazy people want much but get little, while the diligent are prospering.

◄ KEY VERSE ◄

But while he was still speaking these words, a cloud covered them, blotting out the sun, and a voice from the cloud said, *"This* is my beloved Son. Listen to *him."—Mark 9:7*

◄ REFLECTION ◄

The transfiguration revealed Christ's true nature as God's Son. God singled out Jesus from Moses and Elijah as the long-awaited Messiah, with full, divine authority. Moses represented the Law, and Elijah represented the Prophets. Jesus was revealed as the fulfillment of both the Old Testament Law and the prophetic promises. Jesus was not a reincarnation of Elijah or Moses. He was not merely one of the prophets. As God's only Son, he far surpasses all other authority and power.

Throughout your lives together, many voices will try to tell you how to live and how to know God personally. Some of those voices will be helpful; many will not. Be sure to listen to Jesus as your final authority, and then evaluate all other authorities in light of his revelation in Scripture.

◄ MEDITATION ◄

Heavenly Father, reveal the truths of your Word to us so that we may come to know you better each day. Help us recognize false teaching so that we will not be deceived and led away from you. §►

APRIL 15

Jesus Casts Out a Demon
◄§ Mark 9:14-29 §►

At the bottom of the mountain Peter, James, and John found a great crowd surrounding the other nine disciples, as some Jewish leaders argued with them. ¹⁵The crowd watched Jesus in awe as he came toward them, and then ran to greet him. ¹⁶"What's all the argument about?" he asked.

¹⁷One of the men in the crowd spoke up and said, "Teacher, I brought my son for you to heal—he can't talk because he is possessed by a demon. ¹⁸And whenever the demon is in control of him it dashes him to the ground and makes him foam at the mouth and grind his teeth and become rigid. So I begged your disciples to cast out the demon, but they couldn't do it."

¹⁹Jesus said [to his disciples], "Oh, what tiny faith you have; how much longer must I be with you until you believe? How much longer must I be patient with you? Bring the boy to me."

²⁰So they brought the boy, but when he saw Jesus the demon convulsed the child horribly, and he fell to the ground writhing and foaming at the mouth.

²¹"How long has he been this way?" Jesus asked the father.

And he replied, "Since he was very small, [22]and the demon often makes him fall into the fire or into water to kill him. Oh, have mercy on us and do something if you can."

[23]"If I can?" Jesus asked. *"Anything* is possible if you have faith."

[24]The father instantly replied, "I *do* have faith; oh, help me to have *more!*"

[25]When Jesus saw the crowd was growing he rebuked the demon.

"O demon of deafness and dumbness," he said, "I command you to come out of this child and enter him no more!"

[26]Then the demon screamed terribly and convulsed the boy again and left him; and the boy lay there limp and motionless, to all appearance dead. A murmur ran through the crowd—"He is dead." [27]But Jesus took him by the hand and helped him to his feet and he stood up and was all right! [28]Afterwards, when Jesus was alone in the house with his disciples, they asked him, "Why couldn't we cast that demon out?"

[29]Jesus replied, "Cases like this require prayer."

Greetings from Other Believers
◄§ 1 Corinthians 16:19–24 §►

The churches here in Asia send you their loving greetings. Aquila and Priscilla send you their love and so do all the others who meet in their home for their church service. [20]All the friends here have asked me to say "hello" to you for them. And give each other a loving handshake when you meet.

[21]I will write these final words of this letter with my own hand: [22]if anyone does not love the Lord, that person is cursed. Lord Jesus, come! [23]May the love and favor of the Lord Jesus Christ rest upon you. [24]My love to all of you, for we all belong to Christ Jesus.

Sincerely,
Paul

Proverbs for Today
◄§ 13:5–6 §►

A good man hates lies; wicked men lie constantly and come to shame. □ A man's goodness helps him all through life, while evil men are being destroyed by their wickedness.

◢ KEY VERSE ◣

Jesus replied, "Cases like this require prayer." —*Mark 9:29*

◢ REFLECTION ◣

Faith is not something tangible to be taken like medicine. It is an attitude of trusting and believing. But even our ability to believe is a gift from God. No matter how much faith we have, we never reach the point of being self-sufficient. Faith is not stored away like money in the bank. Growing in faith is a constant process of daily renewing our trust in Jesus. Jesus was telling the disciples that they would face difficult situations that could be resolved only through prayer. Prayer is the key that unlocks faith in our lives. Effective prayer needs both an attitude—complete dependence—and an action—asking. Prayer demonstrates our reliance on God as we humbly invite him to fill us with faith and power. Remember that there is no substitute for prayer in your personal lives and in your marriage, especially in difficulties that seem unconquerable.

◢ MEDITATION ◣

Heavenly Father, we thank you that you are always willing to listen to our needs and concerns. We place our complete trust in you and ask that you be the central focus of our lives each day. §►

The Greatest Must Be the Servant of All
§ Mark 9:30–37 §

Leaving that region Jesus and his disciples traveled through Galilee where Jesus tried to avoid all publicity in order to spend more time with his disciples, teaching them. He would say to them, "I, the Messiah, am going to be betrayed and killed and three days later I will return to life again."

[32]But they didn't understand and were afraid to ask him what he meant.

[33]And so they arrived at Capernaum. When they were settled in the house where they were to stay he asked them, "What were you discussing out on the road?"

[34]But they were ashamed to answer, for they had been arguing about which of them was the greatest!

[35]He sat down and called them around him and said, "Anyone wanting to be the greatest must be the least—the servant of all!"

[36]Then he placed a little child among them; and taking the child in his arms he said to them, [37]"Anyone who welcomes a little child like this in my name is welcoming me, and anyone who welcomes me is welcoming my Father who sent me!"

We Pass on God's Comfort to Others
§ 2 Corinthians 1:1–7 §

Dear friends, This letter is from me, Paul, appointed by God to be Jesus Christ's messenger; and from our dear brother Timothy. We are writing to all of you Christians there in Corinth and throughout Greece. [2]May God our Father and the Lord Jesus Christ mightily bless each one of you, and give you peace.

[3,4]What a wonderful God we have—he is the Father of our Lord Jesus Christ, the source of every mercy, and the one who so wonderfully comforts and strengthens us in our hardships and trials. And why does he do this? So that when others are troubled, needing our sympathy and encouragement, we can pass on to them this same help and comfort God has given us. [5]You can be sure that the more we undergo sufferings for Christ, the more he will shower us with his comfort and encouragement. [6,7]We are in deep trouble for bringing you God's comfort and salvation. But in our trouble God has comforted us—and this, too, to help you: to show you from our personal experience how God will tenderly comfort you when you undergo these same sufferings. He will give you the strength to endure.

Proverbs for Today
§ 13:7–8 §

Some rich people are poor, and some poor people have great wealth! □ Being kidnapped and held for ransom never worries the poor man

ᴀ KEY VERSE ᴀ

What a wonderful God we have—he is the Father of our Lord Jesus Christ, the source of every mercy, and the one who so wonderfully comforts and strengthens us in our hardships and trials. And why does he do this? So that when others are troubled, needing our sympathy and encouragement, we can pass on to them this same help and comfort God has given us.—*2 Corinthians 1:3–4*

ᴀ REFLECTION ᴀ

Many people believe that whenever God comforts us, our hardships instantly disappear. But if that were always so, people would turn to God only to be relieved of pain, not to love him. We must understand that comfort can also mean receiving strength, encouragement, and hope to deal with hardships. The more we suffer, the more comfort God can give us. Allow God to comfort you. Remember that every trial you endure will help you help your spouse and other people endure hardships.

ᴀ MEDITATION ᴀ

Heavenly Father, we pray that you will comfort us as we face problems at work and in our home. Help us accept whatever you want for our lives. §

APRIL 17

Entering God's Kingdom Requires Radical Change
⊸§ Mark 9:38–50 §⊸

One of Jesus' disciples, John, told him one day, "Teacher, we saw a man using your name to cast out demons; but we told him not to, for he isn't one of our group."

[39]"Don't forbid him!" Jesus said. "For no one doing miracles in my name will quickly turn against me. [40]Anyone who isn't against us is for us. [41]If anyone so much as gives you a cup of water because you are Christ's—I say this solemnly—he won't lose his reward. [42]But if someone causes one of these little ones who believe in me to lose faith—it would be better for that man if a huge millstone were tied around his neck and he were thrown into the sea.

[43,44]"If your hand does wrong, cut it off. Better live forever with one hand than be thrown into the unquenchable fires of hell with two! [45,46]If your foot carries you toward evil, cut it off! Better be lame and live forever than have two feet that carry you to hell.

[47]"And if your eye is sinful, gouge it out. Better enter the Kingdom of God half blind than have two eyes and see the fires of hell, [48]where the worm never dies, and the fire never goes out— [49]where all are salted with fire.

[50]"Good salt is worthless if it loses its saltiness; it can't season anything. So don't lose your flavor! Live in peace with each other."

Paul's Ministry in Life and in Letters
⊸§ 2 Corinthians 1:8–14 §⊸

I think you ought to know, dear brothers, about the hard time we went through in Asia. We were really crushed and overwhelmed, and feared we would never live through it. [9]We felt we were doomed to die and saw how powerless we were to help ourselves; but that was good, for then we put everything into the hands of God, who alone could save us, for he can even raise the dead. [10]And he did help us, and saved us from a terrible death; yes, and we expect him to do it again and again. [11]But you must help us too, by praying for us. For much thanks and praise will go to God from you who see his wonderful answers to your prayers for our safety!

[12]We are so glad that we can say with utter honesty that in all our dealings we have been pure and sincere, quietly depending upon the Lord for his help, and not on our own skills. And that is even more true, if possible, about the way we have acted toward you. [13,14]My letters have been straightforward and sincere; nothing is written between the lines! And even though you don't know me very well (I hope someday you will), I want you to try to accept me and be proud of me, as you already are to some extent; just as I shall be of you on that day when our Lord Jesus comes back again.

Proverbs for Today
⊸§ 13:9–10 §⊸

The good man's life is full of light. The sinner's road is dark and gloomy. ☐ Pride leads to arguments; be humble, take advice and become wise.

⊸ KEY VERSE ⊸

Pride leads to arguments; be humble, take advice, and become wise.—*Proverbs 13:10*

⊸ REFLECTION ⊸

"I was wrong" and "I need help" are difficult phrases to utter in a marriage because they require humility. Pride is an ingredient in every quarrel you have with your spouse. It stirs up conflict and divides you from the one you pledged to love no matter what the circumstances. Humility, by contrast, heals. Guard against pride. If you find yourself constantly provoking arguments, examine your life for pride. Be open to the advice of others, as well as your spouse, and ask for help when you need it. But most of all, be willing to admit it when you are wrong.

_____ ⚘ MEDITATION ⚘ _____

Heavenly Father, forgive us when we allow our personal feelings to come in the way of our marriage and our relationship with you. Help us always to guard against the sins of pride and arrogance. ⚘

APRIL 18

Jesus' Teachings on Divorce
⚘ Mark 10:1–12 ⚘

Then Jesus left Capernaum and went southward to the Judean borders and into the area east of the Jordan River. And as always there were the crowds; and as usual he taught them.

²Some Pharisees came and asked him, "Do you permit divorce?" Of course they were trying to trap him.

³"What did Moses say about divorce?" Jesus asked them.

⁴"He said it was all right," they replied. "He said that all a man has to do is write his wife a letter of dismissal."

⁵"And why did he say that?" Jesus asked. "I'll tell you why—it was a concession to your hard-hearted wickedness. ⁶,⁷But it certainly isn't God's way. For from the very first he made man and woman to be joined together permanently in marriage; therefore a man is to leave his father and mother, ⁸and he and his wife are united so that they are no longer two, but one. ⁹And no man may separate what God has joined together."

¹⁰Later, when he was alone with his disciples in the house, they brought up the subject again.

¹¹He told them, "When a man divorces his wife to marry someone else, he commits adultery against her. ¹²And if a wife divorces her husband and remarries, she, too, commits adultery."

Paul's Plan to Visit the Corinthians
⚘ 2 Corinthians 1:15–24 ⚘

It was because I was so sure of your understanding and trust that I planned to stop and see you on my way to Macedonia, as well as afterwards when I returned, so that I could be a double blessing to you and so that you could send me on my way to Judea.

¹⁷Then why, you may be asking, did I change my plan? Hadn't I really made up my mind yet? Or am I like a man of the world who says "yes" when he really means "no"? ¹⁸Never! As surely as God is true, I am not that sort of person. My "yes" means "yes."

¹⁹Timothy and Silvanus and I have been telling you about Jesus Christ the Son of God. He isn't one to say "yes" when he means "no." He always does exactly what he says. ²⁰He carries out and fulfills all of God's promises, no matter how many of them there are; and we have told everyone how faithful he is, giving glory to his name. ²¹It is this God who has made you and me into faithful Christians and commissioned us apostles to preach the Good News. ²²He has put his brand upon us—his mark of ownership—and given us his Holy Spirit in our hearts as guarantee that we belong to him, and as the first installment of all that he is going to give us.

²³I call upon this God to witness against me if I am not telling the absolute truth: the reason I haven't come to visit you yet is that I don't want to sadden you with a severe rebuke. ²⁴When I come, although I can't do much to help your faith, for it is strong already, I want to be able to do something about your joy: I want to make you happy, not sad.

Proverbs for Today
❧ 13:11 ❧

Wealth from gambling quickly disappears; wealth from hard work grows.

------- ❧ KEY VERSE ❧ -------

"From the very first he made man and woman to be joined together permanently in marriage; therefore a man is to leave his father and mother, and he and his wife are united so that they are no longer two, but one. And no man may separate what God has joined together."—*Mark 10:6–9*

------- ❧ REFLECTION ❧ -------

God allowed divorce as a concession to people's sinfulness. Divorce was not approved, but it was instituted to protect the injured party in the midst of a bad situation. Unfortunately, many people observed legal traditions that allowed divorce for almost any reason (the cause for divorce being left up to the discretion of the husband). Jesus explained that this was not God's intent; instead, God wants married people to consider their marriage permanent.

Don't enter your marriage with the option of getting out, but be committed to the permanence of the relationship. You'll stand a much better chance of making your marriage work. Don't be hard-hearted like the Pharisees, but be hardheaded in your determination, with God's help, to stay together.

------- ❧ MEDITATION ❧ -------

Heavenly Father, help us to work out any disagreements or differences we may have in our marriage so that we can remain joyfully together as your Word ordains. ❧

APRIL 19

Enter the Kingdom of God like a Child
❧ Mark 10:13–16 ❧

Once when some mothers were bringing their children to Jesus to bless them, the disciples shooed them away, telling them not to bother him.

[14]But when Jesus saw what was happening he was very much displeased with his disciples and said to them, "Let the children come to me, for the Kingdom of God belongs to such as they. Don't send them away! [15]I tell you as seriously as I know how that anyone who refuses to come to God as a little child will never be allowed into his Kingdom."

[16]Then he took the children into his arms and placed his hands on their heads and he blessed them.

Paul's Sorrowful Letter
❧ 2 Corinthians 2:1–4 ❧

"No," I said to myself, "I won't do it. I'll not make them unhappy with another painful visit." [2]For if I make you sad, who is going to make me happy? You are the ones to do it, and how can you if I cause you pain? [3]That is why I wrote as I did in my last letter, so that you will get things straightened out before I come. Then, when I do come, I will not be made sad by the very ones who ought to give me greatest joy. I felt sure that your happiness was so bound up in mine that you would not be happy either, unless I came with joy.

[4]Oh, how I hated to write that letter! It almost broke my heart and I tell you honestly that I cried over it. I didn't want to hurt you, but I had to show you how very much I loved you and cared about what was happening to you.

Proverbs for Today
❧ 13:12–14 ❧

Hope deferred makes the heart sick; but when dreams come true at last, there is life and joy. ☐ Despise God's Word and find yourself in trouble. Obey it and succeed. ☐ The advice of a wise man refreshes like water from a mountain spring. Those accepting it become aware of the pitfalls on ahead.

Oh, how I hated to write that letter! It almost broke my heart, and I tell you honestly that I cried over it. I didn't want to hurt you, but I had to show you how very much I loved you and cared about what was happening to you.—*2 Corinthians 2:4*

_____ ❧ REFLECTION ❧ _____

Paul did not enjoy reprimanding his friends and fellow believers, but he cared enough for the Corinthians to confront them about their wrongdoing. Proverbs 27:6 says that "wounds from a friend are better than kisses from an enemy."

Sometimes the person closest to you—your spouse—makes choices that you know are wrong. If you ignore his or her behavior and let it continue, you aren't showing love. Love means honestly sharing your concerns with those you love. When you don't move quickly to help, you show that you are more concerned about what will happen to you than about what will happen to your partner.

_____ ❧ MEDITATION ❧ _____

Heavenly Father, give us the courage to confront each other when we need to. We also ask that you will give us gracious words so that our message will be as loving and non-judgmental as you are. ❧

APRIL 20

Jesus and the Rich Man
❧ Mark 10:17–31 ❧

As Jesus was starting out on a trip, a man came running to him and knelt down and asked, "Good Teacher, what must I do to get to heaven?"

[18]"Why do you call me good?" Jesus asked. "Only God is truly good! [19]But as for your question—you know the commandments: don't kill, don't commit adultery, don't steal, don't lie, don't cheat, respect your father and mother."

[20]"Teacher," the man replied, "I've never once broken a single one of those laws."

[21]Jesus felt genuine love for this man as he looked at him. "You lack only one thing," he told him; "go and sell all you have and give the money to the poor—and you shall have treasure in heaven—and come, follow me."

[22]Then the man's face fell, and he went sadly away, for he was very rich.

[23]Jesus watched him go, then turned around and said to his disciples, "It's almost impossible for the rich to get into the Kingdom of God!"

[24]This amazed them. So Jesus said it again: "Dear children, how hard it is for those who trust in riches to enter the Kingdom of God. [25]It is easier for a camel to go through the eye of a needle than for a rich man to enter the Kingdom of God."

[26]The disciples were incredulous! "Then who in the world can be saved, if not a rich man?" they asked.

[27]Jesus looked at them intently, then said, "Without God, it is utterly impossible. But with God everything is possible."

[28]Then Peter began to mention all that he and the other disciples had left behind. "We've given up everything to follow you," he said.

[29]And Jesus replied, "Let me assure you that no one has ever given up anything—home, brothers, sisters, mother, father, children, or property—for love of me and to tell others the Good News, [30]who won't be given back, a hundred times over, homes, brothers, sisters, mothers, children, and land—with persecutions!

"All these will be his here on earth, and in the world to come he shall have eternal life. [31]But many people who seem to be important now will be the least important then; and many who are considered least here shall be greatest there."

Reinstate the Repentant Sinner
§ 2 Corinthians 2:5–11 §

Remember that the man I wrote about, who caused all the trouble, has not caused sorrow to me as much as to all the rest of you—though I certainly have my share in it too. I don't want to be harder on him than I should. He has been punished enough by your united disapproval. ⁷Now it is time to forgive him and comfort him. Otherwise he may become so bitter and discouraged that he won't be able to recover. ⁸Please show him now that you still do love him very much.

⁹I wrote to you as I did so that I could find out how far you would go in obeying me. ¹⁰When you forgive anyone, I do too. And whatever I have forgiven (to the extent that this affected me too) has been by Christ's authority, and for your good. ¹¹A further reason for forgiveness is to keep from being outsmarted by Satan; for we know what he is trying to do.

Proverbs for Today
§ 13:15–16 §

A man with good sense is appreciated. A treacherous man must walk a rocky road. □ A wise man thinks ahead; a fool doesn't, and even brags about it!

✦ KEY VERSE ✦

Now it is time to forgive him and comfort him. Otherwise he may become so bitter and discouraged that he won't be able to recover. —*2 Corinthians 2:7*

✦ REFLECTION ✦

It was time to forgive the man who had been punished by the church and had later repented. He now needed friendship and comfort. Church discipline should always allow for restoration. Two mistakes can be made in church discipline—being too lenient with sin and not correcting mistakes, or being too harsh and not forgiving.

As a couple, remember that there is a time to confront and a time to comfort. Don't forget that the purpose of discipline is to restore a person to fellowship with God and others, not to destroy him or her. Be cautious that neither of you allows personal anger to be vented under the guise of correcting a wrong.

✦ MEDITATION ✦

Heavenly Father, show us how we can be a source of encouragement to those who have repented and asked for forgiveness. Help us to work as a couple to restore the person to our church family. §

APRIL 21

The Greatest Must Be the Servant of All
§ Mark 10:32–45 §

Now Jesus and his disciples were on the way to Jerusalem, and Jesus was walking along ahead; and as the disciples were following they were filled with terror and dread.

Taking them aside, Jesus once more began describing all that was going to happen to him when they arrived at Jerusalem.

³³"When we get there," he told them, "I, the Messiah, will be arrested and taken before the chief priests and the Jewish leaders, who will sentence me to die and hand me over to the Romans to be killed. ³⁴They will mock me and spit on me and flog me with their whips and kill me; but after three days I will come back to life again."

³⁵Then James and John, the sons of Zebedee, came over and spoke to him in a low voice. "Master," they said, "we want you to do us a favor."

³⁶"What is it?" he asked.

³⁷"We want to sit on the thrones next to yours in your kingdom," they said, "one at your right and the other at your left!"

³⁸But Jesus answered, "You don't know what you are asking! Are you able to drink from the bitter cup of sorrow I must drink from? Or to be baptized with the baptism of suffering I must be baptized with?"

³⁹"Oh, yes," they said, "we are!"

And Jesus said, "You shall indeed drink from my cup and be baptized with my baptism, ⁴⁰but I do not have the right to place you on thrones next to mine. Those appointments have already been made."

⁴¹When the other disciples discovered what James and John had asked, they were very indignant. ⁴²So Jesus called them to him and said, "As you know, the kings and great men of the earth lord it over the people; ⁴³but among you it is different. Whoever wants to be great among you must be your servant. ⁴⁴And whoever wants to be greatest of all must be the slave of all. ⁴⁵For even I, the Messiah, am not here to be served, but to help others, and to give my life as a ransom for many."

The Fragrance of the Gospel
2 Corinthians 2:12–17

Well, when I got as far as the city of Troas, the Lord gave me tremendous opportunities to preach the Gospel. ¹³But Titus, my dear brother, wasn't there to meet me and I couldn't rest, wondering where he was and what had happened to him. So I said good-bye and went right on to Macedonia to try to find him.

¹⁴But thanks be to God! For through what Christ has done, he has triumphed over us so that now wherever we go he uses us to tell others about the Lord and to spread the Gospel like a sweet perfume. ¹⁵As far as God is concerned there is a sweet, wholesome fragrance in our lives. It is the fragrance of Christ within us, an aroma to both the saved and the unsaved all around us. ¹⁶To those who are not being saved, we seem a fearful smell of death and doom, while to those who know Christ we are a life-giving perfume. But who is adequate for such a task as this? ¹⁷Only those who, like ourselves, are men of integrity, sent by God, speaking with Christ's power, with God's eye upon us. We are not like those hucksters—and there are many of them—whose idea in getting out the Gospel is to make a good living out of it.

Proverbs for Today
13:17–19

An unreliable messenger can cause a lot of trouble. Reliable communication permits progress. ☐ If you refuse criticism you will end in poverty and disgrace; if you accept criticism you are on the road to fame. ☐ It is pleasant to see plans develop. That is why fools refuse to give them up even when they are wrong.

KEY VERSE

An unreliable messenger can cause a lot of trouble. Reliable communication permits progress.—*Proverbs 13:17*

REFLECTION

In Solomon's day, kings had to rely on messengers for information about their country. It was vitally important that these people be trustworthy. Inaccurate information could lead to bloodshed.

Reliable communication is vital in all relationships. If the message received is different from the message sent, relationships, businesses, and diplomatic relations can all break down. This is especially true in marriage. When talking to your spouse, choose your words carefully. When listening, avoid taking action until you clearly understand what your partner means.

MEDITATION

Heavenly Father, give us the patience to wait before we react to each other's words. Help us also to respond with love and kindness to others so that we won't allow misunderstandings to develop.

APRIL 22

Jesus Heals Blind Bartimaeus
Mark 10:46–52

And so Jesus and his disciples reached Jericho. Later, as they left town, a great crowd was following. Now it happened that a blind beggar named Bartimaeus (the son of Timaeus) was sitting beside the road as Jesus was going by.

[47]When Bartimaeus heard that Jesus from Nazareth was near, he began to shout out, "Jesus, Son of David, have mercy on me!"

[48]"Shut up!" some of the people yelled at him.

But he only shouted the louder, again and again, "O Son of David, have mercy on me!"

[49]When Jesus heard him he stopped there in the road and said, "Tell him to come here."

So they called the blind man. "You lucky fellow," they said, "come on, he's calling you!" [50]Bartimaeus yanked off his old coat and flung it aside, jumped up and came to Jesus.

[51]"What do you want me to do for you?" Jesus asked.

"O Teacher," the blind man said, "I want to see!"

[52]And Jesus said to him, "All right, it's done. Your faith has healed you."

And instantly the blind man could see, and followed Jesus down the road!

Law Brings Death, But the Spirit Gives Life
2 Corinthians 3:1–6

Are we beginning to be like those false teachers of yours who must tell you all about themselves and bring long letters of recommendation with them? I think you hardly need someone's letter to tell you about us, do you? And we don't need a recommendation from you, either! [2]The only letter I need is you yourselves! By looking at the good change in your hearts, everyone can see that we have done a good work among you. [3]They can see that you are a letter from Christ, written by us. It is not a letter written with pen and ink, but by the Spirit of the living God; not one carved on stone, but in human hearts.

[4]We dare to say these good things about ourselves only because of our great trust in God through Christ, that he will help us to be true to what we say, [5]and not because we think we can do anything of lasting value by ourselves. Our only power and success comes from God. [6]He is the one who has helped us tell others about his new agreement to save them. We do not tell them that they must obey every law of God or die; but we tell them there is life for them from the Holy Spirit. The old way, trying to be saved by keeping the Ten Commandments, ends in death; in the new way, the Holy Spirit gives them life.

Proverbs for Today
13:20–23

Be with wise men and become wise. Be with evil men and become evil. Curses chase sinners, while blessings chase the righteous! □ When a good man dies, he leaves an inheritance to his grandchildren; but when a sinner dies, his wealth is stored up for the godly. □ A poor man's farm may have good soil, but injustice robs him of its riches.

KEY VERSE

Be with wise men and become wise. Be with evil men and become evil.—*Proverbs 13:20*

REFLECTION

The old saying, "A rotten apple spoils the barrel," is often applied to friendships, and for good reason. Our friends and associates affect us, sometimes profoundly. As a couple and as individuals, be careful whom you choose to be your closest friends. Spend time with people you want to be like—because you and your friends will surely grow to resemble each other.

MEDITATION

Heavenly Father, we ask that you will bring devout Christian friends into our lives who can encourage us, and that you will make us a blessing to them too.

Jesus' Triumphal Entry into Jerusalem
◄§ Mark 11:1–11 §►

As Jesus and his disciples neared Bethphage and Bethany on the outskirts of Jerusalem and came to the Mount of Olives, Jesus sent two of his disciples on ahead.

²"Go into that village over there," he told them, "and just as you enter you will see a colt tied up that has never been ridden. Untie him and bring him here. ³And if anyone asks you what you are doing, just say, 'Our Master needs him and will return him soon.'"

⁴,⁵Off went the two men and found the colt standing in the street, tied outside a house. As they were untying it, some who were standing there demanded, "What are you doing, untying that colt?"

⁶So they said what Jesus had told them to, and then the men agreed.

⁷So the colt was brought to Jesus and the disciples threw their cloaks across its back for him to ride on. ⁸Then many in the crowd spread out their coats along the road before him, while others threw down leafy branches from the fields.

⁹He was in the center of the procession with crowds ahead and behind, and all of them shouting, "Hail to the King!" "Praise God for him who comes in the name of the Lord!" . . . ¹⁰"Praise God for the return of our father David's kingdom . . ." "Hail to the King of the universe!"

¹¹And so he entered Jerusalem and went into the Temple. He looked around carefully at everything and then left—for now it was late in the afternoon—and went out to Bethany with the twelve disciples.

The Old and New Covenants Compared
◄§ 2 Corinthians 3:7–18 §►

Yet that old system of law that led to death began with such glory that people could not bear to look at Moses' face. For as he gave them God's law to obey, his face shone out with the very glory of God—though the brightness was already fading away. ⁸Shall we not expect far greater glory in these days when the Holy Spirit is giving life? ⁹If the plan that leads to doom was glorious, much more glorious is the plan that makes men right with God. ¹⁰In fact, that first glory as it shone from Moses' face is worth nothing at all in comparison with the overwhelming glory of the new agreement. ¹¹So if the old system that faded into nothing was full of heavenly glory, the glory of God's new plan for our salvation is certainly far greater, for it is eternal.

¹²Since we know that this new glory will never go away, we can preach with great boldness, ¹³and not as Moses did, who put a veil over his face so that the Israelis could not see the glory fade away.

¹⁴Not only Moses' face was veiled, but his people's minds and understanding were veiled and blinded too. Even now when the Scripture is read it seems as though Jewish hearts and minds are covered by a thick veil, because they cannot see and understand the real meaning of the Scriptures. For this veil of misunderstanding can be removed only by believing in Christ. ¹⁵Yes, even today when they read Moses' writings their hearts are blind and they think that obeying the Ten Commandments is the way to be saved.

¹⁶But whenever anyone turns to the Lord from his sins, then the veil is taken away. ¹⁷The Lord is the Spirit who gives them life, and where he is there is freedom [from trying to be saved by keeping the laws of God]. ¹⁸But we Christians have no veil over our faces; we can be mirrors that brightly reflect the glory of the Lord. And as the Spirit of the Lord works within us, we become more and more like him.

Proverbs for Today
◄§ 13:24–25 §►

If you refuse to discipline your son, it proves you don't love him; for if you love him you will be prompt to punish him. □ The good man eats to live, while the evil man lives to eat.

We Christians have no veil over our faces; we can be mirrors that brightly reflect the glory of the Lord. And as the Spirit of the Lord works within us, we become more and more like him.—*2 Corinthians 3:18*

────── ✎ REFLECTION ✐ ──────

When Moses came down Mount Sinai with the Ten Commandments, his face glowed from being in God's presence. He put on a veil to keep the people from being terrified by the brightness of his face. Paul adds that this veil also kept them from seeing the glory fade away.

Yet, the glory that the Holy Spirit imparts to every believer is greater both in quality and longevity than that which Moses experienced. The glory we have been promised in the new covenant gradually transforms the believer into a Christlike person. Becoming Christlike is a progressive experience. The more closely we relate to him, the more we become like him.

One of the greatest joys of a Christian marriage is to share in someone else's spiritual development. Encourage each other in your Christian walk.

────── ✎ MEDITATION ✐ ──────

Heavenly Father, we ask that your Spirit will fill us each day with a fresh vitality for our faith and for the work to which you have called us in your Kingdom. ✐

APRIL 24

Jesus Cleanses the Temple
✎ Mark 11:12–25 ✐

The next morning as Jesus and his disciples left Bethany, he felt hungry. [13]A little way off he noticed a fig tree in full leaf, so he went over to see if he could find any figs on it. But no, there were only leaves, for it was too early in the season for fruit.
[14]Then Jesus said to the tree, "You shall never bear fruit again!" And the disciples heard him say it.
[15]When they arrived back to Jerusalem he went to the Temple and began to drive out the merchants and their customers, and knocked over the tables of the moneychangers and the stalls of those selling doves, [16]and stopped everyone from bringing in loads of merchandise.
[17]He told them, "It is written in the Scriptures, 'My Temple is to be a place of prayer for all nations,' but you have turned it into a den of robbers."
[18]When the chief priests and other Jewish leaders heard what he had done they began planning how best to get rid of him. Their problem was their fear of riots because the people were so enthusiastic about Jesus' teaching.

[19]That evening as usual they left the city.
[20]Next morning, as the disciples passed the fig tree he had cursed, they saw that it was withered from the roots! [21]Then Peter remembered what Jesus had said to the tree on the previous day, and exclaimed, "Look, Teacher! The fig tree you cursed has withered!"
[22,23]In reply Jesus said to the disciples, "If you only have faith in God—this is the absolute truth—you can say to this Mount of Olives, 'Rise up and fall into the Mediterranean,' and your command will be obeyed. All that's required is that you really believe and have no doubt! [24]Listen to me! You can pray for *anything,* and *if you believe, you have it;* it's yours! [25]But when you are praying, first forgive anyone you are holding a grudge against, so that your Father in heaven will forgive you your sins too."

Satan Blinds, But God Gives Light
✎ 2 Corinthians 4:1–7 ✐

It is God himself, in his mercy, who has given us this wonderful work [of telling his Good News to others], and so we never give up. [2]We do not try to trick people into believing—we are not interested in fooling anyone. We never try to get anyone to believe that the Bible teaches what it doesn't. All such shameful methods we forego. We stand in the presence of God as we speak and so we tell the truth, as all who know us will agree.

³If the Good News we preach is hidden to anyone, it is hidden from the one who is on the road to eternal death. ⁴Satan, who is the god of this evil world, has made him blind, unable to see the glorious light of the Gospel that is shining upon him, or to understand the amazing message we preach about the glory of Christ, who is God. ⁵We don't go around preaching about ourselves, but about Christ Jesus as Lord. All we say of ourselves is that we are your slaves because of what Jesus has done for us. ⁶For God, who said, "Let there be light in the darkness," has made us understand that it is the brightness of his glory that is seen in the face of Jesus Christ.

⁷But this precious treasure—this light and power that now shine within us —is held in a perishable container, that is, in our weak bodies. Everyone can see that the glorious power within must be from God and is not our own.

Proverbs for Today
⋖§ 14:1–2 §⋗

A wise woman builds her house, while a foolish woman tears hers down by her own efforts. □ To do right honors God; to sin is to despise him.

⋖ KEY VERSE §⋗

But when you are praying, first forgive anyone you are holding a grudge against, so that your Father in heaven will forgive you your sins too. —*Mark 11:25*

⋖ REFLECTION §⋗

There are two parts to the unusual incident that relates to this verse: the cursing of the fig tree and the cleansing of the temple. The cursing of the fig tree was an acted-out parable associated with the cleansing of the temple. The temple was supposed to be a place of worship, but true worship of God had virtually disappeared. The fig tree offered the promise of fruit, but it produced none. Jesus was showing his anger at religious life without substance. If you go through the motions of faith without putting it to work in your life, you are like the fig tree that withered and died. Genuine faith has great potential; ask God to help you bear fruit together for his Kingdom.

⋖ MEDITATION §⋗

Heavenly Father, show us how we can be of service to you and your Kingdom, and give us the strength, wisdom, and faith to persevere in the tasks you give us as a couple. §⋗

APRIL 25

The Parable of the Disloyal Tenants
⋖§ Mark 11:26—12:12 §⋗

By this time Jesus and his disciples had arrived in Jerusalem again, and as he was walking through the Temple area, the chief priests and other Jewish leaders came up to him demanding, "What's going on here? Who gave you the authority to drive out the merchants?"

²⁹Jesus replied, "I'll tell you if you answer one question! ³⁰What about John the Baptist? Was he sent by God, or not? Answer me!"

³¹They talked it over among themselves. "If we reply that God sent him, then he will say, 'All right, why didn't you accept him?' ³²But if we say God didn't send him, then the people will start a riot." (For the people all believed strongly that John was a prophet.)

³³So they said, "We can't answer. We don't know."

To which Jesus replied, "Then I won't answer your question either!"

¹²:¹Here are some of the story-illustrations Jesus gave to the people at that time:

"A man planted a vineyard and built a wall around it and dug a pit for pressing out the grape juice, and built a watchman's tower. Then he leased the farm to tenant farmers and moved to another country. ²At grape-picking time he sent one of his men to collect his share of the crop. ³But the farmers beat up the man and sent him back empty-handed.

⁴"The owner then sent another of his men, who received the same treatment, only worse, for his head was seriously injured. ⁵The next man he sent was killed; and later, others were either beaten or killed, until ⁶there was only one left—his only son. He finally sent him, thinking they would surely give him their full respect.

⁷"But when the farmers saw him coming they said, 'He will own the farm when his father dies. Come on, let's kill him—and then the farm will be ours!' ⁸So they caught him and murdered him and threw his body out of the vineyard.

⁹"What do you suppose the owner will do when he hears what happened? He will come and kill them all, and lease the vineyard to others. ¹⁰Don't you remember reading this verse in the Scriptures? 'The Rock the builders threw away became the cornerstone, the most honored stone in the building! ¹¹This is the Lord's doing and it is an amazing thing to see.'"

¹²The Jewish leaders wanted to arrest him then and there for using this illustration, for they knew he was pointing at them—they were the wicked farmers in his story. But they were afraid to touch him for fear of a mob. So they left him and went away.

Suffering for the Gospel
2 Corinthians 4:8–17

We are pressed on every side by troubles, but not crushed and broken. We are perplexed because we don't know why things happen as they do, but we don't give up and quit. ⁹We are hunted down, but God never abandons us. We get knocked down, but we get up again and keep going. ¹⁰These bodies of ours are constantly facing death just as Jesus did; so it is clear to all that it is only the living Christ within [who keeps us safe].

¹¹Yes, we live under constant danger to our lives because we serve the Lord, but this gives us constant opportunities to show forth the power of Jesus Christ within our dying bodies. ¹²Because of our preaching we face death, but it has resulted in eternal life for you.

¹³We boldly say what we believe [trusting God to care for us], just as the Psalm writer did when he said, "I believe and therefore I speak." ¹⁴We know that the same God who brought the Lord Jesus back from death will also bring us back to life again with Jesus, and present us to him along with you. ¹⁵These sufferings of ours are for your benefit. And the more of you who are won to Christ, the more there are to thank him for his great kindness, and the more the Lord is glorified.

¹⁶That is why we never give up. Though our bodies are dying, our inner strength in the Lord is growing every day. ¹⁷These troubles and sufferings of ours are, after all, quite small and won't last very long. Yet this short time of distress will result in God's richest blessing upon us forever and ever!

Proverbs for Today
14:3–4

A rebel's foolish talk should prick his own pride! But the wise man's speech is respected. □ An empty stable stays clean—but there is no income from an empty stable.

⚜ KEY VERSE ⚜

These troubles and sufferings of ours are, after all, quite small and won't last very long. Yet this short time of distress will result in God's richest blessing upon us forever and ever!—*2 Corinthians 4:17*

⚜ REFLECTION ⚜

Paul suffered many trials as he preached the Good News, but he knew that those trials would one day be over and he would obtain God's many wonderful blessings. Each time you face a seemingly insurmountable problem in your marriage, it's easy to focus on the pain rather than on God's ultimate goal for you. But just as athletes must concentrate on the finish line and ignore their discomfort, you too must focus on the reward for your faith and perseverance. Remember that no matter what happens, your problems are quite small compared to the eternal life that lies ahead.

❧ MEDITATION ❧

Heavenly Father, help us to focus our hearts and minds on the eternal home you have prepared for us, where there will be no sorrow or pain. Give us the faith and strength to face each day refreshed by the future you have for us. ❧

APRIL 26

Jesus Answers the Pharisees and the Sadducees
❧ Mark 12:13–34 ❧

But the Jewish leaders sent other religious and political leaders to talk with Jesus and try to trap him into saying something he could be arrested for.

[14]"Teacher," these spies said, "we know you tell the truth no matter what! You aren't influenced by the opinions and desires of men, but sincerely teach the ways of God. Now tell us, is it right to pay taxes to Rome, or not?"

[15]Jesus saw their trick and said, "Show me a coin and I'll tell you."

[16]When they handed it to him he asked, "Whose picture and title is this on the coin?" They replied, "The emperor's."

[17]"All right," he said, "if it is his, give it to him. But everything that belongs to God must be given to God!" And they scratched their heads in bafflement at his reply.

[18]Then the Sadducees stepped forward—a group of men who say there is no resurrection. Here was their question:

[19]"Teacher, Moses gave us a law that when a man dies without children, the man's brother should marry his widow and have children in his brother's name. [20,21,22]Well, there were seven brothers and the oldest married and died, and left no children. So the second brother married the widow, but soon he died too, and left no children. Then the next brother married her, and died without children, and so on until all were dead, and still there were no children; and last of all, the woman died too.

[23]"What we want to know is this: In the resurrection, whose wife will she be, for she had been the wife of each of them?"

[24]Jesus replied, "Your trouble is that you don't know the Scriptures, and don't know the power of God. [25]For when these seven brothers and the woman rise from the dead, they won't be married—they will be like the angels.

[26]"But now as to whether there will be a resurrection—have you never read in the book of Exodus about Moses and the burning bush? God said to Moses, 'I *am* the God of Abraham, and I *am* the God of Isaac, and I *am* the God of Jacob.'

[27]"God was telling Moses that these men, though dead for hundreds of years, were still very much alive, for he would not have said, 'I *am* the God' of those who don't exist! You have made a serious error."

[28]One of the teachers of religion who was standing there listening to the discussion realized that Jesus had answered well. So he asked, "Of all the commandments, which is the most important?"

[29]Jesus replied, "The one that says, 'Hear, O Israel! The Lord our God is the one and only God. [30]And you must love him with all your heart and soul and mind and strength.'

[31]"The second is: 'You must love others as much as yourself.' No other commandments are greater than these."

[32]The teacher of religion replied, "Sir, you have spoken a true word in saying that there is only one God and no other. [33]And I know it is far more important to love him with all my heart and understanding and strength, and to love others as myself,

than to offer all kinds of sacrifices on the altar of the Temple.''

[34]Realizing this man's understanding, Jesus said to him, ''You are not far from the Kingdom of God.'' And after that, no one dared ask him any more questions.

The Hope of the Resurrection
2 Corinthians 4:18—5:10

So we do not look at what we can see right now, the troubles all around us, but we look forward to the joys in heaven which we have not yet seen. The troubles will soon be over, but the joys to come will last forever.

[5:1]For we know that when this tent we live in now is taken down—when we die and leave these bodies—we will have wonderful new bodies in heaven, homes that will be ours forevermore, made for us by God himself, and not by human hands. [2]How weary we grow of our present bodies. That is why we look forward eagerly to the day when we shall have heavenly bodies which we shall put on like new clothes. [3]For we shall not be merely spirits without bodies. [4]These earthly bodies make us groan and sigh, but we wouldn't like to think of dying and having no bodies at all. We want to slip into our new bodies so that these dying bodies will, as it were, be swallowed up by everlasting life. [5]This is what God has prepared for us and, as a guarantee, he has given us his Holy Spirit.

[6]Now we look forward with confidence to our heavenly bodies, realizing that every moment we spend in these earthly bodies is time spent away from our eternal home in heaven with Jesus. [7]We know these things are true by believing, not by seeing. [8]And we are not afraid, but are quite content to die, for then we will be at home with the Lord. [9]So our aim is to please him always in everything we do, whether we are here in this body or away from this body and with him in heaven. [10]For we must all stand before Christ to be judged and have our lives laid bare—before him. Each of us will receive whatever he deserves for the good or bad things he has done in his earthly body.

Proverbs for Today
14:5–6

A truthful witness never lies; a false witness always lies. □ A mocker never finds the wisdom he claims he is looking for, yet it comes easily to the man with common sense.

KEY VERSE

Jesus replied, ''Your trouble is that you don't know the Scriptures and don't know the power of God. For when these seven brothers and the woman rise from the dead, they won't be married—they will be like the angels.''—*Mark 12:24-25*

REFLECTION

These verses not only indicate that marriage is solely an earthly relationship, they also declare the glory of the Lord. Jesus said that the Sadducees were ignorant of Scripture and, worse, that they didn't understand God's power. Heaven is far beyond our ability to comprehend or imagine (Isaiah 64:4; 1 Corinthians 2:9). We must be careful not to create questions about Heaven that cannot be answered from our human perspective. We need not be afraid of Heaven because of the unknowns. Instead of wondering what God's coming Kingdom will be like, we should concentrate on our relationship with Jesus right now. All that matters is that when we are in the new Kingdom we will be with him. How we live now will make a difference then.

Jesus' statement does not mean that a person will not recognize his or her spouse in the coming Kingdom. It simply means that God's new order will not be an extension of this life—the same physical and natural rules won't apply. In our fallen world, relationships are limited by time, death, and human institutions. But in God's new and restored world, our relationships will be eternal.

MEDITATION

Heavenly Father, we praise you for your divine and infinite power and glory. Keep our minds focused on the eternal things—the things that matter. And keep us from getting mired in questions that we can't answer in this life.

Proud Teachers and a Humble Widow
◄§ Mark 12:35–44 §►

Later, as Jesus was teaching the people in the Temple area, he asked them this question: "Why do your religious teachers claim that the Messiah must be a descendant of King David? [36]For David himself said—and the Holy Spirit was speaking through him when he said it—'God said to my Lord, sit at my right hand until I make your enemies your footstool.' [37]Since David called him his Lord, how can he be his *son?*"

(This sort of reasoning delighted the crowd and they listened to him with great interest.)

[38]Here are some of the other things he taught them at this time:

"Beware of the teachers of religion! For they love to wear the robes of the rich and scholarly, and to have everyone bow to them as they walk through the markets. [39]They love to sit in the best seats in the synagogues, and at the places of honor at banquets— [40]but they shamelessly cheat widows out of their homes and then, to cover up the kind of men they really are, they pretend to be pious by praying long prayers in public. Because of this, their punishment will be the greater."

[41]Then he went over to the collection boxes in the Temple and sat and watched as the crowds dropped in their money. Some who were rich put in large amounts. [42]Then a poor widow came and dropped in two pennies.

[43,44]He called his disciples to him and remarked, "That poor widow has given more than all those rich men put together! For they gave a little of their extra fat, while she gave up her last penny."

New Creations in Christ
◄§ 2 Corinthians 5:11–21 §►

It is because of this solemn fear of the Lord, which is ever present in our minds, that we work so hard to win others. God knows our hearts, that they are pure in this matter, and I hope that, deep within, you really know it too.

[12]Are we trying to pat ourselves on the back again? No, I am giving you some good ammunition! You can use this on those preachers of yours who brag about how well they look and preach, but don't have true and honest hearts. You can boast about us that we, at least, are well intentioned and honest.

[13,14]Are we insane [to say such things about ourselves]? If so, it is to bring glory to God. And if we are in our right minds, it is for your benefit. Whatever we do, it is certainly not for our own profit, but because Christ's love controls us now. Since we believe that Christ died for all of us, we should also believe that we have died to the old life we used to live. [15]He died for all so that all who live—having received eternal life from him—might live no longer for themselves, to please themselves, but to spend their lives pleasing Christ who died and rose again for them. [16]So stop evaluating Christians by what the world thinks about them or by what they seem to be like on the outside. Once I mistakenly thought of Christ that way, merely as a human being like myself. How differently I feel now! [17]When someone becomes a Christian he becomes a brand new person inside. He is not the same any more. A new life has begun!

[18]All these new things are from God who brought us back to himself through what Christ Jesus did. And God has given us the privilege of urging everyone to come into his favor and be reconciled to him. [19]For God was in Christ, restoring the world to himself, no longer counting men's sins against them but blotting them out. This is the wonderful message he has given us to tell others. [20]We are Christ's ambassadors. God is using us to speak to you: we beg you, as though Christ himself were here pleading with you, receive the love he offers you—be reconciled to God. [21]For God took the sinless Christ and poured into him our sins. Then, in exchange, he poured God's goodness into us!

Proverbs for Today

If you are looking for advice, stay away from fools. The wise man looks ahead. The fool attempts to fool himself and won't face facts.

_____ ❧ **KEY VERSE** ❧ _____

When someone becomes a Christian, he becomes a brand new person inside. He is not the same anymore. A new life has begun!—*2 Corinthians 5:17*

_____ ❧ **REFLECTION** ❧ _____

Christians are brand new people on the inside. The Holy Spirit gives them new life, and they are never the same again. They are not merely reformed, rehabilitated, or reeducated—they become new creations, living in vital union with Christ. They do not merely turn over a new leaf; they begin a new life under a new master. The Christian life involves this continual process of transformation by the power of the Holy Spirit. Pray daily that both of you will become more and more like Jesus Christ in your thoughts, attitudes, and actions.

_____ ❧ **MEDITATION** ❧ _____

Heavenly Father, help us to become more like you each day in the activities we do, in the words we say, and in the thoughts that fill our minds. ❧

APRIL 28 _____

Jesus Preaches about the End Times
❧ Mark 13:1–13 ❧

As Jesus was leaving the Temple that day, one of his disciples said, "Teacher, what beautiful buildings these are! Look at the decorated stonework on the walls."

[2]Jesus replied, "Yes, look! For not one stone will be left upon another, except as ruins."

[3,4]And as he sat on the slopes of the Mount of Olives across the valley from Jerusalem, Peter, James, John, and Andrew got alone with him and asked him, "Just when is all this going to happen to the Temple? Will there be some warning ahead of time?"

[5]So Jesus launched into an extended reply. "Don't let anyone mislead you," he said, [6]"for many will come declaring themselves to be your Messiah, and will lead many astray. [7]And wars will break out near and far, but this is not the signal of the end-time.

[8]"For nations and kingdoms will proclaim war against each other, and there will be earthquakes in many lands, and famines. These herald only the early stages of the anguish ahead. [9]But when these things begin to happen, watch out! For you will be in great danger. You will be dragged before the courts, and beaten in the synagogues, and accused before governors and kings of being my followers. This is your opportunity to tell them the Good News. [10]And the Good News must first be made known in every nation before the end-time finally comes. [11]But when you are arrested and stand trial, don't worry about what to say in your defense. Just say what God tells you to. Then you will not be speaking, but the Holy Spirit will.

[12]"Brothers will betray each other to death, fathers will betray their own children, and children will betray their parents to be killed. [13]And everyone will hate you because you are mine. But all who endure to the end without renouncing me shall be saved.

Suffering for the Gospel
❧ 2 Corinthians 6:1–7 ❧

As God's partners we beg you not to toss aside this marvelous message of God's great kindness. [2]For God says, "Your cry came to me at a favorable time, when the doors of welcome were wide open. I helped you on a day when salvation was being offered." Right now God is ready to welcome you. Today he is ready to save you.

³We try to live in such a way that no one will ever be offended or kept back from finding the Lord by the way we act, so that no one can find fault with us and blame it on the Lord. ⁴In fact, in everything we do we try to show that we are true ministers of God.

We patiently endure suffering and hardship and trouble of every kind. ⁵We have been beaten, put in jail, faced angry mobs, worked to exhaustion, stayed awake through sleepless nights of watching, and gone without food. ⁶We have proved ourselves to be what we claim by our wholesome lives and by our understanding of the Gospel and by our patience. We have been kind and truly loving and filled with the Holy Spirit. ⁷We have been truthful, with God's power helping us in all we do. All of the godly man's arsenal—weapons of defense, and weapons of attack—have been ours.

Proverbs for Today
◄§ 14:9–10 §►

The common bond of rebels is their guilt. The common bond of godly people is good will. □ Only the person involved can know his own bitterness or joy—no one else can really share it.

◄§ KEY VERSE §►

The common bond of rebels is their guilt. The common bond of godly people is good will.—*Proverbs 14:9*

◄§ REFLECTION §►

How rarely we find good will around us today. Angry drivers scowl at each other in the streets. People fight to be first in line. Disgruntled employers and employees both demand their rights. But the common bond of God's people should be good will. Those with good will think the best of others and assume that others have good motives and intend to do what is right.

When someone crosses you and you feel your blood pressure rising, ask yourself, "How can I show good will to this person?" Likewise, when your spouse does or says something that gets on your nerves, take a moment to remember all the reasons you fell in love with each other, and focus on the strengths of your marriage and the wonderful times you have had together. Don't harbor ill feelings toward the one person you need more than any other.

◄§ MEDITATION §►

Heavenly Father, help us to keep our emotions under control and to avoid outbursts of anger. §►

APRIL 29

Be Prepared for the End
◄§ Mark 13:14–37 §►

"When you see the horrible thing standing in the Temple —reader, pay attention!—flee, if you can, to the Judean hills. ¹⁵,¹⁶Hurry! If you are on your rooftop porch, don't even go back into the house. If you are out in the fields, don't even return for your money or clothes.

¹⁷"Woe to pregnant women in those days, and to mothers nursing their children. ¹⁸And pray that your flight will not be in winter. ¹⁹For those will be days of such horror as have never been since the beginning of God's creation, nor will ever be again. ²⁰And unless the Lord shortens that time of calamity, not a soul in all the earth will survive. But for the sake of his chosen ones he will limit those days.

²¹"And then if anyone tells you, 'This is the Messiah,' or, 'That one is,' don't pay any attention. ²²For there will be many false Messiahs and false prophets who will do wonderful miracles that would deceive, if possible, even God's own children. ²³Take care! I have warned you!

²⁴"After the tribulation ends, then the sun will grow dim and the moon will not shine, ²⁵and the stars will fall—the heavens will convulse.

²⁶"Then all mankind will see me, the Messiah, coming in the clouds with great power and glory. ²⁷And I will send out the angels to gather together my chosen ones from all over the world—from the farthest bounds of earth and heaven.

²⁸"Now, here is a lesson from a fig tree. When its buds become tender and its leaves begin to sprout, you know that spring has come. ²⁹And when you see these things happening that I've described, you can be sure that my return is very near, that I am right at the door.

³⁰"Yes, these are the events that will signal the end of the age. ³¹Heaven and earth shall disappear, but my words stand sure forever.

³²"However, no one, not even the angels in heaven, nor I myself, knows the day or hour when these things will happen; only the Father knows. ³³And since you don't know when it will happen, stay alert. Be on the watch [for my return].

³⁴"My coming can be compared with that of a man who went on a trip to another country. He laid out his employees' work for them to do while he was gone, and told the gatekeeper to watch for his return.

³⁵,³⁶,³⁷"Keep a sharp lookout! For you do not know when I will come, at evening, at midnight, early dawn or late daybreak. Don't let me find you sleeping. *Watch for my return!* This is my message to you and to everyone else."

Paul's Love for the Corinthians
⋖§ 2 Corinthians 6:8–13 §⋗

We stand true to the Lord whether others honor us or despise us, whether they criticize us or commend us. We are honest, but they call us liars.

⁹The world ignores us, but we are known to God; we live close to death, but here we are, still very much alive. We have been injured but kept from death. ¹⁰Our hearts ache, but at the same time we have the joy of the Lord. We are poor, but we give rich spiritual gifts to others. We own nothing, and yet we enjoy everything.

¹¹Oh, my dear Corinthian friends! I have told you all my feelings; I love you with all my heart. ¹²Any coldness still between us is not because of any lack of love on my part, but because your love is too small and does not reach out to me and draw me in. ¹³I am talking to you now as if you truly were my very own children. Open your hearts to us! Return our love!

Proverbs for Today
⋖§ 14:11–12 §⋗

The work of the wicked will perish; the work of the godly will flourish. Before every man there lies a wide and pleasant road that seems right but ends in death.

⋖ KEY VERSE ⋗

Before every man there lies a wide and pleasant road that seems right but ends in death.—*Proverbs 14:12*

⋖ REFLECTION ⋗

The "wide and pleasant road" seems to offer many options and require few sacrifices. Easy choices, however, should make us take a second look at the possible alternatives. Ask yourselves these questions before rushing to take the easy way out of a situation: Is the solution attractive because it allows us to be lazy? Are we doing this because it will let us continue with our current life-style and perhaps save our reputations? Do we prefer to follow the easy path because it requires no moral restraints? The right choice often requires hard work and self-sacrifice. Don't be trapped by apparent shortcuts.

⋖ MEDITATION ⋗

Heavenly Father, help us to base our decisions in life on the truths in your Word and on the guidance of your Spirit. Forgive us when we allow our desires for instant gratification to keep us from doing what is right. §⋗

Judas Iscariot Betrays Jesus
⋖§ Mark 14:1–11 §⋗

The Passover observance began two days later—an annual Jewish holiday when no bread made with yeast was eaten. The chief priests and other Jewish leaders were still looking for an opportunity to arrest Jesus secretly and put him to death.

²"But we can't do it during the Passover," they said, "or there will be a riot."

³Meanwhile Jesus was in Bethany, at the home of Simon the leper; during supper a woman came in with a beautiful flask of expensive perfume. Then, breaking the seal, she poured it over his head.

⁴,⁵Some of those at the table were indignant among themselves about this "waste," as they called it.

"Why, she could have sold that perfume for a fortune and given the money to the poor!" they snarled.

⁶But Jesus said, "Let her alone; why berate her for doing a good thing? ⁷You always have the poor among you, and they badly need your help, and you can aid them whenever you want to; but I won't be here much longer.

⁸"She has done what she could, and has anointed my body ahead of time for burial. ⁹And I tell you this in solemn truth, that wherever the Good News is preached throughout the world, this woman's deed will be remembered and praised."

¹⁰Then Judas Iscariot, one of his disciples, went to the chief priests to arrange to betray Jesus to them.

¹¹When the chief priests heard why he had come, they were excited and happy and promised him a reward. So he began looking for the right time and place to betray Jesus.

Don't Become One with Unbelievers
⋖§ 2 Corinthians 6:14—7:4 §⋗

Don't be teamed with those who do not love the Lord, for what do the people of God have in common with the people of sin? How can light live with darkness? ¹⁵And what harmony can there be between Christ and the devil? How can a Christian be a partner with one who doesn't believe? ¹⁶And what union can there be between God's temple and idols? For you are God's temple, the home of the living God, and God has said of you, "I will live in them and walk among them, and I will be their God and they shall be my people." ¹⁷That is why the Lord has said, "Leave them; separate yourselves from them; don't touch their filthy things, and I will welcome you, ¹⁸and be a Father to you, and you will be my sons and daughters."

⁷:¹Having such great promises as these, dear friends, let us turn away from everything wrong, whether of body or spirit, and purify ourselves, living in the wholesome fear of God, giving ourselves to him alone. ²Please open your hearts to us again, for not one of you has suffered any wrong from us. Not one of you was led astray. We have cheated no one nor taken advantage of anyone. ³I'm not saying this to scold or blame you, for, as I have said before, you are in my heart forever and I live and die with you. ⁴I have the highest confidence in you, and my pride in you is great. You have greatly encouraged me; you have made me so happy in spite of all my suffering.

Proverbs for Today
⋖§ 14:13–14 §⋗

Laughter cannot mask a heavy heart. When the laughter ends, the grief remains. ☐ The backslider gets bored with himself; the godly man's life is exciting.

──────⋗ KEY VERSE ⋖──────

The backslider gets bored with himself; the godly man's life is exciting.—*Proverbs 14:14*

──────⋗ REFLECTION ⋖──────

When God slips from first place in our lives, everything else loses its meaning. Life seems to be no more than the tiresome process of making money to spend on food, clothing, shelter, and a few luxuries—just getting through the day so we can do the same thing again tomorrow. But when God has first priority in our lives, we soon find ourselves on a lifelong adventure. Even routine projects take on meaning and promise because they hold a greater purpose.

If your lives have become tired and boring, discuss together your mutual relationship with God. The boredom you both are experiencing could be a signal that your priorities have shifted to the wrong side. Get off the bench today and get back into the game of life. After all, it's always exciting to be on the winning team!

∽ MEDITATION ∾

Heavenly Father, forgive us when we become lazy and negative-minded. Help us to focus our energies on furthering your Kingdom. Give our lives meaning by focusing our minds on what matters most: eternity with you. ∾

MAY 1

The Last Supper
∽ Mark 14:12–31 ∾

On the first day of the Passover, the day the lambs were sacrificed, the disciples asked Jesus where he wanted to go to eat the traditional Passover supper. [13]He sent two of them into Jerusalem to make the arrangements.

"As you are walking along," he told them, "you will see a man coming toward you carrying a pot of water. Follow him. [14]At the house he enters, tell the man in charge, 'Our Master sent us to see the room you have ready for us, where we will eat the Passover supper this evening!' [15]He will take you upstairs to a large room all set up. Prepare our supper there."

[16]So the two disciples went on ahead into the city and found everything as Jesus had said, and prepared the Passover.

[17]In the evening Jesus arrived with the other disciples, [18]and as they were sitting around the table eating, Jesus said, "I solemnly declare that one of you will betray me, one of you who is here eating with me."

[19]A great sadness swept over them, and one by one they asked him, "Am I the one?"

[20]He replied, "It is one of you twelve eating with me now. [21]I must die, as the prophets declared long ago; but, oh, the misery ahead for the man by whom I am betrayed. Oh, that he had never been born!"

[22]As they were eating, Jesus took bread and asked God's blessing on it and broke it in pieces and gave it to them and said, "Eat it—this is my body."

[23]Then he took a cup of wine and gave thanks to God for it and gave it to them; and they all drank from it. [24]And he said to them, "This is my blood, poured out for many, sealing the new agreement between God and man. [25]I solemnly declare that I shall never again taste wine until the day I drink a different kind in the Kingdom of God."

[26]Then they sang a hymn and went out to the Mount of Olives.

[27]"All of you will desert me," Jesus told them, "for God has declared through the prophets, 'I will kill the Shepherd, and the sheep will scatter.' [28]But after I am raised to life again, I will go to Galilee and meet you there."

[29]Peter said to him, "I will never desert you no matter what the others do!"

[30]"Peter," Jesus said, "before the cock crows a second time tomorrow morning you will deny me three times."

[31]"No!" Peter exploded. "Not even if I have to die with you! I'll *never* deny you!" And all the others vowed the same.

The Good Report from Titus
◄§ 2 Corinthians 7:5–10 §►

When we arrived in Macedonia there was no rest for us; outside, trouble was on every hand and all around us; within us, our hearts were full of dread and fear. [6]Then God who cheers those who are discouraged refreshed us by the arrival of Titus. [7]Not only was his presence a joy, but also the news that he brought of the wonderful time he had with you. When he told me how much you were looking forward to my visit, and how sorry you were about what had happened, and about your loyalty and warm love for me, well, I overflowed with joy!

[8]I am no longer sorry that I sent that letter to you, though I was very sorry for a time, realizing how painful it would be to you. But it hurt you only for a little while. [9]Now I am glad I sent it, not because it hurt you, but because the pain turned you to God. It was a good kind of sorrow you felt, the kind of sorrow God wants his people to have, so that I need not come to you with harshness. [10]For God sometimes uses sorrow in our lives to help us turn away from sin and seek eternal life. We should never regret his sending it. But the sorrow of the man who is not a Christian is not the sorrow of true repentance and does not prevent eternal death.

Proverbs for Today
◄§ 14:15–16 §►

Only a simpleton believes everything he's told! A prudent man understands the need for proof. A wise man is cautious and avoids danger; a fool plunges ahead with great confidence.

◄ KEY VERSE ◄

God sometimes uses sorrow in our lives to help us turn away from sin and seek eternal life. We should never regret his sending it. But the sorrow of the man who is not a Christian is not the sorrow of true repentance and does not prevent eternal death. *—2 Corinthians 7:10*

◄ REFLECTION ◄

Repentance means being sorry for our sins and changing our behavior. Many people are sorry only for the effects of their sins or for being caught. Compare Peter's remorse and repentance with Judas' bitterness and suicide. Both denied Christ. One repented and was restored to faith and service; the other took his own life.

There are many opportunities to be sorry in marriage. Hurting each other can be all too easy at times. Let sorrow over your offenses motivate you to change how you treat your spouse.

◄ MEDITATION ◄

Heavenly Father, we ask forgiveness for our sins and ask that you will restore us to fellowship with you. §►

MAY 2

Jesus Is Arrested in the Garden of Gethsemane
◄§ Mark 14:32–52 §►

And now Jesus and his disciples came to an olive grove called the Garden of Gethsemane, and he instructed his disciples, "Sit here, while I go and pray."

[33]He took Peter, James and John with him and began to be filled with horror and deepest distress. [34]And he said to them, "My soul is crushed by sorrow to the point of death; stay here and watch with me."

[35]He went on a little further and fell to the ground and prayed that if it were possible the awful hour awaiting him might never come.

[36]"Father, Father," he said, "everything is possible for you. Take away this cup from me. Yet I want your will, not mine."

[37]Then he returned to the three disciples and found them asleep.

"Simon!" he said. "Asleep? Couldn't you watch with me even one hour? [38]Watch with me and pray lest the Tempter overpower you. For though the spirit is willing enough, the body is weak."

[39]And he went away again and prayed, repeating his pleadings. [40]Again he returned to them and found them sleeping, for they were very tired. And they didn't know what to say.

[41]The third time when he returned to them he said, "Sleep on; get your rest! But no! The time for sleep has ended! Look! I am betrayed into the hands of wicked men. [42]Come! Get up! We must go! Look! My betrayer is here!"

[43]And immediately, while he was still speaking, Judas (one of his disciples) arrived with a mob equipped with swords and clubs, sent out by the chief priests and other Jewish leaders.

[44]Judas had told them, "You will know which one to arrest when I go over and greet him. Then you can take him easily." [45]So as soon as they arrived he walked up to Jesus. "Master!" he exclaimed, and embraced him with a great show of friendliness. [46]Then the mob arrested Jesus and held him fast. [47]But someone pulled a sword and slashed at the High Priest's servant, cutting off his ear.

[48]Jesus asked them, "Am I some dangerous robber, that you come like this, armed to the teeth to capture me? [49]Why didn't you arrest me in the Temple? I was there teaching every day. But these things are happening to fulfill the prophecies about me."

[50]Meanwhile, all his disciples had fled. [51,52]There was, however, a young man following along behind, clothed only in a linen nightshirt. When the mob tried to grab him, he escaped, though his clothes were torn off in the process, so that he ran away completely naked.

Paul's Sorrowful Letter
2 Corinthians 7:11–16

Just see how much good this grief from the Lord did for you! You no longer shrugged your shoulders, but became earnest and sincere, and very anxious to get rid of the sin that I wrote you about. You became frightened about what had happened, and longed for me to come and help. You went right to work on the problem and cleared it up [punishing the man who sinned]. You have done everything you could to make it right.

[12]I wrote as I did so the Lord could show how much you really do care for us. That was my purpose even more than to help the man who sinned, or his father to whom he did the wrong.

[13]In addition to the encouragement you gave us by your love, we were made happier still by Titus' joy when you gave him such a fine welcome and set his mind at ease. [14]I told him how it would be—told him before he left me of my pride in you—and you didn't disappoint me. I have always told you the truth and now my boasting to Titus has also proved true! [15]He loves you more than ever when he remembers the way you listened to him so willingly and received him so anxiously and with such deep concern. [16]How happy this makes me, now that I am sure all is well between us again. Once again I can have perfect confidence in you.

Proverbs for Today
14:17–19

A short-tempered man is a fool. He hates the man who is patient. □ The simpleton is crowned with folly; the wise man is crowned with knowledge. □ Evil men shall bow before the godly.

KEY VERSE

Just see how much good this grief from the Lord did for you! You no longer shrugged your shoulders but became earnest and sincere and very anxious to get rid of the sin that I wrote you about. You became frightened about what had happened and longed for me to come and help. You went right to work on the problem and cleared it up [punishing the man who sinned]. You have done everything you could to make it right.—*2 Corinthians 7:11*

REFLECTION

It is difficult to hear that we have sinned, and even more difficult to get past the sin once it has been committed. Paul praised the Corinthians for clearing up an especially troublesome situation in a righteous manner.

Do either of you tend to be defensive when you are confronted with a transgression? Don't let pride keep you from admitting your sins. Accept confrontation as a tool for growth, and do all you can to correct problems that are pointed out to you.

Heavenly Father, help us both be open to change when we are confronted with our sins. And if we should speak to someone else about a sin in his or her life, give us strength, a loving heart, and the right words to say. ❧

MAY 3

Jesus before the Jewish Supreme Court
◄§ Mark 14:53–72 §►

Jesus was led to the High Priest's home where all of the chief priests and other Jewish leaders soon gathered. [54]Peter followed far behind and then slipped inside the gates of the High Priest's residence and crouched beside a fire among the servants.

[55]Inside, the chief priests and the whole Jewish Supreme Court were trying to find something against Jesus that would be sufficient to condemn him to death. But their efforts were in vain. [56]Many false witnesses volunteered, but they contradicted each other.

[57]Finally some men stood up to lie about him and said, [58]"We heard him say, 'I will destroy this Temple made with human hands and in three days I will build another, made without human hands!'" [59]But even then they didn't get their stories straight!

[60]Then the High Priest stood up before the Court and asked Jesus, "Do you refuse to answer this charge? What do you have to say for yourself?"

[61]To this Jesus made no reply.

Then the High Priest asked him. "Are you the Messiah, the Son of God?"

[62]Jesus said, "I am, and you will see me sitting at the right hand of God, and returning to earth in the clouds of heaven."

[63,64]Then the High Priest tore at his clothes and said, "What more do we need? Why wait for witnesses? You have heard his blasphemy. What is your verdict?" And the vote for the death sentence was unanimous.

[65]Then some of them began to spit at him, and they blindfolded him and began to hammer his face with their fists.

"Who hit you that time, you prophet?" they jeered. And even the bailiffs were using their fists on him as they led him away.

[66,67]Meanwhile Peter was below in the courtyard. One of the maids who worked for the High Priest noticed Peter warming himself at the fire.

She looked at him closely and then announced, "*You* were with Jesus, the Nazarene."

[68]Peter denied it. "I don't know what you're talking about!" he said, and walked over to the edge of the courtyard.

Just then, a rooster crowed.

[69]The maid saw him standing there and began telling the others, "There he is! There's that disciple of Jesus!"

[70]Peter denied it again.

A little later others standing around the fire began saying to Peter, "You are, too, one of them, for you are from Galilee!"

[71]He began to curse and swear. "I don't even know this fellow you are talking about," he said.

[72]And immediately the rooster crowed the second time. Suddenly Jesus' words flashed through Peter's mind: "Before the cock crows twice, you will deny me three times." And he began to cry.

Generous Giving Glorifies the Lord
◄§ 2 Corinthians 8:1–8 §►

Now I want to tell you what God in his grace has done for the churches in Macedonia.

²Though they have been going through much trouble and hard times, they have mixed their wonderful joy with their deep poverty, and the result has been an overflow of giving to others. ³They gave not only what they could afford, but far more; and I can testify that they did it because they wanted to, and not because of nagging on my part. ⁴They begged us to take the money so they could share in the joy of helping the Christians in Jerusalem. ⁵Best of all, they went beyond our highest hopes, for their first action was to dedicate themselves to the Lord and to us, for whatever directions God might give to them through us. ⁶They were so enthusiastic about it that we have urged Titus, who encouraged your giving in the first place, to visit you and encourage you to complete your share in this ministry of giving. ⁷You people there are leaders in so many ways—you have so much faith, so many good preachers, so much learning, so much enthusiasm, so much love for us. Now I want you to be leaders also in the spirit of cheerful giving.

⁸I am not giving you an order; I am not saying you must do it, but others are eager for it. This is one way to prove that your love is real, that it goes beyond mere words.

Proverbs for Today
⋅§ 14:20–21 §⋅

Even his own neighbors despise the poor man, while the rich have many "friends." But to despise the poor is to sin. Blessed are those who help them.

_____ ✧ KEY VERSE ✧ _____

You people there are leaders in so many ways—you have so much faith, so many good preachers, so much learning, so much enthusiasm, so much love for us. Now I want you to be leaders also in the spirit of cheerful giving.—*2 Corinthians 8:7*

_____ ✧ REFLECTION ✧ _____

While making his third missionary journey, Paul was collecting money for the impoverished believers in Jerusalem. The churches in Macedonia—Philippi, Thessalonica, and Beroea—gave money even though they were poor, and they gave more than Paul expected. This was sacrificial giving—they were poor themselves, but they wanted to help.

The point of tithing is not so much the amount of money we give, but why and how we give it. God does not want gifts that are given grudgingly or to get something back from him in return. Instead, he wants us to give as these churches did—out of dedication to him, love for fellow believers, the joy of helping those in need, and because it is right. As a couple, how well does your giving measure up to the standards set by the Macedonian churches? Remember all the blessings that God has freely given each of you and respond to him with a glad heart and a willing spirit.

_____ ✧ MEDITATION ✧ _____

Heavenly Father, thank you for the many blessings you have given us. We pray that you will take our tithes and use them to glorify your name and advance your Kingdom. §⋅

MAY 4 _____

Jesus on Trial before Pilate
⋅§ Mark 15:1–21 §⋅

Early in the morning the chief priests, elders and teachers of religion—the entire Supreme Court—met to discuss their next steps. Their decision was to send Jesus under armed guard to Pilate, the Roman governor.

²Pilate asked him, "Are you the King of the Jews?"

"Yes," Jesus replied, "it is as you say."

³,⁴Then the chief priests accused him of many crimes, and Pilate asked him, "Why don't you say something? What about all these charges against you?"

⁵But Jesus said no more, much to Pilate's amazement.

⁶Now, it was Pilate's custom to release one Jewish prisoner each year at Passover time—any prisoner the people requested. ⁷One of the prisoners at that time was Barabbas, convicted along with others for murder during an insurrection.

⁸Now a mob began to crowd in toward Pilate, asking him to release a prisoner as usual.

⁹"How about giving you the 'King of Jews'?" Pilate asked. "Is he the one you want released?" ¹⁰(For he realized by now that this was a frameup, backed by the chief priests because they envied Jesus' popularity.)

¹¹But at this point the chief priests whipped up the mob to demand the release of Barabbas instead of Jesus.

¹²"But if I release Barabbas," Pilate asked them, "what shall I do with this man you call your king?"

¹³They shouted back, "Crucify him!"

¹⁴"But why?" Pilate demanded. "What has he done wrong?" They only roared the louder, "Crucify him!"

¹⁵Then Pilate, afraid of a riot and anxious to please the people, released Barabbas to them. And he ordered Jesus flogged with a leaded whip, and handed him over to be crucified.

¹⁶,¹⁷Then the Roman soldiers took him into the barracks of the palace, called out the entire palace guard, dressed him in a purple robe, and made a crown of long, sharp thorns and put it on his head. ¹⁸Then they saluted, yelling, "Yea! King of the Jews!" ¹⁹And they beat him on the head with a cane, and spat on him and went down on their knees to "worship" him.

²⁰When they finally tired of their sport, they took off the purple robe and put his own clothes on him again, and led him away to be crucified.

²¹Simon of Cyrene, who was coming in from the country just then, was pressed into service to carry Jesus' cross. (Simon is the father of Alexander and Rufus.)

Christ Became Poor for Our Benefit
2 Corinthians 8:9–15

You know how full of love and kindness our Lord Jesus was: though he was so very rich, yet to help you he became so very poor, so that by being poor he could make you rich.

¹⁰I want to suggest that you finish what you started to do a year ago, for you were not only the first to propose this idea, but the first to begin doing something about it. ¹¹Having started the ball rolling so enthusiastically, you should carry this project through to completion just as gladly, giving whatever you can out of whatever you have. Let your enthusiastic idea at the start be equalled by your realistic action now. ¹²If you are really eager to give, then it isn't important how much you have to give. God wants you to give what you have, not what you haven't.

¹³Of course, I don't mean that those who receive your gifts should have an easy time of it at your expense, ¹⁴but you should divide with them. Right now you have plenty and can help them; then at some other time they can share with you when you need it. In this way each will have as much as he needs. ¹⁵Do you remember what the Scriptures say about this? "He that gathered much had nothing left over, and he that gathered little had enough." So you also should share with those in need.

Proverbs for Today
14:22–24

Those who plot evil shall wander away and be lost, but those who plan good shall be granted mercy and quietness. ☐ Work brings profit; talk brings poverty! ☐ Wise men are praised for their wisdom; fools are despised for their folly.

KEY VERSE

Then Pilate, afraid of a riot and anxious to please the people, released Barabbas to them. And he ordered Jesus flogged with a leaded whip, and handed him over to be crucified.—*Mark 15:15*

Although Jesus was innocent according to Roman law, Pilate caved in to political pressure. He abandoned what he knew was right. He tried to second-guess the Jewish leaders and give a decision that would please everyone while keeping himself safe.

When we lay aside God's clear statements of right and wrong and make decisions based on peer pressure, we fall into compromise and lawlessness.

God promises to honor those who do right; not those who make everyone happy. Dedicate your marriage to doing what is pure and holy, and ignore those who pressure you to abandon your convictions and your faith in favor of pleasing those around you.

Heavenly Father, we submit our marriage to you and ask that you give us the strength and courage to do what is right regardless of what others say or think about us. ❧

MAY 5

Jesus Is Crucified
◦§ Mark 15:22–32 §◦

And the Roman soldiers brought Jesus to a place called Golgotha. (Golgotha means skull.) [23]Wine drugged with bitter herbs was offered to him there, but he refused it. [24]And then they crucified him—and threw dice for his clothes.

[25]It was about nine o'clock in the morning when the crucifixion took place.

[26]A signboard was fastened to the cross above his head, announcing his crime. It read, "The King of the Jews."

[27]Two robbers were also crucified that morning, their crosses on either side of his. [28]And so the Scripture was fulfilled that said, "He was counted among evil men."

[29,30]The people jeered at him as they walked by, and wagged their heads in mockery.

"Ha! Look at you now!" they yelled at him. "Sure, you can destroy the Temple and rebuild it in three days! If you're so wonderful, save yourself and come down from the cross."

[31]The chief priests and religious leaders were also standing around joking about Jesus.

"He's quite clever at 'saving' others," they said, "but he can't save himself!"

[32]"Hey there, Messiah!" they yelled at him. "You 'King of Israel'! Come on down from the cross and we'll believe you!"

And even the two robbers dying with him, cursed him.

The Ministry of Titus
◦§ 2 Corinthians 8:16–24 §◦

I am thankful to God that he has given Titus the same real concern for you that I have. [17]He is glad to follow my suggestion that he visit you again—but I think he would have come anyway, for he is very eager to see you! [18]I am sending another well-known brother with him, who is highly praised as a preacher of the Good News in all the churches. [19]In fact, this man was elected by the churches to travel with me to take the gift to Jerusalem. This will glorify the Lord and show our eagerness to help each other. [20]By traveling together we will guard against any suspicion, for we are anxious that no one should find fault with the way we are handling this large gift. [21]God knows we are honest, but I want everyone else to know it too. That is why we have made this arrangement.

[22]And I am sending you still another brother, whom we know from experience to be an earnest Christian. He is especially interested, as he looks forward to this trip, because I have told him all about your eagerness to help.

[23]If anyone asks who Titus is, say that he is my partner, my helper in helping you, and you can also say that the other two brothers represent the assem-

blies here and are splendid examples of those who belong to the Lord.

²⁴Please show your love for me to these men and do for them all that I have publicly boasted you would.

Proverbs for Today
~§ 14:25 §~

A witness who tells the truth saves good men from being sentenced to death, but a false witness is a traitor.

~ KEY VERSE ~

If anyone asks who Titus is, say that he is my partner, my helper in helping you, and you can also say that the other two brothers represent the assemblies here and are splendid examples of those who belong to the Lord.—*2 Corinthians 8:23*

~ REFLECTION ~

Titus was a true disciple of Christ. He was eager to serve, took joy in the growth of others, had integrity, was a servant, and was concerned for the needs of those around him.

As a Christian couple, make a commitment to imitate Titus' qualities. True Christian character means acting as Christ would in all your dealings with people. Don't worry about whether your neighbors have more money than you do or attempt to seek revenge when someone takes advantage of you. Always remember that you are servants of Jesus Christ, and people will look to you—both as individuals and as a couple—as "splendid examples of those who belong to the Lord."

~ MEDITATION ~

Heavenly Father, we ask that you will forgive us when we dishonor your name. Help us to be a blessing to those around us and to serve the needs of your church faithfully. §~

MAY 6

The Death and Burial of Jesus
~§ Mark 15:33–47 §~

About noon, darkness fell across the entire land, lasting until three o'clock that afternoon.
³⁴Then Jesus called out with a loud voice, "Eli, Eli, lama sabachthani?" ("My God, my God, why have you deserted me?")
³⁵Some of the people standing there thought he was calling for the prophet Elijah. ³⁶So one man ran and got a sponge and filled it with sour wine and held it up to him on a stick.
"Let's see if Elijah will come and take him down!" he said.
³⁷Then Jesus uttered another loud cry, and dismissed his spirit.
³⁸And the curtain in the Temple was split apart from top to bottom.
³⁹When the Roman officer standing beside his cross saw how he dismissed his spirit, he exclaimed, "Truly, this was the Son of God!"
⁴⁰Some women were there watching from a distance—Mary Magdalene, Mary (the mother of James the Younger and of Joses), Salome, and others. ⁴¹They and many other Galilean women who were his followers had ministered to him when he was up in Galilee, and had come with him to Jerusalem.
^{42,43}This all happened the day before the Sabbath. Late that afternoon Joseph from Arimathea, an honored member of the Jewish Supreme Court (who personally was eagerly expecting the arrival of God's Kingdom), gathered his courage and went to Pilate and asked for Jesus' body.
⁴⁴Pilate couldn't believe that Jesus was already dead so he called for the Roman officer in charge and asked him. ⁴⁵The officer confirmed the fact, and Pilate told Joseph he could have the body.

⁴⁶Joseph bought a long sheet of linen cloth and, taking Jesus' body down from the cross, wound it in the cloth and laid it in a rock-hewn tomb, and rolled a stone in front of the entrance.

⁴⁷(Mary Magdalene and Mary the mother of Joses were watching as Jesus was laid away.)

Paul's Confidence in the Corinthians
⋅§ 2 Corinthians 9:1–5 ৯•

I realize that I really don't even need to mention this to you, about helping God's people. ²For I know how eager you are to do it, and I have boasted to the friends in Macedonia that you were ready to send an offering a year ago. In fact, it was this enthusiasm of yours that stirred up many of them to begin helping. ³But I am sending these men just to be sure that you really are ready, as I told them you would be, with your money all collected; I don't want it to turn out that this time I was wrong in my boasting about you. ⁴I would be very much ashamed—and so would you—if some of these Macedonian people come with me, only to find that you still aren't ready after all I have told them!

⁵So I have asked these other brothers to arrive ahead of me to see that the gift you promised is on hand and waiting. I want it to be a real gift and not look as if it were being given under pressure.

Proverbs for Today
⋅§ 14:26–27 ৯•

Reverence for God gives a man deep strength; his children have a place of refuge and security. Reverence for the Lord is a fountain of life; its waters keep a man from death.

———————— ⋅◎ KEY VERSE ◎⋅ ————————

Mary Magdalene and Mary the mother of Jesus were watching as Jesus was laid away.—*Mark 15:47*

———————— ⋅◎ REFLECTION ◎⋅ ————————

Because of the lowly status women occupied in ancient Palestine, Mary Magdalene and Mary the mother of Jesus could do very little to help our Lord. They couldn't speak before the Sanhedrin in his defense, they couldn't appeal to Pilate for his release, they couldn't stand against the crowds, and they certainly couldn't overpower the Roman guards. But they did what they could: they stayed at the cross when the disciples had fled in fear and panic; they followed Jesus' body when he was laid in the tomb; and they prepared spices for his burial. Because they used the opportunities they had, they were the first to witness the Resurrection. God blessed their devotion and diligence.

Let these brave and faithful women be an example to you in your marriage. Take advantage of the opportunities you have and do what you can for Christ rather than worrying about what you cannot do. God will honor your efforts and will reward you with his presence throughout eternity.

———————— ⋅◎ MEDITATION ◎⋅ ————————

Heavenly Father, open our eyes so that we can see the needs around us. Help us never to turn down an opportunity to serve you simply because it seems small or unexciting. ৯•

MAY 7 _____

The Resurrection of Jesus
⋅§ Mark 16:1–20 ৯•

The next evening, when the Sabbath ended, Mary Magdalene and Salome and Mary the mother of James went out and purchased embalming spices.

Early the following morning, just at sunrise, they carried them out to the tomb. ³On the way they were discussing how they could ever roll aside the huge stone from the entrance.

⁴But when they arrived they looked up and saw that the stone—a *very* heavy one—was already

moved away and the entrance was open! [5]So they entered the tomb—and there on the right sat a young man clothed in white. The women were startled, [6]but the angel said, "Don't be so surprised. Aren't you looking for Jesus, the Nazarene who was crucified? He isn't here! He has come back to life! Look, that's where his body was lying. [7]Now go and give this message to his disciples including Peter:

"'Jesus is going ahead of you to Galilee. You will see him there, just as he told you before he died!'"

[8]The women fled from the tomb, trembling and bewildered, too frightened to talk.

[9]It was early on Sunday morning when Jesus came back to life, and the first person who saw him was Mary Magdalene—the woman from whom he had cast out seven demons. [10,11]She found the disciples wet-eyed with grief and exclaimed that she had seen Jesus, and he was alive! But they didn't believe her!

[12]Later that day he appeared to two who were walking from Jerusalem into the country, but they didn't recognize him at first because he had changed his appearance. [13]When they finally realized who he was, they rushed back to Jerusalem to tell the others, but no one believed them.

[14]Still later he appeared to the eleven disciples as they were eating together. He rebuked them for their unbelief—their stubborn refusal to believe those who had seen him alive from the dead.

[15]And then he told them, "You are to go into all the world and preach the Good News to everyone, everywhere. [16]Those who believe and are baptized will be saved. But those who refuse to believe will be condemned.

[17]"And those who believe shall use my authority to cast out demons, and they shall speak new languages. [18]They will be able even to handle snakes with safety, and if they drink anything poisonous, it won't hurt them; and they will be able to place their hands on the sick and heal them."

[19]When the Lord Jesus had finished talking with them, he was taken up into heaven and sat down at God's right hand.

[20]And the disciples went everywhere preaching, and the Lord was with them and confirmed what they said by the miracles that followed their messages.

God Prizes Cheerful Givers
⋖ 2 Corinthians 9:6–15 ⋗

But remember this—if you give little, you will get little. A farmer who plants just a few seeds will get only a small crop, but if he plants much, he will reap much. [7]Every one must make up his own mind as to how much he should give. Don't force anyone to give more than he really wants to, for cheerful givers are the ones God prizes. [8]God is able to make it up to you by giving you everything you need and more, so that there will not only be enough for your own needs, but plenty left over to give joyfully to others. [9]It is as the Scriptures say: "The godly man gives generously to the poor. His good deeds will be an honor to him forever."

[10]For God, who gives seed to the farmer to plant, and later on, good crops to harvest and eat, will give you more and more seed to plant and will make it grow so that you can give away more and more fruit from your harvest.

[11]Yes, God will give you much so that you can give away much, and when we take your gifts to those who need them they will break out into thanksgiving and praise to God for your help. [12]So, two good things happen as a result of your gifts—those in need are helped, and they overflow with thanks to God. [13]Those you help will be glad not only because of your generous gifts to themselves and to others, but they will praise God for this proof that your deeds are as good as your doctrine. [14]And they will pray for you with deep fervor and feeling because of the wonderful grace of God shown through you.

[15]Thank God for his Son—his Gift too wonderful for words.

Proverbs for Today
⋖ 14:28–29 ⋗

A growing population is a king's glory; a dwindling nation is his doom. □ A wise man controls his temper. He knows that anger causes mistakes.

A wise man controls his temper. He knows that anger causes mistakes.—*Proverbs 14:29*

_____ ◈ **REFLECTION** ◈ _____

Anger can be like a fire out of control. It can burn us and everything in its path. Anger can divide people. It can push us into hasty decisions that may cause bitterness or guilt. Yet anger, in itself, is not wrong. Anger is a legitimate reaction to injustice and sin; it's a measure of what's important to us. When you feel yourself getting angry, look for the cause. Are you reacting to an evil situation or action that you are going to set right? Or are you responding selfishly to a personal insult? Pray that God will help you control your emotions, channeling legitimate anger into effective action, and conquering selfish feelings through humility and repentance.

_____ ◈ **MEDITATION** ◈ _____

Heavenly Father, help us control our anger. Guide our thoughts and actions so that we won't do or say anything foolish to each other or to others. And show us when anger over someone else's actions should move us to action. ❧

MAY 8 _____

An Angel Predicts John the Baptist's Birth
◅§ Luke 1:1–25 §▻

Dear friend who loves God:

[1,2]Several biographies of Christ have already been written using as their source material the reports circulating among us from the early disciples and other eyewitnesses. [3]However, it occurred to me that it would be well to recheck all these accounts from first to last and after thorough investigation to pass this summary on to you, [4]to reassure you of the truth of all you were taught.

[5]My story begins with a Jewish priest, Zacharias, who lived when Herod was king of Judea. Zacharias was a member of the Abijah division of the Temple service corps. (His wife Elizabeth was, like himself, a member of the priest tribe of the Jews, a descendant of Aaron.) [6]Zacharias and Elizabeth were godly folk, careful to obey all of God's laws in spirit as well as in letter. [7]But they had no children, for Elizabeth was barren; and now they were both very old.

[8,9]One day as Zacharias was going about his work in the Temple—for his division was on duty that week—the honor fell to him by lot to enter the inner sanctuary and burn incense before the Lord. [10]Meanwhile, a great crowd stood outside in the Temple court, praying as they always did during that part of the service when the incense was being burned.

[11,12]Zacharias was in the sanctuary when suddenly an angel appeared, standing to the right of the altar of incense! Zacharias was startled and terrified.

[13]But the angel said, "Don't be afraid, Zacharias! For I have come to tell you that God has heard your prayer, and your wife Elizabeth will bear you a son! And you are to name him John. [14]You will both have great joy and gladness at his birth, and many will rejoice with you. [15]For he will be one of the Lord's great men. He must never touch wine or hard liquor—and he will be filled with the Holy Spirit, even from before his birth! [16]And he will persuade many a Jew to turn to the Lord his God. [17]He will be a man of rugged spirit and power like Elijah, the prophet of old; and he will precede the coming of the Messiah, preparing the people for his arrival. He will soften adult hearts to become like little children's, and will change disobedient minds to the wisdom of faith."

[18]Zacharias said to the angel, "But this is impossible! I'm an old man now, and my wife is also well along in years."

[19]Then the angel said, "I am Gabriel! I stand in the very presence of God. It was he who sent me to you with this good news! [20]And now, because

you haven't believed me, you are to be stricken silent, unable to speak until the child is born. For my words will certainly come true at the proper time."

²¹Meanwhile the crowds outside were waiting for Zacharias to appear and wondered why he was taking so long. ²²When he finally came out, he couldn't speak to them, and they realized from his gestures that he must have seen a vision in the Temple. ²³He stayed on at the Temple for the remaining days of his Temple duties and then returned home. ²⁴Soon afterwards Elizabeth his wife became pregnant and went into seclusion for five months.

²⁵"How kind the Lord is," she exclaimed, "to take away my disgrace of having no children!"

God's Mighty Weapons
⊷§ 2 Corinthians 10:1–6 §⊷

I plead with you—yes, I, Paul—and I plead gently, as Christ himself would do. Yet some of you are saying, "Paul's letters are bold enough when he is far away, but when he gets here he will be afraid to raise his voice!"

²I hope I won't need to show you when I come how harsh and rough I can be. I don't want to carry out my present plans against some of you who seem to think my deeds and words are merely those of an ordinary man. ³It is true that I am an ordinary, weak human being, but I don't use human plans and methods to win my battles. ⁴I use God's mighty weapons, not those made by men, to knock down the devil's strongholds. ⁵These weapons can break down every proud argument against God and every wall that can be built to keep men from finding him. With these weapons I can capture rebels and bring them back to God, and change them into men whose hearts' desire is obedience to Christ. ⁶I will use these weapons against every rebel who re-

mains after I have first used them on you yourselves, and you surrender to Christ.

Proverbs for Today
⊷§ 14:30–31 §⊷

A relaxed attitude lengthens a man's life; jealousy rots it away. □ Anyone who oppresses the poor is insulting God who made them. To help the poor is to honor God.

———— ⊷ **KEY VERSE** §⊷ ————

The angel said, "Don't be afraid, Zacharias! For I have come to tell you that God has heard your prayer, and your wife, Elizabeth, will bear you a son! And you are to name him John."—*Luke 1:13*

———— ⊷ **REFLECTION** §⊷ ————

Zacharias, while offering incense on the altar, was also praying—perhaps for a son or for the coming of the Messiah. In either case, his prayer was answered. He would soon have a son who would prepare the way for the Messiah.

God answers prayer in his own way and in his own time. He worked in an "impossible" situation—Zacharias' wife could not conceive—to bring about the fulfillment of all the prophecies concerning the coming of the Messiah.

If you want to have your prayers answered—whether you and your spouse are hoping for a child or have another important desire—be open to what God can do in impossible situations. Wait for him to work in his way and in his time.

———— ⊷ **MEDITATION** §⊷ ————

Heavenly Father, teach us patience as you reveal your will for our lives in your perfect timing. Let your will be accomplished in our home, and make us thankful no matter how you respond. §⊷

MAY 9

Jesus' Birth Foretold to Mary
⋅§ Luke 1:26–56 §⋅

The following month God sent the angel Gabriel to Nazareth, a village in Galilee, ²⁷to a virgin, Mary, engaged to be married to a man named Joseph, a descendant of King David.

²⁸Gabriel appeared to her and said, "Congratulations, favored lady! The Lord is with you!"

²⁹Confused and disturbed, Mary tried to think what the angel could mean.

³⁰"Don't be frightened, Mary," the angel told her, "for God has decided to wonderfully bless you! ³¹Very soon now, you will become pregnant and have a baby boy, and you are to name him 'Jesus.' ³²He shall be very great and shall be called the Son of God. And the Lord God shall give him the throne of his ancestor David. ³³And he shall reign over Israel forever; his Kingdom shall never end!"

³⁴Mary asked the angel, "But how can I have a baby? I am a virgin."

³⁵The angel replied, "The Holy Spirit shall come upon you, and the power of God shall overshadow you; so the baby born to you will be utterly holy—the Son of God. ³⁶Furthermore, six months ago your Aunt Elizabeth—'the barren one,' they called her—became pregnant in her old age! ³⁷For every promise from God shall surely come true."

³⁸Mary said, "I am the Lord's servant, and I am willing to do whatever he wants. May everything you said come true." And then the angel disappeared.

³⁹,⁴⁰A few days later Mary hurried to the highlands of Judea to the town where Zacharias lived, to visit Elizabeth.

⁴¹At the sound of Mary's greeting, Elizabeth's child leaped within her and she was filled with the Holy Spirit.

⁴²She gave a glad cry and exclaimed to Mary, "You are favored by God above all other women, and your child is destined for God's mightiest praise. ⁴³What an honor this is, that the mother of my Lord should visit me! ⁴⁴When you came in and greeted me, the instant I heard your voice, my baby moved in me for joy! ⁴⁵You believed that God would do what he said; that is why he has given you this wonderful blessing."

⁴⁶Mary responded, "Oh, how I praise the Lord. ⁴⁷How I rejoice in God my Savior! ⁴⁸For he took notice of his lowly servant girl, and now generation after generation forever shall call me blest of God. ⁴⁹For he, the mighty Holy One, has done great things to me. ⁵⁰His mercy goes on from generation to generation, to all who reverence him.

⁵¹"How powerful is his mighty arm! How he scatters the proud and haughty ones! ⁵²He has torn princes from their thrones and exalted the lowly. ⁵³He has satisfied the hungry hearts and sent the rich away with empty hands. ⁵⁴And how he has helped his servant Israel! He has not forgotten his promise to be merciful. ⁵⁵For he promised our fathers—Abraham and his children—to be merciful to them forever."

⁵⁶Mary stayed with Elizabeth about three months and then went back to her own home.

The Shallow Vision of the Corinthians
⋅§ 2 Corinthians 10:7–12 §⋅

The trouble with you is that you look at me and I seem weak and powerless, but you don't look beneath the surface. Yet if anyone can claim the power and authority of Christ, I certainly can. ⁸I may seem to be boasting more than I should about my authority over you—authority to help you, not to hurt you—but I shall make good every claim. ⁹I say this so that you will not think I am just blustering when I scold you in my letters.

¹⁰"Don't bother about his letters," some say. "He sounds big, but it's all noise. When he gets here you will see that there is nothing great about him, and you have never heard a worse preacher!" ¹¹This time my personal presence is going to be just as rough on you as my letters are!

¹²Oh, don't worry, I wouldn't dare say that I am as wonderful as these other men who tell you how good they are! Their trouble is that they are only

comparing themselves with each other, and measuring themselves against their own little ideas. What stupidity!

Proverbs for Today
◦§ 14:32–33 §◦

The godly have a refuge when they die, but the wicked are crushed by their sins. □ Wisdom is enshrined in the hearts of men of common sense, but it must shout loudly before fools will hear it.

_____◦ **KEY VERSE** ◦_____

Mary said, "I am the Lord's servant, and I am willing to do whatever he wants. May everything you said come true."—*Luke 1:38*

_____◦ **REFLECTION** ◦_____

In ancient Palestine a young, unmarried woman who became pregnant could get in serious trouble. Unless the father of the child agreed to marry her, she could remain unmarried for life. If her own father rejected her, she could be forced to beg or, worse, to become a prostitute in order to earn a living. Mary, with her story about being made pregnant by the Holy Spirit, risked being considered crazy as well. Still she said, despite the possible costs, "I am willing." When Mary said that, she didn't know about the tremendous blessing she would receive. She only knew that God was asking her to serve him, and she willingly obeyed.

Don't wait to see the bottom line before responding to God. Offer your lives willingly, even when the results of doing so look distressing. God will honor your faithfulness just as he honored Mary.

_____◦ **MEDITATION** ◦_____

Heavenly Father, whatever your will may be for our lives, grant us peace and courage for the journey you have planned. Help us see beyond our immediate circumstances toward the future, with glad hearts and open minds. §◦

MAY 10

The Birth of John the Baptist
◦§ Luke 1:57–80 §◦

By now Elizabeth's waiting was over, for the time had come for the baby to be born—and it was a boy. [58]The word spread quickly to her neighbors and relatives of how kind the Lord had been to her, and everyone rejoiced.

[59]When the baby was eight days old, all the relatives and friends came for the circumcision ceremony. They all assumed the baby's name would be Zacharias, after his father.

[60]But Elizabeth said, "No! He must be named John!"

[61]"What?" they exclaimed. "There is no one in all your family by that name." [62]So they asked the baby's father, talking to him by gestures.

[63]He motioned for a piece of paper and to everyone's surprise wrote, "His name is *John!*" [64]Instantly Zacharias could speak again, and he began praising God.

[65]Wonder fell upon the whole neighborhood, and the news of what had happened spread through the Judean hills. [66]And everyone who heard about it thought long thoughts and asked, "I wonder what this child will turn out to be? For the hand of the Lord is surely upon him in some special way."

[67]Then his father Zacharias was filled with the Holy Spirit and gave this prophecy:

[68]"Praise the Lord, the God of Israel, for he has come to visit his people and has redeemed them. [69]He is sending us a Mighty Savior from the royal line of his servant David, [70]just as he promised through his holy prophets long ago— [71]someone to save us from our enemies, from all who hate us.

[72,73]"He has been merciful to our ancestors, yes, to Abraham himself, by remembering his sacred

promise to him, [74]and by granting us the privilege of serving God fearlessly, freed from our enemies, [75]and by making us holy and acceptable, ready to stand in his presence forever.

[76]"And you, my little son, shall be called the prophet of the glorious God, for you will prepare the way for the Messiah. [77]You will tell his people how to find salvation through forgiveness of their sins. [78]All this will be because the mercy of our God is very tender, and heaven's dawn is about to break upon us, [79]to give light to those who sit in darkness and death's shadow, and to guide us to the path of peace."

[80]The little boy greatly loved God and when he grew up he lived out in the lonely wilderness until he began his public ministry to Israel.

Boast in the Lord
⋅§ 2 Corinthians 10:13–18 §⋅

But we will not boast of authority we do not have. Our goal is to measure up to God's plan for us, and this plan includes our working there with you. [14]We are not going too far when we claim authority over you, for we were the first to come to you with the Good News concerning Christ. [15]It is not as though we were trying to claim credit for the work someone else has done among you. Instead, we hope that your faith will grow and that, still within the limits set for us, our work among you will be greatly enlarged.

[16]After that, we will be able to preach the Good News to other cities that are far beyond you, where no one else is working; then there will be no question about being in someone else's field. [17]As the Scriptures say, "If anyone is going to boast, let him boast about what the Lord has done and not about himself." [18]When someone boasts about himself and how well he has done, it doesn't count for

much. But when the Lord commends him, that's different!

Proverbs for Today
⋅§ 14:34–35 §⋅

Godliness exalts a nation, but sin is a reproach to any people. ☐ A king rejoices in servants who know what they are doing; he is angry with those who cause trouble.

⋅ KEY VERSE ⋅

We will not boast of authority we do not have. Our goal is to measure up to God's plan for us, and this plan includes our working there with you.—*2 Corinthians 10:13*

⋅ REFLECTION ⋅

Paul criticized the false teachers who tried to prove their goodness by comparing themselves with others rather than with God. When we compare ourselves with others, we may feel proud because we think we're better. But when we measure ourselves against God's standards, it becomes obvious that we're not nearly good enough.

As you look around at neighbors, family members, coworkers, or other couples, resist the temptation to compare yourselves to them. Don't worry about how they live. Instead, continually ask how *you* measure up to what God wants you to be, both as individuals and as a couple, and how *your* thoughts, words, and deeds compare to those of Jesus Christ.

⋅ MEDITATION ⋅

Heavenly Father, help us to live holy and blameless lives. Show us when we begin thinking and doing things that place our interests at the center of our marriage. Give us a Christian home where you and your will come first. §⋅

Jesus Is Born in Bethlehem
Luke 2:1–20

About this time Caesar Augustus, the Roman Emperor, decreed that a census should be taken throughout the nation. ²(This census was taken when Quirinius was governor of Syria.)

³Everyone was required to return to his ancestral home for this registration. ⁴And because Joseph was a member of the royal line, he had to go to Bethlehem in Judea, King David's ancient home—journeying there from the Galilean village of Nazareth. ⁵He took with him Mary, his fiancée, who was obviously pregnant by this time.

⁶And while they were there, the time came for her baby to be born; ⁷and she gave birth to her first child, a son. She wrapped him in a blanket and laid him in a manger, because there was no room for them in the village inn.

⁸That night some shepherds were in the fields outside the village, guarding their flocks of sheep. ⁹Suddenly an angel appeared among them, and the landscape shone bright with the glory of the Lord. They were badly frightened, ¹⁰but the angel reassured them.

"Don't be afraid!" he said. "I bring you the most joyful news ever announced, and it is for everyone! ¹¹The Savior—yes, the Messiah, the Lord—has been born tonight in Bethlehem! ¹²How will you recognize him? You will find a baby wrapped in a blanket, lying in a manger!"

¹³Suddenly, the angel was joined by a vast host of others—the armies of heaven—praising God:

¹⁴"Glory to God in the highest heaven," they sang, "and peace on earth for all those pleasing him."

¹⁵When this great army of angels had returned again to heaven, the shepherds said to each other, "Come on! Let's go to Bethlehem! Let's see this wonderful thing that has happened, which the Lord has told us about."

¹⁶They ran to the village and found their way to Mary and Joseph. And there was the baby, lying in the manger. ¹⁷The shepherds told everyone what had happened and what the angel had said to them about this child. ¹⁸All who heard the shepherds' story expressed astonishment, ¹⁹but Mary quietly treasured these things in her heart and often thought about them.

²⁰Then the shepherds went back again to their fields and flocks, praising God for the visit of the angels, and because they had seen the child, just as the angel had told them.

Paul's Concern for the Corinthians
2 Corinthians 11:1–6

I hope you will be patient with me as I keep on talking like a fool. Do bear with me and let me say what is on my heart. ²I am anxious for you with the deep concern of God himself—anxious that your love should be for Christ alone, just as a pure maiden saves her love for one man only, for the one who will be her husband. ³But I am frightened, fearing that in some way you will be led away from your pure and simple devotion to our Lord, just as Eve was deceived by Satan in the Garden of Eden. ⁴You seem so gullible: you believe whatever anyone tells you even if he is preaching about another Jesus than the one we preach, or a different spirit than the Holy Spirit you received, or shows you a different way to be saved. You swallow it all.

⁵Yet I don't feel that these marvelous "messengers from God," as they call themselves, are any better than I am. ⁶If I am a poor speaker, at least I know what I am talking about, as I think you realize by now, for we have proved it again and again.

Proverbs for Today
15:1–3

A gentle answer turns away wrath, but harsh words cause quarrels. □ A wise teacher makes learning a joy; a rebellious teacher spouts foolishness. □ The Lord is watching everywhere and keeps his eye on both the evil and the good.

I am anxious for you with the deep concern of God himself—anxious that your love should be for Christ alone, just as a pure maiden saves her love for one man only, for the one who will be her husband.—*2 Corinthians 11:2*

REFLECTION

The Corinthians' pure and simple devotion to Christ was being threatened by false teaching. Paul did not want the believers to lose their single-minded love for Christ. Keeping Christ first in our lives can be very difficult when we have so many distractions threatening to sidetrack our faith. Just as Eve lost her focus by listening to the serpent, we too can lose our direction by letting our lives become overcrowded and confused.

Is there anything that threatens your ability to keep Christ first in your lives? Ask yourselves, "How can we minimize the distractions that threaten our devotion to Christ?" Just as you made vows to love, honor, and cherish each other, remember that your commitment to Christ requires that you place him first in your hearts, minds, and home.

MEDITATION

Heavenly Father, we offer our love and devotion to you. Help us to seek your will in all things and not to get side-tracked by the concerns of this world.

MAY 12

Simeon and Anna Recognize Jesus as the Messiah
Luke 2:21–40

Eight days later, at the baby's circumcision ceremony, he was named Jesus, the name given him by the angel before he was even conceived.

[22] When the time came for Mary's purification offering at the Temple, as required by the laws of Moses after the birth of a child, his parents took him to Jerusalem to present him to the Lord; [23] for in these laws God had said, "If a woman's first child is a boy, he shall be dedicated to the Lord."

[24] At that time Jesus' parents also offered their sacrifice for purification—"either a pair of turtledoves or two young pigeons" was the legal requirement. [25] That day a man named Simeon, a Jerusalem resident, was in the Temple. He was a good man, very devout, filled with the Holy Spirit and constantly expecting the Messiah to come soon. [26] For the Holy Spirit had revealed to him that he would not die until he had seen him—God's anointed King. [27] The Holy Spirit had impelled him to go to the Temple that day; and so, when Mary and Joseph arrived to present the baby Jesus to the Lord in obedience to the law, [28] Simeon was there and took the child in his arms, praising God.

[29,30,31] "Lord," he said, "now I can die content! For I have seen him as you promised me I would. I have seen the Savior you have given to the world. [32] He is the Light that will shine upon the nations, and he will be the glory of your people Israel!"

[33] Joseph and Mary just stood there, marveling at what was being said about Jesus.

[34,35] Simeon blessed them but then said to Mary, "A sword shall pierce your soul, for this child shall be rejected by many in Israel, and this to their undoing. But he will be the greatest joy of many others. And the deepest thoughts of many hearts shall be revealed."

[36,37] Anna, a prophetess, was also there in the Temple that day. She was the daughter of Phanuel, of the Jewish tribe of Asher, and was very old, for she had been a widow for eighty-four years following seven years of marriage. She never left the Temple but stayed there night and day, worshiping God by praying and often fasting.

[38] She came along just as Simeon was talking with Mary and Joseph, and she also began thanking God and telling everyone in Jerusalem who had been

awaiting the coming of the Savior that the Messiah had finally arrived.

³⁹When Jesus' parents had fulfilled all the requirements of the Law of God they returned home to Nazareth in Galilee. ⁴⁰There the child became a strong, robust lad, and was known for wisdom beyond his years; and God poured out his blessings on him.

True and False Apostleship
◄§ 2 Corinthians 11:7–15 ß►

Did I do wrong and cheapen myself and make you look down on me because I preached God's Good News to you without charging you anything? ⁸,⁹Instead I "robbed" other churches by taking what they sent me, and using it up while I was with you, so that I could serve you without cost. And when that was gone and I was getting hungry I still didn't ask you for anything, for the Christians from Macedonia brought me another gift. I have never yet asked you for one cent, and I never will. ¹⁰I promise this with every ounce of truth I possess—that I will tell everyone in Greece about it! ¹¹Why? Because I don't love you? God knows I do. ¹²But I will do it to cut out the ground from under the feet of those who boast that they are doing God's work in just the same way we are.

¹³God never sent those men at all; they are "phonies" who have fooled you into thinking they are Christ's apostles. ¹⁴Yet I am not surprised! Satan can change himself into an angel of light, ¹⁵so it is no wonder his servants can do it too, and seem like godly ministers. In the end they will get every bit of punishment their wicked deeds deserve.

Proverbs for Today
◄§ 15:4 ß►

Gentle words cause life and health; griping brings discouragement.

◄ KEY VERSE ►

There the child became a strong, robust lad, and was known for wisdom beyond his years; and God poured out his blessings on him.—*Luke 2:40*

◄ REFLECTION ►

The fact that Jesus demonstrated wisdom beyond his years is not surprising since he stayed in close contact with his Heavenly Father. James 1:5 says that God "is always ready to give a bountiful supply of wisdom to all who ask him."

Regardless of the circumstances you are facing in your marriage, never hesitate to ask God to provide you with wisdom and insight into your particular situation. He is always happy and willing to give wisdom to those who believe. And, like Jesus, you will grow more and more in wisdom each day by walking with God.

◄ MEDITATION ►

Heavenly Father, we pray for wisdom in our marriage and ask that you will give us the insight we need each time we must make a decision together. ß►

MAY 13

Jesus with the Teachers of the Law
◄§ Luke 2:41–52 ß►

When Jesus was twelve years old he accompanied his parents to Jerusalem for the annual Passover Festival, which they attended each year. ⁴³After the celebration was over they started home to Nazareth, but Jesus stayed behind in Jerusalem. His parents didn't miss him the first day, ⁴⁴for they assumed he was with friends among the other travelers. But when he didn't show up that evening, they started to look for him among their relatives and friends; ⁴⁵and when they couldn't find him, they went back to Jerusalem to search for him there.

⁴⁶,⁴⁷Three days later they finally discovered him. He was in the Temple, sitting among the teachers of Law, discussing deep questions with them and

amazing everyone with his understanding and answers.

⁴⁸His parents didn't know what to think. "Son!" his mother said to him. "Why have you done this to us? Your father and I have been frantic, searching for you everywhere."

⁴⁹"But why did you need to search?" he asked. "Didn't you realize that I would be here at the Temple, in my Father's House?" ⁵⁰But they didn't understand what he meant.

⁵¹Then he returned to Nazareth with them and was obedient to them; and his mother stored away all these things in her heart. ⁵²So Jesus grew both tall and wise, and was loved by God and man.

Suffering for Christ—Paul's Validation of Apostleship
❧ 2 Corinthians 11:16–33 ❧

Again I plead, don't think that I have lost my wits to talk like this; but even if you do, listen to me anyway—a witless man, a fool—while I also boast a little as they do. ¹⁷Such bragging isn't something the Lord commanded me to do, for I am acting like a brainless fool. ¹⁸Yet those other men keep telling you how wonderful they are, so here I go: ¹⁹,²⁰(You think you are so wise—yet you listen gladly to those fools; you don't mind at all when they make you their slaves and take everything you have, and take advantage of you, and put on airs, and slap you in the face. ²¹I'm ashamed to say that I'm not strong and daring like that!

But whatever they can boast about—I'm talking like a fool again—I can boast about it, too.)

²²They brag that they are Hebrews, do they? Well, so am I. And they say that they are Israelites, God's chosen people? So am I. And they are descendants of Abraham? Well, I am too.

²³They say they serve Christ? But I have served him far more! (Have I gone mad to boast like this?) I have worked harder, been put in jail oftener, been whipped times without number, and faced death again and again and again. ²⁴Five different times the Jews gave me their terrible thirty-nine lashes. ²⁵Three times I was beaten with rods. Once I was stoned. Three times I was shipwrecked. Once I was in the open sea all night and the whole next day. ²⁶I have traveled many weary miles and have been often in great danger from flooded rivers, and from robbers, and from my own people, the Jews, as well as from the hands of the Gentiles. I have faced grave dangers from mobs in the cities and from death in the deserts and in the stormy seas and from men who claim to be brothers in Christ but are not. ²⁷I have lived with weariness and pain and sleepless nights. Often I have been hungry and thirsty and have gone without food; often I have shivered with cold, without enough clothing to keep me warm.

²⁸Then, besides all this, I have the constant worry of how the churches are getting along: ²⁹Who makes a mistake and I do not feel his sadness? Who falls without my longing to help him? Who is spiritually hurt without my fury rising against the one who hurt him?

³⁰But if I must brag, I would rather brag about the things that show how weak I am. ³¹God, the Father of our Lord Jesus Christ, who is to be praised forever and ever, knows I tell the truth. ³²For instance, in Damascus the governor under King Aretas kept guards at the city gates to catch me; ³³but I was let down by rope and basket from a hole in the city wall, and so I got away! [What popularity!]

Proverbs for Today
❧ 15:5–7 ❧

Only a fool despises his father's advice; a wise son considers each suggestion. ☐ There is treasure in being good, but trouble dogs the wicked. ☐ Only the good can give good advice. Rebels can't.

❧ KEY VERSE ❧

"But why did you need to search?" he asked. "Didn't you realize that I would be here at the Temple, in my Father's House?"—*Luke 2:49*

❧ REFLECTION ❧

Jesus knew he was God's Son, but he did not reject his earthly parents. He went back to Nazareth with them and lived under their authority for another 18 years. God's people do not despise human relationships or family responsibilities. If the Son of God obeyed his human parents, how much more should we honor our family members! Take time each day to pray for your families and show them the respect and love they deserve.

---------- ◈ MEDITATION ◈ ----------

Heavenly Father, we ask that you will bless our families and meet their spiritual and physical needs. ฿

MAY 14

John the Baptist Warns of Coming Judgment
◈ Luke 3:1–18 ฿

In the fifteenth year of the reign of Emperor Tiberius Caesar, a message came from God to John (the son of Zacharias), as he was living out in the deserts. (Pilate was governor over Judea at that time; Herod, over Galilee; his brother Philip, over Iturea and Trachonitis; Lysanias, over Abilene; and Annas and Caiaphas were High Priests.) [3]Then John went from place to place on both sides of the Jordan River, preaching that people should be baptized to show that they had turned to God and away from their sins, in order to be forgiven.

[4]In the words of Isaiah the prophet, John was "a voice shouting from the barren wilderness, 'Prepare a road for the Lord to travel on! Widen the pathway before him! [5]Level the mountains! Fill up the valleys! Straighten the curves! Smooth out the ruts! [6]And then all mankind shall see the Savior sent from God.'"

[7]Here is a sample of John's preaching to the crowds that came for baptism: "You brood of snakes! You are trying to escape hell without truly turning to God! That is why you want to be baptized! [8]First go and prove by the way you live that you really have repented. And don't think you are safe because you are descendants of Abraham. That isn't enough. God can produce children of Abraham from these desert stones! [9]The axe of his judgment is poised over you, ready to sever your roots and cut you down. Yes, every tree that does not produce good fruit will be chopped down and thrown into the fire."

[10]The crowd replied, "What do you want us to do?"

[11]"If you have two coats," he replied, "give one to the poor. If you have extra food, give it away to those who are hungry."

[12]Even tax collectors—notorious for their corruption—came to be baptized and asked, "How shall we prove to you that we have abandoned our sins?"

[13]"By your honesty," he replied. "Make sure you collect no more taxes than the Roman government requires you to."

[14]"And us," asked some soldiers, "what about us?"

John replied, "Don't extort money by threats and violence; don't accuse anyone of what you know he didn't do; and be content with your pay!"

[15]Everyone was expecting the Messiah to come soon, and eager to know whether or not John was he. This was the question of the hour, and was being discussed everywhere.

[16]John answered the question by saying, "I baptize only with water; but someone is coming soon who has far higher authority than mine; in fact, I am not even worthy of being his slave. He will baptize you with fire—with the Holy Spirit. [17]He will separate chaff from grain, and burn up the chaff with eternal fire and store away the grain." [18]He used many such warnings as he announced the Good News to the people.

God's Grace Is Sufficient
◈ 2 Corinthians 12:1–10 ฿

This boasting is all so foolish, but let me go on. Let me tell about the visions I've had, and revelations from the Lord.

[2,3]Fourteen years ago I was taken up to heaven for

a visit. Don't ask me whether my body was there or just my spirit, for I don't know; only God can answer that. But anyway, there I was in paradise, [4]and heard things so astounding that they are beyond a man's power to describe or put in words (and anyway I am not allowed to tell them to others). [5]That experience is something worth bragging about, but I am not going to do it. I am going to boast only about how weak I am and how great God is to use such weakness for his glory. [6]I have plenty to boast about and would be no fool in doing it, but I don't want anyone to think more highly of me than he should from what he can actually see in my life and my message.

[7]I will say this: because these experiences I had were so tremendous, God was afraid I might be puffed up by them; so I was given a physical condition which has been a thorn in my flesh, a messenger from Satan to hurt and bother me, and prick my pride. [8]Three different times I begged God to make me well again.

[9]Each time he said, "No. But I am with you; that is all you need. My power shows up best in weak people." Now I am glad to boast about how weak I am; I am glad to be a living demonstration of Christ's power, instead of showing off my own power and abilities. [10]Since I know it is all for Christ's good, I am quite happy about "the thorn," and about insults and hardships, persecutions and difficulties; for when I am weak, then I am strong—the less I have, the more I depend on him.

Proverbs for Today
~§ 15:8–10 §~

The Lord hates the gifts of the wicked, but delights in the prayers of his people. The Lord despises the deeds of the wicked, but loves those who try to be good. If they stop trying, the Lord will punish them; if they rebel against that punishment, they will die.

KEY VERSE

Each time he said, "No. But I am with you; that is all you need. My power shows up best in weak people." Now I am glad to boast about how weak I am; I am glad to be a living demonstration of Christ's power, instead of showing off my own power and abilities.—*2 Corinthians 12:9*

REFLECTION

Although God did not remove Paul's physical affliction, he promised to demonstrate his power in this faithful apostle. The fact that God's power shows up in weak people should give us courage. When we are blessed with tremendous talents or resources, we are tempted to do God's work on our own, and that leads to pride. We must rely on God for our effectiveness rather than on our own energy, effort, or talent. Our weaknesses not only help develop Christian character, but they also deepen our worship experience. When we admit our weaknesses, we affirm God's strength. When we are weak, when we allow God to fill us with his power, then we are stronger than we could ever be on our own. Depend on God—only his power will make you and your marriage effective for him and allow you both to do work that has lasting value.

MEDITATION

Heavenly Father, we pray that you will show your power in our weaknesses. Help us to be humble about our talents and gifts, acknowledging that they come from you, in order that you may always get the credit for the blessings you so generously give us. §~

The Baptism of Jesus
§ Luke 3:19–23a ঙ

(But after John had publicly criticized Herod, governor of Galilee, for marrying Herodias, his brother's wife, and for many other wrongs he had done, Herod put John in prison, thus adding this sin to all his many others.) [21]Then one day, after the crowds had been baptized, Jesus himself was baptized; and as he was praying, the heavens opened, [22]and the Holy Spirit in the form of a dove settled upon him, and a voice from heaven said, "You are my much loved Son, yes, my delight." [23]Jesus was about thirty years old when he began his public ministry.

Paul's Sacrifice for His Children
§ 2 Corinthians 12:11–15 ঙ

You have made me act like a fool—boasting like this—for you people ought to be writing about me and not making me write about myself. There isn't a single thing these other marvelous fellows have that I don't have too, even though I am really worth nothing at all. [12]When I was there I certainly gave you every proof that I was truly an apostle, sent to you by God himself: for I patiently did many wonders and signs and mighty works among you. [13]The only thing I didn't do for you, that I do everywhere else in all other churches, was to become a burden to you—I didn't ask you to give me food to eat and a place to stay. Please forgive me for this wrong! [14]Now I am coming to you again, the third time; and it is still not going to cost you anything, for I don't want your money. I want *you!* And anyway, you are my children, and little children don't pay for their father's and mother's food—it's the other way around; parents supply food for their children. [15]I am glad to give you myself and all I have for your spiritual good, even though it seems that the more I love you, the less you love me.

Proverbs for Today
§ 15:11 ঙ

The depths of hell are open to God's knowledge. How much more the hearts of all mankind!

KEY VERSE

The depths of hell are open to God's knowledge. How much more the hearts of all mankind!—*Proverbs 15:11*

REFLECTION

Because God is good, many Old Testament people thought hell was hidden from God's sight. In reality, however, nothing is hidden from God. If he can see beyond death, how much more can he know our present wrong motivations and thoughts? How foolish we are when we try to hide our motives and intentions from God!

Don't try to conceal your sins and weaknesses from the Lord. Make a commitment to have a marriage that is open before God, where both of you confess your transgressions, allowing him to place his healing touch on your lives.

MEDITATION

Heavenly Father, forgive us of our sins. We pray that your Holy Spirit will guide us in our confessions and show us when we displease you. ঙ

MAY 16

The Genealogy of Jesus
Luke 3:23b–38

Jesus was known as the son of Joseph.
Joseph's father was Heli;
Heli's father was Matthat;
Matthat's father was Levi;
Levi's father was Melchi;
Melchi's father was Jannai;
Jannai's father was Joseph;
Joseph's father was Mattathias;
Mattathias' father was Amos;
Amos' father was Nahum;
Nahum's father was Esli;
Esli's father was Naggai;
Naggai's father was Maath;
Maath's father was Mattathias;
Mattathias' father was Semein;
Semein's father was Josech;
Josech's father was Joda;
Joda's father was Joanan;
Joanan's father was Rhesa;
Rhesa's father was Zerubbabel;
Zerubbabel's father was Shealtiel;
Shealtiel's father was Neri;
Neri's father was Melchi;
Melchi's father was Addi;
Addi's father was Cosam;
Cosam's father was Elmadam;
Elmadam's father was Er;
Er's father was Joshua;
Joshua's father was Eliezer;
Eliezer's father was Jorim;
Jorim's father was Matthat;
Matthat's father was Levi;
Levi's father was Simeon;
Simeon's father was Judah;
Judah's father was Joseph;
Joseph's father was Jonam;
Jonam's father was Eliakim;
Eliakim's father was Melea;
Melea's father was Menna;
Menna's father was Mattatha;
Mattatha's father was Nathan;
Nathan's father was David;
David's father was Jesse;
Jesse's father was Obed;
Obed's father was Boaz;
Boaz' father was Salmon;
Salmon's father was Nahshon;
Nahshon's father was Amminadab;
Amminadab's father was Admin;
Admin's father was Arni;
Arni's father was Hezron;
Hezron's father was Perez;
Perez' father was Judah;
Judah's father was Jacob;
Jacob's father was Isaac;
Isaac's father was Abraham;
Abraham's father was Terah;
Terah's father was Nahor;
Nahor's father was Serug;
Serug's father was Reu;
Reu's father was Peleg;
Peleg's father was Eber;
Eber's father was Shelah;
Shelah's father was Cainan;
Cainan's father was Arphaxad;
Arphaxad's father was Shem;
Shem's father was Noah;
Noah's father was Lamech;
Lamech's father was Methuselah;
Methuselah's father was Enoch;
Enoch's father was Jared;
Jared's father was Mahalaleel;
Mahalaleel's father was Cainan;
Cainan's father was Enos;
Enos's father was Seth;
Seth's father was Adam;
Adam's father was God.

Paul Fears Another Sorrowful Visit
2 Corinthians 12:16–21

Some of you are saying, "It's true that his visits didn't seem to cost us anything, but he is a sneaky fellow, that Paul, and he fooled us. As sure as anything he must have made money from us some way."

¹⁷But how? Did any of the men I sent to you take advantage of you? ¹⁸When I urged Titus to visit you, and sent our other brother with him, did they make any profit? No, of course not. For we have the same Holy Spirit, and walk in each other's steps, doing things the same way.

¹⁹I suppose you think I am saying all this to get back into your good graces. That isn't it at all. I tell you, with God listening as I say it, that I have said this to help *you,* dear friends—to build you up spiritually and not to help myself. ²⁰For I am afraid that when I come to visit you I won't like what I find, and then you won't like the way I will have to act. I am afraid that I will find you quarreling, and envying each other, and being angry with each other, and acting big, and saying wicked things about each other and whispering behind each other's backs, filled with conceit and disunity. ²¹Yes, I am afraid that when I come God will humble me before you and I will be sad and mourn because many of you who have sinned became sinners and don't even care about the wicked, impure things you have done: your lust and immorality, and the taking of other men's wives.

Proverbs for Today
◄§ 15:12–14 §►

A mocker stays away from wise men because he hates to be scolded. ☐ A happy face means a glad heart; a sad face means a breaking heart. ☐ A wise man is hungry for truth, while the mocker feeds on trash.

---◄ **KEY VERSE** �&.---

Jesus was about thirty years old when he began his public ministry.—*Luke 3:23*

---◄ **REFLECTION** �&.---

Imagine the Savior of the world driving nails in a small-town carpenter's shop until he was 30 years old! It seems incredible that Jesus would have been content to remain in Nazareth all that time, but he patiently trusted the Father's timing for his life and ministry. Thirty was the prescribed age for priests to begin their ministry (Numbers 4:3). Joseph was 30 years old when he began serving the king of Egypt (Genesis 41:46), and David was 30 years old when he began to reign over Judah (2 Samuel 5:4). Age 30, then, was a good time to begin an important task in the Jewish culture.

Like Jesus, make a mutual vow to work within God's timing, resisting the temptation to jump ahead before receiving the Spirit's direction. Are either of you waiting and wondering what your next step should be in life? Don't jump ahead of God, but rather trust him in his perfect timing.

---◄ **MEDITATION** �&.---

Heavenly Father, we submit our lives to you and ask that you will reveal your will to us. Help us not to place our personal agendas ahead of your timing and forgive us when we become fretful and impatient because others seem to be passing us by or appear more successful. §►

MAY 17

Jesus Is Tempted by Satan
◄§ Luke 4:1–13 §►

Then Jesus, full of the Holy Spirit, left the Jordan River, being urged by the Spirit out into the barren wastelands of Judea, where Satan tempted him for forty days. He ate nothing all that time, and was very hungry.

³Satan said, "If you are God's Son, tell this stone to become a loaf of bread."

⁴But Jesus replied, "It is written in the Scriptures, 'Other things in life are much more important than bread!'"

⁵Then Satan took him up and revealed to him all the kingdoms of the world in a moment of time; ^{6,7}and the devil told him, "I will give you all these

splendid kingdoms and their glory—for they are mine to give to anyone I wish—if you will only get down on your knees and worship me."

[8]Jesus replied, "We must worship God, and him alone. So it is written in the Scriptures."

[9,10,11]Then Satan took him to Jerusalem to a high roof of the Temple and said, "If you are the Son of God, jump off! For the Scriptures say that God will send his angels to guard you and to keep you from crashing to the pavement below!"

[12]Jesus replied, "The Scriptures also say, 'Do not put the Lord your God to a foolish test.'"

[13]When the devil had ended all the temptations, he left Jesus for a while and went away.

Paul's Warnings
⋅§ 2 Corinthians 13:1-6 ቈ

This is the third time I am coming to visit you. The Scriptures tell us that if two or three have seen a wrong, it must be punished. [Well, this is my third warning, as I come now for this visit.] [2]I have already warned those who had been sinning when I was there last; now I warn them again, and all others, just as I did then, that this time I come ready to punish severely and I will not spare them.

[3]I will give you all the proof you want that Christ speaks through me. Christ is not weak in his dealings with you, but is a mighty power within you. [4]His weak, human body died on the cross, but now he lives by the mighty power of God. We, too, are weak in our bodies, as he was, but now we live and are strong, as he is, and have all of God's power to use in dealing with you.

[5]Check up on yourselves. Are you really Christians? Do you pass the test? Do you feel Christ's presence and power more and more within you? Or are you just pretending to be Christians when actually you aren't at all? [6]I hope you can agree that I have stood that test and truly belong to the Lord.

Proverbs for Today
⋅§ 15:15-17 ቈ

When a man is gloomy, everything seems to go wrong; when he is cheerful, everything seems right ☐ Better a little with reverence for God, than great treasure and trouble with it. It is better to eat soup with someone you love than steak with someone you hate.

——————⋅§ **KEY VERSE** ቈ——————

When a man is gloomy, everything seems to go wrong; when he is cheerful, everything seems right! —*Proverbs 15:15*

——————⋅§ **REFLECTION** ቈ——————

Our attitudes color our whole personality. We cannot always choose what happens to us, but we can choose our outlook toward each situation. The secret to a Christlike attitude is to fill our minds with good thoughts—thoughts that are true, pure, and lovely; thoughts that dwell on the good things in life (Philippians 4:8). That was Paul's source of joy as he faced imprisonment, and it can be ours as we face the struggles of daily living.

Take a moment each day to reflect on your attitudes, both individually and as a couple. Examine what you allow to enter your minds and what you choose to dwell on. Then consciously choose thoughts and attitudes rooted in the Holy Spirit and in his good gifts. That will give your marriage an infusion of irrepressible joy!

——————⋅§ **MEDITATION** ቈ——————

Heavenly Father, show us when we allow bad attitudes to come between each other, between us and those around us, and between us and you. We offer our thoughts to you and ask that you will shape us according to your will. ቈ

Jesus Teaches in the Synagogues
⊷§ Luke 4:14–30 §⊶

Then Jesus returned to Galilee, full of the Holy Spirit's power. Soon he became well known throughout all that region [15]for his sermons in the synagogues; everyone praised him.

[16]When he came to the village of Nazareth, his boyhood home, he went as usual to the synagogue on Saturday, and stood up to read the Scriptures. [17]The book of Isaiah the prophet was handed to him, and he opened it to the place where it says:

[18,19]"The Spirit of the Lord is upon me; he has appointed me to preach Good News to the poor; he has sent me to heal the brokenhearted and to announce that captives shall be released and the blind shall see, that the downtrodden shall be freed from their oppressors, and that God is ready to give blessings to all who come to him."

[20]He closed the book and handed it back to the attendant and sat down, while everyone in the synagogue gazed at him intently. [21]Then he added, "These Scriptures came true today!"

[22]All who were there spoke well of him and were amazed by the beautiful words that fell from his lips. "How can this be?" they asked. "Isn't this Joseph's son?"

[23]Then he said, "Probably you will quote me that proverb, 'Physician, heal yourself'—meaning, 'Why don't you do miracles here in your home town like those you did in Capernaum?' [24]But I solemnly declare to you that no prophet is accepted in his own home town! [25,26]For example, remember how Elijah the prophet used a miracle to help the widow of Zarephath—a foreigner from the land of Sidon. There were many Jewish widows needing help in those days of famine, for there had been no rain for three and one-half years, and hunger stalked the land; yet Elijah was not sent to them. [27]Or think of the prophet Elisha, who healed Naaman, a Syrian, rather than the many Jewish lepers needing help."

[28]These remarks stung them to fury; [29]and jumping up, they mobbed him and took him to the edge of the hill on which the city was built, to push him over the cliff. [30]But he walked away through the crowd and left them.

Paul's Final Advice and Greetings
⊷§ 2 Corinthians 13:7–14 §⊶

I pray that you will live good lives, not because that will be a feather in our caps, proving that what we teach is right; no, for we want you to do right even if we ourselves are despised. [8]Our responsibility is to encourage the right at all times, not to hope for evil. [9]We are glad to be weak and despised if you are really strong. Our greatest wish and prayer is that you will become mature Christians.

[10]I am writing this to you now in the hope that I won't need to scold and punish when I come; for I want to use the Lord's authority which he has given me, not to punish you but to make you strong.

[11]I close my letter with these last words:

Be happy.

Grow in Christ.

Pay attention to what I have said.

Live in harmony and peace. And may the God of love and peace be with you.

[12]Greet each other warmly in the Lord. [13]All the Christians here send you their best regards. [14]May the grace of our Lord Jesus Christ be with you all. May God's love and the Holy Spirit's friendship be yours.

Paul

Proverbs for Today
⊷§ 15:18–19 §⊶

A quick-tempered man starts fights; a cool-tempered man tries to stop them. □ A lazy fellow has trouble all through life; the good man's path is easy!

_____ ⊷ KEY VERSE ⊶ _____

A lazy fellow has trouble all through life; the good man's path is easy!—*Proverbs 15:19*

The "good man's" life doesn't always seem easy (15:19), but look at the alternatives. Hatred (15:17), bad temper (15:18), and laziness (15:19) cause problems that a godly person does not have to face. By comparison, the Christian life is a smooth, level road because it is built on a solid foundation.

Turn your marriage over to the Lord. If either of you become lazy in your attitude toward each other, your careers, your family, or your commitment to Christ, soon you will experience difficulties in life that may take years to resolve. Live each day with an eye on eternity and seek the guidance of the Holy Spirit in all that you do and say.

─────── ❧ MEDITATION ❧ ───────

Heavenly Father, help us to be obedient to your guidance and direction for our lives. Forgive us when we allow laziness and bad attitudes to steer us away from the path of righteousness. ❧

MAY 19

Jesus Casts Out Demons and Heals Many
❧ Luke 4:31–44 ❧

Then Jesus returned to Capernaum, a city in Galilee, and preached there in the synagogue every Saturday. [32]Here, too, the people were amazed at the things he said. For he spoke as one who knew the truth, instead of merely quoting the opinions of others as his authority.

[33]Once as he was teaching in the synagogue, a man possessed by a demon began shouting at Jesus, [34]"Go away! We want nothing to do with you, Jesus from Nazareth. You have come to destroy us. I know who you are—the Holy Son of God."

[35]Jesus cut him short. "Be silent!" he told the demon. "Come out!" The demon threw the man to the floor as the crowd watched, and then left him without hurting him further.

[36]Amazed, the people asked, "What is in this man's words that even demons obey him?" [37]The story of what he had done spread like wildfire throughout the whole region.

[38]After leaving the synagogue that day, he went to Simon's home where he found Simon's mother-in-law very sick with a high fever. "Please heal her," everyone begged.

[39]Standing at her bedside he spoke to the fever, rebuking it, and immediately her temperature returned to normal and she got up and prepared a meal for them!

[40]As the sun went down that evening, all the villagers who had any sick people in their homes, no matter what their diseases were, brought them to Jesus; and the touch of his hands healed every one! [41]Some were possessed by demons; and the demons came out at his command, shouting, "You are the Son of God." But because they knew he was the Christ, he stopped them and told them to be silent.

[42]Early the next morning he went out into the desert. The crowds searched everywhere for him and when they finally found him they begged him not to leave them, but to stay at Capernaum. [43]But he replied, "I must preach the Good News of the Kingdom of God in other places too, for that is why I was sent." [44]So he continued to travel around preaching in synagogues throughout Judea.

Paul's Greeting and Prayer
❧ Galatians 1:1–5 ❧

From: Paul the missionary and all the other Christians here.

To: The churches of Galatia.

I was not called to be a missionary by any group or agency. My call is from Jesus Christ himself, and from God the Father who raised him from the dead. ³May peace and blessing be yours from God the Father and from the Lord Jesus Christ. ⁴He died for our sins just as God our Father planned, and rescued us from this evil world in which we live. ⁵All glory to God through all the ages of eternity. Amen.

Proverbs for Today
◄§ 15:20–21 §►

A sensible son gladdens his father. A rebellious son saddens his mother. □ If a man enjoys folly, something is wrong! The sensible stay on the pathways of right.

_____ ◢ KEY VERSE ◣ _____

He died for our sins just as God our Father planned, and rescued us from this evil world in which we live.—*Galatians 1:4*

_____ ◢ REFLECTION ◣ _____

God's plan was always to offer humanity a perfect source of salvation through the death and resurrection of his Son, Jesus Christ. As a result, we have been rescued from the power of this evil world—a world ruled by Satan and full of cruelty, tragedy, temptation, and deception. Being saved from the powers of darkness doesn't mean that we are taken out of it, however, but that we are no longer enslaved by it. We have been saved to live holy lives for God, and we have been promised eternity with him. Dedicate your marriage to the Lord and seek his wisdom each day so that your steps will be guided toward righteousness, and so that you won't become ensnared by the lies of this world.

_____ ◢ MEDITATION ◣ _____

Heavenly Father, we thank you for sending your Son, Jesus Christ, to die for our sins and the sins of the world. We pray that you will guide us in all that we do and say, and that our lives will be holy and blameless. §►

MAY 20

The Miracle of a Great Catch
◄§ Luke 5:1–11 §►

One day as Jesus was preaching on the shore of Lake Gennesaret, great crowds pressed in on him to listen to the Word of God. ²He noticed two empty boats standing at the water's edge while the fishermen washed their nets. ³Stepping into one of the boats, Jesus asked Simon, its owner, to push out a little into the water, so that he could sit in the boat and speak to the crowds from there.

⁴When he had finished speaking, he said to Simon, "Now go out where it is deeper and let down your nets and you will catch a lot of fish!"

⁵"Sir," Simon replied, "we worked hard all last night and didn't catch a thing. But if you say so, we'll try again."

⁶And this time their nets were so full that they began to tear! ⁷A shout for help brought their partners in the other boat and soon both boats were filled with fish and on the verge of sinking.

⁸When Simon Peter realized what had happened, he fell to his knees before Jesus and said, "Oh, sir, please leave us—I'm too much of a sinner for you to have around." ⁹For he was awestruck by the size of their catch, as were the others with him, ¹⁰and his partners too—James and John, the sons of Zebedee. Jesus replied, "Don't be afraid! From now on you'll be fishing for the souls of men!"

¹¹And as soon as they landed, they left everything and went with him.

There Is No Other Gospel
◄§ Galatians 1:6–12 §►

I am amazed that you are turning away so soon from God who, in his love and mercy, invited you to share the eternal life he gives through Christ; you are already following a different "way to heaven," which really doesn't go to heaven at all. [7]For there is no other way than the one we showed you; you are being fooled by those who twist and change the truth concerning Christ.

[8]Let God's curses fall on anyone, including myself, who preaches any other way to be saved than the one we told you about; yes, if an angel comes from heaven and preaches any other message, let him be forever cursed. [9]I will say it again: if anyone preaches any other Gospel than the one you welcomed, let God's curse fall upon him.

[10]You can see that I am not trying to please you by sweet talk and flattery; no, I am trying to please God. If I were still trying to please men I could not be Christ's servant.

[11]Dear friends, I solemnly swear that the way to heaven which I preach is not based on some mere human whim or dream. [12]For my message comes from no less a person than Jesus Christ himself, who told me what to say. No one else has taught me.

Proverbs for Today
§ 15:22–23 ᨶ

Plans go wrong with too few counselors; many counselors bring success. □ Everyone enjoys giving good advice, and how wonderful it is to be able to say the right thing at the right time!

KEY VERSE

When Simon Peter realized what had happened, he fell to his knees before Jesus and said, "Oh, sir, please leave us—I'm too much of a sinner for you to have around."—*Luke 5:8*

REFLECTION

Peter was awestruck at this miracle, and his first response was to feel insignificant in comparison to Jesus' greatness. Peter knew Jesus had healed the sick and cast out demons, but he was amazed that Jesus cared about Peter's day-to-day routine and understood his needs.

God's power reaches into every dimension of our lives. As you come to recognize the greatness of God's power expressed in the life of the church, you will find yourselves humbled at the reality of who God is and at the magnitude of his grace toward each of us. If you have not done so already, find a church family that will provide you with the spiritual nourishment you need in your marriage as well as your individual lives.

MEDITATION

Heavenly Father, thank you for being concerned about the small problems and concerns we have. We submit everything to you and ask that you guide us in all our decisions and relationships. ᨶ

MAY 21

Jesus Heals a Leper
§ Luke 5:12–16 ᨶ

One day in a certain village Jesus was visiting, there was a man with an advanced case of leprosy. When he saw Jesus he fell to the ground before him, face downward in the dust, begging to be healed.

"Sir," he said, "if you only will, you can clear me of every trace of my disease."

[13]Jesus reached out and touched the man and said, "Of course I will. Be healed." And the leprosy left him instantly! [14]Then Jesus instructed him to go at once without telling anyone what had happened and be examined by the Jewish priest. "Offer the sacrifice Moses' law requires for lepers who are healed," he said. "This will prove to everyone that you are well." [15]Now the report of his power spread even faster and vast crowds came to hear him preach and to be healed of their diseases.

[16]But he often withdrew to the wilderness for prayer.

Paul Reviews His Conversion
§ Galatians 1:13–24 ই

You know what I was like when I followed the Jewish religion—how I went after the Christians mercilessly, hunting them down and doing my best to get rid of them all. [14]I was one of the most religious Jews of my own age in the whole country, and tried as hard as I possibly could to follow all the old, traditional rules of my religion.

[15]But then something happened! For even before I was born God had chosen me to be his, and called me—what kindness and grace— [16]to reveal his Son within me so that I could go to the Gentiles and show them the Good News about Jesus.

When all this happened to me I didn't go at once and talk it over with anyone else; [17]I didn't go up to Jerusalem to consult with those who were apostles before I was. No, I went away into the deserts of Arabia, and then came back to the city of Damascus. [18]It was not until three years later that I finally went to Jerusalem for a visit with Peter, and stayed there with him for fifteen days. [19]And the only other apostle I met at that time was James, our Lord's brother. [20](Listen to what I am saying, for I am telling you this in the very presence of God. This is exactly what happened—I am not lying to you.) [21]Then after this visit I went to Syria and Cilicia. [22]And still the Christians in Judea didn't even know what I looked like. [23]All they knew was what people were saying, that "our former enemy is now preaching the very faith he tried to wreck." [24]And they gave glory to God because of me.

Proverbs for Today
§ 15:24–26 ই

The road of the godly leads upward, leaving hell behind. □ The Lord destroys the possessions of the proud but cares for widows. □ The Lord hates the thoughts of the wicked but delights in kind words.

⚬ KEY VERSE ⚬

He often withdrew to the wilderness for prayer. —*Luke 5:16*

⚬ REFLECTION ⚬

People were clamoring to hear Jesus preach and have their diseases healed, but Jesus made sure he often withdrew to quiet, solitary places to pray. Many priorities clamor for our attention, and we often run ourselves ragged attending to them. Like Jesus, however, we should take time regularly to withdraw to a quiet place to pray. Strength comes from God, and we can get it only by spending time with him.

While it is important to spend as much quality time as possible with your spouse, be sure you devote a portion of each day alone with God in quiet, contemplative prayer and Bible study. The Lord will refresh both of you in a way that will feed and strengthen your marriage and prepare you for the work to which you each have been called.

⚬ MEDITATION ⚬

Heavenly Father, thank you for the time we can spend with each other. Help us also to give you a regular portion of our day for prayerful devotion alone with you so that we can grow in our knowledge and faith. ই

Jesus Heals a Paralytic
⮜§ Luke 5:17–26 §⮞

One day while Jesus was teaching, some Jewish religious leaders and teachers of the Law were sitting nearby. (It seemed that these men showed up from every village in all Galilee and Judea, as well as from Jerusalem.) And the Lord's healing power was upon him.

[18,19]Then—look! Some men came carrying a paralyzed man on a sleeping mat. They tried to push through the crowd to Jesus but couldn't reach him. So they went up on the roof above him, took off some tiles and lowered the sick man down into the crowd, still on his sleeping mat, right in front of Jesus.

[20]Seeing their faith, Jesus said to the man, "My friend, your sins are forgiven!"

[21]"Who does this fellow think he is?" the Pharisees and teachers of the Law exclaimed among themselves. "This is blasphemy! Who but God can forgive sins?"

[22]Jesus knew what they were thinking, and he replied, "Why is it blasphemy? [23,24]I, the Messiah, have the authority on earth to forgive sins. But talk is cheap—anybody could say that. So I'll prove it to you by healing this man." Then, turning to the paralyzed man, he commanded, "Pick up your stretcher and go on home, for you are healed!"

[25]And immediately, as everyone watched, the man jumped to his feet, picked up his mat and went home praising God! [26]Everyone present was gripped with awe and fear. And they praised God, remarking over and over again, "We have seen strange things today."

Paul Stood Firm for the Gospel
⮜§ Galatians 2:1–5 §⮞

Then fourteen years later I went back to Jerusalem again, this time with Barnabas; and Titus came along too. [2]I went there with definite orders from God to confer with the brothers there about the message I was preaching to the Gentiles. I talked privately to the leaders of the church so that they would all understand just what I had been teaching and, I hoped, agree that it was right. [3]And they did agree; they did not even demand that Titus, my companion, should be circumcised, though he was a Gentile.

[4]Even that question wouldn't have come up except for some so-called "Christians" there—false ones, really—who came to spy on us and see what freedom we enjoyed in Christ Jesus, as to whether we obeyed the Jewish laws or not. They tried to get us all tied up in their rules, like slaves in chains. [5]But we did not listen to them for a single moment, for we did not want to confuse you into thinking that salvation can be earned by being circumcised and by obeying Jewish laws.

Proverbs for Today
⮜§ 15:27–28 §⮞

Dishonest money brings grief to all the family, but hating bribes brings happiness. □ A good man thinks before he speaks; the evil man pours out his evil words without a thought.

⮜ KEY VERSE ⮞

I went there with definite orders from God to confer with the brothers there about the message I was preaching to the Gentiles. I talked privately to the leaders of the church so that they would all understand just what I had been teaching and, I hoped, agree that it was right.—*Galatians 2:2*

⮜ REFLECTION ⮞

Even though God had specifically sent Paul to the Gentiles, Paul was willing to discuss his gospel message with the leaders of the Jerusalem church. That meeting prevented a major split in the church, and it formally acknowledged the apostles' approval of Paul's preaching. Sometimes we avoid talking over conflicts when talking is exactly what we need to do more than anything else. We fear that talking will surface new problems or force an argument. But in the end, marriages stand or fall on communication. Openly discuss your views, actions, and feelings with each other on a regular basis. It will help you prevent a major split.

◈ MEDITATION ◈

Heavenly Father, give us the desire and means to talk to each other as a couple every day. Let our lines of communication always be open, and cause our closeness to grow through your grace and with your blessing. ❧

MAY 23

Jesus Came to Save Sinners
◄§ Luke 5:27–39 §►

Later on as Jesus left the town he saw a tax collector—with the usual reputation for cheating—sitting at a tax collection booth. The man's name was Levi. Jesus said to him, "Come and be one of my disciples!" [28]So Levi left everything, sprang up and went with him.

[29]Soon Levi held a reception in his home with Jesus as the guest of honor. Many of Levi's fellow tax collectors and other guests were there.

[30]But the Pharisees and teachers of the Law complained bitterly to Jesus' disciples about his eating with such notorious sinners.

[31]Jesus answered them, "It is the sick who need a doctor, not those in good health. [32]My purpose is to invite sinners to turn from their sins, not to spend my time with those who think themselves already good enough."

[33]Their next complaint was that Jesus' disciples were feasting instead of fasting. "John the Baptist's disciples are constantly going without food, and praying," they declared, "and so do the disciples of the Pharisees. Why are yours wining and dining?"

[34]Jesus asked, "Do happy men fast? Do wedding guests go hungry while celebrating with the groom? [35]But the time will come when the bridegroom will be killed; then they won't want to eat."

[36]Then Jesus used this illustration: "No one tears off a piece of a new garment to make a patch for an old one. Not only will the new garment be ruined, but the old garment will look worse with a new patch on it! [37]And no one puts new wine into old wineskins, for the new wine bursts the old skins, ruining the skins and spilling the wine. [38]New wine must be put into new wineskins. [39]But no one after drinking the old wine seems to want the fresh and the new. 'The old ways are best,' they say."

The Apostles Accepted Paul's Gospel
◄§ Galatians 2:6–10 §►

And the great leaders of the church who were there had nothing to add to what I was preaching. (By the way, their being great leaders made no difference to me, for all are the same to God.) [7,8,9]In fact, when Peter, James, and John, who were known as the pillars of the church, saw how greatly God had used me in winning the Gentiles, just as Peter had been blessed so greatly in his preaching to the Jews—for the same God gave us each our special gifts—they shook hands with Barnabas and me and encouraged us to keep right on with our preaching to the Gentiles while they continued their work with the Jews. [10]The only thing they did suggest was that we must always remember to help the poor, and I, too, was eager for that.

Proverbs for Today
◄§ 15:29–30 §►

The Lord is far from the wicked, but he hears the prayers of the righteous. □ Pleasant sights and good reports give happiness and health.

◈ KEY VERSE ◈

Seeing their faith, Jesus said to the man, "My friend, your sins are forgiven!"—*Luke 5:20*

In Bible times, many houses were built of stone and had flat roofs made of logs, straw, and mud. Outside stairways led to the roof. The men described in this passage carried their friend up the stairs to the roof, where they took apart as much of the mud and straw mixture as was necessary to lower him through to Jesus.

It wasn't the sick man's faith that impressed Jesus, but the faith of his friends. Jesus responded to their faith and healed the man. For better or worse, our faith affects others. We cannot make another person respond to Christ, but we can do much through our words, actions, and love to give him or her a chance to respond. As a Christian couple, look for opportunities to bring your friends to the living Christ.

────── ✒ MEDITATION ✒ ──────

Heavenly Father, help us to be good witnesses for you to those with whom we come in contact. Help us be a blessing to everyone in your name and for the sake of your Kingdom. ❧

MAY 24

Jesus Is Master of the Sabbath
✦ Luke 6:1–11 ❧

One Sabbath as Jesus and his disciples were walking through some grainfields, they were breaking off the heads of wheat, rubbing off the husks in their hands and eating the grains.

²But some Pharisees said, "That's illegal! Your disciples are harvesting grain, and it's against the Jewish law to work on the Sabbath."

³Jesus replied, "Don't you read the Scriptures? Haven't you ever read what King David did when he and his men were hungry? ⁴He went into the Temple and took the shewbread, the special bread that was placed before the Lord, and ate it—illegal as this was—and shared it with others." ⁵And Jesus added, "I am master even of the Sabbath."

⁶On another Sabbath he was in the synagogue teaching, and a man was present whose right hand was deformed. ⁷The teachers of the Law and the Pharisees watched closely to see whether he would heal the man that day, since it was the Sabbath. For they were eager to find some charge to bring against him.

⁸How well he knew their thoughts! But he said to the man with the deformed hand, "Come and stand here where everyone can see." So he did.

⁹Then Jesus said to the Pharisees and teachers of the Law, "I have a question for you. Is it right to do good on the Sabbath day, or to do harm? To save life, or to destroy it?"

¹⁰He looked around at them one by one and then said to the man, "Reach out your hand." And as he did, it became completely normal again. ¹¹At this, the enemies of Jesus were wild with rage, and began to plot his murder.

Paul Opposed Peter in Antioch
✦ Galatians 2:11–16 ❧

But when Peter came to Antioch I had to oppose him publicly, speaking strongly against what he was doing for it was very wrong. ¹²For when he first arrived he ate with the Gentile Christians [who don't bother with circumcision and the many other Jewish laws]. But afterwards when some Jewish friends of James came, he wouldn't eat with the Gentiles anymore because he was afraid of what these Jewish legalists, who insisted that circumcision was necessary for salvation, would say; ¹³and then all the other Jewish Christians and even Barnabas became hypocrites too, following Peter's example, though they certainly knew better. ¹⁴When I saw what was happening and that they weren't being honest about what they really believed, and weren't following the truth of the Gospel, I said to Peter in front of all the others, "Though you are a Jew by birth, you have long since discarded the Jewish laws; so why, all of a sudden, are you trying to make these Gentiles obey them? [15]You and I are Jews by birth, not mere Gentile sinners, [16]and yet we Jewish Christians know very well that we cannot become right with God by obeying our Jewish laws, but only by faith in Jesus Christ to take away our sins. And so we, too, have trusted Jesus Christ, that we might be accepted by God because of faith—and not because we have obeyed the Jewish laws. For no one will ever be saved by obeying them."

Proverbs for Today
◄§ 15:31–32 §►

If you profit from constructive criticism you will be elected to the wise men's hall of fame. But to reject criticism is to harm yourself and your own best interests.

◄ KEY VERSE ◄

When Peter came to Antioch I had to oppose him publicly, speaking strongly against what he was do-ing, for it was very wrong.—*Galatians 2:11*

◄ REFLECTION ◄

The Judaizers accused Paul of watering down the gospel to make it easier for Gentiles to accept, while Paul accused the Judaizers of nullifying the truth of the gospel by adding conditions to it. The basis of salvation was the issue—is salvation through Christ alone, or does it come through Christ and adher-ence to the law? The argument came to a head when Peter, Paul, some Judaizers, and some Gen-tile Christians all gathered together in Antioch to share a meal. Peter probably thought that by stay-ing aloof from the Gentiles, he was promoting har-mony—he did not want to offend the friends of James. But Paul charged that Peter's action violated the gospel. By joining the Judaizers, Peter implic-itly supported their claim that Christ was not suffi-cient for salvation.

Compromise is an important part of getting along with others, but we should never concede the truth of God's Word. If we feel as though we have to change our Christian beliefs to match those of our companions, we are on dangerous ground. Know which battles are worth fighting. Don't alienate friends or family because of your convic-tions, but also remember that they are watching to see what makes your lives so different. Let your marriage be a blessing and witness to the people you know. They may not agree with you, but they will probably respect your sincerity and be more likely to listen when you present the gospel to them.

◄ MEDITATION ◄

Heavenly Father, help us to never waver in our convic-tions. Grant us the opportunity to share the Good News of salvation with our friends and neighbors so that they may be saved also. §►

MAY 25

Jesus Chooses His Twelve Disciples
◄§ Luke 6:12–16 §►

One day soon afterwards Jesus went out into the mountains to pray, and prayed all night. [13]At day-break he called together his followers and chose twelve of them to be the inner circle of his disciples. (They were appointed as his "apostles," or "mis-sionaries.") [14,15,16]Here are their names:
Simon (he also called him Peter),
Andrew (Simon's brother),
James,
John,
Philip,
Bartholomew,
Matthew,
Thomas,
James (the son of Alphaeus),
Simon (a member of the Zealots, a subversive political party),
Judas (son of James),
Judas Iscariot (who later betrayed him).

Keeping the Law Cannot Bring Salvation
⌁§ Galatians 2:17–21

But what if we trust Christ to save us and then find that we are wrong, and that we cannot be saved without being circumcised and obeying all the other Jewish laws? Wouldn't we need to say that faith in Christ had ruined us? God forbid that anyone should dare to think such things about our Lord. [18]Rather, we are sinners if we start rebuilding the old systems I have been destroying, of trying to be saved by keeping Jewish laws, [19]for it was through reading the Scripture that I came to realize that I could never find God's favor by trying—and failing—to obey the laws. I came to realize that acceptance with God comes by believing in Christ.

[20]I have been crucified with Christ: and I myself no longer live, but Christ lives in me. And the real life I now have within this body is a result of my trusting in the Son of God, who loved me and gave himself for me. [21]I am not one of those who treats Christ's death as meaningless. For if we could be saved by keeping Jewish laws, then there was no need for Christ to die.

Proverbs for Today
⌁§ 15:33 §⌁

Humility and reverence for the Lord will make you both wise and honored.

⌁ KEY VERSE ⌁

At daybreak he called together his followers and chose twelve of them to be the inner circle of his disciples.—*Luke 6:13*

⌁ REFLECTION ⌁

Jesus selected ordinary people to be his disciples, and they were a broad mixture of backgrounds and personalities. They were ordinary people with a high calling. Today, God still calls ordinary people together to build his church, teach the message of salvation, and serve others out of love. Alone we may feel unqualified to serve Christ effectively, but together we make up a group strong enough to serve God in every way. Ask for patience to accept the differences in people in your church, and build on the variety of strengths represented there. Also be thankful for the differences each of you bring to your marriage. Together your unique talents and outlooks on life will make both of you stronger in your relationship and ministry.

⌁ MEDITATION ⌁

Heavenly Father, we thank you for our unique qualities and skills. Forgive us when we become impatient and try to change each other simply to satisfy our personal tastes or needs. Help us to use our individuality as we work together to serve you. §⌁

MAY 26

The Sermon on the Plain
⌁§ Luke 6:17–38 §⌁

When they came down the slopes of the mountain, the disciples stood with Jesus on a large, level area, surrounded by many of his followers who, in turn, were surrounded by the crowds. For people from all over Judea and from Jerusalem and from as far north as the seacoasts of Tyre and Sidon had come to hear him or to be healed. And he cast out many demons. [19]Everyone was trying to touch him, for when they did healing power went out from him and they were cured.

[20]Then he turned to his disciples and said, "What happiness there is for you who are poor, for the Kingdom of God is yours! [21]What happiness there is for you who are now hungry, for you are going to be satisfied! What happiness there is for you who weep, for the time will come when you shall laugh with joy! [22]What happiness it is when others hate you and exclude you and insult you and smear your name because you are mine! [23]When

that happens, rejoice! Yes, leap for joy! For you will have a great reward awaiting you in heaven. And you will be in good company—the ancient prophets were treated that way too!

24"But, oh, the sorrows that await the rich. For they have their only happiness down here. 25They are fat and prosperous now, but a time of awful hunger is before them. Their careless laughter now means sorrow then. 26And what sadness is ahead for those praised by the crowds—for *false* prophets have *always* been praised.

27"Listen, all of you. Love your *enemies*. Do *good* to those who *hate* you. 28Pray for the happiness of those who *curse* you; implore God's blessing on those who *hurt* you.

29"If someone slaps you on one cheek, let him slap the other too! If someone demands your coat, give him your shirt besides. 30Give what you have to anyone who asks you for it; and when things are taken away from you, don't worry about getting them back. 31Treat others as you want them to treat you.

32"Do you think you deserve credit for merely loving those who love you? Even the godless do that! 33And if you do good only to those who do you good—is that so wonderful? Even sinners do that much! 34And if you lend money only to those who can repay you, what good is that? Even the most wicked will lend to their own kind for full return!

35"Love your *enemies*! Do good to *them*! Lend to *them*! And don't be concerned about the fact that they won't repay. Then your reward from heaven will be very great, and you will truly be acting as sons of God: for he is kind to the *unthankful* and to those who are *very wicked*.

36"Try to show as much compassion as your Father does.

37"Never criticize or condemn—or it will all come back on you. Go easy on others; then they will do the same for you. 38For if you give, you will get! Your gift will return to you in full and overflowing measure, pressed down, shaken together to make room for more, and running over. Whatever measure you use to give—large or small—will be used to measure what is given back to you."

The True Children of Abraham
◄§ Galatians 3:1–9 §►

Oh, foolish Galatians! What magician has hypnotized you and cast an evil spell upon you? For you used to see the meaning of Jesus Christ's death as clearly as though I had waved a placard before you with a picture on it of Christ dying on the cross. 2Let me ask you this one question: Did you receive the Holy Spirit by trying to keep the Jewish laws? Of course not, for the Holy Spirit came upon you only after you heard about Christ and trusted him to save you. 3Then have you gone completely crazy? For if trying to obey the Jewish laws never gave you spiritual life in the first place, why do you think that trying to obey them now will make you stronger Christians? 4You have suffered so much for the Gospel. Now are you going to just throw it all overboard? I can hardly believe it!

5I ask you again, does God give you the power of the Holy Spirit and work miracles among you as a result of your trying to obey the Jewish laws? No, of course not. It is when you believe in Christ and fully trust him.

6Abraham had the same experience—God declared him fit for heaven only because he believed God's promises. 7You can see from this that the real children of Abraham are all the men of faith who truly trust in God.

8,9What's more, the Scriptures looked forward to this time when God would save the Gentiles also, through their faith. God told Abraham about this long ago when he said, "I will bless those in every nation who trust in me as you do." And so it is: all who trust in Christ share the same blessing Abraham received.

Proverbs for Today
◄§ 16:1–3 §►

We can make our plans, but the final outcome is in God's hands. We can always "prove" that we are right, but is the Lord convinced? Commit your work to the Lord, then it will succeed.

───── ◢ KEY VERSE ◣ ─────

Commit your work to the Lord, then it will succeed.—*Proverbs 16:3*

People find many ways to commit their work to the Lord wrongly. Some commit their work to the Lord only superficially. They say they are doing a particular project for the Lord, but in reality they are doing it for themselves. Others give God temporary control of their interests, only to take the authority back the moment things stop going the way they expect. Still others commit their task fully to the Lord, and then put forth no effort themselves. They wonder why they do not experience success.

As Christians who have dedicated your lives to the Lord, try to maintain a balance: trusting God as if everything depends on him, while working as if everything depends on you. Think of a specific effort in which you are both involved right now. Have you committed it to the Lord? If not, submit it to him, and work hard to complete the task.

_____ ⋅❀ MEDITATION ❀⋅ _____

Heavenly Father, we submit the authority over the work you have given us into your hands and ask that your Holy Spirit will guide us in our actions. ❧

MAY 27

A Collection of Jesus' Parables
⋅§ Luke 6:39–49 ❧

Here are some of the story-illustrations Jesus used in his sermons: "What good is it for one blind man to lead another? He will fall into a ditch and pull the other down with him. [40]How can a student know more than his teacher? But if he works hard, he may learn as much.

[41]"And why quibble about the speck in someone else's eye—his little fault—when a board is in your own? [42]How can you think of saying to him, 'Brother, let me help you get rid of that speck in your eye,' when you can't see past the board in yours? Hypocrite! First get rid of the board, and then perhaps you can see well enough to deal with his speck!

[43]"A tree from good stock doesn't produce scrub fruit nor do trees from poor stock produce choice fruit. [44]A tree is identified by the kind of fruit it produces. Figs never grow on thorns, or grapes on bramble bushes. [45]A good man produces good deeds from a good heart. And an evil man produces evil deeds from his hidden wickedness. Whatever is in the heart overflows into speech.

[46]"So why do you call me 'Lord' when you won't obey me? [47,48]But all those who come and listen and obey me are like a man who builds a house on a strong foundation laid upon the underlying rock. When the floodwaters rise and break against the house, it stands firm, for it is strongly built.

[49]"But those who listen and don't obey are like a man who builds a house without a foundation. When the floods sweep down against that house, it crumbles into a heap of ruins."

Christ Became a Curse for Us
⋅§ Galatians 3:10–14 ❧

Yes, and those who depend on the Jewish laws to save them are under God's curse, for the Scriptures point out very clearly, "Cursed is everyone who at any time breaks a single one of these laws that are written in God's Book of the Law." [11]Consequently, it is clear that no one can ever win God's favor by trying to keep the Jewish laws, because God has said that the only way we can be right in his sight is by faith. As the prophet Habakkuk says it, "The man who finds life will find it through trusting God." [12]How different from this way of faith is the way of law which says that a man is saved by obeying every law of God, without one slip. [13]But Christ has bought us out from under the doom of that impossible system by taking the curse for our wrongdoing upon himself. For it is written in the Scripture, "Anyone who is hanged on a tree is cursed" [as Jesus was hung upon a wooden cross].

[14]Now God can bless the Gentiles, too, with this same blessing he promised to Abraham; and all of us as Christians can have the promised Holy Spirit through this faith.

Proverbs for Today
~§ 16:4–5 §~

The Lord has made everything for his own purposes—even the wicked, for punishment. □ Pride disgusts the Lord. Take my word for it—*proud men shall be punished.*

~ KEY VERSE ~

And why quibble about the speck in someone else's eye—his little fault—when a board is in your own?—*Luke 6:41*

~ REFLECTION ~

This collection of parables in Luke centers on the appropriate basis for judging the character of one-self and others. We must be very aware of our own shortcomings when we approach others with the intent to "set them straight." We must recognize that we too have areas that need correcting. We should also take care that we are not trying to correct insignificant faults in others when, in reality, we are in greater need of correction. Humility is always important when evaluating others.

True spirituality comes from the heart and must be evidenced by good deeds ("choice fruit"). If our words do not match the true quality of our lives, it is time for self-examination. Seek the guidance of other Christian couples, your pastor, and godly friends and relatives for spiritual correction in your lives. But, most of all, pray that the Holy Spirit will show you when you have done wrong and will remove the "boards" from your eyes.

~ MEDITATION ~

Heavenly Father, forgive us when we are quick to judge the actions of others and slow to examine our own short-comings. Help us to be pure and holy in your sight. §~

MAY 28

Jesus Heals a Roman Soldier's Slave
~§ Luke 7:1–10 §~

When Jesus had finished his sermon he went back into the city of Capernaum.

[2]Just at that time the highly prized slave of a Roman army captain was sick and near death. [3]When the captain heard about Jesus, he sent some respected Jewish elders to ask him to come and heal his slave. [4]So they began pleading earnestly with Jesus to come with them and help the man. They told him what a wonderful person the captain was.

"If anyone deserves your help, it is he," they said, [5]"for he loves the Jews and even paid personally to build us a synagogue!"

[6,7,8]Jesus went with them; but just before arriving at the house, the captain sent some friends to say, "Sir, don't inconvenience yourself by coming to my home, for I am not worthy of any such honor or even to come and meet you. Just speak a word from where you are, and my servant boy will be healed! I know, because I am under the authority of my superior officers, and I have authority over my men. I only need to say 'Go!' and they go; or 'Come!' and they come; and to my slave, 'Do this or that,' and he does it. So just say, 'Be healed!' and my servant will be well again!''

[9]Jesus was amazed. Turning to the crowd he said, "Never among all the Jews in Israel have I met a man with faith like this."

[10]And when the captain's friends returned to his house, they found the slave completely healed.

The Fulfillment of God's Promise to Abraham
~§ Galatians 3:15–20 §~

Dear brothers, even in everyday life a promise made by one man to another, if it is written down and signed, cannot be changed. He cannot decide afterward to do something else instead.

[16]Now, God gave some promises to Abraham and his Child. And notice that it doesn't say the promises were to his *children,* as it would if all his sons—all the Jews—were being spoken of, but to his *Child*—and that, of course, means Christ. [17]Here's what I am trying to say: God's promise to save through faith—and God wrote this promise down and signed it—could not be canceled or changed four hundred and thirty years later when God gave the Ten Commandments. [18]If *obeying those laws* could save us, then it is obvious that this would be a different way of gaining God's favor than Abraham's way, for he simply accepted God's promise.

[19]Well then, why were the laws given? They were added after the promise was given, to show men how guilty they are of breaking God's laws. But this system of law was to last only until the coming of Christ, the Child to whom God's promise was made. (And there is this further difference. God gave his laws to angels to give to Moses, who then gave them to the people; [20]but when God gave his promise to Abraham, he did it by himself alone, without angels or Moses as go-betweens.)

Proverbs for Today
⋖§ 16:6–7 §⋗

Iniquity is atoned for by mercy and truth; evil is avoided by reverence for God. ☐ When a man is trying to please God, God makes even his worst enemies to be at peace with him.

──────── ⋖ **KEY VERSE** ⋗ ────────

It is clear that no one can ever win God's favor by trying to keep the Jewish laws because God has said that the only way we can be right in his sight is by faith. As the prophet Habakkuk says it, "The man who finds life will find it through trusting God." —*Galatians 3:11*

──────── ⋖ **REFLECTION** ⋗ ────────

Trying to be righteous through our own powers and abilities doesn't work. Good intentions such as, "I'll do better next time," or, "I'll never do that again" usually end in failure. Paul pointed to Habakkuk's declaration (in Habakkuk 2:4) that by trusting God—believing in his provision for our sins and living each day in the power of his Spirit—we can break the cycle of failure. Ask the Lord to search your hearts and reveal your shortcomings. When you trust in him, he will reward your sincerity with the strength to live pure and upright lives.

──────── ⋖ **MEDITATION** ⋗ ────────

Heavenly Father, we place our trust in you and ask that you will show us when we have done something that dishonors your name. Give us the wisdom and strength to lead holy and blameless lives. §⋗

MAY 29 ─────────────────────

Jesus Raises a Young Boy from the Dead
⋖§ Luke 7:11–17 §⋗

Not long afterwards Jesus went with his disciples to the village of Nain, with the usual great crowd at his heels. [12]A funeral procession was coming out as he approached the village gate. The boy who had died was the only son of his widowed mother, and many mourners from the village were with her.

[13]When the Lord saw her, his heart overflowed with sympathy. "Don't cry!" he said. [14]Then he walked over to the coffin and touched it, and the bearers stopped. "Laddie," he said, "come back to life again."

[15]Then the boy sat up and began to talk to those around him! And Jesus gave him back to his mother.

[16]A great fear swept the crowd, and they exclaimed with praises to God, "A mighty prophet has risen among us," and, "We have seen the hand of God at work today."

[17]The report of what he did that day raced from end to end of Judea and even out across the borders.

We Are All One in Christ
∙§ Galatians 3:21–29 §∙

Well then, are God's laws and God's promises against each other? Of course not! If we could be saved by his laws, then God would not have had to give us a different way to get out of the grip of sin—for the Scriptures insist we are all its prisoners. The only way out is through faith in Jesus Christ; the way of escape is open to all who believe him.

[23]Until Christ came we were guarded by the law, kept in protective custody, so to speak, until we could believe in the coming Savior. [24]Let me put it another way. The Jewish laws were our teacher and guide until Christ came to give us right standing with God through our faith. [25]But now that Christ has come, we don't need those laws any longer to guard us and lead us to him. [26]For now we are all children of God through faith in Jesus Christ, [27]and we who have been baptized into union with Christ are enveloped by him. [28]We are no longer Jews or Greeks or slaves or free men or even merely men or women, but we are all the same—we are Christians; we are one in Christ Jesus. [29]And now that we are Christ's we are the true descendants of Abraham, and all of God's promises to him belong to us.

Proverbs for Today
∙§ 16:8–9 §∙

A little, gained honestly, is better than great wealth gotten by dishonest means. We should make plans—counting on God to direct us.

∙ KEY VERSE ∙

We are no longer Jews or Greeks or slaves or free men or even merely men or women, but we are all the same—we are Christians; we are one in Christ Jesus.—*Galatians 3:28*

∙ REFLECTION ∙

In Paul's day, many Jewish males greeted each new day by praying, "Lord, I thank you that I am not a Gentile, a slave, or a woman." For Christians, that prayer is inappropriate, because faith in Christ transcends the differences between people (whatever they may be) and makes all believers equal in Christ.

Your marriage is a balanced partnership in which each person is free and equal in God's eyes. Don't let the attitudes of the world negatively effect your relationship. Treat your spouse with love and honor, and be thankful that God has brought you together.

∙ MEDITATION ∙

Heavenly Father, we thank you for our marriage and ask that you will continue to bless us with a loving relationship. While we each are unique individuals, we recognize that we are equal in your sight and pledge our lives to your service. §∙

MAY 30

Jesus Commends John the Baptist's Ministry
∙§ Luke 7:18–35 §∙

The disciples of John the Baptist soon heard of all that Jesus was doing. When they told John about it, [19]he sent two of his disciples to Jesus to ask him, "Are you really the Messiah? Or shall we keep on looking for him?"

[20,21,22]The two disciples found Jesus while he was curing many sick people of their various diseases—healing the lame and the blind and casting out evil spirits. When they asked him John's question, this was his reply: "Go back to John and tell him all you have seen and heard here today: how those who were blind can see. The lame are walking without a limp. The lepers are completely healed. The deaf can hear again. The dead come back to life. And the poor are hearing the Good News. [23]And tell him, 'Blessed is the one who does not lose his faith in me.'"

[24]After they left, Jesus talked to the crowd about John. "Who is this man you went out into the Judean wilderness to see?" he asked. "Did you find him weak as grass, moved by every breath of wind? [25]Did you find him dressed in expensive clothes? No! Men who live in luxury are found in palaces, not out in the wilderness. [26]But did you find a prophet? Yes! And more than a prophet. [27]He is the one to whom the Scriptures refer when they say, 'Look! I am sending my messenger ahead of you, to prepare the way before you.' [28]In all humanity there is no one greater than John. And yet the least citizen of the Kingdom of God is greater than he."

[29]And all who heard John preach—even the most wicked of them—agreed that God's requirements were right, and they were baptized by him. [30]All, that is, except the Pharisees and teachers of Moses' Law. They rejected God's plan for them and refused John's baptism.

[31]"What can I say about such men?" Jesus asked. "With what shall I compare them? [32]They are like a group of children who complain to their friends, 'You don't like it if we play "wedding" and you don't like it if we play "funeral"'! [33]For John the Baptist used to go without food and never took a drop of liquor all his life, and you said, 'He must be crazy!' [34]But I eat my food and drink my wine, and you say, 'What a glutton Jesus is! And he drinks! And has the lowest sort of friends!' [35]But I am sure you can always justify your inconsistencies."

We Are God's Adopted Children
Galatians 4:1-7

But remember this, that if a father dies and leaves great wealth for his little son, that child is not much better off than a slave until he grows up, even though he actually owns everything his father had. [2]He has to do what his guardians and managers tell him to, until he reaches whatever age his father set.

[3]And that is the way it was with us before Christ came. We were slaves to Jewish laws and rituals for we thought they could save us. [4]But when the right time came, the time God decided on, he sent his Son, born of a woman, born as a Jew, [5]to buy freedom for us who were slaves to the law so that he could adopt us as his very own sons. [6]And because we are his sons God has sent the Spirit of his Son into our hearts, so now we can rightly speak of God as our dear Father. [7]Now we are no longer slaves, but God's own sons. And since we are his sons, everything he has belongs to us, for that is the way God planned.

Proverbs for Today
16:10-11

God will help the king to judge the people fairly; there need be no mistakes. □ The Lord demands fairness in every business deal. He established this principle.

KEY VERSE

The Lord demands fairness in every business deal. He established this principle.—*Proverbs 16:11*

REFLECTION

Every worker soon learns what is right, fair, and just in his or her line of work. Whether the job involves buying or selling a product, offering a service, or fashioning raw materials into a finished product, we know what should be and what should not. Sometimes we feel pressure to be less than honest in order to advance ourselves or gain more profit. But if we want to obey God, there is no middle ground: God demands fairness in every business transaction. No amount of rationalizing can excuse a dishonest or unfair business practice. Fairness is not always easy, but it is what God demands.

In your respective jobs, at home, and in your personal dealings, ask the Lord for discernment, strength, and courage to be honest consistently. You will be better witnesses for his Kingdom, and you will promote honesty toward you as well.

Heavenly Father, forgive us when we do things at work or in our home that are unfair, misleading, or even dis- *honest. We know that our lives will be happier when we put our faith into practice during our day-to-day activities and ask that you will keep us from the temptation of taking the easy, but ultimately more painful, route.* ❧

MAY 31

A Sinful Woman Anoints Jesus' Feet
◦§ Luke 7:36–50 §◦

One of the Pharisees asked Jesus to come to his home for lunch and Jesus accepted the invitation. As they sat down to eat, ³⁷a woman of the streets—a prostitute—heard he was there and brought an exquisite flask filled with expensive perfume. ³⁸Going in, she knelt behind him at his feet, weeping, with her tears falling down upon his feet; and she wiped them off with her hair and kissed them and poured the perfume on them.

³⁹When Jesus' host, a Pharisee, saw what was happening and who the woman was, he said to himself, "This proves that Jesus is no prophet, for if God had really sent him, he would know what kind of woman this one is!"

⁴⁰Then Jesus spoke up and answered his thoughts. "Simon," he said to the Pharisee, "I have something to say to you."

"All right, Teacher," Simon replied, "go ahead."

⁴¹Then Jesus told him this story: "A man loaned money to two people—$5,000 to one and $500 to the other. ⁴²But neither of them could pay him back, so he kindly forgave them both, letting them keep the money! Which do you suppose loved him most after that?"

⁴³"I suppose the one who had owed him the most," Simon answered.

"Correct," Jesus agreed.

⁴⁴Then he turned to the woman and said to Simon, "Look! See this woman kneeling here! When I entered your home, you didn't bother to offer me water to wash the dust from my feet, but she has washed them with her tears and wiped them with her hair. ⁴⁵You refused me the customary kiss of greeting, but she has kissed my feet again and again from the time I first came in. ⁴⁶You neglected the usual courtesy of olive oil to anoint my head, but she has covered my feet with rare perfume. ⁴⁷Therefore her sins—and they are many—are forgiven, for she loved me much; but one who is forgiven little, shows little love."

⁴⁸And he said to her, "Your sins are forgiven."

⁴⁹Then the men at the table said to themselves, "Who does this man think he is, going around forgiving sins?"

⁵⁰And Jesus said to the woman, "Your faith has saved you; go in peace."

Do Not Become Enslaved Again
◦§ Galatians 4:8–11 §◦

Before you Gentiles knew God you were slaves to so-called gods that did not even exist. ⁹And now that you have found God (or I should say, now that God has found you) how can it be that you want to go back again and become slaves once more to another poor, weak, useless religion of trying to get to heaven by obeying God's laws? ¹⁰You are trying to find favor with God by what you do or don't do on certain days or months or seasons or years. ¹¹I fear for you. I am afraid that all my hard work for you was worth nothing.

Proverbs for Today
◦§ 16:12–13 §◦

It is a horrible thing for a king to do evil. His right to rule depends upon his fairness. The king rejoices when his people are truthful and fair.

"Therefore her sins—and they are many—are forgiven, for she loved me much; but one who is forgiven little, shows little love."—*Luke 7:47*

Overflowing love is the natural response to forgiveness. But only those who realize the depth of their sin can appreciate the complete forgiveness that God offers them. Jesus has rescued all of his followers, whether they were once extremely wicked or conventionally good, from eternal death.

Are both of you aware of the breadth of God's mercy? Are you grateful for his forgiveness? Do you forgive others no matter what they have done to you? If not, then you have not committed your lives and your home to serving the Lord. Remember that Jesus lived a sinless life but suffered an unjust fate on the cross for your sins. When you hold a grudge, you deny Christ's victory in your lives. On the other hand, when you forgive others, you honor the tremendous sacrifice he made.

Heavenly Father, we praise you for what Jesus did for us on the cross at Calvary. We pray that you will forgive us of our sins and ask that you will help us to offer only love and not condemnation to those who do something unkind or unfair to us. ❧

JUNE 1

Some Disciples of Jesus
❧ Luke 8:1–3 ❧

Not long afterwards Jesus began a tour of the cities and villages of Galilee to announce the coming of the Kingdom of God, and took his twelve disciples with him. ²Some women went along, from whom he had cast out demons or whom he had healed; among them were Mary Magdalene (Jesus had cast out seven demons from her), ³Joanna, Chuza's wife (Chuza was King Herod's business manager and was in charge of his palace and domestic affairs), Susanna, and many others who were contributing from their private means to the support of Jesus and his disciples.

Paul's Longing for Fellowship
❧ Galatians 4:12–20 ❧

Dear brothers, please feel as I do about these things, for I am as free from these chains as you used to be. You did not despise me then when I first preached to you, ¹³even though I was sick when I first brought you the Good News of Christ. ¹⁴But even though my sickness was revolting to you, you didn't reject me and turn me away.

No, you took me in and cared for me as though I were an angel from God, or even Jesus Christ himself.

¹⁵Where is that happy spirit that we felt together then? For in those days I know you would gladly have taken out your own eyes and given them to replace mine if that would have helped me.

¹⁶And now have I become your enemy because I tell you the truth?

¹⁷Those false teachers who are so anxious to win your favor are not doing it for your good. What they are trying to do is to shut you off from me so that you will pay more attention to them. ¹⁸It is a fine thing when people are nice to you with good motives and sincere hearts, especially if they aren't doing it just when I am with you! ¹⁹Oh, my children, how you are hurting me! I am once again suffering for you the pains of a mother waiting for her child to be born—longing for the time when you will finally be filled with Christ. ²⁰How I wish I could be there with you right now and not have to reason with you like this, for at this distance I frankly don't know what to do.

Proverbs for Today
◄§ 16:14–15 §►

The anger of the king is a messenger of death and a wise man will appease it. Many favors are showered on those who please the king.

———————◄ KEY VERSE ◄——————

And now have I become your enemy because I tell you the truth?—*Galatians 4:16*

———————◄ REFLECTION ◄——————

Paul did not gain great popularity when he rebuked the Galatians for the heresy and legalism that had crept into their church. Human nature hasn't changed much—people still get angry when they're scolded. But don't become irritated when someone challenges you. There may be truth in what he or she says. This is especially true when the person is your spouse, since he or she knows you better than anyone else. Receive criticism with humility; carefully think it over. If you discover you need to change an attitude or action, take steps to do it. And don't hold a grudge against the person who told you the truth.

———————◄ MEDITATION ◄——————

Heavenly Father, help us to be humble and to receive advice and criticism from others with an open mind and a willingness to change. ◈►

JUNE 2

The Parable of the Soils
◄§ Luke 8:4–15 §►

One day Jesus gave this illustration to a large crowd that was gathering to hear him—while many others were still on the way, coming from other towns.

⁵"A farmer went out to his field to sow grain. As he scattered the seed on the ground, some of it fell on a footpath and was trampled on; and the birds came and ate it as it lay exposed. ⁶Other seed fell on shallow soil with rock beneath. This seed began to grow, but soon withered and died for lack of moisture. ⁷Other seed landed in thistle patches, and the young grain stalks were soon choked out. ⁸Still other fell on fertile soil; this seed grew and produced a crop one hundred times as large as he had planted." (As he was giving this illustration he said, "If anyone has listening ears, use them now!")

⁹His apostles asked him what the story meant.

¹⁰He replied, "God has granted you to know the meaning of these parables, for they tell a great deal about the Kingdom of God. But these crowds hear the words and do not understand, just as the ancient prophets predicted.

¹¹"This is its meaning: The seed is God's message to men. ¹²The hard path where some seed fell represents the hard hearts of those who hear the words of God, but then the devil comes and steals the words away and prevents people from believing and being saved. ¹³The stony ground represents those who enjoy listening to sermons, but somehow the message never really gets through to them and doesn't take root and grow. They know the message is true, and sort of believe for awhile; but when the hot winds of persecution blow, they lose interest. ¹⁴The seed among the thorns represents those who listen and believe God's words but whose faith afterwards is choked out by worry and riches and the responsibilities and pleasures of life. And so they are never able to help anyone else to believe the Good News.

¹⁵"But the good soil represents honest, good-hearted people. They listen to God's words and cling to them and steadily spread them to others who also soon believe."

The Illustration of Sarah and Hagar
◄§ Galatians 4:21–31 §►

Listen to me, you friends who think you have to obey the Jewish laws to be saved: Why don't you find out what those laws really mean? ²²For it is written that Abraham had two sons, one from his slave-wife and one from his freeborn wife. ²³There was nothing unusual about the birth of the slave-wife's baby. But the baby of the freeborn wife was born only after God had especially promised he would come.

²⁴,²⁵Now this true story is an illustration of God's two ways of helping people. One way was by giving them his laws to obey. He did this on Mount Sinai, when he gave the Ten Commandments to Moses. Mount Sinai, by the way, is called "Mount Hagar" by the Arabs—and in my illustration Abraham's slave-wife Hagar represents Jerusalem, the mother-city of the Jews, the center of that system of trying to please God by trying to obey the Commandments; and the Jews, who try to follow that system, are her slave children. ²⁶But our mother-city is the heavenly Jerusalem, and she is not a slave to Jewish laws.

²⁷That is what Isaiah meant when he prophesied, "Now you can rejoice, O childless woman; you can shout with joy though you never before had a child. For I am going to give you many children—more children than the slave-wife has."

²⁸You and I, dear brothers, are the children that God promised, just as Isaac was. ²⁹And so we who are born of the Holy Spirit are persecuted now by those who want us to keep the Jewish laws, just as Isaac the child of promise was persecuted by Ishmael the slave-wife's son.

³⁰But the Scriptures say that God told Abraham to send away the slave-wife and her son, for the slave-wife's son could not inherit Abraham's home and lands along with the free woman's son. ³¹Dear brothers, we are not slave children, obligated to the Jewish laws, but children of the free woman, acceptable to God because of our faith.

Proverbs for Today
❧ 16:16–17 ❧

How much better is wisdom than gold, and understanding than silver! □ The path of the godly leads away from evil; he who follows that path is safe.

❧ KEY VERSE ❧

A farmer went out to his field to sow grain. As he scattered the seed on the ground, some of it fell on a footpath and was trampled on; and the birds came and ate it as it lay exposed.—*Luke 8:5*

❧ REFLECTION ❧

Why would a farmer allow precious seed to land in the road, on a thorny path, or among rocks? This is not a picture of an irresponsible farmer scattering seeds at random, but of a farmer using the ancient and acceptable method of hand-seeding a large field by casting handfuls as he walks through the field. His goal is to get as much seed as possible to take root in good soil, but there is inevitable waste as some falls or is blown into less productive places. The fact that some of the seed produced no crop was not the fault of the faithful farmer or of the seed. The results depended on the condition of the soil on which the seed fell.

As a Christian couple, it is your responsibility to spread the seeds of salvation through your actions and words. But don't become discouraged when not all your seeds bear fruit. Remember that not every seed lands on good soil; not every person will be open to believing. Simply be faithful in spreading the seeds together. Then rejoice each time one bears fruit for the Kingdom of God.

❧ MEDITATION ❧

Heavenly Father, we pray that you will give us opportunities to spread the Good News of salvation with our friends, neighbors, and coworkers. Give us the courage to speak when we should and the appropriate words to say. ❧

The Illustration of the Lamp
◄§ Luke 8:16–18 §►

[Another time Jesus asked,] "Who ever heard of someone lighting a lamp and then covering it up to keep it from shining? No, lamps are mounted in the open where they can be seen. [17]This illustrates the fact that someday everything [in men's hearts] shall be brought to light and made plain to all. [18]So be careful how you listen; for whoever has, to him shall be given more; and whoever does not have, even what he thinks he has shall be taken away from him."

Freedom from Slavery to Sin
◄§ Galatians 5:1–6 §►

So Christ has made us free. Now make sure that you stay free and don't get all tied up again in the chains of slavery to Jewish laws and ceremonies. [2]Listen to me, for this is serious: *if you are counting on circumcision and keeping the Jewish laws to make you right with God, then Christ cannot save you.* [3]I'll say it again. Anyone trying to find favor with God by being circumcised must always obey every other Jewish law or perish. [4]Christ is useless to you if you are counting on clearing your debt to God by keeping those laws; you are lost from God's grace.

[5]But we by the help of the Holy Spirit are counting on Christ's death to clear away our sins and make us right with God. [6]And we to whom Christ has given eternal life don't need to worry about whether we have been circumcised or not, or whether we are obeying the Jewish ceremonies or not; for all we need is faith working through love.

Proverbs for Today
◄§ 16:18 §►

Pride goes before destruction and haughtiness before a fall.

◈ KEY VERSE ◈

Pride goes before destruction and haughtiness before a fall.—*Proverbs 16:18*

◈ REFLECTION ◈

Proud people take little account of their weaknesses. They think they are above the frailties of common people. In this state of mind they are easily tripped up. Ironically, proud people seldom realize that pride is their problem, although everyone around them is well aware of it. Ask your spouse whether your attitudes are haughty. He or she may help you avoid a fall.

◈ MEDITATION ◈

Heavenly Father, forgive us when we become haughty. Help us never to forget that everything good in us is a gift and blessing from you. §►

Those in the Family of God
◄§ Luke 8:19–21 §►

Once when Jesus' mother and brothers came to see him, they couldn't get into the house where he was teaching, because of the crowds. [20]When Jesus heard they were standing outside and wanted to see him, [21]he remarked, "My mother and my brothers are all those who hear the message of God and obey it."

Freedom to Serve One Another
◄§ Galatians 5:7–15 §►

You were getting along so well. Who has interfered with you to hold you back from following the truth? [8]It certainly isn't God who has done it, for he is the one who has called you to freedom in Christ. [9]But it takes only one wrong person among you to infect all the others.

¹⁰I am trusting the Lord to bring you back to believing as I do about these things. God will deal with that person, whoever he is, who has been troubling and confusing you.

¹¹Some people even say that I myself am preaching that circumcision and Jewish laws are necessary to the plan of salvation. Well, if I preached that, I would be persecuted no more—for that message doesn't offend anyone. The fact that I am still being persecuted proves that I am still preaching salvation through faith in the cross of Christ alone.

¹²I only wish these teachers who want you to cut yourselves by being circumcised would cut themselves off from you and leave you alone!

¹³For, dear brothers, you have been given freedom: not freedom to do wrong, but freedom to love and serve each other. ¹⁴For the whole Law can be summed up in this one command: "Love others as you love yourself." ¹⁵But if instead of showing love among yourselves you are always critical and catty, watch out! Beware of ruining each other.

Proverbs for Today
⋅§ 16:19–20 §⋅

Better poor and humble than proud and rich. □ God blesses those who obey him; happy the man who puts his trust in the Lord.

⋅§ KEY VERSE §⋅

If instead of showing love among yourselves you are always critical and catty, watch out! Beware of ruining each other.—*Galatians 5:15*

⋅§ REFLECTION §⋅

When your attitude toward your spouse is critical and not motivated by love, the chances are quite good that your actions will be unkind. You will stop looking for the good in your husband or wife and see only his or her faults. Soon the unity of your marriage will suffer.

Have you talked behind your spouse's back? Have you found fault with his or her shortcomings instead of praising his or her strengths? Remind yourself of Jesus' command to love others as you love yourself (Matthew 22:39). When you find yourself becoming critical of your spouse, stop and begin treating him or her with loving words and actions. And don't say anything behind his or her back that you wouldn't say in front of it.

⋅§ MEDITATION §⋅

Heavenly Father, we thank you for our marriage. We pray that you will forgive us when we are critical and thoughtless. Help us always to look for the best in each other and to rekindle our love daily. §⋅

JUNE 5

Jesus Calms the Storm
⋅§ Luke 8:22–25 §⋅

One day about that time, as Jesus and his disciples were out in a boat, he suggested that they cross to the other side of the lake. ²³On the way across he lay down for a nap, and while he was sleeping the wind began to rise. A fierce storm developed that threatened to swamp them, and they were in real danger.

²⁴They rushed over and woke him up. "Master, Master, we are sinking!" they screamed.

So he spoke to the storm: "Quiet down," he said, and the wind and waves subsided and all was calm! ²⁵Then he asked them, "Where is your faith?"

And they were filled with awe and fear of him and said to one another, "Who is this man, that even the winds and waves obey him?"

The Spirit and the Flesh Are at War
⋅§ Galatians 5:16–21 §⋅

I advise you to obey only the Holy Spirit's instructions. He will tell you where to go and what to do, and then you won't always be doing the wrong things your evil nature wants you to. ¹⁷For we naturally love to do evil things that are just the opposite from the things that the Holy Spirit tells us to do; and the good things we want to do when the Spirit has his way with us are just the opposite of our natural desires. These two forces within us are constantly fighting each other to win control over us, and our wishes are never free from their pressures. [18]When you are guided by the Holy Spirit you need no longer force yourself to obey Jewish laws.

[19]But when you follow your own wrong inclinations your lives will produce these evil results: impure thoughts, eagerness for lustful pleasure, [20]idolatry, spiritism (that is, encouraging the activity of demons), hatred and fighting, jealousy and anger, constant effort to get the best for yourself, complaints and criticisms, the feeling that everyone else is wrong except those in your own little group—and there will be wrong doctrine, [21]envy, murder, drunkenness, wild parties, and all that sort of thing. Let me tell you again as I have before, that anyone living that sort of life will not inherit the Kingdom of God.

Proverbs for Today
◄§ 16:21–23 §►

The wise man is known by his common sense, and a pleasant teacher is the best. Wisdom is a fountain of life to those possessing it, but a fool's burden is his folly. From a wise mind comes careful and persuasive speech.

◄ KEY VERSE � ►

We naturally love to do evil things that are just the opposite from the things that the Holy Spirit tells us to do; and the good things we want to do when the Spirit has his way with us are just the opposite of our natural desires. These two forces within us are constantly fighting each other to win control over us, and our wishes are never free from their pressures.—*Galatians 5:17*

◄ REFLECTION �a ►

Paul described the two forces at work within us—the Holy Spirit and our evil inclinations. Paul was not saying that these forces are equal. The Holy Spirit is infinitely stronger. The problem is our human weaknesses. Left to our own inclinations, we will always make wrong choices. The only way to achieve freedom from our natural evil desires is through the empowering of the Holy Spirit (see Romans 8:9; Ephesians 4:23; Colossians 3:3–8). Submit your marriage and your lives to the Spirit's guidance. Each time your relationship experiences conflict or friction, he will help you find the way back to peace and harmony. Don't let your relationship with each other depend on your own good will—seek the Holy Spirit's guidance and strength . . . together.

◄ MEDITATION �a ►

Heavenly Father, we ask that your Holy Spirit will fill our hearts and guide us in our lives and in our marriage. §►

JUNE 6

Jesus Casts Out a Legion of Demons
◄§ Luke 8:26–40 §►

So Jesus and his disciples arrived at the other side, in the Gerasene country across the lake from Galilee. [27]As he was climbing out of the boat a man from the city of Gadara came to meet him, a man who had been demon-possessed for a long time. Homeless and naked, he lived in a cemetery among the tombs. [28]As soon as he saw Jesus he shrieked and fell to the ground before him, screaming, "What do you want with me, Jesus, Son of God Most High? Please, I beg you, oh, don't torment me!"

[29]For Jesus was already commanding the demon to leave him. This demon had often taken control of the man so that even when shackled with chains he simply broke them and rushed out into the des-

ert, completely under the demon's power. [30]"What is your name?" Jesus asked the demon. "Legion," they replied—for the man was filled with thousands of them! [31]They kept begging Jesus not to order them into the Bottomless Pit.

[32]A herd of pigs was feeding on the mountainside nearby, and the demons pled with him to let them enter into the pigs. And Jesus said they could. [33]So they left the man and went into the pigs, and immediately the whole herd rushed down the mountainside and fell over a cliff into the lake below, where they drowned. [34]The herdsmen rushed away to the nearby city, spreading the news as they ran.

[35]Soon a crowd came out to see for themselves what had happened and saw the man who had been demon-possessed sitting quietly at Jesus' feet, clothed and sane! And the whole crowd was badly frightened. [36]Then those who had seen it happen told how the demon-possessed man had been healed. [37]And everyone begged Jesus to go away and leave them alone (for a deep wave of fear had swept over them). So he returned to the boat and left, crossing back to the other side of the lake.

[38]The man who had been demon-possessed begged to go too, but Jesus said no.

[39]"Go back to your family," he told him, "and tell them what a wonderful thing God has done for you."

So he went all through the city telling everyone about Jesus' mighty miracle.

[40]On the other side of the lake the crowds received him with open arms, for they had been waiting for him.

The Fruit of the Spirit
Galatians 5:22–26

But when the Holy Spirit controls our lives he will produce this kind of fruit in us: love, joy, peace, patience, kindness, goodness, faithfulness, [23]gentleness and self-control; and here there is no conflict with Jewish laws.

[24]Those who belong to Christ have nailed their natural evil desires to his cross and crucified them there.

[25]If we are living now by the Holy Spirit's power, let us follow the Holy Spirit's leading in every part of our lives. [26]Then we won't need to look for honors and popularity, which lead to jealousy and hard feelings.

Proverbs for Today
16:24

Kind words are like honey—enjoyable and healthful.

KEY VERSE

If we are living now by the Holy Spirit's power, let us follow the Holy Spirit's leading in every part of our lives.—*Galatians 5:25*

REFLECTION

God is interested in every part of your lives, not just the spiritual part. As you live by the Holy Spirit's power, you need to submit every aspect of your emotional, physical, social, intellectual, and vocational experiences and activities to the Lord—including your marriage relationship. God says, "You're saved, so live like it!" The Holy Spirit is the source of your new lives, so walk with him. Don't let anything or anyone else determine your values and standards in any area of your marriage.

MEDITATION

Heavenly Father, we offer our marriage to you and ask that you will guide us in every area of our lives together.

Jesus' Power over Sickness and Death
◄§ Luke 8:41–56 §►

And now a man named Jairus, a leader of a Jewish synagogue, came and fell down at Jesus' feet and begged him to come home with him, ⁴²for his only child was dying, a little girl twelve years old. Jesus went with him, pushing through the crowds.

⁴³,⁴⁴As they went a woman who wanted to be healed came up behind and touched him, for she had been slowly bleeding for twelve years, and could find no cure (though she had spent everything she had on doctors). But the instant she touched the edge of his robe, the bleeding stopped.

⁴⁵"Who touched me?" Jesus asked.

Everyone denied it, and Peter said, "Master, so many are crowding against you. . . ."

⁴⁶But Jesus told him, "No, it was someone who deliberately touched me, for I felt healing power go out from me."

⁴⁷When the woman realized that Jesus knew, she began to tremble and fell to her knees before him and told why she had touched him and that now she was well.

⁴⁸"Daughter," he said to her, "your faith has healed you. Go in peace."

⁴⁹While he was still speaking to her, a messenger arrived from the Jairus' home with the news that the little girl was dead. "She's gone," he told her father; "there's no use troubling the Teacher now."

⁵⁰But when Jesus heard what had happened, he said to the father, "Don't be afraid! Just trust me, and she'll be all right."

⁵¹When they arrived at the house Jesus wouldn't let anyone into the room except Peter, James, John, and the little girl's father and mother. ⁵²The home was filled with mourning people, but he said, "Stop the weeping! She isn't dead; she is only asleep!" ⁵³This brought scoffing and laughter, for they all knew she was dead.

⁵⁴Then he took her by the hand and called, "Get up, little girl!" ⁵⁵And at that moment her life returned and she jumped up! "Give her something to eat!" he said. ⁵⁶Her parents were overcome with happiness, but Jesus insisted that they not tell anyone the details of what had happened.

We Will Reap What We Sow
◄§ Galatians 6:1–10 §►

Dear brothers, if a Christian is overcome by some sin, you who are godly should gently and humbly help him back onto the right path, remembering that next time it might be one of you who is in the wrong. ²Share each other's troubles and problems, and so obey our Lord's command. ³If anyone thinks he is too great to stoop to this, he is fooling himself. He is really a nobody.

⁴Let everyone be sure that he is doing his very best, for then he will have the personal satisfaction of work well done, and won't need to compare himself with someone else. ⁵Each of us must bear some faults and burdens of his own. For none of us is perfect!

⁶Those who are taught the Word of God should help their teachers by paying them.

⁷Don't be misled; remember that you can't ignore God and get away with it: a man will always reap just the kind of crop he sows! ⁸If he sows to please his own wrong desires, he will be planting seeds of evil and he will surely reap a harvest of spiritual decay and death; but if he plants the good things of the Spirit, he will reap the everlasting life which the Holy Spirit gives him. ⁹And let us not get tired of doing what is right, for after a while we will reap a harvest of blessing if we don't get discouraged and give up. ¹⁰That's why whenever we can we should always be kind to everyone, and especially to our Christian brothers.

Proverbs for Today
◄§ 16:25 §►

Before every man there lies a wide and pleasant road he thinks is right, but it ends in death.

Don't be misled; remember that you can't ignore God and get away with it: a man will always reap just the kind of crop he sows!—*Galatians 6:7*

It would certainly be a surprise if you planted corn and pumpkins came up. But it probably would not be a surprise if you gossiped about your friends and soon found them snubbing you in the grocery store. It's a law of life—both physical and spiritual—that you reap what you sow. Every action has a matching consequence.

If you plant selfishness and greed, hoping to please your own desires, you'll reap a crop of sorrow and evil. If, however, you plant seeds of peace and love that are pleasing to God, your harvest will be joy and everlasting life. What kind of seeds are you sowing in your marriage? Plant the ones that will build a stronger, happier, more intimate marriage with each passing year.

Heavenly Father, forgive us when we sow seeds of discord. Help us to put into our relationship what we want to get out of it. ❧

JUNE 8

Jesus Sends Out the Twelve
❧ Luke 9:1–9 ❧

One day Jesus called together his twelve apostles and gave them authority over all demons—power to cast them out—and to heal all diseases. [2]Then he sent them away to tell everyone about the coming of the Kingdom of God and to heal the sick.

[3]"Don't even take along a walking stick," he instructed them, "nor a beggar's bag, nor food, nor money. Not even an extra coat. [4]Be a guest in only one home at each village.

[5]"If the people of a town won't listen to you when you enter it, turn around and leave, demonstrating God's anger against it by shaking its dust from your feet as you go."

[6]So they began their circuit of the villages, preaching the Good News and healing the sick.

[7]When reports of Jesus' miracles reached Herod, the governor, he was worried and puzzled, for some were saying, "This is John the Baptist come back to life again"; [8]and others, "It is Elijah or some other ancient prophet risen from the dead." These rumors were circulating all over the land.

[9]"I beheaded John," Herod said, "so who is this man about whom I hear such strange stories?" And he tried to see him.

Paul's Closing Words
❧ Galatians 6:11–18 ❧

I will write these closing words in my own handwriting. See how large I have to make the letters! [12]Those teachers of yours who are trying to convince you to be circumcised are doing it for just one reason: so that they can be popular and avoid the persecution they would get if they admitted that the cross of Christ alone can save. [13]And even those teachers who submit to circumcision don't try to keep the other Jewish laws; but they want you to be circumcised in order that they can boast that you are their disciples.

[14]As for me, God forbid that I should boast about anything except the cross of our Lord Jesus Christ. Because of that cross my interest in all the attractive things of the world was killed long ago, and the world's interest in me is also long dead. [15]It doesn't make any difference now whether we have been circumcised or not; what counts is whether we really have been changed into new and different people.

[16]May God's mercy and peace be upon all of you who live by this principle and upon those everywhere who are really God's own.

[17]From now on please don't argue with me about these things, for I carry on my body the scars of the whippings and wounds from Jesus' enemies that mark me as his slave.

[18]Dear brothers, may the grace of our Lord Jesus Christ be with you all.

Sincerely,
Paul

Proverbs for Today
§ 16:26–27 §

Hunger is good—if it makes you work to satisfy it! □ Idle hands are the devil's workshop; idle lips are his mouthpiece.

KEY VERSE

Idle hands are the devil's workshop; idle lips are his mouthpiece.—*Proverbs 16:27*

REFLECTION

It is amazing how much trouble people can get into when they have nothing to do. Idleness is used by the devil to lead people into wickedness. It is difficult to refuse temptations when your mind and body are inactive.

Keep busy together. Do constructive activities so your idle time doesn't become destructive. Remember that the devil's workshop is most productive when you are not.

MEDITATION

Heavenly Father, help us to be useful servants in your Kingdom. Show us where we are needed and give us the wisdom, knowledge, and confidence to follow your guidance. §

JUNE 9

The Feeding of the Five Thousand
§ Luke 9:10–17 §

After the apostles returned to Jesus and reported what they had done, he slipped quietly away with them toward the city of Bethsaida. [11]But the crowds found out where he was going, and followed. And he welcomed them, teaching them again about the Kingdom of God and curing those who were ill.

[12]Late in the afternoon all twelve of the disciples came and urged him to send the people away to the nearby villages and farms, to find food and lodging for the night. "For there is nothing to eat here in this deserted spot," they said.

[13]But Jesus replied, *"You feed them!"*

"Why, we have only five loaves of bread and two fish among the lot of us," they protested; "or are you expecting us to go and buy enough for this whole mob?" [14]For there were about 5,000 men there!

"Just tell them to sit down on the ground in groups of about fifty each," Jesus replied. [15]So they did.

[16]Jesus took the five loaves and two fish and looked up into the sky and gave thanks; then he broke off pieces for his disciples to set before the crowd. [17]And everyone ate and ate; still, twelve basketfuls of scraps were picked up afterwards!

God's Overflowing Kindness to Us
§ Ephesians 1:1–8 §

Dear Christian friends at Ephesus, ever loyal to the Lord: This is Paul writing to you, chosen by God to be Jesus Christ's messenger. [2]May his blessings and peace be yours, sent to you from God our Father and Jesus Christ our Lord.

[3]How we praise God, the Father of our Lord Jesus Christ, who has blessed us with every blessing in heaven because we belong to Christ.

[4]Long ago, even before he made the world, God chose us to be his very own, through what Christ would do for us; he decided then to make us holy

in his eyes, without a single fault—we who stand before him covered with his love. ⁵His unchanging plan has always been to adopt us into his own family by sending Jesus Christ to die for us. And he did this because he wanted to!

⁶Now all praise to God for his wonderful kindness to us and his favor that he has poured out upon us, because we belong to his dearly loved Son. ⁷So overflowing is his kindness toward us that he took away all our sins through the blood of his Son, by whom we are saved; ⁸and he has showered down upon us the richness of his grace—for how well he understands us and knows what is best for us at all times.

Proverbs for Today
⊰§ 16:28–30 §⊱

An evil man sows strife; gossip separates the best of friends. ☐ Wickedness loves company—and leads others into sin. The wicked man stares into space with pursed lips, deep in thought, planning his evil deeds.

⊰ KEY VERSE §⊱

As for me, God forbid that I should boast about anything except the cross of our Lord Jesus Christ.

Because of that cross, my interest in all the attractive things of the world was killed long ago, and the world's interest in me is also long dead.—*Galatians 6:14*

⊰ REFLECTION §⊱

The world is full of enticements. We are confronted daily not only with subtle cultural pressures, but also with overt propaganda. The only way to escape those destructive influences is to ask God to help us die to them, just as Paul did.

How much do the interests of this world matter to you in your marriage? Do you covet what others have or brag when you own something your friends and neighbors can't afford? If so, your priorities have become tainted by the lies of this world. Pray together that the Holy Spirit will fill your hearts and minds with emotions and desires that are pure and holy.

⊰ MEDITATION §⊱

Heavenly Father, forgive us when we brag about things that have no consequence in your eyes. Help us never to forget that all good things come from you, and that we probably don't need what we can't afford. §⊱

JUNE 10

Peter's Confession
⊰§ Luke 9:18–22 §⊱

One day as Jesus was alone, praying, with his disciples nearby, he came over and asked them, "Who are the people saying I am?"

¹⁹"John the Baptist," they told him, "or perhaps Elijah or one of the other ancient prophets risen from the dead."

²⁰Then he asked them, "Who do you think I am?"

Peter replied, "The Messiah—the Christ of God!"

²¹He gave them strict orders not to speak of this to anyone. ²²"For I, the Messiah, must suffer

much," he said, "and be rejected by the Jewish leaders—the elders, chief priests, and teachers of the Law—and be killed; and three days later I will come back to life again!"

God's Eternal Plan of Redemption
⊰§ Ephesians 1:9–14 §⊱

God has told us his secret reason for sending Christ, a plan he decided on in mercy long ago; ¹⁰and this was his purpose: that when the time is ripe he will gather us all together from wherever we are—in heaven or on earth—to be with him in Christ, forever. ¹¹Moreover, because of what Christ has done we have become gifts to God that he delights in, for as part of God's sovereign plan we were chosen from the beginning to be his, and all things happen just as he decided long ago. [12]God's purpose in this was that we should praise God and give glory to him for doing these mighty things for us, who were the first to trust in Christ.

[13]And because of what Christ did, all you others too, who heard the Good News about how to be saved, and trusted Christ, were marked as belonging to Christ by the Holy Spirit, who long ago had been promised to all of us Christians. [14]His presence within us is God's guarantee that he really will give us all that he promised; and the Spirit's seal upon us means that God has already purchased us and that he guarantees to bring us to himself. This is just one more reason for us to praise our glorious God.

Proverbs for Today
⋖ 16:31–33 ⋗

White hair is a crown of glory and is seen most among the godly. ☐ It is better to be slow-tempered than famous; it is better to have self-control than to control an army. ☐ We toss the coin, but it is the Lord who controls its decision.

⋗ KEY VERSE ⋖

He has showered down upon us the richness of his grace—for how well he understands us and knows what is best for us at all times.—*Ephesians 1:8*

⋗ REFLECTION ⋖

Grace is God's voluntary and loving favor given to those he saves. We can't earn it, nor do we deserve it. No religious or moral effort can gain it, for it comes only from God's mercy and love. Without grace, no person can be saved.

The greatest gift you can receive is God's offer of eternal life. Thank him for the gift of salvation every day. Regularly dedicate your marriage and your lives to serving him so that others will come to know the peace and joy of faith in Christ.

⋗ MEDITATION ⋖

Heavenly Father, we thank you for sending your Son to die on the cross so that we can be saved from our sin. Help us to share the Good News of salvation with those around us so they too can experience the freedom that comes from knowing you as Savior. ⋗

JUNE 11

Take Up Your Cross and Follow Jesus
⋖ Luke 9:23–27 ⋗

Then Jesus said to all, "Anyone who wants to follow me must put aside his own desires and conveniences and carry his cross with him every day and *keep close to me!* [24]Whoever loses his life for my sake will save it, but whoever insists on keeping his life will lose it; [25]and what profit is there in gaining the whole world when it means forfeiting one's self?

[26]"When I, the Messiah, come in my glory and in the glory of the Father and the holy angels, I will be ashamed then of all who are ashamed of me and

of my words now. [27]But this is the simple truth—some of you who are standing here right now will not die until you have seen the Kingdom of God."

Paul's Prayer for the Ephesians
⋖ Ephesians 1:15–23 ⋗

That is why, ever since I heard of your strong faith in the Lord Jesus and of the love you have for Christians everywhere, [16,17]I have never stopped thanking God for you. I pray for you constantly, asking God, the glorious Father of our Lord Jesus Christ, to give you wisdom to see clearly and really understand who Christ is and all that he has done for you. [18]I pray that your hearts will be flooded with light so that you can see something of the future he has called you to share. I want you to realize that God has been made rich because we who are Christ's have been given to him! [19]I pray that you will begin to understand how incredibly great his power is to help those who believe him. It is that same mighty power [20]that raised Christ from the dead and seated him in the place of honor at God's right hand in heaven, [21]far, far above any other king or ruler or dictator or leader. Yes, his honor is far more glorious than that of anyone else either in this world or in the world to come. [22]And God has put all things under his feet and made him the supreme Head of the Church— [23]which is his body, filled with himself, the Author and Giver of everything everywhere.

Proverbs for Today
◄§ 17:1 §►

A dry crust eaten in peace is better than steak every day along with argument and strife.

◦ KEY VERSE ◦

I pray that you will begin to understand how incredibly great his power is to help those who believe him.—*Ephesians 1:19*

◦ REFLECTION ◦

Since the advent of the nuclear age, the world has feared the power of the atom. Yet, as Christians, we belong to the God of the universe, who not only created atomic power but also raised Jesus Christ from the dead.

Do you feel inadequate in any aspect of your lives together? God's incomparable power is available to you as it is for all who believe and trust in him. God has not left you powerless.

◦ MEDITATION ◦

Heavenly Father, we pray you will intercede in each area of our lives, filling our marriage with your infinite power and love. ❧

JUNE 12

The Transfiguration of Jesus
◄§ Luke 9:28–36 §►

Eight days later Jesus took Peter, James, and John with him into the hills to pray. [29]And as he was praying, his face began to shine, and his clothes became dazzling white and blazed with light. [30]Then two men appeared and began talking with him— Moses and Elijah! [31]They were splendid in appearance, glorious to see; and they were speaking of his death at Jerusalem, to be carried out in accordance with God's plan.

[32]Peter and the others had been very drowsy and had fallen asleep. Now they woke up and saw Jesus covered with brightness and glory, and the two men standing with him. [33]As Moses and Elijah were starting to leave, Peter, all confused and not even knowing what he was saying, blurted out, "Master, this is wonderful! We'll put up three shelters—one for you and one for Moses and one for Elijah!"

[34]But even as he was saying this, a bright cloud formed above them; and terror gripped them as it covered them. [35]And a voice from the cloud said, "*This* is my Son, my Chosen One; listen to *him*."

[36]Then, as the voice died away, Jesus was there alone with his disciples. They didn't tell anyone what they had seen until long afterwards.

We Were Dead and Doomed by Our Sins
◄§ Ephesians 2:1–7 §►

Once you were under God's curse, doomed forever for your sins. [2]You went along with the crowd and were just like all the others, full of sin, obeying Satan, the mighty prince of the power of the air, who is at work right now in the hearts of those who are against the Lord. ³All of us used to be just as they are, our lives expressing the evil within us, doing every wicked thing that our passions or our evil thoughts might lead us into. We started out bad, being born with evil natures, and were under God's anger just like everyone else.

⁴But God is so rich in mercy; he loved us so much ⁵that even though we were spiritually dead and doomed by our sins, he gave us back our lives again when he raised Christ from the dead—only by his undeserved favor have we ever been saved— ⁶and lifted us up from the grave into glory along with Christ, where we sit with him in the heavenly realms—all because of what Christ Jesus did. ⁷And now God can always point to us as examples of how very, very rich his kindness is, as shown in all he has done for us through Jesus Christ.

Proverbs for Today
⤳ 17:2–3 ⤶

A wise slave will rule his master's wicked sons and share their estate. □ Silver and gold are purified by fire, but God purifies hearts.

----------- ◦ KEY VERSE ◦ -----------

And a voice from the cloud said, *"This is my Son, my Chosen One; listen to him."—Luke 9:35*

----------- ◦ REFLECTION ◦ -----------

As God's Son, Jesus has his Father's power and authority; thus he should always be trusted and believed. If a person's teaching is true, it will not contradict Jesus' words. Test everything you hear against what Scripture says Jesus said and did, and you will not be led astray.

If you and your spouse are attending a church where the pastor and other church leaders say things that contradict the Word of God, begin praying that the Holy Spirit will guide you to another church home. All Christians need weekly fellowship with other, sincere believers, so don't let friends or family members keep you from attending a church where Jesus is honored as the Son of God.

----------- ◦ MEDITATION ◦ -----------

Heavenly Father, we believe that you sent your Son, Jesus Christ, to die for our sins and the sins of the world. Help us to learn more about you each day and to strengthen our relationships with you. ⤶

JUNE 13

Jesus Heals a Demon-Possessed Boy
⤳ Luke 9:37–43a ⤶

The next day as Jesus and his disciples descended from the hill, a huge crowd met him, ³⁸and a man in the crowd called out to him, "Teacher, this boy here is my only son, ³⁹and a demon keeps seizing him, making him scream; and it throws him into convulsions so that he foams at the mouth; it is always hitting him and hardly ever leaves him alone. ⁴⁰I begged your disciples to cast the demon out, but they couldn't."

⁴¹"O you stubborn faithless people," Jesus said [to his disciples], "how long should I put up with you? Bring him here."

⁴²As the boy was coming the demon knocked him to the ground and threw him into a violent convulsion. But Jesus ordered the demon to come out, and healed the boy and handed him over to his father.

⁴³Awe gripped the people as they saw this display of the power of God.

We Have Been Saved by Grace through Faith
⤳ Ephesians 2:8–13 ⤶

Because of his kindness you have been saved through trusting Christ. And even trusting is not of yourselves; it too is a gift from God. ⁹Salvation is not a reward for the good we have done, so none of us can take any credit for it. [10]It is God himself who has made us what we are and given us new lives from Christ Jesus; and long ages ago he planned that we should spend these lives in helping others.

[11]Never forget that once you were heathen, and that you were called godless and "unclean" by the Jews. (But their hearts, too, were still unclean, even though they were going through the ceremonies and rituals of the godly, for they circumcised themselves as a sign of godliness.) [12]Remember that in those days you were living utterly apart from Christ; you were enemies of God's children and he had promised you no help. You were lost, without God, without hope.

[13]But now you belong to Christ Jesus, and though you once were far away from God, now you have been brought very near to him because of what Jesus Christ has done for you with his blood.

Proverbs for Today
⋅§ 17:4–5 ⋅

The wicked enjoy fellowship with others who are wicked; liars enjoy liars. ☐ Mocking the poor is mocking the God who made them. He will punish those who rejoice at others' misfortunes.

⋅ KEY VERSE ⋅

Now you belong to Christ Jesus, and though you once were far away from God, now you have been brought very near to him because of what Jesus Christ has done for you with his blood.—*Ephesians 2:13*

⋅ REFLECTION ⋅

Jews and Gentiles alike could be guilty of spiritual pride—Jews for thinking their ceremonies elevated them above everyone else, and Gentiles for forgetting the hopelessness of their condition apart from Christ. Spiritual pride blinds us to our own sins and magnifies the faults of others.

Be careful not to become proud of what God has done for you. Instead, humbly thank God for every good thing you are and have, and encourage others who might be struggling in their faith. Don't put distance between you and your spouse with an air of superiority.

⋅ MEDITATION ⋅

Heavenly Father, forgive us when we become arrogant about the work you have done in our lives. Help us to remain humble and not to develop self-righteous pride that can separate us from each other and from those around us. ⋅

JUNE 14

Servanthood Is the Measure of Greatness
⋅§ Luke 9:43b–50 ⋅

Meanwhile, as the people were exclaiming over all the wonderful things he was doing, Jesus said to his disciples, [44]"Listen to me and remember what I say. I, the Messiah, am going to be betrayed." [45]But the disciples didn't know what he meant, for their minds had been sealed and they were afraid to ask him.

[46]Now came an argument among them as to which of them would be greatest [in the coming Kingdom]! [47]But Jesus knew their thoughts, so he stood a little child beside him [48]and said to them,

"Anyone who takes care of a little child like this is caring for me! And whoever cares for me is caring for God who sent me. Your care for others is the measure of your greatness." [49]His disciple John came to him and said, "Master, we saw someone using your name to cast out demons. And we told him not to. After all, he isn't in our group."

[50]But Jesus said, "You shouldn't have done that! For anyone who is not against you is for you."

Christ Is the Way of Peace
⋅§ Ephesians 2:14–22 ⋅

For Christ himself is our way of peace. He has made peace between us Jews and you Gentiles by making us all one family, breaking down the wall of contempt that used to separate us. [15]By his death he ended the angry resentment between us, caused by the Jewish laws which favored the Jews and excluded the Gentiles, for he died to annul that whole system of Jewish laws. Then he took the two groups that had been opposed to each other and made them parts of himself; thus he fused us together to become one new person, and at last there was peace. [16]As parts of the same body, our anger against each other has disappeared, for both of us have been reconciled to God. And so the feud ended at last at the cross. [17]And he has brought this Good News of peace to you Gentiles who were very far away from him, and to us Jews who were near. [18]Now all of us, whether Jews or Gentiles, may come to God the Father with the Holy Spirit's help because of what Christ has done for us.

[19]Now you are no longer strangers to God and foreigners to heaven, but you are members of God's very own family, citizens of God's country, and you belong in God's household with every other Christian.

[20]What a foundation you stand on now: the apostles and the prophets; and the cornerstone of the building is Jesus Christ himself! [21]We who believe are carefully joined together with Christ as parts of a beautiful, constantly growing temple for God. [22]And you also are joined with him and with each other by the Spirit, and are part of this dwelling place of God.

Proverbs for Today
⊸§ 17:6 §⊸

An old man's grandchildren are his crowning glory. A child's glory is his father.

⊸ KEY VERSE ⊸

His disciple John came to him and said, "Master, we saw someone using your name to cast out demons. And we told him not to. After all, he isn't in our group."—*Luke 9:49*

⊸ REFLECTION ⊸

The disciples were jealous. Nine of them together had been unable to cast out a single demon (Luke 9:40), but when they saw a man who was not one of their group casting out evil spirits, they told him to stop.

Our pride is hurt when someone else succeeds where we have failed, but Jesus says there is no room for such jealousy when it comes to the spiritual warfare against his Kingdom. Share Jesus' open-arms attitude to Christian workers outside your group of friends, church, or family. The church should be united in its efforts of bringing the message of hope and love to a hurting world. Don't let personal agendas get in the way of the work God has called each of you to do.

⊸ MEDITATION ⊸

Heavenly Father, forgive us when we allow the sin of pride to separate us from you and from those around us. Help us to keep our hearts and minds focused on what is truly important—leading others into your Kingdom. ⧼⧽

JUNE 15

Would-Be Disciples
⊸§ Luke 9:51–62 §⊸

As the time drew near for his return to heaven, Jesus moved steadily onward toward Jerusalem with an iron will.

[52]One day he sent messengers ahead to reserve rooms for them in a Samaritan village. [53]But they were turned away! The people of the village refused to have anything to do with them because they were headed for Jerusalem.

[54]When word came back of what had happened, James and John said to Jesus, "Master, shall we order fire down from heaven to burn them up?" [55]But

Jesus turned and rebuked them, [56]and they went on to another village.

[57]As they were walking along someone said to Jesus, "I will always follow you no matter where you go."

[58]But Jesus replied, "Remember, I don't even own a place to lay my head. Foxes have dens to live in, and birds have nests, but I, the Messiah, have no earthly home at all."

[59]Another time, when he invited a man to come with him and to be his disciple, the man agreed—but wanted to wait until his father's death.

[60]Jesus replied, "Let those without eternal life concern themselves with things like that. Your duty is to come and preach the coming of the Kingdom of God to all the world."

[61]Another said, "Yes, Lord, I will come, but first let me ask permission of those at home."

[62]But Jesus told him, "Anyone who lets himself be distracted from the work I plan for him is not fit for the Kingdom of God."

Paul's Special Mission to Gentiles
Ephesians 3:1–7

I Paul, the servant of Christ, am here in jail because of you—for preaching that you Gentiles are a part of God's house. [2,3]No doubt you already know that God has given me this special work of showing God's favor to you Gentiles, as I briefly mentioned before in one of my letters. God himself showed me this secret plan of his, that the Gentiles, too, are included in his kindness. [4]I say this to explain to you how I know about these things. [5]In olden times God did not share this plan with his people, but now he has revealed it by the Holy Spirit to his apostles and prophets.

[6]And this is the secret: that the Gentiles will have their full share with the Jews in all the riches inherited by God's sons; both are invited to belong to his Church, and all of God's promises of mighty blessings through Christ apply to them both when they accept the Good News about Christ and what he has done for them. [7]God has given me the wonderful privilege of telling everyone about this plan of his; and he has given me his power and special ability to do it well.

Proverbs for Today
17:7–8

Truth from a rebel or lies from a king are both unexpected. ☐ A bribe works like magic. Whoever uses it will prosper!

KEY VERSE

I, Paul, the servant of Christ, am here in jail because of you—for preaching that you Gentiles are a part of God's house.—*Ephesians 3:1*

REFLECTION

Even though he was under arrest, Paul maintained his firm belief that God was in control of all that happened to him. His faith never wavered even in the worst of circumstances.

Do either of you let the annoyances of daily living convince you that God has lost control of this world? Like Paul, remember that no matter what happens, God is directing both the world's affairs and your circumstances. God understands your needs and will never forsake you, even in the darkest of situations.

MEDITATION

Heavenly Father, we thank you for never turning your back on us, even when our own actions have caused us problems and heartaches. Continue to bless our marriage and help us to live daily for you.

Jesus Sends out Seventy Disciples
◄§ Luke 10:1–24 §►

The Lord now chose seventy other disciples and sent them on ahead in pairs to all the towns and villages he planned to visit later.

[2]These were Jesus' instructions to them: "Plead with the Lord of the harvest to send out more laborers to help you, for the harvest is so plentiful and the workers so few. [3]Go now, and remember that I am sending you out as lambs among wolves. [4]Don't take any money with you, or a beggar's bag, or even an extra pair of shoes. And don't waste time along the way.

[5]"Whenever you enter a home, give it your blessing. [6]If it is worthy of the blessing, the blessing will stand; if not, the blessing will return to you.

[7]"When you enter a village, don't shift around from home to home, but stay in one place, eating and drinking without question whatever is set before you. And don't hesitate to accept hospitality, for the workman is worthy of his wages!

[8,9]"If a town welcomes you, follow these two rules:

(1) Eat whatever is set before you.
(2) Heal the sick; and as you heal them, say, 'The Kingdom of God is very near you now.'

[10]"But if a town refuses you, go out into its streets and say, [11]'We wipe the dust of your town from our feet as a public announcement of your doom. Never forget how close you were to the Kingdom of God!' [12]Even wicked Sodom will be better off than such a city on the Judgment Day. [13]What horrors await you, you cities of Chorazin and Bethsaida! For if the miracles I did for you had been done in the cities of Tyre and Sidon, their people would have sat in deep repentance long ago, clothed in sackcloth and throwing ashes on their heads to show their remorse. [14]Yes, Tyre and Sidon will receive less punishment on the Judgment Day than you. [15]And you people of Capernaum, what shall I say about you? Will you be exalted to heaven? No, you shall be brought down to hell."

[16]Then he said to the disciples, "Those who welcome you are welcoming me. And those who reject you are rejecting me. And those who reject me are rejecting God who sent me."

[17]When the seventy disciples returned, they joyfully reported to him, "Even the demons obey us when we use your name."

[18]"Yes," he told them, "I saw Satan falling from heaven as a flash of lightning! [19]And I have given you authority over all the power of the Enemy, and to walk among serpents and scorpions and to crush them. Nothing shall injure you! [20]However, the important thing is not that demons obey you, but that your names are registered as citizens of heaven."

[21]Then he was filled with the joy of the Holy Spirit and said, "I praise you, O Father, Lord of heaven and earth, for hiding these things from the intellectuals and worldly wise and for revealing them to those who are as trusting as little children. Yes, thank you, Father, for that is the way you wanted it. [22]I am the Agent of my Father in everything; and no one really knows the Son except the Father, and no one really knows the Father except the Son and those to whom the Son chooses to reveal him."

[23]Then, turning to the twelve disciples, he said quietly, "How privileged you are to see what you have seen. [24]Many a prophet and king of old has longed for these days, to see and hear what you have seen and heard!"

Jews and Gentiles Are One Family in the Church
◄§ Ephesians 3:8–13 §►

Just think! Though I did nothing to deserve it, and though I am the most useless Christian there is, yet I was the one chosen for this special joy of telling the Gentiles the Glad News of the endless treasures available to them in Christ; [9]and to explain to everyone that God is the Savior of the Gentiles too, just as he who made all things had secretly planned from the very beginning.

¹⁰And his reason? To show to all the rulers in heaven how perfectly wise he is when all of his family—Jews and Gentiles alike—are seen to be joined together in his Church, ¹¹in just the way he had always planned it through Jesus Christ our Lord.

¹²Now we can come fearlessly right into God's presence, assured of his glad welcome when we come with Christ and trust in him.

¹³So please don't lose heart at what they are doing to me here. It is for you I am suffering and you should feel honored and encouraged.

Proverbs for Today
<s> 17:9–11 &>

Love forgets mistakes; nagging about them parts the best of friends. □ A rebuke to a man of common sense is more effective than a hundred lashes on the back of a rebel. □ The wicked live for rebellion; they shall be severely punished.

❧ KEY VERSE ❧

Love forgets mistakes; nagging about them parts the best of friends.—*Proverbs 17:9*

❧ REFLECTION ❧

Forgetting mistakes is necessary to any relationship. It is tempting, especially in an argument, to bring up all the mistakes the other person has ever made. Love, however, mentions none of it—difficult though that may be. In your marriage, try never to bring anything into an argument that is unrelated to the topic being discussed. As you each grow to be like Christ, you will learn to forget the confessed mistakes of the past.

❧ MEDITATION ❧

Heavenly Father, just as you have forgiven us of past sins, help us to forget the past mistakes we have made and not to hold them against each other. &>

JUNE 17

The Story of the Good Samaritan
<s> Luke 10:25–37 &>

One day an expert on Moses' laws came to test Jesus' orthodoxy by asking him this question: "Teacher, what does a man need to do to live forever in heaven?"

²⁶Jesus replied, "What does Moses' law say about it?"

²⁷"It says," he replied, "that you must love the Lord your God with all your heart, and with all your soul, and with all your strength, and with all your mind. And you must love your neighbor just as much as you love yourself."

²⁸"Right!" Jesus told him. *"Do this and you shall live!"*

²⁹The man wanted to justify (his lack of love for some kinds of people), so he asked, "Which neighbors?"

³⁰Jesus replied with an illustration: "A Jew going on a trip from Jerusalem to Jericho was attacked by bandits. They stripped him of his clothes and money and beat him up and left him lying half dead beside the road.

³¹"By chance a Jewish priest came along; and when he saw the man lying there, he crossed to the other side of the road and passed him by. ³²A Jewish Temple-assistant walked over and looked at him lying there, but then went on.

³³"But a despised Samaritan came along, and when he saw him, he felt deep pity. ³⁴Kneeling beside him the Samaritan soothed his wounds with medicine and bandaged them. Then he put the man on his donkey and walked along beside him till they came to an inn, where he nursed him through the night. ³⁵The next day he handed the innkeeper two twenty-dollar bills and told him to take care of the man. 'If his bill runs higher than that,' he said, 'I'll pay the difference the next time I am here.'

³⁶"Now which of these three would you say was a neighbor to the bandits' victim?"

³⁷The man replied, "The one who showed him some pity."

Then Jesus said, "Yes, now go and do the same."

Paul Prays for the Ephesians
⋖§ Ephesians 3:14–21 §⋗

When I think of the wisdom and scope of his plan I fall down on my knees and pray to the Father of all the great family of God—some of them already in heaven and some down here on earth— ¹⁶that out of his glorious, unlimited resources he will give you the mighty inner strengthening of his Holy Spirit. ¹⁷And I pray that Christ will be more and more at home in your hearts, living within you as you trust in him. May your roots go down deep into the soil of God's marvelous love; ¹⁸,¹⁹and may you be able to feel and understand, as all God's children should, how long, how wide, how deep, and how high his love really is; and to experience this love for yourselves, though it is so great that you will never see the end of it or fully know or understand it. And so at last you will be filled up with God himself.

²⁰Now glory be to God who by his mighty power at work within us is able to do far more than we would ever dare to ask or even dream of—infinitely beyond our highest prayers, desires, thoughts, or hopes. ²¹May he be given glory forever and ever through endless ages because of his master plan of salvation for the Church through Jesus Christ.

Proverbs for Today
⋖§ 17:12–13 §⋗

It is safer to meet a bear robbed of her cubs than a fool caught in his folly. ☐ If you repay evil for good, a curse is upon your home.

─────── ⋗ KEY VERSE ⋖ ───────

When I think of the wisdom and scope of his plan, I fall down on my knees and pray to the Father of all the great family of God—some of them already in heaven and some down here on earth.—*Ephesians 3:14–15*

─────── ⋗ REFLECTION ⋖ ───────

The great family of God includes all who have believed in him in the past, all who believe in the present, and all who will believe in the future. We are all a family because we have the same Father. He is the source of all creation, the rightful owner of everything. God promises his love and power to his family, the church (Ephesians 3:16–21). If you want to receive God's blessings in your marriage, stay in contact with other believers in the body of Christ.

─────── ⋗ MEDITATION ⋖ ───────

Heavenly Father, we thank you that we are part of your eternal family. We pray that you will bring other Christian couples into our lives so that we can encourage and minister to each other. §⋗

JUNE 18

Mary and Martha
⋖§ Luke 10:38–42 §⋗

As Jesus and the disciples continued on their way to Jerusalem they came to a village where a woman named Martha welcomed them into her home. ³⁹Her sister Mary sat on the floor, listening to Jesus as he talked.

⁴⁰But Martha was the jittery type, and was worrying over the big dinner she was preparing.

She came to Jesus and said, "Sir, doesn't it seem unfair to you that my sister just sits here while I do all the work? Tell her to come and help me."

⁴¹But the Lord said to her, "Martha, dear friend, you are so upset over all these details! ⁴²There is really only one thing worth being concerned about.

Mary has discovered it—and I won't take it away from her!''

We Are One Body in Christ
<del>	</del>⥊ Ephesians 4:1–10 ⠾

I beg you—I, a prisoner here in jail for serving the Lord—to live and act in a way worthy of those who have been chosen for such wonderful blessings as these. ²Be humble and gentle. Be patient with each other, making allowance for each other's faults because of your love. ³Try always to be led along together by the Holy Spirit, and so be at peace with one another.

⁴We are all parts of one body, we have the same Spirit, and we have all been called to the same glorious future. ⁵For us there is only one Lord, one faith, one baptism, ⁶and we all have the same God and Father who is over us all and in us all, and living through every part of us. ⁷However, Christ has given each of us special abilities—whatever he wants us to have out of his rich storehouse of gifts.

⁸The Psalmist tells about this, for he says that when Christ returned triumphantly to heaven after his resurrection and victory over Satan, he gave generous gifts to men. ⁹Notice that it says he returned to heaven. This means that he had first come down from the heights of heaven, far down to the lowest parts of the earth. ¹⁰The same one who came down is the one who went back up, that he might fill all things everywhere with himself, from the very lowest to the very highest.

Proverbs for Today
⥊ 17:14–15 ⠾

It is hard to stop a quarrel once it starts, so don't let it begin. □ The Lord despises those who say that bad is good, and good is bad.

KEY VERSE

Be humble and gentle. Be patient with each other, making allowance for each other's faults because of your love.—*Ephesians 4:2*

REFLECTION

No one is ever going to be perfect here on earth, so we should accept and love others in spite of their failings. When either of you sees faults in others, be patient and gentle. Is there another couple whose actions or personalities really annoy you? Rather than dwelling on their weaknesses or looking for faults, pray for them. Then do even more—spend time with them and see if you can encourage them, whether in their walk with the Lord or in their journey toward him.

MEDITATION

Heavenly Father, forgive us when we become annoyed with other couples. Help us to be a blessing to them and to see past their apparent faults so we can encourage and help them. ⠾

JUNE 19

Jesus Instructs His Followers about Prayer
⥊ Luke 11:1–13 ⠾

Once when Jesus had been out praying, one of his disciples came to him as he finished and said, ''Lord, teach us a prayer to recite just as John taught one to his disciples.''

²And this is the prayer he taught them: ''Father, may your name be honored for its holiness; send your Kingdom soon. ³Give us our food day by day. ⁴And forgive our sins—for we have forgiven those who sinned against us. And don't allow us to be tempted.''

⁵,⁶Then, teaching them more about prayer, he used this illustration: ''Suppose you went to a friend's house at midnight, wanting to borrow three loaves of bread. You would shout up to him,

<del>	</del><del>	</del>
<del>	</del>⥊ 220 ⠾

'A friend of mine has just arrived for a visit and I've nothing to give him to eat.' [7]He would call down from his bedroom, 'Please don't ask me to get up. The door is locked for the night and we are all in bed. I just can't help you this time.'

[8]"But I'll tell you this—though he won't do it as a friend, if you keep knocking long enough he will get up and give you everything you want—just because of your persistence. [9]And so it is with prayer—keep on asking and you will keep on getting; keep on looking and you will keep on finding; knock and the door will be opened. [10]Everyone who asks, receives; all who seek, find; and the door is opened to everyone who knocks.

[11]"You men who are fathers—if your boy asks for bread, do you give him a stone? If he asks for fish, do you give him a snake? [12]If he asks for an egg, do you give him a scorpion? [Of course not!]

[13]"And if even sinful persons like yourselves give children what they need, don't you realize that your heavenly Father will do at least as much, and give the Holy Spirit to those who ask for him?"

God Has Gifted the Church
❧ Ephesians 4:11–16 ❧

Some of us have been given special ability as apostles; to others he has given the gift of being able to preach well; some have special ability in winning people to Christ, helping them to trust him as their Savior; still others have a gift for caring for God's people as a shepherd does his sheep, leading and teaching them in the ways of God.

[12]Why is it that he gives us these special abilities to do certain things best? It is that God's people will be equipped to do better work for him, building up the Church, the body of Christ, to a position of strength and maturity; [13]until finally we all believe alike about our salvation and about our Savior, God's Son, and all become full-grown in the Lord—yes, to the point of being filled full with Christ.

[14]Then we will no longer be like children, forever changing our minds about what we believe because someone has told us something different, or has cleverly lied to us and made the lie sound like the truth. [15,16]Instead, we will lovingly follow the truth at all times—speaking truly, dealing truly, living truly —and so become more and more in every way like Christ who is the Head of his body, the Church. Under his direction the whole body is fitted together perfectly, and each part in its own special way helps the other parts, so that the whole body is healthy and growing and full of love.

Proverbs for Today
❧ 17:16 ❧

It is senseless to pay tuition to educate a rebel who has no heart for truth.

❧ KEY VERSE ❧

"And so it is with prayer—keep on asking and you will keep on getting; keep on looking and you will keep on finding; knock and the door will be opened."—*Luke 11:9*

❧ REFLECTION ❧

When Jesus began to teach his disciples about prayer, he gave them a pattern to follow—a model prayer, in other words. Notice the order in this prayer. First Jesus praises God; then he makes his requests. Praising God first puts us in the right frame of mind to tell him about our needs. Too often our prayers are more like shopping lists than conversations.

Jesus also made forgiving others a central part of our relationship with God. God has forgiven our sins therefore we must forgive those who have wronged us. To remain unforgiving shows that we have not understood how we ourselves, along with all other human beings, need to be forgiven.

Think of someone who has said or done something that made either or both of you angry. Have you truly forgiven that person, or do you still carry a grudge? Your communion with God in prayer is directly affected by your relationships. Pray for the offending person, forgive him or her, and try to reestablish the friendship.

❧ MEDITATION ❧

Heavenly Father, we offer to you the prayer you taught your disciples (recite the Lord's Prayer together). ❧

JUNE 20

The Kingdom of God and the Kingdom of Satan
❧ Luke 11:14–28 ❧

Once, when Jesus cast out a demon from a man who couldn't speak, his voice returned to him. The crowd was excited and enthusiastic, [15]but some said, "No wonder he can cast them out. He gets his power from Satan, the king of demons!" [16]Others asked for something to happen in the sky to prove his claim of being the Messiah.

[17]He knew the thoughts of each of them, so he said, "Any kingdom filled with civil war is doomed; so is a home filled with argument and strife. [18]Therefore, if what you say is true, that Satan is fighting against himself by empowering me to cast out his demons, how can his kingdom survive? [19]And if I am empowered by Satan, what about your own followers? For they cast out demons! Do you think this proves they are possessed by Satan? Ask *them* if you are right! [20]But if I am casting out demons because of power from God, it proves that the Kingdom of God has arrived.

[21]"For when Satan, strong and fully armed, guards his palace, it is safe— [22]until someone stronger and better-armed attacks and overcomes him and strips him of his weapons and carries off his belongings.

[23]"Anyone who is not for me is against me; if he isn't helping me, he is hurting my cause.

[24]"When a demon is cast out of a man, it goes to the deserts, searching there for rest; but finding none, it returns to the person it left, [25]and finds that its former home is all swept and clean. [26]Then it goes and gets seven other demons more evil than itself, and they all enter the man. And so the poor fellow is seven times worse off than he was before."

[27]As he was speaking, a woman in the crowd called out, "God bless your mother—the womb from which you came, and the breasts that gave you suck!"

[28]He replied, "Yes, but even more blessed are all who hear the Word of God and put it into practice."

Throw Off the Old and Clothe Yourself with the New
❧ Ephesians 4:17–24 ❧

Let me say this, then, speaking for the Lord: Live no longer as the unsaved do, for they are blinded and confused. Their closed hearts are full of darkness; they are far away from the life of God because they have shut their minds against him, and they cannot understand his ways. [19]They don't care anymore about right and wrong and have given themselves over to impure ways. They stop at nothing, being driven by their evil minds and reckless lusts.

[20]But that isn't the way Christ taught you! [21]If you have really heard his voice and learned from him the truths concerning himself, [22]then throw off your old evil nature—the old you that was a partner in your evil ways—rotten through and through, full of lust and sham.

[23]Now your attitudes and thoughts must all be constantly changing for the better. [24]Yes, you must be a new and different person, holy and good. Clothe yourself with this new nature.

Proverbs for Today
❧ 17:17–18 ❧

A true friend is always loyal, and a brother is born to help in time of need. □ It is poor judgment to countersign another's note, to become responsible for his debts.

❧ KEY VERSE ❧

As he was speaking, a woman in the crowd called out, "God bless your mother—the womb from which you came, and the breasts that gave you suck!" He replied, "Yes, but even more blessed are all who hear the Word of God and put it into practice."—*Luke 11:27-28*

❧ REFLECTION ❧

Jesus was speaking to people who were placing extremely high value on family relationships. Their genealogies were important guarantees that they were part of God's chosen people. A man's value came from his ancestors, and a woman's value came from the sons she bore. Jesus' response to the woman meant that a person's individual decisions are more important than his or her place on the family tree, not that his mother, Mary, wasn't important. Consistent with Luke's emphasis on Jesus' ministry to women, Jesus' response also showed that a woman is important for more than her repro-

ductive ability. Remember, while it is important to honor and love your biological mothers, whether they are living or have passed away, it is also vital to listen to and care for the godly men and women in your spiritual family, the church.

⚘ MEDITATION ⚘

Heavenly Father, thank you for our spiritual elders. Let us be a blessing to them, just as they have encouraged and nurtured our Christian faith and our marriage. ❧

JUNE 21

The Sign of Jonah
❦ Luke 11:29–36 ❧

As the crowd pressed in upon Jesus, he preached them this sermon: "These are evil times, with evil people. They keep asking for some strange happening in the skies [to prove I am the Messiah], but the only proof I will give them is a miracle like that of Jonah, whose experiences proved to the people of Nineveh that God had sent him. My similar experience will prove that God has sent me to these people.

31"And at the Judgment Day the Queen of Sheba shall arise and point her finger at this generation, condemning it, for she went on a long, hard journey to listen to the wisdom of Solomon; but one far greater than Solomon is here [and few pay any attention].

32"The men of Nineveh, too, shall arise and condemn this nation, for they repented at the preaching of Jonah; and someone far greater than Jonah is here [but this nation won't listen].

33"No one lights a lamp and hides it! Instead, he puts it on a lampstand to give light to all who enter the room. 34Your eyes light up your inward being. A pure eye lets sunshine into your soul. A lustful eye shuts out the light and plunges you into darkness. 35So watch out that the sunshine isn't blotted out. 36If you are filled with light within, with no dark corners, then your face will be radiant too, as though a floodlight is beamed upon you."

Paul's Commands for Christian Living
❦ Ephesians 4:25–32 ❧

Stop lying to each other; tell the truth, for we are parts of each other and when we lie to each other we are hurting ourselves. 26If you are angry, don't sin by nursing your grudge. Don't let the sun go down with you still angry—get over it quickly; 27for when you are angry you give a mighty foothold to the devil.

28If anyone is stealing he must stop it and begin using those hands of his for honest work so he can give to others in need. 29Don't use bad language. Say only what is good and helpful to those you are talking to, and what will give them a blessing.

30Don't cause the Holy Spirit sorrow by the way you live. Remember, he is the one who marks you to be present on that day when salvation from sin will be complete.

31Stop being mean, bad-tempered and angry. Quarreling, harsh words, and dislike of others should have no place in your lives. 32Instead, be kind to each other, tenderhearted, forgiving one another, just as God has forgiven you because you belong to Christ.

Proverbs for Today
❦ 17:19–21 ❧

Sinners love to fight; boasting is looking for trouble. □ An evil man is suspicious of everyone and tumbles into constant trouble. ☐ It's no fun to be a rebel's father.

"Your eyes light up your inward being. A pure eye lets sunshine into your soul. A lustful eye shuts out the light and plunges you into darkness."—*Luke 11:34*

————— ⚬ **REFLECTION** ⚬ —————

Lust is the unnatural or greedy desire for anything, not just sex. The world makes it very easy to become trapped by this deadly sin. Advertisers, the media, and the film industry all capitalize on humanity's sinful inclination to covet the things of the flesh. The only hope of escape is the light of Christ. Faith in him will make your eyes more sensitive to sin as the light of his presence radiates through your lives. If either of you finds it difficult to see the Lord in your marriage, check your vision. It may be that sinful desires are blinding you to Christ.

————— ⚬ **MEDITATION** ⚬ —————

Heavenly Father, we ask that you will shine your holy light on our marriage so that we can see the things that are displeasing to you. Help us to reflect your radiance to others so that they will not become mired in the deadly sins of this world. ⚬

JUNE 22

Jesus Denounces the Pharisees
⚬ Luke 11:37–54 ⚬

As Jesus was speaking, one of the Pharisees asked him home for a meal. When Jesus arrived, he sat down to eat without first performing the ceremonial washing required by Jewish custom. This greatly surprised his host.

[39] Then Jesus said to him, "You Pharisees wash the outside, but inside you are still dirty—full of greed and wickedness! [40] Fools! Didn't God make the inside as well as the outside? [41] Purity is best demonstrated by generosity.

[42] "But woe to you Pharisees! For though you are careful to tithe even the smallest part of your income, you completely forget about justice and the love of God. You should tithe, yes, but you should not leave these other things undone.

[43] "Woe to you Pharisees! For how you love the seats of honor in the synagogues and the respectful greetings from everyone as you walk through the markets! [44] Yes, awesome judgment is awaiting you. For you are like hidden graves in a field. Men go by you with no knowledge of the corruption they are passing."

[45] "Sir," said an expert in religious law who was standing there, "you have insulted my profession, too, in what you just said."

[46] "Yes," said Jesus, "the same horrors await you! For you crush men beneath impossible religious demands—demands that you yourselves would never think of trying to keep. [47] Woe to you! For you are exactly like your ancestors who killed the prophets long ago. [48] Murderers! You agree with your fathers that what they did was right—you would have done the same yourselves.

[49] "This is what God says about you: 'I will send prophets and apostles to you, and you will kill some of them and chase away the others.'

[50] "And you of this generation will be held responsible for the murder of God's servants from the founding of the world— [51] from the murder of Abel to the murder of Zechariah who perished between the altar and the sanctuary. Yes, it will surely be charged against you.

[52] "Woe to you experts in religion! For you hide the truth from the people. You won't accept it for yourselves, and you prevent others from having a chance to believe it."

[53,54] The Pharisees and legal experts were furious; and from that time on they plied him fiercely with a host of questions, trying to trap him into

saying something for which they could have him arrested.

Follow Christ's Example of Self-Sacrifice
e§ Ephesians 5:1–9 §e

Follow God's example in everything you do just as a much loved child imitates his father. ²Be full of love for others, following the example of Christ who loved you and gave himself to God as a sacrifice to take away your sins. And God was pleased, for Christ's love for you was like sweet perfume to him.

³Let there be no sex sin, impurity or greed among you. Let no one be able to accuse you of any such things. ⁴Dirty stories, foul talk and coarse jokes—these are not for you. Instead, remind each other of God's goodness and be thankful.

⁵You can be sure of this: The Kingdom of Christ and of God will never belong to anyone who is impure or greedy, for a greedy person is really an idol worshiper—he loves and worships the good things of this life more than God. ⁶Don't be fooled by those who try to excuse these sins, for the terrible wrath of God is upon all those who do them. ⁷Don't even associate with such people. ⁸For though once your heart was full of darkness, now it is full of light from the Lord, and your behavior should show it! ⁹Because of this light within you, you should do only what is good and right and true.

Proverbs for Today

A cheerful heart does good like medicine, but a broken spirit makes one sick.

◈ KEY VERSE ◈

Follow God's example in everything you do just as a much-loved child imitates his father.—*Ephesians 5:1*

◈ REFLECTION ◈

Children love to imitate their parents. That's why mothers and fathers have to be careful what they say or do, since it will effect the words and actions of their offspring.

Just as children imitate their parents, we should imitate Christ. His great love for us led him to make the ultimate sacrifice so that we might have eternal life. The love you show for others should be of the same kind—a love that goes beyond affection to self-sacrificing service that guards against doing things that will hinder your Christian witness.

◈ MEDITATION ◈

Heavenly Father, help us to be loving servants to those around us. We pray that others will see your love through our words and actions. §e

JUNE 23

Jesus Gives Warnings
e§ Luke 12:1–12 §e

Meanwhile the crowds grew until thousands upon thousands were milling about and crushing each other. Jesus turned now to his disciples and warned them, "More than anything else, beware of these Pharisees and the way they pretend to be good when they aren't. But such hypocrisy cannot be hidden forever. ²It will become as evident as yeast in dough. ³Whatever they have said in the dark shall be heard in the light, and what you have whispered in the inner rooms shall be broadcast from the housetops for all to hear!

⁴"Dear friends, don't be afraid of these who want to murder you. They can only kill the body; they have no power over your souls. ⁵But I'll tell you whom to fear—fear God who has the power to kill and then cast into hell.

⁶"What is the price of five sparrows? A couple of pennies? Not much more than that. Yet God does not forget a single one of them. ⁷And he knows the number of hairs on your head! Never fear, you are

far more valuable to him than a whole flock of sparrows.

⁸"And I assure you of this: I, the Messiah, will publicly honor you in the presence of God's angels if you publicly acknowledge me here on earth as your Friend. ⁹But I will deny before the angels those who deny me here among men. ¹⁰(Yet those who speak against me may be forgiven—while those who speak against the Holy Spirit shall never be forgiven.)

¹¹"And when you are brought to trial before these Jewish rulers and authorities in the synagogues, don't be concerned about what to say in your defense, ¹²for the Holy Spirit will give you the right words even as you are standing there."

Do Things That Please God
⋖§ Ephesians 5:10–20 ᗒᎧ

Learn as you go along what pleases the Lord. ¹¹Take no part in the worthless pleasures of evil and darkness, but instead, rebuke and expose them. ¹²It would be shameful even to mention here those pleasures of darkness which the ungodly do. ¹³But when you expose them, the light shines in upon their sin and shows it up, and when they see how wrong they really are, some of them may even become children of light! ¹⁴That is why God says in the Scriptures, "Awake, O sleeper, and rise up from the dead; and Christ shall give you light."

¹⁵,¹⁶So be careful how you act; these are difficult days. Don't be fools; be wise: make the most of every opportunity you have for doing good. ¹⁷Don't act thoughtlessly, but try to find out and do whatever the Lord wants you to. ¹⁸Don't drink too much wine, for many evils lie along that path; be filled instead with the Holy Spirit, and controlled by him.

¹⁹Talk with each other much about the Lord, quoting psalms and hymns and singing sacred songs, making music in your hearts to the Lord. ²⁰Always give thanks for everything to our God and Father in the name of our Lord Jesus Christ.

Proverbs for Today
⋖§ 17:23 ᗒᎧ

It is wrong to accept a bribe to twist justice.

———————ᗒ KEY VERSE ᗒ———————

Always give thanks for everything to our God and Father in the name of our Lord Jesus Christ.—*Ephesians 5:20*

——————ᗒ REFLECTION ᗒ——————

Whenever either of you feels down, you may *both* find it difficult to give thanks to the Lord for what he has done for you. But don't become discouraged. God can bring good out of any circumstance if we love him and are committed to working for his Kingdom (Romans 8:28). Thank God not for your problems, but for the strength that he is building in your marriage through the difficult experiences you endure together. You can be sure that God's perfect love will see you through.

——————ᗒ MEDITATION ᗒ——————

Heavenly Father, we praise you for being greater than the circumstances in our lives—both the good things, that bless us daily, and the difficulties that help us build patience and endurance. ᗒᎧ

JUNE 24 _____

Jesus Teaches in Parables
⋖§ Luke 12:13–34 ᗒᎧ

Then someone called from the crowd, "Sir, please tell my brother to divide my father's estate with me."

¹⁴But Jesus replied, "Man, who made me a judge over you to decide such things as that? ¹⁵Beware! Don't always be wishing for what you don't have. For real life and real living are not related to how rich we are."

¹⁶Then he gave an illustration: "A rich man had a fertile farm that produced fine crops. ¹⁷In fact, his barns were full to overflowing—he couldn't get

everything in. He thought about his problem, [18]and finally exclaimed, 'I know—I'll tear down my barns and build bigger ones! Then I'll have room enough. [19]And I'll sit back and say to myself, "Friend, you have enough stored away for years to come. Now take it easy! Wine, women, and song for you!"'

[20]"But God said to him, 'Fool! Tonight you die. Then who will get it all?'

[21]"Yes, every man is a fool who gets rich on earth but not in heaven."

[22]Then turning to his disciples he said, "Don't worry about whether you have enough food to eat or clothes to wear. [23]For life consists of far more than food and clothes. [24]Look at the ravens—they don't plant or harvest or have barns to store away their food, and yet they get along all right—for God feeds them. And you are far more valuable to him than any birds!

[25]"And besides, what's the use of worrying? What good does it do? Will it add a single day to your life? Of course not! [26]And if worry can't even do such little things as that, what's the use of worrying over bigger things?

[27]"Look at the lilies! They don't toil and spin, and yet Solomon in all his glory was not robed as well as they are. [28]And if God provides clothing for the flowers that are here today and gone tomorrow, don't you suppose that he will provide clothing for you, you doubters? [29]And don't worry about food—what to eat and drink; don't worry at all that God will provide it for you. [30]All mankind scratches for its daily bread, but your heavenly Father knows your needs. [31]He will always give you all you need from day to day if you will make the Kingdom of God your primary concern.

[32]"So don't be afraid, little flock. For it gives your Father great happiness to give you the Kingdom. [33]Sell what you have and give to those in need. This will fatten your purses in heaven! And the purses of heaven have no rips or holes in them. Your treasures there will never disappear; no thief can steal them; no moth can destroy them. [34]Wherever your treasure is, there your heart and thoughts will also be.

Submit to One Another
⋅§ Ephesians 5:21–33 ࠂ⋅

Honor Christ by submitting to each other. [22]You wives must submit to your husbands' leadership in the same way you submit to the Lord. [23]For a husband is in charge of his wife in the same way Christ is in charge of his body the Church. (He gave his very life to take care of it and be its Savior!) [24]So you wives must willingly obey your husbands in everything, just as the Church obeys Christ.

[25]And you husbands, show the same kind of love to your wives as Christ showed to the Church when he died for her, [26]to make her holy and clean, washed by baptism and God's Word; [27]so that he could give her to himself as a glorious Church without a single spot or wrinkle or any other blemish, being holy and without a single fault. [28]That is how husbands should treat their wives, loving them as parts of themselves. For since a man and his wife are now one, a man is really doing himself a favor and loving himself when he loves his wife! [29,30]No one hates his own body but lovingly cares for it, just as Christ cares for his body the Church, of which we are parts.

[31](That the husband and wife are one body is proved by the Scripture which says, "A man must leave his father and mother when he marries, so that he can be perfectly joined to his wife, and the two shall be one.") [32]I know this is hard to understand, but it is an illustration of the way we are parts of the body of Christ.

[33]So again I say, a man must love his wife as a part of himself; and the wife must see to it that she deeply respects her husband—obeying, praising and honoring him.

Proverbs for Today
⋅§ 17:24–25 ࠂ⋅

Wisdom is the main pursuit of sensible men, but a fool's goals are at the ends of the earth! □ A rebellious son is a grief to his father and a bitter blow to his mother.

──────── ๏ KEY VERSE ๏ ────────

Honor Christ by submitting to each other.—*Ephesians 5:21*

Submission is an often misused word. It does not mean becoming a doormat. Christ—at whose name "every knee shall bow in heaven and on earth and under the earth" (Philippians 2:10)—submitted his will to the Father for the salvation of the world. We honor Christ by following his example. When we submit to God, we become more willing to obey his command to submit to others—that is, to subordinate our rights to theirs.

In a marriage relationship, both husband and wife are called to submission. For the wife, this means willingly following her husband's leadership in Christ. For the husband, it means putting aside his own interests in order to care for his wife. Submission is rarely a problem in homes where both husband and wife have a strong relationship with Christ and where each is concerned for the happiness of the other. Honor Christ in your home by submitting to each other.

──────── ❧ MEDITATION ❧ ────────

Heavenly Father, we submit our lives to you just as we submit our love to each other. Help us never to take our marriage vows lightly and always to consider the other person first. ❧

JUNE 25

Be Prepared for the Lord's Return
❧ Luke 12:35–48 ❧

"Be prepared—all dressed and ready— ³⁶for your Lord's return from the wedding feast. Then you will be ready to open the door and let him in the moment he arrives and knocks. ³⁷There will be great joy for those who are ready and waiting for his return. He himself will seat them and put on a waiter's uniform and serve them as they sit and eat! ³⁸He may come at nine o'clock at night—or even at midnight. But whenever he comes there will be joy for his servants who are ready!

³⁹"Everyone would be ready for him if they knew the exact hour of his return—just as they would be ready for a thief if they knew when he was coming. ⁴⁰So be ready all the time. For I, the Messiah, will come when least expected."

⁴¹Peter asked, "Lord, are you talking just to us or to everyone?"

⁴²,⁴³,⁴⁴And the Lord replied, "I'm talking to any faithful, sensible man whose master gives him the responsibility of feeding the other servants. If his master returns and finds that he has done a good job, there will be a reward—his master will put him in charge of all he owns.

⁴⁵"But if the man begins to think, 'My Lord won't be back for a long time,' and begins to whip the men and women he is supposed to protect, and to spend his time at drinking parties and in drunkenness— ⁴⁶well, his master will return without notice and remove him from his position of trust and assign him to the place of the unfaithful. ⁴⁷He will be severely punished, for though he knew his duty he refused to do it.

⁴⁸"But anyone who is not aware that he is doing wrong will be punished only lightly. Much is required from those to whom much is given, for their responsibility is greater.

Instructions to Parents and Children
❧ Ephesians 6:1–4 ❧

Children, obey your parents; this is the right thing to do because God has placed them in authority over you. ²Honor your father and mother. This is the first of God's Ten Commandments that ends with a promise. ³And this is the promise: that if you honor your father and mother, yours will be a long life, full of blessing.

⁴And now a word to you parents. Don't keep on scolding and nagging your children, making them angry and resentful. Rather, bring them up with the loving discipline the Lord himself approves, with suggestions and godly advice.

Proverbs for Today

How short-sighted to fine the godly for being good! And to punish nobles for being honest!

·ᴥ KEY VERSE ᴥ·

Children, obey your parents; this is the right thing to do because God has placed them in authority over you.—*Ephesians 6:1*

·ᴥ REFLECTION ᴥ·

If our faith in Christ is real, it will usually prove itself at home, in our relationships with those who know us best. Children and parents have a responsibility to each other. Children should honor their parents even if the parents are demanding and un-fair. Parents should gently care for their children, even if the children are disobedient and unpleasant.

Ideally, of course, Christian parents and Christian children will relate to each other with thoughtfulness and love. This will happen if they put the others' interests above their own. If God has blessed your marriage with children, remember that their lives are in your hands, especially during their formative years. Their happiness and well-being is your responsibility, and their needs should always come first.

·ᴥ MEDITATION ᴥ·

Heavenly Father, we pray for the children of the world, knowing that you consider their lives precious. We thank you for Christian families in which young people are brought up to love and serve you and to carry on the work of your Kingdom. &

JUNE 26

Jesus Came to Bring Division
&る Luke 12:49–59 &

"I have come to bring fire to the earth, and, oh, that my task were completed! [50]There is a terrible baptism ahead of me, and how I am pent up until it is accomplished!

[51]"Do you think I have come to give peace to the earth? *No!* Rather, strife and division! [52]From now on families will be split apart, three in favor of me, and two against—or perhaps the other way around. [53]A father will decide one way about me; his son, the other; mother and daughter will disagree; and the decision of an honored mother-in-law will be spurned by her daughter-in-law."

[54]Then he turned to the crowd and said, "When you see clouds beginning to form in the west, you say, 'Here comes a shower.' And you are right.

[55]"When the south wind blows you say, 'Today will be a scorcher.' And it is. [56]Hypocrites! You interpret the sky well enough, but you refuse to notice the warnings all around you about the crisis ahead. [57]Why do you refuse to see for yourselves what is right?

[58]"If you meet your accuser on the way to court, try to settle the matter before it reaches the judge, lest he sentence you to jail; [59]for if that happens you won't be free again until the last penny is paid in full."

Instructions to Slaves and Masters
&る Ephesians 6:5–9 &

Slaves, obey your masters; be eager to give them your very best. Serve them as you would Christ. [6,7]Don't work hard only when your master is watching and then shirk when he isn't looking; work hard and with gladness all the time, as though working for Christ, doing the will of God with all your hearts. [8]Remember, the Lord will pay you for each good thing you do, whether you are slave or free.

[9]And you slave owners must treat your slaves right, just as I have told them to treat you. Don't keep threatening them; remember, you yourselves

are slaves to Christ; you have the same Master they do, and he has no favorites.

Proverbs for Today

The man of few words and settled mind is wise; therefore, even a fool is thought to be wise when he is silent. It pays him to keep his mouth shut.

✦ KEY VERSE ✦

"From now on families will be split apart, three in favor of me, and two against—or perhaps the other way around."—*Luke 12:52*

✦ REFLECTION ✦

In these strange and unsettling words, Jesus revealed that following him often results in conflict. He demands a response, and close groups can be torn apart when some choose to follow him and others refuse to do so. There is no middle ground with Jesus. Loyalties must be declared and commitments made, sometimes to the severing of other relationships. Life is easiest when a family is united in its belief in Christ, but this often does not happen. While it may be the most difficult decision either of you will have to make, as believers you must be willing to risk losing your family's approval if you want to follow Jesus Christ.

✦ MEDITATION ✦

Heavenly Father, we pray that you will touch the hearts of those in our families who don't know you as their Savior. Give us the opportunity to show them how your love has changed our lives, and how you can change theirs too.

JUNE 27

Jesus Calls the People to Repent
Luke 13:1-9

About this time Jesus was informed that Pilate had butchered some Jews from Galilee as they were sacrificing at the Temple in Jerusalem.

[2]"Do you think they were worse sinners than other men from Galilee?" he asked. "Is that why they suffered? [3]Not at all! And don't you realize that you also will perish unless you leave your evil ways and turn to God?

[4]"And what about the eighteen men who died when the Tower of Siloam fell on them? Were they the worst sinners in Jerusalem? [5]Not at all! And you, too, will perish unless you repent."

[6]Then he used this illustration: "A man planted a fig tree in his garden and came again and again to see if he could find any fruit on it, but he was always disappointed. [7]Finally he told his gardener to cut it down. 'I've waited three years and there hasn't been a single fig!' he said. 'Why bother with it any longer? It's taking up space we can use for something else.'

[8]"'Give it one more chance,' the gardener answered. 'Leave it another year, and I'll give it special attention and plenty of fertilizer. [9]If we get figs next year, fine; if not, I'll cut it down.'"

The Whole Armor of God
Ephesians 6:10-17

Last of all I want to remind you that your strength must come from the Lord's mighty power within you. [11]Put on all of God's armor so that you will be able to stand safe against all strategies and tricks of Satan. [12]For we are not fighting against people made of flesh and blood, but against persons without bodies—the evil rulers of the unseen world, those mighty satanic beings and great evil princes of darkness who rule this world; and against huge numbers of wicked spirits in the spirit world.

[13]So use every piece of God's armor to resist the enemy whenever he attacks, and when it is all over, you will still be standing up.

[14]But to do this, you will need the strong belt of

truth and the breastplate of God's approval. [15]Wear shoes that are able to speed you on as you preach the Good News of peace with God. [16]In every battle you will need faith as your shield to stop the fiery arrows aimed at you by Satan. [17]And you will need the helmet of salvation and the sword of the Spirit—which is the Word of God.

Proverbs for Today
⊸§ 18:1 §⊶

The selfish man quarrels against every sound principle of conduct by demanding his own way.

_____⊸ KEY VERSE §⊶_____

The selfish man quarrels against every sound principle of conduct by demanding his own way.—*Proverbs 18:1*

_____⊸ REFLECTION §⊶_____

Our society values assertiveness. And the truth is, at times everyone must be aggressive if he or she is to survive in the workplace, on the highway, or in the check-out line. But assertiveness can become selfishness if it is not tempered by love. God's people should put others before themselves; they should be humble and seek to serve rather than to be served.

That attitude is especially important in marriage. Chances are good that one of you is naturally more aggressive than the other. There isn't anything wrong with that; it simply means that your temperaments can compliment each other. Yet in every decision you make together, you should seek common ground together until you are both satisfied. Remember, there is a fine line between aggressiveness and selfishness. If neither of you crosses that line, your marriage will be loving and harmonious, even when you disagree.

_____⊸ MEDITATION §⊶_____

Heavenly Father, help us always to place your will and each other's needs first in our marriage. §⊶

JUNE 28

A Healing on the Sabbath
⊸§ Luke 13:10–17 §⊶

One Sabbath as Jesus was teaching in a synagogue, [11]he saw a seriously handicapped woman who had been bent double for eighteen years and was unable to straighten herself.

[12]Calling her over to him Jesus said, "Woman, you are healed of your sickness!" [13]He touched her, and instantly she could stand straight. How she praised and thanked God!

[14]But the local Jewish leader in charge of the synagogue was very angry about it because Jesus had healed her on the Sabbath day. "There are six days of the week to work," he shouted to the crowd. "Those are the days to come for healing, not on the Sabbath!"

[15]But the Lord replied, "You hypocrite! You work on the Sabbath! Don't you untie your cattle from their stalls on the Sabbath and lead them out for water? [16]And is it wrong for me, just because it is the Sabbath day, to free this Jewish woman from the bondage in which Satan has held her for eighteen years?"

[17]This shamed his enemies. And all the people rejoiced at the wonderful things he did.

Pray Earnestly in the Spirit

Pray all the time. Ask God for anything in line with the Holy Spirit's wishes. Plead with him, reminding him of your needs, and keep praying earnestly for all Christians everywhere. [19]Pray for me, too, and ask God to give me the right words as I boldly tell others about the Lord, and as I explain to them that his salvation is for the Gentiles too. [20]I am in chains now for preaching this message from God. But pray that I will keep on speaking out boldly for him even here in prison, as I should.

²¹Tychicus, who is a much loved brother and faithful helper in the Lord's work, will tell you all about how I am getting along. ²²I am sending him to you for just this purpose, to let you know how we are and be encouraged by his report.

²³May God give peace to you, my Christian brothers, and love, with faith from God the Father and the Lord Jesus Christ. ²⁴May God's grace and blessing be upon all who sincerely love our Lord Jesus Christ.

Sincerely,
Paul

Proverbs for Today
⋅§ 18:2–3 §⋅

A rebel doesn't care about the facts. All he wants to do is yell. □ Sin brings disgrace.

May God's grace and blessing be upon all who sincerely love our Lord Jesus Christ.—*Ephesians 6:24*

This letter was written to the church at Ephesus, but it was also meant for circulation among other churches. In this epistle, Paul presents the supremacy of Christ, gives information on both the nature of the church and on how church members should live, and stresses the unity of all believers—male, female, parent, child, master, slave—regardless of sex, nationality, or social rank.

The home, like the church, is a difficult place to live the Christian life, because our real personalities come through to those who know us well. Close relationships between imperfect people can lead to trouble—or to increased faith and a deeper reliance on the Lord. You can each build unity in your home and marriage through willing submission to Christ's leadership and humble service to one another.

Heavenly Father, we ask that you will fill our home with unity and love. Help us also to be a source of harmony in our church so that your work can be carried out to its fullest. §⋅

JUNE 29

Illustrations of the Kingdom of God
⋅§ Luke 13:18–22 §⋅

Now Jesus began teaching them again about the Kingdom of God: "What is the Kingdom like?" he asked. "How can I illustrate it? ¹⁹It is like a tiny mustard seed planted in a garden; soon it grows into a tall bush and the birds live among its branches.

²⁰,²¹"It is like yeast kneaded into dough, which works unseen until it has risen high and light."

²²He went from city to city and village to village, teaching as he went, always pressing onward toward Jerusalem.

God Will Finish the Work He Began
⋅§ Philippians 1:1–6 §⋅

From: Paul and Timothy, slaves of Jesus Christ.
To: The pastors and deacons and all the Christians in the city of Philippi.

²May God bless you all. Yes, I pray that God our Father and the Lord Jesus Christ will give each of you his fullest blessings, and his peace in your hearts and your lives. ³All my prayers for you are full of praise to God! ⁴When I pray for you, my heart is full of joy, ⁵because of all your wonderful help in making known the Good News about Christ from the time you first heard it until now. ⁶And I am sure that God who began the good work within you will

keep right on helping you grow in his grace until his task within you is finally finished on that day when Jesus Christ returns.

Proverbs for Today
◄§ 18:4–5 §►

A wise man's words express deep streams of thought. ☐ It is wrong for a judge to favor the wicked and condemn the innocent.

──────── ◙ KEY VERSE ◙ ────────

When I pray for you, my heart is full of joy.—*Philippians 1:4*

──────── ◙ REFLECTION ◙ ────────

This is the first of many times Paul used the word *joy* in his letter to the church at Philippi. Here he wrote that the Philippians were a source of joy when he prayed. By helping Paul, the Philippians were also helping serve the cause of Christ. They were willing to be used by God for whatever task he had in store for them.

As a Christian couple, you can be a source of joy. By having confidence in God's sovereign care for you, and always being willing to help others, you become living witnesses of Christ's love to those who don't know him as Savior. You also become a source of comfort and assurance to other Christians who, like Paul, need to be regularly encouraged in their faith—even if they are leaders in the church.

──────── ◙ MEDITATION ◙ ────────

Heavenly Father, help us to be a source of joy. Let us be a blessing to those who need encouragement, and a source of ministry to those who have not given their lives to you. ◄►

JUNE 30

The Narrow Way
◄§ Luke 13:23–30 §►

Someone asked Jesus, ''Will only a few be saved?''

And he replied, [24,25]''The door to heaven is narrow. Work hard to get in, for the truth is that many will try to enter but when the head of the house has locked the door, it will be too late. Then if you stand outside knocking, and pleading, 'Lord, open the door for us,' he will reply, 'I do not know you.'

[26]'' 'But we ate with you, and you taught in our streets,' you will say.

[27]''And he will reply, 'I tell you, I don't know you. You can't come in here, guilty as you are. Go away.'

[28]''And there will be great weeping and gnashing of teeth as you stand outside and see Abraham, Isaac, Jacob, and all the prophets within the Kingdom of God— [29]for people will come from all over the world to take their places there. [30]And note this: some who are despised now will be greatly honored then; and some who are highly thought of now will be least important then.''

Paul's Love for the Philippians
◄§ Philippians 1:7–11 §►

How natural it is that I should feel as I do about you, for you have a very special place in my heart. We have shared together the blessings of God, both when I was in prison and when I was out, defending the truth and telling others about Christ. [8]Only God knows how deep is my love and longing for you—with the tenderness of Jesus Christ. [9]My prayer for you is that you will overflow more and more with love for others, and at the same time keep on growing in spiritual knowledge and insight, [10]for I want you always to see clearly the difference between right and wrong, and to be inwardly clean, no one being able to criticize you from now until our Lord returns. [11]May you always be doing those good, kind things which show that you are a child of God, for this will bring much praise and glory to the Lord.

Proverbs for Today
§ 18:6–7 §

A fool gets into constant fights. His mouth is his undoing! His words endanger him.

_____ *KEY VERSE* _____

I want you always to see clearly the difference between right and wrong, and to be inwardly clean, no one being able to criticize you from now until our Lord returns.—*Philippians 1:10*

_____ *REFLECTION* _____

Christians should be discerning in their life-style choices. We must allow the Holy Spirit to help us differentiate between right and wrong, good and evil, vital and trivial. This is to help us avoid the criticism of unbelievers and to keep us from compromising our Christian morals and values (Hebrews 5:14).

Don't allow your friends, family, or coworkers to pressure you to do what Scripture says is wrong. Others may criticize you for your convictions, but many will respect your integrity and willingness to take a moral stand. When they begin searching for answers to life's questions, they will know that you can both be trusted, and they will turn to you for answers.

_____ *MEDITATION* _____

Heavenly Father, thank you for the presence of the Holy Spirit in our lives to show us what is right and wrong. We pray that you will help us to be consistent and faithful witnesses to the truths of your Word, and that we will never be hypocritical. §

JULY 1 _____

Jesus Laments over Jerusalem
§ Luke 13:31–35 §

A few minutes later some Pharisees said to Jesus, "Get out of here if you want to live, for King Herod is after you!"

[32]Jesus replied, "Go tell that fox that I will keep on casting out demons and doing miracles of healing today and tomorrow; and the third day I will reach my destination. [33]Yes, today, tomorrow, and the next day! For it wouldn't do for a prophet of God to be killed except in Jerusalem!

[34]"O Jerusalem, Jerusalem! The city that murders the prophets. The city that stones those sent to help her. How often I have wanted to gather your children together even as a hen protects her brood under her wings, but you wouldn't let me. [35]And now—now your house is left desolate. And you will never again see me until you say, 'Welcome to him who comes in the name of the Lord.'"

Paul Rejoices at the Preaching of the Good News
§ Philippians 1:12–18 §

And I want you to know this, dear brothers: Everything that has happened to me here has been a great boost in getting out the Good News concerning Christ. [13]For everyone around here, including all the soldiers over at the barracks, knows that I am in chains simply because I am a Christian. [14]And because of my imprisonment many of the Christians here seem to have lost their fear of chains! Somehow my patience has encouraged them and they have become more and more bold in telling others about Christ.

[15]Some, of course, are preaching the Good News because they are jealous of the way God has used me. They want reputations as fearless preachers! But others have purer motives, [16,17]preaching because they love me, for they know that the Lord has brought me here to use me to defend the Truth.

And some preach to make me jealous, thinking that their success will add to my sorrows here in jail! [18]But whatever their motive for doing it, the fact remains that the Good News about Christ is being preached and I am glad.

Proverbs for Today
⋅§ 18:8 ও⋅

What dainty morsels rumors are. They are eaten with great relish!

I want you to know this, dear brothers: Everything that has happened to me here has been a great boost in getting out the Good News concerning Christ.—*Philippians 1:12*

————————⋅ REFLECTION ও⋅————————

Being imprisoned would cause many people to become bitter or to give up, but Paul saw it as one more opportunity to spread the Good News of Christ. He realized that his current circumstances weren't as important as what he did with them. Turning a bad situation into a good one, he reached out to the Roman soldiers and encouraged those Christians who were afraid of persecution.

You and your partner may not be in prison, but you still have plenty of opportunities to be discouraged—times of indecision, financial burdens, family conflict, church conflict, or the loss of your jobs. How you act in such situations reflects what you believe. Like Paul, look for opportunities to demonstrate your faith even in bad situations. Whether or not the situation improves, your faith and your marriage will grow stronger.

————————⋅ MEDITATION ও⋅————————

Heavenly Father, we turn our conflicts and concerns over to you and ask that you will continue to give us strength and encouragement during our times of difficulty. ও

JULY 2

Jesus Heals on the Sabbath
⋅§ Luke 14:1–6 ও⋅

One Sabbath as Jesus was in the home of a member of the Jewish Council, the Pharisees were watching him like hawks to see if he would heal a man who was present who was suffering from dropsy.

[3]Jesus said to the Pharisees and legal experts standing around, "Well, is it within the Law to heal a man on the Sabbath day, or not?"

[4]And when they refused to answer, Jesus took the sick man by the hand and healed him and sent him away.

[5]Then he turned to them: "Which of you doesn't work on the Sabbath?" he asked. "If your cow falls into a pit, don't you proceed at once to get it out?"

[6]Again they had no answer.

Honor Christ in Both Life and Death
⋅§ Philippians 1:19–30 ও⋅

I am going to keep on being glad, for I know that as you pray for me, and as the Holy Spirit helps me, this is all going to turn out for my good. [20]For I live in eager expectation and hope that I will never do anything that will cause me to be ashamed of myself but that I will always be ready to speak out boldly for Christ while I am going through all these trials here, just as I have in the past; and that I will always be an honor to Christ, whether I live or whether I must die. [21]For to me, living means opportunities for Christ, and dying—well, that's better yet! [22]But if living will give me more opportunities to win people to Christ, then I really don't know which is better, to live or die! [23]Sometimes I want to live and at other times I don't, for I long to go and be with Christ. How much happier for *me* than being here!

²⁴But the fact is that I can be of more help to *you* by staying!

²⁵Yes, I am still needed down here and so I feel certain I will be staying on earth a little longer, to help you grow and become happy in your faith; ²⁶my staying will make you glad and give you reason to glorify Christ Jesus for keeping me safe, when I return to visit you again.

²⁷But whatever happens to me, remember always to live as Christians should, so that, whether I ever see you again or not, I will keep on hearing good reports that you are standing side by side with one strong purpose—to tell the Good News ²⁸fearlessly, no matter what your enemies may do. They will see this as a sign of their downfall, but for you it will be a clear sign from God that he is with you, and that he has given you eternal life with him. ²⁹For to you has been given the privilege not only of trusting him but also of suffering for him. ³⁰We are in this fight together. You have seen me suffer for him in the past; and I am still in the midst of a great and terrible struggle now, as you know so well.

Proverbs for Today
◆§ 18:9–10 §◆

A lazy man is brother to the saboteur. □ The Lord is a strong fortress. The godly run to him and are safe.

KEY VERSE

When they refused to answer, Jesus took the sick man by the hand and healed him and sent him away.—*Luke 14:4*

REFLECTION

By healing this man on the Sabbath, Jesus was rejecting the Pharisaic tradition that did not allow for this. The Pharisees were more concerned for their traditions than they were for following the intent of God's Sabbath law. The Sabbath law was intended for restoration, not oppression. Jesus was giving this man rest by restoring him to full health—relieving him from the burden of his disease.

Remember that as a Christian couple you must always show love and mercy toward one another and to those with whom you come into contact. Such responses should always take precedence over rigidly keeping rules and regulations.

MEDITATION

Heavenly Father, help us to show love and compassion toward others and not to worry about what it will mean to our standing in the community or what others may say or think. §◆

JULY 3

The Privilege of Entering the Kingdom of God
◆§ Luke 14:7–24 §◆

When Jesus noticed that all who came to the dinner were trying to sit near the head of the table, he gave them this advice: ⁸"If you are invited to a wedding feast, don't always head for the best seat. For if someone more respected than you shows up, ⁹the host will bring him over to where you are sitting and say, 'Let this man sit here instead.' And you, embarrassed, will have to take whatever seat is left at the foot of the table!

¹⁰"Do this instead—start at the foot; and when your host sees you he will come and say, 'Friend, we have a better place than this for you!' Thus you will be honored in front of all the other guests. ¹¹For everyone who tries to honor himself shall be humbled; and he who humbles himself shall be honored." ¹²Then he turned to his host. "When you put on a dinner," he said, "don't invite friends, brothers, relatives, and rich neighbors! For they will return the invitation. ¹³Instead, invite the poor, the crippled, the lame, and the blind. ¹⁴Then at the resurrection of the godly, God will

reward you for inviting those who can't repay you."

¹⁵Hearing this, a man sitting at the table with Jesus exclaimed, "What a privilege it would be to get into the Kingdom of God!"

¹⁶Jesus replied with this illustration: "A man prepared a great feast and sent out many invitations. ¹⁷When all was ready, he sent his servant around to notify the guests that it was time for them to arrive. ¹⁸But they all began making excuses. One said he had just bought a field and wanted to inspect it, and asked to be excused. ¹⁹Another said he had just bought five pair of oxen and wanted to try them out. ²⁰Another had just been married and for that reason couldn't come.

²¹"The servant returned and reported to his master what they had said. His master was angry and told him to go quickly into the streets and alleys of the city and to invite the beggars, crippled, lame, and blind. ²²But even then, there was still room.

²³" 'Well, then,' said his master, 'go out into the country lanes and out behind the hedges and urge anyone you find to come, so that the house will be full. ²⁴For none of those I invited first will get even the smallest taste of what I had prepared for them.' "

Christ Is Our Model of Humility
⋙ Philippians 2:1–11 ⋘

Is there any such thing as Christians cheering each other up? Do you love me enough to want to help me? Does it mean anything to you that we are brothers in the Lord, sharing the same Spirit? Are your hearts tender and sympathetic at all? ²Then make me truly happy by loving each other and agreeing wholeheartedly with each other, working together with one heart and mind and purpose.

³Don't be selfish; don't live to make a good impression on others. Be humble, thinking of others as better than yourself. ⁴Don't just think about your own affairs, but be interested in others, too, and in what they are doing.

⁵Your attitude should be the kind that was shown us by Jesus Christ, ⁶who, though he was God, did not demand and cling to his rights as God, ⁷but laid aside his mighty power and glory, taking the disguise of a slave and becoming like men. ⁸And he humbled himself even further, going so far as actually to die a criminal's death on a cross.

⁹Yet it was because of this that God raised him up to the heights of heaven and gave him a name which is above every other name, ¹⁰that at the name of Jesus every knee shall bow in heaven and on earth and under the earth, ¹¹and every tongue shall confess that Jesus Christ is Lord, to the glory of God the Father.

Proverbs for Today
⋙ 18:11–12 ⋘

The rich man thinks of his wealth as an impregnable defense, a high wall of safety. What a dreamer! □ Pride ends in destruction; humility ends in honor.

⋙ KEY VERSE ⋘

Make me truly happy by loving each other and agreeing wholeheartedly with each other, working together with one heart and mind and purpose. —*Philippians 2:2*

⋙ REFLECTION ⋘

Many people—even Christians—live only to please themselves or to make a good impression on others. This is self-centered living. If people are concerned only for themselves, seeds of discord are sown. Paul therefore stressed spiritual unity, asking the Philippians to love one another and to work together with one heart and purpose. When we work together, caring for the problems of those around us as if they were our own, we demonstrate Christ's example of putting others first. This brings unity in the Body of Christ.

Don't be concerned about making a good impression or pleasing yourself to the point where you strain your relationship with your spouse or with others in God's family. Let the Spirit of God work through you to attract fellow believers to himself and to be an encouragement to your husband or wife.

_____ ◈ MEDITATION ◈ _____

Heavenly Father, we pray that you will help us encourage each other and be an example of unity. ◈

JULY 4

The Cost of Discipleship
◈ Luke 14:25–35 ◈

Great crowds were following Jesus. He turned around and addressed them as follows: [26]"Anyone who wants to be my follower must love me far more than he does his own father, mother, wife, children, brothers, or sisters—yes, more than his own life—otherwise he cannot be my disciple. [27]And no one can be my disciple who does not carry his own cross and follow me.

[28]"But don't begin until you count the cost. For who would begin construction of a building without first getting estimates and then checking to see if he has enough money to pay the bills? [29]Otherwise he might complete only the foundation before running out of funds. And then how everyone would laugh!

[30]" 'See that fellow there?' they would mock. 'He started that building and ran out of money before it was finished!'

[31]"Or what king would ever dream of going to war without first sitting down with his counselors and discussing whether his army of 10,000 is strong enough to defeat the 20,000 men who are marching against him?

[32]"If the decision is negative, then while the enemy troops are still far away, he will send a truce team to discuss terms of peace. [33]So no one can become my disciple unless he first sits down and counts his blessings—and then renounces them all for me.

[34]"What good is salt that has lost its saltiness? [35]Flavorless salt is fit for nothing—not even for fertilizer. It is worthless and must be thrown out. Listen well, if you would understand my meaning."

Be a Light to the World
◈ Philippians 2:12–18 ◈

Dearest friends, when I was there with you, you were always so careful to follow my instructions. And now that I am away you must be even more careful to do the good things that result from being saved, obeying God with deep reverence, shrinking back from all that might displease him. [13]For God is at work within you, helping you want to obey him, and then helping you do what he wants.

[14]In everything you do, stay away from complaining and arguing, [15]so that no one can speak a word of blame against you. You are to live clean, innocent lives as children of God in a dark world full of people who are crooked and stubborn. Shine out among them like beacon lights, [16]holding out to them the Word of Life.

Then when Christ returns how glad I will be that my work among you was so worthwhile. [17]And if my lifeblood is, so to speak, to be poured out over your faith which I am offering up to God as a sacrifice—that is, if I am to die for you—even then I will be glad, and will share my joy with each of you. [18]For you should be happy about this, too, and rejoice with me for having this privilege of dying for you.

Proverbs for Today
◈ 18:13 ◈

What a shame—yes, how stupid!—to decide before knowing the facts!

God is at work within you, helping you want to obey him, and then helping you do what he wants. —*Philippians 2:13*

God has not left you alone in your struggles to do his will. He wants to come alongside you and help meet the challenges of your career, ministry, and marriage. He will help you want to obey him and then give you the power to do it. The secret to changing your life and marriage is to submit to his control and let him work through you on a daily basis.

Heavenly Father, we submit our marriage to you and ask that you will place in both of our hearts a keen and earnest desire to love and serve you. ❧

JULY 5

A Lost Sheep and a Lost Coin
✺ Luke 15:1–10 ✺

Dishonest tax collectors and other notorious sinners often came to listen to Jesus' sermons; ²but this caused complaints from the Jewish religious leaders and the experts on Jewish law because he was associating with such despicable people—even eating with them!

³,⁴So Jesus used this illustration: "If you had a hundred sheep and one of them strayed away and was lost in the wilderness, wouldn't you leave the ninety-nine others to go and search for the lost one until you found it? ⁵And then you would joyfully carry it home on your shoulders. ⁶When you arrived you would call together your friends and neighbors to rejoice with you because your lost sheep was found.

⁷"Well, in the same way heaven will be happier over one lost sinner who returns to God than over ninety-nine others who haven't strayed away!

⁸"Or take another illustration: A woman has ten valuable silver coins and loses one. Won't she light a lamp and look in every corner of the house and sweep every nook and cranny until she finds it? ⁹And then won't she call in her friends and neighbors to rejoice with her? ¹⁰In the same way there is joy in the presence of the angels of God when one sinner repents."

Timothy and Epaphroditus
✺ Philippians 2:19–3:1 ✺

If the Lord is willing, I will send Timothy to see you soon. Then when he comes back he can cheer me up by telling me all about you and how you are getting along. ²⁰There is no one like Timothy for having a real interest in you; ²¹everyone else seems to be worrying about his own plans and not those of Jesus Christ. ²²But you know Timothy. He has been just like a son to me in helping me preach the Good News. ²³I hope to send him to you just as soon as I find out what is going to happen to me here. ²⁴And I am trusting the Lord that soon I myself may come to see you.

²⁵Meanwhile, I thought I ought to send Epaphroditus back to you. You sent him to help me in my need; well, he and I have been real brothers, working and battling side by side. ²⁶Now I am sending him home again, for he has been homesick for all of you and upset because you heard that he was ill. ²⁷And he surely was; in fact, he almost died. But God had mercy on him, and on me too, not allowing me to have this sorrow on top of everything else.

²⁸So I am all the more anxious to get him back to you again, for I know how thankful you will be to see him, and that will make me happy and lighten all my cares. ²⁹Welcome him in the Lord with great joy, and show your appreciation, ³⁰for he risked his life for the work of Christ and was at the

point of death while trying to do for me the things you couldn't do because you were far away.

³:¹Whatever happens, dear friends, be glad in the Lord. I never get tired of telling you this and it is good for you to hear it again and again.

Proverbs for Today
◄§ 18:14–15 ℈►

A man's courage can sustain his broken body, but when courage dies, what hope is left? □ The intelligent man is always open to new ideas. In fact, he looks for them.

————— ◢ KEY VERSE ◣ —————

There is joy in the presence of the angels of God when one sinner repents.—*Luke 15:10*

————— ◢ REFLECTION ◣ —————

Palestinian women received ten silver coins as a wedding gift. These coins held sentimental value like that of a wedding ring, and to lose one was very upsetting. Just as a husband or wife would rejoice at finding a lost ring, so the angels rejoice over a "found" repentant sinner. Each individual is precious to God. The Lord grieves over every loss and rejoices whenever one of his children is found and brought into his Kingdom.

————— ◢ MEDITATION ◣ —————

Heavenly Father, help us to share your concern for lost people. ℈►

JULY 6

The Prodigal Son
◄§ Luke 15:11–32 ℈►

To further illustrate the point, Jesus told the crowds this story: "A man had two sons. ¹²When the younger told his father, 'I want my share of your estate now, instead of waiting until you die!' his father agreed to divide his wealth between his sons.

¹³"A few days later this younger son packed all his belongings and took a trip to a distant land, and there wasted all his money on parties and prostitutes. ¹⁴About the time his money was gone a great famine swept over the land, and he began to starve. ¹⁵He persuaded a local farmer to hire him to feed his pigs. ¹⁶The boy became so hungry that even the pods he was feeding the swine looked good to him. And no one gave him anything.

¹⁷"When he finally came to his senses, he said to himself, 'At home even the hired men have food enough and to spare, and here I am, dying of hunger! ¹⁸I will go home to my father and say, "Father, I have sinned against both heaven and you, ¹⁹and am no longer worthy of being called your son. Please take me on as a hired man."'

²⁰"So he returned home to his father. And while he was still a long distance away, his father saw him coming, and was filled with loving pity and ran and embraced him and kissed him.

²¹"His son said to him, 'Father, I have sinned against heaven and you, and am not worthy of being called your son—'

²²"But his father said to the slaves, 'Quick! Bring the finest robe in the house and put it on him. And a jeweled ring for his finger; and shoes! ²³And kill the calf we have in the fattening pen. We must celebrate with a feast, ²⁴for this son of mine was dead and has returned to life. He was lost and is found.' So the party began.

²⁵"Meanwhile, the older son was in the fields working; when he returned home, he heard dance music coming from the house, ²⁶and he asked one of the servants what was going on.

²⁷"'Your brother is back,' he was told, 'and your father has killed the calf we were fattening and has prepared a great feast to celebrate his coming home again unharmed.'

²⁸"The older brother was angry and wouldn't go in. His father came out and begged him, ²⁹but he replied, 'All these years I've worked hard for you and never once refused to do a single thing you told me to; and in all that time you never gave me even one young goat for a feast with my friends. ³⁰Yet when this son of yours comes back after spending your money on prostitutes, you celebrate by killing the finest calf we have on the place.'

³¹"'Look, dear son,' his father said to him, 'you and I are very close, and everything I have is yours. ³²But it is right to celebrate. For he is your brother; and he was dead and has come back to life! He was lost and is found!'"

Paul's Jewish Heritage
⊷§ Philippians 3:2–7 §⊶

Watch out for those wicked men—dangerous dogs, I call them—who say you must be circumcised to be saved. ³For it isn't the *cutting of our bodies* that makes us children of God; it is *worshiping him with our spirits.* That is the only true "circumcision." We Christians glory in what Christ Jesus has done for us and realize that we are helpless to save ourselves.

⁴Yet if anyone ever had reason to hope that he could save himself, it would be I. If others could be saved by what they are, certainly I could! ⁵For I went through the Jewish initiation ceremony when I was eight days old, having been born into a pure-blooded Jewish home that was a branch of the old original Benjamin family. So I was a real Jew if there ever was one! What's more, I was a member of the Pharisees who demand the strictest obedience to every Jewish law and custom. ⁶And sincere? Yes, so much so that I greatly persecuted the Church; and I tried to obey every Jewish rule and regulation right down to the very last point.

⁷But all these things that I once thought very worthwhile—now I've thrown them all away so that I can put my trust and hope in Christ alone.

Proverbs for Today
⊷§ 18:16–18 §⊶

A gift does wonders; it will bring you before men of importance! □ Any story sounds true until someone tells the other side and sets the record straight. □ A coin toss ends arguments and settles disputes between powerful opponents.

⊷ KEY VERSE §⊶

I will go home to my father and say, "Father, I have sinned against both heaven and you, and am no longer worthy of being called your son. Please take me on as a hired man."—*Luke 15:18–19*

⊷ REFLECTION §⊶

Some people need to hit bottom before they will come to their senses. The Prodigal Son's attitude was based on a desire to live as he pleased. That is not so different from the attitudes of most people in our world today. It may take great sorrow and tragedy to cause them to look up to the only One who can help them.

Are you trying to live life your way, selfishly pushing aside anything that gets in your way—including your spouse? Don't be foolish—stop and look before you hit bottom, and save yourself and your family much grief.

⊷ MEDITATION §⊶

Heavenly Father, help us to live holy lives that are a blessing to your Kingdom. Guide our steps so that we can avoid bringing sorrow and pain to each other and to those around us. §⊶

JULY 7

The Story of the Dishonest Accountant
Luke 16:1–14

Jesus now told this story to his disciples: "A rich man hired an accountant to handle his affairs, but soon a rumor went around that the accountant was thoroughly dishonest.

2"So his employer called him in and said, 'What's this I hear about your stealing from me? Get your report in order, for you are to be dismissed.'

3"The accountant thought to himself, 'Now what? I'm through here, and I haven't the strength to go out and dig ditches, and I'm too proud to beg. 4I know just the thing! And then I'll have plenty of friends to take care of me when I leave!'

5,6"So he invited each one who owed money to his employer to come and discuss the situation. He asked the first one, 'How much do you owe him?' 'My debt is 850 gallons of olive oil,' the man replied. 'Yes, here is the contract you signed,' the accountant told him. 'Tear it up and write another one for half that much!'

7"'And how much do you owe him?' he asked the next man. 'A thousand bushels of wheat,' was the reply. 'Here,' the accountant said, 'take your note and replace it with one for only 800 bushels!'

8"The rich man had to admire the rascal for being so shrewd. And it is true that the citizens of this world are more clever [in dishonesty!] than the godly are. 9But shall I tell *you* to act that way, to buy friendship through cheating? Will this ensure your entry into an everlasting home in heaven? 10*No!* For unless you are honest in small matters, you won't be in large ones. If you cheat even a little, you won't be honest with greater responsibilities. 11And if you are untrustworthy about worldly wealth, who will trust you with the true riches of heaven? 12And if you are not faithful with other people's money, why should you be entrusted with money of your own?

13"For neither you nor anyone else can serve two masters. You will hate one and show loyalty to the other, or else the other way around—you will be enthusiastic about one and despise the other. You cannot serve both God and money."

14The Pharisees, who dearly loved their money, naturally scoffed at all this.

The Value of Knowing Christ
Philippians 3:8–12

Yes, everything else is worthless when compared with the priceless gain of knowing Christ Jesus my Lord. I have put aside all else, counting it worth less than nothing, in order that I can have Christ, 9and become one with him, no longer counting on being saved by being good enough or by obeying God's laws, but by trusting Christ to save me; for God's way of making us right with himself depends on faith—counting on Christ alone. 10Now I have given up everything else—I have found it to be the only way to really know Christ and to experience the mighty power that brought him back to life again, and to find out what it means to suffer and to die with him. 11So, whatever it takes, I will be one who lives in the fresh newness of life of those who are alive from the dead.

12I don't mean to say I am perfect. I haven't learned all I should even yet, but I keep working toward that day when I will finally be all that Christ saved me for and wants me to be.

Proverbs for Today
18:19

It is harder to win back the friendship of an offended brother than to capture a fortified city. His anger shuts you out like iron bars.

❧ KEY VERSE ❧

Unless you are honest in small matters, you won't be in large ones. If you cheat even a little, you won't be honest with greater responsibilities. And if you are untrustworthy about worldly wealth, who will trust you with the true riches of heaven? —*Luke 16:10–11*

—————◙ REFLECTION ◙—————
Our integrity is severely tested in money matters. God calls us to be honest even in the small details that we tend to rationalize away. Heaven's riches are far more valuable than earthly wealth—but if we are untrustworthy with our earthly wealth (no matter how much or little we have), we are certainly unfit to handle the vast riches of God's Kingdom. If you encourage each other to have integrity in small matters, you will have the character it takes to have it when you must make crucial decisions.

—————◙ MEDITATION ◙—————
Heavenly Father, we submit our financial affairs to your guidance and direction. Help us to be good stewards of the blessings you have given us so that we can be worthy of whatever you have in store for us in the future. ❧

JULY 8

Lazarus and the Rich Man
❧ Luke 16:15–31 ❧

Then Jesus said to the Pharisees, "You wear a noble, pious expression in public, but God knows your evil hearts. Your pretense brings you honor from the people, but it is an abomination in the sight of God. [16]Until John the Baptist began to preach, the laws of Moses and the messages of the prophets were your guides. But John introduced the Good News that the Kingdom of God would come soon. And now eager multitudes are pressing in. [17]But that doesn't mean that the Law has lost its force in even the smallest point. It is as strong and unshakable as heaven and earth.

[18]"So anyone who divorces his wife and marries someone else commits adultery, and anyone who marries a divorced woman commits adultery."

[19]"There was a certain rich man," Jesus said, "who was splendidly clothed and lived each day in mirth and luxury. [20]One day Lazarus, a diseased beggar, was laid at his door. [21]As he lay there longing for scraps from the rich man's table, the dogs would come and lick his open sores. [22]Finally the beggar died and was carried by the angels to be with Abraham in the place of the righteous dead. The rich man also died and was buried, [23]and his soul went into hell. There, in torment, he saw Lazarus in the far distance with Abraham.

[24]" 'Father Abraham,' he shouted, 'have some pity! Send Lazarus over here if only to dip the tip of his finger in water and cool my tongue, for I am in anguish in these flames.'

[25]"But Abraham said to him, 'Son, remember that during your lifetime you had everything you wanted, and Lazarus had nothing. So now he is here being comforted and you are in anguish. [26]And besides, there is a great chasm separating us, and anyone wanting to come to you from here is stopped at its edge; and no one over there can cross to us.'

[27]"Then the rich man said, 'O Father Abraham, then please send him to my father's home— [28]for I have five brothers—to warn them about this place of torment lest they come here when they die.'

[29]"But Abraham said, 'The Scriptures have warned them again and again. Your brothers can read them any time they want to.'

[30]"The rich man replied, 'No, Father Abraham, they won't bother to read them. But if someone is sent to them from the dead, then they will turn from their sins.'

[31]"But Abraham said, 'If they won't listen to

Moses and the prophets, they won't listen even though someone rises from the dead.' "

Forget the Past and Strive for the Goal
◄§ Philippians 3:13–16 §►

No, dear brothers, I am still not all I should be but I am bringing all my energies to bear on this one thing: Forgetting the past and looking forward to what lies ahead, ¹⁴I strain to reach the end of the race and receive the prize for which God is calling us up to heaven because of what Christ Jesus did for us.

¹⁵I hope all of you who are mature Christians will see eye-to-eye with me on these things, and if you disagree on some point, I believe that God will make it plain to you— ¹⁶if you fully obey the truth you have.

Proverbs for Today
◄§ 18:20–21 §►

Ability to give wise advice satisfies like a good meal! □ Those who love to talk will suffer the consequences. Men have died for saying the wrong thing!

◄§ KEY VERSE §►

"Anyone who divorces his wife and marries someone else commits adultery, and anyone who marries a divorced woman commits adultery."—*Luke 16:18*

◄§ REFLECTION §►

Most religious leaders of Jesus' day permitted a man to divorce his wife for almost any reason. Jesus' words about divorce went beyond Moses' (Deuteronomy 24:1–4). Stricter than any of the then current schools of thought, Jesus shocked his hearers (see Matthew 19:10) just as he shakes today's readers. Jesus says in unmistakable terms that marriage is a lifetime commitment. To leave your spouse for another person may be legal, but it is adultery in God's eyes. As you think about marriage, remember that God intends it to be a permanent commitment.

◄§ MEDITATION §►

Heavenly Father, we submit to you the vows we made when we were married and ask that you will sanctify our love so that we will never be tempted to commit adultery by forsaking each other. §►

JULY 9

Temptation and Forgiveness
◄§ Luke 17:1–4 §►

"There will always be temptations to sin," Jesus said one day to his disciples, "but woe to the man who does the tempting. ²,³If he were thrown into the sea with a huge rock tied to his neck, he would be far better off than facing the punishment in store for those who harm these little children's souls. I am warning you!

"Rebuke your brother if he sins, and forgive him if he is sorry. ⁴Even if he wrongs you seven times a day and each time turns again and asks forgiveness, forgive him."

Our Homeland Is in Heaven
◄§ Philippians 3:17–21 §►

Dear brothers, pattern your lives after mine and notice who else lives up to my example. ¹⁸For I have told you often before, and I say it again now with tears in my eyes, there are many who walk along the Christian road who are really enemies of the cross of Christ. ¹⁹Their future is eternal loss, for their god is their appetite: they are proud of what they should be ashamed of; and all they think about is this life here on earth. ²⁰But our homeland is in heaven, where our Savior the Lord Jesus Christ is; and we are looking forward to his return from there.

[21]When he comes back he will take these dying bodies of ours and change them into glorious bodies like his own, using the same mighty power that he will use to conquer all else everywhere.

Proverbs for Today
⹂ 18:22 ⹂

The man who finds a wife finds a good thing; she is a blessing to him from the Lord.

⹂ KEY VERSE ⹂

The man who finds a wife finds a good thing; she is a blessing to him from the Lord.—*Proverbs 18:22*

⹂ REFLECTION ⹂

When you announce marriage plans, don't expect praise from the world. These days, a lot of people view a permanent tie to one person as a foolish surrender of freedom. But today's emphasis on individual freedom is misguided. Commitment to permanent relationships produces strong marriages, strong marriages produce strong children, and healthy families are the backbone of healthy nations. God created marriage, and he pronounced it good. Live accordingly and seek his approval, not the approval of others.

⹂ MEDITATION ⹂

Heavenly Father, we thank you for our marriage and ask that you will continue to bless our life together. ⹂

JULY 10

Jesus Teaches about Faith
⹂ Luke 17:5–10 ⹂

One day the apostles said to the Lord, "We need more faith; tell us how to get it."

[6]"If your faith were only the size of a mustard seed," Jesus answered, "it would be large enough to uproot that mulberry tree over there and send it hurtling into the sea! Your command would bring immediate results! [7,8,9]When a servant comes in from plowing or taking care of sheep, he doesn't just sit down and eat, but first prepares his master's meal and serves him his supper before he eats his own. And he is not even thanked, for he is merely doing what he is supposed to do. [10]Just so, if you merely obey me, you should not consider yourselves worthy of praise. For you have simply done your duty!"

Rejoice in the Lord Always
⹂ Philippians 4:1–7 ⹂

Dear brother Christians, I love you and long to see you, for you are my joy and my reward for my work. My beloved friends, stay true to the Lord.

[2]And now I want to plead with those two dear women, Euodias and Syntyche. Please, please, with the Lord's help, quarrel no more—be friends again. [3]And I ask you, my true teammate, to help these women, for they worked side by side with me in telling the Good News to others; and they worked with Clement, too, and the rest of my fellow workers whose names are written in the Book of Life.

[4]Always be full of joy in the Lord; I say it again, rejoice! [5]Let everyone see that you are unselfish and considerate in all you do. Remember that the Lord is coming soon. [6]Don't worry about anything; instead, pray about everything; tell God your needs and don't forget to thank him for his answers. [7]If you do this you will experience God's peace, which is far more wonderful than the human mind can understand. His peace will keep your thoughts and your hearts quiet and at rest as you trust in Christ Jesus.

Proverbs for Today
⹂ 18:23–24 ⹂

The poor man pleads and the rich man answers with insults. ☐ There are "friends" who pretend to be friends, but there is a friend who sticks closer than a brother.

───────── ❧ **KEY VERSE** ❧ ─────────

Don't worry about anything; instead, pray about everything; tell God your needs, and don't forget to thank him for his answers.—*Philippians 4:6*

───────── ❧ **REFLECTION** ❧ ─────────

Imagine never having to worry about anything! It seems like an impossibility—we all have worries on the job, in our homes, at school. But God's advice is to turn your worries into prayers. Do you want to worry less? Then pray more! Whenever you start to worry, share your concerns with your spouse, and stop and pray.

───────── ❧ **MEDITATION** ❧ ─────────

Heavenly Father, we turn all of our cares and worries over to you and ask that you forgive us when we doubt your ability to meet our needs. ❧

JULY 11 _____

Jesus Heals Ten Lepers
❧ Luke 17:11–19 ❧

As Jesus and his disciples continued onward toward Jerusalem, they reached the border between Galilee and Samaria, ¹²and as they entered a village there, ten lepers stood at a distance, ¹³crying out, "Jesus, sir, have mercy on us!"

¹⁴He looked at them and said, "Go to the Jewish priest and show him that you are healed!" And as they were going, their leprosy disappeared.

¹⁵One of them came back to Jesus, shouting, "Glory to God, I'm healed!" ¹⁶He fell flat on the ground in front of Jesus, face downward in the dust, thanking him for what he had done. This man was a despised Samaritan.

¹⁷Jesus asked, "Didn't I heal ten men? Where are the nine? ¹⁸Does only this foreigner return to give glory to God?"

¹⁹And Jesus said to the man, "Stand up and go; your faith has made you well."

Think about Pure and Lovely Things
❧ Philippians 4:8–14 ❧

And now, brothers, as I close this letter let me say this one more thing: Fix your thoughts on what is true and good and right. Think about things that are pure and lovely, and dwell on the fine, good things in others. Think about all you can praise God for and be glad about. ⁹Keep putting into practice all you learned from me and saw me doing, and the God of peace will be with you.

¹⁰How grateful I am and how I praise the Lord that you are helping me again. I know you have always been anxious to send what you could, but for a while you didn't have the chance. ¹¹Not that I was ever in need, for I have learned how to get along happily whether I have much or little. ¹²I know how to live on almost nothing or with everything. I have learned the secret of contentment in every situation, whether it be a full stomach or hunger, plenty or want; ¹³for I can do everything God asks me to with the help of Christ who gives me the strength and power. ¹⁴But even so, you have done right in helping me in my present difficulty.

Proverbs for Today
❧ 19:1–3 ❧

Better be poor and honest than rich and dishonest. ☐ It is dangerous and sinful to rush into the unknown. A man may ruin his chances by his own foolishness and then blame it on the Lord!

───────── ❧ **KEY VERSE** ❧ ─────────

I know how to live on almost nothing or with everything. I have learned the secret of contentment in every situation, whether it be a full stomach or hunger, plenty or want.—*Philippians 4:12*

Paul was content because he could see life from God's point of view. He focused on what he was supposed to do, not on what he felt he should have done. He had his priorities straight and was grateful for everything God had given him. Often the desire for more or better possessions is really a longing to fill an empty place in one's life.

As a couple, to what are you drawn when you feel empty inside? Seek God and his Kingdom first and you will never feel the emptiness shared by those who are concerned only with the things of this world.

◦ MEDITATION ◦

Heavenly Father, we thank you for everything you have freely provided us in our marriage. Forgive us when we covet the possessions of others, and help us always to be satisfied with what we have. ❧

JULY 12

Instructions about the Last Days
❧ Luke 17:20–37 ❧

One day the Pharisees asked Jesus, "When will the Kingdom of God begin?" Jesus replied, "The Kingdom of God isn't ushered in with visible signs. [21]You won't be able to say, 'It has begun here in this place or there in that part of the country.' For the Kingdom of God is within you."

[22]Later he talked again about this with his disciples. "The time is coming when you will long for me to be with you even for a single day, but I won't be here," he said. [23]"Reports will reach you that I have returned and that I am in this place or that; don't believe it or go out to look for me. [24]For when I return, you will know it beyond all doubt. It will be as evident as the lightning that flashes across the skies. [25]But first I must suffer terribly and be rejected by this whole nation.

[26]"[When I return] the world will be [as indifferent to the things of God] as the people were in Noah's day. [27]They ate and drank and married—everything just as usual right up to the day when Noah went into the ark and the flood came and destroyed them all.

[28]"And the world will be as it was in the days of Lot: people went about their daily business—eating and drinking, buying and selling, farming and building— [29]until the morning Lot left Sodom.

Then fire and brimstone rained down from heaven and destroyed them all. [30]Yes, it will be 'business as usual' right up to the hour of my return.

[31]"Those away from home that day must not return to pack; those in the fields must not return to town— [32]remember what happened to Lot's wife! [33]Whoever clings to his life shall lose it, and whoever loses his life shall save it. [34]That night two men will be asleep in the same room, and one will be taken away, the other left. [35,36]Two women will be working together at household tasks; one will be taken, the other left; and so it will be with men working side by side in the fields."

[37]"Lord, where will they be taken?" the disciples asked.

Jesus replied, "Where the body is, the vultures gather!"

Paul Thanks the Philippians for Their Gift
❧ Philippians 4:15–23 ❧

As you well know, when I first brought the Gospel to you and then went on my way, leaving Macedonia, only you Philippians became my partners in giving and receiving. No other church did this. [16]Even when I was over in Thessalonica you sent help twice. [17]But though I appreciate your gifts, what makes me happiest is the well-earned reward you will have because of your kindness.

¹⁸At the moment I have all I need—more than I need! I am generously supplied with the gifts you sent me when Epaphroditus came. They are a sweet-smelling sacrifice that pleases God well. ¹⁹And it is he who will supply all your needs from his riches in glory, because of what Christ Jesus has done for us. ²⁰Now unto God our Father be glory forever and ever. Amen.

Sincerely,
Paul

P.S.

²¹Say "hello" for me to all the Christians there; the brothers with me send their greetings too. ²²And all the other Christians here want to be remembered to you, especially those who work in Caesar's palace. ²³The blessings of our Lord Jesus Christ be upon your spirits.

Proverbs for Today
◦§ 19:4–5 §◦

A wealthy man has many "friends"; the poor man has none left. ☐ Punish false witnesses. Track down liars.

◦ KEY VERSE ◦

One day the Pharisees asked Jesus, "When will the Kingdom of God begin?" Jesus replied, "The Kingdom of God isn't ushered in with visible signs. You won't be able to say, 'It has begun here in this place or there in that part of the country.' For the Kingdom of God is within you."—*Luke 17:20–21*

◦ REFLECTION ◦

The Kingdom of God is not like an earthly kingdom, with geographical boundaries. Instead, it consists of the work of God's Spirit in people's lives and relationships. Just as in Jesus' day, we must resist looking to institutions or programs for evidence of the progress of God's Kingdom. Instead, we should look for what God is doing in people's lives. Allow God to instill the truth of his Word in your marriage so that your lives can be a witness to his Kingdom among your friends, family, and co-workers.

◦ MEDITATION ◦

Heavenly Father, help us to be worthy servants of your Kingdom. Prepare our hearts and minds so that we are always ready to be faithful witnesses for you. §◦

JULY 13

An Illustration on Prayer
◦§ Luke 18:1–8 §◦

One day Jesus told his disciples a story to illustrate their need for constant prayer and to show them that they must keep praying until the answer comes.

²"There was a city judge," he said, "a very godless man who had great contempt for everyone. ³A widow of that city came to him frequently to appeal for justice against a man who had harmed her. ^{4,5}The judge ignored her for a while, but eventually she got on his nerves.

"'I fear neither God nor man,' he said to himself, 'but this woman bothers me. I'm going to see that she gets justice, for she is wearing me out with her constant coming!'"

⁶Then the Lord said, "If even an evil judge can be worn down like that, ⁷don't you think that God will surely give justice to his people who plead with him day and night? ⁸Yes! He will answer them quickly! But the question is: When I, the Messiah, return, how many will I find who have faith [and are praying]?"

Paul Thanks God for the Colossians
◦§ Colossians 1:1–6 §◦

From: Paul, chosen by God to be Jesus Christ's messenger, and from Brother Timothy.

²*To:* The faithful Christian brothers—God's people—in the city of Colosse.

May God our Father shower you with blessings and fill you with his great peace.

³Whenever we pray for you we always begin by giving thanks to God the Father of our Lord Jesus Christ, ⁴for we have heard how much you trust the Lord, and how much you love his people. ⁵And you are looking forward to the joys of heaven, and have been ever since the Gospel first was preached to you. ⁶The same Good News that came to you is going out all over the world and changing lives everywhere, just as it changed yours that very first day you heard it and understood about God's great kindness to sinners.

Proverbs for Today
◅§ 19:6–7 §▻

Many beg favors from a man who is generous; everyone is his friend! □ A poor man's own brothers turn away from him in embarrassment; how much more his friends! He calls after them, but they are gone.

───────── ◦ KEY VERSE ◦ ─────────

One day Jesus told his disciples a story to illustrate their need for constant prayer and to show them that they must keep praying until the answer comes.—*Luke 18:1*

───────── ◦ REFLECTION ◦ ─────────

To repeat our prayers until the answer comes does not mean endless repetition or painfully long prayer sessions. Constant prayer means keeping our requests continually before God as we live for him day by day, always believing that he will answer. When we live by faith, we have the persistence not to give up when our lives become difficult. God may delay answering, but his delays always have good reasons, and we must not confuse them with neglect. Pray faithfully each day as a couple. As you persist in prayer, you will grow in character, faith, and hope.

───────── ◦ MEDITATION ◦ ─────────

Heavenly Father, we thank you that we can come to you as a couple with our needs and concerns. Help us to remain faithful with our prayers, trusting in you and in your perfect timing. ❧

JULY 14

The Pharisee and the Tax Collector
◅§ Luke 18:9–17 §▻

Then Jesus told this story to some who boasted of their virtue and scorned everyone else:

¹⁰"Two men went to the Temple to pray. One was a proud, self-righteous Pharisee, and the other a cheating tax collector. ¹¹The proud Pharisee 'prayed' this prayer: 'Thank God, I am not a sinner like everyone else, especially like that tax collector over there! For I never cheat, I don't commit adultery, ¹²I go without food twice a week, and I give to God a tenth of everything I earn.'

¹³"But the corrupt tax collector stood at a distance and dared not even lift his eyes to heaven as he prayed, but beat upon his chest in sorrow, exclaiming, 'God, be merciful to me, a sinner.' ¹⁴I tell you, this sinner, not the Pharisee, returned home forgiven! For the proud shall be humbled, but the humble shall be honored."

¹⁵One day some mothers brought their babies to him to touch and bless. But the disciples told them to go away.

¹⁶,¹⁷Then Jesus called the children over to him and said to the disciples, "Let the little children come to me! Never send them away! For the Kingdom of God belongs to men who have hearts as trusting as these little children's. And anyone who doesn't have their kind of faith will never get within the Kingdom's gates."

Epaphras' Good Report
⇜§ Colossians 1:7–10 §⇝

Epaphras, our much-loved fellow worker, was the one who brought you this Good News. He is Jesus Christ's faithful slave, here to help us in your place. ⁸And he is the one who has told us about the great love for others which the Holy Spirit has given you.

⁹So ever since we first heard about you we have kept on praying and asking God to help you understand what he wants you to do; asking him to make you wise about spiritual things; ¹⁰and asking that the way you live will always please the Lord and honor him, so that you will always be doing good, kind things for others, while all the time you are learning to know God better and better.

Proverbs for Today
⇜§ 19:8–9 §⇝

He who loves wisdom loves his own best interest and will be a success. □ A false witness shall be punished and a liar shall be caught.

⇜§ KEY VERSE §⇝

He is the one who has told us about the great love for others that the Holy Spirit has given you.—*Colossians 1:8*

⇜§ REFLECTION §⇝

Because of their love for one another, Christians can have an impact that goes far beyond their neighborhoods and communities. Christian love comes from the Holy Spirit (see Galatians 5:22). The Bible speaks of it as an action and attitude, not just an emotion. It is a by-product of our new life in Christ (see Romans 5:5 and 1 Corinthians 13). Christians have no excuse for not loving others. As a Christian couple, don't base your love on what feels right at the time; instead, respond in prayerful consideration of what is in the best interests of others.

⇜§ MEDITATION §⇝

Heavenly Father, we pray that your Holy Spirit will guide us in all that we do and say to others. Help us to share your love with a world that so desperately needs it. ⇝

JULY 15

Jesus and the Rich Man
⇜§ Luke 18:18–30 §⇝

Once a Jewish religious leader asked Jesus this question: "Good sir, what shall I do to get to heaven?"

¹⁹"Do you realize what you are saying when you call me 'good'?" Jesus asked him. "Only God is truly good, and no one else.

²⁰"But as to your question, you know what the ten commandments say—don't commit adultery, don't murder, don't steal, don't lie, honor your parents, and so on." ²¹The man replied, "I've obeyed every one of these laws since I was a small child."

²²"There is still one thing you lack," Jesus said. "Sell all you have and give the money to the poor—it will become treasure for you in heaven—and come, follow me."

²³But when the man heard this he went sadly away, for he was very rich.

²⁴Jesus watched him go and then said to his disciples, "How hard it is for the rich to enter the Kingdom of God! ²⁵It is easier for a camel to go through the eye of a needle than for a rich man to enter the Kingdom of God."

²⁶Those who heard him say this exclaimed, "If it is that hard, how can *anyone* be saved?"

²⁷He replied, "God can do what men can't!"

²⁸And Peter said, "We have left our homes and followed you."

²⁹"Yes," Jesus replied, "and everyone who has done as you have, leaving home, wife, brothers,

parents, or children for the sake of the Kingdom of God, ³⁰will be repaid many times over now, as well as receiving eternal life in the world to come."

Prayerful Response to Epaphras' Report
⮩ Colossians 1:11–14 ⮨

We are praying, too, that you will be filled with his mighty, glorious strength so that you can keep going no matter what happens—always full of the joy of the Lord, ¹²and always thankful to the Father who has made us fit to share all the wonderful things that belong to those who live in the Kingdom of light. ¹³For he has rescued us out of the darkness and gloom of Satan's kingdom and brought us into the Kingdom of his dear Son, ¹⁴who bought our freedom with his blood and forgave us all our sins.

Proverbs for Today
⮩ 19:10–12 ⮨

It doesn't seem right for a fool to succeed or for a slave to rule over princes! ☐ A wise man restrains his anger and overlooks insults. This is to his credit. ☐ The king's anger is as dangerous as a lion's. But his approval is as refreshing as the dew on grass.

⮩ KEY VERSE ⮨

Ever since we first heard about you we have kept on praying and asking God to help you understand what he wants you to do.—*Colossians 1:9a*

⮩ REFLECTION ⮨

Sometimes we wonder how to pray for missionaries and other leaders we have never met. Paul had never met the Colossians, but he faithfully prayed for them. This prayer of his teaches us how to pray for others whether we know them or not. We can ask that they: (1) understand God's will, (2) gain spiritual wisdom, (3) live lives pleasing and honoring to God, (4) do kind things for others, (5) know God better and better, (6) be filled with God's strength, (7) endure in faith, (8) stay full of Christ's joy, and (9) always be thankful. All believers have those same basic needs. If during prayer together you aren't sure how to pray for each other, for a family member, or for someone God has placed on your hearts, remember Paul's prayer for the Colossians.

⮩ MEDITATION ⮨

Heavenly Father, teach us how to pray for each other and for those around us. We also ask that your Holy Spirit will guide us when we pray for those who serve you, for those who lead our nation, and for others we know but have never met. ⮨

JULY 16

Jesus Predicts His Death
⮩ Luke 18:31–34 ⮨

Gathering the Twelve around him, Jesus told them, "As you know, we are going to Jerusalem. And when we get there, all the predictions of the ancient prophets concerning me will come true. ³²I will be handed over to the Gentiles to be mocked and treated shamefully and spat upon, ³³and lashed and killed. And the third day I will rise again."

³⁴But they didn't understand a thing he said. He seemed to be talking in riddles.

The Exact Image of the Unseen God
⮩ Colossians 1:15–19 ⮨

Christ is the exact likeness of the unseen God. He existed before God made anything at all, and, in fact, ¹⁶Christ himself is the Creator who made everything in heaven and earth, the things we can see and the things we can't; the spirit world with its kings and kingdoms, its rulers and authorities; all were made by Christ for his own use and glory. ¹⁷He was before all else began and it is his power that holds everything together. ¹⁸He is the Head of the body made up of his people—that is, his Church—which he began; and he is the Leader of all those who arise from the dead, so that he is first in everything; [19]for God wanted all of himself to be in his Son.

Proverbs for Today
~§ 19:13–14 §~

A rebellious son is a calamity to his father, and a nagging wife annoys like constant dripping. ☐ A father can give his sons homes and riches, but only the Lord can give them understanding wives.

————— ~♦ KEY VERSE ♦~ —————

Christ himself is the Creator who made everything in heaven and earth, the things we can see and the things we can't; the spirit world with its kings and kingdoms, its rulers and authorities; all were made by Christ for his own use and glory.—*Colossians 1:16*

————— ~♦ REFLECTION ♦~ —————

Many false teachers in the early church believed that the physical world was evil and therefore could not have been created by God. If Christ were God, they further reasoned, he would only be in charge of the spiritual world. But Paul explained that both the spiritual and physical worlds were created by Christ and are under Christ's authority. Jesus Christ has no equal and no rival.

Submit everything in your lives to the Lord. Many Christian couples limit their relationship with God to church on Sunday and a quick prayer before dinners. God wants to participate in every activity of your lives, including your jobs, your financial decisions, your friendships, and even your entertainment choices. By placing him in a spiritual box, you deny yourselves the blessings, guidance, and love he wants to share with you.

————— ~♦ MEDITATION ♦~ —————

Heavenly Father, we ask that you will touch every aspect of our lives and bless us with your infinite wisdom and perfect guidance. §~

JULY 17

Jesus Heals a Blind Man
~§ Luke 18:35–43 §~

As Jesus and his disciples approached Jericho, a blind man was sitting beside the road, begging from travelers. [36]When he heard the noise of a crowd going past, he asked what was happening. [37]He was told that Jesus from Nazareth was going by, [38]so he began shouting, "Jesus, Son of David, have mercy on me!"

[39]The crowds ahead of Jesus tried to hush the man, but he only yelled the louder, "Son of David, have mercy on me!"

[40]When Jesus arrived at the spot, he stopped. "Bring the blind man over here," he said. [41]Then Jesus asked the man, "What do you want?"

"Lord," he pleaded, "I want to see!"

[42]And Jesus said, "All right, begin seeing! Your faith has healed you."

[43]And instantly the man could see, and followed Jesus, praising God. And all who saw it happen praised God too.

The Reconciling Cross of Christ
~§ Colossians 1:20–23 §~

It was through what his Son did that God cleared a path for everything to come to him—all things in heaven and on earth—for Christ's death on the cross has made peace with God for all by his blood. [21]This includes you who were once so far away from God. You were his enemies and hated him and were separated from him by your evil thoughts and actions, yet now he has brought you back as his friends. ²²He has done this through the death on the cross of his own human body, and now as a result Christ has brought you into the very presence of God, and you are standing there before him with nothing left against you—nothing left that he could even chide you for; ²³the only condition is that you fully believe the Truth, standing in it steadfast and firm, strong in the Lord, convinced of the Good News that Jesus died for you, and never shifting from trusting him to save you. This is the wonderful news that came to each of you and is now spreading all over the world. And I, Paul, have the joy of telling it to others.

Proverbs for Today
§ 19:15–16 &

A lazy man sleeps soundly—and he goes hungry! □ Keep the commandments and keep your life; despising them means death.

KEY VERSE

As they approached Jericho, a blind man was sitting beside the road, begging from travelers.—*Luke 18:35*

REFLECTION

Beggars in ancient Palestine often waited along the roads near cities, because that was where they would be able to contact the most people. Usually handicapped in some way, they were unable to earn a living. Medical help was not available for their problems, and the people of that era tended to ignore their obligation to care for the needy (Leviticus 25:35–38). Thus beggars had little hope of escaping their degrading way of life. But this blind beggar took hope in the Messiah. He shamelessly cried out for Jesus' attention, and Jesus said that the beggar's faith made him see.

As a Christian couple never forget that regardless of how desperate your situation may seem, you can call out to Jesus in faith and he will help you. This includes resolving the major decisions in your lives—such as whether to start a family, change careers, or buy a home—and overcoming the stresses of daily living—such as not having enough money to pay your bills. God loved you so much that he sent his Son to die for your sins. Be assured that he cares enough to answer your prayers in his perfect timing and manner.

MEDITATION

Heavenly Father, we submit our needs and concerns to you and ask that you will give us comfort, guidance, and resolution. We also pray that you will help us to accept whatever your will is for our lives. &

JULY 18

Salvation Comes to Zacchaeus' Home
§ Luke 19:1–10 &

As Jesus was passing through Jericho, a man named Zacchaeus, one of the most influential Jews in the Roman tax-collecting business (and, of course, a very rich man), ³tried to get a look at Jesus, but he was too short to see over the crowds. ⁴So he ran ahead and climbed into a sycamore tree beside the road, to watch from there.

⁵When Jesus came by he looked up at Zacchaeus and called him by name! ''Zacchaeus!'' he said.

''Quick! Come down! For I am going to be a guest in your home today!''

⁶Zacchaeus hurriedly climbed down and took Jesus to his house in great excitement and joy.

⁷But the crowds were displeased. ''He has gone to be the guest of a notorious sinner,'' they grumbled.

⁸Meanwhile, Zacchaeus stood before the Lord and said, ''Sir, from now on I will give half my wealth to the poor, and if I find I have overcharged anyone on his taxes, I will penalize myself by giving him back four times as much!''

9,10Jesus told him, "This shows that salvation has come to this home today. This man was one of the lost sons of Abraham, and I, the Messiah, have come to search for and to save such souls as his."

Christ in You, the Hope of Glory
⋅§ Colossians 1:24–29 §⋅

But part of my work is to suffer for you; and I am glad, for I am helping to finish up the remainder of Christ's sufferings for his body, the Church.

25God has sent me to help his Church and to tell his secret plan to you Gentiles. 26,27He has kept this secret for centuries and generations past, but now at last it has pleased him to tell it to those who love him and live for him, and the riches and glory of his plan are for you Gentiles too. And this is the secret: *that Christ in your hearts is your only hope of glory.*

28So everywhere we go we talk about Christ to all who will listen, warning them and teaching them as well as we know how. We want to be able to present each one to God, perfect because of what Christ has done for each of them. 29This is my work, and I can do it only because Christ's mighty energy is at work within me.

Proverbs for Today
⋅§ 19:17 §⋅

When you help the poor you are lending to the Lord—and he pays wonderful interest on your loan!

⋅❧ KEY VERSE ❧⋅

Everywhere we go we talk about Christ to all who will listen, warning them and teaching them as well as we know how. We want to be able to present each one to God, perfect because of what Christ has done for each of them.—*Colossians 1:28*

⋅❧ REFLECTION ❧⋅

Much is made these days about the characteristics and flaws that make up a dysfunctional personality. Many people believe that if they eliminate their quirks and eccentricities then they will be perfect. The word *perfect* means *mature* or *complete,* not *flawless.* Perfection can only be achieved when you grow daily in your faith.

When you seek the direction of the Holy Spirit in every aspect of your lives together, then you both will be striving toward perfection. That is the only way either of you will find satisfaction in your jobs, contentment in your personal time, happiness in your marriage, or fulfillment in your relationship with the Lord.

⋅❧ MEDITATION ❧⋅

Heavenly Father, although we know that your Son was the only person who lived a sinless life, we pray that you will help us strive toward spiritual perfection and to resist temptations when they come our way. §⋅

JULY 19

The Nobleman and His Assistants
⋅§ Luke 19:11–27 §⋅

And because Jesus was nearing Jerusalem, he told a story to correct the impression that the Kingdom of God would begin right away.

12"A nobleman living in a certain province was called away to the distant capital of the empire to be crowned king of his province. 13Before he left he called together ten assistants and gave them each $2,000 to invest while he was gone. 14But some of his people hated him and sent him their declaration of independence, stating that they had rebelled and would not acknowledge him as their king.

15"Upon his return he called in the men to whom he had given the money, to find out what they had done with it, and what their profits were.

16"The first man reported a tremendous gain—ten times as much as the original amount!

17"'Fine!' the king exclaimed. 'You are a good man. You have been faithful with the little I entrusted to you, and as your reward, you shall be governor of ten cities.'

18"The next man also reported a splendid gain—five times the original amount.

19"'All right!' his master said. 'You can be governor over five cities.'

20"But the third man brought back only the money he had started with. 'I've kept it safe,' he said, 21"because I was afraid [you would demand my profits], for you are a hard man to deal with, taking what isn't yours and even confiscating the crops that others plant.' 22"You vile and wicked slave,' the king roared. 'Hard, am I? That's exactly how I'll be toward you! If you knew so much about me and how tough I am, 23then why didn't you deposit the money in the bank so that I could at least get some interest on it?'

24"Then turning to the others standing by he ordered, 'Take the money away from him and give it to the man who earned the most.'

25"'But, sir,' they said, 'he has enough already!'

26"'Yes,' the king replied, 'but it is always true that those who have, get more, and those who have little, soon lose even that. 27And now about these enemies of mine who revolted—bring them in and execute them before me.'"

Treasures of Wisdom and Knowledge
❧ Colossians 2:1–10 ❧

I wish you could know how much I have struggled in prayer for you and for the church at Laodicea, and for my many other friends who have never known me personally. 2This is what I have asked of God for you: that you will be encouraged and knit together by strong ties of love, and that you will have the rich experience of knowing Christ with real certainty and clear understanding. *For God's secret plan, now at last made known, is Christ himself.* 3In him lie hidden all the mighty, untapped treasures of wisdom and knowledge.

4I am saying this because I am afraid that someone may fool you with smooth talk. 5For though I am far away from you my heart is with you, happy because you are getting along so well, happy be-

cause of your strong faith in Christ. 6And now just as you trusted Christ to save you, trust him, too, for each day's problems; live in vital union with him. 7Let your roots grow down into him and draw up nourishment from him. See that you go on growing in the Lord, and become strong and vigorous in the truth you were taught. Let your lives overflow with joy and thanksgiving for all he has done.

8Don't let others spoil your faith and joy with their philosophies, their wrong and shallow answers built on men's thoughts and ideas, instead of on what Christ has said. 9For in Christ there is all of God in a human body; 10*so you have everything when you have Christ,* and you are filled with God through your union with Christ. He is the highest Ruler, with authority over every other power.

Proverbs for Today
❧ 19:18–19 ❧

Discipline your son in his early years while there is hope. If you don't you will ruin his life. ☐ A short-tempered man must bear his own penalty; you can't do much to help him. If you try once you must try a dozen times!

―――――― ❧ KEY VERSE ❧ ――――――

Let your roots grow down into him and draw up nourishment from him. See that you go on growing in the Lord, and become strong and vigorous in the truth you were taught.—*Colossians 2:7a*

―――――― ❧ REFLECTION ❧ ――――――

Paul described the survival and growth of plants to illustrate the relationship that Christians should have with the Savior. Just as a flower draws nourishment from the soil through its roots, so we receive our life-giving strength from the Lord. The more we draw life from him, the less we will be fooled by those who wrongly claim to have life's answers.

Throughout your marriage you will receive advice and counsel from many different people, each with different life experiences and points of view.

Be sure always to use Scripture and the guidance of the Holy Spirit to judge what they have said. While godly people can be used in a wonderful way to counsel and encourage others, your first source of spiritual nourishment must be the One who died on the cross for your sins.

⚜ MEDITATION ⚜

Heavenly Father, help us to grow stronger each day in our faith and commitment to you. Guide us in our daily activities so that we might be a blessing to those around us in your name and for the sake of your Kingdom. ⤳

JULY 20

Jesus' Triumphal Entry into Jerusalem
⚜ Luke 19:28–40 ⚜

After telling this story, Jesus went on toward Jerusalem, walking along ahead of his disciples. [29]As they came to the towns of Bethphage and Bethany, on the Mount of Olives, he sent two disciples ahead, [30]with instructions to go to the next village, and as they entered they were to look for a donkey tied beside the road. It would be a colt, not yet broken for riding.

"Untie him," Jesus said, "and bring him here. [31]And if anyone asks you what you are doing, just say, 'The Lord needs him.'"

[32]They found the colt as Jesus said, [33]and sure enough, as they were untying it, the owners demanded an explanation.

"What are you doing?" they asked. "Why are you untying our colt?"

[34]And the disciples simply replied, "The Lord needs him!" [35]So they brought the colt to Jesus and threw some of their clothing across its back for Jesus to sit on.

[36,37]Then the crowds spread out their robes along the road ahead of him, and as they reached the place where the road started down from the Mount of Olives, the whole procession began to shout and sing as they walked along, praising God for all the wonderful miracles Jesus had done.

[38]"God has given us a King!" they exulted. "Long live the King! Let all heaven rejoice! Glory to God in the highest heavens!"

[39]But some of the Pharisees among the crowd said, "Sir, rebuke your followers for saying things like that!"

[40]He replied, "If they keep quiet, the stones along the road will burst into cheers!"

Our Sins Have Been Nailed to the Cross
⚜ Colossians 2:11–15 ⚜

When you came to Christ he set you free from your evil desires, not by a bodily operation of circumcision but by a spiritual operation, the baptism of your souls. [12]For in baptism you see how your old, evil nature died with him and was buried with him; and then you came up out of death with him into a new life because you trusted the Word of the mighty God who raised Christ from the dead.

[13]You were dead in sins, and your sinful desires were not yet cut away. Then he gave you a share in the very life of Christ, for he forgave all your sins, [14]and blotted out the charges proved against you, the list of his commandments which you had not obeyed. He took this list of sins and destroyed it by nailing it to Christ's cross. [15]In this way God took away Satan's power to accuse you of sin, and God openly displayed to the whole world Christ's triumph at the cross where your sins were all taken away.

Proverbs for Today
⚜ 19:20–21 ⚜

Get all the advice you can and be wise the rest of your life. ☐ Man proposes, but God disposes.

⚜ KEY VERSE ⚜

In this way God took away Satan's power to accuse you of sin, and God openly displayed to the whole world Christ's triumph at the cross where your sins were all taken away.—*Colossians 2:15*

✍ REFLECTION ✍

Before you and your spouse became Christians, your basic inclination and nature was to sin. As Christians, however, you have new natures. God has crucified your old rebellious dispositions (Romans 6:6) and replaced them with new spirits (Colossians 3:9–10). Your penalties for sin died with Christ on the cross. God has declared you *not guilty,* and you need no longer live under sin's power. Remember, though, that God won't take you out of the world or make you robots—you will still feel like sinning, and sometimes will sin. The difference is that before you were saved, you were slaves to your sinful nature, but now you can choose to live for Christ (see Galatians 2:20).

✍ MEDITATION ✍

Heavenly Father, we thank you for freeing us from bondage to sin and its destructive results. Help us to live daily for you and give us opportunities to share the Good News of salvation with others. ✍

JULY 21

Jesus Weeps over Jerusalem
✍ Luke 19:41-48 ✍

But as Jesus and his disciples came closer to Jerusalem and he saw the city ahead, he began to cry. ⁴²"Eternal peace was within your reach and you turned it down," he wept, "and now it is too late. ⁴³Your enemies will pile up earth against your walls and encircle you and close in on you, ⁴⁴and crush you to the ground, and your children within you; your enemies will not leave one stone upon another—for you have rejected the opportunity God offered you."

⁴⁵Then he entered the Temple and began to drive out the merchants from their stalls, ⁴⁶saying to them, "The Scriptures declare, 'My Temple is a place of prayer; but you have turned it into a den of thieves.'"

⁴⁷After that he taught daily in the Temple, but the chief priests and other religious leaders and the business community were trying to find some way to get rid of him. ⁴⁸But they could think of nothing, for he was a hero to the people—they hung on every word he said.

Don't Allow Yourself to Be Enslaved by Legalism
✍ Colossians 2:16-23 ✍

So don't let anyone criticize you for what you eat or drink, or for not celebrating Jewish holidays and feasts or new moon ceremonies or Sabbaths. ¹⁷For these were only temporary rules that ended when Christ came. They were only shadows of the real thing—of Christ himself. ¹⁸Don't let anyone declare you lost when you refuse to worship angels, as they say you must. They have seen a vision, they say, and know you should. These proud men (though they claim to be so humble) have a very clever imagination. ¹⁹But they are not connected to Christ, the Head to which all of us who are his body are joined; for we are joined together by his strong sinews and we grow only as we get our nourishment and strength from God.

²⁰Since you died, as it were, with Christ and this has set you free from following the world's ideas of how to be saved—by doing good and obeying various rules—why do you keep right on following them anyway, still bound by such rules as ²¹not eating, tasting, or even touching certain foods? ²²Such rules are mere human teachings, for food was made to be eaten and used up. ²³These rules may seem good, for rules of this kind require strong devotion and are humiliating and hard on the body, but they have no effect when it comes to conquering a person's evil thoughts and desires. They only make him proud.

Proverbs for Today
_{◦§ 19:22–23 ◦▷}

Kindness makes a man attractive. And it is better to be poor than dishonest. □ Reverence for God gives life, happiness, and protection from harm.

◦ KEY VERSE ◦

These rules may seem good, for rules of this kind require strong devotion and are humiliating and hard on the body, but they have no effect when it comes to conquering a person's evil thoughts and desires. They only make him proud.—*Colossians 2:23*

◦ REFLECTION ◦

So many people become involved in religious cults today. The tragic consequences are destroyed careers, marriages, and lives. You and your spouse can guard against false religions by asking these questions of any religious group: (1) Does it stress man-made rules and taboos rather than God's grace? (2) Does it foster a critical spirit about others, or does it exercise discipline discreetly and lovingly? (3) Does it stress formulas, secret knowledge, or special visions more than the Word of God? (4) Does it elevate self-righteousness—honoring those who keep the rules—rather than elevating Christ? (5) Does it reject Christ's universal church, claiming to be an elite group? (6) Does it teach humiliation of the body as a means to spiritual growth rather than focusing on the growth of the whole person? (7) Does it disregard the family rather than holding it in high regard as the Bible does? If the answer to any of these questions is yes, then you need to reject the teachings of the leaders of the cult and pray that God will lead you to a fellowship of believers who obey the truths of God's Word.

◦ MEDITATION ◦

Heavenly Father, help us to always maintain fellowship with a church that upholds you and your Word. We pray for those who become ensnared by the false teachings of cults and ask that you will help them see the difference between the light of truth and the darkness of falsehoods. ◦▷

JULY 22

The Story of the Disloyal Tenants
_{◦§ Luke 20:1–19 ◦▷}

On one of those days when Jesus was teaching and preaching the Good News in the Temple, he was confronted by the chief priests and other religious leaders and councilmen. [2]They demanded to know by what authority he had driven out the merchants from the Temple.

[3]"I'll ask you a question before I answer," he replied. [4]"Was John sent by God, or was he merely acting under his own authority?"

[5]They talked it over among themselves. "If we say his message was from heaven, then we are trapped because he will ask, 'Then why didn't you believe him?' [6]But if we say John was not sent from God, the people will mob us, for they are convinced that he was a prophet." [7]Finally they replied, "We don't know!"

[8]And Jesus responded, "Then I won't answer your question either."

[9]Now he turned to the people again and told them this story: "A man planted a vineyard and rented it out to some farmers, and went away to a distant land to live for several years. [10]When harvest time came, he sent one of his men to the farm to collect his share of the crops. But the tenants beat him up and sent him back empty-handed. [11]Then he sent another, but the same thing happened; he was beaten up and insulted and sent away without collecting. [12]A third man was sent and the same thing happened. He, too, was wounded and chased away.

[13]"'What shall I do?' the owner asked himself.

'I know! I'll send my cherished son. Surely they will show respect for him.'

[14]"But when the tenants saw his son, they said, 'This is our chance! This fellow will inherit all the land when his father dies. Come on. Let's kill him, and then it will be ours.' [15]So they dragged him out of the vineyard and killed him.

"What do you think the owner will do? [16]I'll tell you—he will come and kill them and rent the vineyard to others."

"But they would never do a thing like that," his listeners protested.

[17]Jesus looked at them and said, "Then what does the Scripture mean where it says, 'The Stone rejected by the builders was made the cornerstone'?" [18]And he added, "Whoever stumbles over that Stone shall be broken; and those on whom it falls will be crushed to dust."

[19]When the chief priests and religious leaders heard about this story he had told, they wanted him arrested immediately, for they realized that he was talking about them. They were the wicked tenants in his illustration. But they were afraid that if they themselves arrested him there would be a riot. So they tried to get him to say something that could be reported to the Roman governor as reason for arrest by him.

Set Your Heart on Heaven Where Christ Is
⮜§ Colossians 3:1–8 §⮞

Since you became alive again, so to speak, when Christ arose from the dead, now set your sights on the rich treasures and joys of heaven where he sits beside God in the place of honor and power. [2]Let heaven fill your thoughts; don't spend your time worrying about things down here. [3]You should have as little desire for this world as a dead person does. Your real life is in heaven with Christ and God. [4]And when Christ who is our real life comes back again, you will shine with him and share in all his glories.

[5]Away then with sinful, earthly things; deaden the evil desires lurking within you; have nothing to do with sexual sin, impurity, lust and shameful desires; don't worship the good things of life, for that is idolatry. [6]God's terrible anger is upon those who do such things. [7]You used to do them when your life was still part of this world; [8]but now is the time to cast off and throw away all these rotten garments of anger, hatred, cursing, and dirty language.

Proverbs for Today
⮜§ 19:24–25 §⮞

Some men are so lazy they won't even feed themselves! □ Punish a mocker and others will learn from his example. Reprove a wise man and he will be the wiser.

⮜ KEY VERSE ⮞

Punish a mocker and others will learn from his example. Reprove a wise man, and he will be the wiser.—*Proverbs 19:25*

⮜ REFLECTION ⮞

There is a significant difference between the person who learns from the advice of others and someone who refuses to accept correction. How we respond to guidance determines whether or not we will grow in wisdom. The next time someone offers you counsel, make a point of listening carefully to all that is said. You just might learn something. This is especially true when the advisor is your spouse. After all, who knows your strengths and weaknesses better than the person with whom you share your hopes, fears, dreams, and ideas each day?

⮜ MEDITATION ⮞

Heavenly Father, help us to be open to the insight of other people. We also pray that your Holy Spirit will guide both of us so that we can help each other during decisive times when effective counsel is needed. §⮞

JULY 23

It Is Right to Pay Taxes
◆§ Luke 20:20–26 §◆

Watching their opportunity, the religious leaders sent secret agents pretending to be honest men. [21]They said to Jesus, "Sir, we know what an honest teacher you are. You always tell the truth and don't budge an inch in the face of what others think, but teach the ways of God. [22]Now tell us—is it right to pay taxes to the Roman government or not?"

[23]He saw through their trickery and said, [24]"Show me a coin. Whose portrait is this on it? And whose name?"

They replied, "Caesar's—the Roman emperor's."

[25]He said, "Then give the emperor all that is his—and give to God all that is his!"

[26]Thus their attempt to outwit him before the people failed; and marveling at his answer, they were silent.

Principles for Holy Living
◆§ Colossians 3:9–13 §◆

Don't tell lies to each other; it was your old life with all its wickedness that did that sort of thing; now it is dead and gone. [10]You are living a brand new kind of life that is continually learning more and more of what is right, and trying constantly to be more and more like Christ who created this new life within you. [11]In this new life one's nationality or race or education or social position is unimportant; such things mean nothing. Whether a person has Christ is what matters, and he is equally available to all.

[12]Since you have been chosen by God who has given you this new kind of life, and because of his deep love and concern for you, you should practice tenderhearted mercy and kindness to others. Don't worry about making a good impression on them but be ready to suffer quietly and patiently. [13]Be gentle and ready to forgive; never hold grudges. Remember, the Lord forgave you, so you must forgive others.

Proverbs for Today
◆§ 19:26 §◆

A son who mistreats his father or mother is a public disgrace.

◆ KEY VERSE ◆

You are living a brand new kind of life that is continually learning more and more of what is right, and trying constantly to be more and more like Christ who created this new life within you.—*Colossians 3:10*

◆ REFLECTION ◆

Every Christian is part of a spiritual continuing education program. The more we know of Christ and his work, the more we are being changed into his likeness. Because this process is lifelong, we must never stop learning and obeying. There is no justification for drifting along, but there is an incentive to find the rich treasures of growing in Christ. It takes practice, review, patience, and concentration to keep in line with God's will. Make a daily commitment to spend time alone with the Lord. While it is important to pray and study God's Word together as a couple, it is equally vital that you develop a deep, personal relationship with God.

◆ MEDITATION ◆

Heavenly Father, we pray that you will help us to mature in our relationship with you. We ask that you will interact in our lives, individually and in each aspect of our marriage. §◆

Jesus Answers the Religious Leaders
§ Luke 20:27–47 §

Then some Sadducees—men who believed that death is the end of existence, that there is no resurrection— ²⁸came to Jesus with this:

"The laws of Moses state that if a man dies without children, the man's brother shall marry the widow and their children will legally belong to the dead man, to carry on his name. ²⁹We know of a family of seven brothers. The oldest married and then died without any children. ³⁰His brother married the widow and he, too, died. Still no children. ³¹And so it went, one after the other, until each of the seven had married her and died, leaving no children. ³²Finally the woman died also. ³³Now here is our question: Whose wife will she be in the resurrection? For all of them were married to her!"

³⁴,³⁵Jesus replied, "Marriage is for people here on earth, but when those who are counted worthy of being raised from the dead get to heaven, they do not marry. ³⁶And they never die again; in these respects they are like angels, and are sons of God, for they are raised up in new life from the dead.

³⁷,³⁸"But as to your real question—whether or not there is a resurrection—why, even the writings of Moses himself prove this. For when he describes how God appeared to him in the burning bush, he speaks of God as 'the God of Abraham, the God of Isaac, and the God of Jacob.' To say that the Lord *is* some person's God means that person is *alive*, not dead! So from God's point of view, all men are living."

³⁹"Well said, sir!" remarked some of the experts in the Jewish law who were standing there. ⁴⁰And that ended their questions, for they dared ask no more!

⁴¹Then he presented *them* with a question. "Why is it," he asked, "that Christ, the Messiah, is said to be a descendant of King David? ⁴²,⁴³For David himself wrote in the book of Psalms: 'God said to my Lord, the Messiah, "Sit at my right hand until I place your enemies beneath your feet."' ⁴⁴How can the Messiah be both David's son and David's God at the same time?"

⁴⁵Then, with the crowds listening, he turned to his disciples and said, ⁴⁶"Beware of these experts in religion, for they love to parade in dignified robes and to be bowed to by the people as they walk along the street. And how they love the seats of honor in the synagogues and at religious festivals! ⁴⁷But even while they are praying long prayers with great outward piety, they are planning schemes to cheat widows out of their property. Therefore God's heaviest sentence awaits these men."

Let the Peace of Christ Rule in Your Hearts
§ Colossians 3:14–17 §

Most of all, let love guide your life, for then the whole church will stay together in perfect harmony. ¹⁵Let the peace of heart which comes from Christ be always present in your hearts and lives, for this is your responsibility and privilege as members of his body. And always be thankful.

¹⁶Remember what Christ taught and let his words enrich your lives and make you wise; teach them to each other and sing them out in psalms and hymns and spiritual songs, singing to the Lord with thankful hearts. ¹⁷And whatever you do or say, let it be as a representative of the Lord Jesus, and come with him into the presence of God the Father to give him your thanks.

Proverbs for Today
§ 19:27–29 §

Stop listening to teaching that contradicts what you know is right. □ A worthless witness cares nothing for truth—he enjoys his sinning too much. □ Mockers and rebels shall be severely punished.

◦ KEY VERSE ◦

Jesus replied, "Marriage is for people here on earth, but when those who are counted worthy of being raised from the dead get to heaven, they do not marry. And they never die again; in these respects they are like angels, and are sons of God, for they are raised up in new life from the dead."—*Luke 20:34–35*

Jesus' statement does not mean that people will not recognize their partners in heaven. It simply means that we must not think of heaven as an extension of life as we now know it. Our relationships in this life are limited by time, death, and sin. We don't know everything about our resurrection life, but Jesus affirms that relationships will be different from what we are used to here and now. Don't be discouraged that you won't have the same relationship with each other after you die. Instead, be filled with joy, because you have someone to love and care for in this life. And don't forget that you have the assurance of a glorious eternity with the Savior.

── ❧ MEDITATION ❧ ──

Heavenly Father, we praise you for our lives together and thank you for sending your Son to die for our sins so that we might have eternal life in your presence. ❧

JULY 25

The Poor Widow
❧ Luke 21:1–4 ❧

As Jesus stood in the Temple, he was watching the rich tossing their gifts into the collection box. ²Then a poor widow came by and dropped in two small copper coins.

³"Really," he remarked, "this poor widow has given more than all the rest of them combined. ⁴For they have given a little of what they didn't need, but she, poor as she is, has given everything she has."

Paul's Commands for Community Life
❧ Colossians 3:18—4:1 ❧

You wives, submit yourselves to your husbands, for that is what the Lord has planned for you. ¹⁹And you husbands must be loving and kind to your wives and not bitter against them, nor harsh.

²⁰You children must always obey your fathers and mothers, for that pleases the Lord. ²¹Fathers, don't scold your children so much that they become discouraged and quit trying.

²²You slaves must always obey your earthly masters, not only trying to please them when they are watching you but all the time; obey them willingly because of your love for the Lord and because you want to please him. ²³Work hard and cheerfully at all you do, just as though you were working for the Lord and not merely for your masters, ²⁴remembering that it is the Lord Christ who is going to pay you, giving you your full portion of all he owns. He is the one you are really working for. ²⁵And if you don't do your best for him, he will pay you in a way that you won't like—for he has no special favorites who can get away with shirking.

⁴:¹You slave owners must be just and fair to all your slaves. Always remember that you, too, have a Master in heaven who is closely watching you.

Proverbs for Today
❧ 20:1 ❧

Wine gives false courage; hard liquor leads to brawls; what fools men are to let it master them, making them reel drunkenly down the street!

You wives, submit yourselves to your husbands, for that is what the Lord has planned for you. And you husbands must be loving and kind to your wives and not bitter against them nor harsh.—*Colossians 3:18–19*

In his letters Paul described three relationships in the home: (1) husbands and wives, (2) parents and children, and (3) masters and slaves. Fortunately today the evil practice of slavery is no longer a part of our culture. But the principles for families still apply. In each case there is mutual responsibility to submit and love, to obey and encourage, to work hard and be fair. Examine your marriage carefully. Are you relating to each other in the way God intended? Ask God to show each of you how you can be more loving and kind to your spouse.

❦ MEDITATION ❦

Heavenly Father, forgive us when we fail to demonstrate an unselfish, caring attitude toward each other. Help us to be willing to submit to one another in love and to the direction of the Holy Spirit in earnest devotion. ❧

JULY 26

The Signs of the Last Days
❧ Luke 21:5–19 ❧

Some of Jesus' disciples began talking about the beautiful stonework of the Temple and the memorial decorations on the walls.

⁶But Jesus said, "The time is coming when all these things you are admiring will be knocked down, and not one stone will be left on top of another; all will become one vast heap of rubble."

⁷"Master!" they exclaimed. "When? And will there be any warning ahead of time?"

⁸He replied, "Don't let anyone mislead you. For many will come announcing themselves as the Messiah, and saying, 'The time has come.' But don't believe them! ⁹And when you hear of wars and insurrections beginning, don't panic. True, wars must come, but the end won't follow immediately—¹⁰for nation shall rise against nation and kingdom against kingdom, ¹¹and there will be great earthquakes, and famines in many lands, and epidemics, and terrifying things happening in the heavens.

¹²"But before all this occurs, there will be a time of special persecution, and you will be dragged into synagogues and prisons and before kings and governors for my name's sake. ¹³But as a result, the Messiah will be widely known and honored. ¹⁴Therefore, don't be concerned about how to answer the charges against you, ¹⁵for I will give you the right words and such logic that none of your opponents will be able to reply! ¹⁶Even those closest to you—your parents, brothers, relatives, and friends will betray you and have you arrested; and some of you will be killed. ¹⁷And everyone will hate

you because you are mine and are called by my name. ¹⁸But not a hair of your head will perish! ¹⁹For if you stand firm, you will win your souls.

Be Diligent in Prayer
❧ Colossians 4:2–6 ❧

Don't be weary in prayer; keep at it; watch for God's answers and remember to be thankful when they come. ³Don't forget to pray for us too, that God will give us many chances to preach the Good News of Christ for which I am here in jail. ⁴Pray that I will be bold enough to tell it freely and fully, and make it plain, as, of course, I should.

⁵Make the most of your chances to tell others the Good News. Be wise in all your contacts with them. ⁶Let your conversation be gracious as well as sensible, for then you will have the right answer for everyone.

Proverbs for Today
❧ 20:2–3 ❧

The king's fury is like that of a roaring lion; to rouse his anger is to risk your life. □ It is an honor for a man to stay out of a fight. Only fools insist on quarreling.

❦ KEY VERSE ❦

It is an honor for a man to stay out of a fight. Only fools insist on quarreling.—*Proverbs 20:3*

❦ REFLECTION ❦

People who are truly confident of their strength do not need to parade it around. A brave person does not look for chances to prove his or her bravery. A resourceful person can find a way out of a fight.

Too many people consider themselves successful at marriage because they think they know how to "handle" their spouse. Usually they abuse them physically or verbally until their husband or wife simply gives up and either leaves or withdraws into a shell. Don't let your marriage become a torment to the person you pledged to love and honor. Demonstrate that you are both people of character and integrity by placing the needs and feelings of the other person first.

—————————— ⚜ **MEDITATION** ⚜ ——————————

Heavenly Father, we pray that your Holy Spirit will guide us in all that we say and do so that our words and actions create an atmosphere of harmony in our home. We thank you for our marriage and ask that you will maintain a loving attitude in our hearts. ⚜

JULY 27 _____

Be Ready for Christ's Return
⚜ Luke 21:20–38 ⚜

"But when you see Jerusalem surrounded by armies, then you will know that the time of its destruction has arrived. [21]Then let the people of Judea flee to the hills. Let those in Jerusalem try to escape, and those outside the city must not attempt to return. [22]For those will be days of God's judgment, and the words of the ancient Scriptures written by the prophets will be abundantly fulfilled. [23]Woe to expectant mothers in those days, and those with tiny babies. For there will be great distress upon this nation and wrath upon this people. [24]They will be brutally killed by enemy weapons, or sent away as exiles and captives to all the nations of the world; and Jerusalem shall be conquered and trampled down by the Gentiles until the period of Gentile triumph ends in God's good time.

[25]"Then there will be strange events in the skies—warnings, evil omens and portents in the sun, moon and stars; and down here on earth the nations will be in turmoil, perplexed by the roaring seas and strange tides. [26]The courage of many people will falter because of the fearful fate they see coming upon the earth, for the stability of the very heavens will be broken up. [27]Then the peoples of the earth shall see me, the Messiah, coming in a cloud with power and great glory. [28]So when all these things begin to happen, stand straight and look up! For your salvation is near."

[29]Then he gave them this illustration: "Notice the fig tree, or any other tree. [30]When the leaves come out, you know without being told that summer is near. [31]In the same way, when you see the events taking place that I've described you can be just as sure that the Kingdom of God is near.

[32]"I solemnly declare to you that when these things happen, the end of this age has come. [33]And though all heaven and earth shall pass away, yet my words remain forever true.

[34,35]"Watch out! Don't let my sudden coming catch you unawares; don't let me find you living in careless ease, carousing and drinking, and occupied with the problems of this life, like all the rest of the world. [36]Keep a constant watch. And pray that if possible you may arrive in my presence without having to experience these horrors."

[37,38]Every day Jesus went to the Temple to teach, and the crowds began gathering early in the morning to hear him. And each evening he returned to spend the night on the Mount of Olives.

Greetings from Paul's Christian Friends
⚜ Colossians 4:7–18 ⚜

Tychicus, our much loved brother, will tell you how I am getting along. He is a hard worker and serves the Lord with me. [8]I have sent him on this special trip just to see how you are, and to comfort and encourage you. [9]I am also sending Onesimus, a faithful and much loved brother, one of your own people. He and Tychicus will give you all the latest news.

[10]Aristarchus, who is with me here as a prisoner, sends you his love, and so does Mark, a relative of Barnabas. And as I said before, give Mark a hearty welcome if he comes your way. [11]Jesus Justus also sends his love. These are the only Jewish Christians working with me here, and what a comfort they have been!

[12]Epaphras, from your city, a servant of Christ Jesus, sends you his love. He is always earnestly praying for you, asking God to make you strong and perfect and to help you know his will in everything you do. [13]I can assure you that he has worked hard for you with his prayers, and also for the Christians in Laodicea and Hierapolis.

[14]Dear doctor Luke sends his love, and so does Demas.

[15]Please give my greeting to the Christian friends at Laodicea, and to Nymphas, and to those who meet in his home. [16]By the way, after you have read this letter will you pass it on to the church at Laodicea? And read the letter I wrote to them. [17]And say to Archippus, "Be sure that you do all the Lord has told you to."

[18]Here is my own greeting in my own handwriting: Remember me here in jail. May God's blessings surround you.

Sincerely,
Paul

Proverbs for Today
⋞§ 20:4–6 §⋟

If you won't plow in the cold, you won't eat at the harvest. ☐ Though good advice lies deep within a counselor's heart, the wise man will draw it out. ☐ Most people will tell you what loyal friends they are, but are they telling the truth?

⋞ KEY VERSE ⋟

If you won't plow in the cold, you won't eat at the harvest.

⋞ REFLECTION ⋟

From the time you were small children, you've heard warnings like this: if you don't study, you'll fail the test; if you don't save, you won't have money when you need it; if you spend more time with your friends than with your spouse, then you soon won't have a spouse to go home to. God wants us to anticipate future needs and prepare for them. We can't expect him to come to our rescue when we cause our own problems through lack of planning. He provides for us, but he also expects us to be responsible. Don't take anything in your marriage for granted. Love is a seed that, once planted, must be carefully tended if it is to grow and bloom.

⋞ MEDITATION ⋟

Heavenly Father, we thank you for our marriage and ask your Holy Spirit to guide us in our thoughts, words, and actions so that we will be a loving source of encouragement for each other. ⋟

JULY 28

The Last Supper
⋞§ Luke 22:1–23 §⋟

And now the Passover celebration was drawing near—the Jewish festival when only bread made without yeast was used. [2]The chief priests and other religious leaders were actively plotting Jesus' murder, trying to find a way to kill him without starting a riot—a possibility they greatly feared.

[3]Then Satan entered into Judas Iscariot, who was one of the twelve disciples, [4]and he went over to the chief priests and captains of the Temple guards to discuss the best way to betray Jesus to them. [5]They were, of course, delighted to know that he

was ready to help them and promised him a reward. [6]So he began to look for an opportunity for them to arrest Jesus quietly when the crowds weren't around.

[7]Now the day of the Passover celebration arrived, when the Passover lamb was killed and eaten with the unleavened bread. [8]Jesus sent Peter and John ahead to find a place to prepare their Passover meal.

[9]"Where do you want us to go?" they asked.

[10]And he replied, "As soon as you enter Jerusalem, you will see a man walking along carrying a pitcher of water. Follow him into the house he enters, [11]and say to the man who lives there, 'Our Teacher says for you to show us the guest room where he can eat the Passover meal with his disciples.' [12]He will take you upstairs to a large room all ready for us. That is the place. Go ahead and prepare the meal there."

[13]They went off to the city and found everything just as Jesus had said, and prepared the Passover supper.

[14]Then Jesus and the others arrived, and at the proper time all sat down together at the table; [15]and he said, "I have looked forward to this hour with deep longing, anxious to eat this Passover meal with you before my suffering begins. [16]For I tell you now that I won't eat it again until what it represents has occurred in the Kingdom of God."

[17]Then he took a glass of wine, and when he had given thanks for it, he said, "Take this and share it among yourselves. [18]For I will not drink wine again until the Kingdom of God has come."

[19]Then he took a loaf of bread; and when he had thanked God for it, he broke it apart and gave it to them, saying, "This is my body, given for you. Eat it in remembrance of me."

[20]After supper he gave them another glass of wine, saying, "This wine is the token of God's new agreement to save you—an agreement sealed with the blood I shall pour out to purchase back your souls. [21]But here at this table, sitting among us as a friend, is the man who will betray me. [22]I must die. It is part of God's plan. But, oh, the horror awaiting that man who betrays me."

[23]Then the disciples wondered among themselves which of them would ever do such a thing.

Paul Commends the Thessalonians' Faith
◆§ 1 Thessalonians 1:1–10 ◆

From: Paul, Silas and Timothy.

To: The Church at Thessalonica—to you who belong to God the Father and the Lord Jesus Christ: May blessing and peace of heart be your rich gifts from God our Father, and from Jesus Christ our Lord.

[2]We always thank God for you and pray for you constantly. [3]We never forget your loving deeds as we talk to our God and Father about you, and your strong faith and steady looking forward to the return of our Lord Jesus Christ.

[4]We know that God has chosen you, dear brothers, much beloved of God. [5]For when we brought you the Good News, it was not just meaningless chatter to you; no, you listened with great interest. What we told you produced a powerful effect upon you, for the Holy Spirit gave you great and full assurance that what we said was true. And you know how our very lives were further proof to you of the truth of our message. [6]So you became our followers and the Lord's; for you received our message with joy from the Holy Spirit in spite of the trials and sorrows it brought you.

[7]Then you yourselves became an example to all the other Christians in Greece. [8]And now the Word of the Lord has spread out from you to others everywhere, far beyond your boundaries, for wherever we go we find people telling us about your remarkable faith in God. We don't need to tell *them* about it, [9]for *they* keep telling *us* about the wonderful welcome you gave us, and how you turned away from your idols to God so that now the living and true God only is your Master. [10]And they speak of how you are looking forward to the return of God's Son from heaven—Jesus, whom God brought back to life—and he is our only Savior from God's terrible anger against sin.

Proverbs for Today
◆§ 20:7 ◆

It is a wonderful heritage to have an honest father.

When we brought you the Good News, it was not just meaningless chatter to you; no, you listened with great interest. What we told you produced a powerful effect upon you, for the Holy Spirit gave you great and full assurance that what we said was true. And you know how our very lives were further proof to you of the truth of our message. —*1 Thessalonians 1:5*

~ REFLECTION ~

Paul said, "our very lives were further proof." The Thessalonians could see that what Paul, Silas, and Timothy were preaching was true be- cause they lived it. Do your lives confirm or contradict what you say you believe? Is your marriage an encouragement to other Christian couples and a witness for those who are searching for an answer to the conflicts and problems in their lives? If not, then words about what you believe will be meaningless to them. Put your faith and words into action so that your lives and marriage will be living proof of God's perfect love and truth.

~ MEDITATION ~

Heavenly Father, we pray that you will help us be consistent in our words and deeds so that others can see the joy of your salvation through our lives. ~

JULY 29

A Leader Must Be a Servant
~ Luke 22:24–30 ~

And the disciples began to argue among themselves as to who would have the highest rank [in the coming Kingdom].

²⁵Jesus told them, "In this world the kings and great men order their slaves around, and the slaves have no choice but to like it! ²⁶But among you, the one who serves you best will be your leader. ²⁷Out in the world the master sits at the table and is served by his servants. But not here! For I am your servant. ²⁸Nevertheless, because you have stood true to me in these terrible days, ²⁹and because my Father has granted me a Kingdom, I, here and now, grant you the right ³⁰to eat and drink at my table in that Kingdom; and you will sit on thrones judging the twelve tribes of Israel.

Paul Reviews His Ministry to the Thessalonians
~ 1 Thessalonians 2:1–8 ~

You yourselves know, dear brothers, how worthwhile that visit was. ²You know how badly we had been treated at Philippi just before we came to you, and how much we suffered there. Yet God gave us the courage to boldly repeat the same message to you, even though we were surrounded by enemies. ³So you can see that we were not preaching with any false motives or evil purposes in mind; we were perfectly straightforward and sincere.

⁴For we speak as messengers from God, trusted by him to tell the truth; we change his message not one bit to suit the taste of those who hear it; for we serve God alone, who examines our hearts' deepest thoughts. ⁵Never once did we try to win you with flattery, as you very well know, and God knows we were not just pretending to be your friends so that you would give us money! ⁶As for praise, we have never asked for it from you or anyone else, although as apostles of Christ we certainly had a right to some honor from you. ⁷But we were as gentle among you as a mother feeding and caring for her own children. ⁸We loved you dearly—so dearly that we gave you not only God's message, but our own lives too.

Proverbs for Today
~ 20:8–10 ~

A king sitting as judge weighs all the evidence carefully, distinguishing the true from false. □ Who can ever say, "I have cleansed my heart; I am sinless"? □ The Lord despises every kind of cheating.

_____ ◦ KEY VERSE ◦ _____

You know how badly we had been treated at Philippi just before we came to you and how much we suffered there. Yet God gave us the courage to boldly repeat the same message to you, even though we were surrounded by enemies.—*1 Thessalonians 2:2*

_____ ◦ REFLECTION ◦ _____

The Thessalonians knew that Paul had been imprisoned in Philippi just before coming to Thessalonica (see Acts 16:11—17:1). Fear of imprisonment did not keep Paul from preaching the Good News. He placed his desire to serve God and witness to others above any personal interests or fears.

If God is asking you to do something, either individually or as a couple, he will give you the strength and courage to do it in spite of the obstacles that block your way. Paul knew that, in spite of the personal costs, nothing brings greater joy and satisfaction than following the will of God. Don't let the fleeting concerns of this world, or even friends and family, keep you from experiencing the exhilaration of serving the Lord.

_____ ◦ MEDITATION ◦ _____

Heavenly Father, we submit our marriage to you and ask that you will give us the wisdom, strength, ability, and faith to serve you in whatever ministry you have chosen for us. ◦

JULY 30 _____

Jesus Predicts Peter's Denial
◦ Luke 22:31–34 ◦

"Simon, Simon, Satan has asked to have you, to sift you like wheat, ³²but I have pleaded in prayer for you that your faith should not completely fail. So when you have repented and turned to me again, strengthen and build up the faith of your brothers."

³³Simon said, "Lord, I am ready to go to jail with you, and even to die with you."

³⁴But Jesus said, "Peter, let me tell you something. Between now and tomorrow morning when the rooster crows, you will deny me three times, declaring that you don't even know me."

Paul's Work among the Thessalonians
◦ 1 Thessalonians 2:9–13 ◦

Don't you remember, dear brothers, how hard we worked among you? Night and day we toiled and sweated to earn enough to live on so that our expenses would not be a burden to anyone there, as we preached God's Good News among you. ¹⁰You yourselves are our witnesses—as is God—that we have been pure and honest and faultless toward every one of you. ¹¹We talked to you as a father to his own children—don't you remember?—pleading with you, encouraging you and even demanding ¹²that your daily lives should not embarrass God, but bring joy to him who invited you into his Kingdom to share his glory.

¹³And we will never stop thanking God for this: that when we preached to you, you didn't think of the words we spoke as being just our own, but you accepted what we said as the very Word of God—which, of course, it was—and it changed your lives when you believed it.

Proverbs for Today
◦ 20:11 ◦

The character of even a child can be known by the way he acts—whether what he does is pure and right.

_____ ◦ KEY VERSE ◦ _____

"Simon, Simon, Satan has asked to have you, to sift you like wheat, but I have pleaded in prayer for you that your faith should not completely fail. So when you have repented and turned to me again, strengthen and build up the faith of your brothers."—*Luke 22:31–32*

Satan wanted to crush Peter like wheat. He hoped to find only chaff and blow it away. But Jesus assured Peter that his faith, though it would falter, would not be destroyed. It would be renewed, and Peter would become a leader.

In the same way, we often fall short of what God demands of us. But when we turn to God, he restores us and deepens our faith. Turn to him daily as a couple. Set aside a regular time for prayer and Bible reading together so that your faith and understanding will grow, and so that you will both be able to withstand Satan's temptations and tests.

── ◦ **MEDITATION** ◦ ──

Heavenly Father, help us to organize our daily activities so that we always have time for you. Give us insight into your Word and an ever-deepening understanding of your will for our lives. ❧

JULY 31

Jesus Prepares the Disciples for His Death
❧ Luke 22:35–38 ❧

Then Jesus asked his disciples, "When I sent you out to preach the Good News and you were without money, duffle bag, or extra clothing, how did you get along?"

"Fine," they replied.

36"But now," he said, "take a duffle bag if you have one, and your money. And if you don't have a sword, better sell your clothes and buy one! 37For the time has come for this prophecy about me to come true: 'He will be condemned as a criminal!' Yes, everything written about me by the prophets will come true."

38"Master," they replied, "we have two swords among us."

"Enough!" he said.

Persecuted for Spreading the Gospel
❧ 1 Thessalonians 2:14–3:4 ❧

And then, dear brothers, you suffered what the churches in Judea did, persecution from your own countrymen, just as they suffered from their own people the Jews. 15After they had killed their own prophets, they even executed the Lord Jesus; and now they have brutally persecuted us and driven us out. They are against both God and man, 16trying to keep us from preaching to the Gentiles for fear some might be saved; and so their sins continue to grow. But the anger of God has caught up with them at last.

17Dear brothers, after we left you and had been away from you but a very little while (though our hearts never left you), we tried hard to come back to see you once more. 18We wanted very much to come and I, Paul, tried again and again, but Satan stopped us. 19For what is it we live for, that gives us hope and joy and is our proud reward and crown? It is you! Yes, you will bring us much joy as we stand together before our Lord Jesus Christ when he comes back again. 20For you are our trophy and joy.

3:1Finally, when I could stand it no longer, I decided to stay alone in Athens 2,3and send Timothy, our brother and fellow worker, God's minister, to visit you to strengthen your faith and encourage you, and to keep you from becoming fainthearted in all the troubles you were going through. (But of course you know that such troubles are a part of God's plan for us Christians. 4Even while we were still with you we warned you ahead of time that suffering would soon come—and it did.)

Proverbs for Today
❧ 20:12 ❧

If you have good eyesight and good hearing, thank God who gave them to you.

Finally, when I could stand it no longer, I decided to stay alone in Athens and send Timothy, our brother and fellow worker, God's minister, to visit you to strengthen your faith and encourage you and to keep you from becoming fainthearted in all the troubles you were going through. (But of course you know that such troubles are a part of God's plan for us Christians.)—*1 Thessalonians 3:1–3*

REFLECTION

Some people think that troubles are always caused by sin or a lack of faith. But troubles can also be a part of God's plan. Going through trials can develop character (James 1:2–4), patience (Romans 5:3–5), and sensitivity toward others (2 Corinthi-ans 1:3–7). Problems are unavoidable for people in an ungodly world. Any troubles either of you have may be a sign of effective Christian living.

Some people turn to God hoping to escape suffering on earth. Rather than promising escape from suffering, God gives us power to grow through our sufferings. The Christian life is marked by obedience to Christ despite temptation and hardship. Ask God to give you faith and courage during times of hardship and he will help you overcome any adversity and make you both stronger in the process.

MEDITATION

Heavenly Father, we pray that you will give us strength and encouragement when we face difficult times. Forgive us when our faith wavers when things don't go the way we want and help us to never forget that you are in control of all things. ❧

AUGUST 1

Judas Betrays Jesus
❧ Luke 22:39–54 ❧

Then, accompanied by the disciples, Jesus left the upstairs room and went as usual to the Mount of Olives. [40]There he told them, "Pray God that you will not be overcome by temptation."

[41,42]He walked away, perhaps a stone's throw, and knelt down and prayed this prayer: "Father, if you are willing, please take away this cup of horror from me. But I want your will, not mine." [43]Then an angel from heaven appeared and strengthened him, [44]for he was in such agony of spirit that he broke into a sweat of blood, with great drops falling to the ground as he prayed more and more earnestly. [45]At last he stood up again and returned to the disciples—only to find them asleep, exhausted from grief.

[46]"Asleep!" he said. "Get up! Pray God that you will not fall when you are tempted."

[47]But even as he said this, a mob approached, led by Judas, one of his twelve disciples. Judas walked over to Jesus and kissed him on the cheek in friendly greeting.

[48]But Jesus said, "Judas, how can you do this—betray the Messiah with a kiss?"

[49]When the other disciples saw what was about to happen, they exclaimed, "Master, shall we fight? We brought along the swords!" [50]And one of them slashed at the High Priest's servant, and cut off his right ear.

[51]But Jesus said, "Don't resist any more." And he touched the place where the man's ear had been and restored it. [52]Then Jesus addressed the chief priests and captains of the Temple guards and the religious leaders who headed the mob. "Am I a robber," he asked, "that you have come armed with swords and clubs to get me? [53]Why didn't you arrest me in the Temple? I was there every day. But this is your moment—the time when Satan's power reigns supreme."

[54]So they seized him and led him to the High Priest's residence, and Peter followed at a distance.

Timothy's Good Report
·§ 1 Thessalonians 3:5–8 ℰ·

As I was saying, when I could bear the suspense no longer I sent Timothy to find out whether your faith was still strong. I was afraid that perhaps Satan had gotten the best of you and that all our work had been useless. [6]And now Timothy has just returned and brings the welcome news that your faith and love are as strong as ever, and that you remember our visit with joy and want to see us just as much as we want to see you. [7]So we are greatly comforted, dear brothers, in all of our own crushing troubles and suffering here, now that we know you are standing true to the Lord. [8]We can bear anything as long as we know that you remain strong in him.

Proverbs for Today
·§ 20:13–15 ℰ·

If you love sleep, you will end in poverty. Stay awake, work hard, and there will be plenty to eat! ☐ "Utterly worthless!" says the buyer as he haggles over the price. But afterwards he brags about his bargain! ☐ Good sense is far more valuable than gold or precious jewels.

·◈ KEY VERSE ◈·

We can bear anything as long as we know that you remain strong in him.—*1 Thessalonians 3:8*

·◈ REFLECTION ◈·

Paul was encouraged by Timothy's report concerning the Thessalonian Christians. These young believers were standing firm in the faith despite fierce persecution. In the midst of trouble or pressure, believers should encourage each other. Compliments, expressions of thanks, and support for those who are wavering in the faith help to build up fellow believers. When your marriage partner is going through a difficult time, don't become impatient or alarmed. Pray for and with your spouse, encouraging him or her in the faith.

·◈ MEDITATION ◈·

Heavenly Father, give us a love for each other that is strong during the good times and stronger still during the difficult ones. ℰ·

AUGUST 2

Peter's Denials
·§ Luke 22:55–62 ℰ·

The soldiers lit a fire in the courtyard and sat around it for warmth, and Peter joined them there. [56]A servant girl noticed him in the firelight and began staring at him. Finally she spoke: "This man was with Jesus!"

[57]Peter denied it. "Woman," he said, "I don't even know the man!"

[58]After a while someone else looked at him and said, "You must be one of them!"

"No sir, I am not!" Peter replied.

[59]About an hour later someone else flatly stated, "I know this fellow is one of Jesus' disciples, for both are from Galilee."

[60]But Peter said, "Man, I don't know what you are talking about." And as he said the words, a rooster crowed.

[61]At that moment Jesus turned and looked at Peter. Then Peter remembered what he had said—"Before the rooster crows tomorrow morning, you will deny me three times." [62]And Peter walked out of the courtyard, crying bitterly.

Paul Prays for the Thessalonians
·§ 1 Thessalonians 3:9–13 ℰ·

How can we thank God enough for you and for the joy and delight you have given us in our praying for you? [10]For night and day we pray on and on for you, asking God to let us see you again, to fill up any little cracks there may yet be in your faith.

¹¹May God our Father himself and our Lord Jesus send us back to you again. ¹²And may the Lord make your love to grow and overflow to each other and to everyone else, just as our love does toward you. ¹³This will result in your hearts being made strong, sinless and holy by God our Father, so that you may stand before him guiltless on that day when our Lord Jesus Christ returns with all those who belong to him.

Proverbs for Today
⋑ 20:16–18 ⋐

It is risky to make loans to strangers! □ Some men enjoy cheating, but the cake they buy with such ill-gotten gain will turn to gravel in their mouths. □ Don't go ahead with your plans without the advice of others; don't go to war until they agree.

---------⋑ KEY VERSE ⋐---------

Peter walked out of the courtyard, crying bitterly. —*Luke 22:62*

---------⋑ REFLECTION ⋐---------

Peter wept bitterly, not only because he realized that he had denied his Lord, but also because he had turned away from a very dear friend, a person who had loved and taught him for three years. Peter had said he would never deny Christ—despite Jesus' prediction—but when frightened, he went against all he had boldly promised. Unable to stand up for his Lord for even twelve hours, he had failed as a disciple and a friend. Even though Peter loved Christ, he still failed him.

Love and a promise of commitment are not enough to withstand human error and weakness, no matter how much love we think we may have. Thus we need to be aware of our own breaking points and not become overconfident or self-sufficient in our role of husband or wife. When we fail, we must remember that Christ can use those who recognize their failure. Just as Peter learned from this humiliating experience lessons that would help him in the leadership responsibilities he would soon assume, we can learn from our own humiliating experiences the lessons that Christ wants to teach us.

---------⋑ MEDITATION ⋐---------

Heavenly Father, as you forgive us for our failure to love each other perfectly, allow us to learn from our mistakes so that we will become all that you want us to be. ⋑⋐

AUGUST 3

Jesus Is Tried before the Jewish Supreme Court
⋑ Luke 22:63–71 ⋐

Now the guards in charge of Jesus began mocking him. They blindfolded him and hit him with their fists and asked, "Who hit you that time, prophet?" ⁶⁵And they threw all sorts of other insults at him.

⁶⁶Early the next morning at daybreak the Jewish Supreme Court assembled, including the chief priests and all the top religious authorities of the nation. Jesus was led before this Council, ⁶⁷,⁶⁸and instructed to state whether or not he claimed to be the Messiah.

But he replied, "If I tell you, you won't believe me or let me present my case. ⁶⁹But the time is soon coming when I, the Messiah, shall be enthroned beside Almighty God."

⁷⁰They all shouted, "Then you claim you are the Son of God?"

And he replied, "Yes, I am."

[71]"What need do we have for other witnesses?" they shouted. "For we ourselves have heard him say it."

God's People Should Be Holy
◄§ 1 Thessalonians 4:1–8 ยะ

Let me add this, dear brothers: You already know how to please God in your daily living, for you know the commands we gave you from the Lord Jesus himself. Now we beg you—yes, we demand of you in the name of the Lord Jesus—that you live more and more closely to that ideal. [3,4]For God wants you to be holy and pure, and to keep clear of all sexual sin so that each of you will marry in holiness and honor— [5]not in lustful passion as the heathen do, in their ignorance of God and his ways.

[6]And this also is God's will: that you never cheat in this matter by taking another man's wife, because the Lord will punish you terribly for this, as we have solemnly told you before. [7]For God has not called us to be dirty-minded and full of lust, but to be holy and clean. [8]If anyone refuses to live by these rules he is not disobeying the rules of men but of God who gives his *Holy* Spirit to you.

Proverbs for Today
◄§ 20:19 ยะ

Don't tell your secrets to a gossip unless you want them broadcast to the world.

───────── ◙ KEY VERSE ◙ ─────────

God wants you to be holy and pure and to keep clear of all sexual sin so that each of you will marry in holiness and honor—not in lustful passion as the heathen do, in their ignorance of God and his ways. *—1 Thessalonians 4:3–5*

───────── ◙ REFLECTION ◙ ─────────

Sexual desires and activities must be placed under Christ's control. God created sex for procreation, pleasure, and as an expression of love between a husband and wife. Sexual experience must be limited to the marriage relationship to avoid hurting ourselves, our relationship with God, and our relationships with others.

───────── ◙ MEDITATION ◙ ─────────

Heavenly Father, we dedicate to you this beautiful and fragile gift of sex that you have given us. Keep us pure and faithful to you and to each other. ยะ

AUGUST 4

Pilate Sentences Jesus to Death
◄§ Luke 23:1–25 ยะ

Then the entire Council took Jesus over to Pilate, the governor. [2]They began at once accusing him: "This fellow has been leading our people to ruin by telling them not to pay their taxes to the Roman government and by claiming he is our Messiah—a King."

[3]So Pilate asked him, "Are you their Messiah—their King?"

"Yes," Jesus replied, "it is as you say."

[4]Then Pilate turned to the chief priests and to the mob and said, "So? That isn't a crime!"

[5]Then they became desperate. "But he is causing riots against the government everywhere he goes, all over Judea, from Galilee to Jerusalem!"

[6]"Is he then a Galilean?" Pilate asked.

[7]When they told him yes, Pilate said to take him to King Herod, for Galilee was under Herod's jurisdiction; and Herod happened to be in Jerusalem at the time. [8]Herod was delighted at the opportunity to see Jesus, for he had heard a lot about him and had been hoping to see him perform a miracle.

[9]He asked Jesus question after question, but there was no reply. [10]Meanwhile, the chief priests and the other religious leaders stood there shouting their accusations.

[11]Now Herod and his soldiers began mocking

and ridiculing Jesus; and putting a kingly robe on him, they sent him back to Pilate. [12]That day Herod and Pilate—enemies before—became fast friends.

[13]Then Pilate called together the chief priests and other Jewish leaders, along with the people, [14]and announced his verdict:

"You brought this man to me, accusing him of leading a revolt against the Roman government. I have examined him thoroughly on this point and find him innocent. [15]Herod came to the same conclusion and sent him back to us—nothing this man has done calls for the death penalty. [16]I will therefore have him scourged with leaded thongs, and release him."

[17,18]But now a mighty roar rose from the crowd as with one voice they shouted. "Kill him, and release Barabbas to us!" [19](Barabbas was in prison for starting an insurrection in Jerusalem against the government, and for murder.) [20]Pilate argued with them, for he wanted to release Jesus. [21]But they shouted, "Crucify him! Crucify him!"

[22]Once more, for the third time, he demanded, "Why? What crime has he committed? I have found no reason to sentence him to death. I will therefore scourge him and let him go." [23]But they shouted louder and louder for Jesus' death, and their voices prevailed.

[24]So Pilate sentenced Jesus to die as they demanded. [25]And he released Barabbas, the man in prison for insurrection and murder, at their request. But he delivered Jesus over to them to do with as they would.

Christian Ambition
◄§ 1 Thessalonians 4:9–12 §►

But concerning the pure brotherly love that there should be among God's people, I don't need to say very much, I'm sure! For God himself is teaching you to love one another. [10]Indeed, your love is already strong toward all the Christian brothers throughout your whole nation. Even so, dear friends, we beg you to love them more and more. [11]This should be your ambition: to live a quiet life, minding your own business and doing your own work, just as we told you before. [12]As a result, people who are not Christians will trust and respect you, and you will not need to depend on others for enough money to pay your bills.

Proverbs for Today
◄§ 20:20–21 §►

God puts out the light of the man who curses his father or mother. □ Quick wealth is not a blessing in the end.

───────◈ KEY VERSE ◈───────

This should be your ambition: to live a quiet life, minding your own business and doing your own work, just as we told you before.—*1 Thessalonians 4:11*

───────◈ REFLECTION ◈───────

This is part of what it means to live as a Christian—to be responsible in all areas of life. This especially includes your marriage and home. You can hardly be effective when you share your faith with others if people don't respect you. Work together to be a faithful and positive force in society.

───────◈ MEDITATION ◈───────

Heavenly Father, we ask you to help us gain more self-control so that we can live a quiet life, minding our own business, and doing our own work. Do not allow us to slip in our responsibility to each other. §►

AUGUST 5

Jesus Is Crucified
❦ Luke 23:26–43 ❧

As the crowd led Jesus away to his death, Simon of Cyrene, who was just coming into Jerusalem from the country, was forced to follow, carrying Jesus' cross. ²⁷Great crowds trailed along behind, and many grief-stricken women.

²⁸But Jesus turned and said to them, "Daughters of Jerusalem, don't weep for me, but for yourselves and for your children. ²⁹For the days are coming when the women who have no children will be counted fortunate indeed. ³⁰Mankind will beg the mountains to fall on them and crush them, and the hills to bury them. ³¹For if such things as this are done to me, the Living Tree, what will they do to you?"

³²,³³Two others, criminals, were led out to be executed with him at a place called "The Skull." There all three were crucified—Jesus on the center cross, and the two criminals on either side.

³⁴"Father, forgive these people," Jesus said, "for they don't know what they are doing."

And the soldiers gambled for his clothing, throwing dice for each piece. ³⁵The crowd watched. And the Jewish leaders laughed and scoffed. "He was so good at helping others," they said, "let's see him save himself if he is really God's Chosen One, the Messiah."

³⁶The soldiers mocked him, too, by offering him a drink—of sour wine. ³⁷And they called to him, "If you are the King of the Jews, save yourself!"

³⁸A signboard was nailed to the cross above him with these words: "This is the King of the Jews."

³⁹One of the criminals hanging beside him scoffed, "So you're the Messiah, are you? Prove it by saving yourself—and us, too, while you're at it!"

⁴⁰,⁴¹But the other criminal protested. "Don't you even fear God when you are dying? We deserve to die for our evil deeds, but this man hasn't done one thing wrong." ⁴²Then he said, "Jesus, remember me when you come into your Kingdom."

⁴³And Jesus replied, "Today you will be with me in Paradise. This is a solemn promise."

The Hope of the Resurrection
❦ 1 Thessalonians 4:13—5:3 ❧

And now, dear brothers, I want you to know what happens to a Christian when he dies so that when it happens, you will not be full of sorrow, as those are who have no hope. ¹⁴For since we believe that Jesus died and then came back to life again, we can also believe that when Jesus returns, God will bring back with him all the Christians who have died.

¹⁵I can tell you this directly from the Lord: that we who are still living when the Lord returns will not rise to meet him ahead of those who are in their graves. ¹⁶For the Lord himself will come down from heaven with a mighty shout and with the soul-stirring cry of the archangel and the great trumpet-call of God. And the believers who are dead will be the first to rise to meet the Lord. ¹⁷Then we who are still alive and remain on the earth will be caught up with them in the clouds to meet the Lord in the air and remain with him forever. ¹⁸So comfort and encourage each other with this news.

⁵:¹When is all this going to happen? I really don't need to say anything about that, dear brothers, ²for you know perfectly well that no one knows. That day of the Lord will come unexpectedly like a thief in the night. ³When people are saying, "All is well, everything is quiet and peaceful"—then, all of a sudden, disaster will fall upon them as suddenly as a woman's birth pains begin when her child is born. And these people will not be able to get away anywhere—there will be no place to hide.

Proverbs for Today
❦ 20:22–23 ❧

Don't repay evil for evil. Wait for the Lord to handle the matter. ☐ The Lord loathes all cheating and dishonesty.

❧ KEY VERSE ❧

The Lord loathes all cheating and dishonesty.
—*Proverbs 20:23*

❦ 275 ❧

Dishonesty is a difficult sin to avoid because it can save us many uncomfortable moments. It is easy to cheat if we think no one (even our spouse) is looking. But dishonesty affects the very core of a person. It makes him or her untrustworthy and untrusting. It eventually makes a person unable to relate to others.

Don't take dishonesty lightly. Even the smallest portion of dishonesty contains enough of the poison of deceit to kill your spiritual life as well as your marriage. If there is any unconfessed dishonesty in your life, tell God about it now. He is ready to forgive you. If you discover that your spouse has been dishonest with you, forgive him or her.

–§ MEDITATION §–

Heavenly Father, may we strive for honesty in everything that we say and do, building each other up in the truth of your love. ❦

AUGUST 6

Jesus' Death and Burial
–§ Luke 23:44–56 ❦

By now it was noon, and darkness fell across the whole land for three hours, until three o'clock. [45]The light from the sun was gone—and suddenly the thick veil hanging in the Temple split apart.

[46]Then Jesus shouted, "Father, I commit my spirit to you," and with those words he died.

[47]When the captain of the Roman military unit handling the executions saw what had happened, he was stricken with awe before God and said, "Surely this man was innocent."

[48]And when the crowd that came to see the crucifixion saw that Jesus was dead they went home in deep sorrow. [49]Meanwhile, Jesus' friends, including the women who had followed him down from Galilee, stood in the distance watching.

[50,51,52]Then a man named Joseph, a member of the Jewish Supreme Court, from the city of Arimathea in Judea, went to Pilate and asked for the body of Jesus. He was a godly man who had been expecting the Messiah's coming and had not agreed with the decision and actions of the other Jewish leaders. [53]So he took down Jesus' body and wrapped it in a long linen cloth and laid it in a new, unused tomb hewn into the rock [at the side of a hill]. [54]This was done late on Friday afternoon, the day of preparation for the Sabbath.

[55]As the body was taken away, the women from Galilee followed and saw it carried into the tomb.

[56]Then they went home and prepared spices and ointments to embalm him; but by the time they were finished it was the Sabbath, so they rested all that day as required by the Jewish law.

Live in the Light of Jesus' Coming
–§ 1 Thessalonians 5:4–11 ❦

But, dear brothers, you are not in the dark about these things, and you won't be surprised as by a thief when that day of the Lord comes. [5]For you are all children of the light and of the day, and do not belong to darkness and night. [6]So be on your guard, not asleep like the others. Watch for his return and stay sober. [7]Night is the time for sleep and the time when people get drunk. [8]But let us who live in the light keep sober, protected by the armor of faith and love, and wearing as our helmet the happy hope of salvation.

[9]For God has not chosen to pour out his anger upon us, but to save us through our Lord Jesus Christ; [10]he died for us so that we can live with him forever, whether we are dead or alive at the time of his return. [11]So encourage each other to build each other up, just as you are already doing.

Proverbs for Today
–§ 20:24–25 ❦

Since the Lord is directing our steps, why try to understand everything that happens along the way?

☐ It is foolish and rash to make a promise to the Lord before counting the cost.

---------- ❧ **KEY VERSE** ❧ ----------

Encourage each other to build each other up, just as you are already doing.—*1 Thessalonians 5:11*

---------- ❧ **REFLECTION** ❧ ----------

As you near the end of a foot race, your legs ache, your throat burns, and your whole body cries out for you to stop. This is when cheering friends and fans are most valuable. Their encouragement helps you push through the pain to the finish. In the same way, husbands and wives should encourage each other. A word of encouragement offered at the right moment can be the difference between finishing well and collapsing along the way. Observe your mate closely. Be sensitive to one another's need for encouragement, and offer supportive words and actions.

---------- ❧ **MEDITATION** ❧ ----------

Heavenly Father, encourage us as we encourage each other. ❧

AUGUST 7

Jesus Rises from the Dead
❧ Luke 24:1–12 ❧

But very early on Sunday morning the women from Galilee took the ointments to the tomb— [2]and found that the huge stone covering the entrance had been rolled aside. [3]So they went in—but the Lord Jesus' body was gone.

[4]They stood there puzzled, trying to think what could have happened to it. Suddenly two men appeared before them, clothed in shining robes so bright their eyes were dazzled. [5]The women were terrified and bowed low before them.

Then the men asked, "Why are you looking in a tomb for someone who is alive? [6,7]He isn't here! He has come back to life again! Don't you remember what he told you back in Galilee—that the Messiah must be betrayed into the power of evil men and be crucified and that he would rise again the third day?"

[8]Then they remembered, [9]and rushed back to Jerusalem to tell his eleven disciples—and everyone else—what had happened. [10](The women who went to the tomb were Mary Magdalene and Joanna and Mary the mother of James, and several others.) [11]But the story sounded like a fairy tale to the men—they didn't believe it.

[12]However, Peter ran to the tomb to look. Stooping, he peered in and saw the empty linen wrappings; and then he went back home again, wondering what had happened.

Paul's Commands for Holy Living
❧ 1 Thessalonians 5:12–22 ❧

Dear brothers, honor the officers of your church who work hard among you and warn you against all that is wrong. [13]Think highly of them and give them your wholehearted love because they are straining to help you. And remember, no quarreling among yourselves.

[14]Dear brothers, warn those who are lazy; comfort those who are frightened; take tender care of those who are weak; and be patient with everyone. [15]See that no one pays back evil for evil, but always try to do good to each other and to everyone else. [16]Always be joyful. [17]Always keep on praying. [18]No matter what happens, always be thankful, for this is God's will for you who belong to Christ Jesus. [19]Do not smother the Holy Spirit. [20]Do not scoff at those who prophesy, [21]but test everything that is said to be sure it is true, and if it is, then accept it. [22]Keep away from every kind of evil.

Proverbs for Today
❧ 20:26–27 ❧

A wise king stamps out crime by severe punishment. ☐ A man's conscience is the Lord's searchlight exposing his hidden motives.

Dear brothers, warn those who are lazy, comfort those who are frightened, take tender care of those who are weak, and be patient with everyone. —*1 Thessalonians 5:14*

⊷ REFLECTION ⊷

Don't lie down with the lazy; warn them. Don't yell at the frightened; comfort them. At times it's difficult to distinguish between laziness and fear. Two people may be doing nothing—one because he is lazy and the other out of fear of doing something wrong. One of the keys to a good marriage is sensitivity: sensing the condition of your mate and offering the appropriate remedy for each situation. You can't effectively help until you know the problem, so listen patiently. You can't apply the right medicine until you know what kind of wound needs to be treated.

⊷ MEDITATION ⊷

Heavenly Father, open our ears so that we can listen to each other more effectively. Open our hearts so that we can be more patient. ⊷

AUGUST 8

Jesus' Emmaus Road Appearance
⊷ Luke 24:13–34 ⊷

That same day, Sunday, two of Jesus' followers were walking to the village of Emmaus, seven miles out of Jerusalem. [14]As they walked along they were talking of Jesus' death, [15]when suddenly Jesus himself came along and joined them and began walking beside them. [16]But they didn't recognize him, for God kept them from it.

[17]"You seem to be in a deep discussion about something," he said. "What are you so concerned about?" They stopped short, sadness written across their faces. [18]And one of them, Cleopas, replied, "You must be the only person in Jerusalem who hasn't heard about the terrible things that happened there last week."

[19]"What things?" Jesus asked.

"The things that happened to Jesus, the Man from Nazareth," they said. "He was a Prophet who did incredible miracles and was a mighty Teacher, highly regarded by both God and man. [20]But the chief priests and our religious leaders arrested him and handed him over to the Roman government to be condemned to death, and they crucified him. [21]We had thought he was the glorious Messiah and that he had come to rescue Israel.

"And now, besides all this—which happened three days ago— [22,23]some women from our group of his followers were at his tomb early this morning and came back with an amazing report that his body was missing, and that they had seen some angels there who told them Jesus is alive! [24]Some of our men ran out to see, and sure enough, Jesus' body was gone, just as the women had said."

[25]Then Jesus said to them, "You are such foolish, foolish people! You find it so hard to believe all that the prophets wrote in the Scriptures! [26]Wasn't it clearly predicted by the prophets that the Messiah would have to suffer all these things before entering his time of glory?"

[27]Then Jesus quoted them passage after passage from the writings of the prophets, beginning with the book of Genesis and going right on through the Scriptures, explaining what the passages meant and what they said about himself.

[28]By this time they were nearing Emmaus and the end of their journey. Jesus would have gone on, [29]but they begged him to stay the night with them, as it was getting late. So he went home with them. [30]As they sat down to eat, he asked God's blessing on the food and then took a small loaf of bread and broke it and was passing it over to them, [31]when suddenly—it was as though their eyes were opened—they recognized him! And at that moment he disappeared!

[32]They began telling each other how their hearts had felt strangely warm as he talked with them and explained the Scriptures during the walk down the

road. [33,34]Within the hour they were on their way back to Jerusalem, where the eleven disciples and the other followers of Jesus greeted them with these words, "The Lord has really risen! He appeared to Peter!"

Paul's Prayer and Final Greetings
⋖§ 1 Thessalonians 5:23–28 §⋗

May the God of peace himself make you entirely pure and devoted to God; and may your spirit and soul and body be kept strong and blameless until that day when our Lord Jesus Christ comes back again. [24]God, who called you to become his child, will do all this for you, just as he promised. [25]Dear brothers, pray for us. [26]Shake hands for me with all the brothers there. [27]I command you in the name of the Lord to read this letter to all the Christians. [28]And may rich blessings from our Lord Jesus Christ be with you, every one.

Sincerely,
Paul

Proverbs for Today
⋖§ 20:28–30 §⋗

If a king is kind, honest and fair, his kingdom stands secure. □ The glory of young men is their strength; of old men, their experience. □ Punishment that hurts chases evil from the heart.

_____⋖ **KEY VERSE** §⋗_____

They began telling each other how their hearts had felt strangely warm as he talked with them and explained the Scriptures during the walk down the road.—*Luke 24:32*

_____⋖ **REFLECTION** §⋗_____

The two disciples returning to Emmaus missed the significance of history's greatest event because they focused on their disappointments and problems—so much so that they didn't realize that they had been walking in the wrong direction—away from the fellowship of believers in Jerusalem. We are likely to miss Jesus and withdraw from the strength found in our spouse when we become preoccupied with our dashed hopes and frustrated plans. Only when you are looking for Jesus in the midst of your home will you experience the power and help he can bring to your marriage.

_____⋖ **MEDITATION** §⋗_____

Heavenly Father, may we be poised and ready to receive any blessing that you are anxious to give us. §⋗

AUGUST 9

The Ascension of Jesus
⋖§ Luke 24:35–53 §⋗

Then the two from Emmaus told their story of how Jesus had appeared to them as they were walking along the road and how they had recognized him as he was breaking the bread.

[36]And just as they were telling about it, Jesus himself was suddenly standing there among them, and greeted them. [37]But the whole group was terribly frightened, thinking they were seeing a ghost!

[38]"Why are you frightened?" he asked. "Why do you doubt that it is really I? [39]Look at my hands! Look at my feet! You can see that it is I, myself! Touch me and make sure that I am not a ghost! For ghosts don't have bodies, as you see that I do!" [40]As he spoke, he held out his hands for them to see [the marks of the nails], and showed them [the wounds in] his feet.

[41]Still they stood there undecided, filled with joy and doubt.

Then he asked them, "Do you have anything here to eat?"

[42]They gave him a piece of broiled fish, [43]and he ate it as they watched!

[44]Then he said, "When I was with you before, don't you remember my telling you that everything written about me by Moses and the prophets and in the Psalms must all come true?" [45]Then he

opened their minds to understand at last these many Scriptures! [46]And he said, "Yes, it was written long ago that the Messiah must suffer and die and rise again from the dead on the third day; [47]and that this message of salvation should be taken from Jerusalem to all the nations: *There is forgiveness of sins for all who turn to me*. [48]You have seen these prophecies come true.

[49]"And now I will send the Holy Spirit upon you, just as my Father promised. Don't begin telling others yet—stay here in the city until the Holy Spirit comes and fills you with power from heaven."

[50]Then Jesus led them out along the road to Bethany, and lifting his hands to heaven, he blessed them, [51]and then began rising into the sky, and went on to heaven. [52]And they worshiped him, and returned to Jerusalem filled with mighty joy, [53]and were continually in the Temple, praising God.

Paul Encourages the Thessalonians
2 Thessalonians 1:1–12

From: Paul, Silas and Timothy.

To: The church of Thessalonica—kept safe in God our Father and in the Lord Jesus Christ.

[2]May God the Father and the Lord Jesus Christ give you rich blessings and peace-filled hearts and minds.

[3]Dear brothers, giving thanks to God for you is not only the right thing to do, but it is our duty to God, because of the really wonderful way your faith has grown, and because of your growing love for each other. [4]We are happy to tell other churches about your patience and complete faith in God, in spite of all the crushing troubles and hardships you are going through.

[5]This is only one example of the fair, just way God does things, for he is using your sufferings to make you ready for his Kingdom, [6]while at the same time he is preparing judgment and punishment for those who are hurting you.

[7]And so I would say to you who are suffering, God will give you rest along with us when the Lord Jesus appears suddenly from heaven in flaming fire with his mighty angels, [8]bringing judgment on those who do not wish to know God, and who re-fuse to accept his plan to save them through our Lord Jesus Christ. [9]They will be punished in everlasting hell, forever separated from the Lord, never to see the glory of his power, [10]when he comes to receive praise and admiration because of all he has done for his people, his saints. And you will be among those praising him, because you have believed what we told you about him.

[11]And so we keep on praying for you that our God will make you the kind of children he wants to have—will make you as good as you wish you could be!—rewarding your faith with his power. [12]Then everyone will be praising the name of the Lord Jesus Christ because of the results they see in you; and your greatest glory will be that you belong to him. The tender mercy of our God and of the Lord Jesus Christ has made all this possible for you.

Proverbs for Today
21:1–2

Just as water is turned into irrigation ditches, so the Lord directs the king's thoughts. He turns them wherever he wants to. ☐ We can justify our every deed but God looks at our motives.

KEY VERSE

We can justify our every deed, but God looks at our motives.—*Proverbs 21:2*

REFLECTION

People can find an excuse for doing almost anything, but God looks behind the excuse to the motives. We often have to make difficult choices in our marriage when the right action is difficult to discern. We can help ourselves make such decisions by trying to identify our motives first, and then asking, "Would God be pleased with my real reasons for doing this?" God is not pleased when we do good deeds only to get something back.

MEDITATION

Heavenly Father, forgive us for personal motives that have strayed from your teachings. Draw us closer to you so that we can please you with the hidden reasons behind our good deeds.

Christian, the Word Made Flesh
John 1:1–14

Before anything else existed, there was Christ, with God. He has always been alive and is himself God. [3]He created everything there is—nothing exists that he didn't make. [4]Eternal life is in him, and this life gives light to all mankind. [5]His life is the light that shines through the darkness—and the darkness can never extinguish it.

[6,7]God sent John the Baptist as a witness to the fact that Jesus Christ is the true Light. [8]John himself was not the Light; he was only a witness to identify it.

[9]Later on, the one who is the true Light arrived to shine on everyone coming into the world.

[10]But although he made the world, the world didn't recognize him when he came. [11,12]Even in his own land and among his own people, the Jews, he was not accepted. Only a few would welcome and receive him. But to all who received him, he gave the right to become children of God. All they needed to do was to trust him to save them. [13]All those who believe this are reborn!—not a physical rebirth resulting from human passion or plan—but from the will of God.

[14]And Christ became a human being and lived here on earth among us and was full of loving forgiveness and truth. And some of us have seen his glory—the glory of the only Son of the heavenly Father!

Don't Be Deceived
2 Thessalonians 2:1–6

And now, what about the coming again of our Lord Jesus Christ, and our being gathered together to meet him? Please don't be upset and excited, dear brothers, by the rumor that this day of the Lord has already begun. If you hear of people having visions and special messages from God about this, or letters that are supposed to have come from me, don't believe them. [3]Don't be carried away and deceived regardless of what they say.

For that day will not come until two things happen: first, there will be a time of great rebellion against God, and then the man of rebellion will come—the son of hell. [4]He will defy every god there is, and tear down every other object of adoration and worship. He will go in and sit as God in the temple of God, claiming that he himself is God. [5]Don't you remember that I told you this when I was with you? [6]And you know what is keeping him from being here already; for he can come only when his time is ready.

Proverbs for Today
21:3

God is more pleased when we are just and fair than when we give him gifts.

KEY VERSE

We keep on praying for you, that our God will make you the kind of children he wants to have—will make you as good as you wish you could be!—rewarding your faith with his power.—*2 Thessalonians 1:11*

REFLECTION

When we truly love God, we are repeatedly disappointed in our performance. We want to be good, and yet we are unable to do so. God's purpose for all believers is to make them the kind of children he wants to have. As our faith in God increases, God increases the power available in us to do good. If you want God's power in your marriage, believe in his ability to do good rather than in yours. God will make you better than you ever thought you could be.

MEDITATION

Heavenly Father, we accept the power of your Holy Spirit in our marriage as you teach us each day how to have more faith in you.

AUGUST 11

John Proclaims Jesus as the Messiah
⋅§ John 1:15–34 ⋅

John pointed Jesus out to the people, telling the crowds, "This is the one I was talking about when I said, 'Someone is coming who is greater by far than I am—for he existed long before I did!'" [16]We have all benefited from the rich blessings he brought to us—blessing upon blessing heaped upon us! [17]For Moses gave us only the Law with its rigid demands and merciless justice, while Jesus Christ brought us loving forgiveness as well. [18]No one has ever actually seen God, but, of course, his only Son has, for he is the companion of the Father and has told us all about him.

[19]The Jewish leaders sent priests and assistant priests from Jerusalem to ask John whether he claimed to be the Messiah.

[20]He denied it flatly. "I am not the Christ," he said.

[21]"Well then, who are you?" they asked. "Are you Elijah?"

"No," he replied.

"Are you the Prophet?"

"No."

[22]"Then who are you? Tell us, so we can give an answer to those who sent us. What do you have to say for yourself?"

[23]He replied, "I am a voice from the barren wilderness, shouting as Isaiah prophesied, 'Get ready for the coming of the Lord!'"

[24,25]Then those who were sent by the Pharisees asked him, "If you aren't the Messiah or Elijah or the Prophet, what right do you have to baptize?"

[26]John told them, "I merely baptize with water, but right here in the crowd is someone you have never met, [27]who will soon begin his ministry among you, and I am not even fit to be his slave."

[28]This incident took place at Bethany, a village on the other side of the Jordan River where John was baptizing.

[29]The next day John saw Jesus coming toward him and said, "Look! There is the Lamb of God who takes away the world's sin! [30]He is the one I was talking about when I said, 'Soon a man far greater than I am is coming, who existed long before me!' [31]I didn't know he was the one, but I am here baptizing with water in order to point him out to the nation of Israel."

[32]Then John told about seeing the Holy Spirit in the form of a dove descending from heaven and resting upon Jesus.

[33]"I didn't know he was the one," John said again, "but at the time God sent me to baptize he told me, 'When you see the Holy Spirit descending and resting upon someone—he is the one you are looking for. He is the one who baptizes with the Holy Spirit.' [34]I saw it happen to this man, and I therefore testify that he is the Son of God."

The Man of Rebellion
⋅§ 2 Thessalonians 2:7–17 ⋅

As for the work this man of rebellion and hell will do when he comes, it is already going on, but he himself will not come until the one who is holding him back steps out of the way. [8]Then this wicked one will appear, whom the Lord Jesus will burn up with the breath of his mouth and destroy by his presence when he returns. [9]This man of sin will come as Satan's tool, full of satanic power, and will trick everyone with strange demonstrations, and will do great miracles. [10]He will completely fool those who are on their way to hell because they have said "no" to the Truth; they have refused to believe it and love it, and let it save them, [11]so God will allow them to believe lies with all their hearts, [12]and all of them will be justly judged for believing falsehood, refusing the Truth, and enjoying their sins. [13]But we must forever give thanks to God for you, our brothers loved by the Lord, because God chose from the very first to give you salvation, cleansing you by the work of the Holy Spirit and by your trusting in the Truth. [14]Through

⋅§ 282 ⋅

us he told you the Good News. Through us he called you to share in the glory of our Lord Jesus Christ.

¹⁵With all these things in mind, dear brothers, stand firm and keep a strong grip on the truth that we taught you in our letters and during the time we were with you.

¹⁶May our Lord Jesus Christ himself and God our Father, who has loved us and given us everlasting comfort and hope which we don't deserve, ¹⁷comfort your hearts with all comfort, and help you in every good thing you say and do.

Proverbs for Today
◄§ 21:4 §►

Pride, lust, and evil actions are all sin.

◈ KEY VERSE ◈

"I saw it happen to this man, and I therefore testify that he is the Son of God."—*John 1:34*

◈ REFLECTION ◈

John the Baptist's job was to point people to Jesus, the Messiah for whom they were looking. Today people are looking for someone to give them security in an insecure world. Many people believe that security can be found in their spouse and in their home. Don't forget that Christ is the One whom you seek.

◈ MEDITATION ◈

Heavenly Father, thank you for the gift of my spouse to keep me company through this journey that leads me closer to you. Help us keep our eyes on Christ. §►

AUGUST 12

Jesus Calls Some of His Disciples
◄§ John 1:35–51 §►

The following day as John was standing with two of his disciples, ³⁶Jesus walked by. John looked at him intently and then declared, "See! There is the Lamb of God!"

³⁷Then John's two disciples turned and followed Jesus.

³⁸Jesus looked around and saw them following. "What do you want?" he asked them.

"Sir," they replied, "where do you live?"

³⁹"Come and see," he said. So they went with him to the place where he was staying and were with him from about four o'clock that afternoon until the evening. ⁴⁰(One of these men was Andrew, Simon Peter's brother.)

⁴¹Andrew then went to find his brother Peter and told him, "We have found the Messiah!" ⁴²And he brought Peter to meet Jesus.

Jesus looked intently at Peter for a moment and then said, "You are Simon, John's son—but you shall be called Peter, the rock!"

⁴³The next day Jesus decided to go to Galilee. He found Philip and told him, "Come with me." ⁴⁴(Philip was from Bethsaida, Andrew and Peter's home town.)

⁴⁵Philip now went off to look for Nathanael and told him, "We have found the Messiah!—the very person Moses and the prophets told about! His name is Jesus, the son of Joseph from Nazareth!"

⁴⁶"Nazareth!" exclaimed Nathanael. "Can anything good come from there?"

"Just come and see for yourself," Philip declared.

⁴⁷As they approached, Jesus said, "Here comes an honest man—a true son of Israel."

⁴⁸"How do you know what I am like?" Nathanael demanded.

And Jesus replied, "I could see you under the fig tree before Philip found you."

⁴⁹Nathanael replied, "Sir, you are the Son of God—the King of Israel!"

⁵⁰Jesus asked him, "Do you believe all this just because I told you I had seen you under the fig tree? You will see greater proofs than this. ⁵¹You will even see heaven open and the angels of God coming back and forth to me, the Messiah."

Paul Requests Prayer
2 Thessalonians 3:1–5

Finally, dear brothers, as I come to the end of this letter I ask you to pray for us. Pray first that the Lord's message will spread rapidly and triumph wherever it goes, winning converts everywhere as it did when it came to you. [2]Pray too that we will be saved out of the clutches of evil men, for not everyone loves the Lord. [3]But the Lord is faithful; he will make you strong and guard you from satanic attacks of every kind. [4]And we trust the Lord that you are putting into practice the things we taught you, and that you always will. [5]May the Lord bring you into an ever deeper understanding of the love of God and of the patience that comes from Christ.

Proverbs for Today
21:5–7

Steady plodding brings prosperity; hasty speculation brings poverty. □ Dishonest gain will never last, so why take the risk? □ Because the wicked are unfair, their violence boomerangs and destroys them.

KEY VERSE

Steady plodding brings prosperity; hasty speculation brings poverty.—*Proverbs 21:5*

REFLECTION

If there were one quick and easy step to a prosperous and successful marriage, everyone would take it. Yet God's word reveals that only steady plodding does the trick. Diligence does not come naturally to most people. It is a result of strong character. Don't look for quick fixes and easy answers. Be a faithful and diligent spouse over a lifetime.

MEDITATION

Heavenly Father, help us be diligent in the day-to-day work that our marriage requires.

AUGUST 13

Jesus Turns Water into Wine
John 2:1–12

Two days later Jesus' mother was a guest at a wedding in the village of Cana in Galilee, [2]and Jesus and his disciples were invited too. [3]The wine supply ran out during the festivities, and Jesus' mother came to him with the problem.

[4]"I can't help you now," he said. "It isn't yet my time for miracles."

[5]But his mother told the servants, "Do whatever he tells you to."

[6]Six stone waterpots were standing there; they were used for Jewish ceremonial purposes and held perhaps twenty to thirty gallons each. [7,8]Then Jesus told the servants to fill them to the brim with water. When this was done he said, "Dip some out and take it to the master of ceremonies."

[9]When the master of ceremonies tasted the water that was now wine, not knowing where it had come from (though, of course, the servants did), he called the bridegroom over.

[10]"This is wonderful stuff!" he said. "You're different from most. Usually a host uses the best wine first, and afterwards, when everyone is full and doesn't care, then he brings out the less expensive brands. But you have kept the best for the last!"

[11]This miracle at Cana in Galilee was Jesus' first public demonstration of his heaven-sent power. And his disciples believed that he really was the Messiah.

[12]After the wedding he left for Capernaum for a few days with his mother, brothers, and disciples.

An Admonishment against Laziness
2 Thessalonians 3:6–18

Now here is a command, dear brothers, given in the name of our Lord Jesus Christ by his authority: Stay away from any Christian who spends his days in laziness and does not follow the ideal of hard work we set up for you. ⁷For you well know that you ought to follow our example: you never saw us loafing; ⁸we never accepted food from anyone without buying it; we worked hard day and night for the money we needed to live on, in order that we would not be a burden to any of you. ⁹It wasn't that we didn't have the right to ask you to feed us, but we wanted to show you, firsthand, how you should work for your living. ¹⁰Even while we were still there with you we gave you this rule: "He who does not work shall not eat."

¹¹Yet we hear that some of you are living in laziness, refusing to work, and wasting your time in gossiping. ¹²In the name of the Lord Jesus Christ we appeal to such people—we command them—to quiet down, get to work, and earn their own living. ¹³And to the rest of you I say, dear brothers, never be tired of doing right.

¹⁴If anyone refuses to obey what we say in this letter, notice who he is and stay away from him, that he may be ashamed of himself. ¹⁵Don't think of him as an enemy, but speak to him as you would to a brother who needs to be warned.

¹⁶May the Lord of peace himself give you his peace no matter what happens. The Lord be with you all.

¹⁷Now here is my greeting which I am writing with my own hand, as I do at the end of all my letters, for proof that it really is from me. This is in my own handwriting. ¹⁸May the blessing of our Lord Jesus Christ be upon you all.

Sincerely,
Paul

Proverbs for Today
⋅§ 21:8–10 §⋅

A man is known by his actions. An evil man lives an evil life; a good man lives a godly life. ☐ It is better to live in the corner of an attic than with a crabby woman in a lovely home. ☐ An evil man loves to harm others; being a good neighbor is out of his line.

⋅ KEY VERSE ⋅

We hear that some of you are living in laziness, refusing to work, and wasting your time in gossiping. In the name of the Lord Jesus Christ we appeal to such people—we command them—to quiet down, get to work, and earn their own living. And to the rest of you I say, dear brothers, never be tired of doing right.—*2 Thessalonians 3:11–13*

⋅ REFLECTION ⋅

Gossip is tantalizing. It is exciting to hear, making us feel like insiders, and it's fun to pass on, giving us a feeling of power. But gossip tears people down and distracts us from our responsibilities. If you often find your nose in other people's business, you most likely are not keeping up with the responsibilities in your own home. Look for a task to do for Christ or for your family and get to work.

⋅ MEDITATION ⋅

Heavenly Father, forgive us for wasting our time in idle chatter and meaningless activities that don't glorify your kingdom. ❧

AUGUST 14

Jesus Clears the Temple
⋅§ John 2:13–25 §⋅

Then it was time for the annual Jewish Passover celebration, and Jesus went to Jerusalem.

¹⁴In the Temple area he saw merchants selling cattle, sheep, and doves for sacrifices, and money-changers behind their counters. ¹⁵Jesus made a whip from some ropes and chased them all out, and drove out the sheep and oxen, scattering the

moneychangers' coins over the floor and turning over their tables! [16]Then, going over to the men selling doves, he told them, "Get these things out of here. Don't turn my Father's House into a market!"

[17]Then his disciples remembered this prophecy from the Scriptures: "Concern for God's House will be my undoing."

[18]"What right have you to order them out?" the Jewish leaders demanded. "If you have this authority from God, show us a miracle to prove it."

[19]"All right," Jesus replied, "this is the miracle I will do for you: Destroy this sanctuary and in three days I will raise it up!"

[20]"What!" they exclaimed. "It took forty-six years to build this Temple, and you can do it in three days?" [21]But by "this sanctuary" he meant his body. [22]After he came back to life again, the disciples remembered his saying this and realized that what he had quoted from the Scriptures really did refer to him, and had all come true!

[23]Because of the miracles he did in Jerusalem at the Passover celebration, many people were convinced that he was indeed the Messiah. [24,25]But Jesus didn't trust them, for he knew mankind to the core. No one needed to tell him how changeable human nature is!

Paul Warns about False Teachers
◄§ 1 Timothy 1:1–5 §►

From: Paul, a missionary of Jesus Christ, sent out by the direct command of God our Savior and by Jesus Christ our Lord—our only hope.

[2]*To:* Timothy.

Timothy, you are like a son to me in the things of the Lord. May God our Father and Jesus Christ our Lord show you his kindness and mercy and give you great peace of heart and mind.

[3,4]As I said when I left for Macedonia, please stay there in Ephesus and try to stop the men who are teaching such wrong doctrine. Put an end to their myths and fables, and their idea of being saved by finding favor with an endless chain of angels leading up to God—wild ideas that stir up questions and arguments instead of helping people accept God's plan of faith. [5]What I am eager for is that all the Christians there will be filled with love that comes from pure hearts, and that their minds will be clean and their faith strong.

Proverbs for Today
◄§ 21:11–12 §►

The wise man learns by listening; the simpleton can learn only by seeing scorners punished. □ God, the Righteous One, knows what is going on in the homes of the wicked, and will bring the wicked to judgment.

◄ KEY VERSE ◄

The wise man learns by listening; the simpleton can learn only by seeing scorners punished.—*Proverbs 21:11*

◄ REFLECTION ◄

It is usually less painful to learn from others' mistakes than from our own. We can do this by listening to their advice and through watching what happens to them—by keeping our mouths shut and our eyes open. Take counsel from others instead of plunging ahead and learning the hard way.

◄ MEDITATION ◄

Heavenly Father, help us to be students of those around us, watching and learning from them. §►

Nicodemus Visits Jesus at Night
⋖ John 3:1–21 ⋗

After dark one night a Jewish religious leader named Nicodemus, a member of the sect of the Pharisees, came for an interview with Jesus. "Sir," he said, "we all know that God has sent you to teach us. Your miracles are proof enough of this."

³Jesus replied, "With all the earnestness I possess I tell you this: Unless you are born again, you can never get into the Kingdom of God."

⁴"Born again!" exclaimed Nicodemus. "What do you mean? How can an old man go back into his mother's womb and be born again?"

⁵Jesus replied, "What I am telling you so earnestly is this: Unless one is born of water and the Spirit, he cannot enter the Kingdom of God. ⁶Men can only reproduce human life, but the Holy Spirit gives new life from heaven; ⁷so don't be surprised at my statement that you must be born again! ⁸Just as you can hear the wind but can't tell where it comes from or where it will go next, so it is with the Spirit. We do not know on whom he will next bestow this life from heaven."

⁹"What do you mean?" Nicodemus asked.

¹⁰,¹¹Jesus replied, "You, a respected Jewish teacher, and yet you don't understand these things? I am telling you what I know and have seen—and yet you won't believe me. ¹²But if you don't even believe me when I tell you about such things as these that happen here among men, how can you possibly believe if I tell you what is going on in heaven? ¹³For only I, the Messiah, have come to earth and will return to heaven again. ¹⁴And as Moses in the wilderness lifted up the bronze image of a serpent on a pole, even so I must be lifted up upon a pole, ¹⁵so that anyone who believes in me will have eternal life. ¹⁶For God loved the world so much that he gave his only Son so that anyone who believes in him shall not perish but have eternal life. ¹⁷God did not send his Son into the world to condemn it, but to save it.

¹⁸"There is no eternal doom awaiting those who trust him to save them. But those who don't trust him have already been tried and condemned for not believing in the only Son of God. ¹⁹Their sentence is based on this fact: that the Light from heaven came into the world, but they loved the darkness more than the Light, for their deeds were evil. ²⁰They hated the heavenly Light because they wanted to sin in the darkness. They stayed away from that Light for fear their sins would be exposed and they would be punished. ²¹But those doing right come gladly to the Light to let everyone see that they are doing what God wants them to."

The Purpose of the Law
⋖ 1 Timothy 1:6–11 ⋗

But these teachers have missed this whole idea and spend their time arguing and talking foolishness. ⁷They want to become famous as teachers of the laws of Moses when they haven't the slightest idea what those laws really show us. ⁸Those laws are good when used as God intended. ⁹But they were not made for us, whom God has saved; they are for sinners who hate God, have rebellious hearts, curse and swear, attack their fathers and mothers, and murder. ¹⁰,¹¹Yes, these laws are made to identify as sinners all who are immoral and impure: homosexuals, kidnappers, liars, and all others who do things that contradict the glorious Good News of our blessed God, whose messenger I am.

Proverbs for Today
⋖ 21:13 ⋗

He who shuts his ears to the cries of the poor will be ignored in his own time of need.

⋗ KEY VERSE ⋖

God loved the world so much that he gave his only Son so that anyone who believes in him shall not perish but have eternal life.—*John 3:16*

The entire gospel comes to a focus in this verse. True love is not lazy or self-centered; it reaches out and draws others in. God sets the pattern of true love, the basis for all love relationships—if you love someone dearly, you are willing to pay dearly for that person's well-being. God paid dearly with the life of his Son, the highest price he could pay. Jesus accepted our punishment, paid the price for our sins, and then offered us the new life he bought for us. When we share the gospel with others, our love must be like his—willingly giving up our own comfort and security so that others might join us in receiving God's love.

_____ ❦ MEDITATION ❦ _____

Heavenly Father, thank you for paying the ultimate price for our salvation. We are overwhelmed by your love. Please help us to share your love and message of Christ with others. ❧

AUGUST 16 _____

John the Baptist Testifies of Jesus
❧ John 3:22–36 ❧

Afterwards Jesus and his disciples left Jerusalem and stayed for a while in Judea and baptized there. [23,24]At this time John the Baptist was not yet in prison. He was baptizing at Aenon, near Salim, because there was plenty of water there. [25]One day someone began an argument with John's disciples, telling them that Jesus' baptism was best. [26]So they came to John and said, "Master, the man you met on the other side of the Jordan River—the one you said was the Messiah—he is baptizing too, and everybody is going over there instead of coming here to us."

[27]John replied, "God in heaven appoints each man's work. [28]My work is to prepare the way for that man so that everyone will go to him. You yourselves know how plainly I told you that I am not the Messiah. I am here to prepare the way for him—that is all. [29]The crowds will naturally go to the main attraction—the bride will go where the bridegroom is! A bridegroom's friends rejoice with him. I am the Bridegroom's friend, and I am filled with joy at his success. [30]He must become greater and greater, and I must become less and less.

[31]"He has come from heaven and is greater than anyone else. I am of the earth, and my understanding is limited to the things of earth. [32]He tells what he has seen and heard, but how few believe what he tells them! [33,34]Those who believe him discover that God is a fountain of truth. For this one—sent by God—speaks God's words, for God's Spirit is upon him without measure or limit. [35]The Father loves this man because he is his Son, and God has given him everything there is. [36]And all who trust him—God's Son—to save them have eternal life; those who don't believe and obey him shall never see heaven, but the wrath of God remains upon them."

The Greatest of Sinners
❧ 1 Timothy 1:12–17 ❧

How thankful I am to Christ Jesus our Lord for choosing me as one of his messengers, and giving me the strength to be faithful to him, [13]even though I used to scoff at the name of Christ. I hunted down his people, harming them in every way I could. But God had mercy on me because I didn't know what I was doing, for I didn't know Christ at that time. [14]Oh, how kind our Lord was, for he showed me how to trust him and become full of the love of Christ Jesus.

[15]How true it is, and how I long that everyone should know it, that Christ Jesus came into the world to save sinners—and I was the greatest of them all. [16]But God had mercy on me so that Christ Jesus could use me as an example to show everyone how patient he is with even the worst sinners, so that others will realize that they, too, can have everlasting life. [17]Glory and honor to God forever and

ever. He is the King of the ages, the unseen one who never dies; he alone is God, and full of wisdom. Amen.

Proverbs for Today
§ 21:14–16 ⮞

An angry man is silenced by giving him a gift! □ A good man loves justice, but it is a calamity to evil-doers. □ The man who strays away from common sense will end up dead!

◦ KEY VERSE ◦

Oh, how kind our Lord was, for he showed me how to trust him and become full of the love of Christ Jesus.—*1 Timothy 1:14*

◦ REFLECTION ◦

When we become Christians, we often feel that our love for Jesus and others is inadequate. But we can be confident that Christ will give us the faith and love we need. Even with our weak faith, we must demonstrate genuine love toward others. Christ will increase both our faith and love as our relationship with him deepens.

◦ MEDITATION ◦

Heavenly Father, at times our faith seems so weak. Please give us strength to trust you more. ⮞

AUGUST 17

Jesus Talks to a Woman at the Well
§ John 4:1–30 ⮞

When the Lord knew that the Pharisees had heard about the greater crowds coming to him than to John to be baptized and to become his disciples—(though Jesus himself didn't baptize them, but his disciples did)— [3]he left Judea and returned to the province of Galilee.

[4]He had to go through Samaria on the way, [5,6]and around noon as he approached the village of Sychar, he came to Jacob's Well, located on the parcel of ground Jacob gave to his son Joseph. Jesus was tired from the long walk in the hot sun and sat wearily beside the well.

[7]Soon a Samaritan woman came to draw water, and Jesus asked her for a drink. [8]He was alone at the time as his disciples had gone into the village to buy some food. [9]The woman was surprised that a Jew would ask a "despised Samaritan" for anything—usually they wouldn't even speak to them!—and she remarked about this to Jesus.

[10]He replied, "If you only knew what a wonderful gift God has for you, and who I am, you would ask me for some *living* water!"

[11]"But you don't have a rope or a bucket," she said, "and this is a very deep well! Where would you get this living water? [12]And besides, are you greater than our ancestor Jacob? How can you offer better water than this which he and his sons and cattle enjoyed?"

[13]Jesus replied that people soon became thirsty again after drinking this water. [14]"But the water I give them," he said, "becomes a perpetual spring within them, watering them forever with eternal life."

[15]"Please, sir," the woman said, "give me some of that water! Then I'll never be thirsty again and won't have to make this long trip out here every day."

[16]"Go and get your husband," Jesus told her.

[17,18]"But I'm not married," the woman replied.

"All too true!" Jesus said. "For you have had five husbands, and you aren't even married to the man you're living with now."

[19]"Sir," the woman said, "you must be a prophet. [20]But say, tell me, why is it that you Jews insist that Jerusalem is the only place of worship, while we Samaritans claim it is here [at Mount Gerazim], where our ancestors worshiped?"

[21-24]Jesus replied, "The time is coming, ma'am,

when we will no longer be concerned about whether to worship the Father here or in Jerusalem. For it's not *where* we worship that counts, but *how* we worship—is our worship spiritual and real? Do we have the Holy Spirit's help? For God is Spirit, and we must have his help to worship as we should. The Father wants this kind of worship from us. But you Samaritans know so little about him, worshiping blindly, while we Jews know all about him, for salvation comes to the world through the Jews."

[25]The woman said, "Well, at least I know that the Messiah will come—the one they call Christ—and when he does, he will explain everything to us."

[26]Then Jesus told her, "I am the Messiah!"

[27]Just then his disciples arrived. They were surprised to find him talking to a woman, but none of them asked him why, or what they had been discussing.

[28,29]Then the woman left her waterpot beside the well and went back to the village and told everyone, "Come and meet a man who told me everything I ever did! Can this be the Messiah?" [30]So the people came streaming from the village to see him.

Fight the Lord's Battles
1 Timothy 1:18–20

Now, Timothy, my son, here is my command to you: Fight well in the Lord's battles, just as the Lord told us through his prophets that you would. [19]Cling tightly to your faith in Christ and always keep your conscience clear, doing what you know is right. For some people have disobeyed their consciences and have deliberately done what they knew was wrong. It isn't surprising that soon they lost their faith in Christ after defying God like that. [20]Hymenaeus and Alexander are two examples of

this. I had to give them over to Satan to punish them until they could learn not to bring shame to the name of Christ.

Proverbs for Today
21:17–18

A man who loves pleasure becomes poor; wine and luxury are not the way to riches! □ The wicked will finally lose; the righteous will finally win.

KEY VERSE

Cling tightly to your faith in Christ and always keep your conscience clear, doing what you know is right. For some people have disobeyed their consciences and have deliberately done what they knew was wrong. It isn't surprising that soon they lost their faith in Christ after defying God like that. —*1 Timothy 1:19*

REFLECTION

How can you keep your conscience clear? Treasure your faith in Christ more than anything else and do what you know is right. Each time you deliberately ignore your conscience, you are hardening your heart. Soon your capacity to tell right from wrong will disappear. But when you walk with God, he is able to speak to you through your conscience, letting you know the difference between right and wrong. Be sure to act on those inner tugs to do what is right—then your conscience will remain clear.

MEDITATION

Heavenly Father, help us to notice your tugs at our hearts, through our consciences. Keep our hearts soft and sensitive so that we will know the difference between right and wrong.

The Harvest
⧫§ John 4:31–42 §⧫

Meanwhile, the disciples were urging Jesus to eat. [32]"No," he said, "I have some food you don't know about."

[33]"Who brought it to him?" the disciples asked each other.

[34]Then Jesus explained: "My nourishment comes from doing the will of God who sent me, and from finishing his work. [35]Do you think the work of harvesting will not begin until the summer ends four months from now? Look around you! Vast fields of human souls are ripening all around us, and are ready now for reaping. [36]The reapers will be paid good wages and will be gathering eternal souls into the granaries of heaven! What joys await the sower and the reaper, both together! [37]For it is true that one sows and someone else reaps. [38]I sent you to reap where you didn't sow; others did the work, and you received the harvest."

[39]Many from the Samaritan village believed he was the Messiah because of the woman's report: "He told me everything I ever did!" [40,41]When they came out to see him at the well, they begged him to stay at their village; and he did, for two days, long enough for many of them to believe in him after hearing him. [42]Then they said to the woman, "Now we believe because we have heard him ourselves, not just because of what you told us. He is indeed the Savior of the world."

Instructions for Worship
⧫§ 1 Timothy 2:1–8 §⧫

Here are my directions: Pray much for others; plead for God's mercy upon them; give thanks for all he is going to do for them.

[2]Pray in this way for kings and all others who are in authority over us, or are in places of high responsibility, so that we can live in peace and quietness, spending our time in godly living and thinking much about the Lord. [3]This is good and pleases God our Savior, [4]for he longs for all to be saved and to understand this truth: [5]*That God is on one side and all the people on the other side, and Christ Jesus, himself man, is between them to bring them together, [6]by giving his life for all mankind.*

This is the message which at the proper time God gave to the world. [7]And I have been chosen—this is the absolute truth—as God's minister and missionary to teach this truth to the Gentiles, and to show them God's plan of salvation through faith.

[8]So I want men everywhere to pray with holy hands lifted up to God, free from sin and anger and resentment.

Proverbs for Today
⧫§ 21:19–20 §⧫

Better to live in the desert than with a quarrelsome, complaining woman. ☐ The wise man saves for the future, but the foolish man spends whatever he gets.

⧫ KEY VERSE ⧫

The wise man saves for the future, but the foolish man spends whatever he gets.—*Proverbs 21:20*

⧫ REFLECTION ⧫

Easy credit has many couples living on the verge of bankruptcy. The desire to meet high expectations and accumulate more pushes them to spend every penny they earn, and they stretch their credit to the limit. But anyone who spends all he has is spending more than he can afford. A wise couple puts money aside for when they may have less. God approves of foresight and restraint. Take time to examine your life-style to see whether all your spending is pleasing to God, and whether some is merely indulging your cravings.

⧫ MEDITATION ⧫

Heavenly Father, please give us the wisdom that we need to use our money most effectively. §⧫

AUGUST 19

Jesus Heals the Son of a Government Official
⋖§ John 4:43–54 §⋗

At the end of the two days' stay Jesus went on into Galilee. Jesus used to say, "A prophet is honored everywhere except in his own country!" [45]But the Galileans welcomed him with open arms, for they had been in Jerusalem at the Passover celebration and had seen some of his miracles.

[46,47]In the course of his journey through Galilee he arrived at the town of Cana, where he had turned the water into wine. While he was there, a man in the city of Capernaum, a government official, whose son was very sick, heard that Jesus had come from Judea and was traveling in Galilee. This man went over to Cana, found Jesus, and begged him to come to Capernaum with him and heal his son, who was now at death's door.

[48]Jesus asked, "Won't any of you believe in me unless I do more and more miracles?"

[49]The official pled, "Sir, please come now before my child dies."

[50]Then Jesus told him, "Go back home. Your son is healed!" And the man believed Jesus and started home. [51]While he was on his way, some of his servants met him with the news that all was well—his son had recovered. [52]He asked them when the lad had begun to feel better, and they replied, "Yesterday afternoon at about one o'clock his fever suddenly disappeared!" [53]Then the father realized it was the same moment that Jesus had told him, "Your son is healed." And the officer and his entire household believed that Jesus was the Messiah.

[54]This was Jesus' second miracle in Galilee after coming from Judea.

Women in the Church
⋖§ 1 Timothy 2:9–15 §⋗

And the women should be the same way, quiet and sensible in manner and clothing. Christian women should be noticed for being kind and good, not for the way they fix their hair or because of their jewels or fancy clothes. [11]Women should listen and learn quietly and humbly.

[12]I never let women teach men or lord it over them. Let them be silent in your church meetings. [13]Why? Because God made Adam first, and afterwards he made Eve. [14]And it was not Adam who was fooled by Satan, but Eve, and sin was the result. [15]So God sent pain and suffering to women when their children are born, but he will save their souls if they trust in him, living quiet, good, and loving lives.

Proverbs for Today
⋖§ 21:21–22 §⋗

The man who tries to be good, loving and kind finds life, righteousness and honor. ☐ The wise man conquers the strong man and levels his defenses.

⋖ KEY VERSE ⋗

God made Adam first, and afterwards he made Eve. And it was not Adam who was fooled by Satan, but Eve, and sin was the result.—*1 Timothy 2:13–14*

⋗ REFLECTION ⋖

In previous letters Paul had discussed male/female roles in marriage (Ephesians 5:21–33; Colossians 3:18–19). Here he wrote about male/female roles within the church. Some scholars see these verses about Adam and Eve as an illustration of what was happening in the Ephesian church. Just as Eve had been deceived in the Garden of Eden, so the women in the church were being deceived by false teachers. And just as Adam was the first human created by God, so the men in the church in Ephesus should be the first to speak and teach because they had had more experience in learning the things of God. This view stresses that Paul's teaching here is not universal, but applies to churches with similar problems. Other scholars, however, say that the roles Paul points out are God's design for his created order; that God established these roles to maintain harmony in both the family and the church. It is important to pray together as you seek God's will for your relationship with each other as husband and wife.

_____ ❧ MEDITATION ❧ _____

Heavenly Father, allow our hearts and ears to open up to your voice as you speak to us through your word. Help us not to become so entrenched in "roles" that we forget to love each other. ❧

AUGUST 20

A Healing at Bethesda Pool
❧ John 5:1–24 ❧

Afterwards Jesus returned to Jerusalem for one of the Jewish religious holidays. ²Inside the city, near the Sheep Gate, was Bethesda Pool, with five covered platforms or porches surrounding it. ³Crowds of sick folks—lame, blind, or with paralyzed limbs—lay on the platforms (waiting for a certain movement of the water, ⁴for an angel of the Lord came from time to time and disturbed the water, and the first person to step down into it afterwards was healed).

⁵One of the men lying there had been sick for thirty-eight years. ⁶When Jesus saw him and knew how long he had been ill, he asked him, "Would you like to get well?"

⁷"I can't," the sick man said, "for I have no one to help me into the pool at the movement of the water. While I am trying to get there, someone else always gets in ahead of me."

⁸Jesus told him, "Stand up, roll up your sleeping mat and go on home!"

⁹Instantly, the man was healed! He rolled up the mat and began walking!

But it was on the Sabbath when this miracle was done. ¹⁰So the Jewish leaders objected. They said to the man who was cured, "You can't work on the Sabbath! It's illegal to carry that sleeping mat!"

¹¹"The man who healed me told me to," was his reply.

¹²"Who said such a thing as that?" they demanded.

¹³The man didn't know, and Jesus had disappeared into the crowd. ¹⁴But afterwards Jesus found him in the Temple and told him, "Now you are well; don't sin as you did before, or something even worse may happen to you."

¹⁵Then the man went to find the Jewish leaders and told them it was Jesus who had healed him.

¹⁶So they began harassing Jesus as a Sabbath breaker.

¹⁷But Jesus replied, "My Father constantly does good, and I'm following his example."

¹⁸Then the Jewish leaders were all the more eager to kill him because in addition to disobeying their Sabbath laws, he had spoken of God as his Father, thereby making himself equal with God.

¹⁹Jesus replied, "The Son can do nothing by himself. He does only what he sees the Father doing, and in the same way. ²⁰For the Father loves the Son, and tells him everything he is doing; and the Son will do far more awesome miracles than this man's healing. ²¹He will even raise from the dead anyone he wants to, just as the Father does. ²²And the Father leaves all judgment of sin to his Son, ²³so that everyone will honor the Son, just as they honor the Father. But if you refuse to honor God's Son, whom he sent to you, then you are certainly not honoring the Father.

²⁴"I say emphatically that anyone who listens to my message and believes in God who sent me has eternal life, and will never be damned for his sins, but has already passed out of death into life.

Requirements for Church Leadership
❧ 1 Timothy 3:1–7 ❧

It is a true saying that if a man wants to be a pastor he has a good ambition. ²For a pastor must be a good man whose life cannot be spoken against. He must have only one wife, and he must be hard working and thoughtful, orderly, and full of good deeds. He must enjoy having guests in his home, and must be a good Bible teacher. ³He must not be a drinker or quarrelsome, but he must be gentle and kind, and not be one who loves money. ⁴He must have a well-behaved family, with children who obey quickly and quietly. ⁵For if a man can't make his own little family behave, how can he help the whole church?

⁶The pastor must not be a new Christian, because he might be proud of being chosen so soon, and pride comes before a fall. (Satan's downfall is an example.) ⁷Also, he must be well spoken of by people outside the church—those who aren't Christians—so that Satan can't trap him with many accusations, and leave him without freedom to lead his flock.

Proverbs for Today
⋖ 21:23–24 ⋗

Keep your mouth closed and you'll stay out of trouble. ☐ Mockers are proud, haughty and arrogant.

⋖ KEY VERSE ⋗

He must have a well-behaved family, with children who obey quickly and quietly. For if a man can't make his own little family behave, how can he help the whole church?—*1 Timothy 3:4–5*

⋖ REFLECTION ⋗

Christian workers and volunteers sometimes make the mistake of thinking their work is so important that they are justified in ignoring their families. Spiritual leadership, however, must begin at home. If a person is not willing to care for, discipline, and teach his or her children, he or she is not qualified to lead the church.

⋖ MEDITATION ⋗

Heavenly Father, may we not become so busy trying to impress others with our spiritual leadership abilities that we forget where true leadership begins. ⋗

AUGUST 21

Jesus Is the Son of God
⋖ John 5:25–47 ⋗

"And I solemnly declare that the time is coming, in fact, it is here, when the dead shall hear my voice—the voice of the Son of God—and those who listen shall live. ²⁶The Father has life in himself, and has granted his Son to have life in himself, ²⁷and to judge the sins of all mankind because he is the Son of Man. ²⁸Don't be so surprised! Indeed the time is coming when all the dead in their graves shall hear the voice of God's Son, ²⁹and shall rise again—those who have done good, to eternal life; and those who have continued in evil, to judgment.

³⁰"But I pass no judgment without consulting the Father. I judge as I am told. And my judgment is absolutely fair and just, for it is according to the will of God who sent me and is not merely my own.

³¹"When I make claims about myself they aren't believed, ³²,³³but someone else, yes, John the Bap-

tist, is making these claims for me too. You have gone out to listen to his preaching, and I can assure you that all he says about me is true! ³⁴But the truest witness I have is not from a man, though I have reminded you about John's witness so that you will believe in me and be saved. ³⁵John shone brightly for a while, and you benefited and rejoiced, ³⁶but I have a greater witness than John. I refer to the miracles I do; these have been assigned me by the Father, and they prove that the Father has sent me. ³⁷And the Father himself has also testified about me, though not appearing to you personally, or speaking to you directly. ³⁸But you are not listening to him, for you refuse to believe me—the one sent to you with God's message.

³⁹"You search the Scriptures, for you believe they give you eternal life. And the Scriptures point to me! ⁴⁰Yet you won't come to me so that I can give you this life eternal!

41,42"Your approval or disapproval means nothing to me, for as I know so well, you don't have God's love within you. 43I know, because I have come to you representing my Father and you refuse to welcome me, though you readily enough receive those who aren't sent from him, but represent only themselves! 44No wonder you can't believe! For you gladly honor each other, but you don't care about the honor that comes from the only God!

45"Yet it is not I who will accuse you of this to the Father—Moses will! Moses, on whose laws you set your hopes of heaven. 46For you have refused to believe Moses. He wrote about me, but you refuse to believe him, so you refuse to believe in me. 47And since you don't believe what he wrote, no wonder you don't believe me either."

The Requirements for Deacons
⋐ 1 Timothy 3:8–15 ⋑

The deacons must be the same sort of good, steady men as the pastors. They must not be heavy drinkers and must not be greedy for money. 9They must be earnest, wholehearted followers of Christ who is the hidden Source of their faith. 10Before they are asked to be deacons they should be given other jobs in the church as a test of their character and ability, and if they do well, then they may be chosen as deacons.

11Their wives must be thoughtful, not heavy drinkers, not gossipers, but faithful in everything they do. 12Deacons should have only one wife and they should have happy, obedient families. 13Those who do well as deacons will be well rewarded both by respect from others and also by developing their own confidence and bold trust in the Lord.

14I am writing these things to you now, even though I hope to be with you soon, 15so that if I don't come for awhile you will know what kind of men you should choose as officers for the church of the living God, which contains and holds high the truth of God.

Proverbs for Today
⋐ 21:25–26 ⋑

The lazy man longs for many things but his hands refuse to work. He is greedy to get, while the godly love to give!

☙ KEY VERSE ❧

Their wives must be thoughtful, not heavy drinkers, not gossipers, but faithful in everything they do.—*1 Timothy 3:11*

☙ REFLECTION ❧

Some have translated *wives* as *women helpers* or *deaconesses*. It is unclear whether this verse refers to wives of deacons or female leaders of the church (such as Phoebe, the deacon mentioned in Romans 16:1). In either case, God expects the behavior of prominent women in the church to be just as responsible as that of prominent men.

☙ MEDITATION ❧

Heavenly Father, help us to remember that a godly life is more important than impressing people with Christian work. ❧

AUGUST 22

The Feeding of the Five Thousand
⋐ John 6:1–15 ⋑

After this, Jesus crossed over the Sea of Galilee, also known as the Sea of Tiberias. 2-5And a huge crowd, many of them pilgrims on their way to Jeru-salem for the annual Passover celebration, were following him wherever he went, to watch him heal the sick. So when Jesus went up into the hills and sat down with his disciples around him, he soon saw a great multitude of people climbing the hill, looking for him.

Turning to Philip he asked, "Philip, where can we buy bread to feed all these people?" ⁶(He was testing Philip, for he already knew what he was going to do.)

⁷Philip replied, "It would take a fortune to begin to do it!"

⁸,⁹Then Andrew, Simon Peter's brother, spoke up. "There's a youngster here with five barley loaves and a couple of fish! But what good is that with all this mob?"

¹⁰"Tell everyone to sit down," Jesus ordered. And all of them—the approximate count of the men only was 5,000—sat down on the grassy slopes. ¹¹Then Jesus took the loaves and gave thanks to God and passed them out to the people. Afterwards he did the same with the fish. And everyone ate until full!

¹²"Now gather the scraps," Jesus told his disciples, "so that nothing is wasted." ¹³And twelve baskets were filled with the leftovers!

¹⁴When the people realized what a great miracle had happened, they exclaimed, "Surely, he is the Prophet we have been expecting!"

¹⁵Jesus saw that they were ready to take him by force and make him their king, so he went higher into the mountains alone.

Godly Living in the Last Times
⋞ 1 Timothy 3:16—4:6 ⋟

It is quite true that the way to live a godly life is not an easy matter. But the answer lies in Christ, who came to earth as a man, was proved spotless and pure in his Spirit, was served by angels, was preached among the nations, was accepted by men everywhere and was received up again to his glory in heaven.

⁴:¹But the Holy Spirit tells us clearly that in the last times some in the church will turn away from Christ and become eager followers of teachers with devil-inspired ideas. ²These teachers will tell lies with straight faces and do it so often that their consciences won't even bother them.

³They will say it is wrong to be married and wrong to eat meat, even though God gave these things to well-taught Christians to enjoy and be thankful for. ⁴For everything God made is good, and we may eat it gladly if we are thankful for it, ⁵and if we ask God to bless it, for it is made good by the Word of God and prayer.

⁶If you explain this to the others you will be doing your duty as a worthy pastor who is fed by faith and by the true teaching you have followed.

Proverbs for Today
⋞ 21:27 ⋟

God loathes the gifts of evil men, especially if they are trying to bribe him!

⋞ KEY VERSE ⋟

God loathes the gifts of evil men, especially if they are trying to bribe him!—*Proverbs 21:27*

⋞ REFLECTION ⋟

How do couples try to bribe God? Often they go to church, tithe, or volunteer, not because of their love and devotion to God, but because they hope God will bless them in return. But God has made it very clear that he desires obedience and love more than religious ritual (see 1 Samuel 15:22). God does not want our sacrifices of time, energy, and money alone; he wants our hearts—our complete love and devotion. We may be able to bribe people (Proverbs 21:14), but we cannot bribe God.

⋞ MEDITATION ⋟

Heavenly Father, before you we stand naked. We cannot hide behind our good deeds, for you see our motives. Teach us to love you completely. Let us learn what true love and devotion are all about so that we may love each other more completely. ⋟

Jesus Walks on the Water
⊸§ John 6:16–21 §⊷

That evening Jesus' disciples went down to the shore to wait for him. ¹⁷But as darkness fell and Jesus still hadn't come back, they got into the boat and headed out across the lake toward Capernaum. ¹⁸,¹⁹But soon a gale swept down upon them as they rowed, and the sea grew very rough. They were three or four miles out when suddenly they saw Jesus walking toward the boat! They were terrified, ²⁰but he called out to them and told them not to be afraid. ²¹Then they were willing to let him in, and immediately the boat was where they were going!

Exercise Yourself Spiritually
⊸§ 1 Timothy 4:7–11 §⊷

Don't waste time arguing over foolish ideas and silly myths and legends. Spend your time and energy in the exercise of keeping spiritually fit. ⁸Bodily exercise is all right, but spiritual exercise is much more important and is a tonic for all you do. So exercise yourself spiritually and practice being a better Christian, because that will help you not only now in this life, but in the next life too. ⁹,¹⁰This is the truth and everyone should accept it. We work hard and suffer much in order that people will believe it, for our hope is in the living God who died for all, and particularly for those who have accepted his salvation.

¹¹Teach these things and make sure everyone learns them well.

Proverbs for Today

No one believes a liar, but everyone respects the words of an honest man. □ An evil man is stubborn, but a godly man will reconsider.

⊸ KEY VERSE ⊷
Soon a gale swept down upon them as they rowed, and the sea grew very rough. They were three or four miles out when suddenly they saw Jesus walking toward the boat! They were terrified, but he called out to them and told them not to be afraid. —*John 6:18–20*

⊸ REFLECTION ⊷
The terrified disciples thought they were seeing a ghost (Matthew 14:26). But if they had learned from all they had already seen Jesus do, they would have accepted this miracle. They were frightened—they didn't expect Jesus to come, and they weren't prepared for his help. Faith is a mind-set that *expects* God to act. When we live with this expectation, we can overcome our fears. Is there a problem in your marriage that you just can't muddle through? Are you afraid that you or your spouse will never become more like Christ? Expect the presence of Christ in your home. Prepare yourselves for God's help in your hour of need. Accept the miracles that Christ is anxious to perform for you.

⊸ MEDITATION ⊷
Heavenly Father, right now we are terrified by our own personal need. Give us the faith that you will work a miracle within our marriage by overcoming our fears. ⊷

AUGUST 24

Jesus Is the True Bread from Heaven
§ John 6:22–46 §

The next morning, back across the lake, crowds began gathering on the shore [waiting to see Jesus]. For they knew that he and his disciples had come over together and that the disciples had gone off in their boat, leaving him behind. Several small boats from Tiberias were nearby, ²⁴so when the people saw that Jesus wasn't there, nor his disciples, they got into the boats and went across to Capernaum to look for him.

²⁵When they arrived and found him, they said, "Sir, how did you get here?" ²⁶Jesus replied, "The truth of the matter is that you want to be with me because I fed you, not because you believe in me. ²⁷But you shouldn't be so concerned about perishable things like food. No, spend your energy seeking the eternal life that I, the Messiah, can give you. For God the Father has sent me for this very purpose."

²⁸They replied, "What should we do to satisfy God?"

²⁹Jesus told them, "This is the will of God, that you believe in the one he has sent."

³⁰,³¹They replied, "You must show us more miracles if you want us to believe you are the Messiah. Give us free bread every day, like our fathers had while they journeyed through the wilderness! As the Scriptures say, 'Moses gave them bread from heaven.'"

³²Jesus said, "Moses didn't give it to them. My Father did. And now he offers you true Bread from heaven. ³³The true Bread is a Person—the one sent by God from heaven, and he gives life to the world."

³⁴"Sir," they said, "give us that bread every day of our lives!"

³⁵Jesus replied, "I am the Bread of Life. No one coming to me will ever be hungry again. Those believing in me will never thirst. ³⁶But the trouble is, as I have told you before, you haven't believed even though you have seen me. ³⁷But some will come to me—those the Father has given me—and I will never, never reject them. ³⁸For I have come here from heaven to do the will of God who sent me, not to have my own way. ³⁹And this is the will of God, that I should not lose even one of all those he has given me, but that I should raise them to eternal life at the Last Day. ⁴⁰For it is my Father's will that everyone who sees his Son and believes on him should have eternal life—that I should raise him at the Last Day."

⁴¹Then the Jews began to murmur against him because he claimed to be the Bread from heaven.

⁴²"What?" they exclaimed. "Why, he is merely Jesus the son of Joseph, whose father and mother we know. What is this he is saying, that he came down from heaven?"

⁴³But Jesus replied, "Don't murmur among yourselves about my saying that. ⁴⁴For no one can come to me unless the Father who sent me draws him to me, and at the Last Day I will cause all such to rise again from the dead. ⁴⁵As it is written in the Scriptures, 'They shall all be taught of God.' Those the Father speaks to, who learn the truth from him, will be attracted to me. ⁴⁶(Not that anyone actually sees the Father, for only I have seen him.)

Role Models for God's Flock
§ 1 Timothy 4:12—5:2 §

Don't let anyone think little of you because you are young. Be their ideal; let them follow the way you teach and live; be a pattern for them in your love, your faith, and your clean thoughts. ¹³Until I get there, read and explain the Scriptures to the church; preach God's Word.

¹⁴Be sure to use the abilities God has given you through his prophets when the elders of the church laid their hands upon your head. ¹⁵Put these abilities to work; throw yourself into your tasks so that everyone may notice your improvement and progress. ¹⁶Keep a close watch on all you do and think. Stay true to what is right and God will bless you and use you to help others.

⁵:¹Never speak sharply to an older man, but plead

with him respectfully just as though he were your own father. Talk to the younger men as you would to much loved brothers. ²Treat the older women as mothers, and the girls as your sisters, thinking only pure thoughts about them.

Proverbs for Today
⊷§ 21:30–31 §⊷

No one, regardless of how shrewd or well-advised he is, can stand against the Lord. □ Go ahead and prepare for the conflict, but victory comes from God.

────────⊷ KEY VERSE §⊷────────

Go ahead and prepare for the conflict, but victory comes from God.—*Proverbs 21:31*

────────⊷ REFLECTION §⊷────────

All our preparation is useless without God, but even with God's help we still must do our part and prepare. His control of the outcome does not negate our responsibilities. God may want you to write a book, but you must learn to write. God may want to use you in foreign missions, but you must learn the language. God may want to use your marriage to accomplish his plans, but you must learn to love each other. God will accomplish his purposes, but maybe not through us if we aren't well prepared.

────────⊷ MEDITATION §⊷────────

Heavenly Father, as we individually grow in our relationship with Jesus may we also grow together as a couple, representing what you can do through people who are willing to submit their marriage and their home to you. §⊷

AUGUST 25

Jesus Alone Has the Words of Eternal Life
⊷§ John 6:47–71 §⊷

"How earnestly I tell you this—anyone who believes in me already has eternal life! ⁴⁸⁻⁵¹Yes, I am the Bread of Life! When your fathers in the wilderness ate bread from the skies, they all died. But the Bread from heaven gives eternal life to everyone who eats it. I am that Living Bread that came down out of heaven. Anyone eating this Bread shall live forever; this Bread is my flesh given to redeem humanity."

⁵²Then the Jews began arguing with each other about what he meant. "How can this man give us his flesh to eat?" they asked.

⁵³So Jesus said it again, "With all the earnestness I possess I tell you this: Unless you eat the flesh of the Messiah and drink his blood, you cannot have eternal life within you. ⁵⁴But anyone who does eat my flesh and drink my blood has eternal life, and I will raise him at the Last Day. ⁵⁵For my flesh is the true food, and my blood is the true drink. ⁵⁶Everyone who eats my flesh and drinks my blood is in me, and I in him. ⁵⁷I live by the power of the living Father who sent me, and in the same way those who partake of me shall live because of me! ⁵⁸I am the true Bread from heaven; and anyone who eats this Bread shall live forever, and not die as your fathers did—though they ate bread from heaven." ⁵⁹(He preached this sermon in the synagogue in Capernaum.)

⁶⁰Even his disciples said, "This is very hard to understand. Who can tell what he means?"

⁶¹Jesus knew within himself that his disciples were complaining and said to them, "Does *this* offend you? ⁶²Then what will you think if you see me, the Messiah, return to heaven again? ⁶³Only the Holy Spirit gives eternal life. Those born only once, with physical birth, will never receive this gift. But now I have told you how to get this true spiritual life. ⁶⁴But some of you don't believe me." (For

Jesus knew from the beginning who didn't believe and knew the one who would betray him.)

⁶⁵And he remarked, "That is what I meant when I said that no one can come to me unless the Father attracts him to me."

⁶⁶At this point many of his disciples turned away and deserted him.

⁶⁷Then Jesus turned to the Twelve and asked, "Are you going too?"

⁶⁸Simon Peter replied, "Master, to whom shall we go? You alone have the words that give eternal life, ⁶⁹and we believe them and know you are the holy Son of God."

⁷⁰Then Jesus said, "I chose the twelve of you, and one is a devil." ⁷¹He was speaking of Judas, son of Simon Iscariot, one of the Twelve, who would betray him.

Helping Older Widows in the Church
◄§ 1 Timothy 5:3–10 §►

The church should take loving care of women whose husbands have died, if they don't have anyone else to help them. ⁴But if they have children or grandchildren, these are the ones who should take the responsibility, for kindness should begin at home, supporting needy parents. This is something that pleases God very much.

⁵The church should care for widows who are poor and alone in the world, if they are looking to God for his help and spending much time in prayer; ⁶but not if they are spending their time running around gossiping, seeking only pleasure and thus ruining their souls. ⁷This should be your church rule so that the Christians will know and do what is right.

⁸But anyone who won't care for his own relatives when they need help, especially those living in his own family, has no right to say he is a Christian. Such a person is worse than the heathen.

⁹A widow who wants to become one of the special church workers should be at least sixty years old and have been married only once. ¹⁰She must be well thought of by everyone because of the good she has done. Has she brought up her children well? Has she been kind to strangers as well as to other Christians? Has she helped those who are sick and hurt? Is she always ready to show kindness?

Proverbs for Today
◄§ 22:1 §►

If you must choose, take a good name rather than great riches; for to be held in loving esteem is better than silver and gold.

◄ KEY VERSE ◄

Anyone who won't care for his own relatives when they need help, especially those living in his own family, has no right to say he is a Christian. Such a person is worse than the heathen.—*1 Timothy 5:8*

◄ REFLECTION ◄

Almost everyone has relatives—family of some kind. Family relationships are extremely important in God's eyes. God says that a person who neglects his or her family responsibilities should not call himself or herself a Christian. In what ways are you meeting the needs of those in your family circle?

◄ MEDITATION ◄

Heavenly Father, give us the strength, wisdom, love, and patience needed to support and care for our families. Also, give us a sense of humor so that we don't miss the opportunities for joy that you have given us. §►

Jesus at the Feast of Tabernacles
§ John 7:1–13 &

After this, Jesus went to Galilee, going from village to village, for he wanted to stay out of Judea where the Jewish leaders were plotting his death. [2]But soon it was time for the Tabernacle Ceremonies, one of the annual Jewish holidays, [3]and Jesus' brothers urged him to go to Judea for the celebration.

"Go where more people can see your miracles!" they scoffed. [4]"You can't be famous when you hide like this! If you're so great, prove it to the world!" [5]For even his brothers didn't believe in him.

[6]Jesus replied, "It is not the right time for me to go now. But you can go anytime and it will make no difference, [7]for the world can't hate you; but it does hate me, because I accuse it of sin and evil. [8]You go on, and I'll come later when it is the right time." [9]So he remained in Galilee.

[10]But after his brothers had left for the celebration, then he went too, though secretly, staying out of the public eye. [11]The Jewish leaders tried to find him at the celebration and kept asking if anyone had seen him. [12]There was a lot of discussion about him among the crowds. Some said, "He's a wonderful man," while others said, "No, he's duping the public." [13]But no one had the courage to speak out for him in public for fear of reprisals from the Jewish leaders.

Instructions to Younger Widows
§ 1 Timothy 5:11–16 &

The younger widows should not become members of this special group because after awhile they are likely to disregard their vow to Christ and marry again. [12]And so they will stand condemned because they broke their first promise. [13]Besides, they are likely to be lazy and spend their time gossiping around from house to house, getting into other people's business. [14]So I think it is better for these younger widows to marry again and have children, and take care of their own homes; then no one will be able to say anything against them. [15]For I am afraid that some of them have already turned away from the church and been led astray by Satan.

[16]Let me remind you again that a widow's relatives must take care of her, and not leave this to the church to do. Then the church can spend its money for the care of widows who are all alone and have nowhere else to turn.

Proverbs for Today
§ 22:2–4 &

The rich and the poor are alike before the Lord who made them all. □ A prudent man foresees the difficulties ahead and prepares for them; the simpleton goes blindly on and suffers the consequences. □ True humility and respect for the Lord lead a man to riches, honor and long life.

⚞ KEY VERSE ⚟

It is not the right time for me to go now. But you can go anytime and it will make no difference, for the world can't hate you; but it does hate me, because I accuse it of sin and evil.—*John 7:6–7*

⚞ REFLECTION ⚟

Because the world hated Jesus, we who follow him can expect that many people will hate us also. If things are going too well, ask if you are following Jesus as you should. We can be grateful if life goes well, but not at the cost of following Jesus halfheartedly or not at all. As our society becomes more removed from the church and Christianity, you will find more and more opportunities for you and your spouse to set an example of godliness. Are you up to the task?

⚞ MEDITATION ⚟

Heavenly Father, may those who live in darkness see your light reflected in our lives. &

AUGUST 27

Jesus Preaches in the Temple
◄§ John 7:14–36 ►

Then, midway through the festival, Jesus went up to the Temple and preached openly. [15]The Jewish leaders were surprised when they heard him. "How can he know so much when he's never been to our schools?" they asked.

[16]So Jesus told them, "I'm not teaching you my own thoughts, but those of God who sent me. [17]If any of you really determines to do God's will, then you will certainly know whether my teaching is from God or is merely my own. [18]Anyone presenting his own ideas is looking for praise for himself, but anyone seeking to honor the one who sent him is a good and true person. [19]None of *you* obeys the laws of Moses! So why pick on *me* for breaking them? Why kill *me* for this?"

[20]The crowd replied, "You're out of your mind! Who's trying to kill you?"

[21,22,23]Jesus replied, "I worked on the Sabbath by healing a man, and you were surprised. But you work on the Sabbath, too, whenever you obey Moses' law of circumcision (actually, however, this tradition of circumcision is older than the Mosaic law); for if the correct time for circumcising your children falls on the Sabbath, you go ahead and do it, as you should. So why should I be condemned for making a man completely well on the Sabbath? [24]Think this through and you will see that I am right."

[25]Some of the people who lived there in Jerusalem said among themselves, "Isn't this the man they are trying to kill? [26]But here he is preaching in public, and they say nothing to him. Can it be that our leaders have learned, after all, that he really is the Messiah? [27]But how could he be? For we know where this man was born; when Christ comes, he will just appear and no one will know where he comes from."

[28]So Jesus, in a sermon in the Temple, called out, "Yes, you know me and where I was born and raised, but I am the representative of one you don't know, and he is Truth. [29]I know him because I was with him, and he sent me to you."

[30]Then the Jewish leaders sought to arrest him; but no hand was laid on him, for God's time had not yet come.

[31]Many among the crowds at the Temple believed on him. "After all," they said, "what miracles do you expect the Messiah to do that this man hasn't done?"

[32]When the Pharisees heard that the crowds were in this mood, they and the chief priests sent officers to arrest Jesus. [33]But Jesus told them, "[Not yet!] I am to be here a little longer. Then I shall return to the one who sent me. [34]You will search for me but not find me. And you won't be able to come where I am!"

[35]The Jewish leaders were puzzled by this statement. "Where is he planning to go?" they asked. "Maybe he is thinking of leaving the country and going as a missionary among the Jews in other lands, or maybe even to the Gentiles! [36]What does he mean about our looking for him and not being able to find him, and, 'You won't be able to come where I am'?"

Honor Church Leaders
◄§ 1 Timothy 5:17–25 ►

Pastors who do their work well should be paid well and should be highly appreciated, especially those who work hard at both preaching and teaching. [18]For the Scriptures say, "Never tie up the mouth of an ox when it is treading out the grain— let him eat as he goes along!" And in another place, "Those who work deserve their pay!"

[19]Don't listen to complaints against the pastor unless there are two or three witnesses to accuse him. [20]If he has really sinned, then he should be rebuked in front of the whole church so that no one else will follow his example.

[21]I solemnly command you in the presence of God and the Lord Jesus Christ and of the holy angels to do this whether the pastor is a special friend of yours or not. All must be treated exactly the

same. ²²Never be in a hurry about choosing a pastor; you may overlook his sins and it will look as if you approve of them. Be sure that you yourself stay away from all sin. ²³(By the way, this doesn't mean you should completely give up drinking wine. You ought to take a little sometimes as medicine for your stomach because you are sick so often.)

²⁴Remember that some men, even pastors, lead sinful lives and everyone knows it. In such situations you can do something about it. But in other cases only the judgment day will reveal the terrible truth. ²⁵In the same way, everyone knows how much good some pastors do, but sometimes their good deeds aren't known until long afterward.

Proverbs for Today
⋅§ 22:5–6 §⋅

The rebel walks a thorny, treacherous road; the man who values his soul will stay away. Teach a child to choose the right path, and when he is older he will remain upon it.

Anyone presenting his own ideas is looking for praise for himself, but anyone seeking to honor the one who sent him is a good and true person.—*John 7:18*

Have you ever listened to counselors, pastors, or other religious leaders speak about marriage and family relationships and wondered if they were telling the truth? Test them: (1) ask if their words agree with or contradict the Bible; and (2) ask if their words point to Christ or to themselves. You will not be misled if you understand the Word of God and obey his commandments.

Heavenly Father, as we work to make a marriage that is pleasing to you, keep us sensitive to the weaknesses of others so that our example will not lead anyone away from you. Keep us grounded in the Bible and committed to our prayer life together so that we will not be deceived. ⋅§

Rivers of Living Water
⋅§ John 7:37–53 §⋅

On the last day, the climax of the holidays, Jesus shouted to the crowds, "If anyone is thirsty, let him come to me and drink. ³⁸For the Scriptures declare that rivers of living water shall flow from the inmost being of anyone who believes in me." ³⁹(He was speaking of the Holy Spirit, who would be given to everyone believing in him; but the Spirit had not yet been given, because Jesus had not yet returned to his glory in heaven.)

⁴⁰When the crowds heard him say this, some of them declared, "This man surely is the prophet who will come just before the Messiah." ⁴¹,⁴²Others said, "He *is* the Messiah." Still others, "But he *can't* be! Will the Messiah come from *Galilee?* For the Scriptures clearly state that the Messiah will be born of the royal line of David, in *Bethlehem,* the village where David was born." ⁴³So the crowd was divided about him. ⁴⁴And some wanted him arrested, but no one touched him.

⁴⁵The Temple police who had been sent to arrest him returned to the chief priests and Pharisees. "Why didn't you bring him in?" they demanded.

⁴⁶"He says such wonderful things!" they mumbled. "We've never heard anything like it."

⁴⁷"So you also have been led astray?" the Pharisees mocked. ⁴⁸"Is there a single one of us Jewish rulers or Pharisees who believes he is the Messiah? ⁴⁹These stupid crowds do, yes; but what do they know about it? A curse upon them anyway!"

⁵⁰Then Nicodemus spoke up. (Remember him? He was the Jewish leader who came secretly to interview Jesus.) ⁵¹"Is it legal to convict a man before he is even tried?" he asked.

⁵²They replied, "Are you a wretched Galilean

too? Search the Scriptures and see for yourself—no prophets will come from Galilee!''

[53]Then the meeting broke up and everybody went home.

Instructions to Masters and Slaves
◄§ 1 Timothy 6:1–5 §►

Christian slaves should work hard for their owners and respect them; never let it be said that Christ's people are poor workers. Don't let the name of God or his teaching be laughed at because of this. [2]If their owner is a Christian, that is no excuse for slowing down; rather they should work all the harder because a brother in the faith is being helped by their efforts.

Teach these truths, Timothy, and encourage all to obey them.

[3]Some may deny these things, but they are the sound, wholesome teachings of the Lord Jesus Christ and are the foundation for a godly life. [4]Anyone who says anything different is both proud and stupid. He is quibbling over the meaning of Christ's words and stirring up arguments ending in jealousy and anger, which only lead to name-calling, accusations, and evil suspicions. [5]These arguers—their minds warped by sin—don't know how to tell the truth; to them the Good News is just a means of making money. Keep away from them.

Proverbs for Today
◄§ 22:7 §►

Just as the rich rule the poor, so the borrower is servant to the lender.

KEY VERSE

Just as the rich rule the poor, so the borrower is servant to the lender.—*Proverbs 22:7*

REFLECTION

Marriage poses some enticements and expenses that are not always easy to meet. What couple doesn't desire a nice home and all of the expensive trappings everyone expects of good, responsible, successful citizens? Things themselves are not wrong, but they can turn our lives upside down if we over-extend our credit by borrowing money that we can't reasonably pay back. This doesn't mean you should never borrow. It warns us, however, never to take on a loan without the ability to repay it. A loan you can handle is enabling; a loan you can't handle is enslaving. The borrower must realize that until the loan is repaid, he or she is a servant to the lender.

MEDITATION

Heavenly Father, may we consistently seek your wisdom concerning our financial matters so that we will only be slaves of Christ and not slaves to creditors. §►

AUGUST 29 ⸻

Jesus Forgives an Adulterous Woman
◄§ John 8:1–11 §►

Jesus returned to the Mount of Olives, [2]but early the next morning he was back again at the Temple. A crowd soon gathered, and he sat down and talked to them. [3]As he was speaking, the Jewish leaders and Pharisees brought a woman caught in adultery and placed her out in front of the staring crowd.

[4]"Teacher," they said to Jesus, "this woman was caught in the very act of adultery. [5]Moses' law says to kill her. What about it?''

[6]They were trying to trap him into saying something they could use against him, but Jesus stooped down and wrote in the dust with his finger. [7]They kept demanding an answer, so he stood up again and said, "All right, hurl the stones at her until she dies. But only he who never sinned may throw the first!''

[8]Then he stooped down again and wrote some more in the dust. [9]And the Jewish leaders slipped

away one by one, beginning with the eldest, until only Jesus was left in front of the crowd with the woman.

¹⁰Then Jesus stood up again and said to her, "Where are your accusers? Didn't even one of them condemn you?"

¹¹"No, sir," she said.

And Jesus said, "Neither do I. Go and sin no more."

Paul Defines True Riches
◄§ 1 Timothy 6:6–12 §►

Do you want to be truly rich? You already are if you are happy and good. ⁷After all, we didn't bring any money with us when we came into the world, and we can't carry away a single penny when we die. ⁸So we should be well satisfied without money if we have enough food and clothing. ⁹But people who long to be rich soon begin to do all kinds of wrong things to get money, things that hurt them and make them evil-minded and finally send them to hell itself. ¹⁰For the love of money is the first step toward all kinds of sin. Some people have even turned away from God because of their love for it, and as a result have pierced themselves with many sorrows.

¹¹Oh, Timothy, you are God's man. Run from all these evil things and work instead at what is right and good, learning to trust him and love others, and to be patient and gentle. ¹²Fight on for God. Hold tightly to the eternal life which God has given

you, and which you have confessed with such a ringing confession before many witnesses.

Proverbs for Today
◄§ 22:8–9 §►

The unjust tyrant will reap disaster and his reign of terror shall end. ☐ Happy is the generous man, the one who feeds the poor.

────── ◄ KEY VERSE ► ──────

They kept demanding an answer, so he stood up again and said, "All right, hurl the stones at her until she dies. But only he who never sinned may throw the first!"—*John 8:7*

────── ◄ REFLECTION ► ──────

This is a significant statement about judging others. By mentioning the throwing of stones, Jesus could not be accused of being against the law. But by saying that only a sinless person could throw the first stone, he highlighted the importance of compassion and forgiveness. When your spouse is caught in sin, are you quick to pass judgment? To do so is to act as though you have never sinned. Only God, who is perfect, has the right to judge. Our role is to show forgiveness and compassion.

────── ◄ MEDITATION ► ──────

Heavenly Father, forgive me for my sin against you. Give me the spirit of forgiveness so that I can show compassion toward my husband or wife and forgive him or her. §►

AUGUST 30

Jesus' Testimony Is from God the Father
◄§ John 8:12–31a §►

Later, in one of his talks, Jesus said to the people, "I am the Light of the world. So if you follow me, you won't be stumbling through the darkness, for living light will flood your path."

¹³The Pharisees replied, "You are boasting—and lying!"

¹⁴Jesus told them, "These claims are true even

though I make them concerning myself. For I know where I came from and where I am going, but you don't know this about me. ¹⁵You pass judgment on me without knowing the facts. I am not judging you now; ¹⁶but if I were, it would be an absolutely correct judgment in every respect, for I have with me the Father who sent me. ¹⁷Your laws say that if two men agree on something that has happened, their witness is accepted as fact. ¹⁸Well,

I am one witness, and my Father who sent me is the other."

¹⁹"Where is your father?" they asked.

Jesus answered, "You don't know who I am, so you don't know who my Father is. If you knew me, then you would know him too."

²⁰Jesus made these statements while in the section of the Temple known as the Treasury. But he was not arrested, for his time had not yet run out.

²¹Later he said to them again, "I am going away; and you will search for me, and die in your sins. And you cannot come where I am going."

²²The Jews asked, "Is he planning suicide? What does he mean, 'You cannot come where I am going'?"

²³Then he said to them, "You are from below; I am from above. You are of this world; I am not. ²⁴That is why I said that you will die in your sins; for unless you believe that I am the Messiah, the Son of God, you will die in your sins."

²⁵"Tell us who you are," they demanded.

He replied, "I am the one I have always claimed to be. ²⁶I could condemn you for much and teach you much, but I won't, for I say only what I am told to by the one who sent me; and he is Truth." ²⁷But they still didn't understand that he was talking to them about God.

²⁸So Jesus said, "When you have killed the Messiah, then you will realize that I am he and that I have not been telling you my own ideas, but have spoken what the Father taught me. ²⁹And he who sent me is with me—he has not deserted me—for I always do those things that are pleasing to him."

³⁰,³¹Then many of the Jewish leaders who heard him say these things began believing him to be the Messiah.

Fulfill Your Calling
❧ 1 Timothy 6:13–16 ☙

I command you before God who gives life to all, and before Christ Jesus who gave a fearless testi-mony before Pontius Pilate, ¹⁴that you fulfill all he has told you to do, so that no one can find fault with you from now until our Lord Jesus Christ returns. ¹⁵For in due season Christ will be revealed from heaven by the blessed and only Almighty God, the King of kings and Lord of lords, ¹⁶who alone can never die, who lives in light so terrible that no human being can approach him. No mere man has ever seen him, nor ever will. Unto him be honor and everlasting power and dominion forever and ever. Amen.

Proverbs for Today
❧ 22:10–12 ☙

Throw out the mocker, and you will be rid of tension, fighting and quarrels. ☐ He who values grace and truth is the king's friend. ☐ The Lord preserves the upright but ruins the plans of the wicked.

❧ KEY VERSE ☙

The Lord preserves the upright but ruins the plans of the wicked.—*Proverbs 22:12*

❧ REFLECTION ☙

It takes discipline, determination, and hard work to maintain a godly marriage, but God protects and rewards those who make the commitment to follow him. The wicked may seem to have an easier time of it, but in the long run their plans fail and their lives amount to nothing. Don't expect a lasting, successful marriage if you resist God.

❧ MEDITATION ☙

Heavenly Father, thank you for your constant guidance in our relationship. Although our lives are not perfect, we thank you for your protection from things we can not see as well as those things that we do see. ☙

Jesus Is the Eternal Son Sent from God
John 8:31b–59

Jesus said to them, "You are truly my disciples if you live as I tell you to, [32]and you will know the truth, and the truth will set you free."

[33]"But we are descendants of Abraham," they said, "and have never been slaves to any man on earth! What do you mean, 'set free'?"

[34]Jesus replied, "You are slaves of sin, every one of you. [35]And slaves don't have rights, but the Son has every right there is! [36]So if the Son sets you free, you will indeed be free—[37](Yes, I realize that you are descendants of Abraham!) And yet some of you are trying to kill me because my message does not find a home within your hearts. [38]I am telling you what I saw when I was with my Father. But you are following the advice of *your* father."

[39]"Our father is Abraham," they declared.

"No!" Jesus replied, "for if he were, you would follow his good example. [40]But instead you are trying to kill me—and all because I told you the truth I heard from God. Abraham wouldn't do a thing like that! [41]No, you are obeying your *real* father when you act that way."

They replied, "We were not born out of wedlock—our true Father is God himself."

[42]Jesus told them, "If that were so, then you would love me, for I have come to you from God. I am not here on my own, but he sent me. [43]Why can't you understand what I am saying? It is because you are prevented from doing so! [44]For you are the children of your father the devil and you love to do the evil things he does. He was a murderer from the beginning and a hater of truth—there is not an iota of truth in him. When he lies, it is perfectly normal; for he is the father of liars. [45]And so when I tell the truth, you just naturally don't believe it!

[46]"Which of you can truthfully accuse me of one single sin? [No one!] And since I am telling you the truth, why don't you believe me? [47]Anyone whose Father is God listens gladly to the words of God. Since you don't, it proves you aren't his children."

[48]"You Samaritan! Foreigner! Devil!" the Jewish leaders snarled. "Didn't we say all along you were possessed by a demon?"

[49]"No," Jesus said, "I have no demon in me. For I honor my Father—and you dishonor me. [50]And though I have no wish to make myself great, God wants this for me and judges [those who reject me]. [51]With all the earnestness I have I tell you this—no one who obeys me shall ever die!"

[52]The leaders of the Jews said, "Now we know you are possessed by a demon. Even Abraham and the mightiest prophets died, and yet you say that obeying you will keep a man from dying! [53]So you are greater than our father Abraham, who died? And greater than the prophets, who died? Who do you think you are?" [54]Then Jesus told them this: "If I am merely boasting about myself, it doesn't count. But it is my Father—and you claim him as your God—who is saying these glorious things about me. [55]But you do not even know him. I do. If I said otherwise, I would be as great a liar as you! But it is true—I know him and fully obey him. [56]Your father Abraham rejoiced to see my day. He knew I was coming and was glad."

[57]*The Jewish leaders:* "You aren't even fifty years old—sure, you've seen Abraham!"

[58]*Jesus:* "The absolute truth is that I was in existence before Abraham was ever born!"

[59]At that point the Jewish leaders picked up stones to kill him. But Jesus was hidden from them, and walked past them and left the Temple.

Paul's Instructions to the Rich
1 Timothy 6:17–21

Tell those who are rich not to be proud and not to trust in their money, which will soon be gone, but their pride and trust should be in the living God who always richly gives us all we need for our enjoyment. [18]Tell them to use their money to do good. They should be rich in good works and should give happily to those in need, always being ready to share with others whatever God has given them. [19]By doing this they will be storing up real treasure for themselves in heaven—it is the only safe investment for eternity! And they will be living a fruitful Christian life down here as well.

²⁰Oh, Timothy, don't fail to do these things that God entrusted to you. Keep out of foolish arguments with those who boast of their "knowledge" and thus prove their lack of it. ²¹Some of these people have missed the most important thing in life—they don't know God. May God's mercy be upon you.

Sincerely,
Paul

Proverbs for Today
≈§ 22:13 ≈

The lazy man is full of excuses. "I can't go to work!" he says. "If I go outside I might meet a lion in the street and be killed!"

——— ∂ KEY VERSE ∂ ———

Tell those who are rich not to be proud and not to trust in their money, which will soon be gone, but their pride and trust should be in the living God who always richly gives us all we need for our enjoyment.—*1 Timothy 6:17*

∂ **REFLECTION** ∂

Ephesus was a wealthy city, and the Ephesian church probably had many wealthy members. Paul advised Timothy to deal with that reality by teaching that the possession of riches carries great responsibility. Those who have money must be generous, not arrogant, because they have a lot to give. They must be careful not to put their trust in money instead of in the living God for their security.

Despite overwhelming evidence to the contrary, most couples live as though money will bring happiness. Rich people craving greater riches can be caught in an endless cycle that only ends in ruin and destruction.

How can couples keep away from the love of money? (1) Realize that one day riches will all be gone (1 Timothy 6:7, 17); (2) be content with what you have (6:8); (3) monitor what you are willing to do or to sacrifice to get more money (6:9–10); (4) love each other more than money (6:11); (5) love God's work more than money (6:11); (6) freely share what you have (6:18).

∂ **MEDITATION** ∂

Heavenly Father, as we grow each day in our love for you as well as our love for each other may we continue to keep money in its proper perspective. ≈

SEPTEMBER 1

Jesus Heals a Blind Man
≈§ John 9:1–12 ≈

As Jesus was walking along, he saw a man blind from birth.

²"Master," his disciples asked him, "why was this man born blind? Was it a result of his own sins or those of his parents?"

³"Neither," Jesus answered. "But to demonstrate the power of God. ⁴All of us must quickly carry out the tasks assigned us by the one who sent me, for there is little time left before the night falls and all work comes to an end. ⁵But while I am still here in the world, I give it my light."

⁶Then he spat on the ground and made mud from the spittle and smoothed the mud over the blind man's eyes, ⁷and told him, "Go and wash in the Pool of Siloam" (the word "Siloam" means "Sent"). So the man went where he was sent and washed and came back seeing!

⁸His neighbors and others who knew him as a blind beggar asked each other, "Is this the same fellow—that beggar?"

⁹Some said yes, and some said no. "It can't be

the same man," they thought, "but he surely looks like him!"

And the beggar said, "I *am* the same man!"

[10]Then they asked him how in the world he could see. What had happened?

[11]And he told them, "A man they call Jesus made mud and smoothed it over my eyes and told me to go to the Pool of Siloam and wash off the mud. I did, and I can see!"

[12]"Where is he now?" they asked.

"I don't know," he replied.

Paul Encourages Timothy to Be Faithful
~§ 2 Timothy 1:1–8 §~

From: Paul, Jesus Christ's missionary, sent out by God to tell men and women everywhere about the eternal life he has promised them through faith in Jesus Christ.

[2]*To:* Timothy, my dear son. May God the Father and Christ Jesus our Lord shower you with his kindness, mercy and peace.

[3]How I thank God for you, Timothy. I pray for you every day, and many times during the long nights I beg my God to bless you richly. He is my fathers' God, and mine, and my only purpose in life is to please him.

[4]How I long to see you again. How happy I would be, for I remember your tears as we left each other.

[5]I know how much you trust the Lord, just as your mother Eunice and your grandmother Lois do; and I feel sure you are still trusting him as much as ever.

[6]This being so, I want to remind you to stir into flame the strength and boldness that is in you, that entered into you when I laid my hands upon your head and blessed you. [7]For the Holy Spirit, God's gift, does not want you to be afraid of people, but to be wise and strong, and to love them and enjoy being with them.

[8]If you will stir up this inner power, you will never be afraid to tell others about our Lord, or to let them know that I am your friend even though I am here in jail for Christ's sake. You will be ready to suffer with me for the Lord, for he will give you strength in suffering.

Proverbs for Today
~§ 22:14 §~

A prostitute is a dangerous trap; those cursed of God are caught in it.

~ø KEY VERSE ø~

I know how much you trust the Lord, just as your mother Eunice and your grandmother Lois do; and I feel sure you are still trusting him as much as ever. —*2 Timothy 1:5*

~ø REFLECTION ø~

Timothy's mother and grandmother, Eunice and Lois, were early Christian converts, possibly through Paul's ministry in their home city, Lystra (Acts 16:1). They communicated their strong Christian faith to Timothy, even though his father was probably not a believer. Don't hide your light at home; families are fertile fields for planting gospel seeds. Let your parents, children, spouse, brothers, and sisters know of your faith in Jesus, and be sure they see Christ's love, helpfulness, and joy in you.

~ø MEDITATION ø~

Heavenly Father, forgive us for finding it easier to share your light and truth with those people that who don't know us very well. May we become so much like you that our families will not be able to keep from noticing the intriguing and wonderful things you are doing in our lives. §~

SEPTEMBER 2

A Pharisaic Investigation
❧ John 9:13–41 ❧

Then some people took the man [whom Jesus had healed] to the Pharisees. [14]Now as it happened, this all occurred on a Sabbath. [15]Then the Pharisees asked him all about it. So he told them how Jesus had smoothed the mud over his eyes, and when it was washed away, he could see!

[16]Some of them said, "Then this fellow Jesus is not from God, because he is working on the Sabbath."

Others said, "But how could an ordinary sinner do such miracles?" So there was a deep division of opinion among them.

[17]Then the Pharisees turned on the man who had been blind and demanded, "This man who opened your eyes—who do you say he is?"

"I think he must be a prophet sent from God," the man replied.

[18]The Jewish leaders wouldn't believe he had been blind, until they called in his parents [19]and asked them, "Is this your son? Was he born blind? If so, how can he see?"

[20]His parents replied, "We know this is our son and that he was born blind, [21]but we don't know what happened to make him see, or who did it. He is old enough to speak for himself. Ask him."

[22,23]They said this in fear of the Jewish leaders who had announced that anyone saying Jesus was the Messiah would be excommunicated.

[24]So for the second time they called in the man who had been blind and told him, "Give the glory to God, not to Jesus, for we know Jesus is an evil person."

[25]"I don't know whether he is good or bad," the man replied, "but I know this: *I was blind, and now I see!*"

[26]"But what did he do?" they asked. "How did he heal you?"

[27]"Look!" the man exclaimed. "I told you once; didn't you listen? Why do you want to hear it again? Do you want to become his disciples too?"

[28]Then they cursed him and said, "You are his disciple, but we are disciples of Moses. [29]We know God has spoken to Moses, but as for this fellow, we don't know anything about him."

[30]"Why, that's very strange!" the man replied. "He can heal blind men, and yet you don't know anything about him! [31]Well, God doesn't listen to evil men, but he has open ears to those who worship him and do his will. [32]Since the world began there has never been anyone who could open the eyes of someone born blind. [33]If this man were not from God, he couldn't do it."

[34]"You illegitimate bastard, you!" they shouted. "Are you trying to teach *us?*" And they threw him out.

[35]When Jesus heard what had happened, he found the man and said, "Do you believe in the Messiah?"

[36]The man answered, "Who is he, sir, for I want to."

[37]"You have seen him," Jesus said, "and he is speaking to you!"

[38]"Yes, Lord," the man said, "I believe!" And he worshiped Jesus.

[39]Then Jesus told him, "I have come into the world to give sight to those who are spiritually blind and to show those who think they see that they are blind."

[40]The Pharisees who were standing there asked, "Are you saying we are blind?"

[41]"If you were blind, you wouldn't be guilty," Jesus replied. "But your guilt remains because you claim to know what you are doing.

Stand Firm for the Gospel
❧ 2 Timothy 1:9–14 ❧

It is he who saved us and chose us for his holy work, not because we deserved it but because that was his plan long before the world began—to show his love and kindness to us through Christ. [10]And now he has made all of this plain to us by the coming of our Savior Jesus Christ, who broke the power of death and showed us the way of everlasting life through trusting him. ¹¹And God has chosen me to be his missionary, to preach to the Gentiles and teach them.

¹²That is why I am suffering here in jail and I am certainly not ashamed of it, for I know the one in whom I trust, and I am sure that he is able to safely guard all that I have given him until the day of his return.

¹³Hold tightly to the pattern of truth I taught you, especially concerning the faith and love Christ Jesus offers you. ¹⁴Guard well the splendid, God-given ability you received as a gift from the Holy Spirit who lives within you.

Proverbs for Today
~§ 22:15 ଈ~

A youngster's heart is filled with rebellion, but punishment will drive it out of him.

—————— ✍ KEY VERSE ଈ——————

Hold tightly to the pattern of truth I taught you, especially concerning the faith and love Christ Jesus offers you. Guard well the splendid, God-given

ability you received as a gift from the Holy Spirit who lives within you.—*2 Timothy 1:13–14*

—————— ✍ REFLECTION ଈ——————

Timothy was in a time of transition. He had been Paul's bright young helper; soon he would be on his own as leader of a difficult, but critically important, church. Although his responsibilities were changing, Timothy was not without help. He had everything he needed to face the future, if he would hold on tightly to it. Throughout your marriage, you will face many difficult transitions: children, the death of loved ones, an empty nest, retirement, sickness, etc. It is good to follow Paul's advice to Timothy and look back at your experience. Who is the foundation of your faith? What gifts has the Holy Spirit given you as a couple? How can you work together to build on the foundation that has already been laid, using the gifts you have already been given? How can this period of transition become an example of God's presence in your lives?

—————— ✍ MEDITATION ଈ——————

Heavenly Father, help us to guard our faith and to use well the gifts you have given us. ଈ

SEPTEMBER 3

Jesus Is the Good Shepherd
~§ John 10:1–21 ଈ~

"Anyone refusing to walk through the gate into a sheepfold, who sneaks over the wall, must surely be a thief! ²For a shepherd comes through the gate. ³The gatekeeper opens the gate for him, and the sheep hear his voice and come to him; and he calls his own sheep by name and leads them out. ⁴He walks ahead of them; and they follow him, for they recognize his voice. ⁵They won't follow a stranger but will run from him, for they don't recognize his voice."

⁶Those who heard Jesus use this illustration didn't understand what he meant, ⁷so he explained it to them.

"I am the Gate for the sheep," he said. ⁸"All others who came before me were thieves and robbers. But the true sheep did not listen to them. ⁹Yes, I am the Gate. Those who come in by way of the Gate will be saved and will go in and out and find green pastures. ¹⁰The thief's purpose is to steal, kill and destroy. My purpose is to give life in all its fullness.

¹¹"I am the Good Shepherd. The Good Shepherd lays down his life for the sheep. ¹²A hired man will run when he sees a wolf coming and will leave the sheep, for they aren't his and he isn't their shepherd. And so the wolf leaps on them and scatters the flock. ¹³The hired man runs because he is hired and has no real concern for the sheep.

¹⁴"I am the Good Shepherd and know my own sheep, and they know me, ¹⁵just as my Father knows me and I know the Father; and I lay down my life for the sheep. ¹⁶I have other sheep, too, in another fold. I must bring them also, and they will heed my voice; and there will be one flock with one Shepherd.

¹⁷"The Father loves me because I lay down my life that I may have it back again. ¹⁸No one can kill me without my consent—I lay down my life voluntarily. For I have the right and power to lay it down when I want to and also the right and power to take it again. For the Father has given me this right."

¹⁹When he said these things, the Jewish leaders were again divided in their opinions about him. ²⁰Some of them said, "He has a demon or else is crazy. Why listen to a man like that?"

²¹Others said, "This doesn't sound to us like a man possessed by a demon! Can a demon open the eyes of blind men?"

The Blessing of Onesiphorus
⊸§ 2 Timothy 1:15–18 §⊷

As you know, all the Christians who came here from Asia have deserted me; even Phygellus and Hermogenes are gone. ¹⁶May the Lord bless Onesiphorus and all his family, because he visited me and encouraged me often. His visits revived me like a breath of fresh air, and he was never ashamed of my being in jail. ¹⁷In fact, when he came to Rome he searched everywhere trying to find me, and finally did. ¹⁸May the Lord give him a special blessing at the day of Christ's return. And you know better than I can tell you how much he helped me at Ephesus.

Proverbs for Today
⊸§ 22:16 §⊷

He who gains by oppressing the poor or by bribing the rich shall end in poverty.

⊸ KEY VERSE ⊷

"Anyone refusing to walk through the gate into a sheepfold, who sneaks over the wall, must surely be a thief!"—*John 10:1*

⊸ REFLECTION ⊷

At night, sheep were often gathered into a sheepfold to protect them from thieves, weather, or wild animals. The sheepfolds were caves, sheds, or open areas surrounded by walls made of stones or branches. The shepherd often slept in the fold to protect the sheep. Christians have their own shepherd—Jesus. Just as a shepherd cares for his sheep, Jesus, the Good Shepherd, cares for his flock. The prophet Ezekiel, in predicting the coming of the Messiah, called him a Shepherd (Ezekiel 34:23). If you trust in Christ, he is in your shepherd, protecting you and your family from evil.

⊸ MEDITATION ⊷

Heavenly Father, thank you for protecting us in the day as well as in the evening hours. §⊷

SEPTEMBER 4

Jesus Is God's Son
⊸§ John 10:22–42 §⊷

It was winter, and Jesus was in Jerusalem at the time of the Dedication Celebration. He was at the Temple, walking through the section known as Solomon's Hall. ²⁴The Jewish leaders surrounded him and asked, "How long are you going to keep us in suspense? If you are the Messiah, tell us plainly."

²⁵"I have already told you, and you don't believe me," Jesus replied. "The proof is in the miracles I do in the name of my Father. ²⁶But you don't believe me because you are not part of my flock. ²⁷My sheep recognize my voice, and I know them, and they follow me. ²⁸I give them eternal life and they shall never perish. No one shall snatch them away from me, ²⁹for my Father has given them to me,

and he is more powerful than anyone else, so no one can kidnap them from me. [30]I and the Father are one."

[31]Then again the Jewish leaders picked up stones to kill him.

[32]Jesus said, "At God's direction I have done many a miracle to help the people. For which one are you killing me?"

[33]They replied, "Not for any good work, but for blasphemy; you, a mere man, have declared yourself to be God."

[34,35,36]"In your own Law it says that men are gods!" he replied. "So if the Scripture, which cannot be untrue, speaks of those as gods to whom the message of God came, do you call it blasphemy when the one sanctified and sent into the world by the Father says, 'I am the Son of God'? [37]Don't believe me unless I do miracles of God. [38]But if I do, believe them even if you don't believe me. Then you will become convinced that the Father is in me, and I in the Father."

[39]Once again they started to arrest him. But he walked away and left them, [40]and went beyond the Jordan River to stay near the place where John was first baptizing. [41]And many followed him.

"John didn't do miracles," they remarked to one another, "but all his predictions concerning this man have come true." [42]And many came to the decision that he was the Messiah.

Suffer As a Good Soldier of Christ
§ 2 Timothy 2:1–7 ß

Oh, Timothy, my son, be strong with the strength Christ Jesus gives you. [2]For you must teach others those things you and many others have heard me speak about. Teach these great truths to trustworthy men who will, in turn, pass them on to others.

[3]Take your share of suffering as a good soldier of Jesus Christ, just as I do, [4]and as Christ's soldier do not let yourself become tied up in worldly affairs, for then you cannot satisfy the one who has enlisted you in his army. [5]Follow the Lord's rules for doing his work, just as an athlete either follows the rules or is disqualified and wins no prize. [6]Work hard, like a farmer who gets paid well if he raises a large crop. [7]Think over these three illustrations, and may the Lord help you to understand how they apply to you.

Proverbs for Today
§ 22:17–19 ß

Listen to this wise advice; follow it closely, for it will do you good, and you can pass it on to others: *Trust in the Lord.*

---
§ KEY VERSE ß

O Timothy, my son, be strong with the strength Christ Jesus gives you.—*2 Timothy 2:1*

---
§ REFLECTION ß

Timothy would face suffering as he preached and taught, but Paul told him that he should be willing to take it for the sake of Christ. Christian leaders are not the only ones to suffer. Soldiers, athletes, farmers, and spouses all must discipline themselves and be willing to sacrifice to achieve the results they want. Like soldiers, we have to give up worldly security and endure rigorous discipline. Like athletes, we must train hard and follow the rules. Like farmers, we must work hard whenever necessary. We keep going in spite of suffering because of the promise of victory, the vision of winning, and the hope of harvest. As a married couple, you must develop an endurance that allows your love to grow and develop over a period of years, becoming stronger with the passage of time and events. All your suffering is made worthwhile by your goal of glorifying God through your lives and through your relationships, winning people to Christ, and one day living eternally with him.

---
§ MEDITATION ß

Heavenly Father, help us to work hard at our relationship. Please strengthen our bond so that nothing can sever it. ß

SEPTEMBER 5

Lazarus Dies
◄§ John 11:1–29 §►

Do you remember Mary, who poured the costly perfume on Jesus' feet and wiped them with her hair? Well, her brother Lazarus, who lived in Bethany with Mary and her sister Martha, was sick. ³So the two sisters sent a message to Jesus telling him, "Sir, your good friend is very, very sick."

⁴But when Jesus heard about it he said, "The purpose of his illness is not death, but for the glory of God. I, the Son of God, will receive glory from this situation."

⁵Although Jesus was very fond of Martha, Mary, and Lazarus, ⁶he stayed where he was for the next two days and made no move to go to them. ⁷Finally, after the two days, he said to his disciples, "Let's go to Judea."

⁸But his disciples objected. "Master," they said, "only a few days ago the Jewish leaders in Judea were trying to kill you. Are you going there again?"

⁹Jesus replied, "There are twelve hours of daylight every day, and during every hour of it a man can walk safely and not stumble. ¹⁰Only at night is there danger of a wrong step, because of the dark."

¹¹Then he said, "Our friend Lazarus has gone to sleep, but now I will go and waken him!"

¹²,¹³The disciples, thinking Jesus meant Lazarus was having a good night's rest, said, "That means he is getting better!" But Jesus meant Lazarus had died.

¹⁴Then he told them plainly, "Lazarus is dead. ¹⁵And for your sake, I am glad I wasn't there, for this will give you another opportunity to believe in me. Come, let's go to him."

¹⁶Thomas, nicknamed "The Twin," said to his fellow disciples, "Let's go too—and die with him."

¹⁷When they arrived at Bethany, they were told that Lazarus had already been in his tomb for four days. ¹⁸Bethany was only a couple of miles down the road from Jerusalem, ¹⁹and many of the Jewish leaders had come to pay their respects and to console Martha and Mary on their loss. ²⁰When Martha got word that Jesus was coming, she went to meet him. But Mary stayed at home.

²¹Martha said to Jesus, "Sir, if you had been here, my brother wouldn't have died. ²²And even now it's not too late, for I know that God will bring my brother back to life again, if you will only ask him to."

²³Jesus told her, "Your brother will come back to life again."

²⁴"Yes," Martha said, "when everyone else does, on Resurrection Day."

²⁵Jesus told her, "I am the one who raises the dead and gives them life again. Anyone who believes in me, even though he dies like anyone else, shall live again. ²⁶He is given eternal life for believing in me and shall never perish. Do you believe this, Martha?"

²⁷"Yes, Master," she told him. "I believe you are the Messiah, the Son of God, the one we have so long awaited."

²⁸Then she left him and returned to Mary and, calling her aside from the mourners, told her, "He is here and wants to see you." ²⁹So Mary went to him at once.

Suffering for Christ
◄§ 2 Timothy 2:8–15a §►

Don't ever forget the wonderful fact that Jesus Christ was a Man, born into King David's family; and that he was God, as shown by the fact that he rose again from the dead. ⁹It is because I have preached these great truths that I am in trouble here and have been put in jail like a criminal. But the Word of God is not chained, even though I am. ¹⁰I am more than willing to suffer if that will bring salvation and eternal glory in Christ Jesus to those God has chosen.

¹¹I am comforted by this truth, that when we suffer and die for Christ it only means that we will begin living with him in heaven. ¹²And if we think that our present service for him is hard, just remember that some day we are going to sit with

him and rule with him. But if we give up when we suffer, and turn against Christ, then he must turn against us. [13]Even when we are too weak to have any faith left, he remains faithful to us and will help us, for he cannot disown us who are part of himself, and he will always carry out his promises to us.

[14]Remind your people of these great facts, and command them in the name of the Lord not to argue over unimportant things. Such arguments are confusing and useless, and even harmful. [15]Work hard so God can say to you, "Well done."

Proverbs for Today
&5 22:20–21 &w

In the past, haven't I been right? Then believe what I am telling you now, and share it with others.

KEY VERSE

When Jesus heard about [Lazarus's illness] he said, "The purpose of his illness is not death, but for the glory of God. I, the Son of God, will receive glory from this situation."—*John 11:4*

REFLECTION

Any difficult situation a couple faces can ultimately bring glory to God because God can bring good out of any bad situation. When trouble comes, do you whine, complain, and blame God, or do you see your problems as opportunities to honor him? When you find yourself in difficulties, ask God to bring good from your situation.

MEDITATION

Heavenly Father, forgive us for the grumbling and complaining that we have done. Take our lives and allow them to glorify your Son, Jesus. &w

SEPTEMBER 6

Jesus Raises Lazarus from the Dead
&5 John 11:30–46 &w

Now Jesus had stayed outside the village, at the place where Martha met him. [31]When the Jewish leaders who were at the house trying to console Mary saw her leave so hastily, they assumed she was going to Lazarus' tomb to weep; so they followed her.

[32]When Mary arrived where Jesus was, she fell down at his feet, saying, "Sir, if you had been here, my brother would still be alive."

[33]When Jesus saw her weeping and the Jewish leaders wailing with her, he was moved with indignation and deeply troubled. [34]"Where is he buried?" he asked them.

They told him, "Come and see." [35]Tears came to Jesus' eyes.

[36]"They were close friends," the Jewish leaders said. "See how much he loved him."

[37,38]But some said, "This fellow healed a blind man—why couldn't he keep Lazarus from dying?"

And again Jesus was moved with deep anger. Then they came to the tomb. It was a cave with a heavy stone rolled across its door.

[39]"Roll the stone aside," Jesus told them.

But Martha, the dead man's sister, said, "By now the smell will be terrible, for he has been dead four days."

[40]"But didn't I tell you that you will see a wonderful miracle from God if you believe?" Jesus asked her.

[41]So they rolled the stone aside. Then Jesus looked up to heaven and said, "Father, thank you for hearing me. [42](You always hear me, of course, but I said it because of all these people standing here, so that they will believe you sent me.)" [43]Then he shouted, "Lazarus, come out!"

[44]And Lazarus came—bound up in the gravecloth, his face muffled in a head swath. Jesus told them, "Unwrap him and let him go!"

⁴⁵And so at last many of the Jewish leaders who were with Mary and saw it happen, finally believed on him. ⁴⁶But some went away to the Pharisees and reported it to them.

Be a Good Student of God's Word
❧ 2 Timothy 2:15b–21 ❧

Be a good workman, one who does not need to be ashamed when God examines your work. Know what his Word says and means. ¹⁶Steer clear of foolish discussions which lead people into the sin of anger with each other. ¹⁷Things will be said that will burn and hurt for a long time to come. Hymenaeus and Philetus, in their love of argument, are men like that. ¹⁸They have left the path of truth, preaching the lie that the resurrection of the dead has already occurred; and they have weakened the faith of some who believe them.

¹⁹But God's truth stands firm like a great rock, and nothing can shake it. It is a foundation stone with these words written on it: "The Lord knows those who are really his," and "A person who calls himself a Christian should not be doing things that are wrong."

²⁰In a wealthy home there are dishes made of gold and silver as well as some made from wood and clay. The expensive dishes are used for guests, and the cheap ones are used in the kitchen or to put garbage in. ²¹If you stay away from sin you will be like one of these dishes made of purest gold—the very best in the house—so that Christ himself can use you for his highest purposes.

Proverbs for Today
❧ 22:22–23 ❧

Don't rob the poor and sick! For the Lord is their defender. If you injure them he will punish you.

―――――― ❧ KEY VERSE ❧ ――――――

Work hard so God can say to you, "Well done." Be a good workman, one who does not need to be ashamed when God examines your work. Know what his Word says and means.—*2 Timothy 2:15*

―――――― ❧ REFLECTION ❧ ――――――

Life on earth is not a script that we act out. It is a time of deciding whether we will live for God or not, and then living out what we have decided. Because God will examine what kind of workers we have been for him, couples should build their lives on his Word and integrate his Word into their lives—it alone tells us how to live for God and serve him, building a godly home in the process. Couples who ignore the Bible will certainly be ashamed at the judgment. Consistent and diligent study of God's Word is vital, or else we will be lulled into neglecting God and our true purpose for living.

―――――― ❧ MEDITATION ❧ ――――――

Heavenly Father, as we spend time each day devoting ourselves to the study of your Word, may our home be a place that is pleasing to you. ❧

SEPTEMBER 7 ―――――――――――――――

The Prophecy of the High Priest
❧ John 11:47–57 ❧

Then the chief priests and Pharisees convened a council to discuss the situation.

"What are we going to do?" they asked each other. "For this man certainly does miracles. ⁴⁸If we let him alone the whole nation will follow him— and then the Roman army will come and kill us and take over the Jewish government."

⁴⁹And one of them, Caiaphas, who was High Priest that year, said, "You stupid idiots— ⁵⁰let this one man die for the people—why should the whole nation perish?"

⁵¹This prophecy that Jesus should die for the entire nation came from Caiaphas in his position as

High Priest—he didn't think of it by himself, but was inspired to say it. ⁵²It was a prediction that Jesus' death would not be for Israel only, but for all the children of God scattered around the world. ⁵³So from that time on the Jewish leaders began plotting Jesus' death.

⁵⁴Jesus now stopped his public ministry and left Jerusalem; he went to the edge of the desert, to the village of Ephraim, and stayed there with his disciples.

⁵⁵The Passover, a Jewish holy day, was near, and many country people arrived in Jerusalem several days early so that they could go through the cleansing ceremony before the Passover began. ⁵⁶They wanted to see Jesus, and as they gossiped in the Temple, they asked each other, "What do you think? Will he come for the Passover?" ⁵⁷Meanwhile the chief priests and Pharisees had publicly announced that anyone seeing Jesus must report him immediately so that they could arrest him.

Flee Evil Desires
⋖§ 2 Timothy 2:22–26 §⋗

Run from anything that gives you the evil thoughts that young men often have, but stay close to anything that makes you want to do right. Have faith and love, and enjoy the companionship of those who love the Lord and have pure hearts. ²³Again I say, don't get involved in foolish arguments which only upset people and make them angry. ²⁴God's people must not be quarrelsome; they must be gentle, patient teachers of those who are wrong. ²⁵Be humble when you are trying to teach those who are mixed up concerning the truth. For if you talk meekly and courteously to them they are more likely, with God's help, to turn away from their wrong ideas and believe what is true. ²⁶Then they will come to their senses and escape from Satan's trap of slavery to sin which he uses to catch them whenever he likes, and then they can begin doing the will of God.

Proverbs for Today
⋖§ 22:24–25 §⋗

Keep away from angry, short-tempered men, lest you learn to be like them and endanger your soul.

⌐ KEY VERSE ⌐

Run from anything that gives you the evil thoughts that young men often have, but stay close to anything that makes you want to do right. Have faith and love, and enjoy the companionship of those who love the Lord and have pure hearts.—*2 Timothy 2:22*

⌐ REFLECTION ⌐

Running away is sometimes cowardly. But wise people realize that removing oneself from temptation is often prudent. Timothy, a young man, was warned to run from anything that produced evil thoughts (1 Timothy 6:11). Perhaps you experience a recurring temptation that is difficult to resist. Remove yourself from the situation and seek the support of your spouse in staying away from situations that tempt you. In a spiritual battle, knowing when to run is as important as knowing when and how to fight.

⌐ MEDITATION ⌐

Heavenly Father, we know that you understand temptation because your only Son, Jesus, was tempted. Give us swift and agile feet that will take us far from places and things that tempt us beyond our level of endurance. ❧

SEPTEMBER 8

Mary Anoints Jesus' Feet
◄§ John 12:1–11 ৶►

Six days before the Passover ceremonies began, Jesus arrived in Bethany where Lazarus was—the man he had brought back to life. ²A banquet was prepared in Jesus' honor. Martha served, and Lazarus sat at the table with him. ³Then Mary took a jar of costly perfume made from essence of nard, and anointed Jesus' feet with it and wiped them with her hair. And the house was filled with fragrance.

⁴But Judas Iscariot, one of his disciples—the one who would betray him—said, ⁵"That perfume was worth a fortune. It should have been sold and the money given to the poor." ⁶Not that he cared for the poor, but he was in charge of the disciples' funds and often dipped into them for his own use!

⁷Jesus replied, "Let her alone. She did it in preparation for my burial. ⁸You can always help the poor, but I won't be with you very long."

⁹When the ordinary people of Jerusalem heard of his arrival, they flocked to see him and also to see Lazarus—the man who had come back to life again. ¹⁰Then the chief priests decided to kill Lazarus too, ¹¹for it was because of him that many of the Jewish leaders had deserted and believed in Jesus as their Messiah.

The Character of the Last Days
◄§ 2 Timothy 3:1–10a ৶►

You may as well know this too, Timothy, that in the last days it is going to be very difficult to be a Christian. ²For people will love only themselves and their money; they will be proud and boastful, sneering at God, disobedient to their parents, ungrateful to them, and thoroughly bad. ³They will be hardheaded and never give in to others; they will be constant liars and troublemakers and will think nothing of immorality. They will be rough and cruel, and sneer at those who try to be good. ⁴They will betray their friends; they will be hotheaded,

puffed up with pride, and prefer good times to worshiping God. ⁵They will go to church, yes, but they won't really believe anything they hear. Don't be taken in by people like that.

⁶They are the kind who craftily sneak into other people's homes and make friendships with silly, sin-burdened women and teach them their new doctrines. ⁷Women of that kind are forever following new teachers, but they never understand the truth. ⁸And these teachers fight truth just as Jannes and Jambres fought against Moses. They have dirty minds, warped and twisted, and have turned against the Christian faith.

⁹But they won't get away with all this forever. Some day their deceit will be well known to everyone, as was the sin of Jannes and Jambres.

¹⁰But you know from watching me that I am not that kind of person.

Proverbs for Today
◄§ 22:26–27 ৶►

Unless you have the extra cash on hand, don't countersign a note. Why risk everything you own? They'll even take your bed!

◄ KEY VERSE ◄

They are the kind who craftily sneak into other people's homes and make friendships with silly, sin-burdened women and teach them their new doctrines. Women of that kind are forever following new teachers, but they never understand the truth.—*2 Timothy 3:6–7*

◄ REFLECTION ◄

Because of their cultural background, women in the Ephesian church had had no formal religious training. They enjoyed their new freedom to study Christian truths, but their eagerness to learn made them a target for false teachers. Paul warned Timothy to watch out for men who would take advantage of these women. Couples need to grow in their knowledge of the Word, because ignorance can make them vulnerable to deception. Who do you allow to come into your home and share their beliefs with you? What television shows, movies, and books do you read?

❧ MEDITATION ❧

Heavenly Father, let us grow daily in the knowledge of your Word so that we will not be deceived. ❧

SEPTEMBER 9

The Crowd Hails Jesus As King
❧ John 12:12–19 ❧

The next day, the news that Jesus was on the way to Jerusalem swept through the city, and a huge crowd of Passover visitors [13]took palm branches and went down the road to meet him, shouting, "The Savior! God bless the King of Israel! Hail to God's Ambassador!"

[14]Jesus rode along on a young donkey, fulfilling the prophecy that said: [15]"Don't be afraid of your King, people of Israel, for he will come to you meekly, sitting on a donkey's colt!"

[16](His disciples didn't realize at the time that this was a fulfillment of prophecy; but after Jesus returned to his glory in heaven, then they noticed how many prophecies of Scripture had come true before their eyes.)

[17]And those in the crowd who had seen Jesus call Lazarus back to life were telling all about it. [18]That was the main reason why so many went out to meet him—because they had heard about this mighty miracle.

[19]Then the Pharisees said to each other, "We've lost. Look—the whole world has gone after him!"

God's Word Can Equip Us for Righteousness
❧ 2 Timothy 3:10b–17 ❧

You know what I believe and the way I live and what I want. You know my faith in Christ and how I have suffered. You know my love for you, and my patience. [11]You know how many troubles I have had as a result of my preaching the Good News. You know about all that was done to me while I was visiting in Antioch, Iconium and Lystra, but the Lord delivered me. [12]Yes, and those who decide to please Christ Jesus by living godly lives will suffer at the hands of those who hate him. [13]In fact, evil men and false teachers will become worse and worse, deceiving many, they themselves having been deceived by Satan.

[14]But you must keep on believing the things you have been taught. You know they are true for you know that you can trust those of us who have taught you. [15]You know how, when you were a small child, you were taught the holy Scriptures; and it is these that make you wise to accept God's salvation by trusting in Christ Jesus. [16]The whole Bible was given to us by inspiration from God and is useful to teach us what is true and to make us realize what is wrong in our lives; it straightens us out and helps us do what is right. [17]It is God's way of making us well prepared at every point, fully equipped to do good to everyone.

Proverbs for Today
❧ 22:28–29 ❧

Do not move the ancient boundary marks. That is stealing. □ Do you know a hard-working man? He shall be successful and stand before kings!

❧ KEY VERSE ❧

His disciples didn't realize at the time that this was a fulfillment of prophecy; but after Jesus returned to his glory in heaven, then they noticed how many prophecies of Scripture had come true before their eyes.—*John 12:16*

❧ REFLECTION ❧

After Jesus' resurrection, the disciples understood many of the prophecies they had missed along the way. Jesus' words and actions took on new meaning and made more sense to them than before. In retrospect, these disciples saw how Jesus had led them into a deeper and better understanding of his truth. Stop now and think about the events in your lives together that have led up to where you are now. How has God led you to this point? As you grow older, you can look back and see God's involvement in your home and in your relationship more clearly than you do now. Let this truth encourage you to live for Christ today.

───────────── ❧ MEDITATION ❧ ─────────────

Heavenly Father, thank you for your faithful presence in every moment of our lives because it is a fulfillment of your grace and love. ❧

SEPTEMBER 10 _____

Jesus Predicts His Death
❧ John 12:20–36 ❧

Some Greeks who had come to Jerusalem to attend the Passover [21]paid a visit to Philip, who was from Bethsaida, and said, "Sir, we want to meet Jesus." [22]Philip told Andrew about it, and they went together to ask Jesus.

[23,24]Jesus replied that the time had come for him to return to his glory in heaven, and that "I must fall and die like a kernel of wheat that falls into the furrows of the earth. Unless I die I will be alone—a single seed. But my death will produce many new wheat kernels—a plentiful harvest of new lives. [25]If you love your life down here—you will lose it. If you despise your life down here—you will exchange it for eternal glory.

[26]"If these Greeks want to be my disciples, tell them to come and follow me, for my servants must be where I am. And if they follow me, the Father will honor them. [27]Now my soul is deeply troubled. Shall I pray, 'Father, save me from what lies ahead'? But that is the very reason why I came! [28]Father, bring glory and honor to your name."

Then a voice spoke from heaven saying, "I have already done this, and I will do it again." [29]When the crowd heard the voice, some of them thought it was thunder, while others declared an angel had spoken to him.

[30]Then Jesus told them, "The voice was for your benefit, not mine. [31]The time of judgment for the world has come—and the time when Satan, the prince of this world, shall be cast out. [32]And when I am lifted up [on the cross], I will draw everyone to me." [33]He said this to indicate how he was going to die.

[34]"Die?" asked the crowd. "We understood that the Messiah would live forever and never die. Why are you saying he will die? What Messiah are you talking about?"

[35]Jesus replied, "My light will shine out for you just a little while longer. Walk in it while you can, and go where you want to go before the darkness falls, for then it will be too late for you to find your way. [36]Make use of the Light while there is still time; then you will become light bearers."

After saying these things, Jesus went away and was hidden from them.

Paul's Charge to Timothy
❧ 2 Timothy 4:1–4 ❧

And so I solemnly urge you before God and before Christ Jesus—who will some day judge the living and the dead when he appears to set up his Kingdom— [2]to preach the Word of God urgently at all times, whenever you get the chance, in season and out, when it is convenient and when it is not. Correct and rebuke your people when they need it, encourage them to do right, and all the time be feeding them patiently with God's Word.

[3]For there is going to come a time when people won't listen to the truth, but will go around looking for teachers who will tell them just what they want to hear. [4]They won't listen to what the Bible says but will blithely follow their own misguided ideas.

Proverbs for Today
⌁§ 23:1–3 ε~

When dining with a rich man, be on your guard and don't stuff yourself, though it all tastes so good; for he is trying to bribe you, and no good is going to come of his invitation.

⌁ KEY VERSE ε~

There is going to come a time when people won't listen to the truth but will go around looking for teachers who will tell them just what they want to hear. They won't listen to what the Bible says but will blithely follow their own misguided ideas.—2 Timothy 4:3–4

⌁ REFLECTION ε~

It is difficult to accept correction; to be told we have to change. But no matter how much the truth hurts, we must be willing to listen to it so we can obey God fully. As you draw closer to God and to your spouse through prayer and the reading of God's Word, some passages of Scripture may make you feel uncomfortable because they challenge your way of dealing with each other. Whenever this happens, go before the Lord and ask him to help you face the challenge together. Don't be too lazy or afraid to obey God's Word.

⌁ MEDITATION ε~

Heavenly Father, give us the courage to change when we are confronted with your Word. ε~

SEPTEMBER 11

Isaiah Predicted Unbelief
⌁§ John 12:37–50 ε~

But despite all the miracles Jesus had done, most of the people would not believe he was the Messiah. [38]This is exactly what Isaiah the prophet had predicted: "Lord, who will believe us? Who will accept God's mighty miracles as proof?" [39]But they couldn't believe, for as Isaiah also said: [40]"God has blinded their eyes and hardened their hearts so that they can neither see nor understand nor turn to me to heal them." [41]Isaiah was referring to Jesus when he made this prediction, for he had seen a vision of the Messiah's glory.

[42]However, even many of the Jewish leaders believed him to be the Messiah but wouldn't admit it to anyone because of their fear that the Pharisees would excommunicate them from the synagogue; [43]for they loved the praise of men more than the praise of God.

[44]Jesus shouted to the crowds, "If you trust me, you are really trusting God. [45]For when you see me, you are seeing the one who sent me. [46]I have come as a Light to shine in this dark world, so that all who put their trust in me will no longer wander in the darkness. [47]If anyone hears me and doesn't obey me, I am not his judge—for I have come to save the world and not to judge it. [48]But all who reject me and my message will be judged at the Day of Judgment by the truths I have spoken. [49]For these are not my own ideas, but I have told you what the Father said to tell you. [50]And I know his instructions lead to eternal life; so whatever he tells me to say, I say!"

Paul Realizes That His End Is Near
⌁§ 2 Timothy 4:5–8 ε~

Stand steady, and don't be afraid of suffering for the Lord. Bring others to Christ. Leave nothing undone that you ought to do.

[6]I say this because I won't be around to help you very much longer. My time has almost run out. Very soon now I will be on my way to heaven. [7]I have fought long and hard for my Lord, and through it all I have kept true to him. And now the time has come for me to stop fighting and rest. [8]In heaven a crown is waiting for me which the Lord, the righteous Judge, will give me on that great day of his return. And not just to me, but

to all those whose lives show that they are eagerly looking forward to his coming back again.

Proverbs for Today
◄§ 23:4–5 §►

Don't weary yourself trying to get rich. Why waste your time? For riches can disappear as though they had the wings of a bird!

KEY VERSE

Don't weary yourself trying to get rich. Why waste your time? For riches can disappear as though they had the wings of a bird!—*Proverbs 23:4–5*

REFLECTION

We have all heard of couples who have won millions of dollars and then lost it all. Even the average couple can spend an inheritance—or a paycheck—with lightning speed and have little to show for it. Don't spend your time chasing earthly treasures. Instead, store up treasures in heaven, for such treasures will never be lost.

MEDITATION

Heavenly Father, let us spend our energies and our resources helping your Kingdom grow. §►

SEPTEMBER 12

Jesus Washes the Disciples' Feet
◄§ John 13:1–20 §►

Jesus knew on the evening of Passover Day that it would be his last night on earth before returning to his Father. During supper the devil had already suggested to Judas Iscariot, Simon's son, that this was the night to carry out his plan to betray Jesus. Jesus knew that the Father had given him everything and that he had come from God and would return to God. And how he loved his disciples! ⁴So he got up from the supper table, took off his robe, wrapped a towel around his loins, ⁵poured water into a basin, and began to wash the disciples' feet and to wipe them with the towel he had around him.

⁶When he came to Simon Peter, Peter said to him, "Master, you shouldn't be washing our feet like this!"

⁷Jesus replied, "You don't understand now why I am doing it; some day you will."

⁸"No," Peter protested, "you shall never wash my feet!"

"But if I don't, you can't be my partner," Jesus replied.

⁹Simon Peter exclaimed, "Then wash my hands and head as well—not just my feet!"

¹⁰Jesus replied, "One who has bathed all over needs only to have his feet washed to be entirely clean. Now you are clean—but that isn't true of everyone here." ¹¹For Jesus knew who would betray him. That is what he meant when he said, "Not all of you are clean."

¹²After washing their feet he put on his robe again and sat down and asked, "Do you understand what I was doing? ¹³You call me 'Master' and 'Lord,' and you do well to say it, for it is true. ¹⁴And since I, the Lord and Teacher, have washed your feet, you ought to wash each other's feet. ¹⁵I have given you an example to follow: do as I have done to you. ¹⁶How true it is that a servant is not greater than his master. Nor is the messenger more important than the one who sends him. ¹⁷You know these things—now do them! That is the path of blessing.

¹⁸"I am not saying these things to all of you; I know so well each one of you I chose. The Scripture declares, 'One who eats supper with me will betray me,' and this will soon come true. ¹⁹I tell you this now so that when it happens, you will believe on me.

²⁰"Truly, anyone welcoming my messenger is welcoming me. And to welcome me is to welcome the Father who sent me."

Paul's Final Instructions and Greetings
⮕ 2 Timothy 4:9–22 ⮔

Please come as soon as you can, ¹⁰for Demas has left me. He loved the good things of this life and went to Thessalonica. Crescens has gone to Galatia, Titus to Dalmatia. ¹¹Only Luke is with me. Bring Mark with you when you come, for I need him. ¹²(Tychicus is gone too, as I sent him to Ephesus.) ¹³When you come, be sure to bring the coat I left at Troas with Brother Carpus, and also the books, but especially the parchments.

¹⁴Alexander the coppersmith has done me much harm. The Lord will punish him, ¹⁵but be careful of him, for he fought against everything we said.

¹⁶The first time I was brought before the judge no one was here to help me. Everyone had run away. I hope that they will not be blamed for it. ¹⁷But the Lord stood with me and gave me the opportunity to boldly preach a whole sermon for all the world to hear. And he saved me from being thrown to the lions. ¹⁸Yes, and the Lord will always deliver me from all evil and will bring me into his heavenly Kingdom. To God be the glory forever and ever. Amen.

¹⁹Please say "hello" for me to Priscilla and Aquila and those living at the home of Onesiphorus. ²⁰Erastus stayed at Corinth, and I left Trophimus sick at Miletus.

²¹Do try to be here before winter. Eubulus sends you greetings, and so do Pudens, Linus, Claudia, and all the others. ²²May the Lord Jesus Christ be with your spirit.

Farewell,
Paul

Proverbs for Today
⮕ 23:6–8 ⮔

Don't associate with evil men; don't long for their favors and gifts. Their kindness is a trick; they want to use you as their pawn. The delicious food they serve will turn sour in your stomach and you will vomit it, and have to take back your words of appreciation for their "kindness."

_____ ⮕ KEY VERSE ⮔ _____

The Lord stood with me and gave me the opportunity to boldly preach a whole sermon for all the world to hear. And he saved me from being thrown to the lions.—*2 Timothy 4:17*

_____ ⮕ REFLECTION ⮔ _____

With his mentor in prison and his church in turmoil, Timothy was not feeling brave at all. Paul may have been subtly telling him, "The Lord has called you to preach, and he will give you the courage to do so." There are moments in every marriage when a husband or wife does not feel brave; the house is in turmoil and your spouse seems distant while loneliness sets in. Yet God always gives us the strength to do what he has commanded. This strength may not be evident, however, until we step out in faith and actually begin doing the task. Stepping in to faithfully serve that person we have promised to love and cherish "till death us do part" may allow the Lord to reveal the strength he has already given you.

_____ ⮕ MEDITATION ⮔ _____

Heavenly Father, when our own strength is not enough give us the courage that we need to keep going. ⮔

SEPTEMBER 13

Judas Betrays Jesus
§ John 13:21–38 §

Now Jesus was in great anguish of spirit and ex-claimed, "Yes, it is true—one of you will betray me." [22]The disciples looked at each other, wonder-ing whom he could mean. [23]Since I was sitting next to Jesus at the table, being his closest friend, [24]Si-mon Peter motioned to me to ask him who it was who would do this terrible deed.

[25]So I turned and asked him, "Lord, who is it?"

[26]He told me, "It is the one I honor by giving the bread dipped in the sauce."

And when he had dipped it, he gave it to Judas, son of Simon Iscariot.

[27]As soon as Judas had eaten it, Satan entered into him. Then Jesus told him, "Hurry—do it now."

[28]None of the others at the table knew what Jesus meant. [29]Some thought that since Judas was their treasurer, Jesus was telling him to go and pay for the food or to give some money to the poor. [30]Judas left at once, going out into the night.

[31]As soon as Judas left the room, Jesus said, "My time has come; the glory of God will soon sur-round me—and God shall receive great praise be-cause of all that happens to me. [32]And God shall give me his own glory, and this so very soon. [33]Dear, dear children, how brief are these moments before I must go away and leave you! Then, though you search for me, you cannot come to me—just as I told the Jewish leaders.

[34]"And so I am giving a new commandment to you now—love each other just as much as I love you. [35]Your strong love for each other will prove to the world that you are my disciples."

[36]Simon Peter said, "Master, where are you going?"

And Jesus replied, "You can't go with me now; but you will follow me later."

[37]"But why can't I come now?" he asked, "for I am ready to die for you."

[38]Jesus answered, "Die for me? No—three times before the cock crows tomorrow morning, you will deny that you even know me!

Titus Appointed to Strengthen the Churches
§ Titus 1:1–6 §

From: Paul, the slave of God and the messenger of Jesus Christ.

I have been sent to bring faith to those God has chosen and to teach them to know God's truth—the kind of truth that changes lives—so that they can have eternal life, which God promised them be-fore the world began—and he cannot lie. [3]And now in his own good time he has revealed this Good News and permits me to tell it to everyone. By command of God our Savior I have been trusted to do this work for him.

[4]*To:* Titus, who is truly my son in the affairs of the Lord.

May God the Father and Christ Jesus our Savior give you his blessings and his peace. [5]I left you there on the island of Crete so that you could do whatever was needed to help strengthen each of its churches, and I asked you to appoint pastors in every city who would follow the instructions I gave you. [6]The men you choose must be well thought of for their good lives; they must have only one wife and their children must love the Lord and not have a reputation for being wild or disobedient to their parents.

Proverbs for Today
§ 23:9–11 §

Don't waste your breath on a rebel. He will de-spise the wisest advice. □ Don't steal the land of defenseless orphans by moving their ancient boundary marks, for their Redeemer is strong; he himself will accuse you.

§ KEY VERSE §

"I am giving a new commandment to you now—love each other just as much as I love you. Your strong love for each other will prove to the world that you are my disciples."—*John 13:34–35*

Jesus says that our love will prove that we are his disciples. Do people see petty bickering, jealousy, and division in your home? Or do they know you are Jesus' followers by your love for each other?

Heavenly Father, thank you for this gift of love that you have given us. We dedicate it to your service so that others will see how wonderful you are. ᴥ►

SEPTEMBER 14

Jesus Is the Way to the Father
◄ᴥ John 14:1–14 ᴥ►

"Let not your heart be troubled. You are trusting God, now trust in me. [2,3]There are many homes up there where my Father lives, and I am going to prepare them for your coming. When everything is ready, then I will come and get you, so that you can always be with me where I am. If this weren't so, I would tell you plainly. [4]And you know where I am going and how to get there."

[5]"No, we don't," Thomas said. "We haven't any idea where you are going, so how can we know the way?"

[6]Jesus told him, "I am the Way—yes, and the Truth and the Life. No one can get to the Father except by means of me. [7]If you had known who I am, then you would have known who my Father is. From now on you know him—and have seen him!"

[8]Philip said, "Sir, show us the Father and we will be satisfied."

[9]Jesus replied, "Don't you even yet know who I am, Philip, even after all this time I have been with you? Anyone who has seen me has seen the Father! So why are you asking to see him? [10]Don't you believe that I am in the Father and the Father is in me? The words I say are not my own but are from my Father who lives in me. And he does his work through me. [11]Just believe it—that I am in the Father and the Father is in me. Or else believe it because of the mighty miracles you have seen me do.

[12,13]"In solemn truth I tell you, anyone believing in me shall do the same miracles I have done, and even greater ones, because I am going to be with the Father. You can ask him for *anything,* using my name, and I will do it, for this will bring praise to the Father because of what I, the Son, will do for you. [14]Yes, ask *anything,* using my name, and I will do it!

Requirements for Church Leadership
◄ᴥ Titus 1:7–16 ᴥ►

These pastors must be men of blameless lives because they are God's ministers. They must not be proud or impatient; they must not be drunkards or fighters or greedy for money. [8]They must enjoy having guests in their homes and must love all that is good. They must be sensible men, and fair. They must be clean minded and level headed. [9]Their belief in the truth which they have been taught must be strong and steadfast, so that they will be able to teach it to others and show those who disagree with them where they are wrong.

[10]For there are many who refuse to obey; this is especially true among those who say that all Christians must obey the Jewish laws. But this is foolish talk; it blinds people to the truth, [11]and it must be stopped. Already whole families have been turned away from the grace of God. Such teachers are only after your money. [12]One of their own men, a prophet from Crete, has said about them, "These men of Crete are all liars; they are like lazy animals,

living only to satisfy their stomachs." [13]And this is true. So speak to the Christians there as sternly as necessary to make them strong in the faith, [14]and to stop them from listening to Jewish folk tales and the demands of men who have turned their backs on the truth.

[15]A person who is pure of heart sees goodness and purity in everything; but a person whose own heart is evil and untrusting finds evil in everything, for his dirty mind and rebellious heart color all he sees and hears. [16]Such persons claim they know God, but from seeing the way they act, one knows they don't. They are rotten and disobedient, worthless so far as doing anything good is concerned.

Proverbs for Today
◄§ 23:12 §►

Don't refuse to accept criticism; get all the help you can.

◄§ KEY VERSE §►

Don't refuse to accept criticism; get all the help you can.—*Proverbs 23:12*

◄§ REFLECTION §►

Did you know that one of your greatest resources for wisdom and instruction may come from that person who lives with you day in and day out? Although a spouse can fall into the habit of nagging, there is also a bit of truth in the words that we really don't want to hear. The world is full of people who think they know everything; they don't want to be instructed, and they think that learning from others shows weakness. They are wrong. Listening to others is a sign of wisdom. Refusing to learn from others, even your spouse, can be a great mistake. It can cause a person who could have been successful to fall flat on his or her face.

◄§ MEDITATION §►

Heavenly Father, may we accept criticism with an open mind and a loving heart. §►

SEPTEMBER 15 _____

The Comforter
◄§ John 14:15–31 §►

"If you love me, obey me; and I will ask the Father and he will give you another Comforter, and he will never leave you. [17]He is the Holy Spirit, the Spirit who leads into all truth. The world at large cannot receive him, for it isn't looking for him and doesn't recognize him. But you do, for he lives with you now and some day shall be in you. [18]No, I will not abandon you or leave you as orphans in the storm—I will come to you. [19]In just a little while I will be gone from the world, but I will still be present with you. For I will live again—and you will too. [20]When I come back to life again, you will know that I am in my Father, and you in me, and I in you. [21]The one who obeys me is the one who loves me; and because he loves me, my Father will

love him; and I will too, and I will reveal myself to him."

[22]Judas (not Judas Iscariot, but his other disciple with that name) said to him, "Sir, why are you going to reveal yourself only to us disciples and not to the world at large?"

[23]Jesus replied, "Because I will only reveal myself to those who love me and obey me. The Father will love them too, and we will come to them and live with them. [24]Anyone who doesn't obey me doesn't love me. And remember, I am not making up this answer to your question! It is the answer given by the Father who sent me.

[25]"I am telling you these things now while I am still with you. [26]But when the Father sends the Comforter instead of me—and by the Comforter I mean the Holy Spirit—he will teach you much, as

well as remind you of everything I myself have told you.

27"I am leaving you with a gift—peace of mind and heart! And the peace I give isn't fragile like the peace the world gives. So don't be troubled or afraid. 28Remember what I told you—I am going away, but I will come back to you again. If you really love me, you will be very happy for me, for now I can go to the Father, who is greater than I am. 29I have told you these things before they happen so that when they do, you will believe [in me].

30"I don't have much more time to talk to you, for the evil prince of this world approaches. He has no power over me, 31but I will freely do what the Father requires of me so that the world will know that I love the Father. Come, let's be going.

Community Life within the Church
❧ Titus 2:1–10 ❧

But as for you, speak up for the right living that goes along with true Christianity. 2Teach the older men to be serious and unruffled; they must be sensible, knowing and believing the truth and doing everything with love and patience.

3Teach the older women to be quiet and respectful in everything they do. They must not go around speaking evil of others and must not be heavy drinkers, but they should be teachers of goodness. 4These older women must train the younger women to live quietly, to love their husbands and their children, 5and to be sensible and clean minded, spending their time in their own homes, being kind and obedient to their husbands, so that the Christian faith can't be spoken against by those who know them.

6In the same way, urge the young men to behave carefully, taking life seriously. 7And here you yourself must be an example to them of good deeds of every kind. Let everything you do reflect your love of the truth and the fact that you are in dead earnest about it. 8Your conversation should be so sensible and logical that anyone who wants to argue will be ashamed of himself because there won't be anything to criticize in anything you say!

9Urge slaves to obey their masters and to try their best to satisfy them. They must not talk back, 10nor steal, but must show themselves to be entirely trustworthy. In this way they will make people want to believe in our Savior and God.

Proverbs for Today
❧ 23:13–14 ❧

Don't fail to correct your children; discipline won't hurt them! They won't die if you use a stick on them! Punishment will keep them out of hell.

❧ KEY VERSE ❧

Teach the older women to be quiet and respectful in everything they do. They must not go around speaking evil of others and must not be heavy drinkers, but they should be teachers of goodness. These older women must train the younger women to live quietly, to love their husbands and their children, and to be sensible and clean minded, spending their time in their own homes, being kind and obedient to their husbands so that the Christian faith can't be spoken against by those who know them. In the same way, urge the young men to behave carefully, taking life seriously.—*Titus 2:3–6*

❧ REFLECTION ❧

Women who were new Christians were to learn how to have harmony in the home by watching older women who had been Christians for some time. We have the same need today. Younger wives and mothers should learn to live in a Christian manner—loving their husbands and caring for their children—through observing exemplary women of God. If you are an older Christian, can you be confident that your example is motivating younger believers to live in a way that honors God?

The advice given to young men was very important. In ancient Greek society, the role of the husband and father was not viewed as a nurturing role, but merely a functional one. Many young men today have been raised in families where the father neglected his responsibilities to his wife and children. The few husbands and fathers who are good examples of Christian living in their families are extremely important role models for young men who need to see how it is done more than to be told how to do it.

❧ MEDITATION ❧

Heavenly Father, thank you for the different functions of a husband and wife that work so beautifully together to form one home. Guide us as we continue to grow into the godly husband and wife that you would have us to be. ❧

SEPTEMBER 16

The Vine and the Branches
❧ John 15:1–15 ❧

"I am the true Vine, and my Father is the Gardener. ²He lops off every branch that doesn't produce. And he prunes those branches that bear fruit for even larger crops. ³He has already tended you by pruning you back for greater strength and usefulness by means of the commands I gave you. ⁴Take care to live in me, and let me live in you. For a branch can't produce fruit when severed from the vine. Nor can you be fruitful apart from me.

⁵"Yes, I am the Vine; you are the branches. Whoever lives in me and I in him shall produce a large crop of fruit. For apart from me you can't do a thing. ⁶If anyone separates from me, he is thrown away like a useless branch, withers, and is gathered into a pile with all the others and burned. ⁷But if you stay in me and obey my commands, you may ask any request you like, and it will be granted! ⁸My true disciples produce bountiful harvests. This brings great glory to my Father.

⁹"I have loved you even as the Father has loved me. Live within my love. ¹⁰When you obey me you are living in my love, just as I obey my Father and live in his love. ¹¹I have told you this so that you will be filled with my joy. Yes, your cup of joy will overflow! ¹²I demand that you love each other as much as I love you. ¹³And here is how to measure it—the greatest love is shown when a person lays down his life for his friends; ¹⁴and you are my friends if you obey me. ¹⁵I no longer call you slaves, for a master doesn't confide in his slaves; now you are my friends, proved by the fact that I have told you everything the Father told me.

Salvation Is Available to Everyone
❧ Titus 2:11–15 ❧

For the free gift of eternal salvation is now being offered to everyone; ¹²and along with this gift comes the realization that God wants us to turn from godless living and sinful pleasures and to live good, God-fearing lives day after day, ¹³looking forward to that wonderful time we've been expecting, when his glory shall be seen—the glory of our great God and Savior Jesus Christ. ¹⁴He died under God's judgment against our sins, so that he could rescue us from constant falling into sin and make us his very own people, with cleansed hearts and real enthusiasm for doing kind things for others. ¹⁵You must teach these things and encourage your people to do them, correcting them when necessary as one who has every right to do so. Don't let anyone think that what you say is not important.

Proverbs for Today
❧ 23:15–16 ❧

My son, how I will rejoice if you become a man of common sense. Yes, my heart will thrill to your thoughtful, wise words.

❧ KEY VERSE ❧

"I have told you this so that you will be filled with my joy. Yes, your cup of joy will overflow!"—*John 15:11*

When things are going well, couples feel good and secure. When problems come—bad circumstances, family conflict, money problems—couples can feel the stress in their relationship. True joy transcends these waves of circumstance so the relationship can survive too. And joy comes from a consistent relationship with Jesus Christ. When our lives are intertwined with Christ's, he will help us walk through adversity without sinking into lows and manage prosperity without moving into deceptive highs. The joy of living with Jesus Christ daily keeps us *together* as well as level-headed through the highs and lows of our circumstances.

Heavenly Father, fill us with your joy. May our home overflow with your joy. ❧

SEPTEMBER 17

Be Prepared for Persecution
❧ John 15:16–27 ❧

"You didn't choose me! I chose you! I appointed you to go and produce lovely fruit always, so that no matter what you ask for from the Father, using my name, he will give it to you. [17]I demand that you love each other, [18]for you get enough hate from the world! But then, it hated me before it hated you. [19]The world would love you if you belonged to it; but you don't—for I chose you to come out of the world, and so it hates you. [20]Do you remember what I told you? 'A slave isn't greater than his master!' So since they persecuted me, naturally they will persecute you. And if they had listened to me, they would listen to you! [21]The people of the world will persecute you because you belong to me, for they don't know God who sent me.

[22]"They would not be guilty if I had not come and spoken to them. But now they have no excuse for their sin. [23]Anyone hating me is also hating my Father. [24]If I hadn't done such mighty miracles among them they would not be counted guilty. But as it is, they saw these miracles and yet they hated both of us—me and my Father. [25]This has fulfilled what the prophets said concerning the Messiah, 'They hated me without reason.'

[26]"But I will send you the Comforter—the Holy Spirit, the source of all truth. He will come to you from the Father and will tell you all about me. [27]And you also must tell everyone about me, because you have been with me from the beginning.

Be Obedient to the Government
❧ Titus 3:1–8 ❧

Remind your people to obey the government and its officers, and always to be obedient and ready for any honest work. [2]They must not speak evil of anyone, nor quarrel, but be gentle and truly courteous to all.

[3]Once we, too, were foolish and disobedient; we were misled by others and became slaves to many evil pleasures and wicked desires. Our lives were full of resentment and envy. We hated others and they hated us.

[4]But when the time came for the kindness and love of God our Savior to appear, [5]then he saved us—not because we were good enough to be saved, but because of his kindness and pity—by washing away our sins and giving us the new joy of the indwelling Holy Spirit [6]whom he poured out upon us with wonderful fullness—and all because of what Jesus Christ our Savior did [7]so that he could declare us good in God's eyes—all because of his great kindness; and now we can share in the wealth of the eternal life he gives us, and we are eagerly looking forward to receiving it. [8]These things I have told you are all true. Insist on them so that Christians will be careful to do good deeds

all the time, for this is not only right, but it brings results.

Proverbs for Today
23:17–18

Don't envy evil men but continue to reverence the Lord all the time, for surely you have a wonderful future ahead of you. There is hope for you yet!

KEY VERSE

"I demand that you love each other, for you get enough hate from the world! But then, it hated me before it hated you."—*John 15:17–18*

REFLECTION

Christian couples will get plenty of hatred from the world; from other Christian couples they need love and support. Do you allow small problems to get in the way of loving other believers? Jesus commands that you love them, and he will give both of you the strength to do it.

MEDITATION

Heavenly Father, we pray for our Christian friends. If they have a need that you would like to meet through us, keep us open to your guidance so that we will not miss the opportunity to encourage them in their faith.

SEPTEMBER 18

The Promise to Send the Holy Spirit
John 16:1–15

"I have told you these things so that you won't be staggered [by all that lies ahead.] [2]For you will be excommunicated from the synagogues, and indeed the time is coming when those who kill you will think they are doing God a service. [3]This is because they have never known the Father or me. [4]Yes, I'm telling you these things now so that when they happen you will remember I warned you. I didn't tell you earlier because I was going to be with you for a while longer.

[5]"But now I am going away to the one who sent me; and none of you seems interested in the purpose of my going; none wonders why. [6]Instead you are only filled with sorrow. [7]But the fact of the matter is that it is best for you that I go away, for if I don't, the Comforter won't come. If I do, he will—for I will send him to you.

[8]"And when he has come he will convince the world of its sin, and of the availability of God's goodness, and of deliverance from judgment. [9]The world's sin is unbelief in me; [10]there is righteousness available because I go to the Father and you shall see me no more; [11]there is deliverance from judgment because the prince of this world has already been judged.

[12]"Oh, there is so much more I want to tell you, but you can't understand it now. [13]When the Holy Spirit, who is truth, comes, he shall guide you into all truth, for he will not be presenting his own ideas, but will be passing on to you what he has heard. He will tell you about the future. [14]He shall praise me and bring me great honor by showing you my glory. [15]All the Father's glory is mine; this is what I mean when I say that he will show you my glory.

Stay Away from Arguments
Titus 3:9–15

Don't get involved in arguing over unanswerable questions and controversial theological ideas; keep out of arguments and quarrels about obedience to Jewish laws, for this kind of thing isn't worthwhile; it only does harm. [10]If anyone is causing divisions among you, he should be given a first and second warning. After that have nothing more to do with him, [11]for such a person has a wrong sense of values. He is sinning, and he knows it.

[12]I am planning to send either Artemas or Tychi-

cus to you. As soon as one of them arrives, please try to meet me at Nicopolis as quickly as you can, for I have decided to stay there for the winter. [13]Do everything you can to help Zenas the lawyer and Apollos with their trip; see that they are given everything they need. [14]For our people must learn to help all who need their assistance, that their lives will be fruitful.

[15]Everybody here sends greetings. Please say "hello" to all of the Christian friends there. May God's blessings be with you all.

Sincerely,
Paul

Proverbs for Today
§ 23:19–21 §

O my son, be wise and stay in God's paths; don't carouse with drunkards and gluttons, for they are on their way to poverty. And remember that too much sleep clothes a man with rags.

_____ ◈ KEY VERSE ◈ _____

If anyone is causing divisions among you, he should be given a first and second warning. After that have nothing more to do with him, for such a person has a wrong sense of values. He is sinning, and he knows it.—*Titus 3:10–11*

_____ ◈ REFLECTION ◈ _____

God warns us against petty quarrels and discussions that lead to foolishness. When arguments like this develop, it is best to turn the discussion back to a track that is going somewhere or politely excuse yourself from the discussion. While this passage is about unity in the church, God also wants unity between husbands and wives. Thus, a person must also be warned when he or she is causing division between a couple. This warning should not be a heavy-handed action, but should correct the individual's divisive nature and restore him or her to fellowship.

_____ ◈ MEDITATION ◈ _____

Heavenly Father, when we face people or situations that threaten to divide us send your Holy Spirit to give us the wisdom that we need to handle the situation. ❧

SEPTEMBER 19

Jesus Predicts His Death and Resurrection
§ John 16:16–33 §

"In just a little while I will be gone, and you will see me no more; but just a little while after that, and you will see me again!"

[17,18]"Whatever is he saying?" some of his disciples asked. "What is this about 'going to the Father'? We don't know what he means."

[19]Jesus realized they wanted to ask him so he said, "Are you asking yourselves what I mean? [20]The world will greatly rejoice over what is going to happen to me, and you will weep. But your weeping shall suddenly be turned to wonderful joy [when you see me again]. [21]It will be the same joy as that of a woman in labor when her child is born—her anguish gives place to rapturous joy and the pain is forgotten. [22]You have sorrow now, but I will see you again and then you will rejoice; and no one can rob you of that joy. [23]At that time you won't need to ask me for anything, for you can go directly to the Father and ask him, and he will give you what you ask for because you use my name. [24]You haven't tried this before, [but begin now]. Ask, using my name, and you will receive, and your cup of joy will overflow.

[25]"I have spoken of these matters very guardedly, but the time will come when this will not be necessary and I will tell you plainly all about the Father. [26]Then you will present your petitions over my signature! And I won't need to ask the Father to grant you these requests, [27]for the Father himself loves you dearly because you love me and believe that I

came from the Father. ²⁸Yes, I came from the Father into the world and will leave the world and return to the Father."

²⁹"At last you are speaking plainly," his disciples said, "and not in riddles. ³⁰Now we understand that you know everything and don't need anyone to tell you anything. From this we believe that you came from God."

³¹"Do you finally believe this?" Jesus asked. ³²"But the time is coming—in fact, it is here—when you will be scattered, each one returning to his own home, leaving me alone. Yet I will not be alone, for the Father is with me. ³³I have told you all this so that you will have peace of heart and mind. Here on earth you will have many trials and sorrows; but cheer up, for I have overcome the world."

Paul Gives Thanks for Philemon
Philemon 1:1–7

From: Paul, in jail for preaching the Good News about Jesus Christ, and from Brother Timothy.

To: Philemon, our much loved fellow worker, and to the church that meets in your home, and to Apphia our sister, and to Archippus who like myself is a soldier of the cross.

³May God our Father and the Lord Jesus Christ give you his blessings and his peace.

⁴I always thank God when I am praying for you, dear Philemon, ⁵because I keep hearing of your love and trust in the Lord Jesus and in his people. ⁶And I pray that as you share your faith with others it will grip their lives too, as they see the wealth of good things in you that come from Christ Jesus. ⁷I myself have gained much joy and comfort from your love, my brother, because your kindness has so often refreshed the hearts of God's people.

Proverbs for Today
23:22

Listen to your father's advice and don't despise an old mother's experience.

KEY VERSE

I myself have gained much joy and comfort from your love, my brother, because your kindness has so often refreshed the hearts of God's people.—*Philemon 1:7*

REFLECTION

Paul reflected on Philemon's kindness, love, and comfort. Philemon had opened his heart and his home to the church. We should do likewise, opening ourselves and our homes to others, offering Christian fellowship to refresh people's spirits.

MEDITATION

Heavenly Father, we dedicate our home to your service. May it be a place where other Christians can be refreshed and comforted.

SEPTEMBER 20

Jesus Prays for His Followers
John 17:1–26

When Jesus had finished saying all these things he looked up to heaven and said, "Father, the time has come. Reveal the glory of your Son so that he can give the glory back to you. ²For you have given him authority over every man and woman in all the earth. He gives eternal life to each one you have given him. ³And this is the way to have eternal life— by knowing you, the only true God, and Jesus Christ, the one you sent to earth! ⁴I brought glory to you here on earth by doing everything you told me to. ⁵And now, Father, reveal my glory as I stand in your presence, the glory we shared before the world began.

⁶"I have told these men all about you. They were in the world, but then you gave them to me. Actually, they were always yours, and you gave them to me; and they have obeyed you. ⁷Now they know that everything I have is a gift from you, ⁸for I have

passed on to them the commands you gave me; and they accepted them and know of a certainty that I came down to earth from you, and they believe you sent me.

9"My plea is not for the world but for those you have given me because they belong to you. 10And all of them, since they are mine, belong to you; and you have given them back to me with everything else of yours, and so *they are my glory!* 11Now I am leaving the world, and leaving them behind, and coming to you. Holy Father, keep them in your own care—all those you have given me—so that they will be united just as we are, with none missing. 12During my time here I have kept safe within your family all of these you gave me. I guarded them so that not one perished, except the son of hell, as the Scriptures foretold.

13"And now I am coming to you. I have told them many things while I was with them so that they would be filled with my joy. 14I have given them your commands. And the world hates them because they don't fit in with it, just as I don't. 15I'm not asking you to take them out of the world, but to keep them safe from Satan's power. 16They are not part of this world any more than I am. 17Make them pure and holy through teaching them your words of truth. 18As you sent me into the world, I am sending them into the world, 19and I consecrate myself to meet their need for growth in truth and holiness.

20"I am not praying for these alone but also for the future believers who will come to me because of the testimony of these. 21My prayer for all of them is that they will be of one heart and mind, just as you and I are, Father—that just as you are in me and I am in you, so they will be in us, and the world will believe you sent me.

22"I have given them the glory you gave me—the glorious unity of being one, as we are— 23I in them and you in me, all being perfected into one—so that the world will know you sent me and will understand that you love them as much as you love me. 24Father, I want them with me—these you've given me—so that they can see my glory. You gave me the glory because you loved me before the world began!

25"O righteous Father, the world doesn't know you, but I do; and these disciples know you sent me. 26And I have revealed you to them, and will keep on revealing you so that the mighty love you have for me may be in them, and I in them.''

Paul's Plea for Onesimus
Philemon 1:8-25

Now I want to ask a favor of you. I could demand it of you in the name of Christ because it is the right thing for you to do, but I love you and prefer just to ask you—I, Paul, an old man now, here in jail for the sake of Jesus Christ. 10My plea is that you show kindness to my child Onesimus, whom I won to the Lord while here in my chains. 11Onesimus (whose name means ''Useful'') hasn't been of much use to you in the past, but now he is going to be of real use to both of us. 12I am sending him back to you, and with him comes my own heart.

13I really wanted to keep him here with me while I am in these chains for preaching the Good News, and you would have been helping me through him, 14but I didn't want to do it without your consent. I didn't want you to be kind because you had to but because you wanted to. 15Perhaps you could think of it this way: that he ran away from you for a little while so that now he can be yours forever, 16no longer only a slave, but something much better—a beloved brother, especially to me. Now he will mean much more to you too, because he is not only a servant but also your brother in Christ.

17If I am really your friend, give him the same welcome you would give to me if I were the one who was coming. 18If he has harmed you in any way or stolen anything from you, charge me for it. 19I will pay it back (I, Paul, personally guarantee this by writing it here with my own hand) but I won't mention how much you owe me! The fact is, you even owe me your very soul! 20Yes, dear brother, give me joy with this loving act and my weary heart will praise the Lord.

21I've written you this letter because I am positive that you will do what I ask and even more!

22Please keep a guest room ready for me, for I am hoping that God will answer your prayers and let me come to you soon.

²³Epaphras my fellow prisoner, who is also here for preaching Christ Jesus, sends you his greetings. ²⁴So do Mark, Aristarchus, Demas and Luke, my fellow workers.

²⁵The blessings of our Lord Jesus Christ be upon your spirit.

Paul

Proverbs for Today
≈§ 23:23 §≈

Get the facts at any price, and hold on tightly to all the good sense you can get.

≈ KEY VERSE ≈

Now I want to ask a favor of you. I could demand it of you in the name of Christ because it is the right thing for you to do, but I love you and prefer just to ask you—I, Paul, an old man now, here in jail for the sake of Jesus Christ.—*Philemon 1:8–9*

≈ REFLECTION ≈

Since Paul was an elder and an apostle, he could have used his authority over Philemon, commanding him to deal kindly with his runaway slave. But Paul based his request not on his own authority, but on Philemon's Christian commitment. Paul wanted Philemon's heartfelt, not grudging, obedience. When you know something is right and you have the power to demand it, do you appeal to your authority, or to your spouse's commitment? Here Paul provides a good example of how to deal with a possible conflict between Christian friends and couples.

≈ MEDITATION ≈

Heavenly Father, when there is a conflict that we are involved in, whether it is between us or others, help us to resolve it in a manner pleasing to you. ≈

SEPTEMBER 21

Jesus Is Arrested in the Garden
≈§ John 18:1–14 §≈

After saying these things Jesus crossed the Kidron ravine with his disciples and entered a grove of olive trees. ²Judas, the betrayer, knew this place, for Jesus had gone there many times with his disciples.

³The chief priests and Pharisees had given Judas a squad of soldiers and police to accompany him. Now with blazing torches, lanterns, and weapons they arrived at the olive grove.

⁴,⁵Jesus fully realized all that was going to happen to him. Stepping forward to meet them he asked, "Whom are you looking for?"

"Jesus of Nazareth," they replied.

"I am he," Jesus said. ⁶And as he said it, they all fell backwards to the ground!

⁷Once more he asked them, "Whom are you searching for?"

And again they replied, "Jesus of Nazareth."

⁸"I told you I am he," Jesus said; "and since I am the one you are after, let these others go." ⁹He did this to carry out the prophecy he had just made, "I have not lost a single one of those you gave me. . . ."

¹⁰Then Simon Peter drew a sword and slashed off the right ear of Malchus, the High Priest's servant.

¹¹But Jesus said to Peter, "Put your sword away. Shall I not drink from the cup the Father has given me?"

¹²So the Jewish police, with the soldiers and their lieutenant, arrested Jesus and tied him. ¹³First they took him to Annas, the father-in-law of Caiaphas, the High Priest that year. ¹⁴Caiaphas was the one who told the other Jewish leaders, "Better that one should die for all."

God's Son Is Greater Than Angels
≈§ Hebrews 1:1–14 §≈

Long ago God spoke in many different ways to our fathers through the prophets [in visions, dreams, and even face to face], telling them little by little about his plans.

²But now in these days he has spoken to us through his Son to whom he has given everything, and through whom he made the world and everything there is.

³God's Son shines out with God's glory, and all that God's Son is and does marks him as God. He regulates the universe by the mighty power of his command. He is the one who died to cleanse us and clear our record of all sin, and then sat down in highest honor beside the great God of heaven.

⁴Thus he became far greater than the angels, as proved by the fact that his name "Son of God," which was passed on to him from his Father, is far greater than the names and titles of the angels. ⁵,⁶For God never said to any angel, "You are my Son, and today I have given you the honor that goes with that name." But God said it about Jesus. Another time he said, "I am his Father and he is my Son." And still another time—when his first-born Son came to earth—God said, "Let all the angels of God worship him."

⁷God speaks of his angels as messengers swift as the wind and as servants made of flaming fire; ⁸but of his Son he says, "Your Kingdom, O God, will last forever and ever; its commands are always just and right. ⁹You love right and hate wrong; so God, even your God, has poured out more gladness upon you than on anyone else."

¹⁰God also called him "Lord" when he said, "Lord, in the beginning you made the earth, and the heavens are the work of your hands. ¹¹They will disappear into nothingness, but you will remain forever. They will become worn out like old clothes, ¹²and some day you will fold them up and replace them. But you yourself will never change, and your years will never end."

¹³And did God ever say to an angel, as he does to his Son, "Sit here beside me in honor until I crush all your enemies beneath your feet"?

¹⁴No, for the angels are only spirit-messengers sent out to help and care for those who are to receive his salvation.

Proverbs for Today
◆§ 23:24–25 §◆

The father of a godly man has cause for joy—what pleasure a wise son is! So give your parents joy!

KEY VERSE

Then Simon Peter drew a sword and slashed off the right ear of Malchus, the High Priest's servant. But Jesus said to Peter, "Put your sword away. Shall I not drink from the cup the Father has given me?" —*John 18:10–11*

REFLECTION

Trying to protect Jesus, Peter drew a sword and wounded one of the temple police. But Jesus told him to put away his sword and allow God's plan to unfold. At times it is tempting to take matters into our own hands, to force the issue. Instead we must trust God to work out his plan. When you find yourself in this situation, step back and remember that God has a plan for your life and marriage that you do not know about. Think of it—if Peter had had his way, Jesus would not have gone to the cross, and God's plan of redemption would have been halted.

MEDITATION

Heavenly Father, thank you for having a plan for our lives. As we draw closer to you, Lord, let us put our own plans aside to make room for your plans which are higher and nobler. §◆

SEPTEMBER 22

Peter's Denials
◄§ John 18:15–27 §►

Simon Peter followed along behind, as did another of the disciples who was acquainted with the High Priest. So that other disciple was permitted into the courtyard along with Jesus, [16]while Peter stood outside the gate. Then the other disciple spoke to the girl watching at the gate, and she let Peter in. [17]The girl asked Peter, "Aren't you one of Jesus' disciples?"

"No," he said, "I am not!"

[18]The police and the household servants were standing around a fire they had made, for it was cold. And Peter stood there with them, warming himself.

[19]Inside, the High Priest began asking Jesus about his followers and what he had been teaching them.

[20]Jesus replied, "What I teach is widely known, for I have preached regularly in the synagogue and Temple; I have been heard by all the Jewish leaders and teach nothing in private that I have not said in public. [21]Why are you asking me this question? Ask those who heard me. You have some of them here. They know what I said."

[22]One of the soldiers standing there struck Jesus with his fist. "Is that the way to answer the High Priest?" he demanded.

[23]"If I lied, prove it," Jesus replied. "Should you hit a man for telling the truth?"

[24]Then Annas sent Jesus, bound, to Caiaphas the High Priest.

[25]Meanwhile, as Simon Peter was standing by the fire, he was asked again, "Aren't you one of his disciples?"

"Of course not," he replied.

[26]But one of the household slaves of the High Priest—a relative of the man whose ear Peter had cut off—asked, "Didn't I see you out there in the olive grove with Jesus?"

[27]Again Peter denied it. And immediately a rooster crowed.

Do Not Drift Away from the Truth
◄§ Hebrews 2:1–4 §►

So we must listen very carefully to the truths we have heard, or we may drift away from them. [2]For since the messages from angels have always proved true and people have always been punished for disobeying them, [3]what makes us think that we can escape if we are indifferent to this great salvation announced by the Lord Jesus himself, and passed on to us by those who heard him speak?

[4]God always has shown us that these messages are true by signs and wonders and various miracles and by giving certain special abilities from the Holy Spirit to those who believe; yes, God has assigned such gifts to each of us.

Proverbs for Today
◄§ 23:26–28 §►

O my son, trust my advice—stay away from prostitutes. For a prostitute is a deep and narrow grave. Like a robber, she waits for her victims as one after another become unfaithful to their wives.

◄ KEY VERSE ◄

We must listen very carefully to the truths we have heard, or we may drift away from them.—*Hebrews 2:1*

◄ REFLECTION ◄

Listening is hard work. It involves our minds, bodies, and senses. Listening to Christ means not merely hearing, but also responding in obedience (see James 1:22–25). Couples must persevere in their obedience to Christ. Even though you may get tired and begin to lose patience, God is still there for you.

◄ MEDITATION ◄

Heavenly Father, speak to us in a clear voice so that we will be able to draw closer to you. §►

SEPTEMBER 23

Jesus Is Tried before Pilate
◆§ John 18:28–40 §◆

Jesus' trial before Caiaphas ended in the early hours of the morning. Next he was taken to the palace of the Roman governor. His accusers wouldn't go in themselves for that would "defile" them, they said, and they wouldn't be allowed to eat the Passover lamb. ²⁹So Pilate, the governor, went out to them and asked, "What is your charge against this man? What are you accusing him of doing?"

³⁰"We wouldn't have arrested him if he weren't a criminal!" they retorted.

³¹"Then take him away and judge him yourselves by your own laws," Pilate told them.

"But we want him crucified," they demanded, "and your approval is required." ³²This fulfilled Jesus' prediction concerning the method of his execution.

³³Then Pilate went back into the palace and called for Jesus to be brought to him. "Are you the King of the Jews?" he asked him.

³⁴" 'King' as *you* use the word or as the *Jews* use it?" Jesus asked.

³⁵"Am I a Jew?" Pilate retorted. "Your own people and their chief priests brought you here. Why? What have you done?"

³⁶Then Jesus answered, "I am not an earthly king. If I were, my followers would have fought when I was arrested by the Jewish leaders. But my Kingdom is not of the world."

³⁷Pilate replied, "But you are a king then?"

"Yes," Jesus said. "I was born for that purpose. And I came to bring truth to the world. All who love the truth are my followers."

³⁸"What is truth?" Pilate exclaimed. Then he went out again to the people and told them, "He is not guilty of any crime. ³⁹But you have a custom of asking me to release someone from prison each year at Passover. So if you want me to, I'll release the 'King of the Jews.' "

⁴⁰But they screamed back. "No! Not this man, but Barabbas!" Barabbas was a robber.

Jesus' Suffering and Death Secured Salvation
◆§ Hebrews 2:5–10 §◆

And the future world we are talking about will not be controlled by angels. ⁶No, for in the book of Psalms David says to God, "What is mere man that you are so concerned about him? And who is this Son of Man you honor so highly? ⁷For though you made him lower than the angels for a little while, now you have crowned him with glory and honor. ⁸And you have put him in complete charge of everything there is. Nothing is left out."

We have not yet seen all of this take place, ⁹but we do see Jesus—who for awhile was a little lower than the angels—crowned now by God with glory and honor because he suffered death for us. Yes, because of God's great kindness, Jesus tasted death for everyone in all the world.

¹⁰And it was right and proper that God, who made everything for his own glory, should allow Jesus to suffer, for in doing this he was bringing vast multitudes of God's people to heaven; for his suffering made Jesus a perfect Leader, one fit to bring them into their salvation.

Proverbs for Today
◆§ 23:29–35 §◆

Whose heart is filled with anguish and sorrow? Who is always fighting and quarreling? Who is the man with bloodshot eyes and many wounds? It is the one who spends long hours in the taverns, trying out new mixtures. Don't let the sparkle and the smooth taste of strong wine deceive you. For in the end it bites like a poisonous serpent; it stings like an adder. You will see hallucinations and have delirium tremens, and you will say foolish, silly things that would embarrass you no end when sober. You will stagger like a sailor tossed at sea, clinging to a swaying mast. And afterwards you will say, "I didn't even know it when they beat me up. . . . Let's go and have another drink!"

"Then take him away and judge him yourselves by your own laws," Pilate told them.—*John 18:31*

Pilate made four attempts to deal with Jesus: (1) he tried to put the responsibility on someone else (John 18:31); (2) he tried to find a way of escape so he could release Jesus (18:39); (3) he tried to compromise with the people, beating Jesus rather than handing him over to die (19:1–3); and (4) he appealed to the sympathy of the accusers (19:15). Everyone has a responsibility to decide what he or she will do with Jesus. Pilate tried to let everyone else decide—and in the end, he lost. Your spouse cannot decide what you will do with Jesus. If you want a close relationship with Jesus, it is your responsibility. Your husband or wife cannot do it for you.

Heavenly Father, as we grow closer to you, on an individual level, deepen our commitment to each other and to our marriage. ❧

SEPTEMBER 24

The People Demand Jesus' Crucifixion
❧ John 19:1–15 ❧

Then Pilate laid open Jesus' back with a leaded whip, ²and the soldiers made a crown of thorns and placed it on his head and robed him in royal purple. ³"Hail, 'King of the Jews!' " they mocked, and struck him with their fists.

⁴Pilate went outside again and said to the Jews, "I am going to bring him out to you now, but understand clearly that I find him *not guilty.*"

⁵Then Jesus came out wearing the crown of thorns and the purple robe. And Pilate said, "Behold the man!"

⁶At sight of him the chief priests and Jewish officials began yelling, "Crucify! Crucify!"

"*You* crucify him," Pilate said. "I find him *not guilty.*"

⁷They replied, "By our laws he ought to die because he called himself the Son of God."

⁸When Pilate heard this, he was more frightened than ever. ⁹He took Jesus back into the palace again and asked him, "Where are you from?" but Jesus gave no answer.

¹⁰"You won't talk to me?" Pilate demanded. "Don't you realize that I have the power to release you or to crucify you?"

¹¹Then Jesus said, "You would have no power at all over me unless it were given to you from above. So those who brought me to you have the greater sin."

¹²Then Pilate tried to release him, but the Jewish leaders told him, "If you release this man, you are no friend of Caesar's. Anyone who declares himself a king is a rebel against Caesar."

¹³At these words Pilate brought Jesus out to them again and sat down at the judgment bench on the stone-paved platform. ¹⁴It was now about noon of the day before Passover.

And Pilate said to the Jews, "Here is your king!"

¹⁵"Away with him," they yelled. "Away with him—crucify him!"

"What? Crucify your king?" Pilate asked.

"We have no king but Caesar," the chief priests shouted back.

Christ Came As a Human Being
❧ Hebrews 2:11–15 ❧

We who have been made holy by Jesus, now have the same Father he has. That is why Jesus is not ashamed to call us his brothers. ¹²For he says in the book of Psalms, "I will talk to my brothers about God my Father, and together we will sing his praises." ¹³At another time he said, "I will put my trust in God along with my brothers." And at still another time, "See, here am I and the children God gave me."

¹⁴Since we, God's children, are human beings—

made of flesh and blood—he became flesh and blood too by being born in human form; for only as a human being could he die and in dying break the power of the devil who had the power of death. [15]Only in that way could he deliver those who through fear of death have been living all their lives as slaves to constant dread.

Proverbs for Today
◄§ 24:1–2 §►

Don't envy godless men; don't even enjoy their company. For they spend their days plotting violence and cheating.

KEY VERSE

Only in that way could he deliver those who through fear of death have been living all their lives as slaves to constant dread.—*Hebrews 2:15*

REFLECTION

Christ's death and resurrection free us from the fear of death because death has been defeated. Do some of your loved ones need the freedom from the fear of death that only Christ can give? All who live in dread of death should have the opportunity to know the truth of Christ's victory. How can both of you share this understanding with family members?

MEDITATION

Heavenly Father, thank you for this wonderful freedom from the fear of death. When we are faced with death in our families give us your strength and comfort so that we can share this freedom with others. ☙

SEPTEMBER 25

Jesus Is Crucified
◄§ John 19:16–30 §►

Then Pilate gave Jesus to the soldiers to be crucified.

[17]So they had him at last, and he was taken out of the city, carrying his cross to the place known as "The Skull," in Hebrew, "Golgotha." [18]There they crucified him and two others with him, one on either side, with Jesus between them. [19]And Pilate posted a sign over him reading, "Jesus of Nazareth, the King of the Jews." [20]The place where Jesus was crucified was near the city; and the signboard was written in Hebrew, Latin, and Greek, so that many people read it.

[21]Then the chief priests said to Pilate, "Change it from 'The King of the Jews' to '*He said,* I am King of the Jews.'"

[22]Pilate replied, "What I have written, I have written. It stays exactly as it is."

[23,24]When the soldiers had crucified Jesus, they put his garments into four piles, one for each of them. But they said, "Let's not tear up his robe,"

for it was seamless. "Let's throw dice to see who gets it." This fulfilled the Scripture that says,

"They divided my clothes among them, and cast lots for my robe." [25]So that is what they did.

Standing near the cross were Jesus' mother, Mary, his aunt, the wife of Cleopas, and Mary Magdalene. [26]When Jesus saw his mother standing there beside me, his close friend, he said to her, "He is your son."

[27]And to me he said, "She is your mother!" And from then on I took her into my home.

[28]Jesus knew that everything was now finished, and to fulfill the Scriptures said, "I'm thirsty." [29]A jar of sour wine was sitting there, so a sponge was soaked in it and put on a hyssop branch and held up to his lips.

[30]When Jesus had tasted it, he said, "It is finished," and bowed his head and dismissed his spirit.

Jesus Is Our Merciful High Priest
◄§ Hebrews 2:16–3:6 §►

We all know he did not come as an angel but as a human being—yes, a Jew. [17]And it was necessary for Jesus to be like us, his brothers, so that he could be our merciful and faithful High Priest before God, a Priest who would be both merciful to us and faithful to God in dealing with the sins of the people. [18]For since he himself has now been through suffering and temptation, he knows what it is like when we suffer and are tempted, and he is wonderfully able to help us.

[3:1]Therefore, dear brothers whom God has set apart for himself—you who are chosen for heaven—I want you to think now about this Jesus who is God's Messenger and the High Priest of our faith.

[2]For Jesus was faithful to God who appointed him High Priest, just as Moses also faithfully served in God's house. [3]But Jesus has far more glory than Moses, just as a man who builds a fine house gets more praise than his house does. [4]And many people can build houses, but only God made everything.

[5]Well, Moses did a fine job working in God's house, but he was only a servant; and his work was mostly to illustrate and suggest those things that would happen later on. [6]But Christ, God's faithful Son, is in complete charge of God's house. And we Christians are God's house—he lives in us!—if we keep up our courage firm to the end, and our joy and our trust in the Lord.

Proverbs for Today
24:3–4

Any enterprise is built by wise planning, becomes strong through common sense, and profits wonderfully by keeping abreast of the facts.

KEY VERSE

When Jesus saw his mother standing there beside me, his close friend, he said to her, "He is your son." And to me he said, "She is your mother!" And from then on I took her into my home.—*John 19:26–27*

REFLECTION

Even while dying on the cross, Jesus was concerned about his family. He instructed John to care for Mary, his mother. Our families are precious gifts from God, and we should value and care for them under all circumstances. What can you do today to show your love to your family?

MEDITATION

Heavenly Father, teach us to show love to each other and to our families.

SEPTEMBER 26

Jesus' Burial
John 19:31–42

The Jewish leaders didn't want the victims hanging there the next day, which was the Sabbath (and a very special Sabbath at that, for it was the Passover), so they asked Pilate to order the legs of the men broken to hasten death; then their bodies could be taken down. [32]So the soldiers came and broke the legs of the two men crucified with Jesus; [33]but when they came to him, they saw that he was dead already, so they didn't break his. [34]However, one of the soldiers pierced his side with a spear, and blood and water flowed out. [35]I saw all this myself and have given an accurate report so that you also can believe. [36,37]The soldiers did this in fulfillment of the Scripture that says, "Not one of his bones shall be broken," and, "They shall look on him whom they pierced."

[38]Afterwards Joseph of Arimathea, who had been a secret disciple of Jesus for fear of the Jewish leaders, boldly asked Pilate for permission to take Jesus' body down; and Pilate told him to go ahead. So he came and took it away. [39]Nicodemus, the man who had come to Jesus at night, came too, bringing a hundred pounds of embalming ointment made from myrrh and aloes. [40]Together they wrapped Jesus' body in a long linen cloth saturated with the

spices, as is the Jewish custom of burial. [41]The place of crucifixion was near a grove of trees, where there was a new tomb, never used before. [42]And so, because of the need for haste before the Sabbath, and because the tomb was close at hand, they laid him there.

God's Anger against the Israelites
Hebrews 3:7–14

And since Christ is so much superior, the Holy Spirit warns us to listen to him, to be careful to hear his voice today and not let our hearts become set against him, as the people of Israel did. They steeled themselves against his love and complained against him in the desert while he was testing them. [9]But God was patient with them forty years, though they tried his patience sorely; he kept right on doing his mighty miracles for them to see. [10]"But," God says, "I was very angry with them, for their hearts were always looking somewhere else instead of up to me, and they never found the paths I wanted them to follow."

[11]Then God, full of this anger against them, bound himself with an oath that he would never let them come to his place of rest.

[12]Beware then of your own hearts, dear brothers, lest you find that they, too, are evil and unbelieving and are leading you away from the living God. [13]Speak to each other about these things every day while there is still time, so that none of you will become hardened against God, being blinded by the glamor of sin. [14]For if we are faithful to the end, trusting God just as we did when we first became Christians, we will share in all that belongs to Christ.

Proverbs for Today
24:5

A wise man is mightier than a strong man. Wisdom is mightier than strength.

_____ KEY VERSE _____

Afterwards Joseph of Arimathea, who had been a secret disciple of Jesus for fear of the Jewish leaders, boldly asked Pilate for permission to take Jesus' body down; and Pilate told him to go ahead. So he came and took it away. Nicodemus, the man who had come to Jesus at night, came too, bringing a hundred pounds of embalming ointment made from myrrh and aloes.—*John 19:38–39*

_____ REFLECTION _____

Joseph of Arimathea and Nicodemus were secret followers of Jesus. They were afraid to make this known because of their positions in the Jewish community. Joseph was a leader and honored member of the Supreme Court. Nicodemus, also a member of the Court, had come to Jesus by night (John 3:1) and later had tried to defend him before the other religious leaders (7:50–52). Yet they risked their reputations to bury Jesus' body. Are the two of you secret believers? Would you risk your reputation because of your allegiance to Jesus? Do you hide your faith from your friends, neighbors, and coworkers? This is an appropriate time to step out of hiding and declare your allegiance to Christ.

_____ MEDITATION _____

Heavenly Father, help us to boldly proclaim your Word!

SEPTEMBER 27

The Resurrection of Jesus
❧ John 20:1–18 ❧

Early Sunday morning, while it was still dark, Mary Magdalene came to the tomb and found that the stone was rolled aside from the entrance.

²She ran and found Simon Peter and me and said, "They have taken the Lord's body out of the tomb, and I don't know where they have put him!"

³,⁴We ran to the tomb to see; I outran Peter and got there first, ⁵and stooped and looked in and saw the linen cloth lying there, but I didn't go in. ⁶Then Simon Peter arrived and went on inside. He also noticed the cloth lying there, ⁷while the swath that had covered Jesus' head was rolled up in a bundle and was lying at the side. ⁸Then I went in too, and saw, and believed [that he had risen]— ⁹for until then we hadn't realized that the Scriptures said he would come to life again!

¹⁰We went on home, ¹¹and by that time Mary had returned to the tomb and was standing outside crying. And as she wept, she stooped and looked in ¹²and saw two white-robed angels sitting at the head and foot of the place where the body of Jesus had been lying.

¹³"Why are you crying?" the angels asked her.

"Because they have taken away my Lord," she replied, "and I don't know where they have put him."

¹⁴She glanced over her shoulder and saw someone standing behind her. It was Jesus, but she didn't recognize him!

¹⁵"Why are you crying?" he asked her. "Whom are you looking for?"

She thought he was the gardener. "Sir," she said, "if you have taken him away, tell me where you have put him, and I will go and get him."

¹⁶"Mary!" Jesus said. She turned toward him.

"Master!" she exclaimed.

¹⁷"Don't touch me," he cautioned, "for I haven't yet ascended to the Father. But go find my brothers and tell them that I ascend to my Father and your Father, my God and your God."

¹⁸Mary Magdalene found the disciples and told them, "I have seen the Lord!" Then she gave them his message.

Now Is the Time to Listen to God
❧ Hebrews 3:15–19 ❧

But *now* is the time. Never forget the warning, "*Today* if you hear God's voice speaking to you, do not harden your hearts against him, as the people of Israel did when they rebelled against him in the desert."

¹⁶And who were those people I speak of, who heard God's voice speaking to them but then rebelled against him? They were the ones who came out of Egypt with Moses their leader. ¹⁷And who was it who made God angry for all those forty years? These same people who sinned and as a result died in the wilderness. ¹⁸And to whom was God speaking when he swore with an oath that they could never go into the land he had promised his people? He was speaking to all those who disobeyed him. ¹⁹And why couldn't they go in? Because they didn't trust him.

Proverbs for Today
❧ 24:6–7 ❧

Don't go to war without wise guidance; there is safety in many counselors. ☐ Wisdom is too much for a rebel. He'll not be chosen as a counselor!

❧ KEY VERSE ❧

Don't go to war without wise guidance; there is safety in many counselors.—*Proverbs 24:6*

❧ REFLECTION ❧

In any major decision concerning college, marriage, career, children, etc., it doesn't show weakness to ask for advice. It shows foolishness *not* to ask for it. Find good advisers before making any big decision.

❧ MEDITATION ❧

Heavenly Father, as we try to live so that others will see your glory in us, lead us to the right people when we need counsel from other experienced Christians. ❧

Resurrection Appearances
◄§ John 20:19–31 §►

That evening the disciples were meeting behind locked doors, in fear of the Jewish leaders, when suddenly Jesus was standing there among them! After greeting them, ²⁰he showed them his hands and side. And how wonderful was their joy as they saw their Lord!

²¹He spoke to them again and said, "As the Father has sent me, even so I am sending you." ²²Then he breathed on them and told them, "Receive the Holy Spirit. ²³If you forgive anyone's sins, they are forgiven. If you refuse to forgive them, they are unforgiven."

²⁴One of the disciples, Thomas, "The Twin," was not there at the time with the others. ²⁵When they kept telling him, "We have seen the Lord," he replied, "I won't believe it unless I see the nail wounds in his hands—and put my fingers into them—and place my hand into his side."

²⁶Eight days later the disciples were together again, and this time Thomas was with them. The doors were locked; but suddenly, as before, Jesus was standing among them and greeting them.

²⁷Then he said to Thomas, "Put your finger into my hands. Put your hand into my side. Don't be faithless any longer. Believe!"

²⁸"My Lord and my God!" Thomas said.

²⁹Then Jesus told him, "You believe because you have seen me. But blessed are those who haven't seen me and believe anyway."

³⁰,³¹Jesus' disciples saw him do many other miracles besides the ones told about in this book, but these are recorded so that you will believe that he is the Messiah, the Son of God, and that believing in him you will have life.

Entrance into God's Rest
◄§ Hebrews 4:1–6 §►

Although God's promise still stands—his promise that all may enter his place of rest—we ought to tremble with fear because some of you may be on the verge of failing to get there after all. ²For this wonderful news—the message that God wants to save us—has been given to us just as it was to those who lived in the time of Moses. But it didn't do them any good because they didn't believe it. They didn't mix it with faith. ³For only we who believe God can enter into his place of rest. He has said, "I have sworn in my anger that those who don't believe me will never get in," even though he has been ready and waiting for them since the world began.

⁴We know he is ready and waiting because it is written that God rested on the seventh day of creation, having finished all that he had planned to make.

⁵Even so they didn't get in, for God finally said, "They shall never enter my rest." ⁶Yet the promise remains and some get in—but not those who had the first chance, for they disobeyed God and failed to enter.

Proverbs for Today
◄§ 24:8 §►

To plan evil is as wrong as doing it.

◄§ KEY VERSE §►

To plan evil is as wrong as doing it.—*Proverbs 24:8*

◄§ REFLECTION §►

Planning evil can be as wrong as doing it because what you think determines what you will do. Jesus made this clear when he said that lust makes a man guilty of adultery (Matthew 5:27–28). Even the way we think about the opposite sex is important to God and reflects the intent of our hearts. God wants us to have pure lives as well as pure sex lives; planning evil spoils the purity even if the evil has not yet been committed. Should you say, "Then I might as well go ahead and do it, because I've already planned it"? No. You may be guilty planning the act, but at least you have not yet damaged other people. Stop and ask God to forgive you and put you on a different path.

━━━━━━━━ ❧ **MEDITATION** ❦ ━━━━━━━━

Heavenly Father, sanctify every part of our minds and hearts so that sin will not have a chance to grow in our thoughts. ❧

SEPTEMBER 29 _____

Jesus Appears to His Disciples Again
❦ John 21:1–14 ❧

Later Jesus appeared again to the disciples beside the Lake of Galilee. This is how it happened:
²A group of us were there—Simon Peter, Thomas, "The Twin," Nathanael from Cana in Galilee, my brother James and I and two other disciples.
³Simon Peter said, "I'm going fishing."
"We'll come too," we all said. We did, but caught nothing all night. ⁴At dawn we saw a man standing on the beach but couldn't see who he was.
⁵He called, "Any fish, boys?"
"No," we replied.
⁶Then he said, "Throw out your net on the right-hand side of the boat, and you'll get plenty of them!" So we did, and couldn't draw in the net because of the weight of the fish, there were so many!
⁷Then I said to Peter, "It is the Lord!" At that, Simon Peter put on his tunic (for he was stripped to the waist) and jumped into the water [and swam ashore]. ⁸The rest of us stayed in the boat and pulled the loaded net to the beach, about 300 feet away. ⁹When we got there, we saw that a fire was kindled and fish were frying over it, and there was bread.
¹⁰"Bring some of the fish you've just caught," Jesus said. ¹¹So Simon Peter went out and dragged the net ashore. By his count there were 153 large fish; and yet the net hadn't torn.
¹²"Now come and have some breakfast!" Jesus said; and none of us dared ask him if he really was the Lord, for we were quite sure of it. ¹³Then Jesus went around serving us the bread and fish.

¹⁴This was the third time Jesus had appeared to us since his return from the dead.

The Power of God's Word
❦ Hebrews 4:7–13 ❧

But he has set another time for coming in, and that time is now. He announced this through King David long years after man's first failure to enter, saying in the words already quoted, "Today when you hear him calling, do not harden your hearts against him."
⁸This new place of rest he is talking about does not mean the land of Israel that Joshua led them into. If that were what God meant, he would not have spoken long afterwards about "today" being the time to get in. ⁹So there is a full complete rest *still waiting* for the people of God. ¹⁰Christ has already entered there. He is resting from his work, just as God did after the creation. ¹¹Let us do our best to go into that place of rest, too, being careful not to disobey God as the children of Israel did, thus failing to get in.
¹²For whatever God says to us is full of living power: it is sharper than the sharpest dagger, cutting swift and deep into our innermost thoughts and desires with all their parts, exposing us for what we really are. ¹³He knows about everyone, everywhere. Everything about us is bare and wide open to the all-seeing eyes of our living God; nothing can be hidden from him to whom we must explain all that we have done.

Proverbs for Today
⊸§ 24:9–10 ɞ⊷

The rebel's schemes are sinful, and the mocker is the scourge of all mankind. ☐ You are a poor specimen if you can't stand the pressure of adversity.

----------⊸ KEY VERSE ⊷----------

You are a poor specimen if you can't stand the pressure of adversity.—*Proverbs 24:10*

----------⊸ REFLECTION ⊷----------

Adversity in your marriage can be useful. It shows who you really are; what kind of character you have developed. In addition, it helps your relationship grow stronger. When Jeremiah questioned God because of the adversity he faced, the Lord asked how he ever expected to face big challenges if the little ones wearied him (Jeremiah 12:5). Don't complain about your problems. The adversity you face today is training you to be strong for the more difficult situations you and your spouse will face in the future.

----------⊸ MEDITATION ⊷----------

Heavenly Father, thank you for the strength that you are giving us and for the opportunity to grow as a couple. ɞ⊷

SEPTEMBER 30

Jesus Commands Peter to Feed His Sheep
⊸§ John 21:15–25 ɞ⊷

After breakfast Jesus said to Simon Peter, "Simon, son of John, do you love me more than these others?"

"Yes," Peter replied, "You know I am your friend."

"Then feed my lambs," Jesus told him.

[16]Jesus repeated the question: "Simon, son of John, do you *really* love me?"

"Yes, Lord," Peter said, "you know I am your friend."

"Then take care of my sheep," Jesus said.

[17]Once more he asked him, "Simon, son of John, are you even my friend?"

Peter was grieved at the way Jesus asked the question this third time. "Lord, you know my heart; you know I am," he said.

Jesus said, "Then feed my little sheep. [18]When you were young, you were able to do as you liked and go wherever you wanted to; but when you are old, you will stretch out your hands and others will direct you and take you where you don't want to go." [19]Jesus said this to let him know what kind of death he would die to glorify God. Then Jesus told him, "Follow me."

[20]Peter turned around and saw the disciple Jesus loved following, the one who had leaned around at supper that time to ask Jesus, "Master, which of us will betray you?" [21]Peter asked Jesus, "What about him, Lord? What sort of death will he die?"

[22]Jesus replied, "If I want him to live until I return, what is that to you? *You* follow me."

[23]So the rumor spread among the brotherhood that that disciple wouldn't die! But that isn't what Jesus said at all! He only said, "If I want him to live until I come, what is that to you?"

[24]*I am that disciple!* I saw these events and have recorded them here. And we all know that my account of these things is accurate.

[25]And I suppose that if all the other events in Jesus' life were written, the whole world could hardly contain the books!

Jesus Understands Our Weaknesses
⊸§ Hebrews 4:14–5:6 ɞ⊷

But Jesus the Son of God is our great High Priest who has gone to heaven itself to help us; therefore let us never stop trusting him. [15]This High Priest of ours understands our weaknesses, since he had the same temptations we do, though he never once gave way to them and sinned. [16]So let us come boldly to the very throne of God and stay there to receive his mercy and to find grace to help us in our times of need.

[5:1]The Jewish high priest is merely a man like anyone else, but he is chosen to speak for all other men in their dealings with God. He presents their gifts to God and offers to him the blood of animals that are sacrificed to cover the sins of the people and his own sins too. And because he is a man he can deal gently with other men, though they are foolish and ignorant, for he, too, is surrounded with the same temptations and understands their problems very well.

[4]Another thing to remember is that no one can be a high priest just because he wants to be. He has to be called by God for this work in the same way God chose Aaron.

[5]That is why Christ did not elect himself to the honor of being High Priest; no, he was chosen by God. God said to him, "My Son, today I have honored you." [6]And another time God said to him, "You have been chosen to be a priest forever, with the same rank as Melchizedek."

Proverbs for Today
24:11–12

Rescue those who are unjustly sentenced to death; don't stand back and let them die. Don't try to disclaim responsibility by saying you didn't know about it. For God, who knows all hearts, knows yours, and he knows you knew! And he will reward everyone according to his deeds.

KEY VERSE

Let us come boldly to the very throne of God and stay there to receive his mercy and to find grace to help us in our times of need.—*Hebrews 4:16*

REFLECTION

Prayer is our approach to God. Some couples do it meekly with heads hung, afraid to ask God to meet their needs. Others pray flippantly with little thought. Join hands with each other and come with reverence, for God is your King. But come with bold assurance, for he is also your friend and Counselor.

MEDITATION

Heavenly Father, thank you for hearing and answering all of our prayers.

OCTOBER 1 _____

Jesus Ascends to Heaven
Acts 1:1–13

Dear friend who loves God:

In my first letter I told you about Jesus' life and teachings and how he returned to heaven after giving his chosen apostles further instructions from the Holy Spirit. [3]During the forty days after his crucifixion he appeared to the apostles from time to time, actually alive, and proved to them in many ways that it was really he himself they were seeing. And on these occasions he talked to them about the Kingdom of God.

[4]In one of these meetings he told them not to leave Jerusalem until the Holy Spirit came upon them in fulfillment of the Father's promise, a matter he had previously discussed with them.

[5]"John baptized you with water," he reminded them, "but you shall be baptized with the Holy Spirit in just a few days."

[6]And another time when he appeared to them, they asked him, "Lord, are you going to free Israel [from Rome] now and restore us as an independent nation?"

[7]"The Father sets those dates," he replied, "and they are not for you to know. [8]But when the Holy Spirit has come upon you, you will receive power to testify about me with great effect, to the people in Jerusalem, throughout Judea, in Samaria, and to

the ends of the earth, about my death and resurrection."

⁹It was not long afterwards that he rose into the sky and disappeared into a cloud, leaving them staring after him. ¹⁰As they were straining their eyes for another glimpse, suddenly two white-robed men were standing there among them, ¹¹and said, "Men of Galilee, why are you standing here staring at the sky? Jesus has gone away to heaven, and some day, just as he went, he will return!"

¹²They were at the Mount of Olives when this happened, so now they walked the half mile back to Jerusalem ¹³and held a prayer meeting in an upstairs room of the house where they were staying.

Jesus Learned Obedience through Suffering
⋖§ Hebrews 5:7–10 §⋗

Yet while Christ was here on earth he pleaded with God, praying with tears and agony of soul to the only one who would save him from [premature] death. And God heard his prayers because of his strong desire to obey God at all times.

⁸And even though Jesus was God's Son, he had to learn from experience what it was like to obey, when obeying meant suffering. ⁹It was after he had proved himself perfect in this experience that Jesus became the Giver of eternal salvation to all those who obey him. ¹⁰For remember that God has chosen him to be a High Priest with the same rank as Melchizedek.

Proverbs for Today
⋖§ 24:13–14 §⋗

My son, honey whets the appetite, and so does wisdom! When you enjoy becoming wise, there is hope for you! A bright future lies ahead!

❧ KEY VERSE ❧

"When the Holy Spirit has come upon you, you will receive power to testify about me with great effect, to the people in Jerusalem, throughout Judea, in Samaria, and to the ends of the earth, about my death and resurrection."—*Acts 1:8*

❧ REFLECTION ❧

Jesus promised the apostles that they would receive power to witness after they had received the Holy Spirit. Notice the progression: (1) they received the Holy Spirit, (2) he gave them power, and (3) they witnessed with extraordinary results. Often we try to reverse the order and witness by our own power and authority. Witnessing is not showing what we can do for God, but showing and telling what God has done for us. Allow God to work in your marriage so that you can tell others how wonderful he is.

❧ MEDITATION ❧

Heavenly Father, send your Holy Spirit to our home. Let us receive your power to testify to other couples about what you have done for us and what you can do for them. ❧

OCTOBER 2

Matthias Is Chosen to Be an Apostle
⋖§ Acts 1:14–26 §⋗

Here is the list of those who were present at the meeting:

Peter,
John, James,
Andrew,
Philip, Thomas,
Bartholomew,

Matthew,
James (son of Alphaeus),
Simon (also called "The Zealot"),
Judas (son of James),
and the brothers of Jesus.
Several women, including Jesus' mother, were
     also there.

¹⁵This prayer meeting went on for several days. During this time, on a day when about 120 people

were present, Peter stood up and addressed them as follows:

[16]"Brothers, it was necessary for the Scriptures to come true concerning Judas, who betrayed Jesus by guiding the mob to him, for this was predicted long ago by the Holy Spirit, speaking through King David. [17]Judas was one of us, chosen to be an apostle just as we were. [18]He bought a field with the money he received for his treachery and falling headlong there, he burst open, spilling out his bowels. [19]The news of his death spread rapidly among all the people of Jerusalem, and they named the place 'The Field of Blood.' [20]King David's prediction of this appears in the Book of Psalms, where he says, 'Let his home become desolate with no one living in it.' And again, 'Let his work be given to someone else to do.'

[21,22]"So now we must choose someone else to take Judas' place and to join us as witnesses of Jesus' resurrection. Let us select someone who has been with us constantly from our first association with the Lord—from the time he was baptized by John until the day he was taken from us into heaven."

[23]The assembly nominated two men: Joseph Justus (also called Barsabbas) and Matthias. [24,25]Then they all prayed for the right man to be chosen. "O Lord," they said, "you know every heart; show us which of these men you have chosen as an apostle to replace Judas the traitor, who has gone on to his proper place."

[26]Then they drew straws, and in this manner Matthias was chosen and became an apostle with the other eleven.

Maturity Versus Immaturity
Hebrews 5:11–14

There is much more I would like to say along these lines, but you don't seem to listen, so it's hard to make you understand.

[12,13]You have been Christians a long time now, and you ought to be teaching others, but instead you have dropped back to the place where you need someone to teach you all over again the very first principles in God's Word. You are like babies who can drink only milk, not old enough for solid food. And when a person is still living on milk it shows he isn't very far along in the Christian life, and doesn't know much about the difference between right and wrong. He is still a baby-Christian! [14]You will never be able to eat solid spiritual food and understand the deeper things of God's Word until you become better Christians and learn right from wrong by practicing doing right.

Proverbs for Today
24:15–16

O evil man, leave the upright man alone, and quit trying to cheat him out of his rights. Don't you know that this good man, though you trip him up seven times, will each time rise again? But one calamity is enough to lay you low.

KEY VERSE

Then they all prayed for the right man to be chosen. "O Lord," they said, "you know every heart; show us which of these men you have chosen as an apostle to replace Judas the traitor, who has gone on to his proper place."—*Acts 1:24-25*

REFLECTION

The apostles had to choose a replacement for Judas Iscariot. They outlined specific criteria for making the choice. When the "finalists" had been chosen, the apostles prayed, asking God to guide the selection process. This gives couples a good example of how to proceed when making important decisions. Set up criteria consistent with the Bible, examine the alternatives, and pray for wisdom and guidance to reach a wise decision.

MEDITATION

Heavenly Father, you know our hearts and minds. Show us what you want us to do.

The Coming of the Holy Spirit at Pentecost
◄§ Acts 2:1–13 §►

Seven weeks had gone by since Jesus' death and resurrection, and the Day of Pentecost had now arrived. As the believers met together that day, ²suddenly there was a sound like the roaring of a mighty windstorm in the skies above them and it filled the house where they were meeting. ³Then, what looked like flames or tongues of fire appeared and settled on their heads. ⁴And everyone present was filled with the Holy Spirit and began speaking in languages they didn't know, for the Holy Spirit gave them this ability.

⁵Many godly Jews were in Jerusalem that day for the religious celebrations, having arrived from many nations. ⁶And when they heard the roaring in the sky above the house, crowds came running to see what it was all about, and were stunned to hear their own languages being spoken by the disciples.

⁷"How can this be?" they exclaimed. "For these men are all from Galilee, ⁸and yet we hear them speaking all the native languages of the lands where we were born! ⁹Here we are—Parthians, Medes, Elamites, men from Mesopotamia, Judea, Cappadocia, Pontus, Ausia, ¹⁰Phrygia, Pamphylia, Egypt, the Cyrene language areas of Libya, visitors from Rome—both Jews and Jewish converts—¹¹Cretans, and Arabians. And we all hear these men telling in our own languages about the mighty miracles of God!"

¹²They stood there amazed and perplexed. "What can this mean?" they asked each other.

¹³But others in the crowd were mocking. "They're drunk, that's all!" they said.

Go Beyond Elementary Principles
◄§ Hebrews 6:1–6 §►

Let us stop going over the same old ground again and again, always teaching those first lessons about Christ. Let us go on instead to other things and become mature in our understanding, as strong Christians ought to be. Surely we don't need to speak further about the foolishness of trying to be saved by being good, or about the necessity of faith in God; ²you don't need further instruction about baptism and spiritual gifts and the resurrection of the dead and eternal judgment.

³The Lord willing, we will go on now to other things.

⁴There is no use trying to bring you back to the Lord again if you have once understood the Good News and tasted for yourself the good things of heaven and shared in the Holy Spirit, ⁵and know how good the Word of God is, and felt the mighty powers of the world to come, ⁶and then have turned against God. You cannot bring yourself to repent again if you have nailed the Son of God to the cross again by rejecting him, holding him up to mocking and to public shame.

Proverbs for Today
◄§ 24:17–20 §►

Do not rejoice when your enemy meets trouble. Let there be no gladness when he falls—for the Lord may be displeased with you and stop punishing him! Don't envy the wicked. Don't covet his riches. For the evil man has no future; his light will be snuffed out.

◢ KEY VERSE ◣

What looked like flames or tongues of fire appeared and settled on their heads. And everyone present was filled with the Holy Spirit and began speaking in languages they didn't know, for the Holy Spirit gave them this ability.—*Acts 2:3–4*

◢ REFLECTION ◣

God made his presence known to this group of believers in a spectacular way—roaring wind, fire, and his Holy Spirit. Would you like God to reveal himself to you in such recognizable ways? Beware of forcing your expectations on God. When the prophet Elijah (of the Old Testament) needed a message from God, there was a mighty wind, then an earthquake, and finally a fire, but God's message came in a gentle whisper (1 Kings 19:11–13). God may use dramatic methods to work in your marriage—or he may speak in gentle whispers. Wait patiently and listen for his message, however he gives it.

———— *MEDITATION* ————

Heavenly Father, fill us with your Holy Spirit. Prepare us to hear your voice, whether it be loud and dramatic or soft and gentle.

OCTOBER 4 _____

Peter's Sermon
Acts 2:14–39

Then Peter stepped forward with the eleven apostles, and shouted to the crowd, "Listen, all of you, visitors and residents of Jerusalem alike! [15]Some of you are saying these men are drunk! It isn't true! It's much too early for that! People don't get drunk by 9 A.M.! [16]No! What you see this morning was predicted centuries ago by the prophet Joel— [17]'In the last days,' God said, 'I will pour out my Holy Spirit upon all mankind, and your sons and daughters shall prophesy, and your young men shall see visions, and your old men dream dreams. [18]Yes, the Holy Spirit shall come upon all my servants, men and women alike, and they shall prophesy. [19]And I will cause strange demonstrations in the heavens and on the earth—blood and fire and clouds of smoke; [20]the sun shall turn black and the moon blood-red before that awesome Day of the Lord arrives. [21]But anyone who asks for mercy from the Lord shall have it and shall be saved.'

[22]"O men of Israel, listen! God publicly endorsed Jesus of Nazareth by doing tremendous miracles through him, as you well know. [23]But God, following his prearranged plan, let you use the Roman government to nail him to the cross and murder him. [24]Then God released him from the horrors of death and brought him back to life again, for death could not keep this man within its grip.

[25]"King David quoted Jesus as saying:

'I know the Lord is always with me. He is helping me. God's mighty power supports me.
[26]No wonder my heart is filled with joy and my tongue shouts his praises! For I know all will be well with me in death—
[27]You will not leave my soul in hell or let the body of your Holy Son decay.
[28]You will give me back my life, and give me wonderful joy in your presence.'

[29]"Dear brothers, think! David wasn't referring to himself when he spoke these words I have quoted, for he died and was buried, and his tomb is still here among us. [30]But he was a prophet, and knew God had promised with an unbreakable oath that one of David's own descendants would [be the Messiah and] sit on David's throne. [31]David was looking far into the future and predicting the Messiah's resurrection, and saying that the Messiah's soul would not be left in hell and his body would not decay. [32]He was speaking of Jesus, and we all are witnesses that Jesus rose from the dead.

[33]"And now he sits on the throne of highest honor in heaven, next to God. And just as promised, the Father gave him the authority to send the Holy Spirit—with the results you are seeing and hearing today. [34]"[No, David was not speaking of himself in these words of his I have quoted], for he never ascended into the skies. Moreover, he further stated, 'God spoke to my Lord, the Messiah, and said to him, Sit here in honor beside me [35]until I bring your enemies into complete subjection.'

[36]"Therefore I clearly state to everyone in Israel that God has made this Jesus you crucified to be the Lord, the Messiah!"

[37]These words of Peter's moved them deeply, and they said to him and to the other apostles, "Brothers, what should we do?"

³⁸And Peter replied, "Each one of you must turn from sin, return to God, and be baptized in the name of Jesus Christ for the forgiveness of your sins; then you also shall receive this gift, the Holy Spirit. ³⁹For Christ promised him to each one of you who has been called by the Lord our God, and to your children and even to those in distant lands!"

The Example of Abraham
◄§ Hebrews 6:7–15 §►

When a farmer's land has had many showers upon it and good crops come up, that land has experienced God's blessing upon it. ⁸But if it keeps on having crops of thistles and thorns, the land is considered no good and is ready for condemnation and burning off.

⁹Dear friends, even though I am talking like this I really don't believe that what I am saying applies to you. I am confident you are producing the good fruit that comes along with your salvation. ¹⁰For God is not unfair. How can he forget your hard work for him, or forget the way you used to show your love for him—and still do—by helping his children? ¹¹And we are anxious that you keep right on loving others as long as life lasts, so that you will get your full reward.

¹²Then, knowing what lies ahead for you, you won't become bored with being a Christian, nor become spiritually dull and indifferent, but you will be anxious to follow the example of those who receive all that God has promised them because of their strong faith and patience.

¹³For instance, there was God's promise to Abraham: God took an oath in his own name, since there was no one greater to swear by, ¹⁴that he would bless Abraham again and again, and give him a son and make him the father of a great nation of people. ¹⁵Then Abraham waited patiently until finally God gave him a son, Isaac, just as he had promised.

Proverbs for Today
◄§ 24:21–22 §►

My son, watch your step before the Lord and the king, and don't associate with radicals. For you will go down with them to sudden disaster, and who knows where it all will end?

◄ KEY VERSE ►

These words of Peter's moved them deeply, and they said to him and to the other apostles, "Brothers, what should we do?"—*Acts 2:37*

◄ REFLECTION ►

Peter had been an unstable leader during Jesus' ministry. His bravado was his downfall, even causing him to deny that he knew Jesus (Matthew 26:70–72). But Christ forgave Peter and restored him after his denial. This was a new Peter, humble but bold. His confidence came from the Holy Spirit, who made him a powerful and dynamic speaker. Have you ever felt as if your marriage has been so filled with mistakes and struggles that God could never use it to glorify him? No matter what sins you have committed, God has promised that if you admit your sins to him and turn away from those sins, he will forgive you and make you useful to his kingdom. Confess your sins and allow God to forgive you and effectively use you and your marriage in his service.

◄ MEDITATION ►

Heavenly Father, forgive us for the sins that we have committed against each other and ultimately you. Restore any aspect of our marriage that is not pleasing to you so that it can be dedicated to your service. §►

OCTOBER 5

The Fellowship of the Jerusalem Church
Acts 2:40–47

Then Peter preached a long sermon, telling about Jesus and strongly urging all his listeners to save themselves from the evils of their nation. [41]And those who believed Peter were baptized—about 3,000 in all! [42]They joined with the other believers in regular attendance at the apostles' teaching sessions and at the Communion services and prayer meetings.

[43]A deep sense of awe was on them all, and the apostles did many miracles.

[44]And all the believers met together constantly and shared everything with each other, [45]selling their possessions and dividing with those in need. [46]They worshiped together regularly at the Temple each day, met in small groups in homes for Communion, and shared their meals with great joy and thankfulness, [47]praising God. The whole city was favorable to them, and each day God added to them all who were being saved.

The Assurance of God's Promises
Hebrews 6:16–20

When a man takes an oath, he is calling upon someone greater than himself to force him to do what he has promised, or to punish him if he later refuses to do it; the oath ends all argument about it. [17]God also bound himself with an oath, so that those he promised to help would be perfectly sure and never need to wonder whether he might change his plans.

[18]He has given us both his promise and his oath, two things we can completely count on, for it is impossible for God to tell a lie. Now all those who flee to him to save them can take new courage when they hear such assurances from God; now they can know without doubt that he will give them the salvation he has promised them.

[19]This certain hope of being saved is a strong and trustworthy anchor for our souls, connecting us with God himself behind the sacred curtains of heaven, [20]where Christ has gone ahead to plead for us from his position as our High Priest, with the honor and rank of Melchizedek.

Proverbs for Today
24:23–25

It is wrong to sentence the poor, and let the rich go free. ☐ He who says to the wicked, "You are innocent," shall be cursed by many people of many nations; but blessings shall be showered on those who rebuke sin fearlessly.

KEY VERSE

God also bound himself with an oath, so that those he promised to help would be perfectly sure and never need to wonder whether he might change his plans.—*Hebrews 6:17*

REFLECTION

God's promises are unchangeable and trustworthy because God is unchangeable and trustworthy. When he promised Abraham a son, God took an oath in his own name. The oath was as good as his name, and his name was as good as his divine nature. In a world that is constantly shifting and changing, couples can rest on the solid and secure sameness of God. Do you fear the changes that you see around you? Do not be afraid. God will not let you go.

MEDITATION

Heavenly Father, we confidently rest on your unchanging grace.

Peter Heals a Man Who Could not Walk
◄§ Acts 3:1–26 §►

Peter and John went to the Temple one afternoon to take part in the three o'clock daily prayer meeting. [2]As they approached the Temple, they saw a man lame from birth carried along the street and laid beside the Temple gate—the one called The Beautiful Gate—as was his custom every day. [3]As Peter and John were passing by, he asked them for some money.

[4]They looked at him intently, and then Peter said, "Look here!"

[5]The lame man looked at them eagerly, expecting a gift.

[6]But Peter said, "We don't have any money for you! But I'll give you something else! I command you in the name of Jesus Christ of Nazareth, *walk!*"

[7,8]Then Peter took the lame man by the hand and pulled him to his feet. And as he did, the man's feet and ankle-bones were healed and strengthened so that he came up with a leap, stood there a moment and began walking! Then, walking, leaping, and praising God, he went into the Temple with them.

[9]When the people inside saw him walking and heard him praising God, [10]and realized he was the lame beggar they had seen so often at The Beautiful Gate, they were inexpressibly surprised! [11]They all rushed out to Solomon's Hall, where he was holding tightly to Peter and John! Everyone stood there awed by the wonderful thing that had happened.

[12]Peter saw his opportunity and addressed the crowd. "Men of Israel," he said, "what is so surprising about this? And why look at us as though we by our own power and godliness had made this man walk? [13]For it is the God of Abraham, Isaac, Jacob and of all our ancestors who has brought glory to his servant Jesus by doing this. I refer to the Jesus whom you rejected before Pilate, despite Pilate's determination to release him. [14]You didn't want him freed—this holy, righteous one. Instead you demanded the release of a murderer. [15]And you killed the Author of Life; but God brought him back to life again. And John and I are witnesses of this fact, for after you killed him we saw him alive!

[16]"Jesus' name has healed this man—and you know how lame he was before. Faith in Jesus' name—faith given us from God—has caused this perfect healing.

[17]"Dear brothers, I realize that what you did to Jesus was done in ignorance; and the same can be said of your leaders. [18]But God was fulfilling the prophecies that the Messiah must suffer all these things. [19]Now change your mind and attitude to God and turn to him so he can cleanse away your sins and send you wonderful times of refreshment from the presence of the Lord [20]and send Jesus your Messiah back to you again. [21,22]For he must remain in heaven until the final recovery of all things from sin, as prophesied from ancient times. Moses, for instance, said long ago, 'The Lord God will raise up a Prophet among you, who will resemble me! Listen carefully to everything he tells you. [23]Anyone who will not listen to him shall be utterly destroyed.'

[24]"Samuel and every prophet since have all spoken about what is going on today. [25]You are the children of those prophets; and you are included in God's promise to your ancestors to bless the entire world through the Jewish race—that is the promise God gave to Abraham. [26]And as soon as God had brought his servant to life again, he sent him first of all to you men of Israel, to bless you by turning you back from your sins."

Melchizedek Is Greater Than the Levitical Priesthood
◄§ Hebrews 7:1–11 §►

This Melchizedek was king of the city of Salem, and also a priest of the Most High God. When Abraham was returning home after winning a great battle against many kings, Melchizedek met him and blessed him; [2]then Abraham took a tenth of all he had won in the battle and gave it to Melchizedek.

Melchizedek's name means "Justice," so he is

the King of Justice; and he is also the King of Peace because of the name of his city, Salem, which means "Peace." ³Melchizedek had no father or mother and there is no record of any of his ancestors. He was never born and he never died but his life is like that of the Son of God—a priest forever.

⁴See then how great this Melchizedek is:

(a)Even Abraham, the first and most honored of all God's chosen people, gave Melchizedek a tenth of the spoils he took from the kings he had been fighting. ⁵One could understand why Abraham would do this if Melchizedek had been a Jewish priest, for later on God's people were required by law to give gifts to help their priests because the priests were their relatives. ⁶But Melchizedek was not a relative, and yet Abraham paid him.

(b)Melchizedek placed a blessing upon mighty Abraham, ⁷and as everyone knows, a person who has the power to bless is always greater than the person he blesses.

⁸(c)The Jewish priests, though mortal, received tithes; but we are told that Melchizedek lives on.

⁹(d)One might even say that Levi himself (the ancestor of all Jewish priests, of all who receive tithes), paid tithes to Melchizedek through Abraham. ¹⁰For although Levi wasn't born yet, the seed from which he came was in Abraham when Abraham paid the tithes to Melchizedek.

¹¹(e)If the Jewish priests and their laws had been able to save us, why then did God need to send Christ as a priest with the rank of Melchizedek, instead of sending someone with the rank of Aaron—the same rank all other priests had?

Proverbs for Today
◄§ 24:26 §►

It is an honor to receive a frank reply.

─────── ◄ KEY VERSE ◄ ───────

"Now change your mind and attitude to God and turn to him so he can cleanse away your sins and send you wonderful times of refreshment from the presence of the Lord and send Jesus your Messiah back to you again."—*Acts 3:19–20*

─────── ◄ REFLECTION ◄ ───────

When we repent, God promises not only to wipe away our sin, but also to bring spiritual refreshment. At first repentance may seem painful because it is hard to give up certain sins. But God will give you a better way. As Hosea promised, "Let us press on to know him, and he will respond to us as surely as the coming of dawn or the rain of early spring" (Hosea 6:3). Do you feel a need for refreshment in your marriage? God is anxious to respond to you.

─────── ◄ MEDITATION ◄ ───────

Heavenly Father, we are thirsty for your presence in our marriage and in our home. §►

OCTOBER 7 _____

Peter's Defense before the Jewish Supreme Court
◄§ Acts 4:1–22 §►

While Peter and John were talking to the people, the chief priests, the captain of the Temple police, and some of the Sadducees came over to them, ²very disturbed that Peter and John were claiming that Jesus had risen from the dead. ³They arrested them and since it was already evening, jailed them overnight. ⁴But many of the people who heard their message believed it, so that the number of believers now reached a new high of about 5,000 men!

⁵The next day it happened that the Council of all the Jewish leaders was in session in Jerusalem—⁶Annas the High Priest was there, and Caiaphas, John, Alexander, and others of the High Priest's relatives. ⁷So the two disciples were brought in before them.

"By what power, or by whose authority have you done this?" the Council demanded.

[8]Then Peter, filled with the Holy Spirit, said to them, "Honorable leaders and elders of our nation, [9]if you mean the good deed done to the cripple, and how he was healed, [10]let me clearly state to you and to all the people of Israel that it was done in the name and power of Jesus from Nazareth, the Messiah, the man you crucified—but God raised back to life again. It is by his authority that this man stands here healed! [11]For Jesus the Messiah is (the one referred to in the Scriptures when they speak of) a 'stone discarded by the builders which became the capstone of the arch.' [12]There is salvation in no one else! Under all heaven there is no other name for men to call upon to save them."

[13]When the Council saw the boldness of Peter and John, and could see that they were obviously uneducated non-professionals, they were amazed and realized what being with Jesus had done for them! [14]And the Council could hardly discredit the healing when the man they had healed was standing right there beside them! [15]So they sent them out of the Council chamber and conferred among themselves.

[16]"What shall we do with these men?" they asked each other. "We can't deny that they have done a tremendous miracle, and everybody in Jerusalem knows about it. [17]But perhaps we can stop them from spreading their propaganda. We'll tell them that if they do it again we'll really throw the book at them." [18]So they called them back in, and told them never again to speak about Jesus.

[19]But Peter and John replied, "You decide whether God wants us to obey you instead of him! [20]We cannot stop telling about the wonderful things we saw Jesus do and heard him say."

[21]The Council then threatened them further, and finally let them go because they didn't know how to punish them without starting a riot. For everyone was praising God for this wonderful miracle—[22]the healing of a man who had been lame for forty years.

Jesus Is a High Priest Like Melchizedek
✧ Hebrews 7:12–22 ✧

And when God sends a new kind of priest, his law must be changed to permit it. As we all know, Christ did not belong to the priest-tribe of Levi, but came from the tribe of Judah, which had not been chosen for priesthood; Moses had never given them that work. [15]So we can plainly see that God's method changed, for Christ, the new High Priest who came with the rank of Melchizedek, [16]did not become a priest by meeting the old requirement of belonging to the tribe of Levi, but on the basis of power flowing from a life that cannot end. [17]And the Psalmist points this out when he says of Christ, "You are a priest forever with the rank of Melchizedek."

[18]Yes, the old system of priesthood based on family lines was canceled because it didn't work. It was weak and useless for saving people. [19]It never made anyone really right with God. But now we have a far better hope, for Christ makes us acceptable to God, and now we may draw near to him.

[20]God took an oath that Christ would always be a Priest, [21]although he never said that of other priests. Only to Christ he said, "The Lord has sworn and will never change his mind: You are a Priest forever, with the rank of Melchizedek." [22]Because of God's oath, Christ can guarantee forever the success of this new and better arrangement.

Proverbs for Today
✧ 24:27 ✧

Develop your business first before building your house.

✧ KEY VERSE ✧

Develop your business first before building your house.—*Proverbs 24:27*

✧ REFLECTION ✧

We should do things in their proper order. If a farmer builds his house in the spring, he misses the planting season. If a businessperson invests his or her money in a house while the business is struggling, he or she may lose both. It is possible to work hard and still lose everything if the work is done in the wrong sequence. Don't become impatient with the strengthening and building of your marriage. Remember that God is the foundation of your home and he will build upon it one brick at a time.

─────── * MEDITATION * ───────

Heavenly Father, thank you for the patience that you are giving us to enjoy each step that will take us toward a strong and godly marriage. ❧

OCTOBER 8 ─────────────────

The Jerusalem Believers Unite in Prayer
❧ Acts 4:23–37 ❧

As soon as they were freed, Peter and John found the other disciples and told them what the Council had said.

24Then all the believers united in this prayer:

"O Lord, Creator of heaven and earth and of the sea and everything in them— 25,26you spoke long ago by the Holy Spirit through our ancestor King David, your servant, saying, 'Why do the heathen rage against the Lord, and the foolish nations plan their little plots against Almighty God? The kings of the earth unite to fight against him, and against the anointed Son of God!'

27"That is what is happening here in this city today! For Herod the king, and Pontius Pilate the governor, and all the Romans—as well as the people of Israel—are united against Jesus, your anointed Son, your holy servant. 28They won't stop at anything that you in your wise power will let them do. 29And now, O Lord, hear their threats, and grant to your servants great boldness in their preaching, 30and send your healing power, and may miracles and wonders be done by the name of your holy servant Jesus."

31After this prayer, the building where they were meeting shook and they were all filled with the Holy Spirit and boldly preached God's message.

32All the believers were of one heart and mind, and no one felt that what he owned was his own; everyone was sharing. 33And the apostles preached powerful sermons about the resurrection of the Lord Jesus, and there was warm fellowship among all the believers, 34,35and no poverty—for all who owned land or houses sold them and brought the money to the apostles to give to others in need.

36For instance, there was Joseph (the one the apostles nicknamed "Barny the Preacher"! He was of the tribe of Levi, from the island of Cyprus). 37He was one of those who sold a field he owned and brought the money to the apostles for distribution to those in need.

Jesus Is a Priest Forever
❧ Hebrews 7:23–28 ❧

Under the old arrangement there had to be many priests, so that when the older ones died off, the system could still be carried on by others who took their places.

24But Jesus lives forever and continues to be a Priest so that no one else is needed. 25He is able to save completely all who come to God through him. Since he will live forever, he will always be there to remind God that he has paid for their sins with his blood.

26He is, therefore, exactly the kind of High Priest we need; for he is holy and blameless, unstained by sin, undefiled by sinners, and to him has been given the place of honor in heaven. 27He never needs the daily blood of animal sacrifices, as other priests did, to cover over first their own sins and then the sins of the people; for he finished all sacrifices, once and for all, when he sacrificed himself on the cross. 28Under the old system, even the high priests were weak and sinful men who could not keep from doing wrong, but later God appointed by his oath his Son who is perfect forever.

Proverbs for Today
◄§ 24:28–29 §►

Don't testify spitefully against an innocent neighbor. Why lie about him? Don't say, "Now I can pay him back for all his meanness to me!"

After this prayer, the building where they were meeting shook, and they were all filled with the Holy Spirit and boldly preached God's message. —*Acts 4:31*

Notice how the believers prayed. First they praised God; then they told God their specific problem and asked for his help. They did not ask God to remove the problem, but to help them deal with it. This is a model for you to follow when you pray for your marriage. You may ask God to remove your problems, and he may choose to do so; but you must recognize that often he will leave the problem in place and give you the grace to deal with it. In the process you will draw closer to God and closer to each other.

Heavenly Father, thank you for who you are and for answering our prayers. Help us to accept your answers. ☙

OCTOBER 9

Ananias and Sapphira Are Judged
◄§ Acts 5:1–11 §►

But there was a man named Ananias (with his wife Sapphira) who sold some property, ²and brought only part of the money, claiming it was the full price. (His wife had agreed to this deception.) ³But Peter said, "Ananias, Satan has filled your heart. When you claimed this was the full price, you were lying to the Holy Spirit. ⁴The property was yours to sell or not, as you wished. And after selling it, it was yours to decide how much to give. How could you do a thing like this? You weren't lying to us, but to God."

⁵As soon as Ananias heard these words, he fell to the floor, dead! Everyone was terrified, ⁶and the younger men covered him with a sheet and took him out and buried him.

⁷About three hours later his wife came in, not knowing what had happened. ⁸Peter asked her, "Did you people sell your land for such and such a price?"

"Yes," she replied, "we did."

⁹And Peter said, "How could you and your hus-band even think of doing a thing like this—conspiring together to test the Spirit of God's ability to know what is going on? Just outside that door are the young men who buried your husband, and they will carry you out too."

¹⁰Instantly she fell to the floor, dead, and the young men came in and, seeing that she was dead, carried her out and buried her beside her husband. ¹¹Terror gripped the entire church and all others who heard what had happened.

Christ, the Priest of a New Covenant
◄§ Hebrews 8:1–6 §►

What we are saying is this: Christ, whose priest-hood we have just described, is our High Priest, and is in heaven at the place of greatest honor next to God himself. ²He ministers in the temple in heaven, the true place of worship built by the Lord and not by human hands.

³And since every high priest is appointed to offer gifts and sacrifices, Christ must make an offering too. ⁴The sacrifice he offers is far better than those offered by the earthly priests. (But even so, if he

were here on earth he wouldn't even be permitted to be a priest, because down here the priests still follow the old Jewish system of sacrifices.) [5]Their work is connected with a mere earthly model of the real tabernacle in heaven; for when Moses was getting ready to build the tabernacle, God warned him to follow exactly the pattern of the heavenly tabernacle as shown to him on Mount Sinai. [6]But Christ, as a Minister in heaven, has been rewarded with a far more important work than those who serve under the old laws, because the new agreement which he passes on to us from God contains far more wonderful promises.

Proverbs for Today
◆§ 24:30–34 §◆

I walked by the field of a certain lazy fellow and saw that it was overgrown with thorns, and covered with weeds; and its walls were broken down. Then, as I looked, I learned this lesson: "A little extra sleep, A little more slumber, A little folding of the hands to rest" means that poverty will break in upon you suddenly like a robber, and violently like a bandit.

━━━━━◆ KEY VERSE ◆━━━━━

There was a man named Ananias (with his wife Sapphira) who sold some property and brought only part of the money, claiming it was the full price. (His wife had agreed to this deception.)—*Acts 5:1–2*

━━━━━◆ REFLECTION ◆━━━━━

Dishonesty and covetousness are destructive in a marriage, preventing the Holy Spirit from working effectively. The sin Ananias and Sapphira committed was not stinginess or holding back part of the money—they could choose whether or not to sell the land they owned and how much money to give. Their sin was lying to God and to God's people—saying that they had given the whole amount while holding back some for themselves, trying to make themselves appear more generous than they really were. If you lie to try to deceive God and his people, you will destroy your testimony for Christ.

━━━━━◆ MEDITATION ◆━━━━━

Heavenly Father, examine our hearts today. If you see any dishonesty or covetousness in us, dig it out so that you can use us. §◆

OCTOBER 10

An Angel Rescues the Apostles from Jail
◆§ Acts 5:12–25 §◆

Meanwhile, the apostles were meeting regularly at the Temple in the area known as Solomon's Hall, and they did many remarkable miracles among the people. [13]The other believers didn't dare join them, though, but all had the highest regard for them. [14]And more and more believers were added to the Lord, crowds both of men and women. [15]Sick people were brought out into the streets on beds and mats so that at least Peter's shadow would fall across some of them as he went by! [16]And crowds came in from the Jerusalem suburbs, bringing their sick folk and those possessed by demons; and every one of them was healed.

[17]The High Priest and his relatives and friends among the Sadducees reacted with violent jealousy [18]and arrested the apostles, and put them in the public jail.

[19]But an angel of the Lord came at night, opened the gates of the jail and brought them out. Then he told them, [20]"Go over to the Temple and preach about this Life!"

[21]They arrived at the Temple about daybreak, and immediately began preaching! Later that morning the High Priest and his courtiers arrived at the Temple, and, convening the Jewish Council and the en-

tire Senate, they sent for the apostles to be brought for trial. ²²But when the police arrived at the jail, the men weren't there, so they returned to the Council and reported, ²³"The jail doors were locked, and the guards were standing outside, but when we opened the gates, no one was there!"

²⁴When the police captain and the chief priests heard this, they were frantic, wondering what would happen next and where all this would end! ²⁵Then someone arrived with the news that the men they had jailed were out in the Temple, preaching to the people!

The Old Agreement Versus the New Agreement
⋖§ Hebrews 8:7–13 §⋗

The old agreement didn't even work. If it had, there would have been no need for another to replace it. ⁸But God himself found fault with the old one, for he said, "The day will come when I will make a new agreement with the people of Israel and the people of Judah. ⁹This new agreement will not be like the old one I gave to their fathers on the day when I took them by the hand to lead them out of the land of Egypt; they did not keep their part in that agreement, so I had to cancel it. ¹⁰But this is the new agreement I will make with the people of Israel, says the Lord: I will write my laws in their minds so that they will know what I want them to do without my even telling them, and these laws will be in their hearts so that they will want to obey them, and I will be their God and they shall be my people. ¹¹And no one then will need to speak to his friend or neighbor or brother, saying, 'You, too, should know the Lord,' because everyone, great and small, will know me already. ¹²And I will be merciful to them in their wrongdoings, and I will remember their sins no more."

¹³God speaks of these new promises, of this new agreement, as taking the place of the old one; for the old one is out of date now and has been put aside forever.

Proverbs for Today
⋖§ 25:1–5 §⋗

These proverbs of Solomon were discovered and copied by the aides of King Hezekiah of Judah: It is God's privilege to conceal things, and the king's privilege to discover and invent. You cannot understand the height of heaven, the size of the earth, or all that goes on in the king's mind! □ When you remove dross from silver, you have sterling ready for the silversmith. When you remove corrupt men from the king's court, his reign will be just and fair.

KEY VERSE

More and more believers were added to the Lord, crowds both of men and women.—*Acts 5:14*

REFLECTION

What makes Christianity attractive? It is easy to be drawn to churches because of programs, good speakers, size, beautiful facilities, fellowship, or marriage classes. Believers were attracted to the early church by God's power and miracles; the generosity, sincerity, honesty, and unity of the members; and the character of the leaders. How did you and your spouse choose the church you attend? How do your standards differ from those of the believers in the early church? God wants to add to his church, not just increase the number of programs or congregations.

MEDITATION

Heavenly Father, thank you for the example of the believers in the early church. Help us become more like them in our commitment to involvement in our local church. ৶

OCTOBER 11

The Apostles Suffer Persecution
◆§ Acts 5:26–42 §◆

The police captain went with his officers and arrested the apostles (without violence, for they were afraid the people would kill them if they roughed up the disciples) and brought them in before the Council.

²⁸"Didn't we tell you never again to preach about this Jesus?" the High Priest demanded. "And instead you have filled all Jerusalem with your teaching and intend to bring the blame for this man's death on us!"

²⁹But Peter and the apostles replied, "We must obey God rather than men. ³⁰The God of our ancestors brought Jesus back to life again after you had killed him by hanging him on a cross. ³¹Then, with mighty power, God exalted him to be a Prince and Savior, so that the people of Israel would have an opportunity for repentance, and for their sins to be forgiven. ³²And we are witnesses of these things, and so is the Holy Spirit, who is given by God to all who obey him."

³³At this, the Council was furious, and decided to kill them. ³⁴But one of their members, a Pharisee named Gamaliel (an expert on religious law and very popular with the people), stood up and requested that the apostles be sent outside the Council chamber while he talked.

³⁵Then he addressed his colleagues as follows:

"Men of Israel, take care what you are planning to do to these men! ³⁶Some time ago there was that fellow Theudas, who pretended to be someone great. About 400 others joined him, but he was killed, and his followers were harmlessly dispersed.

³⁷"After him, at the time of the taxation, there was Judas of Galilee. He drew away some people as disciples, but he also died, and his followers scattered.

³⁸"And so my advice is, leave these men alone. If what they teach and do is merely on their own, it will soon be overthrown. ³⁹But if it is of God, you will not be able to stop them, lest you find yourselves fighting even against God."

⁴⁰The Council accepted his advice, called in the apostles, had them beaten, and then told them never again to speak in the name of Jesus, and finally let them go. ⁴¹They left the Council chamber rejoicing that God had counted them worthy to suffer dishonor for his name. ⁴²And every day, in the Temple and in their home Bible classes, they continued to teach and preach that Jesus is the Messiah.

The Furniture of the Earthly Tabernacle
◆§ Hebrews 9:1–10 §◆

Now in that first agreement between God and his people there were rules for worship and there was a sacred tent down here on earth. Inside this place of worship there were two rooms. The first one contained the golden candlestick and a table with special loaves of holy bread upon it; this part was called the Holy Place. ³Then there was a curtain and behind the curtain was a room called the Holy of Holies. ⁴In that room there were a golden incense-altar and the golden chest, called the ark of the covenant, completely covered on all sides with pure gold. Inside the ark were he tablets of stone with the Ten Commandments written on them, and a golden jar with some manna in it, and Aaron's wooden cane that budded. ⁵Above the golden chest were statues of angels called the cherubim—the guardians of God's glory—with their wings stretched out over the ark's golden cover, called the mercy seat. But enough of such details.

⁶Well, when all was ready the priests went in and out of the first room whenever they wanted to, doing their work. ⁷But only the high priest went into the inner room, and then only once a year, all alone, and always with blood which he sprinkled on the mercy seat as an offering to God to cover his own mistakes and sins, and the mistakes and sins of all the people.

⁸And the Holy Spirit uses all this to point out to us that under the old system the common people could not go into the Holy of Holies as long as the outer room and the entire system it represents were still in use.

⁹This has an important lesson for us today. For under the old system, gifts and sacrifices were offered, but these failed to cleanse the hearts of the people who brought them. ¹⁰For the old system dealt only with certain rituals—what foods to eat and drink, rules for washing themselves, and rules about this and that. The people had to keep these rules to tide them over until Christ came with God's new and better way.

Proverbs for Today
⋙ 25:6–7 ⋘

Don't demand an audience with the king as though you were some powerful prince. It is better to wait for an invitation rather than to be sent back to the end of the line, publicly disgraced!

⋙ KEY VERSE ⋘

Every day, in the Temple and in their home Bible classes, they continued to teach and preach that Jesus is the Messiah.—*Acts 5:42*

⋙ REFLECTION ⋘

Home Bible studies are not new. The apostles had to teach in homes because the synagogues and the temple were not open to their teaching. Home Bible studies met the needs of believers and also introduced new people to the Christian faith. During later times of persecution, this became the primary method of passing on Bible knowledge. Christians throughout the world still meet in homes, whether to escape persecution or merely to extend hospitality to one another. How can you use your home to reach others for Christ?

⋙ MEDITATION ⋘

Heavenly Father, thank you for the freedom that we have to teach and preach inside and outside our home. Prod us so that we will take advantage of every opportunity that you give us to share the gospel with others. ⋘

OCTOBER 12

The Church Appoints Seven Deacons
⋙ Acts 6:1–7 ⋘

But with the believers multiplying rapidly, there were rumblings of discontent. Those who spoke only Greek complained that their widows were being discriminated against, that they were not being given as much food, in the daily distribution, as the widows who spoke Hebrew. ²So the Twelve called a meeting of all the believers.

"We should spend our time preaching, not administering a feeding program," they said. ³"Now look around among yourselves, dear brothers, and select seven men, wise and full of the Holy Spirit, who are well thought of by everyone; and we will put them in charge of this business. ⁴Then we can spend our time in prayer, preaching, and teaching."

⁵This sounded reasonable to the whole assembly, and they elected the following:

Stephen (a man unusually full of faith and the Holy Spirit),
Philip,
Prochorus,
Nicanor,
Timon,
Parmenas,
Nicolaus of Antioch (a Gentile convert to the Jewish faith, who had become a Christian).
⁶These seven were presented to the apostles, who prayed for them and laid their hands on them in blessing.

⁷God's message was preached in ever-widening circles, and the number of disciples increased vastly in Jerusalem; and many of the Jewish priests were converted too.

Our High Priest Died for Our Sins
‹§ Hebrews 9:11–15 §›

He came as High Priest of this better system which we now have. He went into that greater, perfect tabernacle in heaven, not made by men nor part of this world, [12]and once for all took blood into that inner room, the Holy of Holies, and sprinkled it on the mercy seat; but it was not the blood of goats and calves. No, he took his own blood, and with it he, by himself, made sure of our eternal salvation.

[13]And if under the old system the blood of bulls and goats and the ashes of young cows could cleanse men's bodies from sin, [14]just think how much more surely the blood of Christ will transform our lives and hearts. His sacrifice frees us from the worry of having to obey the old rules, and makes us want to serve the living God. For by the help of the eternal Holy Spirit, Christ willingly gave himself to God to die for our sins—he being perfect, without a single sin or fault. [15]Christ came with this new agreement so that all who are invited may come and have forever all the wonders God has promised them. For Christ died to rescue them from the penalty of the sins they had committed while still under that old system.

Proverbs for Today
‹§ 25:8–10 §›

Don't be hot-headed and rush to court! You may start something you can't finish and go down before your neighbor in shameful defeat. So discuss the matter with him privately. Don't tell anyone else, lest he accuse you of slander and you can't withdraw what you said.

─────── ‹§ **KEY VERSE** §› ───────

With the believers multiplying rapidly, there were rumblings of discontent. Those who spoke only Greek complained that their widows were being discriminated against, that they were not being given as much food in the daily distribution as the widows who spoke Hebrew.—*Acts 6:1*

─────── ‹§ **REFLECTION** §› ───────

When we read the descriptions of the early church—the miracles, the sharing, and the generosity—we may wish we could have been a part of that "ideal" church. But in reality, they had problems just as we do today. No church has ever been or will ever be perfect until Christ and his church are united at his Second Coming. All churches have problems. If your church's shortcomings distress you and your spouse, ask yourselves: "Would a perfect church let us be members?" Then do what you can to make your church better. A church does not have to be perfect to be faithful. As a couple you have gifts that can be used by God in various areas of ministry. Offer these gifts in service to him where you are.

─────── ‹§ **MEDITATION** §› ───────

Heavenly Father, help us see what we can do to be part of the solutions in our church and not the problems. §›

OCTOBER 13 _____

Stephen's Speech before the Jewish Supreme Court
‹§ Acts 6:8–7:16 §›

Stephen, the man so full of faith and the Holy Spirit's power, did spectacular miracles among the people.

[9]But one day some of the men from the Jewish cult of "The Freedmen" started an argument with him, and they were soon joined by Jews from Cyrene, Alexandria in Egypt, and the Turkish provinces of Cilicia, and Ausia. [10]But none of them was able to stand against Stephen's wisdom and spirit.

[11]So they brought in some men to lie about him, claiming they had heard Stephen curse Moses, and even God.

[12]This accusation roused the crowds to fury against Stephen, and the Jewish leaders arrested him and brought him before the Council. [13]The lying witnesses testified again that Stephen was constantly speaking against the Temple and against the laws of Moses.

[14]They declared, "We have heard him say that this fellow Jesus of Nazareth will destroy the Temple, and throw out all of Moses' laws." [15]At this point everyone in the Council chamber saw Stephen's face become as radiant as an angel's!

[7:1]Then the High Priest asked him, "Are these accusations true?"

[2]This was Stephen's lengthy reply: "The glorious God appeared to our ancestor Abraham in Iraq before he moved to Syria, [3]and told him to leave his native land, to say good-bye to his relatives and to start out for a country that God would direct him to. [4]So he left the land of the Chaldeans and lived in Haran, in Syria, until his father died. Then God brought him here to the land of Israel, [5]but gave him no property of his own, not one little tract of land.

"However, God promised that eventually the whole country would belong to him and his descendants—though as yet he had no children! [6]But God also told him that these descendants of his would leave the land and live in a foreign country and there become slaves for 400 years. [7]'But I will punish the nation that enslaves them,' God told him, 'and afterwards my people will return to this land of Israel and worship me here.'

[8]"God also gave Abraham the ceremony of circumcision at that time, as evidence of the covenant between God and the people of Abraham. And so Isaac, Abraham's son, was circumcised when he was eight days old. Isaac became the father of Jacob, and Jacob was the father of the twelve patriarchs of the Jewish nation. [9]These men were very jealous of Joseph and sold him to be a slave in Egypt. But God was with him, [10]and delivered him out of all of his anguish, and gave him favor before Pharaoh, king of Egypt. God also gave Joseph unusual wisdom, so that Pharaoh appointed him governor over all Egypt, as well as putting him in charge of all the affairs of the palace.

[11]"But a famine developed in Egypt and Canaan and there was great misery for our ancestors. When their food was gone, [12]Jacob heard that there was still grain in Egypt, so he sent his sons to buy some. [13]The second time they went, Joseph revealed his identity to his brothers, and they were introduced to Pharaoh. [14]Then Joseph sent for his father Jacob and all his brothers' families to come to Egypt, seventy-five persons in all. [15]So Jacob came to Egypt, where he died, and all his sons. [16]All of them were taken to Shechem and buried in the tomb Abraham bought from the sons of Hamor, Shechem's father.

Sacrifice under the Old Agreement
Hebrews 9:16–23

Now, if someone dies and leaves a will—a list of things to be given away to certain people when he dies—no one gets anything until it is proved that the person who wrote the will is dead. [17]The will goes into effect only after the death of the person who wrote it. While he is still alive no one can use it to get any of those things he has promised them.

[18]That is why blood was sprinkled [as proof of Christ's death] before even the first agreement could go into effect. [19]For after Moses had given the people all of God's laws, he took the blood of calves and goats, along with water, and sprinkled the blood over the book of God's laws and over all the people, using branches of hyssop bushes and scarlet wool to sprinkle with. [20]Then he said, "This is the blood that marks the beginning of the agreement between you and God, the agreement God commanded me to make with you." [21]And in the same way he sprinkled blood on the sacred tent and on whatever instruments were used for worship. [22]In fact we can say that under the old agreement almost everything was cleansed by sprinkling it with blood, and without the shedding of blood there is no forgiveness of sins.

[23]That is why the sacred tent down here on earth, and everything in it—all copied from things in heaven—all had to be made pure by Moses in this way, by being sprinkled with the blood of animals. But the real things in heaven, of which these down

here are copies, were made pure with far more precious offerings.

Proverbs for Today
◄§ 25:11–14 §►

Timely advice is as lovely as gold apples in a silver basket. □ It is a badge of honor to accept valid criticism. □ A faithful employee is as refreshing as a cool day in the hot summertime. □ One who doesn't give the gift he promised is like a cloud blowing over a desert without dropping any rain.

◄§ KEY VERSE §►

One who doesn't give the gift he promised is like a cloud blowing over a desert without dropping any rain.—*Proverbs 25:14*

◄§ REFLECTION §►

All churches, missions organizations, and Christian groups depend on the gifts of people to keep their ministries going. But many people who promise to give to them fail to keep their promises. The Bible is clear about the effect this has on those involved in the ministry. If you pledge to give, make every effort to follow through. If you don't give, pray with your spouse over the amount of money that God wants you to give, and obey his leading in this area.

◄§ MEDITATION §►

Heavenly Father, because you have given us everything that we have, we want to give something back to you. Lead us to those ministries that can use our help. §►

OCTOBER 14

Stephen's Speech—the Life of Moses
◄§ Acts 7:17–43 §►

"As the time drew near when God would fulfill his promise to Abraham to free his descendants from slavery, the Jewish people greatly multiplied in Egypt; but then a king was crowned who had no respect for Joseph's memory. [19]This king plotted against our race, forcing parents to abandon their children in the fields.

[20]"About that time Moses was born—a child of divine beauty. His parents hid him at home for three months, [21]and when at last they could no longer keep him hidden, and had to abandon him, Pharaoh's daughter found him and adopted him as her own son, [22]and taught him all the wisdom of the Egyptians, and he became a mighty prince and orator.

[23]"One day as he was nearing his fortieth birthday, it came into his mind to visit his brothers, the people of Israel. [24]During this visit he saw an Egyptian mistreating a man of Israel. So Moses killed the Egyptian. [25]Moses supposed his brothers would realize that God had sent him to help them, but they didn't.

[26]"The next day he visited them again and saw two men of Israel fighting. He tried to be a peacemaker. 'Gentlemen,' he said, 'you are brothers and shouldn't be fighting like this! It is wrong!'

[27]"But the man in the wrong told Moses to mind his own business. 'Who made *you* a ruler and judge over us?' he asked. [28]'Are you going to kill me as you killed that Egyptian yesterday?'

[29]"At this, Moses fled the country, and lived in the land of Midian, where his two sons were born.

[30]"Forty years later, in the desert near Mount Sinai, an Angel appeared to him in a flame of fire in a bush. [31]Moses saw it and wondered what it was, and as he ran to see, the voice of the Lord called out to him, [32]'I am the God of your ancestors—of Abraham, Isaac and Jacob.' Moses shook with terror and dared not look.

[33]"And the Lord said to him, 'Take off your shoes, for you are standing on holy ground. [34]I have seen the anguish of my people in Egypt and have heard their cries. I have come down to deliver

them. Come, I will send you to Egypt.' ³⁵And so God sent back the same man his people had previously rejected by demanding, 'Who made *you* a ruler and judge over us?' Moses was sent to be their ruler and savior. ³⁶And by means of many remarkable miracles he led them out of Egypt and through the Red Sea, and back and forth through the wilderness for forty years.

³⁷"Moses himself told the people of Israel, 'God will raise up a Prophet much like me from among your brothers.' ³⁸How true this proved to be, for in the wilderness, Moses was the go-between—the mediator between the people of Israel and the Angel who gave them the Law of God—the Living Word—on Mount Sinai.

³⁹"But our fathers rejected Moses and wanted to return to Egypt. ⁴⁰They told Aaron, 'Make idols for us, so that we will have gods to lead us back; for we don't know what has become of this Moses, who brought us out of Egypt.' ⁴¹So they made a calf-idol and sacrificed to it, and rejoiced in this thing they had made.

⁴²"Then God turned away from them and gave them up, and let them serve the sun, moon and stars as their gods! In the book of Amos' prophecies the Lord God asks, 'Was it to me you were sacrificing during those forty years in the desert, Israel? ⁴³No, your real interest was in your heathen gods—Sakkuth, and the star god Kaiway, and in all the images you made. So I will send you into captivity far away beyond Babylon.'

Christ Conquered the Power of Sin
◄§ Hebrews 9:24–28 §►

For Christ has entered into heaven itself, to appear now before God as our Friend. It was not in the earthly place of worship that he did this, for that was merely a copy of the real temple in heaven. ²⁵Nor has he offered himself again and again, as the high priest down here on earth offers animal blood

in the Holy of Holies each year. ²⁶If that had been necessary, then he would have had to die again and again, ever since the world began. But no! He came once for all, at the end of the age, to put away the power of sin forever by dying for us.

²⁷And just as it is destined that men die only once, and after that comes judgment, ²⁸so also Christ died only once as an offering for the sins of many people; and he will come again, but not to deal again with our sins.

This time he will come bringing salvation to all those who are eagerly and patiently waiting for him.

Proverbs for Today
◄§ 25:15 §►

Be patient and you will finally win, for a soft tongue can break hard bones.

◄ KEY VERSE ►

Christ has entered into heaven itself to appear now before God as our Friend. It was not in the earthly place of worship that he did this, for that was merely a copy of the real temple in heaven.—*Hebrews 9:24*

◄ REFLECTION ►

Amidst references to priests, tabernacles, sacrifices, and other ideas unfamiliar to us, we come to this description of Christ as our friend. We can relate to this role and be encouraged by it. Christ is our friend; he stands with us and for us; he is on our side at God's side. Whatever you may be facing, Jesus stands beside you as a friend. He will encourage you and lift you up if you will only let him.

◄ MEDITATION ►

Thank you, Jesus, for being our friend; for being *for us!* §►

OCTOBER 15

Stephen Is Martyred
Acts 7:44–60

"Our ancestors carried along with them a portable Temple, or Tabernacle, through the wilderness. In it they kept the stone tablets with the Ten Commandments written on them. This building was constructed in exact accordance with the plan shown to Moses by the Angel. [45]Years later, when Joshua led the battles against the Gentile nations, this Tabernacle was taken with them into their new territory, and used until the time of King David.

[46]"God blessed David greatly, and David asked for the privilege of building a permanent Temple for the God of Jacob. [47]But it was Solomon who actually built it. [48,49]However, God doesn't live in temples made by human hands. 'The heaven is my throne,' says the Lord through his prophets, 'and earth is my footstool. What kind of home could you build?' asks the Lord. 'Would I stay in it? [50]Didn't I make both heaven and earth?'

[51]"You stiff-necked heathen! Must you forever resist the Holy Spirit? But your fathers did, and so do you! [52]Name one prophet your ancestors didn't persecute! They even killed the ones who predicted the coming of the Righteous One—the Messiah whom you betrayed and murdered. [53]Yes, and you deliberately destroyed God's Laws, though you received them from the hands of angels."

[54]The Jewish leaders were stung to fury by Stephen's accusation, and ground their teeth in rage. [55]But Stephen, full of the Holy Spirit, gazed steadily upward into heaven and saw the glory of God and Jesus standing at God's right hand. [56]And he told them, "Look, I see the heavens opened and Jesus the Messiah standing beside God, at his right hand!"

[57]Then they mobbed him, putting their hands over their ears, and drowning out his voice with their shouts, [58]and dragged him out of the city to stone him. The official witnesses—the executioners—took off their coats and laid them at the feet of a young man named Paul.

[59]And as the murderous stones came hurtling at him, Stephen prayed, "Lord Jesus, receive my spirit." [60]And he fell to his knees, shouting, "Lord, don't charge them with this sin!" and with that, he died.

Christ Died Once for All
Hebrews 10:1–10

The old system of Jewish laws gave only a dim foretaste of the good things Christ would do for us. The sacrifices under the old system were repeated again and again, year after year, but even so they could never save those who lived under their rules. [2]If they could have, one offering would have been enough; the worshipers would have been cleansed once for all, and their feeling of guilt would be gone.

[3]But just the opposite happened: those yearly sacrifices reminded them of their disobedience and guilt instead of relieving their minds. [4]For it is not possible for the blood of bulls and goats really to take away sins.

[5]That is why Christ said, as he came into the world, "O God, the blood of bulls and goats cannot satisfy you, so you have made ready this body of mine for me to lay as a sacrifice upon your altar. [6]You were not satisfied with the animal sacrifices, slain and burnt before you as offerings for sin. [7]Then I said, 'See, I have come to do your will, to lay down my life, just as the Scriptures said that I would.'"

[8]After Christ said this, about not being satisfied with the various sacrifices and offerings required under the old system, [9]he then added, "Here I am. I have come to give my life."

He cancels the first system in favor of a far better one. [10]Under this new plan we have been forgiven and made clean by Christ's dying for us once and for all.

Proverbs for Today
25:16

Do you like honey? Don't eat too much of it, or it will make you sick!

"God doesn't live in temples made by human hands. 'The heaven is my throne,' says the Lord through his prophets, 'and earth is my footstool. What kind of home could you build?' asks the Lord. 'Would I stay in it?' "—*Acts 7:48–49*

────── ❧ REFLECTION ❧ ──────

Stephen had been accused of speaking against the temple (6:13). Although he recognized the impor-tance of the temple, he knew that it was not more important than God. God is not limited; he doesn't live only in a sanctuary, but wherever hearts of faith are open to receive him. Are you open to receiving Christ into your home and into your marriage?

────── ❧ MEDITATION ❧ ──────

Heavenly Father, prepare our lives and home to receive you. Live in us and through us. ❧

OCTOBER 16

Many in Samaria Become Believers
❧ Acts 8:1–25 ❧

Paul was in complete agreement with the killing of Stephen.

And a great wave of persecution of the believers began that day, sweeping over the church in Jerusa-lem, and everyone except the apostles fled into Ju-dea and Samaria. [2](But some godly Jews came and with great sorrow buried Stephen.) [3]Paul was like a wild man, going everywhere to devastate the believ-ers, even entering private homes and dragging out men and women alike and jailing them.

[4]But the believers who had fled Jerusalem went everywhere preaching the Good News about Jesus! [5]Philip, for instance, went to the city of Samaria and told the people there about Christ. [6]Crowds listened intently to what he had to say because of the miracles he did. [7]Many evil spirits were cast out, screaming as they left their victims, and many who were paralyzed or lame were healed, [8]so there was much joy in that city!

[9,10,11]A man named Simon had formerly been a sorcerer there for many years; he was a very influen-tial, proud man because of the amazing things he could do—in fact, the Samaritan people often spoke of him as the Messiah. [12]But now they believed Philip's message that Jesus was the Messiah, and his words concerning the Kingdom of God; and many men and women were baptized. [13]Then Simon himself believed and was baptized and began fol-lowing Philip wherever he went, and was amazed by the miracles he did.

[14]When the apostles back in Jerusalem heard that the people of Samaria had accepted God's message, they sent down Peter and John. [15]As soon as they arrived, they began praying for these new Christians to receive the Holy Spirit, [16]for as yet he had not come upon any of them. For they had only been baptized in the name of the Lord Jesus. [17]Then Pe-ter and John laid their hands upon these believers, and they received the Holy Spirit.

[18]When Simon saw this—that the Holy Spirit was given when the apostles placed their hands upon people's heads—he offered money to buy this power.

[19]"Let me have this power too," he exclaimed, "so that when I lay my hands on people, they will receive the Holy Spirit!"

[20]But Peter replied, "Your money perish with you for thinking God's gift can be bought! [21]You can have no part in this, for your heart is not right before God. [22]Turn from this great wickedness and pray. Perhaps God will yet forgive your evil thoughts— [23]for I can see that there is jealousy and sin in your heart."

[24]"Pray for me," Simon exclaimed, "that these terrible things won't happen to me."

[25]After testifying and preaching in Samaria, Peter and John returned to Jerusalem, stopping at several Samaritan villages along the way to preach the Good News to them too.

Christ Opened a New and Living Way
§ Hebrews 10:11–22 §

Under the old agreement the priests stood before the altar day after day offering sacrifices that could never take away our sins. ¹²But Christ gave himself to God for our sins as one sacrifice for all time, and then sat down in the place of highest honor at God's right hand, ¹³waiting for his enemies to be laid under his feet. ¹⁴For by that one offering he made forever perfect in the sight of God all those whom he is making holy.

¹⁵And the Holy Spirit testifies that this is so, for he has said, ¹⁶"This is the agreement I will make with the people of Israel, though they broke their first agreement: I will write my laws into their minds so that they will always know my will, and I will put my laws in their hearts so that they will want to obey them." ¹⁷And then he adds, "I will never again remember their sins and lawless deeds."

¹⁸Now, when sins have once been forever forgiven and forgotten, there is no need to offer more sacrifices to get rid of them.

¹⁹And so, dear brothers, now we may walk right into the very Holy of Holies where God is, because of the blood of Jesus. ²⁰This is the fresh, new, life-giving way which Christ has opened up for us by tearing the curtain—his human body—to let us into the holy presence of God.

²¹And since this great High Priest of ours rules over God's household, ²²let us go right in, to God himself, with true hearts fully trusting him to receive us, because we have been sprinkled with Christ's blood to make us clean, and because our bodies have been washed with pure water.

Proverbs for Today
§ 25:17 §

Don't visit your neighbor too often, or you will outwear your welcome!

_____ KEY VERSE _____

"Pray for me," Simon exclaimed, "that these terrible things won't happen to me."—*Acts 8:24*

_____ REFLECTION _____

Do you remember the last time your spouse rebuked you harshly? Were you hurt? Angry? Defensive? Learn a lesson from Simon and his reaction to Peter's rebuke. He exclaimed, "Pray for me!" If you are rebuked for a serious mistake, it is for your good. Admit your error, repent quickly, and ask for prayer.

_____ MEDITATION _____

Heavenly Father, help us be honest with each other and open to helpful criticism. §

OCTOBER 17 _____

Philip Tells the Ethiopian Eunuch about Jesus
§ Acts 8:26–40 §

But as for Philip, an angel of the Lord said to him, "Go over to the road that runs from Jerusalem through the Gaza Desert, arriving around noon." ²⁷So he did, and who should be coming down the road but the Treasurer of Ethiopia, a eunuch of great authority under Candace the queen. He had gone to Jerusalem to worship at the Temple, ²⁸and was now returning in his chariot, reading aloud from the book of the prophet Isaiah.

²⁹The Holy Spirit said to Philip, "Go over and walk along beside the chariot."

³⁰Philip ran over and heard what he was reading and asked, "Do you understand it?"

³¹"Of course not!" the man replied. "How can I when there is no one to instruct me?" And he begged Philip to come up into the chariot and sit with him.

^{32}The passage of Scripture he had been reading from was this:

"He was led as a sheep to the slaughter, and as a lamb is silent before the shearers, so he opened not his mouth; ^{33}in his humiliation, justice was denied him; and who can express the wickedness of the people of his generation? For his life is taken from the earth."

^{34}The eunuch asked Philip, "Was Isaiah talking about himself or someone else?"

^{35}So Philip began with this same Scripture and then used many others to tell him about Jesus.

^{36}As they rode along, they came to a small body of water, and the eunuch said, "Look! Water! Why can't I be baptized?"

^{37}"You can," Philip answered, "if you believe with all your heart."

And the eunuch replied, "I believe that Jesus Christ is the Son of God."

^{38}He stopped the chariot, and they went down into the water and Philip baptized him. ^{39}And when they came up out of the water, the Spirit of the Lord caught away Philip, and the eunuch never saw him again, but went on his way rejoicing. ^{40}Meanwhile, Philip found himself at Azotus! He preached the Good News there and in every city along the way, as he traveled to Caesarea.

Let Us Serve One Another
⋖§ Hebrews 10:23–25 ଈ

Now we can look forward to the salvation God has promised us. There is no longer any room for doubt, and we can tell others that salvation is ours, for there is no question that he will do what he says.

^{24}In response to all he has done for us, let us outdo each other in being helpful and kind to each other and in doing good.

^{25}Let us not neglect our church meetings, as some people do, but encourage and warn each other, especially now that the day of his coming back again is drawing near.

Proverbs for Today
⋖§ 25:18–19 ଈ

Telling lies about someone is as harmful as hitting him with an axe, or wounding him with a sword, or shooting him with a sharp arrow. ☐ Putting confidence in an unreliable man is like chewing with a sore tooth, or trying to run on a broken foot.

KEY VERSE

Telling lies about someone is as harmful as hitting him with an axe, or wounding him with a sword, or shooting him with a sharp arrow.—*Proverbs 25:18*

REFLECTION

Lying is vicious. Its effects can be as permanent as those of a stab wound. The next time you are tempted to pass on a bit of gossip, imagine yourself striking the victim of your remarks with an axe. This image may shock you into silence. Have you told a lie to your spouse or about your spouse recently? Confess this lie to the Lord and also to your husband or wife.

MEDITATION

Heavenly Father, please heal any wounds that have been caused by a lie that one of us has told. ଈ

Paul's Conversion
ᑫ§ Acts 9:1–19a §ᑫ

But Paul, threatening with every breath and eager to destroy every Christian, went to the High Priest in Jerusalem. [2]He requested a letter addressed to synagogues in Damascus, requiring their cooperation in the persecution of any believers he found there, both men and women, so that he could bring them in chains to Jerusalem.

[3]As he was nearing Damascus on this mission, suddenly a brilliant light from heaven spotted down upon him! [4]He fell to the ground and heard a voice saying to him, "Paul! Paul! Why are you persecuting me?"

[5]"Who is speaking, sir?" Paul asked.

And the voice replied, "I am Jesus, the one you are persecuting! [6]Now get up and go into the city and await my further instructions."

[7]The men with Paul stood speechless with surprise, for they heard the sound of someone's voice but saw no one! [8,9]As Paul picked himself up off the ground, he found that he was blind. He had to be led into Damascus and was there three days, blind, going without food and water all that time.

[10]Now there was in Damascus a believer named Ananias. The Lord spoke to him in a vision, calling, "Ananias!"

"Yes, Lord!" he replied.

[11]And the Lord said, "Go over to Straight Street and find the house of a man named Judas and ask there for Paul of Tarsus. He is praying to me right now, for [12]I have shown him a vision of a man named Ananias coming in and laying his hands on him so that he can see again!"

[13]"But Lord," exclaimed Ananias, "I have heard about the terrible things this man has done to the believers in Jerusalem! [14]And we hear that he has arrest warrants with him from the chief priests, authorizing him to arrest every believer in Damascus!"

[15]But the Lord said, "Go and do what I say. For Paul is my chosen instrument to take my message to the nations and before kings, as well as to the people of Israel. [16]And I will show him how much he must suffer for me."

[17]So Ananias went over and found Paul and laid his hands on him and said, "Brother Paul, the Lord Jesus, who appeared to you on the road, has sent me so that you may be filled with the Holy Spirit and get your sight back."

[18]Instantly (it was as though scales fell from his eyes) Paul could see, and was immediately baptized. [19]Then he ate and was strengthened.

A Warning Against Apostasy
ᑫ§ Hebrews 10:26–31 §ᑫ

If anyone sins deliberately by rejecting the Savior after knowing the truth of forgiveness, this sin is not covered by Christ's death; there is no way to get rid of it. [27]There will be nothing to look forward to but the terrible punishment of God's awful anger which will consume all his enemies. [28]A man who refused to obey the laws given by Moses was killed without mercy if there were two or three witnesses to his sin. [29]Think how much more terrible the punishment will be for those who have trampled underfoot the Son of God and treated his cleansing blood as though it were common and unhallowed, and insulted and outraged the Holy Spirit who brings God's mercy to his people.

[30]For we know him who said, "Justice belongs to me; I will repay them"; who also said, "The Lord himself will handle these cases." [31]It is a fearful thing to fall into the hands of the living God.

Proverbs for Today
ᑫ§ 25:20–22 §ᑫ

Being happy-go-lucky around a person whose heart is heavy is as bad as stealing his jacket in cold weather, or rubbing salt in his wounds. ☐ If your enemy is hungry, give him food! If he is thirsty, give him something to drink! This will make him feel ashamed of himself, and God will reward you.

ᔔ KEY VERSE ᔔ

The Lord said, "Go and do what I say. For Paul is my chosen instrument to take my message to the nations and before kings, as well as to the people of Israel. And I will show him how much he must suffer for me."—*Acts 9:15–16*

-------- ❧ REFLECTION ❧ --------

Many young couples are attracted to Christianity because of the emphasis placed on family and the promise of a better life. But Christianity involves not only great blessings but often great suffering too. The apostle Paul would suffer for his faith (see 2 Corinthians 11:23–27). God calls us to commitment, not to comfort. He promises to be with us through suffering and hardship, not to spare us from them.

-------- ❧ MEDITATION ❧ --------

Heavenly Father, give us the courage to follow you in all circumstances and no matter what the cost. ❧

OCTOBER 19

Paul Preaches the Good News about Jesus
❧ Acts 9:19b–31 ❧

Paul stayed with the believers in Damascus for a few days [20]and went at once to the synagogue to tell everyone there the Good News about Jesus—that he is indeed the Son of God!

[21]All who heard him were amazed. "Isn't this the same man who persecuted Jesus' followers so bitterly in Jerusalem?" they asked. "And we understand that he came here to arrest them all and take them in chains to the chief priests."

[22]Paul became more and more fervent in his preaching, and the Damascus Jews couldn't withstand his proofs that Jesus was indeed the Christ.

[23]After a while the Jewish leaders determined to kill him. [24]But Paul was told about their plans, that they were watching the gates of the city day and night prepared to murder him. [25]So during the night some of his converts let him down in a basket through an opening in the city wall!

[26]Upon arrival in Jerusalem he tried to meet with the believers, but they were all afraid of him. They thought he was faking! [27]Then Barnabas brought him to the apostles and told them how Paul had seen the Lord on the way to Damascus, what the Lord had said to him, and all about his powerful preaching in the name of Jesus. [28]Then they accepted him, and after that he was constantly with the believers [29]and preached boldly in the name of the Lord. But then some Greek-speaking Jews with whom he had argued plotted to murder him. [30]However, when the other believers heard about his danger, they took him to Caesarea and then sent him to his home in Tarsus.

[31]Meanwhile, the church had peace throughout Judea, Galilee and Samaria, and grew in strength and numbers. The believers learned how to walk in the fear of the Lord and in the comfort of the Holy Spirit.

Remember Your Eternal Reward
❧ Hebrews 10:32–39 ❧

Don't ever forget those wonderful days when you first learned about Christ. Remember how you kept right on with the Lord even though it meant terrible suffering. [33]Sometimes you were laughed at and beaten, and sometimes you watched and sympathized with others suffering the same things. [34]You suffered with those thrown into jail, and you were actually joyful when all you owned was taken from you, knowing that better things were awaiting you in heaven, things that would be yours forever.

[35]Do not let this happy trust in the Lord die away, no matter what happens. Remember your reward! [36]You need to keep on patiently doing God's will if you want him to do for you all that he has promised. [37]His coming will not be delayed much longer. [38]And those whose faith has made them good in God's sight must live by faith, trusting him

in everything. Otherwise, if they shrink back, God will have no pleasure in them.

[39]But we have never turned our backs on God and sealed our fate. No, our faith in him assures our souls' salvation.

Proverbs for Today
25:23–24

As surely as a wind from the north brings cold, just as surely a retort causes anger! □ It is better to live in a corner of an attic than in a beautiful home with a cranky, quarrelsome woman.

KEY VERSE

As surely as a wind from the north brings cold, just as surely a retort causes anger!—*Proverbs 25:23*

REFLECTION

It is hard to keep your mouth shut when your spouse speaks rudely to you, but answering back can sometimes be a sure step into a full-scale argument. Plan ahead of time how you will respond—either speaking softly or saying nothing at all. If you control your tongue, you may be able to prevent an angry explosion.

MEDITATION

Heavenly Father, our tongues can be either vicious weapons or soothing ointments. Forgive us for the unkind things we say to each other in the heat of the moment. Help us to control our tongues.

OCTOBER 20

Peter Heals Aeneas
Acts 9:32–35

Peter traveled from place to place to visit them, and in his travels came to the believers in the town of Lydda. [33]There he met a man named Aeneas, paralyzed and bedridden for eight years.

[34]Peter said to him, ''Aeneas! Jesus Christ has healed you! Get up and make your bed.'' And he was healed instantly. [35]Then the whole population of Lydda and Sharon turned to the Lord when they saw Aeneas walking around.

Faith
Hebrews 11:1–6

What is faith? It is the confident assurance that something we want is going to happen. It is the certainty that what we hope for is waiting for us, even though we cannot see it up ahead. [2]Men of God in days of old were famous for their faith.

[3]By faith—by believing God—we know that the world and the stars—in fact, all things—were made at God's command; and that they were all made from things that can't be seen.

[4]It was by faith that Abel obeyed God and brought an offering that pleased God more than Cain's offering did. God accepted Abel and proved it by accepting his gift; and though Abel is long dead, we can still learn lessons from him about trusting God.

[5]Enoch trusted God too, and that is why God took him away to heaven without dying; suddenly he was gone because God took him. Before this happened God had said how pleased he was with Enoch. [6]You can never please God without faith, without depending on him. Anyone who wants to come to God must believe that there is a God and that he rewards those who sincerely look for him.

Proverbs for Today
25:25–27

Good news from far away is like cold water to the thirsty. □ If a godly man compromises with the wicked, it is like polluting a fountain or muddying a spring. □ Just as it is harmful to eat too much honey, so also it is bad for men to think about all the honors they deserve!

KEY VERSE

Just as it is harmful to eat too much honey, so also it is bad for men to think about all the honors they deserve!—*Proverbs 25:27*

REFLECTION

Dwelling on honors or the appreciation you deserve from your spouse can only be harmful. It can make you resentful, bitter, discouraged, or angry, and it will harm your relationship. Pining for what you think you should receive may make you miss honors you are already receiving.

MEDITATION

Heavenly Father, thank you for my spouse and for the many things that he or she so generously gives to me.

OCTOBER 21

Peter Raises Dorcas from the Dead
Acts 9:36–43

In the city of Joppa there was a woman named Dorcas ("Gazelle"), a believer who was always doing kind things for others, especially for the poor. [37]About this time she became ill and died. Her friends prepared her for burial and laid her in an upstairs room. [38]But when they learned that Peter was nearby at Lydda, they sent two men to beg him to return with them to Joppa. [39]This he did; as soon as he arrived, they took him upstairs where Dorcas lay. The room was filled with weeping widows who were showing one another the coats and other garments Dorcas had made for them. [40]But Peter asked them all to leave the room; then he knelt and prayed. Turning to the body he said, "Get up, Dorcas," and she opened her eyes! And when she saw Peter, she sat up! [41]He gave her his hand and helped her up and called in the believers and widows, presenting her to them.

[42]The news raced through the town, and many believed in the Lord. [43]And Peter stayed a long time in Joppa, living with Simon, the tanner.

The Faith of Noah, Abraham, and Sarah
Hebrews 11:7–12

Noah was another who trusted God. When he heard God's warning about the future, Noah believed him even though there was then no sign of a flood, and wasting no time, he built the ark and saved his family. Noah's belief in God was in direct contrast to the sin and disbelief of the rest of the world—which refused to obey—and because of his faith he became one of those whom God has accepted.

[8]Abraham trusted God, and when God told him to leave home and go far away to another land which he promised to give him, Abraham obeyed. Away he went, not even knowing where he was going. [9]And even when he reached God's promised land, he lived in tents like a mere visitor, as did Isaac and Jacob, to whom God gave the same promise. [10]Abraham did this because he was confidently waiting for God to bring him to that strong heavenly city whose designer and builder is God.

[11]Sarah, too, had faith, and because of this she was able to become a mother in spite of her old age, for she realized that God, who gave her his promise, would certainly do what he said. [12]And so a whole nation came from Abraham, who was too old to have even one child—a nation with so many millions of people that, like the stars of the sky and the sand on the ocean shores, there is no way to count them.

Proverbs for Today
25:28

A man without self-control is as defenseless as a city with broken-down walls.

Noah was another who trusted God. When he heard God's warning about the future, Noah believed him even though there was then no sign of a flood, and wasting no time, he built the ark and saved his family. Noah's belief in God was in direct contrast to the sin and disbelief of the rest of the world—which refused to obey—and because of his faith he became one of those whom God has accepted.—*Hebrews 11:7*

◦§ REFLECTION ◦&

Noah experienced what it meant to be different from his neighbors. God commanded him to build a huge boat in the middle of dry land. Although God's command seemed foolish, Noah obeyed. Noah's obedience made him appear strange to his neighbors. As you obey God in your marriage, don't be surprised if others consider you odd. Your obedience makes their disobedience stand out. Remember, if God asks you to do something, he will give you the necessary strength to carry out that task.

◦§ MEDITATION ◦&

Heavenly Father, you have given us specific instructions for a Christ-centered home and marriage. Help us to be like Noah in our obedience. &

OCTOBER 22

God Gives Visions to Peter and Cornelius
◦§ Acts 10:1–23a &

In Caesarea there lived a Roman army officer, Cornelius, a captain of an Italian regiment. [2]He was a godly man, deeply reverent, as was his entire household. He gave generously to charity and was a man of prayer. [3]While wide awake one afternoon he had a vision—it was about three o'clock—and in this vision he saw an angel of God coming toward him.

"Cornelius!" the angel said.

[4]Cornelius stared at him in terror. "What do you want, sir?" he asked the angel.

And the angel replied, "Your prayers and charities have not gone unnoticed by God! [5,6]Now send some men to Joppa to find a man named Simon Peter, who is staying with Simon, the tanner, down by the shore, and ask him to come and visit you."

[7]As soon as the angel was gone, Cornelius called two of his household servants and a godly soldier, one of his personal bodyguard, [8]and told them what had happened and sent them off to Joppa.

[9,10]The next day, as they were nearing the city, Peter went up on the flat roof of his house to pray. It was noon and he was hungry, but while lunch was being prepared, he fell into a trance. [11]He saw the sky open, and a great canvas sheet, suspended by its four corners, settle to the ground. [12]In the sheet were all sorts of animals, snakes and birds [forbidden to the Jews for food].

[13]Then a voice said to him, "Go kill and eat any of them you wish."

[14]"Never, Lord," Peter declared, "I have never in all my life eaten such creatures, for they are forbidden by our Jewish laws."

[15]The voice spoke again, "Don't contradict God! If he says something is kosher, then it is."

[16]The same vision was repeated three times. Then the sheet was pulled up again to heaven.

[17]Peter was very perplexed. What could the vision mean? What was he supposed to do?

Just then the men sent by Cornelius had found the house and were standing outside at the gate, [18]inquiring whether this was the place where Simon Peter lived!

[19]Meanwhile, as Peter was puzzling over the vision, the Holy Spirit said to him, "Three men have come to see you. [20]Go down and meet them and go with them. All is well, I have sent them."

[21]So Peter went down. "I'm the man you're

looking for," he said. "Now what is it you want?"

²²Then they told him about Cornelius the Roman officer, a good and godly man, well thought of by the Jews, and how an angel had instructed him to send for Peter to come and tell him what God wanted him to do.

²³So Peter invited them in and lodged them overnight.

Faith in God's Promises
⊷§ Hebrews 11:13–16 §⊷

These men of faith I have mentioned died without ever receiving all that God had promised them; but they saw it all awaiting them on ahead and were glad, for they agreed that this earth was not their real home but that they were just strangers visiting down here. ¹⁴And quite obviously when they talked like that, they were looking forward to their real home in heaven.

¹⁵If they had wanted to, they could have gone back to the good things of this world. ¹⁶But they didn't want to. They were living for heaven. And now God is not ashamed to be called their God, for he has made a heavenly city for them.

Proverbs for Today
⊷§ 26:1–2 §⊷

Honor doesn't go with fools any more than snow with summertime or rain with harvest time! □ An undeserved curse has no effect. Its intended victim will be no more harmed by it than by a sparrow or swallow flitting through the sky.

⊷ KEY VERSE ⊷

Sarah, too, had faith, and because of this she was able to become a mother in spite of her old age, for she realized that God, who gave her his promise, would certainly do what he said. And so a whole nation came from Abraham, who was too old to have even one child—a nation with so many millions of people that, like the stars of the sky and the sand on the ocean shores, there is no way to count them.—*Hebrews 11:11–12*

⊷ REFLECTION ⊷

Sarah was Abraham's wife. They were unable to have children through many years of their marriage. God promised Abraham a son, but Sarah doubted that she could become pregnant in her old age. At first she laughed, not so much from a lack of faith in what God could do as from doubt about what he could do through *her*. Eventually Sarah believed that God would do what he said he would do. What parts of your life seem to be "on hold" right now? Waiting may be a part of God's plan for you and your marriage.

⊷ MEDITATION ⊷

Heavenly Father, help us to wait patiently for you to answer our prayers. And help us to accept your answers. §⊷

OCTOBER 23

The Good News Is for Gentiles Also
⊷§ Acts 10:23b–48 §⊷

The next day Peter went with [Cornelius' men], accompanied by some other believers from Joppa.

²⁴They arrived in Caesarea the following day, and Cornelius was waiting for him, and had called together his relatives and close friends to meet Peter.

²⁵As Peter entered his home, Cornelius fell to the floor before him in worship.

²⁶But Peter said, "Stand up! I'm not a god!"

²⁷So he got up and they talked together for a while and then went in where the others were assembled.

²⁸Peter told them, "You know it is against the Jewish laws for me to come into a Gentile home like this. But God has shown me in a vision that I

should never think of anyone as inferior. ²⁹So I came as soon as I was sent for. Now tell me what you want."

³⁰Cornelius replied, "Four days ago I was praying as usual at this time of the afternoon, when suddenly a man was standing before me clothed in a radiant robe! ³¹He told me, 'Cornelius, your prayers are heard and your charities have been noticed by God! ³²Now send some men to Joppa and summon Simon Peter, who is staying in the home of Simon, a tanner, down by the shore.' ³³So I sent for you at once, and you have done well to come so soon. Now here we are, waiting before the Lord, anxious to hear what he has told you to tell us!"

³⁴Then Peter replied, "I see very clearly that the Jews are not God's only favorites! ³⁵In every nation he has those who worship him and do good deeds and are acceptable to him. ^{36,37}I'm sure you have heard about the Good News for the people of Israel—that there is peace with God through Jesus, the Messiah, who is Lord of all creation. This message has spread all through Judea, beginning with John the Baptist in Galilee. ³⁸And you no doubt know that Jesus of Nazareth was anointed by God with the Holy Spirit and with power, and he went around doing good and healing all who were possessed by demons, for God was with him.

³⁹"And we apostles are witnesses of all he did throughout Israel and in Jerusalem, where he was murdered on a cross. ^{40,41}But God brought him back to life again three days later and showed him to certain witnesses God had selected beforehand—not to the general public, but to us who ate and drank with him after he rose from the dead. ⁴²And he sent us to preach the Good News everywhere and to testify that Jesus is ordained of God to be the Judge of all—living and dead. ⁴³And all the prophets have written about him, saying that everyone who believes in him will have their sins forgiven through his name."

⁴⁴Even as Peter was saying these things, the Holy Spirit fell upon all those listening! ⁴⁵The Jews who came with Peter were amazed that the gift of the Holy Spirit would be given to Gentiles too! ^{46,47}But there could be no doubt about it, for they heard them speaking in tongues and praising God.

Peter asked, "Can anyone object to my baptizing them, now that they have received the Holy Spirit just as we did?" ⁴⁸So he did, baptizing them in the name of Jesus, the Messiah. Afterwards Cornelius begged him to stay with them for several days.

God's Testing of Abraham
◄§ Hebrews 11:17–20 §►

While God was testing him, Abraham still trusted in God and his promises, and so he offered up his son Isaac, and was ready to slay him on the altar of sacrifice; ¹⁸yes, to slay even Isaac, through whom God had promised to give Abraham a whole nation of descendants!

¹⁹He believed that if Isaac died God would bring him back to life again; and that is just about what happened, for as far as Abraham was concerned, Isaac was doomed to death, but he came back again alive! ²⁰It was by faith that Isaac knew God would give future blessings to his two sons, Jacob and Esau.

Proverbs for Today
◄§ 26:3–5 §►

Guide a horse with a whip, a donkey with a bridle, and a rebel with a rod to his back! When arguing with a rebel, don't use foolish arguments as he does, or you will become as foolish as he is! Prick his conceit with silly replies!

◄ KEY VERSE ►

The Jews who came with Peter were amazed that the gift of the Holy Spirit would be given to Gentiles too!—*Acts 10:45*

◄ REFLECTION ►

Cornelius and Peter were very different from each other. Cornelius was wealthy, a Gentile, and a military man. Peter was a Jewish fisherman turned preacher. But God's plan included both of them. In Cornelius' house that day, a new chapter in Christian history was written as a Jewish Christian leader and a Gentile Christian convert each discovered something significant about God at work in the other person. Cornelius needed Peter and his gospel to know he could be saved. Peter needed Cornelius and his salvation experience to know that Gentiles were included in God's plan. You and your spouse also need each other to understand how God works. What can you learn about God from your husband or wife?

---------- ❧ MEDITATION ❧ ----------

Heavenly Father, thank you for putting us—two very different people—together. Help us to be open to what you are teaching us through each other. ❧

OCTOBER 24

Peter Defends His Preaching to the Gentiles
❧ Acts 11:1-18 ❧

Soon the news reached the apostles and other brothers in Judea that Gentiles also were being converted! [2]But when Peter arrived back in Jerusalem, the Jewish believers argued with him.

[3]"You fellowshiped with Gentiles and even ate with them," they accused.

[4]Then Peter told them the whole story. [5]"One day in Joppa," he said, "while I was praying, I saw a vision—a huge sheet, let down by its four corners from the sky. [6]Inside the sheet were all sorts of animals, reptiles and birds [which we are not to eat]. [7]And I heard a voice say, 'Kill and eat whatever you wish.'

[8]" 'Never, Lord,' I replied. 'For I have never yet eaten anything forbidden by our Jewish laws!'

[9]"But the voice came again, 'Don't say it isn't right when God declares it is!'

[10]"This happened *three times* before the sheet and all it contained disappeared into heaven. [11]Just then three men who had come to take me with them to Caesarea arrived at the house where I was staying! [12]The Holy Spirit told me to go with them and not to worry about their being Gentiles! These six brothers here accompanied me, and we soon arrived at the home of the man who had sent the messengers. [13]He told us how an angel had appeared to him and told him to send messengers to Joppa to find Simon Peter! [14]He will tell you how you and all your household can be saved!' the angel had told him.

[15]"Well, I began telling them the Good News, but just as I was getting started with my sermon, the Holy Spirit fell on them, just as he fell on us at the beginning! [16]Then I thought of the Lord's words when he said, 'Yes, John baptized with water, but you shall be baptized with the Holy Spirit.' [17]And since it was *God* who gave these Gentiles the same gift he gave us when we believed on the Lord Jesus Christ, who was I to argue?''

[18]When the others heard this, all their objections were answered and they began praising God! "Yes," they said, "God has given to the Gentiles, too, the privilege of turning to him and receiving eternal life!"

The Faith of Jacob, Joseph, and Moses' Parents
❧ Hebrews 11:21-23 ❧

By faith Jacob, when he was old and dying, blessed each of Joseph's two sons as he stood and prayed, leaning on the top of his cane.

[22]And it was by faith that Joseph, as he neared the end of his life, confidently spoke of God bringing the people of Israel out of Egypt; and he was so sure of it that he made them promise to carry his bones with them when they left!

[23]Moses' parents had faith too. When they saw that God had given them an unusual child, they trusted that God would save him from the death the king commanded, and they hid him for three months, and were not afraid.

Proverbs for Today
❧ 26:6-8 ❧

To trust a rebel to convey a message is as foolish as cutting off your feet and drinking poison! In the mouth of a fool a proverb becomes as useless as a paralyzed leg. Honoring a rebel will backfire like a stone tied to a slingshot!

Moses' parents had faith too. When they saw that God had given them an unusual child, they trusted that God would save him from the death the king commanded, and they hid him for three months and were not afraid.—*Hebrews 11:23*

∞ REFLECTION ∞

Moses' parents trusted God for their son's life. They were not merely proud parents, they were believers who had faith that God would care for him. As a parent, have you trusted God enough to take care of your children? What about other family members? God has a plan for every person, and your important task is to pray for your children and prepare them to do the work God has planned for them to do. Faith allows us to entrust our children and our spouse to God.

∞ MEDITATION ∞

Heavenly Father, just as you had a plan for Moses, we know that you have a plan for us. Thank you for caring for us when it seems that no one else does. We commit ourselves and our relationship to you. ∞

OCTOBER 25

Barnabas and Paul Become Partners in Evangelism
∞ Acts 11:19–30 ∞

Meanwhile, the believers who fled from Jerusalem during the persecution after Stephen's death traveled as far as Phoenicia, Cyprus, and Antioch, scattering the Good News, but only to Jews. [20]However, some of the believers who went to Antioch from Cyprus and Cyrene also gave their message about the Lord Jesus to some Greeks. [21]And the Lord honored this effort so that large numbers of these Gentiles became believers.

[22]When the church at Jerusalem heard what had happened, they sent Barnabas to Antioch to help the new converts. [23]When he arrived and saw the wonderful things God was doing, he was filled with excitement and joy, and encouraged the believers to stay close to the Lord, whatever the cost. [24]Barnabas was a kindly person, full of the Holy Spirit and strong in faith. As a result large numbers of people were added to the Lord.

[25]Then Barnabas went on to Tarsus to hunt for Paul. [26]When he found him, he brought him back to Antioch; and both of them stayed there for a full year, teaching the many new converts. (It was there at Antioch that the believers were first called "Christians.")

[27]During this time some prophets came down from Jerusalem to Antioch, [28]and one of them, named Agabus, stood up in one of the meetings to predict by the Spirit that a great famine was coming upon the land of Israel. (This was fulfilled during the reign of Claudius.) [29]So the believers decided to send relief to the Christians in Judea, each giving as much as he could. [30]This they did, consigning their gifts to Barnabas and Paul to take to the elders of the church in Jerusalem.

The Faith of Moses
∞ Hebrews 11:24–29 ∞

It was by faith that Moses, when he grew up, refused to be treated as the grandson of the king, but chose to share ill-treatment with God's people instead of enjoying the fleeting pleasures of sin. [26]He thought that it was better to suffer for the promised Christ than to own all the treasures of Egypt, for he was looking forward to the great reward that God would give him. [27]And it was because he trusted God that he left the land of Egypt and wasn't afraid of the king's anger. Moses kept right on going; it seemed as though he could see God right there with him. ²⁸And it was because he believed God would save his people that he commanded them to kill a lamb as God had told them to and sprinkle the blood on the doorposts of their homes, so that God's terrible Angel of Death could not touch the oldest child in those homes, as he did among the Egyptians.

²⁹The people of Israel trusted God and went right through the Red Sea as though they were on dry ground. But when the Egyptians chasing them tried it, they all were drowned.

Proverbs for Today
◄§ 26:9–12 §►

A rebel will misapply an illustration so that its point will no more be felt than a thorn in the hand of a drunkard. □ The master may get better work from an untrained apprentice than from a skilled rebel! □ As a dog returns to his vomit, so a fool repeats his folly. □ There is one thing worse than a fool, and that is a man who is conceited.

_____ ◈ KEY VERSE ◈ _____

A rebel will misapply an illustration so that its point will no more be felt than a thorn in the hand of a drunkard.—*Proverbs 26:9*

_____ ◈ REFLECTION ◈ _____

One way to avoid learning is to refuse to see where an illustration touches your life. Instead of taking its point to heart, a rebel will apply it to his or her spouse, church, employer, or whoever he or she is rebelling against. The next time you find yourself saying, "My husband/wife should really pay attention to that," stop and ask whether there is a message in it for you.

_____ ◈ MEDITATION ◈ _____

Heavenly Father, let us hear your voice and realize that you are speaking to us and not about someone else. §►

OCTOBER 26

An Angel Rescues Peter from Prison
◄§ Acts 12:1–25 §►

About that time King Herod moved against some of the believers, ²and killed the apostle James (John's brother). ³When Herod saw how much this pleased the Jewish leaders, he arrested Peter during the Passover celebration ⁴and imprisoned him, placing him under the guard of sixteen soldiers. Herod's intention was to deliver Peter to the Jews for execution after the Passover. ⁵But earnest prayer was going up to God from the church for his safety all the time he was in prison.

⁶The night before he was to be executed, he was asleep, double-chained between two soldiers with others standing guard before the prison gate, ⁷when suddenly there was a light in the cell and an angel of the Lord stood beside Peter! The angel slapped him on the side to awaken him and said, "Quick! Get up!" And the chains fell off his wrists! ⁸Then the angel told him, "Get dressed and put on your shoes." And he did. "Now put on your coat and follow me!" the angel ordered.

⁹So Peter left the cell, following the angel. But all the time he thought it was a dream or vision, and didn't believe it was really happening. ¹⁰They passed the first and second cell blocks and came to the iron gate to the street, and this opened to them of its own accord! So they passed through and walked along together for a block, and then the angel left him.

¹¹Peter finally realized what had happened! "It's really true!" he said to himself. "The Lord has sent his angel and saved me from Herod and from what the Jews were hoping to do to me!"

¹²After a little thought he went to the home of Mary, mother of John Mark, where many were gathered for a prayer meeting.

¹³He knocked at the door in the gate, and a girl named Rhoda came to open it. ¹⁴When she recognized Peter's voice, she was so overjoyed that she ran back inside to tell everyone that Peter was standing outside in the street. ¹⁵They didn't believe her. "You're out of your mind," they said. When she insisted they decided, "It must be his angel. [They must have killed him.]"

¹⁶Meanwhile Peter continued knocking. When they finally went out and opened the door, their surprise knew no bounds. ¹⁷He motioned for them to quiet down and told them what had happened and how the Lord had brought him out of jail. "Tell James and the others what happened," he said—and left for safer quarters.

¹⁸At dawn, the jail was in great commotion. What had happened to Peter? ¹⁹When Herod sent for him and found that he wasn't there, he had the sixteen guards arrested, court-martialed and sentenced to death. Afterwards he left to live in Caesarea for a while.

²⁰While he was in Caesarea, a delegation from Tyre and Sidon arrived to see him. He was highly displeased with the people of those two cities, but the delegates made friends with Blastus, the royal secretary, and asked for peace, for their cities were economically dependent upon trade with Herod's country. ²¹An appointment with Herod was granted, and when the day arrived he put on his royal robes, sat on his throne and made a speech to them. ²²At its conclusion the people gave him a great ovation, shouting, "It is the voice of a god and not of a man!"

²³Instantly, an angel of the Lord struck Herod with a sickness so that he was filled with maggots and died—because he accepted the people's worship instead of giving the glory to God.

²⁴God's Good News was spreading rapidly and there were many new believers.

²⁵Barnabas and Paul now visited Jerusalem and, as soon as they had finished their business, returned to Antioch, taking John Mark with them.

Heroes of Faith
✙§ Hebrews 11:30–40 §✙

It was faith that brought the walls of Jericho tumbling down after the people of Israel had walked around them seven days, as God had commanded them. ³¹By faith—because she believed in God and his power—Rahab the harlot did not die with all the others in her city when they refused to obey God, for she gave a friendly welcome to the spies.

³²Well, how much more do I need to say? It would take too long to recount the stories of the faith of Gideon and Barak and Samson and Jephthah and David and Samuel and all the other prophets. ³³These people all trusted God and as a result won battles, overthrew kingdoms, ruled their people well, and received what God had promised them; they were kept from harm in a den of lions, ³⁴and in a fiery furnace. Some, through their faith, escaped death by the sword. Some were made strong again after they had been weak or sick. Others were given great power in battle; they made whole armies turn and run away. ³⁵And some women, through faith, received their loved ones back again from death. But others trusted God and were beaten to death, preferring to die rather than turn from God and be free—trusting that they would rise to a better life afterwards.

³⁶Some were laughed at and their backs cut open with whips, and others were chained in dungeons. ³⁷,³⁸Some died by stoning and some by being sawed in two; others were promised freedom if they would renounce their faith, then were killed with the sword. Some went about in skins of sheep and goats, wandering over deserts and mountains, hiding in dens and caves. They were hungry and sick and ill-treated—too good for this world. ³⁹And these men of faith, though they trusted God and won his approval, none of them received all that God had promised them; ⁴⁰for God wanted them to wait and share the even better rewards that were prepared for us.

Proverbs for Today
◆§ 26:13–16 &◆

The lazy man won't go out and work. "There might be a lion outside!" he says. He sticks to his bed like a door to its hinges! He is too tired even to lift his food from his dish to his mouth! Yet in his own opinion he is smarter than seven wise men.

◆ KEY VERSE ◆

Barnabas and Paul now visited Jerusalem and as soon as they had finished their business, returned to Antioch, taking John Mark with them.—*Acts 12:25*

◆ REFLECTION ◆

John Mark was Barnabas' nephew. His mother, Mary, often opened her home to the apostles, so John Mark would have been exposed to most of the teachers and teachings of the early church. John Mark later joined Paul and Barnabas on their first missionary journey, but for unknown reasons, left them in the middle of the trip. John Mark was criticized for abandoning the mission, but he wrote the Gospel of Mark and was later acclaimed by Paul as a vital help in the growth of the early church (2 Timothy 4:11). Although you can sometimes see the mistakes your spouse makes, remember that no one is perfect. Give each other time to grow.

◆ MEDITATION ◆

Heavenly Father, as we attempt to live for you as a Christian couple, help us realize that it is not the mistakes that we make that are so important but what we learn from the mistakes as we overcome them. &◆

OCTOBER 27

Barnabas and Paul Are Sent Out to Preach
◆§ Acts 13:1–12 &◆

Among the prophets and teachers of the church at Antioch were Barnabas and Symeon (also called "The Black Man"), Lucius (from Cyrene), Manaen (the foster-brother of King Herod), and Paul. [2]One day as these men were worshiping and fasting the Holy Spirit said, "Dedicate Barnabas and Paul for a special job I have for them." [3]So after more fasting and prayer, the men laid their hands on them—and sent them on their way.

[4]Directed by the Holy Spirit they went to Seleucia and then sailed for Cyprus. [5]There, in the town of Salamis, they went to the Jewish synagogue and preached. (John Mark went with them as their assistant.)

[6,7]Afterwards they preached from town to town across the entire island until finally they reached Paphos where they met a Jewish sorcerer, a fake prophet named Bar-Jesus. He had attached himself to the governor, Sergius Paulus, a man of considerable insight and understanding. The governor invited Barnabas and Paul to visit him, for he wanted to hear their message from God. [8]But the sorcerer, Elymas (his name in Greek), interfered and urged the governor to pay no attention to what Paul and Barnabas said, trying to keep him from trusting the Lord.

[9]Then Paul, filled with the Holy Spirit, glared angrily at the sorcerer and said, [10]"You son of the devil, full of every sort of trickery and villainy, enemy of all that is good, will you never end your opposition to the Lord? [11]And now God has laid his hand of punishment upon you, and you will be stricken awhile with blindness."

Instantly mist and darkness fell upon him, and he began wandering around begging for someone to take his hand and lead him. [12]When the governor saw what happened he believed and was astonished at the power of God's message.

Let Us Run the Race God Has Set for Us
◆§ Hebrews 12:1–4 &◆

Since we have such a huge crowd of men of faith watching us from the grandstands, let us strip off anything that slows us down or holds us back, and especially those sins that wrap themselves so tightly around our feet and trip us up; and let us run with patience the particular race that God has set before us.

²Keep your eyes on Jesus, our leader and instructor. He was willing to die a shameful death on the cross because of the joy he knew would be his afterwards; and now he sits in the place of honor by the throne of God.

³If you want to keep from becoming fainthearted and weary, think about his patience as sinful men did such terrible things to him. ⁴After all, you have never yet struggled against sin and temptation until you sweat great drops of blood.

Proverbs for Today
◄§ 26:17 §►

Yanking a dog's ears is no more foolish than interfering in an argument that isn't any of your business.

◄§ KEY VERSE §►

Since we have such a huge crowd of men of faith watching us from the grandstands, let us strip off anything that slows us down or holds us back, and especially those sins that wrap themselves so tightly around our feet and trip us up; and let us run with patience the particular race that God has set before us.—*Hebrews 12:1*

◄§ REFLECTION §►

A Christian marriage requires hard work. It requires us to give up whatever endangers our relationship with God and with our spouse, to focus on running patiently, and to struggle against sin with the power of the Holy Spirit. To maintain a Christian marriage, each person must constantly focus on his or her relationship with Jesus. We will stumble if we look away from him and at ourselves or at the circumstances surrounding us.

◄§ MEDITATION §►

Heavenly Father, help us to work hard at our marriage and to stay focused on you. §►

OCTOBER 28

A Trip to Antioch of Pisidia
◄§ Acts 13:13–23 §►

Now Paul and those with him left Paphos by ship for Turkey, landing at the port town of Perga. There John deserted them and returned to Jerusalem. ¹⁴But Barnabas and Paul went on to Antioch, a city in the province of Pisidia.

On the Sabbath they went into the synagogue for the services. ¹⁵After the usual readings from the Books of Moses and from the Prophets, those in charge of the service sent them this message: "Brothers, if you have any word of instruction for us come and give it!"

¹⁶So Paul stood, waved a greeting to them and began. "Men of Israel," he said, "and all others here who reverence God, [let me begin my remarks with a bit of history].

¹⁷"The God of this nation Israel chose our ancestors and honored them in Egypt by gloriously leading them out of their slavery. ¹⁸And he nursed them through forty years of wandering around in the wilderness. ¹⁹,²⁰Then he destroyed seven nations in Canaan, and gave Israel their land as an inheritance. Judges ruled for about 450 years, and were followed by Samuel the prophet.

²¹"Then the people begged for a king, and God gave them Saul (son of Kish), a man of the tribe of Benjamin, who reigned for forty years. ²²But God removed him and replaced him with David as king, a man about whom God said, 'David (son of Jesse) is a man after my own heart, for he will obey me.'

[23]And it is one of King David's descendants, Jesus, who is God's promised Savior of Israel!

God Disciplines All of His Children
§ Hebrews 12:5–11 §

And have you quite forgotten the encouraging words God spoke to you, his child? He said, "My son, don't be angry when the Lord punishes you. Don't be discouraged when he has to show you where you are wrong. [6]For when he punishes you, it proves that he loves you. When he whips you it proves you are really his child."

[7]Let God train you, for he is doing what any loving father does for his children. Whoever heard of a son who was never corrected? [8]If God doesn't punish you when you need it, as other fathers punish their sons, then it means that you aren't really God's son at all—that you don't really belong in his family. [9]Since we respect our fathers here on earth, though they punish us, should we not all the more cheerfully submit to God's training so that we can begin really to live?

[10]Our earthly fathers trained us for a few brief years, doing the best for us that they knew how, but God's correction is always right and for our best good, that we may share his holiness. [11]Being punished isn't enjoyable while it is happening—it hurts! But afterwards we can see the result, a quiet growth in grace and character.

Proverbs for Today
§ 26:18–19 §

A man who is caught lying to his neighbor and says, "I was just fooling," is like a madman throwing around firebrands, arrows and death!

KEY VERSE

Being punished isn't enjoyable while it is happening—it hurts! But afterwards we can see the result, a quiet growth in grace and character.—*Hebrews 12:11*

REFLECTION

We may respond to discipline in several ways: (1) we can accept it with resignation; (2) we can accept it with self-pity, thinking we really don't deserve it; (3) we can be angry and resent God for it; or (4) we can accept it gratefully as the appropriate response toward a loving Father. What is God teaching you through your marriage? What is God teaching you about your marriage? What is God teaching you about him?

MEDITATION

Heavenly Father, thank you for the opportunity to grow in grace and character, even when it hurts. §

OCTOBER 29

Paul Preaches to the Jews of Antioch
§ Acts 13:24–44 §

"But before Jesus came, John the Baptist preached the need for everyone in Israel to turn from sin to God. [25]As John was finishing his work he asked, 'Do you think I am the Messiah? No! But he is coming soon—and in comparison with him, I am utterly worthless.'

[26]"Brothers—you sons of Abraham, and also all of you Gentiles here who reverence God—this salvation is for all of us! [27]The Jews in Jerusalem and their leaders fulfilled prophecy by killing Jesus; for they didn't recognize him, or realize that he is the one the prophets had written about, though they heard the prophets' words read every Sabbath. [28]They found no just cause to execute him, but asked Pilate to have him killed anyway. [29]When they had fulfilled all the prophecies concerning his death, he was taken from the cross and placed in a tomb.

[30]"But God brought him back to life again! [31]And he was seen many times during the next few

days by the men who had accompanied him to Jerusalem from Galilee—these men have constantly testified to this in public witness.

[32,33] "And now Barnabas and I are here to bring you this Good News—that God's promise to our ancestors has come true in our own time, in that God brought Jesus back to life again. This is what the second Psalm is talking about when it says concerning Jesus, 'Today I have honored you as my Son.'

[34] "For God had promised to bring him back to life again, no more to die. This is stated in the Scripture that says, 'I will do for you the wonderful thing I promised David.' [35] In another Psalm he explained more fully, saying, 'God will not let his Holy One decay.' [36] This was not a reference to David, for after David had served his generation according to the will of God, he died and was buried, and his body decayed. [37] [No, it was a reference to another]—someone God brought back to life, whose body was not touched at all by the ravages of death.

[38] "Brothers! Listen! In this man Jesus, there is forgiveness for your sins! [39] Everyone who trusts in him is freed from all guilt and declared righteous—something the Jewish law could never do. [40] Oh, be careful! Don't let the prophets' words apply to you. For they said, [41] 'Look and perish, you despisers [of the truth], for I am doing something in your day—something that you won't believe when you hear it announced.' "

[42] As the people left the synagogue that day, they asked Paul to return and speak to them again the next week. [43] And many Jews and godly Gentiles who worshiped at the synagogue followed Paul and Barnabas down the street as the two men urged them to accept the mercies God was offering. [44] The following week almost the entire city turned out to hear them preach the Word of God.

Commands for Christian Living
Hebrews 12:12–17

So take a new grip with your tired hands, stand firm on your shaky legs, [13] and mark out a straight, smooth path for your feet so that those who follow you, though weak and lame, will not fall and hurt themselves, but become strong.

[14] Try to stay out of all quarrels and seek to live a clean and holy life, for one who is not holy will not see the Lord. [15] Look after each other so that not one of you will fail to find God's best blessings. Watch out that no bitterness takes root among you, for as it springs up it causes deep trouble, hurting many in their spiritual lives. [16] Watch out that no one becomes involved in sexual sin or becomes careless about God as Esau did: he traded his rights as the oldest son for a single meal. [17] And afterwards, when he wanted those rights back again, it was too late, even though he wept bitter tears of repentance. So remember, and be careful.

Proverbs for Today
26:20

Fire goes out for lack of fuel, and tensions disappear when gossip stops.

KEY VERSE

Fire goes out for lack of fuel, and tensions disappear when gossip stops.—*Proverbs 26:20*

REFLECTION

Talking about every little irritation only keeps the fires of anger going. Refusing to discuss them cuts the fuel line and makes the fires die out. When your mate irritates you, do you tell someone else? Try cutting off the gossip, and see if your irritation dies from lack of fuel.

MEDITATION

Heavenly Father, teach us to control what we say about each other as well as what we say to each other.

Arguments Against Paul and Barnabas
Acts 13:45–52

But when the Jewish leaders saw the crowds, they were jealous, and cursed and argued against whatever Paul said.

[46]Then Paul and Barnabas spoke out boldly and declared, "It was necessary that this Good News from God should be given first to you Jews. But since you have rejected it, and shown yourselves unworthy of eternal life—well, we will offer it to Gentiles. [47]For this is as the Lord commanded when he said, 'I have made you a light to the Gentiles, to lead them from the farthest corners of the earth to my salvation.'"

[48]When the Gentiles heard this, they were very glad and rejoiced in Paul's message; and as many as wanted eternal life, believed. [49]So God's message spread all through that region. [50]Then the Jewish leaders stirred up both the godly women and the civic leaders of the city and incited a mob against Paul and Barnabas, and ran them out of town. [51]But they shook off the dust of their feet against the town and went on to the city of Iconium. [52]And their converts were filled with joy and with the Holy Spirit.

The Earthly and Heavenly Mount Zion
Hebrews 12:18–24

You have not had to stand face to face with terror, flaming fire, gloom, darkness and a terrible storm, as the Israelites did at Mount Sinai when God gave them his laws. [19]For there was an awesome trumpet blast, and a voice with a message so terrible that the people begged God to stop speaking. [20]They staggered back under God's command that if even an animal touched the mountain it must die. [21]Moses himself was so frightened at the sight that he shook with terrible fear.

[22]But you have come right up into Mount Zion, to the city of the living God, the heavenly Jerusalem, and to the gathering of countless happy angels; [23]and to the church, composed of all those registered in heaven; and to God who is Judge of all; and to the spirits of the redeemed in heaven, already made perfect; [24]and to Jesus himself, who has brought us his wonderful new agreement; and to the sprinkled blood which graciously forgives instead of crying out for vengeance as the blood of Abel did.

Proverbs for Today
26:21–22

A quarrelsome man starts fights as easily as a match sets fire to paper. ☐ Gossip is a dainty morsel eaten with great relish.

KEY VERSE

When the Jewish leaders saw the crowds, they were jealous, and cursed and argued against whatever Paul said.—*Acts 13:45*

REFLECTION

The Jewish leaders brought theological arguments against Paul and Barnabas, but the real reason for their denunciation was jealousy (Acts 5:17). When you see your spouse succeeding where you have failed or receiving affirmation that you crave, sometimes it may be difficult to rejoice with him or her. Jealousy is our natural reaction. But how tragic when our own jealous feelings make us try to stop God's work.

MEDITATION

Heavenly Father, forgive us for any jealousy we may have toward one another. Help us build each other up so that you will be glorified.

OCTOBER 31

The Good News Is Preached at Iconium
⋇ Acts 14:1–7 ⋇

At Iconium, Paul and Barnabas went together to the synagogue and preached with such power that many—both Jews and Gentiles—believed.

²But the Jews who spurned God's message stirred up distrust among the Gentiles against Paul and Barnabas, saying all sorts of evil things about them. ³Nevertheless, they stayed there a long time, preaching boldly, and the Lord proved their message was from him by giving them power to do great miracles. ⁴But the people of the city were divided in their opinion about them. Some agreed with the Jewish leaders, and some backed the apostles.

⁵,⁶When Paul and Barnabas learned of a plot to incite a mob of Gentiles, Jews, and Jewish leaders to attack and stone them, they fled for their lives, going to the cities of Lycaonia, Lystra, Derbe, and the surrounding area, ⁷and preaching the Good News there.

Serve God with Holy Fear and Awe
⋇ Hebrews 12:25–29 ⋇

So see to it that you obey him who is speaking to you. For if the people of Israel did not escape when they refused to listen to Moses, the earthly messenger, how terrible our danger if we refuse to listen to God who speaks to us from heaven! ²⁶When he spoke from Mount Sinai his voice shook the earth, but, "Next time," he says, "I will not only shake the earth, but the heavens too." ²⁷By this he means that he will sift out everything without solid foundations, so that only unshakable things will be left.

²⁸Since we have a Kingdom nothing can destroy, let us please God by serving him with thankful hearts, and with holy fear and awe. ²⁹For our God is a consuming fire.

Proverbs for Today
⋇ 26:23 ⋇

Pretty words may hide a wicked heart, just as a pretty glaze covers a common clay pot.

⋇ KEY VERSE ⋇

Since we have a Kingdom nothing can destroy, let us please God by serving him with thankful hearts and with holy fear and awe.—*Hebrews 12:28*

⋇ REFLECTION ⋇

Many Christian couples are so consumed with the day-to-day necessities of life that serving God becomes secondary. It is important for husbands and wives to remind each other that the world will eventually crumble, and only God's Kingdom will last. Whatever happens here, our future is built on a solid foundation that cannot be destroyed. Build your home on Christ and his unchanging Word.

⋇ MEDITATION ⋇

Heavenly Father, may everyone who enters our home be reminded of God. ⋇

Paul Is Stoned in Lystra
Acts 14:8–20a

While Paul and Barnabas were at Lystra, they came upon a man with crippled feet who had been that way from birth, so he had never walked. [9]He was listening as Paul preached, and Paul noticed him and realized he had faith to be healed. [10]So Paul called to him, "Stand up!" and the man leaped to his feet and started walking!

[11]When the listening crowd saw what Paul had done, they shouted (in their local dialect, of course), "These men are gods in human bodies!" [12]They decided that Barnabas was the Greek god Jupiter, and that Paul, because he was the chief speaker, was Mercury! [13]The local priest of the Temple of Jupiter, located on the outskirts of the city, brought them cartloads of flowers and prepared to sacrifice oxen to them at the city gates before the crowds.

[14]But when Barnabas and Paul saw what was happening they ripped at their clothing in dismay and ran out among the people, shouting, [15]"Men! What are you doing? We are merely human beings like yourselves! We have come to bring you the Good News that you are invited to turn from the worship of these foolish things and to pray instead to the living God who made heaven and earth and sea and everything in them. [16]In bygone days he permitted the nations to go their own ways, [17]but he never left himself without a witness; there were always his reminders—the kind things he did such as sending you rain and good crops and giving you food and gladness."

[18]But even so, Paul and Barnabas could scarcely restrain the people from sacrificing to them!

[19]Yet only a few days later, some Jews arrived from Antioch and Iconium and turned the crowds into a murderous mob that stoned Paul and dragged him out of the city, apparently dead. [20]But as the believers stood around him, he got up and went back into the city!

Live Holy and Obedient Lives
Hebrews 13:1–9

Continue to love each other with true brotherly love. [2]Don't forget to be kind to strangers, for some who have done this have entertained angels without realizing it! [3]Don't forget about those in jail. Suffer with them as though you were there yourself. Share the sorrow of those being mistreated, for you know what they are going through.

[4]Honor your marriage and its vows, and be pure; for God will surely punish all those who are immoral or commit adultery.

[5]Stay away from the love of money; be satisfied with what you have. For God has said, "I will never, *never* fail you nor forsake you." [6]That is why we can say without any doubt or fear, "The Lord is my Helper and I am not afraid of anything that mere man can do to me."

[7]Remember your leaders who have taught you the Word of God. Think of all the good that has come from their lives, and try to trust the Lord as they do.

[8]Jesus Christ is the same yesterday, today, and forever. [9]So do not be attracted by strange, new ideas. Your spiritual strength comes as a gift from God, not from ceremonial rules about eating certain foods—a method which, by the way, hasn't helped those who have tried it!

Proverbs for Today
26:24–26

A man with hate in his heart may sound pleasant enough, but don't believe him; for he is cursing you in his heart. Though he pretends to be so kind, his hatred will finally come to light for all to see.

Honor your marriage and its vows, and be pure; for God will surely punish all those who are immoral or commit adultery.—*Hebrews 13:4*

Real love toward others produces tangible actions: (1) kindness to strangers (Hebrews 13:2); (2) sympathy for those who are in prison and those who have been mistreated (13:3); (3) respect for one's marriage vows (13:4); and (4) satisfaction with what one has (13:5). Make sure your love runs deep enough to affect your hospitality, sympathy, fidelity, and contentment.

Heavenly Father, give us the love toward each other that only you can give. A real love that will easily honor our marriage vows. &8

NOVEMBER 2 _____

Paul and Barnabas Return to Antioch
&8 Acts 14:20b–28 &8

The next day Paul left with Barnabas for Derbe. [21]After preaching the Good News there and making many disciples, they returned again to Lystra, Iconium and Antioch, [22]where they helped the believers to grow in love for God and each other. They encouraged them to continue in the faith in spite of all the persecution, reminding them that they must enter into the Kingdom of God through many tribulations. [23]Paul and Barnabas also appointed elders in every church and prayed for them with fasting, turning them over to the care of the Lord in whom they trusted.

[24]Then they traveled back through Pisidia to Pamphylia, [25]preached again in Perga, and went on to Attalia.

[26]Finally they returned by ship to Antioch, where their journey had begun, and where they had been committed to God for the work now completed. [27]Upon apprival they called together the believers and reported on their trip, telling how God had opened the door of faith to the Gentiles too. [28]And they stayed there with the believers at Antioch for a long while.

Let Us Suffer with Christ
&8 Hebrews 13:10–16 &8

We have an altar—the cross where Christ was sacrificed—where those who continue to seek salvation by obeying Jewish laws can never be helped. [11]Under the system of Jewish laws the high priest brought the blood of the slain animals into the sanctuary as a sacrifice for sin, and then the bodies of the animals were burned outside the city. [12]That is why Jesus suffered and died outside the city, where his blood washed our sins away.

[13]So let us go out to him beyond the city walls [that is, outside the interests of this world, being willing to be despised] to suffer with him there, bearing his shame. [14]For this world is not our home; we are looking forward to our everlasting home in heaven.

[15]With Jesus' help we will continually offer our sacrifice of praise to God by telling others of the glory of his name. [16]Don't forget to do good and to share what you have with those in need, for such sacrifices are very pleasing to him.

Proverbs for Today
&8 26:27 &8

The man who sets a trap for others will get caught in it himself. Roll a boulder down on someone, and it will roll back and crush you.

This world is not our home; we are looking forward to our everlasting home in heaven.—*Hebrews 13:14*

REFLECTION

It can be easy to make your marriage and home the primary focus of your life. But we should not be attached to this world because all that we are and have here is temporary. Only our relationship with God and our service to him will last. Be a help to your spouse in helping him/her focus on the ultimate goal in life—living with God forever in heaven.

MEDITATION

Heavenly Father, thank you for giving us this earthly home to help prepare us for our heavenly home.

NOVEMBER 3

The Jerusalem Church Council
Acts 15:1–21

While Paul and Barnabas were at Antioch, some men from Judea arrived and began to teach the believers that unless they adhered to the ancient Jewish custom of circumcision, they could not be saved. [2]Paul and Barnabas argued and discussed this with them at length, and finally the believers sent them to Jerusalem, accompanied by some local men, to talk to the apostles and elders there about this question. [3]After the entire congregation had escorted them out of the city the delegates went on to Jerusalem, stopping along the way in the cities of Phoenicia and Samaria to visit the believers, telling them—much to everyone's joy—that the Gentiles, too, were being converted.

[4]Arriving in Jerusalem, they met with the church leaders—all the apostles and elders were present—and Paul and Barnabas reported on what God had been doing through their ministry. [5]But then some of the men who had been Pharisees before their conversion stood to their feet and declared that all Gentile converts must be circumcised and required to follow all the Jewish customs and ceremonies.

[6]So the apostles and church elders set a further meeting to decide this question.

[7]At the meeting, after long discussion, Peter stood and addressed them as follows: "Brothers, you all know that God chose me from among you long ago to preach the Good News to the Gentiles, so that they also could believe. [8]God, who knows men's hearts, confirmed the fact that he accepts Gentiles by giving them the Holy Spirit, just as he gave him to us. [9]He made no distinction between them and us, for he cleansed their lives through faith, just as he did ours. [10]And now are you going to correct God by burdening the Gentiles with a yoke that neither we nor our fathers were able to bear? [11]Don't you believe that all are saved the same way, by the free gift of the Lord Jesus?"

[12]There was no further discussion, and everyone now listened as Barnabas and Paul told about the miracles God had done through them among the Gentiles.

[13]When they had finished, James took the floor. "Brothers," he said, "listen to me. [14]Peter has told you about the time God first visited the Gentiles to take from them a people to bring honor to his name. [15]And this fact of Gentile conversion agrees with what the prophets predicted. For instance, listen to this passage from the prophet Amos:

[16]'Afterwards' [says the Lord], 'I will return and renew the broken contract with David, [17]so that Gentiles, too, will find the Lord—all those marked with my name.'
[18]That is what the Lord says, who reveals his plans made from the beginning.

[19]"And so my judgment is that we should not insist that the Gentiles who turn to God must obey our Jewish laws, [20]except that we should write to them to refrain from eating meat sacrificed to idols, from all fornication, and also from eating unbled meat of strangled animals. [21]For these things have been preached against in Jewish synagogues in every city on every Sabbath for many generations."

Final Commands and a Benediction
◄§ Hebrews 13:17–25 §►

Obey your spiritual leaders and be willing to do what they say. For their work is to watch over your souls, and God will judge them on how well they do this. Give them reason to report joyfully about you to the Lord and not with sorrow, for then you will suffer for it too.

¹⁸Pray for us, for our conscience is clear and we want to keep it that way. ¹⁹I especially need your prayers right now so that I can come back to you sooner.

²⁰,²¹And now may the God of peace, who brought again from the dead our Lord Jesus, equip you with all you need for doing his will. May he who became the great Shepherd of the sheep by an everlasting agreement between God and you, signed with his blood, produce in you through the power of Christ all that is pleasing to him. To him be glory forever and ever. Amen.

²²Brethren, please listen patiently to what I have said in this letter, for it is a short one. ²³I want you to know that Brother Timothy is now out of jail; if he comes here soon, I will come with him to see you. ²⁴,²⁵Give my greetings to all your leaders and to the other believers there. The Christians from Italy who are here with me send you their love. God's grace be with you all.

Good-bye.

Proverbs for Today
◄§ 26:28 §►

Flattery is a form of hatred and wounds cruelly.

◄§ KEY VERSE §►

Pray for us, for our conscience is clear and we want to keep it that way. I especially need your prayers right now so that I can come back to you sooner. —*Hebrews 13:18–19*

◄§ REFLECTION §►

The writer of Hebrews recognized the need for prayer. Christian leaders are especially vulnerable to criticism from others, pride if they succeed, depression if they fail, and Satan's constant efforts to nullify their work for God. They desperately need our prayers. Pray for your spiritual leaders daily. It will uplift them and encourage them in their faith.

◄§ MEDITATION §►

Heavenly Father, be with my pastor, spouse, and other spiritual leaders. Help them to be sensitive to your leading and to do your will. §►

NOVEMBER 4

A Letter to Gentile Believers
◄§ Acts 15:22–41 §►

Then the apostles and elders and the whole congregation voted to send delegates to Antioch with Paul and Barnabas, to report on this decision. The men chosen were two of the church leaders—Judas (also called Barsabbas) and Silas.

²³This is the letter they took along with them:

"From: The apostles, elders and brothers at Jerusalem.

"To: The Gentile brothers in Antioch, Syria and Cilicia. Greetings!

²⁴"We understand that some believers from here have upset you and questioned your salvation, but they had no such instructions from us. ²⁵So it seemed wise to us, having unanimously agreed on our decision, to send to you these two official representatives, along with our beloved Barnabas and Paul. ²⁶These men—Judas and Silas, who have risked their lives for the sake of our Lord Jesus Christ—will confirm orally what we have decided concerning your question.

²⁷,²⁸,²⁹"For it seemed good to the Holy Spirit and to us to lay no greater burden of Jewish laws on you than to abstain from eating food offered to idols

and from unbled meat of strangled animals, and, of course, from fornication. If you do this, it is enough. Farewell."

³⁰The four messengers went at once to Antioch, where they called a general meeting of the Christians and gave them the letter. ³¹And there was great joy throughout the church that day as they read it.

³²Then Judas and Silas, both being gifted speakers, preached long sermons to the believers, strengthening their faith. ³³They stayed several days, and then Judas and Silas returned to Jerusalem taking greetings and appreciation to those who had sent them. ³⁴,³⁵Paul and Barnabas stayed on at Antioch to assist several others who were preaching and teaching there.

³⁶Several days later Paul suggested to Barnabas that they return again to Turkey, and visit each city where they had preached before, to see how the new converts were getting along. ³⁷Barnabas agreed, and wanted to take along John Mark. ³⁸But Paul didn't like that idea at all, since John had deserted them in Pamphylia. ³⁹Their disagreement over this was so sharp that they separated. Barnabas took Mark with him and sailed for Cyprus, ⁴⁰,⁴¹while Paul chose Silas and, with the blessing of the believers, left for Syria and Cilicia, to encourage the churches there.

Trials Build Character
§ James 1:1–4 &

From: James, a servant of God and of the Lord Jesus Christ.

To: Jewish Christians scattered everywhere. Greetings!

²Dear brothers, is your life full of difficulties and temptations? Then be happy, ³for when the way is rough, your patience has a chance to grow. ⁴So let it grow, and don't try to squirm out of your problems. For when your patience is finally in full bloom, then you will be ready for anything, strong in character, full and complete.

Proverbs for Today
§ 27:1–2 &

Don't brag about your plans for tomorrow—wait and see what happens. □ Don't praise yourself; let others do it!

_____ ◈ KEY VERSE ◈ _____

Dear brothers, is your life full of difficulties and temptations? Then be happy, for when the way is rough, your patience has a chance to grow.—*James 1:2–3*

_____ ◈ REFLECTION ◈ _____

A couple can't really know the depth of their marriage relationship until they respond to pressure. It is easy to be kind and loving when everything is going well, but can they still be loving when circumstances seem unfair? Instead of complaining about struggles, couples should see them as an opportunity for growth. Thank God for promising to be with you in the rough times. Ask him to help you solve your problems or to give you the strength to endure them.

_____ ◈ MEDITATION ◈ _____

Heavenly Father, thank you for always being with us. Help us to solve our problems or make us strong enough to endure them. &

NOVEMBER 5

A Second Missionary Journey
⊰ Acts 16:1–10 ⊱

Paul and Silas went first to Derbe and then on to Lystra where they met Timothy, a believer whose mother was a Christian Jewess but his father a Greek. ²Timothy was well thought of by the brothers in Lystra and Iconium, ³so Paul asked him to join them on their journey. In deference to the Jews of the area, he circumcised Timothy before they left, for everyone knew that his father was a Greek [and hadn't permitted this before]. ⁴Then they went from city to city, making known the decision concerning the Gentiles, as decided by the apostles and elders in Jerusalem. ⁵So the church grew daily in faith and numbers.

⁶Next they traveled through Phrygia and Galatia, because the Holy Spirit had told them not to go into the Turkish province of Ausia at that time. ⁷Then going along the borders of Mysia they headed north for the province of Bithynia, but again the Spirit of Jesus said no. ⁸So instead they went on through Mysia province to the city of Troas.

⁹That night Paul had a vision. In his dream he saw a man over in Macedonia, Greece, pleading with him, "Come over here and help us." ¹⁰Well, that settled it. We would go to Macedonia, for we could only conclude that God was sending us to preach the Good News there.

God Supplies Wisdom to Those Who Ask
⊰ James 1:5–8 ⊱

If you want to know what God wants you to do, ask him, and he will gladly tell you, for he is always ready to give a bountiful supply of wisdom to all who ask him; he will not resent it. ⁶But when you ask him, be sure that you really expect him to tell you, for a doubtful mind will be as unsettled as a wave of the sea that is driven and tossed by the wind; ⁷,⁸and every decision you then make will be uncertain, as you turn first this way, and then that. If you don't ask with faith, don't expect the Lord to give you any solid answer.

Proverbs for Today
⊰ 27:3 ⊱

A rebel's frustrations are heavier than sand and rocks.

⊰ KEY VERSE ⊱

When you ask him, be sure that you really expect him to tell you, for a doubtful mind will be as unsettled as a wave of the sea that is driven and tossed by the wind; and every decision you then make will be uncertain, as you turn first this way and then that. If you don't ask with faith, don't expect the Lord to give you any solid answer.—*James 1:6–8*

⊰ REFLECTION ⊱

Do you and your spouse find it difficult to make important decisions? At those times, do you lose sleep or patience more easily with each other? If you have ever seen the constant rolling of huge waves at sea, you know how restless they are—subject to the forces of wind, gravity, and tide. Doubt leaves one as unsettled as the restless waves, tossed to and fro. If you want to stop being tossed about, believe that God knows what is best for you. Ask him for wisdom, and trust that he will give it to you. Then your decisions will be sure and solid.

⊰ MEDITATION ⊱

Heavenly Father, erase our doubts and help us trust fully in you and your plan for our lives. ⊱

Lydia Is Converted
Acts 16:11–15

We [Luke, Paul, and his companions] went aboard a boat at Troas, and sailed straight across to Samothrace, and the next day on to Neapolis, [12]and finally reached Philippi, a Roman colony just inside the Macedonian border, and stayed there several days.

[13]On the Sabbath, we went a little way outside the city to a river bank where we understood some people met for prayer; and we taught the Scriptures to some women who came. [14]One of them was Lydia, a saleswoman from Thyatira, a merchant of purple cloth. She was already a worshiper of God and, as she listened to us, the Lord opened her heart and she accepted all that Paul was saying. [15]She was baptized along with all her household and asked us to be her guests. "If you agree that I am faithful to the Lord," she said, "come and stay at my home." And she urged us until we did.

Happy Is the Person Who Endures Temptation
James 1:9–18

A Christian who doesn't amount to much in this world should be glad, for he is great in the Lord's sight. [10,11]But a rich man should be glad that his riches mean nothing to the Lord, for he will soon be gone, like a flower that has lost its beauty and fades away, withered—killed by the scorching summer sun. So it is with rich men. They will soon die and leave behind all their busy activities.

[12]Happy is the man who doesn't give in and do wrong when he is tempted, for afterwards he will get as his reward the crown of life that God has promised those who love him. [13]And remember, when someone wants to do wrong it is never God who is tempting him, for God never wants to do wrong and never tempts anyone else to do it [14]Temptation is the pull of man's own evil thoughts and wishes. [15]These evil thoughts lead to evil actions and afterwards to the death penalty from God. [16]So don't be misled, dear brothers.

[17]But whatever is good and perfect comes to us from God, the Creator of all light, and he shines forever without change or shadow. [18]And it was a happy day for him when he gave us our new lives, through the truth of his Word, and we became, as it were, the first children in his new family.

Proverbs for Today
27:4–6

Jealousy is more dangerous and cruel than anger. □ Open rebuke is better than hidden love! Wounds from a friend are better than kisses from an enemy!

KEY VERSE

On the Sabbath we went a little way outside the city to a riverbank where we understood some people met for prayer; and we taught the Scriptures to some women who came. One of them was Lydia, a saleswoman from Thyatira, a merchant of purple cloth.—*Acts 16:13–14a*

REFLECTION

After following the Holy Spirit's leading into Macedonia, Paul made his first evangelistic contact with a small group of women. Paul never allowed sexual or cultural boundaries to keep him from preaching the gospel. After preaching to these women, Lydia, an influential merchant, believed. This threw open the door for ministry in that region. In the early church God often worked in and through women. Husbands should be careful not to exclude their wives from hearing the gospel, and should support them in participating in the ministry of the church.

MEDITATION

Heavenly Father, help us joyfully spread the good news of your salvation to everyone and to support anyone, regardless of sex, who is doing the same.

NOVEMBER 7

The Conversion of the Philippian Jailer
❧§ Acts 16:16–40 ❧

One day as we [Luke, Paul, and his companions] were going down to the place of prayer beside the river, we met a demon-possessed slave girl who was a fortune-teller, and earned much money for her masters. [17]She followed along behind us shouting, "These men are servants of God and they have come to tell you how to have your sins forgiven."

[18]This went on day after day until Paul, in great distress, turned and spoke to the demon within her. "I command you in the name of Jesus Christ to come out of her," he said. And instantly it left her.

[19]Her masters' hopes of wealth were now shattered; they grabbed Paul and Silas and dragged them before the judges at the marketplace.

[20,21]"These Jews are corrupting our city," they shouted. "They are teaching the people to do things that are against the Roman laws."

[22]A mob was quickly formed against Paul and Silas, and the judges ordered them stripped and beaten with wooden whips. [23]Again and again the rods slashed down across their bared backs; and afterwards they were thrown into prison. The jailer was threatened with death if they escaped, [24]so he took no chances, but put them into the inner dungeon and clamped their feet into the stocks.

[25]Around midnight, as Paul and Silas were praying and singing hymns to the Lord—and the other prisoners were listening— [26]suddenly there was a great earthquake; the prison was shaken to its foundations, all the doors flew open—and the chains of every prisoner fell off! [27]The jailer wakened to see the prison doors wide open, and assuming the prisoners had escaped, he drew his sword to kill himself.

[28]But Paul yelled to him, "Don't do it! We are all here!"

[29]Trembling with fear, the jailer called for lights and ran to the dungeon and fell down before Paul and Silas. [30]He brought them out and begged them, "Sirs, what must I do to be saved?"

[31]They replied, "Believe on the Lord Jesus and you will be saved, and your entire household."

[32]Then they told him and all his household the Good News from the Lord. [33]That same hour he washed their stripes and he and all his family were baptized. [34]Then he brought them up into his house and set a meal before them. How he and his household rejoiced because all were now believers! [35]The next morning the judges sent police officers over to tell the jailer, "Let those men go!" [36]So the jailer told Paul they were free to leave.

[37]But Paul replied, "Oh, no they don't! They have publicly beaten us without trial and jailed us—and we are Roman citizens! So now they want us to leave secretly? Never! Let them come themselves and release us!"

[38]The police officers reported to the judges, who feared for their lives when they heard Paul and Silas were Roman citizens. [39]So they came to the jail and begged them to go, and brought them out and pled with them to leave the city. [40]Paul and Silas then returned to the home of Lydia where they met with the believers and preached to them once more before leaving town.

Become a Doer of the Word
❧§ James 1:19–27 ❧

Dear brothers, don't ever forget that it is best to listen much, speak little, and not become angry; [20]for anger doesn't make us good, as God demands that we must be.

[21]So get rid of all that is wrong in your life, both inside and outside, and humbly be glad for the wonderful message we have received, for it is able to save our souls as it takes hold of our hearts.

[22]And remember, it is a message to obey, not just to listen to. So don't fool yourselves. [23]For if a person just listens and doesn't obey, he is like a man looking at his face in a mirror; [24]as soon as he walks away, he can't see himself anymore or remember what he looks like. [25]But if anyone keeps looking steadily into God's law for free men, he will not only remember it but he will do what it says,

and God will greatly bless him in everything he does.

²⁶Anyone who says he is a Christian but doesn't control his sharp tongue is just fooling himself, and his religion isn't worth much. ²⁷The Christian who is pure and without fault, from God the Father's point of view, is the one who takes care of orphans and widows, and who remains true to the Lord—not soiled and dirtied by his contacts with the world.

Proverbs for Today
⋖ 27:7-9 ⋗

Even honey seems tasteless to a man who is full; but if he is hungry, he'll eat anything! ☐ A man who strays from home is like a bird that wanders from its nest. ☐ Friendly suggestions are as pleasant as perfume.

⋖ KEY VERSE ⋗

Dear brothers, don't ever forget that it is best to listen much, speak little, and not become angry; for anger doesn't make us good, as God demands that we must be.—*James 1:19-20*

⋖ REFLECTION ⋗

When we talk too much and listen too little, we communicate to our husband or wife that we think our ideas are more important than his or hers. God wants us to reverse that process. Put a mental stopwatch on your conversations with your spouse and keep track of how much you talk and how much you listen. In your conversations, does your spouse feel that his or her viewpoints and ideas have value?

⋖ MEDITATION ⋗

Heavenly Father, shut our mouths and open our ears so that we can love each other as we should. ⋗

NOVEMBER 8

Paul and Silas Continue Their Preaching Mission
⋖ Acts 17:1-15 ⋗

Now Paul and Silas traveled through the cities of Amphipolis and Apollonia and came to Thessalonica, where there was a Jewish synagogue. ²As was Paul's custom, he went there to preach, and for three Sabbaths in a row he opened the Scriptures to the people, ³explaining the prophecies about the sufferings of the Messiah and his coming back to life, and proving that Jesus is the Messiah. ⁴Some who listened were persuaded and became converts—including a large number of godly Greek men, and also many important women of the city.

⁵But the Jewish leaders were jealous and incited some worthless fellows from the streets to form a mob and start a riot. They attacked the home of Jason, planning to take Paul and Silas to the City Council for punishment.

⁶Not finding them there, they dragged out Jason and some of the other believers, and took them before the Council instead. "Paul and Silas have turned the rest of the world upside down, and now they are here disturbing our city," they shouted, ⁷"and Jason has let them into his home. They are all guilty of treason, for they claim another king, Jesus, instead of Caesar."

⁸,⁹The people of the city, as well as the judges, were concerned at these reports and let them go only after they had posted bail.

¹⁰That night the Christians hurried Paul and Silas to Beroea, and, as usual, they went to the synagogue to preach. ¹¹But the people of Beroea were more open minded than those in Thessalonica, and gladly listened to the message. They searched the Scriptures day by day to check up on Paul and Silas' statements to see if they were really so. ¹²As a result, many of them believed, including

several prominent Greek women and many men also.

[13]But when the Jews in Thessalonica learned that Paul was preaching in Beroea, they went over and stirred up trouble. [14]The believers acted at once, sending Paul on to the coast, while Silas and Timothy remained behind. [15]Those accompanying Paul went on with him to Athens, and then returned to Beroea with a message for Silas and Timothy to hurry and join him.

Do Not Show Favor to the Rich
◄§ James 2:1–9 §►

Dear brothers, how can you claim that you belong to the Lord Jesus Christ, the Lord of glory, if you show favoritism to rich people and look down on poor people?

[2]If a man comes into your church dressed in expensive clothes and with valuable gold rings on his fingers, and at the same moment another man comes in who is poor and dressed in threadbare clothes, [3]and you make a lot of fuss over the rich man and give him the best seat in the house and say to the poor man, "You can stand over there if you like, or else sit on the floor"—well, [4]judging a man by his wealth shows that you are guided by wrong motives.

[5]Listen to me, dear brothers: God has chosen poor people to be rich in faith, and the Kingdom of Heaven is theirs, for that is the gift God has promised to all those who love him. [6]And yet, of the two strangers, you have despised the poor man. Don't you realize that it is usually the rich men who pick on you and drag you into court? [7]And all too often they are the ones who laugh at Jesus Christ, whose noble name you bear.

[8]Yes indeed, it is good when you truly obey our Lord's command, "You must love and help your neighbors just as much as you love and take care of yourself." [9]But you are breaking this law of our Lord's when you favor the rich and fawn over them; it is sin.

Proverbs for Today
◄§ 27:10 §►

Never abandon a friend—either yours or your father's. Then you won't need to go to a distant relative for help in your time of need.

◄ KEY VERSE ◄

Judging a man by his wealth shows that you are guided by wrong motives.—*James 2:4*

◄ REFLECTION ◄

Many couples dream of riches and financial security. Often we are even partial to rich friends and neighbors because we mistakenly assume that their wealth shows some special blessing by God. But God does not promise earthly rewards or riches, nor does he give riches only to good people; in fact, Christ calls us to be ready to suffer for him and give up everything in order to hold on to eternal life.

◄ MEDITATION ◄

Heavenly Father, may the richness of your love and mercy keep us away from the temptation to think that you will make us rich in material possessions. §►

NOVEMBER 9 _____

Paul's Sermon at the Mars Hill Forum
◄§ Acts 17:16–34 §►

While Paul was waiting for Silas and Timothy in Athens, he was deeply troubled by all the idols he saw everywhere throughout the city. [17]He went to the synagogue for discussions with the Jews and the devout Gentiles, and spoke daily in the public square to all who happened to be there.

[18]He also had an encounter with some of the Epicurean and Stoic philosophers. Their reaction,

when he told them about Jesus and his resurrection, was, "He's a dreamer," or, "He's pushing some foreign religion."

¹⁹But they invited him to the forum at Mars Hill. "Come and tell us more about this new religion," they said, ²⁰"for you are saying some rather startling things and we want to hear more." ²¹(I should explain that all the Athenians as well as the foreigners in Athens seemed to spend all their time discussing the latest new ideas!)

²²So Paul, standing before them at the Mars Hill forum, addressed them as follows:

"Men of Athens, I notice that you are very religious, ²³for as I was out walking I saw your many altars, and one of them had this inscription on it— 'To the Unknown God.' You have been worshiping him without knowing who he is, and now I wish to tell you about him.

²⁴"He made the world and everything in it, and since he is Lord of heaven and earth, he doesn't live in man-made temples; ²⁵and human hands can't minister to his needs—for he has no needs! He himself gives life and breath to everything, and satisfies every need there is. ²⁶He created all the people of the world from one man, Adam, and scattered the nations across the face of the earth. He decided beforehand which should rise and fall, and when. He determined their boundaries.

²⁷"His purpose in all of this is that they should seek after God, and perhaps feel their way toward him and find him—though he is not far from any one of us. ²⁸For in him we live and move and are! As one of your own poets says it, 'We are the sons of God.' ²⁹If this is true, we shouldn't think of God as an idol made by men from gold or silver or chipped from stone. ³⁰God tolerated man's past ignorance about these things, but now he commands everyone to put away idols and worship only him. ³¹For he has set a day for justly judging the world by the man he has appointed, and has pointed him out by bringing him back to life again."

³²When they heard Paul speak of the resurrection of a person who had been dead, some laughed, but others said, "We want to hear more about this later." ³³That ended Paul's discussion with them, ³⁴but a few joined him and became believers. Among them was Dionysius, a member of the City Council, and a woman named Damaris, and others.

Breaking One Commandment Violates the Whole Law
✑ James 2:10–13 ✑

And the person who keeps every law of God, but makes one little slip, is just as guilty as the person who has broken every law there is. ¹¹For the God who said you must not marry a woman who already has a husband, also said you must not murder, so even though you have not broken the marriage laws by committing adultery, but have murdered someone, you have entirely broken God's laws and stand utterly guilty before him.

¹²You will be judged on whether or not you are doing what Christ wants you to. So watch what you do and what you think; ¹³for there will be no mercy to those who have shown no mercy. But if you have been merciful, then God's mercy toward you will win out over his judgment against you.

Proverbs for Today
✑ 27:11 ✑

My son, how happy I will be if you turn out to be sensible! It will be a public honor to me.

✑ KEY VERSE ✑

You will be judged on whether or not you are doing what Christ wants you to. So watch what you do and what you think; for there will be no mercy to those who have shown no mercy. But if you have been merciful, then God's mercy toward you will win out over his judgment against you. —*James 2:12-13*

✑ REFLECTION ✑

Our sins are forgiven by God's mercy alone. We can't earn forgiveness by forgiving others. But when we withhold forgiveness from others after having received it ourselves, we show that we don't understand or appreciate God's mercy toward us. Do you need to forgive your spouse for something that was said or done to you? Do not withhold your forgiveness.

❧ MEDITATION ❧

Heavenly Father, help me to forgive others as you have forgiven me. ❧

NOVEMBER 10

Paul Meets Priscilla and Aquila
❧ Acts 18:1–8 ❧

Then Paul left Athens and went to Corinth. 2,3There he became acquainted with a Jew named Aquila, born in Pontus, who had recently arrived from Italy with his wife, Priscilla. They had been expelled from Italy as a result of Claudius Caesar's order to deport all Jews from Rome. Paul lived and worked with them, for they were tentmakers just as he was.

4Each Sabbath found Paul at the synagogue, trying to convince the Jews and Greeks alike. 5And after the arrival of Silas and Timothy from Macedonia, Paul spent his full time preaching and testifying to the Jews that Jesus is the Messiah. 6But when the Jews opposed him and blasphemed, hurling abuse at Jesus, Paul shook off the dust from his robe and said, "Your blood be upon your own heads—I am innocent—from now on I will preach to the Gentiles."

7After that he stayed with Titus Justus, a Gentile who worshiped God and lived next door to the synagogue. 8However, Crispus, the leader of the synagogue, and all his household believed in the Lord and were baptized—as were many others in Corinth.

Genuine Faith Produces Good Works
❧ James 2:14–26 ❧

Dear brothers, what's the use of saying that you have faith and are Christians if you aren't proving it by helping others? Will *that* kind of faith save anyone? 15If you have a friend who is in need of food and clothing, 16and you say to him, "Well, goodbye and God bless you; stay warm and eat hearty," and then don't give him clothes or food, what good does that do?

17So you see, it isn't enough just to have faith. You must also do good to prove that you have it. Faith that doesn't show itself by good works is no faith at all—it is dead and useless.

18But someone may well argue, "You say the way to God is by faith alone, plus nothing; well, I say that good works are important too, for without good works you can't prove whether you have faith or not; but anyone can see that I have faith by the way I act."

19Are there still some among you who hold that "only believing" is enough? Believing in one God? Well, remember that the demons believe this too—so strongly that they tremble in terror! 20Fool! When will you ever learn that "believing" is useless without *doing* what God wants you to? Faith that does not result in good deeds is not real faith.

21Don't you remember that even our father Abraham was declared good because of what he *did,* when he was willing to obey God, even if it meant offering his son Isaac to die on the altar? 22You see, he was trusting God so much that he was willing to do whatever God told him to; his faith was made complete by what he did, by his actions, his good deeds. 23And so it happened just as the Scriptures say, that Abraham trusted God, and the Lord declared him good in God's sight, and he was even called "the friend of God." 24So you see, a man is saved by what he does, as well as by what he believes.

25Rahab, the prostitute, is another example of this. She was saved because of what she did when she hid those messengers and sent them safely away by a different road. ²⁶Just as the body is dead when there is no spirit in it, so faith is dead if it is not the kind that results in good deeds.

Proverbs for Today
⋘ 27:12 ⋙

A sensible man watches for problems ahead and prepares to meet them. The simpleton never looks, and suffers the consequences.

────────── ⋙ KEY VERSE ⋙──────────

There [Paul] became acquainted with a Jew named Aquila, born in Pontus, who had recently arrived from Italy with his wife, Priscilla. They had been expelled from Italy as a result of Claudius Caesar's order to deport all Jews from Rome. Paul lived and worked with them, for they were tentmakers just as he was.—*Acts 18:2–3*

──────────⋙ REFLECTION ⋙──────────

Some couples know how to make the most of life. They complement each other, utilize each other's strengths, and form an effective team. Their united efforts affect those around them. Aquila and Priscilla were such a couple. They are never mentioned separately in the Bible. In marriage and ministry, they were together.

Priscilla and Aquila met Paul in Corinth during his second missionary journey. They had just been expelled from Rome due to Emperor Claudius' decree against the Jews. Their home was as movable as the tents they made to support themselves, but they opened their home to Paul, and he joined them in tentmaking. Paul shared with them his wealth of spiritual wisdom.

──────────⋙ MEDITATION ⋙──────────

Heavenly Father, as we make the most of this life you have given us, help us form an effective team that will always work to glorify you. ⋙

NOVEMBER 11

Governor Gallio Releases Paul
⋘ Acts 18:9–23 ⋙

One night the Lord spoke to Paul in a vision and told him, "Don't be afraid! Speak out! Don't quit! ¹⁰For I am with you and no one can harm you. Many people here in this city belong to me." ¹¹So Paul stayed there the next year and a half, teaching the truths of God.

¹²But when Gallio became governor of Achaia, the Jews rose in concerted action against Paul and brought him before the governor for judgment. ¹³They accused Paul of "persuading men to worship God in ways that are contrary to Roman law." ¹⁴But just as Paul started to make his defense, Gallio turned to his accusers and said, "Listen, you Jews, if this were a case involving some crime, I would be obliged to listen to you, ¹⁵but since it is merely a bunch of questions of semantics and personalities and your silly Jewish laws, you take care of it. I'm

not interested and I'm not touching it." ¹⁶And he drove them out of the courtroom.

¹⁷Then the mob grabbed Sosthenes, the new leader of the synagogue, and beat him outside the courtroom. But Gallio couldn't have cared less.

¹⁸Paul stayed in the city several days after that and then said good-bye to the Christians and sailed for the coast of Syria, taking Priscilla and Aquila with him. At Cenchreae, Paul had his head shaved according to Jewish custom, for he had taken a vow. ¹⁹Arriving at the port of Ephesus, he left us aboard ship while he went over to the synagogue for a discussion with the Jews. ²⁰They asked him to stay for a few days, but he felt that he had no time to lose.

²¹"I must by all means be at Jerusalem for the holiday," he said. But he promised to return to Ephesus later if God permitted; and so he set sail again.

²²The next stop was at the port of Caesarea from where he visited the church [at Jerusalem] and then

sailed on to Antioch. [23]After spending some time there, he left for Turkey again, going through Galatia and Phrygia visiting all the believers, encouraging them and helping them grow in the Lord.

Controlling the Tongue
◄§ James 3:1–12 §►

Dear brothers, don't be too eager to tell others their faults, for we all make many mistakes; and when we teachers of religion, who should know better, do wrong, our punishment will be greater than it would be for others.

If anyone can control his tongue, it proves that he has perfect control over himself in every other way. [3]We can make a large horse turn around and go wherever we want by means of a small bit in his mouth. [4]And a tiny rudder makes a huge ship turn wherever the pilot wants it to go, even though the winds are strong.

[5]So also the tongue is a small thing, but what enormous damage it can do. A great forest can be set on fire by one tiny spark. [6]And the tongue is a flame of fire. It is full of wickedness, and poisons every part of the body. And the tongue is set on fire by hell itself, and can turn our whole lives into a blazing flame of destruction and disaster.

[7]Men have trained, or can train, every kind of animal or bird that lives and every kind of reptile and fish, [8]but no human being can tame the tongue. It is always ready to pour out its deadly poison. [9]Sometimes it praises our heavenly Father, and sometimes it breaks out into curses against men who are made like God. [10]And so blessing and cursing come pouring out of the same mouth. Dear brothers, surely this is not right! [11]Does a spring of water bubble out first with fresh water and then with bitter water? [12]Can you pick olives from a fig tree, or figs from a grape vine? No, and you can't draw fresh water from a salty pool.

Proverbs for Today
◄§ 27:13 §►

The world's poorest credit risk is the man who agrees to pay a stranger's debts.

◄ KEY VERSE ►

The tongue is a flame of fire. It is full of wickedness, and poisons every part of the body. And the tongue is set on fire by hell itself and can turn our whole lives into a blazing flame of destruction and disaster.—*James 3:6*

◄ REFLECTION ►

James compared the damage the tongue can do to a raging fire—the tongue's wickedness comes from hell itself. The uncontrolled tongue can do terrible damage. Satan uses the tongue to divide people and pit them against one another. Idle words are damaging because they spread destruction quickly, and no one can stop the results once they begin. A few words spoken in anger can greatly harm your marriage. Before you speak, remember that words are like fire—once said, you can't take them back, and you can neither control nor reverse the damage they can cause.

◄ MEDITATION ►

Heavenly Father, give us the power to monitor and control what we say. §►

NOVEMBER 12

Priscilla and Aquila Teach Apollos about Jesus
◄§ Acts 18:24–28 §►

As it happened, a Jew named Apollos, a wonderful Bible teacher and preacher, had just arrived in Ephesus from Alexandria in Egypt. [25,26]While he was in Egypt, someone had told him about John the Baptist and what John had said about Jesus, but that is all he knew. He had never heard the rest of the story! So he was preaching boldly and enthusiastically in the synagogue, ''The Messiah is coming! Get ready to receive him!'' Priscilla and Aquila were there and heard him—and it was a powerful sermon. Afterwards they met with him and explained what had happened to Jesus since the time of John, and all that it meant!

²⁷Apollos had been thinking about going to Greece, and the believers encouraged him in this. They wrote to their fellow-believers there, telling them to welcome him. And upon his arrival in Greece, he was greatly used of God to strengthen the church, ²⁸for he powerfully refuted all the Jewish arguments in public debate, showing by the Scriptures that Jesus is indeed the Messiah.

Heavenly Wisdom and Earthly Ambition
◄§ James 3:13–18 §►

If you are wise, live a life of steady goodness, so that only good deeds will pour forth. And if you don't brag about them, then you will be truly wise! ¹⁴And by all means don't brag about being wise and good if you are bitter and jealous and selfish; that is the worst sort of lie. ¹⁵For jealousy and selfishness are not God's kind of wisdom. Such things are earthly, unspiritual, inspired by the devil. ¹⁶For wherever there is jealousy or selfish ambition, there will be disorder and every other kind of evil.

¹⁷But the wisdom that comes from heaven is first of all pure and full of quiet gentleness. Then it is peace-loving and courteous. It allows discussion and is willing to yield to others; it is full of mercy and good deeds. It is wholehearted and straightforward and sincere. ¹⁸And those who are peacemakers will plant seeds of peace and reap a harvest of goodness.

Proverbs for Today
◄§ 27:14 §►

If you shout a pleasant greeting to a friend too early in the morning, he will count it as a curse!

─────── ◄§ KEY VERSE §► ───────

While [Apollos] was in Egypt, someone had told him about John the Baptist and what John had said about Jesus, but that is all he knew. He had never heard the rest of the story! So he was preaching boldly and enthusiastically in the synagogue, "The Messiah is coming! Get ready to receive him!" Priscilla and Aquila were there and heard him—and it was a powerful sermon. Afterwards they met with him and explained what had happened to Jesus since the time of John, and all that it meant!—*Acts 18:25–26*

─────── ◄§ REFLECTION §► ───────

Apollos had heard only what John the Baptist had said about Jesus, so his message was not the complete story. John focused on repentance from sin, the first step to faith in Christ. Apollos did not know about Jesus' life, crucifixion, and resurrection, nor did he know about the coming of the Holy Spirit. Priscilla and Aquila explained it all to him. Just as God used a married couple to teach Apollos, God can use you as a couple to minister to others.

─────── ◄§ MEDITATION §► ───────

Heavenly Father, use us, just as you used your servants Priscilla and Aquila, to be strong witnesses and to help others grow in their faith. §►

NOVEMBER 13

Paul Preaches to John the Baptist's Disciples
◄§ Acts 19:1–10 §►

While Apollos was in Corinth, Paul traveled through Turkey and arrived in Ephesus, where he found several disciples. ²"Did you receive the Holy Spirit when you believed?" he asked them.

"No," they replied, "we don't know what you mean. What is the Holy Spirit?"

³"Then what beliefs did you acknowledge at your baptism?" he asked.

And they replied, "What John the Baptist taught."

⁴Then Paul pointed out to them that John's baptism was to demonstrate a desire to turn from sin to God and that those receiving his baptism must then go on to believe in Jesus, the one John said would come later.

⁵As soon as they heard this, they were baptized in the name of the Lord Jesus. ⁶Then, when Paul laid his hands upon their heads, the Holy Spirit came on them, and they spoke in other languages and prophesied. ⁷The men involved were about twelve in number.

⁸Then Paul went to the synagogue and preached boldly each Sabbath day for three months, telling what he believed and why, and persuading many to believe in Jesus. ⁹But some rejected his message and publicly spoke against Christ, so he left, refusing to preach to them again. Pulling out the believers, he began a separate meeting at the lecture hall of Tyrannus and preached there daily. ¹⁰This went on for the next two years, so that everyone in the Turkish province of Ausia—both Jews and Greeks—heard the Lord's message.

God Strengthens the Humble and Opposes the Proud
◄§ James 4:1–6 &►

What is causing the quarrels and fights among you? Isn't it because there is a whole army of evil desires within you? ²You want what you don't have, so you kill to get it. You long for what others have, and can't afford it, so you start a fight to take it away from them. And yet the reason you don't have what you want is that you don't ask God for it. ³And even when you do ask you don't get it because your whole aim is wrong—you want only what will give *you* pleasure.

⁴You are like an unfaithful wife who loves her husband's enemies. Don't you realize that making friends with God's enemies—the evil pleasures of this world—makes you an enemy of God? I say it again, that if your aim is to enjoy the evil pleasure of the unsaved world, you cannot also be a friend of God. ⁵Or what do you think the Scripture means when it says that the Holy Spirit, whom God has placed within us, watches over us with tender jealousy? ⁶But he gives us more and more strength to stand against all such evil longings. As the Scripture says, God gives strength to the humble, but sets himself against the proud and haughty.

Proverbs for Today
◄§ 27:15–16 &►

A constant dripping on a rainy day and a cranky woman are much alike! You can no more stop her complaints than you can stop the wind or hold onto anything with oil-slick hands.

◄ KEY VERSE ◄

What is causing the quarrels and fights among you? Isn't it because there is a whole army of evil desires within you?—*James 4:1*

◄ REFLECTION ◄

Quarrels among believers can be harmful. James tells us that these quarrels result from evil desires within us—we want more possessions, more money, higher status, more recognition. We fight and aggressively grab what we want. Instead, we should ask God to help us reign in our selfish desires and trust him to give us what we really need. The cure for evil desires is humility. Pride makes us self-centered and leads us to conclude that we deserve all we can see, touch, or imagine. When you quarrel with your husband or wife, examine your motives. They may not be as pure as you would like to think they are.

◄ MEDITATION ◄

Heavenly Father, send your Holy Spirit to cleanse our relationship of petty quarrels and bickering. &►

Paul Casts Out Demons in Ephesus
⋖§ Acts 19:11–20 §⋗

And God gave Paul the power to do unusual miracles, [12]so that even when his handkerchiefs or parts of his clothing were placed upon sick people, they were healed, and any demons within them came out.

[13]A team of itinerant Jews who were traveling from town to town casting out demons planned to experiment by using the name of the Lord Jesus. The incantation they decided on was this: "I adjure you by Jesus, whom Paul preaches, to come out!" [14]Seven sons of Sceva, a Jewish priest, were doing this. [15]But when they tried it on a man possessed by a demon, the demon replied, "I know Jesus and I know Paul, but who are you?" [16]And he leaped on two of them and beat them up, so that they fled out of his house naked and badly injured.

[17]The story of what happened spread quickly all through Ephesus, to Jews and Greeks alike; and a solemn fear descended on the city, and the name of the Lord Jesus was greatly honored. [18,19]Many of the believers who had been practicing black magic confessed their deeds and brought their incantation books and charms and burned them at a public bonfire. (Someone estimated the value of the books at $10,000.) [20]This indicates how deeply the whole area was stirred by God's message.

Draw Near to God
⋖§ James 4:7–10 §⋗

So give yourselves humbly to God. Resist the devil and he will flee from you. [8]And when you draw close to God, God will draw close to you. Wash your hands, you sinners, and let your hearts be filled with God alone to make them pure and true to him. [9]Let there be tears for the wrong things you have done. Let there be sorrow and sincere grief. Let there be sadness instead of laughter, and gloom instead of joy. [10]Then when you realize your worthlessness before the Lord, he will lift you up, encourage and help you.

Proverbs for Today
⋖§ 27:17 §⋗

A friendly discussion is as stimulating as the sparks that fly when iron strikes iron.

⚬ KEY VERSE ⚬

A friendly discussion is as stimulating as the sparks that fly when iron strikes iron.—*Proverbs 27:17*

⚬ REFLECTION ⚬

An honest, open, and thorough discussion can help a couple see their ideas with new clarity, refine them, and shape them into brilliant insights. This requires a marriage partner who can challenge you and be challenged through discussion that will stimulate thought. The couple that brings their ideas together can help each other become sharper.

⚬ MEDITATION ⚬

Heavenly Father, thank you for a mate who challenges me through thoughtful and intelligent conversation. §⋗

A Riot Erupts at Ephesus
⋖§ Acts 19:21–41 §⋗

Afterwards, Paul felt impelled by the Holy Spirit to go across to Greece before returning to Jerusalem. "And after that," he said, "I must go on to Rome!" [22]He sent his two assistants, Timothy and Erastus, on ahead to Greece while he stayed awhile longer in Turkey.

²³But about that time, a big blowup developed in Ephesus concerning the Christians. ²⁴It began with Demetrius, a silversmith who employed many craftsmen to manufacture silver shrines of the Greek goddess Diana. ²⁵He called a meeting of his men, together with others employed in related trades, and addressed them as follows:

"Gentlemen, this business is our income. ²⁶As you know so well from what you've seen and heard, this man Paul has persuaded many, many people that handmade gods aren't gods at all. As a result, our sales volume is going down! And this trend is evident not only here in Ephesus, but throughout the entire province! ²⁷Of course, I am not only talking about the business aspects of this situation and our loss of income, but also of the possibility that the temple of the great goddess Diana will lose its influence, and that Diana—this magnificent goddess worshiped not only throughout this part of Turkey but all around the world—will be forgotten!"

²⁸At this their anger boiled and they began shouting, "Great is Diana of the Ephesians!"

²⁹A crowd began to gather and soon the city was filled with confusion. Everyone rushed to the amphitheater, dragging along Gaius and Aristarchus, Paul's traveling companions, for trial. ³⁰Paul wanted to go in, but the disciples wouldn't let him. ³¹Some of the Roman officers of the province, friends of Paul, also sent a message to him, begging him not to risk his life by entering.

³²Inside, the people were all shouting, some one thing and some another—everything was in confusion. In fact, most of them didn't even know why they were there.

³³Alexander was spotted among the crowd by some of the Jews and dragged forward. He motioned for silence and tried to speak. ³⁴But when the crowd realized he was a Jew, they started shouting again and kept it up for two hours: "Great is Diana of the Ephesians! Great is Diana of the Ephesians!"

³⁵At last the mayor was able to quiet them down enough to speak. "Men of Ephesus," he said, "everyone knows that Ephesus is the center of the religion of the great Diana, whose image fell down to us from heaven. ³⁶Since this is an indisputable fact, you shouldn't be disturbed no matter what is said, and should do nothing rash. ³⁷Yet you have brought these men here who have stolen nothing from her temple and have not defamed her. ³⁸If Demetrius and the craftsmen have a case against them, the courts are currently in session and the judges can take the case at once. Let them go through legal channels. ³⁹And if there are complaints about other matters, they can be settled at the regular City Council meetings; ⁴⁰for we are in danger of being called to account by the Roman government for today's riot, since there is no cause for it. And if Rome demands an explanation, I won't know what to say."

⁴¹Then he dismissed them, and they dispersed.

Don't Criticize One Another
◄§ James 4:11–12 §►

Don't criticize and speak evil about each other, dear brothers. If you do, you will be fighting against God's law of loving one another, declaring it is wrong. But your job is not to decide whether this law is right or wrong, but to obey it. ¹²Only he who made the law can rightly judge among us. He alone decides to save us or destroy. So what right do you have to judge or criticize others?

Proverbs for Today
◄§ 27:18–20 §►

A workman may eat from the orchard he tends; anyone should be rewarded who protects another's interests. ☐ A mirror reflects a man's face, but what he is really like is shown by the kind of friends he chooses. ☐ Ambition and death are alike in this: neither is ever satisfied.

◙ KEY VERSE ◙

A workman may eat from the orchard he tends; anyone should be rewarded who protects another's interests.—*Proverbs 27:18*

◙ REFLECTION ◙

With all the problems and concerns a leader has, it can be easy to overlook the very person who most deserves attention—your spouse. The person who stands behind you, works hard, and helps you get the job done deserves to share in your success. Be sure that in all your worrying, planning, and organizing, you don't forget the person who is helping you the most.

Paul Raises Eutychus from the Dead
❧ Acts 20:1–12 ☙

When it was all over, Paul sent for the disciples, preached a farewell message to them, said good-bye and left for Greece, [2]preaching to the believers along the way, in all the cities he passed through. [3]He was in Greece three months and was preparing to sail for Syria when he discovered a plot by the Jews against his life, so he decided to go north to Macedonia first.

[4]Several men were traveling with him, going as far as Turkey; they were Sopater of Beroea, the son of Pyrrhus; Aristarchus and Secundus, from Thessalonica; Gaius, from Derbe; and Timothy; and Tychicus and Trophimus, who were returning to their homes in Turkey, [5]and had gone on ahead and were waiting for us at Troas. [6]As soon as the Passover ceremonies ended, we boarded ship at Philippi in northern Greece and five days later arrived in Troas, Turkey, where we stayed a week.

[7]On Sunday, we gathered for a communion service, with Paul preaching. And since he was leaving the next day, he talked until midnight! [8]The upstairs room where we met was lighted with many flickering lamps; [9]and as Paul spoke on and on, a young man named Eutychus, sitting on the window sill, went fast asleep and fell three stories to his death below. [10,11,12]Paul went down and took him into his arms. "Don't worry," he said, "he's all right!" And he was! What a wave of awesome joy swept through the crowd! They all went back upstairs and ate the Lord's Supper together; then Paul preached another long sermon—so it was dawn when he finally left them!

❧ MEDITATION ☙

Heavenly Father, thank you for my spouse and all the work that he/she does to support me. ☙

NOVEMBER 16

Our Lives Are Like the Morning Fog
❧ James 4:13–17 ☙

Look here, you people who say, "Today or tomorrow we are going to such and such a town, stay there a year, and open up a profitable business." [14]How do you know what is going to happen tomorrow? For the length of your lives is as uncertain as the morning fog—now you see it; soon it is gone. [15]What you ought to say is, "If the Lord wants us to, we shall live and do this or that." [16]Otherwise you will be bragging about your own plans, and such self-confidence never pleases God.

[17]Remember, too, that knowing what is right to do and then not doing it is sin.

Proverbs for Today
❧ 27:21–22 ☙

The purity of silver and gold can be tested in a crucible, but a man is tested by his reaction to men's praise. ☐ You can't separate a rebel from his foolishness though you crush him to powder.

❧ KEY VERSE ☙

What you ought to say is, "If the Lord wants us to, we shall live and do this or that."—*James 4:15*

❧ REFLECTION ☙

It is good for a couple to have goals, but goals will disappoint you if you leave God out of them. There is no point in making plans as though God does not exist, because the future is in his hands. What would you like to be doing ten years from now? One year from now? Tomorrow? How might you react if God were to step in and rearrange your plans? Plan ahead, but hold on to your plans lightly. When you put God's desires at the center of your planning, you will not be disappointed. Sit down together and list your goals. Do these goals include God?

───── ✍ **MEDITATION** ✍ ─────

Heavenly Father, we dedicate every moment of our future to you. Guide us and give us wisdom and courage to do your will. ✍

NOVEMBER 17 ─────────────

Paul's Farewell Sermon to the Ephesian Elders
✍ Acts 20:13–38 ✍

Paul was going by land to Assos, and we went on ahead by ship. ¹⁴He joined us there and we sailed together to Mitylene; ¹⁵the next day we passed Chios; the next, we touched at Samos; and a day later we arrived at Miletus.

¹⁶Paul had decided against stopping at Ephesus this time, as he was hurrying to get to Jerusalem, if possible, for the celebration of Pentecost.

¹⁷But when we landed at Miletus, he sent a message to the elders of the church at Ephesus asking them to come down to the boat to meet him.

¹⁸When they arrived he told them, "You men know that from the day I set foot in Turkey until now ¹⁹I have done the Lord's work humbly—yes, and with tears—and have faced grave danger from the plots of the Jews against my life. ²⁰Yet I never shrank from telling you the truth, either publicly or in your homes. ²¹I have had one message for Jews and Gentiles alike—the necessity of turning from sin to God through faith in our Lord Jesus Christ.

²²"And now I am going to Jerusalem, drawn there irresistibly by the Holy Spirit, not knowing what awaits me, ²³except that the Holy Spirit has told me in city after city that jail and suffering lie ahead. ²⁴But life is worth nothing unless I use it for doing the work assigned me by the Lord Jesus—the work of telling others the Good News about God's mighty kindness and love.

²⁵"And now I know that none of you among whom I went about teaching the Kingdom will ever see me again. ²⁶Let me say plainly that no man's blood can be laid at my door, ²⁷for I didn't shrink from declaring all God's message to you.

²⁸"And now beware! Be sure that you feed and shepherd God's flock—his church, purchased with his blood—for the Holy Spirit is holding you responsible as overseers. ²⁹I know full well that after I leave you, false teachers, like vicious wolves, will appear among you, not sparing the flock. ³⁰Some of you yourselves will distort the truth in order to draw a following. ³¹Watch out! Remember the three years I was with you—my constant watchcare over you night and day and my many tears for you.

³²"And now I entrust you to God and his care and to his wonderful words which are able to build your faith and give you all the inheritance of those who are set apart for himself.

³³"I have never been hungry for money or fine clothing— ³⁴you know that these hands of mine worked to pay my own way and even to supply the needs of those who were with me. ³⁵And I was a constant example to you in helping the poor; for I remembered the words of the Lord Jesus, 'It is more blessed to give than to receive.'"

³⁶When he had finished speaking, he knelt and prayed with them, ³⁷and they wept aloud as they embraced him in farewell, ³⁸sorrowing most of all because he said that he would never see them again. Then they accompanied him down to the ship.

Warnings to the Rich
✍ James 5:1–6 ✍

Look here, you rich men, now is the time to cry and groan with anguished grief because of all the terrible troubles ahead of you. ²Your wealth is even now rotting away, and your fine clothes are becoming mere moth-eaten rags. ³The value of your gold and silver is dropping fast, yet it will stand as evidence against you, and eat your flesh like fire. That is what you have stored up for yourselves, to receive on that coming day of judgment. ⁴For listen! Hear the cries of the field workers whom you have cheated of their pay. Their cries have reached the ears of the Lord of Hosts.

⁵You have spent your years here on earth having fun, satisfying your every whim, and now your fat hearts are ready for the slaughter. ⁶You have condemned and killed good men who had no power to defend themselves against you.

Proverbs for Today
⁓§ 27:23–27 §⁓

Riches can disappear fast. And the king's crown doesn't stay in his family forever—so watch your business interests closely. Know the state of your flocks and your herds; then there will be lamb's wool enough for clothing, and goat's milk enough for food for all your household after the hay is harvested, and the new crop appears, and the mountain grasses are gathered in.

―――― ⁓ **KEY VERSE** ⁓ ――――

Life is worth nothing unless I use it for doing the work assigned me by the Lord Jesus—the work of telling others the Good News about God's mighty kindness and love.—*Acts 20:24*

―――― ⁓ **REFLECTION** ⁓ ――――

Many couples feel that they have failed in life unless they are getting a lot out of it: recognition, fun, money, success. But Paul thought life was worth nothing unless he used it for God's work. What he put into life was far more important than what he got out of it. Which is more important to you—what you get out of life, or what you put into it? What is most important to you in your marriage relationship—what you get from your marriage or what you put into it? What does God want you to put into your marriage?

―――― ⁓ **MEDITATION** ⁓ ――――

Heavenly Father, help us to work hard at our marriage and to do the work that you have assigned to us. ⁓

NOVEMBER 18

Paul Arrives in Jerusalem
⁓§ Acts 21:1–17 §⁓

After parting from the Ephesian elders, we [Luke, Paul, and his companions] sailed straight to Cos. The next day we reached Rhodes and then went to Patara. ²There we boarded a ship sailing for the Syrian province of Phoenicia. ³We sighted the island of Cyprus, passed it on our left and landed at the harbor of Tyre, in Syria, where the ship unloaded. ⁴We went ashore, found the local believers and stayed with them a week. These disciples warned Paul—the Holy Spirit prophesying through them—not to go on to Jerusalem. ⁵At the end of the week when we returned to the ship, the entire congregation including wives and children walked down to the beach with us where we prayed and said our farewells. ⁶Then we went aboard and they returned home.

⁷The next stop after leaving Tyre was Ptolemais where we greeted the believers, but stayed only one day. ⁸Then we went on to Caesarea and stayed at the home of Philip the Evangelist, one of the first seven deacons. ⁹He had four unmarried daughters who had the gift of prophecy.

¹⁰During our stay of several days, a man named Agabus, who also had the gift of prophecy, arrived from Judea ¹¹and visited us. He took Paul's belt, bound his own feet and hands with it and said, "The Holy Spirit declares, 'So shall the owner of this belt be bound by the Jews in Jerusalem and turned over to the Romans.'" ¹²Hearing this, all of us—the local believers and his traveling companions—begged Paul not to go on to Jerusalem.

[13]But he said, "Why all this weeping? You are breaking my heart! For I am ready not only to be jailed at Jerusalem, but also to die for the sake of the Lord Jesus." [14]When it was clear that he wouldn't be dissuaded, we gave up and said, "The will of the Lord be done."

[15]So shortly afterwards, we packed our things and left for Jerusalem. [16]Some disciples from Caesarea accompanied us, and on arrival we were guests at the home of Mnason, originally from Cyprus, one of the early believers; [17]and all the believers at Jerusalem welcomed us cordially.

Job, Our Example in Patient Suffering
◄§ James 5:7–12 §►

Now as for you, dear brothers who are waiting for the Lord's return, be patient, like a farmer who waits until the autumn for his precious harvest to ripen. [8]Yes, be patient. And take courage, for the coming of the Lord is near.

[9]Don't grumble about each other, brothers. Are you yourselves above criticism? For see! The great Judge is coming. He is almost here. [Let him do whatever criticizing must be done.]

[10]For examples of patience in suffering, look at the Lord's prophets. [11]We know how happy they are now because they stayed true to him then, even though they suffered greatly for it. Job is an example of a man who continued to trust the Lord in sorrow; from his experiences we can see how the Lord's plan finally ended in good, for he is full of tenderness and mercy.

[12]But most of all, dear brothers, do not swear either by heaven or earth or anything else; just say a simple yes or no, so that you will not sin and be condemned for it.

Proverbs for Today
◄§ 28:1 §►

The wicked flee when no one is chasing them! But the godly are bold as lions!

───── ◢ **KEY VERSE** ◣ ─────

Most of all, dear brothers, do not swear either by heaven or earth or anything else; just say a simple yes or no so that you will not sin and be condemned for it.—*James 5:12*

───── ◢ **REFLECTION** ◣ ─────

A person with a reputation for exaggeration or lying often can't get anyone to believe him or her on his or her word alone. Christians should never become like that. Always be honest so that others will believe your simple yes or no. By avoiding lies, half truths, and omissions of the truth, you will become known as a trustworthy person. Do you tell half truths or exaggerate to your spouse? Be open, honest, and truthful instead—that will build a solid marriage.

───── ◢ **MEDITATION** ◣ ─────

Heavenly Father, teach us to make a practice of telling the truth and not exaggerating or embellishing what we say. §►

NOVEMBER 19 ─────────

A Great Riot in the Jerusalem Temple
◄§ Acts 21:18–36 §►

The second day Paul took us with him to meet with James and the elders of the Jerusalem church. [19]After greetings were exchanged, Paul recounted the many things God had accomplished among the Gentiles through his work.

[20]They praised God but then said, "You know, dear brother, how many thousands of Jews have also believed, and they are all very insistent that Jewish believers must continue to follow the Jewish traditions and customs. [21]Our Jewish Christians here at Jerusalem have been told that you are against the laws of Moses, against our Jewish cus-

toms, and that you forbid the circumcision of their children. ²²Now what can be done? For they will certainly hear that you have come.

²³"We suggest this: We have four men here who are preparing to shave their heads and take some vows. ²⁴Go with them to the Temple and have your head shaved too—and pay for theirs to be shaved.

"Then everyone will know that you approve of this custom for the Hebrew Christians and that you yourself obey the Jewish laws and are in line with our thinking in these matters.

²⁵"As for the Gentile Christians, we aren't asking them to follow these Jewish customs at all—except for the ones we wrote to them about: not to eat food offered to idols, not to eat unbled meat from strangled animals, and not to commit fornication."

²⁶,²⁷So Paul agreed to their request and the next day went with the men to the Temple for the ceremony, thus publicizing his vow to offer a sacrifice seven days later with the others.

The seven days were almost ended when some Jews from Turkey saw him in the Temple and roused a mob against him. They grabbed him, ²⁸yelling, "Men of Israel! Help! Help! This is the man who preaches against our people and tells everybody to disobey the Jewish laws. He even talks against the Temple and defiles it by bringing Gentiles in!" ²⁹(For down in the city earlier that day, they had seen him with Trophimus, a Gentile from Ephesus in Turkey, and assumed that Paul had taken him into the Temple.)

³⁰The whole population of the city was electrified by these accusations and a great riot followed. Paul was dragged out of the Temple, and immediately the gates were closed behind him. ³¹As they were killing him, word reached the commander of the Roman garrison that all Jerusalem was in an uproar. ³²He quickly ordered out his soldiers and officers and ran down among the crowd. When the mob saw the troops coming, they quit beating Paul. ³³The commander arrested him and ordered him bound with double chains. Then he asked the crowd who he was and what he had done. ³⁴Some shouted one thing and some another. When he couldn't find out anything in all the uproar and confusion, he ordered Paul to be taken to the armory. ³⁵As they reached the stairs, the mob grew so violent that the soldiers lifted Paul to their shoulders to protect him, ³⁶and the crowd surged behind shouting, "Away with him, away with him!"

Prayer Offered in Earnest Faith
৵ James 5:13–20 ৵

Is anyone among you suffering? He should keep on praying about it. And those who have reason to be thankful should continually be singing praises to the Lord.

¹⁴Is anyone sick? He should call for the elders of the church and they should pray over him and pour a little oil upon him, calling on the Lord to heal him. ¹⁵And their prayer, if offered in faith, will heal him, for the Lord will make him well; and if his sickness was caused by some sin, the Lord will forgive him.

¹⁶Admit your faults to one another and pray for each other so that you may be healed. The earnest prayer of a righteous man has great power and wonderful results. ¹⁷Elijah was as completely human as we are, and yet when he prayed earnestly that no rain would fall, none fell for the next three and one half years! ¹⁸Then he prayed again, this time that it *would* rain, and down it poured and the grass turned green and the gardens began to grow again.

¹⁹Dear brothers, if anyone has slipped away from God and no longer trusts the Lord and someone helps him understand the Truth again, ²⁰that person who brings him back to God will have saved a wandering soul from death, bringing about the forgiveness of his many sins.

Sincerely,
James

Proverbs for Today
৵ 28:2 ৵

When there is moral rot within a nation, its government topples easily; but with honest, sensible leaders there is stability.

——————— ৵ KEY VERSE ৵ ———————

When there is moral rot within a nation, its government topples easily; but with honest, sensible leaders there is stability.—*Proverbs 28:2*

One person's selfishness quickly affects others. A selfish employee who steals from his company impairs its efficiency. A selfish driver who drinks before taking the wheel makes the state highways unsafe. A selfish spouse who has an adulterous affair often breaks up several families. When enough people live for themselves with little concern for how their actions affect others, the resulting moral rot can topple an entire nation. Are you part of the problem . . . or the solution?

… MEDITATION …

Heavenly Father, forgive me for being so selfish. Help me to be sensitive to the needs of my mate. ›•

NOVEMBER 20

Paul Retells His Conversion
… Acts 21:37—22:16 ›•

As Paul was about to be taken inside, he said to the commander, "May I have a word with you?"

"Do you know Greek?" the commander asked, surprised. "Aren't you that Egyptian who led a rebellion a few years ago and took **4,000** members of the Assassins with him into the desert?"

³⁹"No," Paul replied, "I am a Jew from Tarsus in Cilicia which is no small town. I request permission to talk to these people."

⁴⁰The commander agreed, so Paul stood on the stairs and motioned to the people to be quiet; soon a deep silence enveloped the crowd, and he addressed them in Hebrew as follows:

²²:¹"Brothers and fathers, listen to me as I offer my defense." ²(When they heard him speaking in Hebrew, the silence was even greater.) ³"I am a Jew," he said, "born in Tarsus, a city in Cilicia, but educated here in Jerusalem under Gamaliel, at whose feet I learned to follow our Jewish laws and customs very carefully. I became very anxious to honor God in everything I did, just as you have tried to do today. ⁴And I persecuted the Christians, hounding them to death, binding and delivering both men and women to prison. ⁵The High Priest or any member of the Council can testify that this is so. For I asked them for letters to the Jewish leaders in Damascus, with instructions to let me bring any Christians I found to Jerusalem in chains to be punished.

⁶"As I was on the road, nearing Damascus, suddenly about noon a very bright light from heaven shone around me. ⁷And I fell to the ground and heard a voice saying to me, 'Saul, Saul, why are you persecuting me?'

⁸"'Who is it speaking to me, sir?' I asked. And he replied, 'I am Jesus of Nazareth, the one you are persecuting.' ⁹The men with me saw the light but didn't understand what was said.

¹⁰"And I said, 'What shall I do, Lord?'

"And the Lord told me, 'Get up and go into Damascus, and there you will be told what awaits you in the years ahead.'

¹¹"I was blinded by the intense light, and had to be led into Damascus by my companions. ¹²There a man named Ananias, as godly a man as you could find for obeying the law, and well thought of by all the Jews of Damascus, ¹³came to me, and standing beside me said, 'Brother Saul, receive your sight!' And that very hour I could see him!

¹⁴"Then he told me, 'The God of our fathers has chosen you to know his will and to see the Messiah and hear him speak. ¹⁵You are to take his message everywhere, telling what you have seen and heard. ¹⁶And now, why delay? Go and be baptized, and be cleansed from your sins, calling on the name of the Lord.'

Trials Refine Our Faith
… 1 Peter 1:1–7 ›•

From: Peter, Jesus Christ's missionary.

To: The Jewish Christians driven out of Jerusalem and scattered throughout Pontus, Galatia, Cappadocia, Asia minor, and Bithynia.

²Dear friends, God the Father chose you long ago and knew you would become his children. And the Holy Spirit has been at work in your hearts, cleansing you with the blood of Jesus Christ and making you to please him. May God bless you richly and grant you increasing freedom from all anxiety and fear.

³All honor to God, the God and Father of our Lord Jesus Christ; for it is his boundless mercy that has given us the privilege of being born again, so that we are now members of God's own family. Now we live in the hope of eternal life because Christ rose again from the dead. ⁴And God has reserved for his children the priceless gift of eternal life; it is kept in heaven for you, pure and undefiled, beyond the reach of change and decay. ⁵And God, in his mighty power, will make sure that you get there safely to receive it, because you are trusting him. It will be yours in that coming last day for all to see. ⁶So be truly glad! There is wonderful joy ahead, even though the going is rough for a while down here.

⁷These trials are only to test your faith, to see whether or not it is strong and pure. It is being tested as fire tests gold and purifies it—and your faith is far more precious to God than mere gold; so if your faith remains strong after being tried in the test tube of fiery trials, it will bring you much praise and glory and honor on the day of his return.

Proverbs for Today
⁕§ 28:3–5 ¿◈

When a poor man oppresses those even poorer, he is like an unexpected flood sweeping away their last hope. ☐ To complain about the law is to praise wickedness. To obey the law is to fight evil. ☐ Evil men don't understand the importance of justice, but those who follow the Lord are much concerned about it.

KEY VERSE

These trials are only to test your faith, to see whether or not it is strong and pure. It is being tested as fire tests gold and purifies it—and your faith is far more precious to God than mere gold; so if your faith remains strong after being tried in the test tube of fiery trials, it will bring you much praise and glory and honor on the day of his return. —1 Peter 1:7

REFLECTION

This letter is helpful to Christian couples facing trials. Many Christians around the world are living under governments more repressive than the Roman Empire of the late first century. Christians everywhere are subject to misunderstanding, ridicule, and even harassment by unbelieving friends, employers, and family members. No couple is exempt from catastrophe, pain, illness, or death. But trials, like persecution, can teach us to draw on God's grace. Allow your trials to nudge you toward God, not drive you away from him.

MEDITATION

Heavenly Father, as you purify us through our struggles and trials, make us useful to God. ¿◈

NOVEMBER 21

Paul Is Sentenced to Be Whipped
⁕§ Acts 22:17–29 ¿◈

[Then Paul said] "One day after my return to Jerusalem, while I was praying in the Temple, I fell into a trance and saw a vision of God saying to me, 'Hurry! Leave Jerusalem, for the people here won't believe you when you give them my message.'

¹⁹" 'But Lord,' I argued, 'they certainly know that I imprisoned and beat those in every synagogue who believed on you. ²⁰And when your witness Stephen was killed, I was standing there

agreeing—keeping the coats they laid aside as they stoned him.'

²¹"But God said to me, 'Leave Jerusalem, for I will send you far away to the *Gentiles!*'"

²²The crowd listened until Paul came to that word, then with one voice they shouted, "Away with such a fellow! Kill him! He isn't fit to live!" ²³They yelled and threw their coats in the air and tossed up handfuls of dust.

²⁴So the commander brought him inside and ordered him lashed with whips to make him confess his crime. He wanted to find out why the crowd had become so furious!

²⁵As they tied Paul down to lash him, Paul said to an officer standing there, "Is it legal for you to whip a Roman citizen who hasn't even been tried?"

²⁶The officer went to the commander and asked, "What are you doing? This man is a Roman citizen!"

²⁷So the commander went over and asked Paul, "Tell me, are you a Roman citizen?"

"Yes, I certainly am."

²⁸"I am too," the commander muttered, "and it cost me plenty!"

"But I am a citizen by birth!"

²⁹The soldiers standing ready to lash him, quickly disappeared when they heard Paul was a Roman citizen, and the commander was frightened because he had ordered him bound and whipped.

The Hope of Eternal Life
⋖ 1 Peter 1:8–13 ⋗

You love him even though you have never seen him; though not seeing him, you trust him; and even now you are happy with the inexpressible joy that comes from heaven itself. ⁹And your further reward for trusting him will be the salvation of your souls.

¹⁰This salvation was something the prophets did not fully understand. Though they wrote about it, they had many questions as to what it all could mean. ¹¹They wondered what the Spirit of Christ within them was talking about, for he told them to write down the events which, since then, have

happened to Christ: his suffering, and his great glory afterwards. And they wondered when and to whom all this would happen.

¹²They were finally told that these things would not occur during their lifetime, but long years later, during yours. And now at last this Good News has been plainly announced to all of us. It was preached to us in the power of the same heaven-sent Holy Spirit who spoke to them; and it is all so strange and wonderful that even the angels in heaven would give a great deal to know more about it.

¹³So now you can look forward soberly and intelligently to more of God's kindness to you when Jesus Christ returns.

Proverbs for Today
⋖ 28:6–7 ⋗

Better to be poor and honest than rich and a cheater. □ Young men who are wise obey the law; a son who is a member of a lawless gang is a shame to his father.

───────── ⋗ **KEY VERSE** ⋖ ─────────

They wondered what the Spirit of Christ within them was talking about, for he told them to write down the events which, since then, have happened to Christ: his suffering, and his great glory afterwards. And they wondered when and to whom all this would happen.—*1 Peter 1:11*

───────── ⋗ **REFLECTION** ⋖ ─────────

The Spirit of Christ is another name for the Holy Spirit. Before Jesus left his ministry on earth to return to Heaven, he promised to send his Holy Spirit, the Comforter, to teach, help, and guide his followers (John 14:15–17; 16:7). The Holy Spirit would tell them all about Jesus and reveal his glory (John 15:26; 16:14). The Old Testament prophets, writing under the Holy Spirit's inspiration (2 Peter 1:20–21), described the coming Messiah; the New Testament apostles, through the inspiration of the same Spirit, preached about the crucified and risen Lord.

The Holy Spirit has not left the earth. He is with twentieth century Christians in the same way that he was with the first century Christians. The Holy Spirit is here to help you in all aspects of your life, including your marriage. When you pray together, ask the Holy Spirit to comfort, teach, help, and guide you through your relationship.

You will be amazed when you see him working in your lives.

—————————— ◦ ᴍᴇᴅɪᴛᴀᴛɪᴏɴ ◦ ——————————

We ask you, Holy Spirit, to comfort, guide, and teach us and to strengthen our marriage. Work in and through us as individuals and as a couple. ᔈ

NOVEMBER 22

Paul Appears before the Sanhedrin
ᔈ Acts 22:30—23:11 ᔈ

The next day the commander freed Paul from his chains and ordered the chief priests into session with the Jewish Council. He had Paul brought in before them to try to find out what the trouble was all about.

23:1Gazing intently at the Council, Paul began:

"Brothers, I have always lived before God in all good conscience!"

2Instantly Ananias the High Priest commanded those close to Paul to slap him on the mouth.

3Paul said to him, "God shall slap you, you whitewashed pigpen. What kind of judge are you to break the law yourself by ordering me struck like that?"

4Those standing near Paul said to him, "Is that the way to talk to God's High Priest?"

5"I didn't realize he was the High Priest, brothers," Paul replied, "for the Scriptures say, 'Never speak evil of any of your rulers.'"

6Then Paul thought of something! Part of the Council were Sadducees, and part were Pharisees! So he shouted, "Brothers, I am a Pharisee, as were all my ancestors! And I am being tried here today because I believe in the resurrection of the dead!"

7This divided the Council right down the middle—the Pharisees against the Sadducees— 8for the Sadducees say there is no resurrection or angels or even eternal spirit within us, but the Pharisees believe in all of these.

9So a great clamor arose. Some of the Jewish leaders jumped up to argue that Paul was all right. "We see nothing wrong with him," they shouted. "Perhaps a spirit or angel spoke to him [there on the Damascus road]."

10The shouting grew louder and louder, and the men were tugging at Paul from both sides, pulling him this way and that. Finally the commander, fearing they would tear him apart, ordered his soldiers to take him away from them by force and bring him back to the armory.

11That night the Lord stood beside Paul and said, "Don't worry, Paul; just as you have told the people about me here in Jerusalem, so you must also in Rome."

Be Holy, for God Is Holy
ᔈ 1 Peter 1:14–25 ᔈ

Obey God because you are his children; don't slip back into your old ways—doing evil because you knew no better. 15But be holy now in everything you do, just as the Lord is holy, who invited you to be his child. 16He himself has said, "You must be holy, for I am holy."

17And remember that your heavenly Father to whom you pray has no favorites when he judges. He will judge you with perfect justice for everything you do; so act in reverent fear of him from now on until you get to heaven. 18God paid a ransom to save you from the impossible road to heaven which your fathers tried to take, and the ransom he paid was not mere gold or silver, as you very well know. 19But he paid for you with the precious lifeblood of Christ, the sinless, spotless Lamb of God. 20God chose him for this purpose long before the world began, but only recently was he brought into public view, in these last days, as a blessing to you. ²¹Because of this, your trust can be in God who raised Christ from the dead and gave him great glory. Now your faith and hope can rest in him alone. ²²Now you can have real love for everyone because your souls have been cleansed from selfishness and hatred when you trusted Christ to save you; so see to it that you really do love each other warmly, with all your hearts.

²³For you have a new life. It was not passed on to you from your parents, for the life they gave you will fade away. This new one will last forever, for it comes from Christ, God's ever-living Message to men. ²⁴Yes, our natural lives will fade as grass does when it becomes all brown and dry. All our greatness is like a flower that droops and falls; ²⁵but the Word of the Lord will last forever. And his message is the Good News that was preached to you.

Proverbs for Today
❧ 28:8–10 ❧

Income from exploiting the poor will end up in the hands of someone who pities them. □ God doesn't listen to the prayers of those who flout the law. □ A curse on those who lead astray the godly.

But men who encourage the upright to do good shall be given a worthwhile reward.

❧ KEY VERSE ❧

God doesn't listen to the prayers of those who flout the law.—*Proverbs 28:9*

❧ REFLECTION ❧

God does not listen to our prayers if we intend to go back to our sin as soon as we get off our knees. If we want to forsake our sin and follow him, however, he listens—no matter how bad our sin has been. What closes God's ears is not the depth of our sin, but our secret intention to do it again. How many times have you prayed for that recurring sin in your relationship (anger, lust, jealousy, pride, selfishness) only to find that you keep returning to that same problem again and again? Maybe God isn't listening to your prayers because you really don't want to stop sinning against him.

❧ MEDITATION ❧

Heavenly Father, forgive us for our sins against you, and give us the desire not to sin. ❧

NOVEMBER 23 _____

A Plot against Paul's Life
❧ Acts 23:12–35 ❧

The next morning some forty or more of the Jews got together and bound themselves by a curse neither to eat nor drink until they had killed Paul! ¹⁴Then they went to the chief priests and elders and told them what they had done. ¹⁵"Ask the commander to bring Paul back to the Council again," they requested. "Pretend you want to ask a few more questions. We will kill him on the way."

¹⁶But Paul's nephew got wind of their plan and came to the armory and told Paul.

¹⁷Paul called one of the officers and said, "Take this boy to the commander. He has something important to tell him."

¹⁸So the officer did, explaining, "Paul, the prisoner, called me over and asked me to bring this young man to you to tell you something."

¹⁹The commander took the boy by the hand, and leading him aside asked, "What is it you want to tell me, lad?"

²⁰"Tomorrow," he told him, "the Jews are going to ask you to bring Paul before the Council again, pretending they want to get some more information. ²¹But don't do it! There are more than forty men hiding along the road ready to jump him and kill him. They have bound themselves under a

curse to neither eat nor drink till he is dead. They are out there now, expecting you to agree to their request."

²²"Don't let a soul know you told me this," the commander warned the boy as he left. ²³,²⁴Then the commander called two of his officers and ordered, "Get 200 soldiers ready to leave for Caesarea at nine o'clock tonight! Take 200 spearmen and 70 mounted cavalry. Give Paul a horse to ride and get him safely to Governor Felix."

²⁵Then he wrote this letter to the governor:

²⁶"*From:* Claudius Lysias

"*To:* His Excellency, Governor Felix.

"Greetings!

²⁷"This man was seized by the Jews and they were killing him when I sent the soldiers to rescue him, for I learned that he was a Roman citizen. ²⁸Then I took him to their Council to try to find out what he had done. ²⁹I soon discovered it was something about their Jewish beliefs, certainly nothing worthy of imprisonment or death. ³⁰But when I was informed of a plot to kill him, I decided to send him on to you and will tell his accusers to bring their charges before you."

³¹So that night, as ordered, the soldiers took Paul to Antipatris. ³²They returned to the armory the next morning, leaving him with the cavalry to take him on to Caesarea.

³³When they arrived in Caesarea, they presented Paul and the letter to the governor. ³⁴He read it and then asked Paul where he was from.

"Cilicia," Paul answered.

³⁵"I will hear your case fully when your accusers arrive," the governor told him, and ordered him kept in the prison at King Herod's palace.

We Are Living Building Stones
◄§ 1 Peter 2:1–10 §►

So get rid of your feelings of hatred. Don't just pretend to be good! Be done with dishonesty and jealousy and talking about others behind their backs. ²,³Now that you realize how kind the Lord has been to you, put away all evil, deception, envy, and fraud. Long to grow up into the fullness of your salvation; cry for this as a baby cries for his milk.

⁴Come to Christ, who is the living Foundation of Rock upon which God builds; though men have spurned him, he is very precious to God who has chosen him above all others.

⁵And now you have become living building-stones for God's use in building his house. What's more, you are his holy priests; so come to him—[you who are acceptable to him because of Jesus Christ]—and offer to God those things that please him. ⁶As the Scriptures express it, "See, I am sending Christ to be the carefully chosen, precious Cornerstone of my church, and I will never disappoint those who trust in him."

⁷Yes, he is very precious to you who believe; and to those who reject him, well—"The same Stone that was rejected by the builders has become the Cornerstone, the most honored and important part of the building." ⁸And the Scriptures also say, "He is the Stone that some will stumble over, and the Rock that will make them fall." They will stumble because they will not listen to God's Word, nor obey it, and so this punishment must follow—that they will fall.

⁹But you are not like that, for you have been chosen by God himself—you are priests of the King, you are holy and pure, you are God's very own—all this so that you may show to others how God called you out of the darkness into his wonderful light. ¹⁰Once you were less than nothing; now you are God's own. Once you knew very little of God's kindness; now your very lives have been changed by it.

Proverbs for Today
◄§ 28:11 §►

Rich men are conceited, but their real poverty is evident to the poor.

───────── ◖ KEY VERSE ◗ ─────────

Now you have become living building-stones for God's use in building his house. What's more, you are his holy priests; so come to him—[you who are acceptable to him because of Jesus Christ]—and offer to God those things that please him.—*1 Peter 2:5*

REFLECTION

Peter portrayed the church as a living temple—Christ is the foundation, and each believer is a stone. Paul portrayed the church as a body—Christ is the head, and each believer is a member (see Ephesians 4:15–16). Both pictures emphasize community. One stone is not a temple or even a wall; one body part is useless without the others. In our individualistic society, it is easy to forget our interdependence with other Christians. When God calls you to a task, remember that he is also calling your spouse and others to work with you. Together your individual efforts will be multiplied. Together look for those people and join with them to build a beautiful house for God.

MEDITATION

Heavenly Father, you are teaching us so many things about working together. If you would like for us to work with other people to build your Kingdom, bring us together with those people.

NOVEMBER 24

Accusations Against Paul
Acts 24:1–9

Five days later Ananias the High Priest arrived with some of the Jewish leaders and the lawyer Tertullus, to make their accusations against Paul. [2]When Tertullus was called forward, he laid charges against Paul in the following address to the governor:

"Your Excellency, you have given quietness and peace to us Jews and have greatly reduced the discrimination against us. [3]And for this we are very, very grateful to you. [4]But lest I bore you, kindly give me your attention for only a moment as I briefly outline our case against this man. [5]For we have found him to be a troublemaker, a man who is constantly inciting the Jews throughout the entire world to riots and rebellions against the Roman government. He is a ringleader of the sect known as the Nazarenes. [6]Moreover, he was trying to defile the Temple when we arrested him.

"We would have given him what he justly deserves, [7]but Lysias, the commander of the garrison, came and took him violently away from us, [8]demanding that he be tried by Roman law. You can find out the truth of our accusations by examining him yourself."

[9]Then all the other Jews chimed in, declaring that everything Tertullus said was true.

Live According to God's Will
1 Peter 2:11–16

Dear brothers, you are only visitors here. Since your real home is in heaven I beg you to keep away from the evil pleasures of this world; they are not for you, for they fight against your very souls.

[12]Be careful how you behave among your unsaved neighbors; for then, even if they are suspicious of you and talk against you, they will end up praising God for your good works when Christ returns.

[13]For the Lord's sake, obey every law of your government: those of the king as head of the state, [14]and those of the king's officers, for he has sent them to punish all who do wrong, and to honor those who do right.

[15]It is God's will that your good lives should silence those who foolishly condemn the Gospel without knowing what it can do for them, having never experienced its power. [16]You are free from the law, but that doesn't mean you are free to do wrong. Live as those who are free to do only God's will at all times.

Proverbs for Today
28:12–13

When the godly are successful, everyone is glad. When the wicked succeed, everyone is sad. □ A man who refuses to admit his mistakes can never be successful. But if he confesses and forsakes them, he gets another chance.

✎ KEY VERSE ✎

Be careful how you behave among your unsaved neighbors; for then, even if they are suspicious of you and talk against you, they will end up praising God for your good works when Christ returns. —*1 Peter 2:12*

✎ REFLECTION ✎

If your actions are above reproach, even hostile people will end up praising God. Peter's readers were scattered among Gentiles who were inclined to believe vicious lies about Christians. Even today, Christians, and especially Christian families, are consistently misrepresented in our society. Attractive, gracious, upright behavior on the part of Christian couples could show these rumors to be false and could even win some of the unsaved critics to the Lord's side. Don't write off people because they misunderstand Christianity; instead, show them Christ in your life. The day may come when they will praise him with you.

✎ MEDITATION ✎

Heavenly Father, as we witness to our friends and neighbors, give us the self-control that we will need to be good examples of your grace. ✎

NOVEMBER 25

Paul's Defense before Governor Felix
✎ Acts 24:10–27 ✎

Now it was Paul's turn. The governor motioned for him to rise and speak.

Paul began: "I know, sir, that you have been a judge of Jewish affairs for many years, and this gives me confidence as I make my defense. [11]You can quickly discover that it was no more than twelve days ago that I arrived in Jerusalem to worship at the Temple, [12]and you will discover that I have never incited a riot in any synagogue or on the streets of any city; [13]and these men certainly cannot prove the things they accuse me of doing.

[14]"But one thing I do confess, that I believe in the way of salvation, which they refer to as a sect; I follow that system of serving the God of our ancestors; I firmly believe in the Jewish law and everything written in the books of prophecy; [15]and I believe, just as these men do, that there will be a resurrection of both the righteous and ungodly. [16]Because of this I try with all my strength to always maintain a clear conscience before God and man.

[17]"After several years away, I returned to Jerusalem with money to aid the Jews, and to offer a sacrifice to God. [18]My accusers saw me in the Temple as I was presenting my thank offering. I had shaved my head as their laws required, and there was no crowd around me, and no rioting! But some Jews from Turkey were there [19](who ought to be here if they have anything against me)— [20]but look! Ask these men right here what wrongdoing their Council found in me, [21]except that I said one thing I shouldn't when I shouted out, 'I am here before the Council to defend myself for believing that the dead will rise again!'"

[22]Felix, who knew Christians didn't go around starting riots, told the Jews to wait for the arrival of Lysias, the garrison commander, and then he would decide the case. [23]He ordered Paul to prison but instructed the guards to treat him gently and not to forbid any of his friends from visiting him or bringing him gifts to make his stay more comfortable.

[24]A few days later Felix came with Drusilla, his legal wife, a Jewess. Sending for Paul, they listened as he told them about faith in Christ Jesus. [25]And as he reasoned with them about righteousness and self-control and the judgment to come, Felix was terrified.

"Go away for now," he replied, "and when I

have a more convenient time, I'll call for you again."

²⁶He also hoped that Paul would bribe him, so he sent for him from time to time and talked with him. ²⁷Two years went by in this way; then Felix was succeeded by Porcius Festus. And because Felix wanted to gain favor with the Jews, he left Paul in chains.

Suffering Is a Part of Our Christian Lives
◄§ 1 Peter 2:17-25 §►

Show respect for everyone. Love Christians everywhere. Fear God and honor the government. ¹⁸Servants, you must respect your masters and do whatever they tell you—not only if they are kind and reasonable, but even if they are tough and cruel. ¹⁹Praise the Lord if you are punished for doing right! ²⁰Of course, you get no credit for being patient if you are beaten for doing wrong; but if you do right and suffer for it, and are patient beneath the blows, God is well pleased.

²¹This suffering is all part of the work God has given you. Christ, who suffered for you, is your example. Follow in his steps: ²²He never sinned, never told a lie, ²³never answered back when insulted; when he suffered he did not threaten to get even; he left his case in the hands of God who always judges fairly. ²⁴He personally carried the load of our sins in his own body when he died on the cross, so that we can be finished with sin and live a good life from now on. For his wounds have healed ours! ²⁵Like sheep you wandered away from God, but now you have returned to your Shepherd, the Guardian of your souls who keeps you safe from all attacks.

Proverbs for Today
◄§ 28:14 §►

Blessed is the man who reveres God, but the man who doesn't care is headed for serious trouble.

◄§ KEY VERSE §►

As [Paul] reasoned with them about righteousness and self-control and the judgment to come, Felix was terrified. "Go away for now," he replied, "and when I have a more convenient time, I'll call for you again."—*Acts 24:25*

◄§ REFLECTION §►

Have you ever noticed that it is easy to read Scripture and to feel as though it is speaking to people other than yourself? Maybe it is because you are not applying Scripture to that part of your life where your true nature is revealed—your marriage and family relationships. Paul's talk with Felix became so personal that Felix felt uncomfortable. Felix, like Herod Antipas (Mark 6:17–18), had taken another man's wife. Paul's words were interesting until they focused on "righteousness and self-control and the judgment to come." Many people will be glad to discuss the gospel with you as long as it doesn't touch their lives too personally. When it does, some will resist or run away. But this is what the gospel is all about—God's power to change lives. The gospel is not effective until it moves from principles and doctrine into a life-changing dynamic. When someone resists or runs from your witness, you have made the gospel personal. When you find yourself running from the gospel or unhappy with something that Scripture reveals to you, God may be speaking to you on an intimate level, telling you that it is time to get right with him.

◄§ MEDITATION §►

Heavenly Father, as we read your Word, show us where we need to change. Then give us the openness to face our problems and faults and courage to make the changes you want. §►

Paul Demands a Hearing before Caesar
◄§ Acts 25:1–12 §►

Three days after Festus arrived in Caesarea to take over his new responsibilities, he left for Jerusalem, ²where the chief priests and other Jewish leaders got hold of him and gave him their story about Paul. ³They begged him to bring Paul to Jerusalem at once. (Their plan was to waylay and kill him.) ⁴But Festus replied that since Paul was at Caesarea and he himself was returning there soon, ⁵those with authority in this affair should return with him for the trial.

⁶Eight or ten days later he returned to Caesarea and the following day opened Paul's trial.

⁷On Paul's arrival in court the Jews from Jerusalem gathered around, hurling many serious accusations which they couldn't prove. ⁸Paul denied the charges: "I am not guilty," he said. "I have not opposed the Jewish laws or desecrated the Temple or rebelled against the Roman government."

⁹Then Festus, anxious to please the Jews, asked him, "Are you willing to go to Jerusalem and stand trial before me?"

¹⁰,¹¹But Paul replied, "No! I demand my privilege of a hearing before the Emperor himself. You know very well I am not guilty. If I have done something worthy of death, I don't refuse to die! But if I am innocent, neither you nor anyone else has a right to turn me over to these men to kill me. *I appeal to Caesar.*"

¹²Festus conferred with his advisors and then replied, "Very well! You have appealed to Caesar, and to Caesar you shall go!"

Instructions for Wives
◄§ 1 Peter 3:1–6 §►

Wives, fit in with your husbands' plans; for then if they refuse to listen when you talk to them about the Lord, they will be won by your respectful, pure behavior. Your godly lives will speak to them better than any words.

³Don't be concerned about the outward beauty that depends on jewelry, or beautiful clothes, or hair arrangement. ⁴Be beautiful inside, in your hearts, with the lasting charm of a gentle and quiet spirit which is so precious to God. ⁵That kind of deep beauty was seen in the saintly women of old, who trusted God and fitted in with their husbands' plans.

⁶Sarah, for instance, obeyed her husband Abraham, honoring him as head of the house. And if you do the same, you will be following in her steps like good daughters and doing what is right; then you will not need to fear [offending your husbands].

Proverbs for Today
◄§ 28:15–16 §►

A wicked ruler is as dangerous to the poor as a lion or bear attacking them. Only a stupid prince will oppress his people, but a king will have a long reign if he hates dishonesty and bribes.

◄ KEY VERSE ►

Wives, fit in with your husbands' plans; for then if they refuse to listen when you talk to them about the Lord, they will be won by your respectful, pure behavior. Your godly lives will speak to them better than any words. Don't be concerned about the outward beauty that depends on jewelry, or beautiful clothes, or hair arrangement. Be beautiful inside, in your hearts, with the lasting charm of a gentle and quiet spirit that is so precious to God. —*1 Peter 3:1–4*

◄ REFLECTION ►

In the early church, if a man became a Christian, he usually would bring his whole family into the church with him (see, for example, the story of the conversion of the Philippian jailer in Acts 16:29–33). By contrast, a woman who became a Christian usually would come into the church by herself. Under Roman law, the husband and father had absolute authority over all members of his household, including his wife. If he disapproved of her new beliefs, she could endanger her marriage by demanding her rights as a free woman in Christ. Peter reassured Christian women who were married to unbelievers that they did not have to preach to their husbands. Under the circumstances, their best approach would be loving service—showing their husbands self-giving love of Christ. By being exemplary wives, they would please their husbands. Then, at the very least, the men would allow them to continue practicing their "strange" religion. At best,

their husbands would join them and become Christians too.

A changed life speaks loudly and clearly, and it is often the most effective way to influence a family member. Live your Christian faith quietly and consistently in your home, and your family will see Christ in you.

⚜ MEDITATION ⚜

Heavenly Father, while we are so concerned with the external you are concerned with the internal. Make me a beautiful person on the inside, helping me witness to your love and care through my life. ❧

NOVEMBER 27

Festus Explains Paul's Case
§ Acts 25:13–27 ❧

A few days later King Agrippa arrived with Bernice for a visit with Festus. [14]During their stay of several days Festus discussed Paul's case with the king. "There is a prisoner here," he told him, "whose case was left for me by Felix. [15]When I was in Jerusalem, the chief priests and other Jewish leaders gave me their side of the story and asked me to have him killed. [16]Of course I quickly pointed out to them that Roman law does not convict a man before he is tried. He is given an opportunity to defend himself face to face with his accusers.

[17]"When they came here for the trial, I called the case the very next day and ordered Paul brought in. [18]But the accusations made against him weren't at all what I supposed they would be. [19]It was something about their religion, and about someone called Jesus who died, but Paul insists is alive! [20]I was perplexed as to how to decide a case of this kind and asked him whether he would be willing to stand trial on these charges in Jerusalem. [21]But Paul appealed to Caesar! So I ordered him back to jail until I could arrange to get him to the Emperor."

[22]"I'd like to hear the man myself," Agrippa said. And Festus replied, "You shall—tomorrow!"

[23]So the next day, after the king and Bernice had

arrived at the courtroom with great pomp, accompanied by military officers and prominent men of the city, Festus ordered Paul brought in.

[24]Then Festus addressed the audience: "King Agrippa and all present," he said, "this is the man whose death is demanded both by the local Jews and by those in Jerusalem! [25]But in my opinion he has done nothing worthy of death. However, he appealed his case to Caesar, and I have no alternative but to send him. [26]But what shall I write the Emperor? For there is no real charge against him! So I have brought him before you all, and especially you, King Agrippa, to examine him and then tell me what to write. [27]For it doesn't seem reasonable to send a prisoner to the Emperor without any charges against him!"

Instructions for Husbands
§ 1 Peter 3:7–9 ❧

You husbands must be careful of your wives, being thoughtful of their needs and honoring them as the weaker sex. Remember that you and your wife are partners in receiving God's blessings, and if you don't treat her as you should, your prayers will not get ready answers.

[8]And now this word to all of you: You should be like one big happy family, full of sympathy toward

each other, loving one another with tender hearts and humble minds. ⁹Don't repay evil for evil. Don't snap back at those who say unkind things about you. Instead, pray for God's help for them, for we are to be kind to others, and God will bless us for it.

Proverbs for Today
⊷§ 28:17–18 §⊶

A murderer's conscience will drive him into hell. Don't stop him! ☐ Good men will be rescued from harm, but cheaters will be destroyed.

◦ KEY VERSE ◦

You husbands must be careful of your wives, being thoughtful of their needs and honoring them as the weaker sex. Remember that you and your wife are partners in receiving God's blessings, and if you don't treat her as you should, your prayers will not get ready answers.—*1 Peter 3:7*

◦ REFLECTION ◦

When Peter called women the "weaker sex" he was not implying moral or intellectual inferiority. In-stead, he was recognizing women's physical limitations. Women in his day, if unprotected by men, were vulnerable to attack, abuse, and financial disaster. Women's lives may be easier today, but they are still vulnerable to criminal attack and family abuse. In addition, in spite of increased opportunities in the workplace, most women still earn considerably less than men, and the vast majority of the nations' poor are single mothers and their children. A man who honors his wife as a member of the weaker sex will protect, respect, help, and stay with her. He will not expect her to work full-time both outside and inside the home; he will lighten her load wherever he can. He will be sensitive to her needs, and he will relate to her with courtesy, consideration, insight, and tact.

If a man does not treat his wife kindly, his prayers will become ineffective because a living relationship with God depends on right relationships with others. If a man uses his position to mistreat his wife, his relationship with God will suffer.

◦ MEDITATION ◦

Heavenly Father, bless our marriage. Help us to serve each other in love. §⊶

NOVEMBER 28

Paul's Defense before King Agrippa
⊷§ Acts 26:1–32 §⊶

Then Agrippa said to Paul, "Go ahead. Tell us your story."

So Paul, with many gestures, presented his defense:

²"I am fortunate, King Agrippa," he began, "to be able to present my answer before you, ³for I know you are an expert on Jewish laws and customs. Now please listen patiently!

⁴"As the Jews are well aware, I was given a thorough Jewish training from my earliest childhood in Tarsus and later at Jerusalem, and I lived accordingly. ⁵If they would admit it, they know that I have always been the strictest of Pharisees when it comes to obedience to Jewish laws and customs. ⁶But the real reason behind their accusations is something else—it is because I am looking forward to the fulfillment of God's promise made to our ancestors. ⁷The twelve tribes of Israel strive night and day to attain this same hope I have! Yet, O King, for me it is a crime, they say! ⁸But is it a crime to believe in the resurrection of the dead? Does it seem incredible to you that God can bring men back to life again?

⁹"I used to believe that I ought to do many horrible things to the followers of Jesus of Nazareth. ¹⁰I imprisoned many of the saints in Jerusalem, as authorized by the High Priests; and when they

were condemned to death, I cast my vote against them. [11]I used torture to try to make Christians everywhere curse Christ. I was so violently opposed to them that I even hounded them in distant cities in foreign lands.

[12]"I was on such a mission to Damascus, armed with the authority and commission of the chief priests, [13]when one day about noon, sir, a light from heaven brighter than the sun shone down on me and my companions. [14]We all fell down, and I heard a voice speaking to me in Hebrew, 'Saul, Saul, why are you persecuting me? You are only hurting yourself.'

[15]"'Who are you, sir?' I asked.

"And the Lord replied, 'I am Jesus, the one you are persecuting. [16]Now stand up! For I have appeared to you to appoint you as my servant and my witness. You are to tell the world about this experience and about the many other occasions when I shall appear to you. [17]And I will protect you from both your own people and the Gentiles. Yes, I am going to send you to the Gentiles [18]to open their eyes to their true condition so that they may repent and live in the light of God instead of in Satan's darkness, so that they may receive forgiveness for their sins and God's inheritance along with all people everywhere whose sins are cleansed away, who are set apart by faith in me.'

[19]"And so, O King Agrippa, I was not disobedient to that vision from heaven! [20]I preached first to those in Damascus, then in Jerusalem and through Judea, and also to the Gentiles that all must forsake their sins and turn to God—and prove their repentance by doing good deeds. [21]The Jews arrested me in the Temple for preaching this, and tried to kill me, [22]but God protected me so that I am still alive today to tell these facts to everyone, both great and small. I teach nothing except what the prophets and Moses said— [23]that the Messiah would suffer, and be the First to rise from the dead, to bring light to Jews and Gentiles alike."

[24]Suddenly Festus shouted, "Paul, you are insane. Your long studying has broken your mind!"

[25]But Paul replied, "I am not insane, Most Excellent Festus. I speak words of sober truth. [26]And King Agrippa knows about these things. I speak frankly for I am sure these events are all familiar to him, for they were not done in a corner! [27]King Agrippa, do you believe the prophets? But I know you do—"

[28]Agrippa interrupted him. "With trivial proofs like these, you expect me to become a Christian?"

[29]And Paul replied, "Would to God that whether my arguments are trivial or strong, both you and everyone here in this audience might become the same as I am, except for these chains."

[30]Then the king, the governor, Bernice, and all the others stood and left. [31]As they talked it over afterwards they agreed, "This man hasn't done anything worthy of death or imprisonment."

[32]And Agrippa said to Festus, "He could be set free if he hadn't appealed to Caesar!"

Exhortations to Holy Living
§ 1 Peter 3:10–15 §

If you want a happy, good life, keep control of your tongue, and guard your lips from telling lies. [11]Turn away from evil and do good. Try to live in peace even if you must run after it to catch and hold it! [12]For the Lord is watching his children, listening to their prayers; but the Lord's face is hard against those who do evil.

[13]Usually no one will hurt you for wanting to do good. [14]But even if they should, you are to be envied, for God will reward you for it. [15]Quietly trust yourself to Christ your Lord and if anybody asks why you believe as you do, be ready to tell him, and do it in a gentle and respectful way.

Proverbs for Today
§ 28:19–20 §

Hard work brings prosperity; playing around brings poverty. The man who wants to do right will get a rich reward. But the man who wants to get rich quick will quickly fail.

KEY VERSE

Turn away from evil and do good. Try to live in peace even if you must run after it to catch and hold it!—*1 Peter 3:11*

Too often we see peace as merely the absence of conflict, and we think that a peacemaking spouse must take a passive role. But a spouse who is an effective peacemaker actively pursues peace in the home. He or she builds good relationships, knowing that peace is a by-product of commitment. He or she anticipates problems and deals with them before they occur. When conflicts arise, he or she brings them into the open and deals with them before they grow unmanageable. Sometimes making peace in a marriage can be harder work than waging war.

Heavenly Father, may we maintain peace in our home because we both are pursuing it. ❧

NOVEMBER 29

Paul Begins His Voyage to Rome
❧ Acts 27:1–15 ❧

Arrangements were finally made to start us [Luke, Paul, and his companions] on our way to Rome by ship; so Paul and several other prisoners were placed in the custody of an officer named Julius, a member of the imperial guard. ²We left on a boat which was scheduled to make several stops along the Turkish coast. I should add that Aristarchus, a Greek from Thessalonica, was with us.

³The next day when we docked at Sidon, Julius was very kind to Paul and let him go ashore to visit with friends and receive their hospitality. ⁴Putting to sea from there, we encountered headwinds that made it difficult to keep the ship on course, so we sailed north of Cyprus between the island and the mainland, ⁵and passed along the coast of the provinces of Cilicia and Pamphylia, landing at Myra, in the province of Lycia. ⁶There our officer found an Egyptian ship from Alexandria, bound for Italy, and put us aboard.

⁷,⁸We had several days of rough sailing, and finally neared Cnidus; but the winds had become too strong, so we ran across to Crete, passing the port of Salome. Beating into the wind with great difficulty and moving slowly along the southern coast, we arrived at Fair Havens, near the city of Lasea. ⁹There we stayed for several days. The weather was becoming dangerous for long voyages by then, because it was late in the year, and Paul spoke to the ship's officers about it.

¹⁰"Sirs," he said, "I believe there is trouble ahead if we go on—perhaps shipwreck, loss of cargo, injuries, and death." ¹¹But the officers in charge of the prisoners listened more to the ship's captain and the owner than to Paul. ¹²And since Fair Havens was an exposed harbor—a poor place to spend the winter—most of the crew advised trying to go further up the coast to Phoenix, in order to winter there; Phoenix was a good harbor with only a northwest and southwest exposure.

¹³Just then a light wind began blowing from the south, and it looked like a perfect day for the trip; so they pulled up anchor and sailed along close to shore.

¹⁴,¹⁵But shortly afterwards, the weather changed abruptly and a heavy wind of typhoon strength (a "northeaster," they called it) caught the ship and blew it out to sea. They tried at first to face back to shore but couldn't, so they gave up and let the ship run before the gale.

Do Right, Even When You Suffer For It
❧ 1 Peter 3:16–22 ❧

Do what is right; then if men speak against you, calling you evil names, they will become ashamed of themselves for falsely accusing you when you have only done what is good. ¹⁷Remember, if God wants you to suffer, it is better to suffer for doing good than for doing wrong!

¹⁸Christ also suffered. He died once for the sins of all us guilty sinners, although he himself was in-

nocent of any sin at any time, that he might bring us safely home to God. But though his body died, his spirit lived on, [19]and it was in the spirit that he visited the spirits in prison, and preached to them—[20]spirits of those who, long before in the days of Noah, had refused to listen to God, though he waited patiently for them while Noah was building the ark. Yet only eight persons were saved from drowning in that terrible flood. [21](That, by the way, is what baptism pictures for us: In baptism we show that we have been saved from death and doom by the resurrection of Christ; not because our bodies are washed clean by the water, but because in being baptized we are turning to God and asking him to cleanse our *hearts* from sin.) [22]And now Christ is in heaven, sitting in the place of honor next to God the Father, with all the angels and powers of heaven bowing before him and obeying him.

Proverbs for Today
~§ 28:21–22 ?~

Giving preferred treatment to rich people is a clear case of selling one's soul for a piece of bread.

□ Trying to get rich quick is evil and leads to poverty.

~& KEY VERSE &~

Do what is right; then if men speak against you, calling you evil names, they will become ashamed of themselves for falsely accusing you when you have only done what is good.—*1 Peter 3:16*

~& REFLECTION &~

A Christian couple may not be able to keep people from attacking them, but they can at least stop supplying them with ammunition. As long as the two of you are doing what is right, those accusations will be empty and will only embarrass the people doing the accusing. Keep your conduct above criticism!

~& MEDITATION &~

Heavenly Father, protect us from those people who would like to harm us. Help us to continue to live as you would have us to live. ?~

NOVEMBER 30

Paul Is Shipwrecked on the Way to Rome
~§ Acts 27:16–44 ?~

We [Luke, Paul, and his companions] finally sailed behind a small island named Clauda, where with great difficulty we hoisted aboard the lifeboat that was being towed behind us, [17]and then banded the ship with ropes to strengthen the hull. The sailors were afraid of being driven across to the quicksands of the African coast, so they lowered the topsails and were thus driven before the wind. [18]The next day as the seas grew higher, the crew began throwing the cargo overboard. [19]The following day they threw out the tackle and anything else they could lay their hands on. [20]The terrible storm raged unabated many days, until at last all hope was gone.

[21]No one had eaten for a long time, but finally Paul called the crew together and said, "Men, you should have listened to me in the first place and not left Fair Havens—you would have avoided all this injury and loss! [22]But cheer up! Not one of us will lose our lives, even though the ship will go down.

[23]"For last night an angel of the God to whom I belong and whom I serve stood beside me, [24]and said, 'Don't be afraid, Paul—for you will surely stand trial before Caesar! What's more, God has granted your request and will save the lives of all those sailing with you.' [25]So take courage! For I believe God! It will be just as he said! [26]But we will be shipwrecked on an island."

[27]About midnight on the fourteenth night of the storm, as we were being driven to and fro on the

Adriatic Sea, the sailors suspected land was near. [28]They sounded, and found 120 feet of water below them. A little later they sounded again, and found only ninety feet. [29]At this rate they knew they would soon be driven ashore; and fearing rocks along the coast, they threw out four anchors from the stern and prayed for daylight.

[30]Some of the sailors planned to abandon the ship, and lowered the emergency boat as though they were going to put out anchors from the prow. [31]But Paul said to the soldiers and commanding officer, ''You will all die unless everyone stays aboard.'' [32]So the soldiers cut the ropes and let the boat fall off.

[33]As the darkness gave way to the early morning light, Paul begged everyone to eat. ''You haven't touched food for two weeks,'' he said. [34]''Please eat something now for your own good! For not a hair of your heads shall perish!''

[35]Then he took some hardtack and gave thanks to God before them all, and broke off a piece and ate it. [36]Suddenly everyone felt better and began eating, [37]all two hundred seventy-six of us—for that is the number we had aboard. [38]After eating, the crew lightened the ship further by throwing all the wheat overboard.

[39]When it was day, they didn't recognize the coastline, but noticed a bay with a beach and wondered whether they could get between the rocks and be driven up onto the beach. [40]They finally decided to try. Cutting off the anchors and leaving them in the sea, they lowered the rudders, raised the foresail and headed ashore. [41]But the ship hit a sandbar and ran aground. The bow of the ship stuck fast, while the stern was exposed to the violence of the waves and began to break apart.

[42]The soldiers advised their commanding officer to let them kill the prisoners lest any of them swim ashore and escape. [43]But Julius wanted to spare Paul, so he told them no. Then he ordered all who could swim to jump overboard and make for land, [44]and the rest to try for it on planks and debris from the broken ship. So everyone escaped safely ashore!

Be Ready to Suffer for Christ
1 Peter 4:1–6

Since Christ suffered and underwent pain, you must have the same attitude he did; you must be ready to suffer, too. For remember, when your body suffers, sin loses its power, [2]and you won't be spending the rest of your life chasing after evil desires, but will be anxious to do the will of God. [3]You have had enough in the past of the evil things the godless enjoy—sex sin, lust, getting drunk, wild parties, drinking bouts, and the worship of idols, and other terrible sins.

[4]Of course, your former friends will be very surprised when you don't eagerly join them any more in the wicked things they do, and they will laugh at you in contempt and scorn. [5]But just remember that they must face the Judge of all, living and dead; they will be punished for the way they have lived. [6]That is why the Good News was preached even to those who were dead—killed by the flood—so that although their bodies were punished with death, they could still live in their spirits as God lives.

Proverbs for Today
28:23–24

In the end, people appreciate frankness more than flattery. □ A man who robs his parents and says, ''What's wrong with that?'' is no better than a murderer.

KEY VERSE

Since Christ suffered and underwent pain, you must have the same attitude he did; you must be ready to suffer, too. For remember, when your body suffers, sin loses its power, and you won't be spending the rest of your life chasing after evil desires but will be anxious to do the will of God. —1 Peter 4:1–2

REFLECTION

Some people will do anything to avoid pain. As followers of Christ, however, we should be willing and prepared to do God's will and to suffer for it if necessary. When our bodies are in pain or our lives are in jeopardy, our real values show up clearly, and sinful pleasures seem less important. The same should be true of your marriage. When you are experiencing hurts in your relationship, healing will begin if you work on the problems together, draw-

ing closer to each other and trying to please each other.

--------- ◦§ MEDITATION ◦§ ---------

Heavenly Father, when you allow pain into our lives give us the wisdom and the strength that we will need to deal with it. ◦§

DECEMBER 1 _____

Paul Survives a Bite from a Poisonous Snake
◦§ Acts 28:1–10 ◦§

We [Luke, Paul, and his companions] soon learned that we were on the island of Malta. The people of the island were very kind to us, building a bonfire on the beach to welcome and warm us in the rain and cold.

³As Paul gathered an armful of sticks to lay on the fire, a poisonous snake, driven out by the heat, fastened itself onto his hand! ⁴The people of the island saw it hanging there and said to each other, "A murderer, no doubt! Though he escaped the sea, justice will not permit him to live!"

⁵But Paul shook off the snake into the fire and was unharmed. ⁶The people waited for him to begin swelling or suddenly fall dead; but when they had waited a long time and no harm came to him, they changed their minds and decided he was a god.

⁷Near the shore where we landed was an estate belonging to Publius, the governor of the island. He welcomed us courteously and fed us for three days. ⁸As it happened, Publius' father was ill with fever and dysentery. Paul went in and prayed for him, and laying his hands on him, healed him! ⁹Then all the other sick people in the island came and were cured. ¹⁰As a result we were showered with gifts, and when the time came to sail, people put on board all sorts of things we would need for the trip.

Use Your Gifts to Serve Others
◦§ 1 Peter 4:7–11 ◦§

The end of the world is coming soon. Therefore be earnest, thoughtful men of prayer. ⁸Most

important of all, continue to show deep love for each other, for love makes up for many of your faults. ⁹Cheerfully share your home with those who need a meal or a place to stay for the night.

¹⁰God has given each of you some special abilities; be sure to use them to help each other, passing on to others God's many kinds of blessings. ¹¹Are you called to preach? Then preach as though God himself were speaking through you. Are you called to help others? Do it with all the strength and energy that God supplies, so that God will be glorified through Jesus Christ—to him be glory and power forever and ever. Amen.

Proverbs for Today
◦§ 28:25–26 ◦§

Greed causes fighting; trusting God leads to prosperity. □ A man is a fool to trust himself! But those who use God's wisdom are safe.

--------- ◦§ KEY VERSE ◦§ ---------

A man is a fool to trust himself! But those who use God's wisdom are safe.—*Proverbs 28:26*

--------- ◦§ REFLECTION ◦§ ---------

For many people, the rugged individualist is a hero. We admire the bold, self-directed men and women who know what they want and fight for it. They are self-reliant, neither giving nor asking for advice. What a contrast to God's way. A person can't know the future and can't predict the consequences of his or her choices with certainty. The totally self-reliant person is self-condemned by self-proclaimed independence, but the wise person is protected by dependence on God. Do you depend only on yourself, not needing anyone else? Where does God fit in your marriage relationship? Through dependence on God, your marriage will develop a richness of spirit that you can not obtain through your own efforts.

—————— ⚜ MEDITATION ⚜ ——————

Heavenly Father, help me to be wise and thus rely on you. And give both of us your wisdom as we seek to serve you together. ❧

DECEMBER 2

Paul Lives under Guard in Rome
⚜ Acts 28:11–31 ❧

It was three months after the shipwreck before we [Luke, Paul, and his companions] set sail again, and this time it was in *The Twin Brothers* of Alexandria, a ship that had wintered at the island. [12]Our first stop was Syracuse, where we stayed three days. [13]From there we circled around to Rhegium; a day later a south wind began blowing, so the following day we arrived at Puteoli, [14]where we found some believers! They begged us to stay with them seven days. Then we went on to Rome.

[15]The brothers in Rome had heard we were coming and came to meet us at the Forum on the Appian Way. Others joined us at The Three Taverns. When Paul saw them, he thanked God and took courage.

[16]When we arrived in Rome, Paul was permitted to live wherever he wanted to, though guarded by a soldier.

[17]Three days after his arrival, he called together the local Jewish leaders and spoke to them as follows:

"Brothers, I was arrested by the Jews in Jerusalem and handed over to the Roman government for prosecution, even though I had harmed no one nor violated the customs of our ancestors. [18]The Romans gave me a trial and wanted to release me, for they found no cause for the death sentence demanded by the Jewish leaders. [19]But when the Jews protested the decision, I felt it necessary, with no malice against them, to appeal to Caesar. [20]I asked you to come here today so we could get acquainted and I could tell you that it is because I believe the Messiah has come that I am bound with this chain."

[21]They replied, "We have heard nothing against you! We have had no letters from Judea or reports from those arriving from Jerusalem. [22]But we want to hear what you believe, for the only thing we know about these Christians is that they are denounced everywhere!"

[23]So a time was set and on that day large numbers came to his house. He told them about the Kingdom of God and taught them about Jesus from the Scriptures—from the five books of Moses and the books of prophecy. He began lecturing in the morning and went on into the evening!

[24]Some believed, and some didn't. [25]But after they had argued back and forth among themselves, they left with this final word from Paul ringing in their ears: "The Holy Spirit was right when he said through Isaiah the prophet,

[26]" 'Say to the Jews, "You will hear and see but not understand, [27]for your hearts are too fat and your ears don't listen and you have closed your eyes against understanding, for you don't want to see and hear and understand and turn to me to heal you." ' [28,29]So I want you to realize that this salvation from God is available to the Gentiles too, and they will accept it."

[30]Paul lived for the next two years in his rented house and welcomed all who visited him, [31]telling them with all boldness about the Kingdom of God and about the Lord Jesus Christ; and no one tried to stop him.

We Are Partners with Christ in Suffering
❧ 1 Peter 4:12–19 ❧

Dear friends, don't be bewildered or surprised when you go through the fiery trials ahead, for this is no strange, unusual thing that is going to happen to you. [13]Instead, be really glad—because these trials will make you partners with Christ in his suffering, and afterwards you will have the wonderful joy of sharing his glory in that coming day when it will be displayed.

[14]Be happy if you are cursed and insulted for being a Christian, for when that happens the Spirit of God will come upon you with great glory. [15]Don't let me hear of your suffering for murdering or stealing or making trouble or being a busybody and prying into other people's affairs. [16]But it is no shame to suffer for being a Christian. Praise God for the privilege of being in Christ's family and being called by his wonderful name! [17]For the time has come for judgment, and it must begin first among God's own children. And if even we who are Christians must be judged, what terrible fate awaits those who have never believed in the Lord? [18]If the righteous are barely saved, what chance will the godless have?

[19]So if you are suffering according to God's will, keep on doing what is right and trust yourself to the God who made you, for he will never fail you.

Proverbs for Today
❧ 28:27–28 ❧

If you give to the poor, your needs will be supplied! But a curse upon those who close their eyes to poverty. ☐ When the wicked prosper, good men go away; when the wicked meet disaster, good men return.

_____ ❧ **KEY VERSE** ❧ _____

If you give to the poor, your needs will be supplied! But a curse upon those who close their eyes to poverty.—*Proverbs 28:27*

_____ ❧ **REFLECTION** ❧ _____

God wants us to identify with the needy, not ignore them. The second part of this proverb could be restated, "A blessing on those who open their eyes to human need." If we help others when they are in trouble, they will do whatever they can to return the favor. Paul promises that God will supply all our needs (Philippians 4:19); he does this through other people. Christian couples powerfully witness for Christ when they help supply someone's need.

_____ ❧ **MEDITATION** ❧ _____

Heavenly Father, reveal to us someone's needs that you want to meet through us. ❧

DECEMBER 3 _____

A Greeting and a Doxology
❧ Revelation 1:1–9a ❧

This book unveils some of the future activities soon to occur in the life of Jesus Christ. God permitted him to reveal these things to his servant John in a vision; and then an angel was sent from heaven to explain the vision's meaning. [2]John wrote it all down—the words of God and Jesus Christ and everything he heard and saw.

[3]If you read this prophecy aloud to the church, you will receive a special blessing from the Lord.

Those who listen to it being read and do what it says will also be blessed. For the time is near when these things will all come true.

[4]*From:* John

To: The seven churches in Turkey.

Dear Friends:

May you have grace and peace from God who is, and was, and is to come! and from the seven-fold Spirit before his throne; [5]and from Jesus Christ who faithfully reveals all truth to us. He was the first to rise from death, to die no more. He is far greater than any king in all the earth. All praise to him who always loves us and who set us free from our sins by pouring out his lifeblood for us. ⁶He has gathered us into his Kingdom and made us priests of God his Father. Give to him everlasting glory! He rules forever! Amen!

⁷See! He is arriving, surrounded by clouds; and every eye shall see him—yes, and those who pierced him. And the nations will weep in sorrow and in terror when he comes. Yes! Amen! Let it be so!

⁸"I am the A and the Z, the Beginning and the Ending of all things," says God, who is the Lord, the All Powerful One who is, and was, and is coming again!

⁹It is I, your brother John, a fellow sufferer for the Lord's sake, who am writing this letter to you. I, too, have shared the patience Jesus gives, and we shall share his Kingdom!

Exhortations Concerning Church Leadership
⋙ 1 Peter 5:1-7 ⋘

And now, a word to you elders of the church. I, too, am an elder; with my own eyes I saw Christ dying on the cross; and I, too, will share his glory and his honor when he returns. Fellow elders, this is my plea to you: ²Feed the flock of God; care for it willingly, not grudgingly; not for what you will get out of it, but because you are eager to serve the Lord. ³Don't be tyrants, but lead them by your good example, ⁴and when the Head Shepherd comes, your reward will be a never-ending share in his glory and honor.

⁵You younger men, follow the leadership of those who are older. And all of you serve each other with humble spirits, for God gives special blessings to those who are humble, but sets himself against those who are proud. ⁶If you will humble yourselves under the mighty hand of God, in his good time he will lift you up.

⁷Let him have all your worries and cares, for he is always thinking about you and watching everything that concerns you.

Proverbs for Today
⋙ 29:1 ⋘

The man who is often reproved but refuses to accept criticism will suddenly be broken and never have another chance.

⋙ KEY VERSE ⋘

You younger men, follow the leadership of those who are older. And all of you serve each other with humble spirits, for God gives special blessings to those who are humble, but sets himself against those who are proud.—*1 Peter 5:5*

⋙ REFLECTION ⋘

Both young and old can benefit from Peter's instructions. Pride often keeps elders from trying to understand young people and young people from listening to their elders. Peter told both young and old to be humble and to serve each other. Young men should follow the leadership of older men, who should lead by example.

Respect your elders, listen to those younger than you, and be humble enough to learn from each other. If you are a young husband who needs direction, seek out an experienced elder in your church with a successful Christian home and marriage. And listen closely to this person. If you are a mature Christian with a solid marriage and family, share your experiences with younger husbands so that they can be encouraged by your interest and by the work that God has done in your home.

⋙ MEDITATION ⋘

Heavenly Father, lead us to mentors who can show us how to honor Christ in our home. ⋘

DECEMBER 4

John Has a Vision on the Lord's Day
❧ Revelation 1:9b–20 ❧

I was on the island of Patmos, exiled there for preaching the Word of God, and for telling what I knew about Jesus Christ. [10]It was the Lord's Day and I was worshiping, when suddenly I heard a loud voice behind me, a voice that sounded like a trumpet blast, [11]saying, "I am A and Z, the First and Last!" And then I heard him say, "Write down everything you see, and send your letter to the seven churches in Turkey: to the church in Ephesus, the one in Smyrna, and those in Pergamos, Thyatira, Sardis, Philadelphia, and Laodicea."

[12]When I turned to see who was speaking, there behind me were seven candlesticks of gold. [13]And standing among them was one who looked like Jesus who called himself the Son of Man, wearing a long robe circled with a golden band across his chest. [14]His hair was white as wool or snow, and his eyes penetrated like flames of fire. [15]His feet gleamed like burnished bronze, and his voice thundered like the waves against the shore. [16]He held seven stars in his right hand and a sharp, double-bladed sword in his mouth, and his face shone like the power of the sun in unclouded brilliance.

[17,18]When I saw him, I fell at his feet as dead; but he laid his right hand on me and said, "Don't be afraid! Though I am the First and Last, the Living One who died, who is now alive forevermore, who has the keys of hell and death—don't be afraid! [19]Write down what you have just seen, and what will soon be shown to you. [20]This is the meaning of the seven stars you saw in my right hand, and the seven golden candlesticks: The seven stars are the leaders of the seven churches, and the seven candlesticks are the churches themselves.

Stand Firm in the Midst of Suffering
❧ 1 Peter 5:8–14 ❧

Be careful—watch out for attacks from Satan, your great enemy. He prowls around like a hungry, roaring lion, looking for some victim to tear apart. [9]Stand firm when he attacks. Trust the Lord; and remember that other Christians all around the world are going through these sufferings too.

[10]After you have suffered a little while, our God, who is full of kindness through Christ, will give you his eternal glory. He personally will come and pick you up, and set you firmly in place, and make you stronger than ever. [11]To him be all power over all things, forever and ever. Amen.

[12]I am sending this note to you through the courtesy of Silvanus who is, in my opinion, a very faithful brother. I hope I have encouraged you by this letter for I have given you a true statement of the way God blesses. What I have told you here should help you to stand firmly in his love.

[13]The church here in Rome—she is your sister in the Lord—sends you her greetings; so does my son Mark. [14]Give each other the handshake of Christian love. Peace be to all of you who are in Christ.

Proverbs for Today
❧ 29:2–4 ❧

With good men in authority, the people rejoice; but with the wicked in power, they groan. ☐ A wise son makes his father happy, but a lad who hangs around with prostitutes disgraces him. ☐ A just king gives stability to his nation, but one who demands bribes destroys it.

❧ KEY VERSE ❧

Be careful—watch out for attacks from Satan, your great enemy. He prowls around like a hungry, roaring lion, looking for some victim to tear apart. Stand firm when he attacks. Trust the Lord; and remember that other Christians all around the world are going through these sufferings too.—*1 Peter 5:8–9*

❧ REFLECTION ❧

Lions attack sick, young, and straggling animals; they choose victims that are alone or not alert. God warns us to watch out for Satan when we are suffering or persecuted. When we feel alone, weak, helpless, cut off from other believers, or so focused on our troubles that we forget to watch for danger, we are especially vulnerable to Satan's attacks. Not only does Satan attack individual people, but he also attacks relationships—using people to attack each other. Don't allow Satan to use you to attack your spouse. During times of suffering, seek other Christians for support. Keep your eyes on Christ and resist the devil. Then "he will flee from you" (James 4:7).

——————— ❧ MEDITATION ❧ ———————

Heavenly Father, help us stand firm when Satan attacks our marriage and home. ❧

DECEMBER 5

The Letter to the Church in Ephesus
❧ Revelation 2:1–7 ❧

"Write a letter to the leader of the church at Ephesus and tell him this:

"I write to inform you of a message from him who walks among the churches and holds their leaders in his right hand.

"He says to you: ²I know how many good things you are doing. I have watched your hard work and your patience; I know you don't tolerate sin among your members, and you have carefully examined the claims of those who say they are apostles but aren't. You have found out how they lie. ³You have patiently suffered for me without quitting.

⁴"Yet there is one thing wrong; you don't love me as at first! ⁵Think about those times of your first love (how different now!) and turn back to me again and work as you did before; or else I will come and remove your candlestick from its place among the churches.

⁶"But there is this about you that is good: You hate the deeds of the licentious Nicolaitans, just as I do.

⁷"Let this message sink into the ears of anyone who listens to what the Spirit is saying to the churches: To everyone who is victorious, I will give fruit from the Tree of Life in the Paradise of God.

Seek to Know God and His Will
❧ 2 Peter 1:1–11 ❧

From: Simon Peter, a servant and missionary of Jesus Christ.

To: all of you who have our kind of faith. The faith I speak of is the kind that Jesus Christ our God and Savior gives to us. How precious it is, and how just and good he is to give this same faith to each of us.

²Do you want more and more of God's kindness and peace? Then learn to know him better and better. ³For as you know him better, he will give you, through his great power, everything you need for living a truly good life: he even shares his own glory and his own goodness with us! ⁴And by that same mighty power he has given us all the other rich and wonderful blessings he promised; for instance, the promise to save us from the lust and rottenness all around us, and to give us his own character.

⁵But to obtain these gifts, you need more than faith; you must also work hard to be good, and even that is not enough. For then you must learn to know God better and discover what he wants you to do. ⁶Next, learn to put aside your own desires so that you will become patient and godly, gladly letting God have his way with you. ⁷This will make possible the next step, which is for you to enjoy other people and to like them, and finally you will grow to love them deeply. ⁸The more you go on in this way, the more you will grow strong spiritually and become fruitful and useful to our Lord Jesus Christ. ⁹But anyone who fails to go after these additions to faith is blind indeed, or at least very shortsighted, and has forgotten that God delivered him from the old life of sin so that now he can live a strong, good life for the Lord.

[10]So, dear brothers, work hard to prove that you really are among those God has called and chosen, and then you will never stumble or fall away. [11]And God will open wide the gates of heaven for you to enter into the eternal kingdom of our Lord and Savior Jesus Christ.

Proverbs for Today
◄§ 29:5–8 §►

Flattery is a trap; evil men are caught in it, but good men stay away and sing for joy. □ The good man knows the poor man's rights; the godless don't care. □ Fools start fights everywhere while wise men try to keep peace.

─────── ◄§ **KEY VERSE** §► ───────

"There is one thing wrong; you don't love me as at first! Think about those times of your first love (how different now!) and turn back to me again and work as you did before; or else I will come and remove your candlestick from its place among the churches."—*Revelation 2:4–5*

─────── ◄§ **REFLECTION** §► ───────

The church at Ephesus was once commended for its love for God and others (Ephesians 3:17–19),

but many of the church founders had died, and the second-generation believers had lost their zeal for God. They were a busy church—they did much to benefit one other and the community—but they were acting for the wrong reasons. Work for God is not lasting unless it is based on love for God and others.

Remember the enthusiasm you felt when you fell in love with each other? New believers experience enthusiasm when they realize how wonderful it is to be forgiven. But when we lose sight of the seriousness of sin, we begin to lose the thrill of our forgiveness. In the first steps of your Christian life, you may have had enthusiasm without knowledge. Do you now have knowledge without enthusiasm? Both are necessary if you are to keep love for God and for your spouse intense and untarnished. Do you love God with the same fervor as when you were a new Christian? Do you love each other with the same fervor as when you first fell in love?

─────── ◄§ **MEDITATION** §► ───────

Heavenly Father, forgive us for our lack of enthusiasm in following Christ. Help us to be as devoted to you now as we ever were before. §►

DECEMBER 6 ───────────────

The Letter to the Church in Smyrna
◄§ Revelation 2:8–11 §►

"To the leader of the church in Smyrna write this letter:

"This message is from him who is the First and Last, who was dead and then came back to life. [9]"I know how much you suffer for the Lord, and I know all about your poverty (but you have heavenly riches!). I know the slander of those opposing you, who say that they are Jews—the children of God—but they aren't, for they support the cause of Satan. [10]Stop being afraid of what you are about to suffer—for the devil will soon throw some of you

into prison to test you. You will be persecuted for 'ten days.' Remain faithful even when facing death and I will give you the crown of life—an unending, glorious future. [11]Let everyone who can hear, listen to what the Spirit is saying to the churches: He who is victorious shall not be hurt by the Second Death.

Peter Is an Eyewitness of Christ
◄§ 2 Peter 1:12–18 §►

I plan to keep on reminding you of these things even though you already know them and are really getting along quite well! [13,14]But the Lord Jesus Christ has showed me that my days here on earth are numbered, and I am soon to die. As long as I am still here I intend to keep sending these reminders to you, [15]hoping to impress them so clearly upon you that you will remember them long after I have gone.

[16]For we have not been telling you fairy tales when we explained to you the power of our Lord Jesus Christ and his coming again. My own eyes have seen his splendor and his glory: [17,18]I was there on the holy mountain when he shone out with honor given him by God his Father; I heard that glorious, majestic voice calling down from heaven, saying, "This is my much-loved Son; I am well pleased with him."

Proverbs for Today
✑ 29:9–11 ✑

There's no use arguing with a fool. He only rages and scoffs, and tempers flare. □ The godly pray for those who long to kill them. □ A rebel shouts in anger; a wise man holds his temper in and cools it.

—————— ✑ KEY VERSE ✑ ——————

I plan to keep on reminding you of these things even though you already know them and are really getting along quite well!—*2 Peter 1:12*

—————— ✑ REFLECTION ✑ ——————

Faith is built on a foundation of fundamental truths. We must continually remind ourselves of those truths if we are to keep our commitment to Christ strong. Peter wanted his readers to remember them, so he said he would keep bringing them to mind. It is easy to forget about the basics of the gospel after years of knowing him. Don't let that happen to each other. Help each other remember what Christ has done for you.

—————— ✑ MEDITATION ✑ ——————

Heavenly Father, use us to remind each other of your great love, provision, and rule in our lives. ✑

DECEMBER 7

The Letter to the Church in Pergamos
✑ Revelation 2:12–17 ✑

"Write this letter to the leader of the church in Pergamos:

"This message is from him who wields the sharp and double-bladed sword. [13]I am fully aware that you live in the city where Satan's throne is, at the center of satanic worship; and yet you have remained loyal to me, and refused to deny me, even when Antipas, my faithful witness, was martyred among you by Satan's devotees.

[14]"And yet I have a few things against you. You tolerate some among you who do as Balaam did when he taught Balak how to ruin the people of Israel by involving them in sexual sin and encouraging them to go to idol feasts. [15]Yes, you have some of these very same followers of Balaam among you!

[16]"Change your mind and attitude, or else I will come to you suddenly and fight against them with the sword of my mouth.

[17]"Let everyone who can hear, listen to what the Spirit is saying to the churches: Every one who is victorious shall eat of the hidden manna, the secret nourishment from heaven; and I will give to each a white stone, and on the stone will be engraved a new name that no one else knows except the one receiving it.

God Inspired the Message of the Prophets
✑ 2 Peter 1:19—2:11 ✑

So we have seen and proved that what the prophets said came true. You will do well to pay close attention to everything they have written, for, like lights shining into dark corners, their words help us to understand many things that otherwise would be dark and difficult. But when you consider the wonderful truth of the prophets' words, then the light will dawn in your souls and Christ the Morning Star will shine in your hearts. [20,21]For no prophecy recorded in Scripture was ever thought up by the prophet himself. It was the Holy Spirit within these godly men who gave them true messages from God.

[2:1]But there were false prophets, too, in those days, just as there will be false teachers among you. They will cleverly tell their lies about God, turning against even their Master who bought them; but theirs will be a swift and terrible end. [2]Many will follow their evil teaching that there is nothing wrong with sexual sin. And because of them Christ and his way will be scoffed at.

[3]These teachers in their greed will tell you anything to get hold of your money. But God condemned them long ago and their destruction is on the way. [4]For God did not spare even the angels who sinned, but threw them into hell, chained in gloomy caves and darkness until the judgment day. [5]And he did not spare any of the people who lived in ancient times before the flood except Noah, the one man who spoke up for God, and his family of seven. At that time God completely destroyed the whole world of ungodly men with the vast flood. [6]Later, he turned the cities of Sodom and Gomorrah into heaps of ashes and blotted them off the face of the earth, making them an example for all the ungodly in the future to look back upon and fear.

[7,8]But at the same time the Lord rescued Lot out of Sodom because he was a good man, sick of the terrible wickedness he saw everywhere around him day after day. [9]So also the Lord can rescue you and me from the temptations that surround us, and continue to punish the ungodly until the day of final judgment comes. [10]He is especially hard on those who follow their own evil, lustful thoughts, and those who are proud and willful, daring even to scoff at the Glorious Ones without so much as trembling, [11]although the angels in heaven who stand in the very presence of the Lord, and are far greater in power and strength than these false teachers, never speak out disrespectfully against these evil Mighty Ones.

Proverbs for Today
⋖§ 29:12–14 §⋗

A wicked ruler will have wicked aides on his staff. □ Rich and poor are alike in this: each depends on God for light. □ A king who is fair to the poor shall have a long reign.

◦ KEY VERSE ◦

"I have a few things against you. You tolerate some among you who do as Balaam did when he taught Balak how to ruin the people of Israel by involving them in sexual sin and encouraging them to go to idol feasts."—*Revelation 2:14*

◦ REFLECTION ◦

There is room for differences of opinion among Christians in some areas, but there is no room for heresy or immorality. Your town may not participate in idol feasts, but it probably has pornography, sexual sin, cheating, gossiping, and lying. Don't tolerate sin under the pressure to be open-minded. A Christian couple should be of one mind on all of these issues so that they can be a powerful influence in their community.

◦ MEDITATION ◦

Heavenly Father, there is a lot of work to be done before you return. As we strive to be faithful to you direct our efforts so that we can fight effectively against sin. ❧

The Letter to the Church in Thyatira
Revelation 2:18–29

"Write this letter to the leader of the church in Thyatira:

"This is a message from the Son of God, whose eyes penetrate like flames of fire, whose feet are like glowing brass.

[19]"I am aware of all your good deeds—your kindness to the poor, your gifts and service to them; also I know your love and faith and patience, and I can see your constant improvement in all these things.

[20]"Yet I have this against you: You are permitting that woman Jezebel, who calls herself a prophetess, to teach my servants that sex sin is not a serious matter; she urges them to practice immorality and to eat meat that has been sacrificed to idols. [21]I gave her time to change her mind and attitude, but she refused. [22]Pay attention now to what I am saying: I will lay her upon a sickbed of intense affliction, along with all her immoral followers, unless they turn again to me, repenting of their sin with her; [23]and I will strike her children dead. And all the churches shall know that I am he who searches deep within men's hearts, and minds; I will give to each of you whatever you deserve.

[24,25]"As for the rest of you in Thyatira who have not followed this false teaching ('deeper truths,' as they call them—depths of Satan, really), I will ask nothing further of you; only hold tightly to what you have until I come.

[26]"To every one who overcomes—who to the very end keeps on doing things that please me—I will give power over the nations. [27]You will rule them with a rod of iron just as my Father gave me the authority to rule them; they will be shattered like a pot of clay that is broken into tiny pieces. [28]And I will give you the Morning Star!

[29]"Let all who can hear, listen to what the Spirit says to the churches.

Beware of False Teachers
2 Peter 2:12–22

But false teachers are fools—no better than animals. They do whatever they feel like; born only to be caught and killed, they laugh at the terrifying powers of the underworld which they know so little about; and they will be destroyed along with all the demons and powers of hell.

[13]That is the pay these teachers will have for their sin. For they live in evil pleasures day after day. They are a disgrace and a stain among you, deceiving you by living in foul sin on the side while they join your love feasts as though they were honest men. [14]No woman can escape their sinful stare, and of adultery they never have enough. They make a game of luring unstable women. They train themselves to be greedy; and are doomed and cursed. [15]They have gone off the road and become lost like Balaam, the son of Beor, who fell in love with the money he could make by doing wrong; [16]but Balaam was stopped from his mad course when his donkey spoke to him with a human voice, scolding and rebuking him.

[17]These men are as useless as dried-up springs of water, promising much and delivering nothing; they are as unstable as clouds driven by the storm winds. They are doomed to the eternal pits of darkness. [18]They proudly boast about their sins and conquests, and, using lust as their bait, they lure back into sin those who have just escaped from such wicked living.

[19]"You aren't saved by being good," they say, "so you might as well be bad. Do what you like, be free."

But these very teachers who offer this "freedom" from law are themselves slaves to sin and destruction. For a man is a slave to whatever controls him. [20]And when a person has escaped from the wicked ways of the world by learning about our Lord and Savior Jesus Christ, and then gets tangled up with sin and becomes its slave again, he is worse off than he was before. [21]It would be better if he had never known about Christ at all than to learn of him and then afterwards turn his back on the holy commandments that were given to him. [22]There is an old saying that "A dog comes back to what he has vomited, and a pig is washed only to come back and wallow in the mud again." That is the way it is with those who turn again to their sin.

Proverbs for Today
⋰§ 9:15–17 ও

Scolding and spanking a child helps him to learn. Left to himself, he brings shame to his mother. ☐ When rulers are wicked, their people are too; but good men will live to see the tyrant's downfall. ☐ Discipline your son and he will give you happiness and peace of mind.

──────── ও KEY VERSE ও ────────

"I have this against you: You are permitting that woman Jezebel, who calls herself a prophetess, to teach my servants that sex sin is not a serious matter; she urges them to practice immorality and to eat meat that has been sacrificed to idols."—*Revelation 2:20*

──────── ও REFLECTION ও ────────

Why is sex sin serious? Sex outside marriage always hurts someone. It hurts God because it goes against God's desires for us. It hurts others because it violates the commitments they made. It hurts us because it often brings disease to our bodies and adversely affects our personalities (see 1 Corinthians 6:12–20). Sex sin has tremendous power to destroy families, communities, and even nations because it destroys the relationships on which these institutions are built. God wants to protect us from hurting ourselves and others; thus we are to have no part in sex sin, even if our culture accepts it.

──────── ও MEDITATION ও ────────

Heavenly Father, protect us from sexual thoughts, attitudes, and actions that are sinful. ও

DECEMBER 9 _____

The Letter to the Church in Sardis
⋰§ Revelation 3:1–6 ও

"To the leader of the church in Sardis write this letter:
"This message is sent to you by the one who has the seven-fold Spirit of God and the seven stars.

"I know your reputation as a live and active church, but you are dead. [2]Now wake up! Strengthen what little remains—for even what is left is at the point of death. Your deeds are far from right in the sight of God. [3]Go back to what you heard and believed at first; hold to it firmly and turn to me again. Unless you do, I will come suddenly upon you, unexpected as a thief, and punish you.

[4]"Yet even there in Sardis some haven't soiled their garments with the world's filth; they shall walk with me in white, for they are worthy. [5]Everyone who conquers will be clothed in white, and I will not erase his name from the Book of Life, but I will announce before my Father and his angels that he is mine.

[6]"Let all who can hear, listen to what the Spirit is saying to the churches.

Scoffers in the Last Days
⋰§ 2 Peter 3:1–7 ও

This is my second letter to you, dear brothers, and in both of them I have tried to remind you— if you will let me—about facts you already know: facts you learned from the holy prophets and from us apostles who brought you the words of our Lord and Savior.

[3]First, I want to remind you that in the last days there will come scoffers who will do every wrong they can think of, and laugh at the truth. [4]This will be their line of argument: "So Jesus promised to come back, did he? Then where is he? He'll never come! Why, as far back as anyone can remember

everything has remained exactly as it was since the first day of creation."

⁵,⁶They deliberately forget this fact: that God did destroy the world with a mighty flood, long after he had made the heavens by the word of his command, and had used the waters to form the earth and surround it. ⁷And God has commanded that the earth and the heavens be stored away for a great bonfire at the judgment day, when all ungodly men will perish.

Proverbs for Today
◄§ 29:18 ϡ►

Where there is ignorance of God, crime runs wild; but what a wonderful thing it is for a nation to know and keep his laws.

◄ KEY VERSE ϡ

Where there is ignorance of God, crime runs wild; but what a wonderful thing it is for a nation to know and keep his laws.—*Proverbs 29:18*

◄ REFLECTION ϡ

When a husband or wife does whatever seems "right in his own eyes" (Judges 17:6), the marriage becomes weak. But when even one partner strives to know and keep God's laws, the relationship improves. Build your marriage on a foundation of God's ways.

◄ MEDITATION ϡ

Heavenly Father, help us to follow your ways in our relationship. ϡ►

DECEMBER 10

The Letter to the Church in Philadelphia
◄§ Revelation 3:7–13 ϡ►

"Write this letter to the leader of the church in Philadelphia.

"This message is sent to you by the one who is holy and true, and has the key of David to open what no one can shut and to shut what no one can open.

⁸"I know you well; you aren't strong, but you have tried to obey and have not denied my Name. Therefore I have opened a door to you that no one can shut.

⁹"Note this: I will force those supporting the causes of Satan while claiming to be mine (but they aren't—they are lying) to fall at your feet and acknowledge that you are the ones I love.

¹⁰"Because you have patiently obeyed me despite the persecution, therefore I will protect you from the time of Great Tribulation and temptation, which will come upon the world to test everyone alive. ¹¹Look, I am coming soon! Hold tightly to the little strength you have—so that no one will take away your crown.

¹²"As for the one who conquers, I will make him a pillar in the temple of my God; he will be secure, and will go out no more; and I will write my God's Name on him, and he will be a citizen in the city of my God—the New Jerusalem, coming down from heaven from my God; and he will have my new Name inscribed upon him.

¹³"Let all who can hear, listen to what the Spirit is saying to the churches.

The Day of the Lord
◄§ 2 Peter 3:8–13 ϡ►

But don't forget this, dear friends, that a day or a thousand years from now is like tomorrow to the Lord. ⁹He isn't really being slow about his promised return, even though it sometimes seems that way. But he is waiting, for the good reason that he is not willing that any should perish, and he is giving more time for sinners to repent. ¹⁰The day of the Lord is surely coming, as unexpectedly as a thief, and then the heavens will pass away with a terrible noise and the heavenly bodies will disappear in fire, and the earth and everything on it will be burned up.

[11]And so since everything around us is going to melt away, what holy, godly lives we should be living! [12]You should look forward to that day and hurry it along—the day when God will set the heavens on fire, and the heavenly bodies will melt and disappear in flames. [13]But we are looking forward to God's promise of new heavens and a new earth afterwards, where there will be only goodness.

Proverbs for Today
◄§ 29:19–20 §►

Sometimes mere words are not enough—discipline is needed. For the words may not be heeded. ☐ There is more hope for a fool than for a man of quick temper.

_____◄ KEY VERSE ►_____

You should look forward to that day and hurry it along—the day when God will set the heavens on fire, and the heavenly bodies will melt and disappear in flames.—*2 Peter 3:12*

_____◄ REFLECTION ►_____

How can we "hurry" Christ's return? We really can't. He is waiting so that more people can repent. Thus you should work hard to share the Good News and bring more people to faith in him (see Matthew 24:14).

_____◄ MEDITATION ►_____

Heavenly Father, as we look forward to the day when we will spend eternity with you, help us to spread your Good News to others. §►

DECEMBER 11 _____

The Letter to the Church in Laodicea
◄§ Revelation 3:14–22 §►

"Write this letter to the leader of the church in Laodicea:

"This message is from the one who stands firm, the faithful and true Witness [of all that is or was or evermore shall be], the primeval source of God's creation:

[15]"I know you well—you are neither hot nor cold; I wish you were one or the other! [16]But since you are merely lukewarm, I will spit you out of my mouth!

[17]"You say, 'I am rich, with everything I want; I don't need a thing!' And you don't realize that spiritually you are wretched and miserable and poor and blind and naked.

[18]"My advice to you is to buy pure gold from me, gold purified by fire—only then will you truly be rich. And to purchase from me white garments, clean and pure, so you won't be naked and ashamed; and to get medicine from me to heal your eyes and give you back your sight. [19]I continually discipline and punish everyone I love; so I must punish you, unless you turn from your indifference and become enthusiastic about the things of God.

[20]"Look! I have been standing at the door and I am constantly knocking. If anyone hears me calling him and opens the door, I will come in and fellowship with him and he with me. [21]I will let every one who conquers sit beside me on my throne, just as I took my place with my Father on his throne when I had conquered. [22]Let those who can hear, listen to what the Spirit is saying to the churches."

Prepare For Christ's Coming
◄§ 2 Peter 3:14–18 §►

Dear friends, while you are waiting for these things to happen and for him to come, try hard to live without sinning; and be at peace with everyone so that he will be pleased with you when he returns.

[15,16]And remember why he is waiting. He is giving us time to get his message of salvation out to others. Our wise and beloved brother Paul has

talked about these same things in many of his letters. Some of his comments are not easy to understand, and there are people who are deliberately stupid, and always demand some unusual interpretation—they have twisted his letters around to mean something quite different from what he meant, just as they do the other parts of the Scripture—and the result is disaster for them.

¹⁷I am warning you ahead of time, dear brothers, so that you can watch out and not be carried away by the mistakes of these wicked men, lest you yourselves become mixed up too. ¹⁸But grow in spiritual strength and become better acquainted with our Lord and Savior Jesus Christ. To him be all glory and splendid honor, both now and forevermore. Good-bye.

Peter

Proverbs for Today
⋙ 29:21–22 ⋘

Pamper a servant from childhood, and he will expect you to treat him as a son! □ A hot-tempered man starts fights and gets into all kinds of trouble.

——— ✍ KEY VERSE ✍ ———

"I continually discipline and punish everyone I love; so I must punish you unless you turn from your indifference and become enthusiastic about the things of God."—*Revelation 3:19*

——— ✍ REFLECTION ✍ ———

God would discipline this lukewarm church unless they turned from their indifference toward him. His purpose in discipline is not to punish, but to bring people back to him. Are you lukewarm in your devotion to God? God may discipline you to pull you out of your indifference; but he uses only loving discipline. You can avoid God's discipline by drawing near to him through confession, prayer, worship, and studying his Word. Do you feel distant from God? Ask the Holy Spirit to reignite your faith.

——— ✍ MEDITATION ✍ ———

Heavenly Father, forgive us for our laziness and indifference toward you. Reignite your spiritual fire within us. ⋙

DECEMBER 12

A Vision of God's Throne
⋙ Revelation 4:1–11 ⋘

Then as I looked, I saw a door standing open in heaven, and the same voice I had heard before, that sounded like a mighty trumpet blast, spoke to me and said, "Come up here and I will show you what must happen in the future!"

²And instantly I was, in spirit, there in heaven and saw—oh, the glory of it!—a throne and someone sitting on it! ³Great bursts of light flashed forth from him as from a glittering diamond, or from a shining ruby, and a rainbow glowing like an emerald encircled his throne. ⁴Twenty-four smaller thrones surrounded his, with twenty-four Elders sitting on them; all were clothed in white, with golden crowns upon their heads. ⁵Lightning and thunder issued from the throne, and there were voices in the thunder. Directly in front of his throne were seven lighted lamps representing the seven-fold Spirit of God. ⁶Spread out before it was a shiny crystal sea. Four Living Beings, dotted front and back with eyes, stood at the throne's four sides. ⁷The first of these Living Beings was in the form of a lion; the second looked like an ox; the third had the face of a man; and the fourth, the form of an eagle, with wings spread out as though in flight. ⁸Each of these Living Beings had six wings, and the central sections of their wings were covered with eyes. Day after day and night after night they kept on saying, "Holy, holy, holy, Lord God Almighty—the one who was, and is, and is to come."

⁹And when the Living Beings gave glory and honor and thanks to the one sitting on the throne, who lives forever and ever, ¹⁰the twenty-four Elders fell down before him and worshiped him, the Eternal Living One, and cast their crowns before the throne, singing, ¹¹"O Lord, you are worthy to receive the glory and the honor and the power, for you have created all things. They were created and called into being by your act of will."

An Eyewitness of the Incarnate Christ
⋅§ 1 John 1:1–4 ⩙

Christ was alive when the world began, yet I myself have seen him with my own eyes and listened to him speak. I have touched him with my own hands. He is God's message of life. ²This one who is life from God has been shown to us and we guarantee that we have seen him; I am speaking of Christ, who is eternal Life. He was with the Father and then was shown to us. ³Again I say, we are telling you about what we ourselves have actually seen and heard, so that you may share the fellowship and the joys we have with the Father and with Jesus Christ his son. ⁴And if you do as I say in this letter, then you, too, will be full of joy, and so will we.

Proverbs for Today
⋅§ 29:23 ⩙

Pride ends in a fall, while humility brings honor.

⋅ KEY VERSE ⩙

Again I say, we are telling you about what we ourselves have actually seen and heard, so that you may share the fellowship and the joys we have with the Father and with Jesus Christ his son.—*1 John 1:3*

⋅ REFLECTION ⩙

Just as there are three steps to true Christian fellowship, there are three steps to a strong marriage. First, it is grounded in the testimony of the Word of God. Without this underlying strength, togetherness is impossible. Second, it is mutual, depending on the unity of the husband and wife. Third, it is daily renewed through the Holy Spirit. A godly marriage is social, physical, and spiritual, and it is made possible only by a living relationship with Christ.

⋅ MEDITATION ⩙

Heavenly Father, we praise you for the joys that we can share with each other because of Jesus Christ. ⩙

DECEMBER 13

The Scroll and the Lamb
⋅§ Revelation 5:1–14 ⩙

And I saw a scroll in the right hand of the one who was sitting on the throne, a scroll with writing on the inside and on the back, and sealed with seven seals. ²A mighty angel with a loud voice was shouting out this question: "Who is worthy to break the seals on this scroll, and to unroll it?" ³But no one in all heaven or earth or from among the dead was permitted to open and read it.

⁴Then I wept with disappointment because no one anywhere was worthy; no one could tell us what it said.

⁵But one of the twenty-four Elders said to me, "Stop crying, for look! The Lion of the tribe of Judah, the Root of David, has conquered, and proved himself worthy to open the scroll and to break its seven seals."

⁶I looked and saw a Lamb standing there before the twenty-four Elders, in front of the throne and the Living Beings, and on the Lamb were wounds that once had caused his death. He had seven horns and seven eyes, which represent the seven-fold Spirit of God, sent out into every part of the world. ⁷He stepped forward and took the scroll from the right hand of the one sitting upon the throne. ⁸And as he took the scroll, the twenty-four Elders

fell down before the Lamb, each with a harp and golden vials filled with incense—the prayers of God's people!

⁹They were singing him a new song with these words: "You are worthy to take the scroll and break its seals and open it; for you were slain, and your blood has bought people from every nation as gifts for God. ¹⁰And you have gathered them into a kingdom and made them priests of our God; they shall reign upon the earth."

¹¹Then in my vision I heard the singing of millions of angels surrounding the throne and the Living Beings and the Elders: ¹²"The Lamb is worthy" (loudly they sang it!) "—the Lamb who was slain. He is worthy to receive the power, and the riches, and the wisdom, and the strength, and the honor, and the glory, and the blessing."

¹³And then I heard everyone in heaven and earth and from the dead beneath the earth and in the sea, exclaiming, "The blessing and the honor and the glory and the power belong to the one sitting on the throne, and to the Lamb forever and ever." ¹⁴And the four Living Beings kept saying, "Amen!" And the twenty-four Elders fell down and worshiped him.

Forgiveness through the Blood of Jesus
⋅§ 1 John 1:5–10 ₰

This is the message God has given us to pass on to you: that God is Light and in him is no darkness at all. ⁶So if we say we are his friends, but go on living in spiritual darkness and sin, we are lying. ⁷But if we are living in the light of God's presence, just as Christ does, then we have wonderful fellowship and joy with each other, and the blood of Jesus his Son cleanses us from every sin.

⁸If we say that we have no sin, we are only fooling ourselves, and refusing to accept the truth. ⁹But if we confess our sins to him, he can be depended on to forgive us and to cleanse us from every wrong. [And it is perfectly proper for God to do this for us because Christ died to wash away our sins.] ¹⁰If we claim we have not sinned, we are lying and calling God a liar, *for he says we have sinned*.

Proverbs for Today
⋅§ 29:24–25 ₰

A man who assists a thief must really hate himself! For he knows the consequence but does it anyway. ☐ Fear of man is a dangerous trap, but to trust in God means safety.

KEY VERSE

Fear of man is a dangerous trap, but to trust in God means safety.—*Proverbs 29:25*

REFLECTION

Is your home armed with a burglar alarm? A gun? Easy access to a telephone to dial 911? Fear of human beings can hamper everything you try to do. In extreme forms, it can make you afraid to leave your home. By contrast, fear of God—respect, reverence, and trust—is liberating. Why fear people who can do no eternal harm? Instead, fear God who can turn the harm intended by others into good for those who trust him.

MEDITATION

Heavenly Father, our help comes from you. Don't let us be enslaved to fear of others. ₰

DECEMBER 14

The Lamb Opens the Seals
§ Revelation 6:1–17 §

As I watched, the Lamb broke the first seal and began to unroll the scroll. Then one of the four Living Beings, with a voice that sounded like thunder, said, "Come!"

²I looked, and there in front of me was a white horse. Its rider carried a bow, and a crown was placed upon his head; he rode out to conquer in many battles and win the war.

³Then he unrolled the scroll to the second seal, and broke it open too. And I heard the second Living Being say, "Come!"

⁴This time a red horse rode out. Its rider was given a long sword and the authority to banish peace and bring anarchy to the earth; war and killing broke out everywhere.

⁵When he had broken the third seal, I heard the third Living Being say, "Come!" And I saw a black horse, with its rider holding a pair of balances in his hand. ⁶And a voice from among the four Living Beings said, "A loaf of bread for $20, or three pounds of barley flour, but there is no olive oil or wine."

⁷And when the fourth seal was broken, I heard the fourth Living Being say, "Come!" ⁸And now I saw a pale horse, and its rider's name was Death. And there followed after him another horse whose rider's name was Hell. They were given control of one-fourth of the earth, to kill with war and famine and disease and wild animals.

⁹And when he broke open the fifth seal, I saw an altar, and underneath it all the souls of those who had been martyred for preaching the Word of God and for being faithful in their witnessing. ¹⁰They called loudly to the Lord and said, "O Sovereign Lord, holy and true, how long will it be before you judge the people of the earth for what they've done to us? When will you avenge our blood against those living on the earth?" ¹¹White robes were given to each of them, and they were told to rest a little longer until their other brothers, fellow servants of Jesus, had been martyred on the earth and joined them.

¹²I watched as he broke the sixth seal, and there was a vast earthquake; and the sun became dark like black cloth, and the moon was blood-red. ¹³Then the stars of heaven appeared to be falling to earth—like green fruit from fig trees buffeted by mighty winds. ¹⁴And the starry heavens disappeared as though rolled up like a scroll and taken away; and every mountain and island shook and shifted. ¹⁵The kings of the earth, and world leaders and rich men, and high-ranking military officers, and all men great and small, slave and free, hid themselves in the caves and rocks of the mountains, ¹⁶and cried to the mountains to crush them. "Fall on us," they pleaded, "and hide us from the face of the one sitting on the throne, and from the anger of the Lamb, ¹⁷because the great day of their anger has come, and who can survive it?"

Our Advocate before the Father
§ 1 John 2:1–6 §

My little children, I am telling you this so that you will stay away from sin. But if you sin, there is someone to plead for you before the Father. His name is Jesus Christ, the one who is all that is good and who pleases God completely. ²He is the one who took God's wrath against our sins upon himself, and brought us into fellowship with God; and he is the forgiveness for our sins, and not only ours but all the world's.

³And how can we be sure that we belong to him? By looking within ourselves: are we really trying to do what he wants us to?

⁴Someone may say, "I am a Christian; I am on my way to heaven; I belong to Christ." But if he doesn't do what Christ tells him to, he is a liar. ⁵But those who do what Christ tells them to will learn to love God more and more. That is the way to know whether or not you are a Christian. ⁶Anyone who says he is a Christian should live as Christ did.

Proverbs for Today
§ 29:26–27 §

Do you want justice? Don't fawn on the judge, but ask the Lord for it! □ The good hate the badness of the wicked. The wicked hate the goodness of the good.

He is the one who took God's wrath against our sins upon himself and brought us into fellowship with God; and he is the forgiveness for our sins, and not only ours but all the world's.—*1 John 2:2*

.◦§ REFLECTION §◦.

Sometimes we have a difficult time forgiving others who wrong us. Imagine how hard it would be to tell your spouse that you were willing to forgive no matter what he or she does! This is what God has done for us in Jesus Christ. No one, no matter what he or she has done, is beyond God's forgiveness. All they have to do is turn to Jesus and commit their hearts to him.

.◦§ MEDITATION §◦.

Heavenly Father, forgive us our sins against you. ❧

DECEMBER 15

144,000 Are Marked by God
◦§ Revelation 7:1–17 §◦

Then I saw four angels standing at the four corners of the earth, holding back the four winds from blowing, so that not a leaf rustled in the trees, and the ocean became as smooth as glass. [2]And I saw another angel coming from the east, carrying the Great Seal of the Living God. And he shouted out to those four angels who had been given power to injure earth and sea, [3]"Wait! Don't do anything yet—hurt neither earth nor sea nor trees—until we have placed the Seal of God upon the foreheads of his servants."

[4-8]How many were given this mark? I heard the number—it was 144,000; out of all twelve tribes of Israel, as listed here:

Judah	12,000
Reuben	12,000
Gad	12,000
Asher	12,000
Naphtali	12,000
Manasseh	12,000
Simeon	12,000
Levi	12,000
Issachar	12,000
Zebulun	12,000
Joseph	12,000
Benjamin	12,000

[9]After this I saw a vast crowd, too great to count, from all nations and provinces and languages, standing in front of the throne and before the Lamb, clothed in white, with palm branches in their hands. [10]And they were shouting with a mighty shout, "Salvation comes from our God upon the throne, and from the Lamb."

[11]And now all the angels were crowding around the throne and around the Elders and the four Living Beings, and falling face down before the throne and worshiping God. [12]"Amen!" they said. "Blessing, and glory, and wisdom, and thanksgiving, and honor, and power, and might, be to our God forever and forever. Amen!"

[13]Then one of the twenty-four Elders asked me, "Do you know who these are, who are clothed in white, and where they come from?"

[14]"No, sir," I replied. "Please tell me."

"These are the ones coming out of the Great Tribulation," he said; "they washed their robes and whitened them by the blood of the Lamb. [15]That is why they are here before the throne of God, serving him day and night in his temple. The one sitting on the throne will shelter them; [16]they will never be hungry again, nor thirsty, and they will be fully protected from the scorching noontime heat. [17]For the Lamb standing in front of the throne will feed them and be their Shepherd and lead them to the springs of the Water of Life. And God will wipe their tears away."

Love One Another
◦§ 1 John 2:7–11 §◦

Dear brothers, I am not writing out a new rule for you to obey, for it is an old one you have always had, right from the start. You have heard it all before. [8]Yet it is always new, and works for you just as it did for Christ; and as we obey this commandment, *to love one another,* the darkness in our lives disappears and the new light of life in Christ shines in.

[9]Anyone who says he is walking in the light of Christ but dislikes his fellow man, is still in darkness. [10]But whoever loves his fellow man is "walking in the light" and can see his way without stumbling around in darkness and sin. [11]For he who dislikes his brother is wandering in spiritual darkness and doesn't know where he is going, for the darkness has made him blind so that he cannot see the way.

Proverbs for Today
~§ 30:1–4 §~

These are the messages of Agur, son of Jakeh addressed to Ithiel and Ucal: I am tired out, O God, and ready to die. I am too stupid even to call myself a human being! I cannot understand man, let alone God. Who else but God goes back and forth to heaven? Who else holds the wind in his fists, and wraps up the oceans in his cloak? Who but God has created

the world? If there is any other, what is his name—and his Son's name—if you know it?

---------- ~§ **KEY VERSE** §~ ----------

Dear brothers, I am not writing out a new rule for you to obey, for it is an old one you have always had, right from the start. You have heard it all before. Yet it is always new, and works for you just as it did for Christ; and as we obey this commandment, to *love one another,* the darkness in our lives disappears and the new light of life in Christ shines in.—*1 John 2:7–8*

---------- ~§ **REFLECTION** §~ ----------

Love should be the unifying force and the identifying mark of every Christian marriage. It is the key to walking in the light because we cannot grow spiritually while we harbor hatred within us. A growing relationship with God will result in a growing relationship with your spouse.

---------- ~§ **MEDITATION** §~ ----------

Heavenly Father, it sounds easy to love, but the reality is that we find it easier to love ourselves. Teach us to love each other first. §~

DECEMBER 16 _____

The Seventh Seal and the Trumpets
~§ Revelation 8:1–13 §~

When the Lamb had broken the seventh seal, there was silence throughout all heaven for what seemed like half an hour. [2]And I saw the seven angels that stand before God, and they were given seven trumpets.

[3]Then another angel with a golden censer came and stood at the altar; and a great quantity of incense was given to him to mix with the prayers of God's people, to offer upon the golden altar before the throne. [4]And the perfume of the incense mixed with prayers ascended up to God from the altar where the angel had poured them out.

[5]Then the angel filled the censer with fire from the altar and threw it down upon the earth; and thunder crashed and rumbled, lightning flashed, and there was a terrible earthquake.

[6]Then the seven angels with the seven trumpets prepared to blow their mighty blasts.

[7]The first angel blew his trumpet, and hail and fire mixed with blood were thrown down upon the earth. One-third of the earth was set on fire so that one-third of the trees were burned, and all green grass.

[8,9]Then the second angel blew his trumpet, and what appeared to be a huge burning mountain was thrown into the sea, destroying a third of all the

ships; and a third of the sea turned red as blood; and a third of the fish were killed.

[10]The third angel blew, and a great flaming star fell from heaven upon a third of the rivers and springs. [11]The star was called "Bitterness" because it poisoned a third of all the water on the earth and many people died.

[12]The fourth angel blew his trumpet and immediately a third of the sun was blighted and darkened, and a third of the moon and the stars, so that the daylight was dimmed by a third, and the nighttime darkness deepened. [13]As I watched, I saw a solitary eagle flying through the heavens crying loudly, "Woe, woe, woe to the people of the earth because of the terrible things that will soon happen when the three remaining angels blow their trumpets."

Do Not Love This Evil World
◄§ 1 John 2:12–17 §►

I am writing these things to all of you, my little children, because your sins have been forgiven in the name of Jesus our Savior. [13]I am saying these things to you older men because you really know Christ, the one who has been alive from the beginning. And you young men, I am talking to you because you have won your battle with Satan. And I am writing to you younger boys and girls because you, too, have learned to know God our Father.

[14]And so I say to you fathers who know the eternal God, and to you young men who are strong, with God's Word in your hearts, and have won your struggle against Satan: [15]Stop loving this evil world and all that it offers you, for when you love these things you show that you do not really love God; [16]for all these worldly things, these evil desires—the craze for sex, the ambition to buy everything that appeals to you, and the pride that comes from wealth and importance—these are not from God. They are from this evil world itself. [17]And this world is fading away, and these evil, forbidden things will go with it, but whoever keeps doing the will of God will live forever.

Proverbs for Today
◄§ 30:5–6 §►

Every word of God proves true. He defends all who come to him for protection. Do not add to his words, lest he rebuke you, and you be found a liar.

----------◄ KEY VERSE ►----------

Stop loving this evil world and all that it offers you, for when you love these things you show that you do not really love God.—*1 John 2:15*

----------◄ REFLECTION ►----------

Some people think that worldliness has to do only with external behavior. But worldliness begins in the heart. It is characterized by these three attitudes: (1) lust—preoccupation with gratifying physical desires; (2) materialism—craving and accumulating things and (3) pride—obsession with one's status or importance. When the serpent tempted Eve (see Genesis 3:6), he tempted her in those areas. Also, when the devil tempted Jesus in the wilderness, those were his three areas of attack (Matthew 4:1–11). By contrast, God values self-control, a spirit of generosity, and humble service. It is possible to avoid "worldly pleasures" while still harboring worldly attitudes in one's heart. Does your marriage reflect the world's values or God's values? What values do you emphasize in your home?

----------◄ MEDITATION ►----------

Heavenly Father, forgive us for loving this world. Change us so that we have the values of Christ. §►

DECEMBER 17

Trumpets Announce God's Judgment
◄§ Revelation 9:1–21 §►

Then the fifth angel blew his trumpet and I saw one who was fallen to earth from heaven, and to him was given the key to the bottomless pit. [2]When he opened it, smoke poured out as though from some huge furnace, and the sun and air were darkened by the smoke.

[3]Then locusts came from the smoke and descended onto the earth and were given power to sting like scorpions. [4]They were told not to hurt the grass or plants or trees, but to attack those people who did not have the mark of God on their foreheads. [5]They were not to kill them, but to torture them for five months with agony like the pain of scorpion stings. [6]In those days men will try to kill themselves but won't be able to—death will not come. They will long to die—but death will flee away!

[7]The locusts looked like horses armored for battle. They had what looked like golden crowns on their heads, and their faces looked like men's. [8]Their hair was long like women's, and their teeth were those of lions. [9]They wore breastplates that seemed to be of iron, and their wings roared like an army of chariots rushing into battle. [10]They had stinging tails like scorpions, and their power to hurt, given to them for five months, was in their tails. [11]Their king is the Prince of the bottomless pit whose name in Hebrew is Abaddon, and in Greek, Apollyon [and in English, the Destroyer]

[12]One terror now ends, but there are two more coming!

[13]The sixth angel blew his trumpet and I heard a voice speaking from the four horns of the golden altar that stands before the throne of God, [14]saying to the sixth angel, "Release the four mighty demons held bound at the great River Euphrates." [15]They had been kept in readiness for that year and month and day and hour, and now they were turned loose to kill a third of all mankind. [16]They led an army of 200,000,000 warriors—I heard an announcement of how many there were.

[17,18]I saw their horses spread out before me in my vision; their riders wore fiery-red breastplates, though some were sky-blue and others yellow. The horses' heads looked much like lions', and smoke and fire and flaming sulphur billowed from their mouths, killing one-third of all mankind. [19]Their power of death was not only in their mouths, but in their tails as well, for their tails were similar to serpents' heads that struck and bit with fatal wounds.

[20]But the men left alive after these plagues *still refused to worship God!* They would not renounce their demon-worship, nor their idols made of gold and silver, brass, stone, and wood—which neither see nor hear nor walk! [21]Neither did they change their mind and attitude about all their murders and witchcraft, their immorality and theft.

The Antichrist
◄§ 1 John 2:18–27 §►

Dear children, this world's last hour has come. You have heard about the Antichrist who is coming—the one who is against Christ—and already many such persons have appeared. This makes us all the more certain that the end of the world is near. [19]These "against-Christ" people used to be members of our churches, but they never really belonged with us or else they would have stayed. When they left us it proved that they were not of us at all.

[20]But you are not like that, for the Holy Spirit has come upon you, and you know the truth. [21]So I am not writing to you as to those who need to know the truth, but I warn you as those who can discern the difference between true and false.

[22]And who is the greatest liar? The one who says that Jesus is not Christ. Such a person is antichrist, for he does not believe in God the Father and in his Son. [23]For a person who doesn't believe in Christ, God's Son, can't have God the Father either. But he who has Christ, God's Son, has God the Father also.

[24]So keep on believing what you have been

taught from the beginning. If you do, you will always be in close fellowship with both God the Father and his Son. [25]And he himself has promised us this: *eternal life.*

[26]These remarks of mine about the Antichrist are pointed at those who would dearly love to blindfold you and lead you astray. [27]But you have received the Holy Spirit and he lives within you, in your hearts, so that you don't need anyone to teach you what is right. For he teaches you all things, and he is the Truth, and no liar; and so, just as he has said, you must live in Christ, never to depart from him.

Proverbs for Today
❧ 30:7–9 ❧

O God, I beg two favors from you before I die: First, help me never to tell a lie. Second, give me neither poverty nor riches! Give me just enough to satisfy my needs! For if I grow rich, I may become content without God. And if I am too poor, I may steal, and thus insult God's holy name.

❧ KEY VERSE ❧

These "against-Christ" people used to be members of our churches, but they never really belonged with us or else they would have stayed. When they left us it proved that they were not of us at all. —*1 John 2:19*

REFLECTION

Today many people are Christians more in name than in truth. Perhaps going to church is a family tradition. Maybe they like the social and business contacts they make there. Or going to church is just a long-standing habit, and they have never stopped to ask themselves why they go. Are you really a Christian? Unless you have trusted Christ as Savior, the answer is no. Don't settle for less than the best. Become personally acquainted with Jesus Christ and become his loyal, trustworthy follower.

MEDITATION

Heavenly Father, we renew our relationship with you now. Thank you, Jesus, for coming to die for us. And thank you, Holy Spirit, for living inside us. ❧

DECEMBER 18

A Small Scroll
❧ Revelation 10:1–11 ❧

Then I saw another mighty angel coming down from heaven, surrounded by a cloud, with a rainbow over his head; his face shone like the sun and his feet flashed with fire. [2]And he held open in his hand a small scroll. He set his right foot on the sea and his left foot on the earth, [3]and gave a great shout—it was like the roar of a lion—and the seven thunders crashed their reply.

[4]I was about to write what the thunders said when a voice from heaven called to me, "Don't do it. Their words are not to be revealed."

[5]Then the mighty angel standing on the sea and land lifted his right hand to heaven, [6]and swore by him who lives forever and ever, who created heaven and everything in it and the earth and all that it contains and the sea and its inhabitants, that there should be no more delay, [7]but that when the seventh angel blew his trumpet, then God's veiled plan—mysterious through the ages ever since it was announced by his servants the prophets—would be fulfilled.

[8]Then the voice from heaven spoke to me again, "Go and get the unrolled scroll from the mighty angel standing there upon the sea and land."

[9]So I approached him and asked him to give me the scroll. "Yes, take it and eat it," he said. "At first it will taste like honey, but when you swallow it, it will make your stomach sour!" [10]So I took it from his hand, and ate it! And just as he had said, it was sweet in my mouth but it gave me a stomach ache when I swallowed it.

[11]Then he told me, "You must prophesy further about many peoples, nations, tribes, and kings."

We Are God's Children
◄§ 1 John 2:28–3:6 §►

And now, my little children, stay in happy fellowship with the Lord so that when he comes you will be sure that all is well, and will not have to be ashamed and shrink back from meeting him. [29]Since we know that God is always good and does only right, we may rightly assume that all those who do right are his children.

[3:1]See how very much our heavenly Father loves us, for he allows us to be called his children—think of it—and we really *are!* But since most people don't know God, naturally they don't understand that we are his children. [2]Yes, dear friends, we are already God's children, right now, and we can't even imagine what it is going to be like later on. But we do know this, that when he comes we will be like him, as a result of seeing him as he really is. [3]And everyone who really believes this will try to stay pure because Christ is pure.

[4]But those who keep on sinning are against God, for every sin is done against the will of God. [5]And you know that he became a man so that he could take away our sins, and that there is no sin in him, no missing of God's will at any time in any way. [6]So if we stay close to him, obedient to him, we won't be sinning either; but as for those who keep on sinning, they should realize this: They sin because they have never really known him or become his.

Proverbs for Today
◄§ 30:10 §►

Never falsely accuse a man to his employer, lest he curse you for your sin.

◆ KEY VERSE ◆

Since we know that God is always good and does only right, we may rightly assume that all those who do right are his children.—*1 John 2:29*

◆ REFLECTION ◆

The visible proof of a godly marriage is right behavior. Many couples do some good things but don't have faith in Christ. Others claim to have faith but rarely produce good works. A deficit in either faith or right behavior is cause for shame when Christ returns. Good works cannot produce salvation, but they are necessary proof that true faith has actually occurred. What evidence shows that you belong to Christ?

◆ MEDITATION ◆

Heavenly Father, help us live for you so that others will know we are your children. §►

DECEMBER 19 _____

Two Witnesses
◄§ Revelation 11:1–19 §►

Now I was given a measuring stick and told to go and measure the temple of God, including the inner court where the altar stands, and to count the number of worshipers. [2]"But do not measure the outer court," I was told, "for it has been turned over to the nations. They will trample the Holy City for forty-two months. [3]And I will give power to my two witnesses to prophesy 1,260 days clothed in sackcloth."

[4]These two prophets are the two olive trees, and two candlesticks standing before the God of all the earth. [5]Anyone trying to harm them will be killed by bursts of fire shooting from their mouths. [6]They have power to shut the skies so that no rain will fall during the three and a half years they prophesy, and to turn rivers and oceans to blood, and to send

every kind of plague upon the earth as often as they wish.

⁷When they complete the three and a half years of their solemn testimony, the tyrant who comes out of the bottomless pit will declare war against them and conquer and kill them; ⁸,⁹and for three and a half days their bodies will be exposed in the streets of Jerusalem (the city fittingly described as "Sodom" or "Egypt")—the very place where their Lord was crucified. No one will be allowed to bury them, and people from many nations will crowd around to gaze at them. ¹⁰And there will be a worldwide holiday—people everywhere will rejoice and give presents to each other and throw parties to celebrate the death of the two prophets who had tormented them so much!

¹¹But after three and a half days, the spirit of life from God will enter them and they will stand up! And great fear will fall on everyone. ¹²Then a loud voice will shout from heaven, "Come up!" And they will rise to heaven in a cloud as their enemies watch.

¹³The same hour there will be a terrible earthquake that levels a tenth of the city, leaving 7,000 dead. Then everyone left will, in their terror, give glory to the God of heaven.

¹⁴The second woe is past, but the third quickly follows:

¹⁵For just then the seventh angel blew his trumpet, and there were loud voices shouting down from heaven, "The Kingdom of this world now belongs to our Lord, and to his Christ; and he shall reign forever and ever."

¹⁶And the twenty-four Elders sitting on their thrones before God threw themselves down in worship, saying, ¹⁷"We give thanks, Lord God Almighty, who is and was, for now you have assumed your great power and have begun to reign. ¹⁸The nations were angry with you, but now it is your turn to be angry with them. It is time to judge the dead, and reward your servants—prophets and people alike, all who fear your Name, both great and small—and to destroy those who have caused destruction upon the earth."

¹⁹Then, in heaven, the temple of God was opened and the ark of his covenant could be seen inside. Lightning flashed and thunder crashed and roared, and there was a great hailstorm and the world was shaken by a mighty earthquake.

God's Children Do Not Continue in Sin
✑§ 1 John 3:7–11 §✎

Oh, dear children, don't let anyone deceive you about this: if you are constantly doing what is good, it is because you *are* good, even as he is. ⁸But if you keep on sinning, it shows that you belong to Satan, who since he first began to sin has kept steadily at it. But the Son of God came to destroy these works of the devil. ⁹The person who has been born into God's family does not make a practice of sinning, because now God's life is in him; so he can't keep on sinning, for this new life has been born into him and controls him—he has been *born again*.

¹⁰So now we can tell who is a child of God and who belongs to Satan. Whoever is living a life of sin and doesn't love his brother shows that he is not in God's family; ¹¹for the message to us from the beginning has been that we should love one another.

Proverbs for Today
✑§ 30:11–14 §✎

There are those who curse their father and mother, and feel themselves faultless despite their many sins. They are proud beyond description, arrogant, disdainful. They devour the poor with teeth as sharp as knives!

✑ KEY VERSE ✎

If you keep on sinning, it shows that you belong to Satan, who since he first began to sin has kept steadily at it. But the Son of God came to destroy these works of the devil.—*1 John 3:8*

✑ REFLECTION ✎

John was writing about people who make a habit of sinning and look for ways to justify it. Many people develop stubborn habits. It is in these habits that temptation is strong and we can become weak, giving Satan a foothold. We must deal with these habits honestly rather than make excuses for them.

Couples must take three steps to prevail over sin: (1) seek the power of the Holy Spirit and the Word of God on a daily basis; (2) flee lustful desires; and (3) rely on the help of the Body of Christ—accountability to others and the prayers of others.

────── ❧ **MEDITATION** ❧ ──────

Heavenly Father, we have developed habits that lead us away from you. Please forgive us and teach us to live as you want instead. ❧

DECEMBER 20 ────────────

The Woman and the Dragon
❧ Revelation 12:1–17 ❧

Then a great pageant appeared in heaven, portraying things to come. I saw a woman clothed with the sun, with the moon beneath her feet, and a crown of twelve stars on her head. [2]She was pregnant and screamed in the pain of her labor, awaiting her delivery.

[3]Suddenly a red Dragon appeared, with seven heads and ten horns, and seven crowns on his heads. [4]His tail drew along behind him a third of the stars, which he plunged to the earth. He stood before the woman as she was about to give birth to her child, ready to eat the baby as soon as it was born.

[5]She gave birth to a boy who was to rule all nations with a heavy hand, and he was caught up to God and to his throne. [6]The woman fled into the wilderness, where God had prepared a place for her, to take care of her for 1,260 days.

[7]Then there was war in heaven; Michael and the angels under his command fought the Dragon and his hosts of fallen angels. [8]And the Dragon lost the battle and was forced from heaven. [9]This great Dragon—the ancient serpent called the devil, or Satan, the one deceiving the whole world—was thrown down onto the earth with all his army.

[10]Then I heard a loud voice shouting across the heavens, "It has happened at last! God's salvation and the power and the rule, and the authority of his Christ are finally here; for the Accuser of our brothers has been thrown down from heaven onto earth—he accused them day and night before our God. [11]They defeated him by the blood of the Lamb, and by their testimony; for they did not love their lives but laid them down for him. [12]Rejoice, O heavens! You citizens of heaven, rejoice! Be glad! But woe to you people of the world, for the devil has come down to you in great anger, knowing that he has little time.''

[13]And when the Dragon found himself cast down to earth, he persecuted the woman who had given birth to the child. [14]But she was given two wings like those of a great eagle, to fly into the wilderness to the place prepared for her, where she was cared for and protected from the Serpent, the Dragon, for three and a half years.

[15]And from the Serpent's mouth a vast flood of water gushed out and swept toward the woman in an effort to get rid of her; [16]but the earth helped her by opening its mouth and swallowing the flood! [17]Then the furious Dragon set out to attack the rest of her children—all who were keeping God's commandments and confessing that they belong to Jesus. He stood waiting on an ocean beach.

Effective Love
❧ 1 John 3:12–24 ❧

We are not to be like Cain, who belonged to Satan and killed his brother. Why did he kill him? Because Cain had been doing wrong and he knew very well that his brother's life was better than his. [13]So don't be surprised, dear friends, if the world hates you.

[14]If we love other Christians it proves that we

have been delivered from hell and given eternal life. But a person who doesn't have love for others is headed for eternal death. [15]Anyone who hates his Christian brother is really a murderer at heart; and you know that no one wanting to murder has eternal life within. [16]We know what real love is from Christ's example in dying for us. And so we also ought to lay down our lives for our Christian brothers.

[17]But if someone who is supposed to be a Christian has money enough to live well, and sees a brother in need, and won't help him—how can God's love be within *him*? [18]Little children, let us stop just *saying* we love people; let us *really* love them, and *show it* by our *actions*. [19]Then we will know for sure, by our actions, that we are on God's side, and our consciences will be clear, even when we stand before the Lord. [20]But if we have bad consciences and feel that we have done wrong, the Lord will surely feel it even more, for he knows everything we do.

[21]But, dearly loved friends, if our consciences are clear, we can come to the Lord with perfect assurance and trust, [22]and get whatever we ask for because we are obeying him and doing the things that please him. [23]And this is what God says we must do: Believe on the name of his Son Jesus Christ, and love one another. [24]Those who do what God says—they are living with God and he with them.

We know this is true because the Holy Spirit he has given us tells us so.

Proverbs for Today
৺৯ 30:15–16 ৶৶

There are two things never satisfied, like a leech forever craving more: no, three things! no, four! Hell. The barren womb. A barren desert. Fire.

⊸ KEY VERSE ⊛

We know what real love is from Christ's example in dying for us. And so we also ought to lay down our lives for our Christian brothers.—*1 John 3:16*

⊸ REFLECTION ⊛

A marriage without love is a marriage lacking the presence of Christ. Real love is an action, not a feeling. It produces selfless, sacrificial giving. The greatest act of love anyone can do is to give himself or herself to others. How can you lay down your life for your spouse? Sometimes it is easier to say you'll die for your husband or wife than truly to live for him or her, which involves putting his or her desires first. Show your love with actions rather than only with words.

⊸ MEDITATION ⊛

Heavenly Father, teach us to love each other as you have loved us. ৶৶

DECEMBER 21

A Creature from the Sea
৺৯ Revelation 13:1–18 ৶৶

And now, in my vision, I saw a strange Creature rising up out of the sea. It had seven heads and ten horns, and ten crowns upon its horns. And written on each head were blasphemous names, each one defying and insulting God. [2]This Creature looked like a leopard but had bear's feet and a lion's mouth! And the Dragon gave him his own power and throne and great authority.

[3]I saw that one of his heads seemed wounded beyond recovery—but the fatal wound was healed! All the world marveled at this miracle and followed the Creature in awe. [4]They worshiped the Dragon for giving him such power, and they worshiped the strange Creature. "Where is there anyone as great as he?" they exclaimed. "Who is able to fight against him?"

[5]Then the Dragon encouraged the Creature to speak great blasphemies against the Lord; and gave him authority to control the earth for forty-two

months. [6]All that time he blasphemed God's Name and his temple and all those living in heaven. [7]The Dragon gave him power to fight against God's people and to overcome them, and to rule over all nations and language groups throughout the world. [8]And all mankind—whose names were not written down before the founding of the world in the slain Lamb's Book of Life—worshiped the evil Creature.

[9]Anyone who can hear, listen carefully: [10]The people of God who are destined for prison will be arrested and taken away; those destined for death will be killed. But do not be dismayed, for here is your opportunity for endurance and confidence.

[11]Then I saw another strange animal, this one coming up out of the earth, with two little horns like those of a lamb but a fearsome voice like the Dragon's. [12]He exercised all the authority of the Creature whose death-wound had been healed, whom he required all the world to worship. [13]He did unbelievable miracles such as making fire flame down to earth from the skies while everyone was watching. [14]By doing these miracles, he was deceiving people everywhere. He could do these marvelous things whenever the first Creature was there to watch him. And he ordered the people of the world to make a great statue of the first Creature, who was fatally wounded and then came back to life. [15]He was permitted to give breath to this statue and even make it speak! Then the statue ordered that anyone refusing to worship it must die!

[16]He required everyone—great and small, rich and poor, slave and free—to be tattooed with a certain mark on the right hand or on the forehead. [17]And no one could get a job or even buy in any store without the permit of that mark, which was either the name of the Creature or the code number of his name. [18]Here is a puzzle that calls for careful thought to solve it. Let those who are able, interpret this code: the numerical values of the letters in his name add to 666!

The Incarnation—A Test for Truth
◄§ 1 John 4:1–6 §►

Dearly loved friends, don't always believe everything you hear just because someone says it is a message from God: test it first to see if it really is. For there are many false teachers around, [2]and the way to find out if their message is from the Holy Spirit is to ask: Does it really agree that Jesus Christ, God's Son, actually became man with a human body? If so, then the message is from God. [3]If not, the message is not from God but from one who is against Christ, like the "Antichrist" you have heard about who is going to come, and his attitude of enmity against Christ is already abroad in the world.

[4]Dear young friends, you belong to God and have already won your fight with those who are against Christ, because there is someone in your hearts who is stronger than any evil teacher in this wicked world. [5]These men belong to this world, so, quite naturally, they are concerned about worldly affairs and the world pays attention to them. [6]But we are children of God; that is why only those who have walked and talked with God will listen to us. Others won't. That is another way to know whether a message is really from God; for if it is, the world won't listen to it.

Proverbs for Today
◄§ 30:17 §►

A man who mocks his father and despises his mother shall have his eye plucked out by ravens and eaten by vultures.

◄ KEY VERSE ►

Dearly loved friends, don't always believe everything you hear just because someone says it is a message from God: test it first to see if it really is. For there are many false teachers around, and the way to find out if their message is from the Holy Spirit is to ask: Does it really agree that Jesus Christ, God's Son, actually became man with a human body? If so, then the message is from God.—*1 John 4:1–2*

◄ REFLECTION ►

Many people claim to know God's ideal for marriage and home. Unfortunately, much of what is printed and taught is not true. Christian couples should have faith, but they should not be gullible. Verify every message you hear, even the claims that the message is from God. If the message is truly from God, it will be consistent with the Bible.

◈ MEDITATION ◈

Heavenly Father, help us to be on our guard and to beware of false teachers. ℘

DECEMBER 22

The Lamb Stands on Mount Zion
◄§ Revelation 14:1–7 ℘

Then I saw a Lamb standing on Mount Zion in Jerusalem, and with him were 144,000 who had his Name and his Father's Name written on their foreheads. [2]And I heard a sound from heaven like the roaring of a great waterfall or the rolling of mighty thunder. It was the singing of a choir accompanied by harps.

[3]This tremendous choir—144,000 strong—sang a wonderful new song in front of the throne of God and before the four Living Beings and the twenty-four Elders; and no one could sing this song except those 144,000 who had been redeemed from the earth. [4]For they are spiritually undefiled, pure as virgins, following the Lamb wherever he goes. They have been purchased from among the men on the earth as a consecrated offering to God and the Lamb. [5]No falsehood can be charged against them; they are blameless.

[6]And I saw another angel flying through the heavens, carrying the everlasting Good News to preach to those on earth—to every nation, tribe, language and people.

[7]"Fear God," he shouted, "and extol his greatness. For the time has come when he will sit as Judge. Worship him who made the heaven and the earth, the sea and all its sources."

Let Us Love One Another
◄§ 1 John 4:7–15 ℘

Dear friends, let us practice loving each other, for love comes from God and those who are loving and kind show that they are the children of God, and that they are getting to know him better. [8]But if a person isn't loving and kind, it shows that he doesn't know God—for God is love.

[9]God showed how much he loved us by sending his only Son into this wicked world to bring to us eternal life through his death. [10]In this act we see what real love is: it is not our love for God, but his love for us when he sent his Son to satisfy God's anger against our sins.

[11]Dear friends, since God loved us as much as that, we surely ought to love each other too. [12]For though we have never yet seen God, when we love each other God lives in us and his love within us grows ever stronger. [13]And he has put his own Holy Spirit into our hearts as a proof to us that we are living with him and he with us. [14]And furthermore, we have seen with our own eyes and now tell all the world that God sent his Son to be their Savior. [15]Anyone who believes and says that Jesus is the Son of God has God living in him, and he is living with God.

Proverbs for Today
◄§ 30:18–20 ℘

There are three things too wonderful for me to understand—no, four! How an eagle glides through the sky. How a serpent crawls upon a rock. How a ship finds its way across the heaving ocean. The growth of love between a man and a girl. There is another thing too: how a prostitute can sin and then say, "What's wrong with that?"

◈ KEY VERSE ◈

If a person isn't loving and kind, it shows that he doesn't know God—for God is love.—*1 John 4:8*

John said, "God is love," not, "Love is God." Our world, with its shallow and selfish view of love, has turned these words around and contaminated our understanding of love. The world says that love is what makes a person feel good, and that it is all right to sacrifice moral principles and others' rights in order to obtain such "love." But that isn't real love; it is love's enemy—selfishness. God's love isn't like the love propagated by an evil world. Our definition of love must come from the God who is holy, just, and perfect. Husbands and wives must learn to love as God does.

―――――― ❧ MEDITATION ❧――――――

Heavenly Father, teach us to love as you do and not as the world does. ❧

DECEMBER 23 ――――――――――

Angels Announce the Judgment to Come
❧ Revelation 14:8–20 ❧

Then another angel followed him through the skies, saying, "Babylon is fallen, is fallen—that great city—because she seduced the nations of the world and made them share the wine of her intense impurity and sin."

[9]Then a third angel followed them shouting, "Anyone worshiping the Creature from the sea and his statue and accepting his mark on the forehead or the hand, [10]must drink the wine of the anger of God; it is poured out undiluted into God's cup of wrath. And they will be tormented with fire and burning sulphur in the presence of the holy angels and the Lamb. [11]The smoke of their torture rises forever and ever, and they will have no relief day or night, for they have worshiped the Creature and his statue, and have been tattooed with the code of his name. [12]Let this encourage God's people to endure patiently every trial and persecution, for they are his saints who remain firm to the end in obedience to his commands and trust in Jesus."

[13]And I heard a voice in the heavens above me saying, "Write this down: At last the time has come for his martyrs to enter into their full reward. Yes, says the Spirit, they are blest indeed, for now they shall rest from all their toils and trials; for their good deeds follow them to heaven!" [14]Then the scene changed and I saw a white cloud, and someone sitting on it who looked like Jesus, who was called "The Son of Man," with a crown of solid gold upon his head and a sharp sickle in his hand.

[15]Then an angel came from the temple and called out to him, "Begin to use the sickle, for the time has come for you to reap; the harvest is ripe on the earth." [16]So the one sitting on the cloud swung his sickle over the earth, and the harvest was gathered in. [17]After that another angel came from the temple in heaven, and he also had a sharp sickle.

[18]Just then the angel who has power to destroy the world with fire, shouted to the angel with the sickle, "Use your sickle now to cut off the clusters of grapes from the vines of the earth, for they are fully ripe for judgment." [19]So the angel swung his sickle on the earth and loaded the grapes into the great winepress of God's wrath. [20]And the grapes were trodden in the winepress outside the city, and blood flowed out in a stream 200 miles long and as high as a horse's bridle.

God's Children Live in Love
❧ 1 John 4:16–21 ❧

We know how much God loves us because we have felt his love and because we believe him when he tells us that he loves us dearly. God is love, and anyone who lives in love is living with God and God is living in him. [17]And as we live with Christ, our love grows more perfect and complete; so we will not be ashamed and embarrassed at the day of judgment, but can face him with confidence and joy, because he loves us and we love him too.

[18]We need have no fear of someone who loves us

perfectly; his perfect love for us eliminates all dread of what he might do to us. If we are afraid, it is for fear of what he might do to us, and shows that we are not fully convinced that he really loves us. [19]So you see, our love for him comes as a result of his loving us first.

[20]If anyone says "I love God," but keeps on hating his brother, he is a liar; for if he doesn't love his brother who is right there in front of him, how can he love God whom he has never seen? [21]And God himself has said that one must love not only God, but his brother too.

Proverbs for Today
⋖§ 30:21–23 §⋗

There are three things that make the earth tremble—no, four it cannot stand: A slave who becomes a king. A rebel who prospers. A bitter woman when she finally marries. A servant girl who marries her mistress' husband.

KEY VERSE

If anyone says "I love God," but keeps on hating his brother, he is a liar; for if he doesn't love his brother who is right there in front of him, how can he love God whom he has never seen?—*1 John 4:20*

REFLECTION

It is easy to say we love God when it doesn't cost us anything more than weekly attendance at religious services. But the real test of our love for God is how we treat the people right in front of us—our spouse, family members, and fellow believers. We cannot love God while neglecting those who are created in his image. Do you really love God? Show it by treating your spouse with the highest respect.

MEDITATION

Heavenly Father, help me to love and respect the people you have placed right in front of me—my spouse, my family, and my fellow believers. §⋗

DECEMBER 24

The Song of Moses and the Lamb
⋖§ Revelation 15:1–8 §⋗

And I saw in heaven another mighty pageant showing things to come: Seven angels were assigned to carry down to earth the seven last plagues—and then at last God's anger will be finished.

[2]Spread out before me was what seemed to be an ocean of fire and glass, and on it stood all those who had been victorious over the Evil Creature and his statue and his mark and number. All were holding harps of God, [3,4]and they were singing the song of Moses, the servant of God, and the song of the Lamb:

"Great and marvelous
Are your doings,
Lord God Almighty.
Just and true

Are your ways,
O King of Ages.
Who shall not fear,
O Lord,
And glorify your Name?
For you alone are holy.
All nations will come
And worship before you,
For your righteous deeds
Have been disclosed."

[5]Then I looked and saw that the Holy of Holies of the temple in heaven was thrown wide open!

[6]The seven angels who were assigned to pour out the seven plagues then came from the temple, clothed in spotlessly white linen, with golden belts across their chests. [7]And one of the four Living Beings handed each of them a golden flask filled with the terrible wrath of the Living God who lives forever and forever. [8]The temple was filled with smoke

from his glory and power; and no one could enter until the seven angels had completed pouring out the seven plagues.

Eternal Life Is in God's Son
◄§ 1 John 5:1–15 §►

If you believe that Jesus is the Christ—that he is God's Son and your Savior—then you are a child of God. And all who love the Father love his children too. ²So you can find out how much you love God's children—your brothers and sisters in the Lord—by how much you love and obey God. ³Loving God means doing what he tells us to do, and really, that isn't hard at all; ⁴for every child of God can obey him, defeating sin and evil pleasure by trusting Christ to help him.

⁵But who could possibly fight and win this battle except by believing that Jesus is truly the Son of God? ⁶,⁷,⁸And we know he is, because God said so with a voice from heaven when Jesus was baptized, and again as he was facing death —yes, not only at his baptism but also as he faced death. And the Holy Spirit, forever truthful, says it too. So we have these three witnesses: the voice of the Holy Spirit in our hearts, the voice from heaven at Christ's baptism, and the voice before he died. And they all say the same thing: that Jesus Christ is the Son of God. ⁹We believe men who witness in our courts, and so surely we can believe whatever God declares. And God declares that Jesus is his Son. ¹⁰All who believe this know in their hearts that it is true. If anyone doesn't believe this, he is actually calling God a liar, because he doesn't believe what God has said about his Son.

¹¹And what is it that God has said? That he has given us eternal life, and that this life is in his Son. ¹²So whoever has God's Son has life; whoever does not have his Son, does not have life.

¹³I have written this to you who believe in the Son of God so that you may know you have eternal life. ¹⁴And we are sure of this, that he will listen to us whenever we ask him for anything in line with his will. ¹⁵And if we really know he is listening when we talk to him and make our requests, then we can be sure that he will answer us.

Proverbs for Today
◄§ 30:24–28 §►

There are four things that are small but unusually wise: Ants: they aren't strong, but store up food for the winter. Cliff badgers: delicate little animals who protect themselves by living among the rocks. The locusts: though they have no leader, they stay together in swarms. The lizards: they are easy to catch and kill, yet are found even in king's palaces!

──────◄ KEY VERSE ►──────

If we really know he is listening when we talk to him and make our requests, then we can be sure that he will answer us.—*1 John 5:15*

──────◄ REFLECTION ►──────

The emphasis here is on God's will, not our will. When we communicate with God, we don't demand what we want; rather, we discuss with him what he wants for us. If you will align your prayers to God's will, he will listen. And you can be certain that if he listens, he will answer. Start praying with confidence! God does hear and answer your prayers.

──────◄ MEDITATION ►──────

Heavenly Father, as we pray for each and every area of our lives together, we are confident that you are listening to us and that you will answer. Thank you. §►

Angels Pour Out Plagues upon the Earth
◄§ Revelation 16:1–21 §►

And I heard a mighty voice shouting from the temple to the seven angels, "Now go your ways and empty out the seven flasks of the wrath of God upon the earth."

²So the first angel left the temple and poured out his flask over the earth, and horrible, malignant sores broke out on everyone who had the mark of the Creature and was worshiping his statue.

³The second angel poured out his flask upon the oceans, and they became like the watery blood of a dead man; and everything in all the oceans died.

⁴The third angel poured out his flask upon the rivers and springs and they became blood. ⁵And I heard this angel of the waters declaring, "You are just in sending this judgment, O Holy One, who is and was, ⁶for your saints and prophets have been martyred and their blood poured out upon the earth; and now, in turn, you have poured out the blood of those who murdered them; it is their just reward."

⁷And I heard the angel of the altar say, "Yes, Lord God Almighty, your punishments are just and true."

⁸Then the fourth angel poured out his flask upon the sun, causing it to scorch all men with its fire. ⁹Everyone was burned by this blast of heat, and they cursed the name of God who sent the plagues—they did not change their mind and attitude to give him glory.

¹⁰Then the fifth angel poured out his flask upon the throne of the Creature from the sea, and his kingdom was plunged into darkness. And his subjects gnawed their tongues in anguish, ¹¹and cursed the God of heaven for their pains and sores, but they refused to repent of all their evil deeds.

¹²The sixth angel poured out his flask upon the great River Euphrates and it dried up so that the kings from the east could march their armies westward without hindrance. ¹³And I saw three evil spirits disguised as frogs leap from the mouth of the Dragon, the Creature, and his False Prophet.

¹⁴These miracle-working demons conferred with all the rulers of the world to gather them for battle against the Lord on that great coming Judgment Day of God Almighty.

¹⁵"Take note: I will come as unexpectedly as a thief! Blessed are all who are awaiting me, who keep their robes in readiness and will not need to walk naked and ashamed."

¹⁶And they gathered all the armies of the world near a place called, in Hebrew, Armageddon—the Mountain of Megiddo.

¹⁷Then the seventh angel poured out his flask into the air; and a mighty shout came from the throne of the temple in heaven, saying, "It is finished!" ¹⁸Then the thunder crashed and rolled, and lightning flashed; and there was a great earthquake of a magnitude unprecedented in human history. ¹⁹The great city of "Babylon" split into three sections, and cities around the world fell in heaps of rubble; and so all of "Babylon's" sins were remembered in God's thoughts, and she was punished to the last drop of anger in the cup of the wine of the fierceness of his wrath. ²⁰And islands vanished, and mountains flattened out, ²¹and there was an incredible hailstorm from heaven; hailstones weighing a hundred pounds fell from the sky onto the people below, and they cursed God because of the terrible hail.

God's Children Do Not Continue in Sin
◄§ 1 John 5:16–21 §►

If you see a Christian sinning in a way that does not end in death, you should ask God to forgive him and God will give him life, unless he has sinned that one fatal sin. But there is that one sin which ends in death and if he has done that, there is no use praying for him. ¹⁷Every wrong is a sin, of course. I'm not talking about these ordinary sins; I am speaking of that one that ends in death.

¹⁸No one who has become part of God's family makes a practice of sinning, for Christ, God's Son, holds him securely and the devil cannot get his hands on him. ¹⁹We know that we are children of

God and that all the rest of the world around us is under Satan's power and control. [20]And we know that Christ, God's Son, has come to help us understand and find the true God. And now we are in God because we are in Jesus Christ his Son, who is the only true God; and he is eternal Life.

[21]Dear children, keep away from anything that might take God's place in your hearts. Amen.

Sincerely,
John

Proverbs for Today
§ 30:29–31 §

There are three stately monarchs in the earth—no, four: The lion, king of the animals. He won't turn aside for anyone. The peacock. The male goat. A king as he leads his army.

—————— *KEY VERSE* ——————

Dear children, keep away from anything that might take God's place in your hearts. Amen.—*1 John 5:21*

—————— *REFLECTION* ——————

This verse can also be translated, "Keep yourself from idols." An idol is anything that substitutes for the true faith; anything that robs Christ of his full deity and humanity; any human idea that claims to be more authoritative than the Bible; anything that replaces God as the center of our lives. Is God at the center of your marriage?

—————— *MEDITATION* ——————

Heavenly Father, we dedicate our marriage to you. We ask that the Holy Spirit will dwell in our home and in our relationship. §

DECEMBER 26

The Woman, A Symbol of Babylon
§ Revelation 17:1–18 §

One of the seven angels who had poured out the plagues came over and talked with me. "Come with me," he said, "and I will show you what is going to happen to the Notorious Prostitute, who sits upon the many waters of the world. [2]The kings of the world have had immoral relations with her, and the people of the earth have been made drunk by the wine of her immorality."

[3]So the angel took me in spirit into the wilderness. There I saw a woman sitting on a scarlet animal that had seven heads and ten horns, written all over with blasphemies against God. [4]The woman wore purple and scarlet clothing and beautiful jewelry made of gold and precious gems and pearls, and held in her hand a golden goblet full of obscenities:

[5]A mysterious caption was written on her forehead: "Babylon the Great, Mother of Prostitutes and of Idol Worship Everywhere around the World."

[6]I could see that she was drunk—drunk with the blood of the martyrs of Jesus she had killed. I stared at her in horror.

[7]"Why are you so surprised?" the angel asked. "I'll tell you who she is and what the animal she is riding represents. [8]He was alive but isn't now. And yet, soon he will come up out of the bottomless pit and go to eternal destruction; and the people of earth, whose names have not been written in the Book of Life before the world began, will be dumbfounded at his reappearance after being dead.

[9]"And now think hard: his seven heads represent a certain city built on seven hills where this woman has her residence. [10]They also represent seven kings. Five have already fallen, the sixth now reigns, and the seventh is yet to come, but his reign will be brief. [11]The scarlet animal that died is the eighth king, having reigned before as one of the seven; after his second reign, he too, will go to his doom. [12]His ten horns are ten kings who have not yet risen to power; they will be appointed to their kingdoms for one brief moment, to reign with him. [13]They

will all sign a treaty giving their power and strength to him. ¹⁴Together they will wage war against the Lamb, and the Lamb will conquer them; for he is Lord over all lords, and King of kings, and his people are the called and chosen and faithful ones.

¹⁵"The oceans, lakes and rivers that the woman is sitting on represent masses of people of every race and nation.

¹⁶"The scarlet animal and his ten horns—which represent ten kings who will reign with him—all hate the woman, and will attack her and leave her naked and ravaged by fire. ¹⁷For God will put a plan into their minds, a plan that will carry out his purposes: They will mutually agree to give their authority to the scarlet animal, so that the words of God will be fulfilled. ¹⁸And this woman you saw in your vision represents the great city that rules over the kings of the earth."

To Love One Another Is to Obey God
2 John 1:1–6

From: John, the old Elder of the church.

To: That dear woman Cyria, one of God's very own, and to her children whom I love so much, as does everyone else in the church. ²Since the Truth is in our hearts forever, ³God the Father and Jesus Christ his Son will bless us with great mercy and much peace, and with truth and love.

⁴How happy I am to find some of your children here, and to see that they are living as they should, following the Truth, obeying God's command.

⁵And now I want to urgently remind you, dear friends, of the old rule God gave us right from the beginning, that Christians should love one another. ⁶If we love God, we will do whatever he tells us to.

And he has told us from the very first to love each other.

Proverbs for Today
30:32

If you have been a fool by being proud or plotting evil, don't brag about it—cover your mouth with your hand in shame.

KEY VERSE

If we love God, we will do whatever he tells us to. And he has told us from the very first to love each other.—*2 John 1:6*

REFLECTION

The love Christians should have for one another is a recurrent New Testament theme. This theme is repeated again and again so that we will understand its importance. Love is not an option for Christians, it is a command. True obedience to God is measured by our love for others. But just knowing God's command is not enough. We must put it into practice. We can show love to our spouse in many ways: listening, helping, giving, serving, and refusing to judge. Do you really practice this New Testament love in your marriage? Be honest.

MEDITATION

Heavenly Father, as we practice to obey all of your commandments, let us not forget the most important one of all—to love you with all of our heart, soul, mind, and strength.

DECEMBER 27

The Fall of Babylon
Revelation 18:1–24

After all this I saw another angel come down from heaven with great authority, and the earth grew bright with his splendor.

²He gave a mighty shout, "Babylon the Great is fallen, is fallen; she has become a den of demons, a haunt of devils and every kind of evil spirit. ³For all the nations have drunk the fatal wine of her intense immorality. The rulers of earth have enjoyed themselves with her, and businessmen throughout

the world have grown rich from all her luxurious living.''

[4]Then I heard another voice calling from heaven, ''Come away from her, my people; do not take part in her sins, or you will be punished with her. [5]For her sins are piled as high as heaven and God is ready to judge her for her crimes. [6]Do to her as she has done to you, and more—give double penalty for all her evil deeds. She brewed many a cup of woe for others—give twice as much to her. [7]She has lived in luxury and pleasure—match it now with torments and with sorrows. She boasts, 'I am queen upon my throne. I am no helpless widow. I will not experience sorrow.' [8]Therefore the sorrows of death and mourning and famine shall overtake her in a single day, and she shall be utterly consumed by fire; for mighty is the Lord who judges her.''

[9]And the world leaders, who took part in her immoral acts and enjoyed her favors, will mourn for her as they see the smoke rising from her charred remains. [10]They will stand far off, trembling with fear and crying out, ''Alas, Babylon, that mighty city! In one moment her judgment fell.''

[11]The merchants of the earth will weep and mourn for her, for there is no one left to buy their goods. [12]She was their biggest customer for gold and silver, precious stones, pearls, finest linens, purple silks, and scarlet; and every kind of perfumed wood, and ivory goods and most expensive wooden carvings, and brass and iron and marble; [13]and spices and perfumes and incense, ointment and frankincense, wine, olive oil, and fine flour; wheat, cattle, sheep, horses, chariots, and slaves— and even the souls of men.

[14]''All the fancy things you loved so much are gone,'' they cry. ''The dainty luxuries and splendor that you prized so much will never be yours again. They are gone forever.''

[15]And so the merchants who have become wealthy by selling her these things shall stand at a distance, fearing danger to themselves, weeping and crying, [16]''Alas, that great city, so beautiful— like a woman clothed in finest purple and scarlet linens, decked out with gold and precious stones and pearls! [17]In one moment, all the wealth of the city is gone!''

And all the shipowners and captains of the merchant ships and crews will stand a long way off, [18]crying as they watch the smoke ascend, and saying, ''Where in all the world is there another city such as this?'' [19]And they will throw dust on their heads in their sorrow and say, ''Alas, alas, for that great city! She made us all rich from her great wealth. And now in a single hour all is gone. . . .''

[20]But you, O heaven, rejoice over her fate; and you, O children of God and the prophets and the apostles! For at last God has given judgment against her for you.

[21]Then a mighty angel picked up a boulder shaped like a millstone and threw it into the ocean and shouted, ''Babylon, that great city, shall be thrown away as I have thrown away this stone, and she shall disappear forever. [22]Never again will the sound of music be there—no more pianos, saxophones, and trumpets. No industry of any kind will ever again exist there, and there will be no more milling of the grain. [23]Dark, dark will be her nights; not even a lamp in a window will ever be seen again. No more joyous wedding bells and happy voices of the bridegrooms and the brides. Her businessmen were known around the world and she deceived all nations with her sorceries. [24]And she was responsible for the blood of all the martyred prophets and the saints.''

Beware of False Teachers
◄§ 2 John 1:7-13 §►

Watch out for the false leaders—and there are many of them around—who don't believe that Jesus Christ came to earth as a human being with a body like ours. Such people are against the truth and against Christ. [8]Beware of being like them, and losing the prize that you and I have been working so hard to get. See to it that you win your full reward from the Lord. [9]For if you wander beyond the teaching of Christ, you will leave God behind; while if you are loyal to Christ's teachings, you will have God too. Then you will have both the Father and the Son.

[10]If anyone comes to teach you, and he doesn't believe what Christ taught, don't even invite him into your home. Don't encourage him in any way.

¹¹If you do you will be a partner with him in his wickedness.

¹²Well, I would like to say much more, but I don't want to say it in this letter, for I hope to come to see you soon and then we can talk over these things together and have a joyous time.

¹³Greetings from the children of your sister—another choice child of God.

Sincerely,
John

Proverbs for Today
⋖§ 30:33 §⋗

As the churning of cream yields butter, and a blow to the nose causes bleeding, so anger causes quarrels.

──────── ⋗ KEY VERSE ⋖ ────────

"She has lived in luxury and pleasure—match it now with torments and with sorrows. She boasts, 'I am queen upon my throne. I am no helpless widow. I will not experience sorrow.' "—*Revelation 18:7*

──────── ⋗ REFLECTION ⋖ ────────

Babylon "lived in luxury and pleasure." She boasted, "I am queen upon my throne . . . I will not experience sorrow." The powerful, wealthy people of this world are susceptible to this same attitude. A couple who is financially comfortable often feels invulnerable, secure, and in control, not in need of God or anyone else. That kind of attitude defies God, and God's judgment against it is harsh. If you are financially secure, don't become complacent or deluded by the myth of self-sufficiency. Use your resources to help others and advance God's Kingdom.

──────── ⋗ MEDITATION ⋖ ────────

Heavenly Father, thank you for the resources that you have given us. Help us avoid the temptation to keep everything for ourselves. ⋗

DECEMBER 28

A Vast Crowd in Heaven Praises God
⋖§ Revelation 19:1–21 §⋗

After this I heard the shouting of a vast crowd in heaven, "Hallelujah! Praise the Lord! Salvation is from our God. Honor and authority belong to him alone; ²for his judgments are just and true. He has punished the Great Prostitute who corrupted the earth with her sin; and he has avenged the murder of his servants."

³Again and again their voices rang, "Praise the Lord! The smoke from her burning ascends forever and forever!"

⁴Then the twenty-four Elders and four Living Beings fell down and worshiped God, who was sitting upon the throne, and said, "Amen! Hallelujah! Praise the Lord!"

⁵And out of the throne came a voice that said, "Praise our God, all you his servants, small and great, who fear him."

⁶Then I heard again what sounded like the shouting of a huge crowd, or like the waves of a hundred oceans crashing on the shore, or like the mighty rolling of great thunder, "Praise the Lord. For the Lord our God, the Almighty, reigns. ⁷Let us be glad and rejoice and honor him; for the time has come for the wedding banquet of the Lamb, and his bride has prepared herself. ⁸She is permitted to wear the cleanest and whitest and finest of linens." (Fine linen represents the good deeds done by the people of God.)

⁹And the angel dictated this sentence to me: "Blessed are those who are invited to the wedding feast of the Lamb." And he added, "God himself has stated this."

¹⁰Then I fell down at his feet to worship him, but

he said, "No! Don't! For I am a servant of God just as you are, and as your brother Christians are, who testify of their faith in Jesus. Worship God. The purpose of all prophecy and of all I have shown you is to tell about Jesus."

¹¹Then I saw heaven opened and a white horse standing there; and the one sitting on the horse was named "Faithful and True"—the one who justly punishes and makes war. ¹²His eyes were like flames, and on his head were many crowns. A name was written on his forehead, and only he knew its meaning. ¹³He was clothed with garments dipped in blood, and his title was "The Word of God." ¹⁴The armies of heaven, dressed in finest linen, white and clean, followed him on white horses.

¹⁵In his mouth he held a sharp sword to strike down the nations; he ruled them with an iron grip; and he trod the winepress of the fierceness of the wrath of Almighty God. ¹⁶On his robe and thigh was written this title: "King of Kings and Lord of Lords."

¹⁷Then I saw an angel standing in the sunshine, shouting loudly to the birds, "Come! Gather together for the supper of the Great God! ¹⁸Come and eat the flesh of kings, and captains, and great generals; of horses and riders; and of all humanity, both great and small, slave and free."

¹⁹Then I saw the Evil Creature gathering the governments of the earth and their armies to fight against the one sitting on the horse and his army. ²⁰And the Evil Creature was captured, and with him the False Prophet, who could do mighty miracles when the Evil Creature was present—miracles that deceived all who had accepted the Evil Creature's mark, and who worshiped his statue. Both of them—the Evil Creature and his False Prophet—were thrown alive into the Lake of Fire that burns with sulphur. ²¹And their entire army was killed with the sharp sword in the mouth of the one riding the white horse, and all the birds of heaven were gorged with their flesh.

God's Children Do What Is Right
◅§ 3 John 1:1-15 §►

From: John, the Elder.
To: Dear Gaius, whom I truly love.

²Dear friend, I am praying that all is well with you and that your body is as healthy as I know your soul is. ³Some of the brothers traveling by have made me very happy by telling me that your life stays clean and true, and that you are living by the standards of the Gospel. ⁴I could have no greater joy than to hear such things about my children.

⁵Dear friend, you are doing a good work for God in taking care of the traveling teachers and missionaries who are passing through. ⁶They have told the church here of your friendship and your loving deeds. I am glad when you send them on their way with a generous gift. ⁷For they are traveling for the Lord, and take neither food, clothing, shelter, nor money from those who are not Christians, even though they have preached to them. ⁸So we ourselves should take care of them in order that we may become partners with them in the Lord's work.

⁹I sent a brief letter to the church about this, but proud Diotrephes, who loves to push himself forward as the leader of the Christians there, does not admit my authorityr over him and refuses to listen to me. ¹⁰When I come I will tell you some of the things he is doing and what wicked things he is saying about me and what insulting language he is using. He not only refuses to welcome the missionary travelers himself, but tells others not to, and when they do he tries to put them out of the church.

¹¹Dear friend, don't let this bad example influence you. Follow only what is good. Remember that those who do what is right prove that they are God's children; and those who continue in evil prove that they are far from God. ¹²But everyone, including Truth itself, speaks highly of Demetrius. I myself can say the same for him, and you know I speak the truth.

¹³I have much to say but I don't want to write it, ¹⁴for I hope to see you soon and then we will have much to talk about together. ¹⁵So good-bye for now. Friends here send their love, and please give each of the folks there a special greeting from me.

Sincerely,
John

Proverbs for Today
◄§ 31:1–7 §►

These are the wise sayings of King Lemuel of Massa, taught to him at his mother's knee: O my son, whom I have dedicated to the Lord, do not spend your time with women—the royal pathway to destruction. And it is not for kings, O Lemuel, to drink wine and whiskey. For if they drink they may forget their duties and be unable to give justice to those who are oppressed. Hard liquor is for sick men at the brink of death, and wine for those in deep depression. Let them drink to forget their poverty and misery.

◄ KEY VERSE ◄

If they drink they may forget their duties and be unable to give justice to those who are oppressed. —*Proverbs 31:5*

◄ REFLECTION ◄

Many Christian couples struggle with the place of alcohol in their lives. While many argue that a social drink now and then is not harmful or sinful, Scripture consistently warns against the misuse of alcohol. If you think that it is acceptable for you and your spouse to drink, pray diligently about this matter. While drunkenness might be understandable among unbelievers who are on the brink of death, it is inexcusable for anyone in a leadership position. Alcohol clouds the mind and can lead to injustice and poor decisions. Couples have better things to do than anesthetize themselves with alcohol.

◄ MEDITATION ◄

Heavenly Father, remind us of our duties and help us to fulfill them responsibly. Keep our minds sharp for the ongoing work of your kingdom. §►

DECEMBER 29

Satan Is Bound for a Thousand Years
◄§ Revelation 20:1–15 §►

Then I saw an angel come down from heaven with the key to the bottomless pit and a heavy chain in his hand. [2] He seized the Dragon—that old Serpent, the devil, Satan—and bound him in chains for 1,000 years, [3] and threw him into the bottomless pit, which he then shut and locked, so that he could not fool the nations any more until the thousand years were finished. Afterwards he would be released again for a little while.

[4] Then I saw thrones, and sitting on them were those who had been given the right to judge. And I saw the souls of those who had been beheaded for their testimony about Jesus, for proclaiming the Word of God, and who had not worshiped the Creature or his statue, nor accepted his mark on their foreheads or their hands. They had come to life again and now they reigned with Christ for a thousand years.

[5] This is the First Resurrection. (The rest of the dead did not come back to life until the thousand years had ended.) [6] Blessed and holy are those who share in the First Resurrection. For them the Second Death holds no terrors, for they will be priests of God and of Christ, and shall reign with him a thousand years.

[7] When the thousand years end, Satan will be let out of his prison. [8] He will go out to deceive the nations of the world and gather them together, with Gog and Magog, for battle—a mighty host, numberless as sand along the shore. [9] They will go up across the broad plain of the earth and surround God's people and the beloved city of Jerusalem on every side. But fire from God in heaven will flash down on the attacking armies and consume them.

[10] Then the devil who had betrayed them will again be thrown into the Lake of Fire burning with sulphur where the Creature and False Prophet are,

and they will be tormented day and night forever and ever.

[11] And I saw a great white throne and the one who sat upon it, from whose face the earth and sky fled away, but they found no place to hide. [12] I saw the dead, great and small, standing before God; and The Books were opened, including the Book of Life. And the dead were judged according to the things written in The Books, each according to the deeds he had done. [13] The oceans surrendered the bodies buried in them; and the earth and the underworld gave up the dead in them. Each was judged according to his deeds. [14] And Death and Hell were thrown into the Lake of Fire. This is the Second Death—the Lake of Fire. [15] And if anyone's name was not found recorded in the Book of Life, he was thrown into the Lake of Fire.

Defend God's Truth
◄§ Jude 1:1–7 §►

From: Jude, a servant of Jesus Christ, and a brother of James.

To: Christians everywhere—beloved of God and chosen by him. [2] May you be given more and more of God's kindness, peace, and love.

[3] Dearly loved friends, I had been planning to write you some thoughts about the salvation God has given us, but now I find I must write of something else instead, urging you to stoutly defend the truth which God gave, once for all, to his people to keep without change through the years. [4] I say this because some godless teachers have wormed their way in among you, saying that after we become Christians we can do just as we like without fear of God's punishment. The fate of such people was written long ago, for they have turned against our only Master and Lord, Jesus Christ.

[5] My answer to them is: Remember this fact—which you know already—that the Lord saved a whole nation of people out of the land of Egypt, and then killed every one of them who did not trust and obey him. [6] And I remind you of those angels who were once pure and holy, but turned to a life of sin. Now God has them chained up in prisons of darkness, waiting for the judgment day. [7] And don't forget the cities of Sodom and Gomorrah and their neighboring towns, all full of lust of every kind including lust of men for other men. Those cities were destroyed by fire and continue to be a warning to us that there is a hell in which sinners are punished.

Proverbs for Today
◄§ 31:8–9 §►

You should defend those who cannot help themselves. Yes, speak up for the poor and helpless, and see that they get justice.

◄ KEY VERSE ◄

Dear friend, you are doing a good work for God in taking care of the traveling teachers and missionaries who are passing through.—*3 John 1:5*

◄ REFLECTION ◄

Perhaps you and your spouse have asked yourselves what you can do to minister to other people as a couple. One thing you can do is to invite people into your home for meals—fellow church members, young people, traveling missionaries, those in need, visitors. This is an active and much-appreciated way you can show God's love to others.

◄ MEDITATION ◄

Heavenly Father, make us a hospitable couple. Make us able and willing to open our home to your people. §►

DECEMBER 30

The New Jerusalem
◆§ Revelation 21:1—22:7 §◆

Then I saw a new earth (with no oceans!) and a new sky, for the present earth and sky had disappeared. [2]And I, John, saw the Holy City, the new Jerusalem, coming down from God out of heaven. It was a glorious sight, beautiful as a bride at her wedding.

[3]I heard a loud shout from the throne saying, "Look, the home of God is now among men, and he will live with them and they will be his people; yes, God himself will be among them. [4]He will wipe away all tears from their eyes, and there shall be no more death, nor sorrow, nor crying, nor pain. All of that has gone forever."

[5]And the one sitting on the throne said, "See, I am making all things new!" And then he said to me, "Write this down, for what I tell you is trustworthy and true: [6]It is finished! I am the A and the Z—the Beginning and the End. I will give to the thirsty the springs of the Water of Life—as a gift! [7]Everyone who conquers will inherit all these blessings, and I will be his God and he will be my son. [8]But cowards who turn back from following me, and those who are unfaithful to me, and the corrupt, and murderers, and the immoral, and those conversing with demons, and idol worshipers and all liars—their doom is in the Lake that burns with fire and sulphur. This is the Second Death."

[9]Then one of the seven angels, who had emptied the flasks containing the seven last plagues, came and said to me, "Come with me and I will show you the bride, the Lamb's wife."

[10]In a vision he took me to a towering mountain peak and from there I watched that wondrous city, the holy Jerusalem, descending out of the skies from God. [11]It was filled with the glory of God, and flashed and glowed like a precious gem, crystal clear like jasper. [12]Its walls were broad and high, with twelve gates guarded by twelve angels. And the names of the twelve tribes of Israel were written on the gates. [13]There were three gates on each side—north, south, east, and west. [14]The walls had twelve foundation stones, and on them were written the names of the twelve apostles of the Lamb.

[15]The angel held in his hand a golden measuring stick to measure the city and its gates and walls. [16]When he measured it, he found it was a square as wide as it was long; in fact it was in the form of a cube, for its height was exactly the same as its other dimensions—1,500 miles each way. [17]Then he measured the thickness of the walls and found them to be 216 feet across (the angel called out these measurements to me, using standard units).

[18,19,20]The city itself was pure, transparent gold like glass! The wall was made of jasper, and was built on twelve layers of foundation stones inlaid with gems:

The first layer with jasper;
The second with sapphire;
The third with chalcedony;
The fourth with emerald;
The fifth with sardonyx;
The sixth layer with sardus;
The seventh with chrysolite;
The eighth with beryl;
The ninth with topaz;
The tenth with chrysoprase;
The eleventh with jacinth;
The twelfth with amethyst.

[21]The twelve gates were made of pearls—each gate from a single pearl! And the main street was pure, transparent gold, like glass.

[22]No temple could be seen in the city, for the Lord God Almighty and the Lamb are worshiped in it everywhere. [23]And the city has no need of sun or moon to light it, for the glory of God and of the Lamb illuminate it. [24]Its light will light the nations of the earth, and the rulers of the world will come and bring their glory to it. [25]Its gates never close; they stay open all day long—and there is no night! [26]And the glory and honor of all the nations shall be brought into it. [27]Nothing evil will be permitted in it—no one immoral or dishonest—but only those whose names are written in the Lamb's Book of Life.

[22:1]And he pointed out to me a river of pure

Water of Life, clear as crystal, flowing from the throne of God and the Lamb, ²coursing down the center of the main street. On each side of the river grew Trees of Life, bearing twelve crops of fruit, with a fresh crop each month; the leaves were used for medicine to heal the nations.

³There shall be nothing in the city which is evil; for the throne of God and of the Lamb will be there, and his servants will worship him. ⁴And they shall see his face; and his name shall be written on their foreheads. ⁵And there will be no night there—no need for lamps or sun—for the Lord God will be their light; and they shall reign forever and ever.

⁶,⁷Then the angel said to me, "These words are trustworthy and true: 'I am coming soon!' God, who tells his prophets what the future holds, has sent his angel to tell you this will happen soon. Blessed are those who believe it and all else written in the scroll."

The Punishment of False Teachers
~§ Jude 1:8–16 §~

Yet these false teachers carelessly go right on living their evil, immoral lives, degrading their bodies and laughing at those in authority over them, even scoffing at the Glorious Ones. ⁹Yet Michael, one of the mightiest of the angels, when he was arguing with Satan about Moses' body, did not dare to accuse even Satan, or jeer at him, but simply said, "The Lord rebuke you." ¹⁰But these men mock and curse at anything they do not understand, and, like animals, they do whatever they feel like, thereby ruining their souls.

¹¹Woe upon them! For they follow the example of Cain who killed his brother; and, like Balaam, they will do anything for money; and like Korah, they have disobeyed God and will die under his curse.

¹²When these men join you at the love feasts of the church, they are evil smears among you, laughing and carrying on, gorging and stuffing themselves without a thought for others. They are like clouds blowing over dry land without giving rain, promising much, but producing nothing. They are like fruit trees without any fruit at picking time. They are not only dead, but doubly dead, for they

have been pulled out, roots and all, to be burned.

¹³All they leave behind them is shame and disgrace like the dirty foam left along the beach by the wild waves. They wander around looking as bright as stars, but ahead of them is the everlasting gloom and darkness that God has prepared for them.

¹⁴Enoch, who lived seven generations after Adam, knew about these men and said this about them: "See, the Lord is coming with millions of his holy ones. ¹⁵He will bring the people of the world before him in judgment, to receive just punishment, and to prove the terrible things they have done in rebellion against God, revealing all they have said against him." ¹⁶These men are constant gripers, never satisfied, doing whatever evil they feel like; they are loudmouthed "show-offs," and when they show respect for others, it is only to get something from them in return.

Proverbs for Today
~§ 31:10–24 §~

If you can find a truly good wife, she is worth more than precious gems! Her husband can trust her, and she will richly satisfy his needs. She will not hinder him, but help him all her life. She finds wool and flax and busily spins it. She buys imported foods, brought by ship from distant ports. She gets up before dawn to prepare breakfast for her household, and plans the day's work for her servant girls. She goes out to inspect a field, and buys it; with her own hands she plants a vineyard. She is energetic, a hard worker, and watches for bargains. She works far into the night! She sews for the poor, and generously helps those in need. She has no fear of winter for her household, for she has made warm clothes for all of them. She also upholsters with finest tapestry; her own clothing is beautifully made—a purple gown of pure linen. Her husband is well known, for he sits in the council chamber with the other civic leaders. She makes belted linen garments to sell to the merchants.

────── ✎ KEY VERSE ✎ ──────

If you can find a truly good wife, she is worth more than precious gems! Her husband can trust her, and she will richly satisfy his needs. She will not hinder him but help him all her life.—*Proverbs 31:10–12*

Proverbs has a lot to say about women. How fitting that the book ends with a picture of "the best of them all"—a wife of strong character, great wisdom, many skills, and great compassion.

Some people have the mistaken idea that the ideal wife in the Bible is retiring, servile, and entirely domestic. Not so! She is a conscientious wife and mother. She is also a manufacturer, importer, manager, realtor, farmer, seamstress, upholsterer, and merchant. Her strength and dignity do not come from her amazing achievements, however. They are a result of her reverence for God.

_____ ◦ MEDITATION ◦ _____

Heavenly Father, let me be a help to my husband because of the strength and dignity that you are giving me as I draw closer to you. ◦

DECEMBER 31

The Promise of Jesus' Return
◦§ Revelation 22:8–21 §◦

I, John, saw and heard all these things, and fell down to worship the angel who showed them to me; [9]but again he said, "No, don't do anything like that. I, too, am a servant of Jesus as you are, and as your brothers the prophets are, as well as all those who heed the truth stated in this Book. Worship God alone."

[10]Then he instructed me, "Do not seal up what you have written, for the time of fulfillment is near. [11]And when that time comes, all doing wrong will do it more and more; the vile will become more vile; good men will be better; those who are holy will continue on in greater holiness."

[12]"See, I am coming soon, and my reward is with me, to repay everyone according to the deeds he has done. [13]I am the A and the Z, the Beginning and the End, the First and Last. [14]Blessed forever are all who are washing their robes, to have the right to enter in through the gates of the city, and to eat the fruit from the Tree of Life.

[15]"Outside the city are those who have strayed away from God, and the sorcerers and the immoral and murderers and idolaters, and all who love to lie, and do so.

[16]"I, Jesus, have sent my angel to you to tell the churches all these things. I am both David's Root and his Descendant. I am the bright Morning Star.

[17]The Spirit and the bride say, 'Come.' Let each one who hears them say the same, 'Come.' Let the thirsty one come—anyone who wants to; let him come and drink the Water of Life without charge. [18]And I solemnly declare to everyone who reads this book: If anyone adds anything to what is written here, God shall add to him the plagues described in this book. [19]And if anyone subtracts any part of these prophecies, God shall take away his share in the Tree of Life, and in the Holy City just described.

[20]"He who has said all these things declares: Yes, I am coming soon!"

Amen! Come, Lord Jesus!

[21]The grace of our Lord Jesus Christ be with you all. Amen!

Exhortations to Holy Living
◦§ Jude 1:17–25 §◦

Dear friends, remember what the apostles of our Lord Jesus Christ told you, [18]that in the last times there would come these scoffers whose whole purpose in life is to enjoy themselves in every evil way imaginable. [19]They stir up arguments; they love the evil things of the world; they do not have the Holy Spirit living in them.

[20]But you, dear friends, must build up your lives ever more strongly upon the foundation of our

holy faith, learning to pray in the power and strength of the Holy Spirit.

²¹Stay always within the boundaries where God's love can reach and bless you. Wait patiently for the eternal life that our Lord Jesus Christ in his mercy is going to give you. ²²Try to help those who argue against you. Be merciful to those who doubt. ²³Save some by snatching them as from the very flames of hell itself. And as for others, help them to find the Lord by being kind to them, but be careful that you yourselves aren't pulled along into their sins. Hate every trace of their sin while being merciful to them as sinners.

²⁴,²⁵And now—all glory to him who alone is God, who saves us through Jesus Christ our Lord; yes, splendor and majesty, all power and authority are his from the beginning; his they are and his they evermore shall be. And he is able to keep you from slipping and falling away, and to bring you, sinless and perfect, into his glorious presence with mighty shouts of everlasting joy. Amen.

Jude

Proverbs for Today
⋖§ 31:25–31 §⋗

She is a woman of strength and dignity, and has no fear of old age. When she speaks, her words are wise, and kindness is the rule for everything she says. She watches carefully all that goes on throughout her household, and is never lazy. Her children stand and bless her; so does her husband. He praises her with these words: "There are many fine women in the world, but you are the best of them all!" Charm can be deceptive and beauty doesn't last, but a woman who fears and reverences God shall be greatly praised. Praise her for the many fine things she does. These good deeds of hers shall bring her honor and recognition from people of importance.

⋖ KEY VERSE ⋗

Charm can be deceptive and beauty doesn't last, but a woman who fears and reverences God shall be greatly praised.—*Proverbs 31:30*

⋖ REFLECTION ⋗

Proverbs 31 never mentions what "a truly good wife" looks like. Her attractiveness comes entirely from her character. In our society, where physical appearance counts for so much, this picture goes against the grain.

The wife described in this chapter has outstanding abilities. Her family's social position is high. In fact, she may not be one woman at all—she may be a composite portrait of ideal womanhood. Do not see her as a model to imitate in every detail; your days are not long enough to do everything she does! See her as an inspiration. We can't be just like her, but we can learn from her industry, integrity, and resourcefulness.

⋖ MEDITATION ⋗

Heavenly Father, give me an inner beauty that reflects your love and grace. §⋗